D1499944

PERSONALITY
READINGS IN
THEORY AND RESEARCH

PERSONALITY
READINGS IN
THEORY AND RESEARCH

Third Edition

Edited by

Eugene A. Southwell

Indiana University Northwest

Michael Merbaum

Concordia University

Brooks/Cole Publishing Company
Monterey, California

A Division of Wadsworth Publishing Company, Inc.

Cop. 1
Soc

Printed in the United States of America

10 9 8 7 6 5 4 3 2 1

Library of Congress Cataloging in Publication Data

Southwell, Eugene A   ed.
  Personality.

    Includes bibliographies and index.
    1. Personality—Addresses, essays, lectures.
I. Merbaum, Michael.   II. Title.
BF698.S615   1978   155.2'08   77-20260
ISBN 0-8185-0257-6

Acquisition Editor: *Charles T. Hendrix*
Project Development Editor: *Claire L. Verduin*
Manuscript Editor: *Valerie Faraday Daigen*
Production Editor: *Stephen E. White*
Interior and Cover Design: *Katherine Minerva*
Illustrations: *John Foster*
Cover Illustration: from *The Fair,* an etching by *Helen Breger*
Typesetting: *David R. Sullivan Company, Dallas, Texas*

To
Bill, Kim, Kirk, Tal, and Marc

PREFACE

Although this edition differs significantly from the first (1964) and second (1971) editions in terms of our choice of personality theories to be presented, we are still guided by the strong conviction that a serious study of the field of the psychology of personality must include exposure to original writing. Therefore, in this edition, as in the two previous editions, each personality theory is represented by three papers: first, a theoretical statement by the theorist himself; second, a research paper that either describes the testing of a hypothesis generated by the theoretical statement or illustrates a type of research that is related to the ideas presented in the theoretical paper; and, third, a critique of the theoretical position, an alternative explanation of the research results, or a criticism of the research methodology employed.

Paired with a standard text, this book can suggest to students in an undergraduate course in personality how to think critically about personality theory. For classes in which lectures provide extensive coverage of the various theories, this book can be used alone, as the basic text.

In each chapter, our aim has been to present significant contributions to psychological thought in the form of a compact, internally consistent unit. We hope thereby to give the reader a familiarity not only with the particular theoretical position but also with the research strategies that have been used to test it and with the inevitable dissenting opinions, which enliven the scientific enterprise.

Textbooks in the field of personality theory generally limit themselves to discussions and interpretations of the various personality theories. But, because of the lack of agreement among personality theorists about the facts, and because of the inherent complexity of the subject matter, popular theories tend to be unique creations that reflect the theorist's particular viewpoint, as well as his or her personal convictions regarding science and the nature of human behavior. Only the original theoretical works, by exposing the student not only to the ideas of the theorists but also to their logical arguments and their use of language, can give the student a full appreciation of the uniqueness of each theory.

In order for a theory to remain a useful member of the scientific community, it must bring order and meaning to a realm of observational data; it should also generate hypotheses amenable to testing. This latter feature enables theories to be self-corrective in the light of new evidence, and it makes them useful tools in the search for additional knowledge. But what constitutes the most useful strategy for testing hypotheses is open to debate. Some theorists feel that only through the use of rigorous statistical and experimental controls can theoretical statements be supported or enhanced. Others maintain that thorough observation of the organism in its social milieu is the most useful means of evaluating and elaborating on a particular theoretical view. Although these positions are by no means mutually exclusive, our own bias is firmly toward the former approach, and our choice of research papers reflects that fact.

Theory construction and research design are by no means straightforward processes. Consequently, ideas, observations, and interpretations of data are frequently open to debate. In many instances, the existence of alternative ideas, conflicting observations, and varying interpretations of data generates lively controversy, which in turn sharpens the alertness of the scientific community to relevant issues. It is because we believe that controversy is valuable to science that we have included the critical commentaries, which bear either on the theory or on research designed to test it.

It would be impossible to include in a single volume the writings of all those psychologists who have made impressive contributions to the field of the psychology of personality. Therefore, what we offer is a sample of the theoretical positions that are currently exerting a strong influence on the development of the study of personality.

This book is the result of the cooperation and assistance of many people. We especially wish to thank the authors and publishers who have permitted us to use their material. Although we have modified the titles of some articles to fit the theory-research-critique format of the book, appropriate credit appears in the footnote at the beginning of each selection.

We are also indebted to the psychologists who have used our book over the years and who have been kind enough to review the two previous editions and the manuscript for this edition. In particular, we wish to thank Stephen E. Berger, University of Southern California; Brian C. Hayden, Brown University; Jaques W. Kaswan, Ohio State University; Mark Sherman, Syracuse University; George Stricker, Adelphi University; and Auke Tellegen, University of Minnesota.

Finally, we are especially grateful to Amy Cardaras, Sandra Smith, and Helen Vagnone for their assistance in secretarial and library-research matters.

Eugene A. Southwell
Michael Merbaum

CONTENTS

ix

Part 1
PSYCHOANALYTIC THEORY

One
SIGMUND FREUD

Sigmund Freud (1856–1939) has so influenced the development of contemporary personality theory that one could hardly engage in a study of the topic of personality without first becoming aware of the contributions of this remarkable man. His theory, the most comprehensive yet developed, comprises a network of structural and dynamic concepts so elaborate that no single paper can fully represent it.

(Before proceeding with this chapter, you might find it useful to read the introductory material and the first selection in Chapter Two. Although Chapter Two presents a modification of Freud's theory of personality development—a modification usually called *ego psychology*—the introductory material and the Hartmann paper provide excellent background reading for this chapter.)

The first selection in this chapter is included for two main reasons: (1) to illustrate Freud's clever and persuasive style of thinking and (2) to give background for the third selection in this chapter. The paper is of primarily historical interest and certainly is not illustrative of current methods in the psychoanalytic study of children, as represented by the work of child analysts such as Anna Freud (Freud's daughter), Melanie Klein, Erik Erikson, and others. The paper, "Analysis of a Phobia in a Five-Year-Old Boy" (also known as "The Case of Little Hans"), was first published in 1909 and occupies 147 pages in the standard edition of Freud's collected works. We have reprinted here only the "Discussion" portion of the paper—roughly the last third of it. The first two-thirds of the paper, not reprinted here, consist of some introductory theoretical remarks and a detailed account of the development of Hans's fear (phobia) of horses. Serious students of Freud should read the entire paper.

The case of Little Hans was very significant because it confirmed for Freud (and his followers) the validity of the theory that the Oedipus complex and castration anxiety play important roles in the development of psychoneuroses. Freud's earlier writings about infantile sexuality were based on the psychoanalysis of adults, not children. Following his publication of "Three Essays on the Theory of Sexuality" in 1905, he asked colleagues to make available to him their observations on the sexual lives of children. What he had in mind, in fact, was to test the hypotheses set forth in the 1905 paper. Little Hans's father, a physician and a close friend of Freud's, began sending reports to Freud when Hans was about 3 years of age. At this time, Hans was expressing a strong interest in his penis ("widdler")—the relative sizes of widdlers, their function, who possesses a widdler, masturbation, and procreation (Hans's mother was at the time pregnant with Hans's sister). These reports continued at frequent intervals and were quite detailed in their descriptions of Hans's dialogues with his mother and father (especially with his father). Although the case-history portion of the original paper cannot be presented here because of its length, the reader will find an excellent summary of it in the third paper of this chapter. We suggest that you read those pages before reading Freud's article.

The second paper, by Calvin Hall and Robert L. Van de Castle, presents an experimental test of a hypothesis generated from Freud's theory of the castration complex. The theory follows directly from Freud's earlier writings about infantile sexuality and the Oedipus complex and represents an elaboration on his "Three Essays" and "Little Hans" papers. According to the theory, males develop a fear of losing their penis (castration anxiety), and females develop a desire for a penis (penis envy) and want to deprive the male of his penis (castration wish). According to Freud, these anxieties and wishes are rarely (if ever) expressed directly in the adult and must therefore be investigated indirectly, such as through the analysis of dreams. The Hall and Van de Castle paper presents an attempt to empirically verify the existence of castration anxiety, penis envy, and castration wishes in the dreams of male and female adults. This paper illustrates that one can go about testing psychoanalytic concepts in a way much different from the one Freud employed when he used the Little Hans case to test his theory of infantile sexuality. The Little Hans paper can be described as a *clinical* test of Freudian theory, whereas the Hall and Van de Castle article represents an *experimental* test. As you will see when you read the third (critique) paper in this chapter, from an objective scientific point of view the case of Little Hans leaves much to be desired as "proof" of the validity of psychoanalytic theory.

It is important, when studying the Hall and Van de Castle paper, to compare the *methodology* used with that described in the Little Hans article. After summarizing several previous studies on the content of dreams as a function of the castration complex, the experimenters present two hypotheses to be tested in their study. Note that the hypotheses are stated in such a way that they are amenable to empirical test. That is, they are worded so that the mere operation of counting the frequency of occurrence of dream contents will provide information allowing for the confirmation or rejection of the hypotheses. Specifically, the hypotheses are (1) that the dreams of males and females will differ and (2) that this difference will be in a direction compatible with Freudian theory. Once such predictions have been formulated, one can collect dreams, sort them into three categories (castration anxiety, penis envy, castration wish), and, by comparing the numbers of males and females in each category, *quantitatively* assess the truth or falsity of the hypotheses.

The design of the experiment is straightforward. Hall and Van de Castle asked a large number of male and female college students to record, on a standard report form, their dreams. The instructions for reporting dreams were *standardized* for all the subjects, and the dreams were later scored by the investigators in terms of the presence or absence of the factors of interest.

In research done prior to the study reported here, the experimenters had developed a dream-scoring manual. They had determined that different scorers, following the rules for scoring provided by the manual, have a high degree of agreement in their classification of dream contents. Thus, the dream-scoring system was highly *reliable*, and Hall and Van de Castle could be confident that their assignment of dreams to categories would not be haphazard. In other words, they could be reasonably sure that, if one scorer called a dream a "castration anxiety" dream, other scorers would do the same.

By classifying the dreams according to the sex of the dreamer and the content of the dream, the experimenters produced their *data*: the numbers of males and females falling into each of the three categories of dreams. The researchers then needed to know the *probability* (likelihood) that the ratio of males to females in each category was determined by *chance*. If the number in each category had been determined by chance alone, the experimenters could have expected to find an equal number of males and females having each kind of dream. This is the *null hypothesis*—that there is no statistical difference between males and females in terms of the content of their dreams. To test this hypothesis, Hall and Van de Castle applied the chi-square test—a statistical test designed for this purpose. When, on the basis of the results of this test, the null hypothesis was *rejected*, the experimenters were free to accept their first hypothesis—that there is a difference between males and females in terms of the content of their dreams. All that remained was to observe the direction of the difference; this was in line with their second hypothesis.

As you study the "Discussion" portion of the Hall and Van de Castle article, note that the authors consider other ways of analyzing their data and that they consider alternative theories that would also predict the results of their experiment. Although no experiment is an end in itself, the research paper presented here is an excellent example of the interplay of theory, research, and critique—a process that is the hallmark of the scientific method.

An explanation of a phenomenon that is couched in specific theoretical terms often invites disagreement. Freud's psychoanalytic theory is no exception, as is evident from the third selection in this chapter. Joseph Wolpe and Stanley Rachman attack Freud's interpretation of the case of Little Hans and present a trenchant criticism of his theoretical analysis from the standpoint of what they term "scientific objectivism." The authors are especially critical of the *method* of data collection utilized by Freud (the anecdotal reports by Hans's father), questioning the scientific value of data collected in this fashion. They question the *reliability* of the father's reports as well as the accuracy of Hans's testimony. In this regard it would be useful for the reader to compare Freud's method of data collection with the method described in the Hall and Van de Castle study. Recall that Hall and Van de Castle were careful to assess the reliability of the "testimony" provided by their method of dream scoring, whereas in the Little Hans case only one person reported observations of Little Hans, and thus there is no way to evaluate the reliability of these reports. Further, in Wolpe and Rachman's analysis of the reports by Hans's father, they note that many of Hans's statements reflect ideas suggested to him by the father; and, on two occasions, the father presented his own interpretation of Hans's behavior as "fact," thereby substantiating the assertion made by many of Freud's critics that psychoanalytic theory is "self-validating" in the sense that patients learn to report events that confirm the theory's predictions.

Following their critical appraisal of Freud's method of hypothesis-testing and their conclusion that, in light of these shortcomings, Freud's acceptance of the data as confirmation of his theory of phobia development was not warranted, they go on to present an alternative explanation of the development of Hans's phobia, using the principles of classical (Pavlovian) conditioning.

SUGGESTIONS FOR FURTHER READING

For the student interested in Freud's life and work, the three-volume biography *The Life and Work of Sigmund Freud* (Basic Books, 1953–1957), by Ernest Jones, is highly recommended. There is also a one-volume abridged edition available, published in 1961 by Doubleday, abridged by Lionel L. Trilling and Steven Marcus. An excellent paperback presentation of psychoanalytic theory is the small book by G. S. Blum, *Psychodynamics: The Science of Unconscious Mental Forces*, published by Brooks/Cole in 1966.

For Freud's works in translation, *The Standard Edition of the Complete Psychological Works*, edited by James Strachey and published by Hogarth Press, should be consulted.

Students who read German should consult the *Gesammelte Werke, Chronologisch Geordnet*, edited by Anna Freud and published by the Imago Publishing Company.

The Psychoanalytic Theory of Neurosis, by Otto Fenichel, published by Norton, is difficult reading but worth the effort for the student who is seriously interested in the psychoanalytic technique of psychotherapy.

The now old but still worthwhile monograph by Robert Sears, *Survey of Objective Studies of Psychoanalytic Concepts* (published in 1943 by the Social Science Research Council) is well worth reading for a picture of how some American psychologists have attempted to test Freudian theory.

Finally, *Critical Essays on Psychoanalysis*, edited by Stanley Rachman and published by Pergamon Press, presents some provocative articles critical of psychoanalysis.

Sigmund Freud
THE CASE OF LITTLE HANS

I shall now proceed to examine this observation of the development and resolution of a phobia in a boy under five years of age, and I shall have to do so from three points of view. In the first place I shall consider how far it supports the assertions which I put forward in my *Three Essays on the Theory of Sexuality* (1905). Secondly, I shall consider to what extent it can contribute towards our understanding of this very frequent form of disorder. And thirdly, I shall consider whether it can be made to shed any light upon the mental life of children or to afford any criticism of our educational aims.

(I)

My impression is that the picture of a child's sexual life presented in this observation of little Hans agrees very well with the account I gave of it (basing my views upon psycho-analytic examinations of adults) in my *Three Essays*. But before going into the details of this agreement I must deal with two objections which will be raised against my making use of the present analysis for this purpose. The first objection is to the effect that Hans was not a normal child, but (as events—the illness itself, in fact—showed) had a predisposition to neurosis, and was a young "degenerate"; it would be illegitimate, therefore, to apply to other, normal children conclusions which might perhaps be true of him. I shall postpone consideration of this objection, since it only limits the value of the observation, and does not completely nullify it. According to the second and more uncompromising objection, an analysis of a child conducted by his father, who went to work instilled with *my* theoretical views and infected with *my* prejudices, must be entirely devoid of any objective worth. A child, it will be said, is necessarily highly suggestible, and in regard to no one, perhaps, more than to his own father; he will allow anything to be forced upon him, out of gratitude to his father for taking so much notice of him; none of his assertions can have any evidential value, and everything he produces in the way of associations, phantasies, and dreams will naturally take the direction into which they are being urged by every possible means. Once more, in short, the whole thing is simply "suggestion"—the only difference being that in the case of a child it can be unmasked much more easily than in that of an adult.

A singular thing. I can remember, when I first began to meddle in the conflict of scientific opinions twenty-two years ago, with what derision the older generation of neurologists and psychiatrists of those days received assertions about suggestion and its

From Sigmund Freud, *The Standard Edition of the Complete Psychological Works*, ed. J. Strachey, 24 vols. (London: Hogarth Press, 1953–66), Vol. 10, pp. 101–147; also in *The Collected Papers of Sigmund Freud*, ed. E. Jones, 5 vols. (New York: Basic Books, 1959), Vol. 3, pp. 243–287. Reprinted by permission of the publishers.

effects. Since then the situation has fundamentally changed. The former aversion has been converted into an only too ready acceptance; and this has happened not only as a consequence of the impression which the work of Liébeault and Bernheim and their pupils could not fail to create in the course of these two decades, but also because it has since been discovered how great an economy of thought can be effected by the use of the catchword "suggestion." Nobody knows and nobody cares what suggestion is, where it comes from, or when it arises,—it is enough that everything awkward in the region of psychology can be labelled "suggestion." I do not share the view which is at present fashionable that assertions made by children are invariably arbitrary and untrustworthy. The arbitrary has no existence in mental life. The untrustworthiness of the assertions of children is due to the predominance of their imagination, just as the untrustworthiness of the assertions of grown-up people is due to the predominance of their prejudices. For the rest, even children do not lie without a reason, and on the whole they are more inclined to a love of truth than are their elders. If we were to reject little Hans's statements root and branch we should certainly be doing him a grave injustice. On the contrary, we can quite clearly distinguish from one another the occasions on which he was falsifying the facts or keeping them back under the compelling force of a resistance, the occasions on which, being undecided himself, he agreed with his father (so that what he said must not be taken as evidence), and the occasions on which, freed from every pressure, he burst into a flood of information about what was really going on inside him and about things which until then no one but himself had known. Statements made by adults offer no greater certainty. It is a regrettable fact that no account of a psycho-analysis can reproduce the impressions received by the analyst as he conducts it, and that a final sense of conviction can never be obtained from reading about it but only from directly experiencing it. But this disability attaches in an equal degree to analyses of adults.

Little Hans is described by his parents as a cheerful, straightforward child, and so he should have been, considering the education given him by his parents, which consisted essentially in the omission of our usual educational sins. So long as he was able to carry on his researches in a state of happy *naïveté*, without a suspicion of the conflicts which were soon to arise out of them, he kept nothing back; and the observations made during the period before the phobia admit of no doubt or demur. It was with the outbreak of the illness and during the analysis that discrepancies began to make their appearance between what he said and what he thought; and this was partly because unconscious material, which he was unable to master all at once, was forcing itself upon him, and partly because the content of his thoughts provoked reservations on account of his relation to his parents. It is my unbiased opinion that these difficulties, too, turned out no greater than in many analyses of adults.

It is true that during the analysis Hans had to be told many things that he could not say himself, that he had to be presented with thoughts which he had so far shown no signs of possessing, and that his attention had to be turned in the direction from which his father was expecting something to come. This detracts from the evidential value of the analysis; but the procedure is the same in every case. For a psycho-analysis is not an impartial scientific investigation, but a therapeutic measure. Its essence is not to prove anything, but merely to alter something. In a psycho-analysis the physician always gives his patient (sometimes to a greater and sometimes to a less extent) the conscious anticipatory ideas by the help of which he is put in a position to recognize and to grasp the unconscious material. For there are some patients who need more of such assistance and some who need less; but there are none who get through without some of it. Slight disorders may perhaps be brought to an end by the subject's unaided efforts, but never a neurosis—a thing which has set itself up against the ego as an element alien to it. To get the better of such an element another person must be brought in, and in so far as that other person can be of assistance the neurosis will be curable. If it is in the very nature of any neurosis to turn away from the "other person"—and this seems to be one of the characteristics of the states grouped together under the name of dementia praecox—then for that very reason such a state will be incurable by any efforts of ours. It is true that a child, on account of the small development of his intellectual systems, requires especially energetic assistance. But, after all, the information which the physician gives his patient is itself derived in its turn from analytical experience; and indeed it is sufficiently convincing if, at the cost of this intervention by the physician, we are enabled to discover the structure of the pathogenic material and simultaneously to dissipate it.

And yet, even during the analysis, the small patient gave evidence of enough independence to acquit him upon the charge of "suggestion." Like all other children, he applied his childish sexual theories to the material before him without having received any encouragement to do so. These theories are extremely remote from the adult mind. Indeed, in this instance I actually omitted to warn Hans's father that the boy would be bound to approach the subject of childbirth by way of the excretory complex. This negligence on my part, though it led to an obscure phase in the analysis, was nevertheless the means of producing a good piece of evidence of the genuineness and independence of Hans's mental processes. He suddenly became occupied with "lumf," without his father, who is supposed to have been practising suggestion upon him, having the least idea how he had arrived at that subject or what was going to come of it. Nor can his father be saddled with any responsibility for the production of the two plumber phantasies, which arose out of Hans's early acquired "castration complex." And I must here confess that, out of theoretical interest, I entirely concealed from Hans's father my expectation that there would turn out to be some such connection, so as not to interfere with the value of a piece of evidence such as does not often come within one's grasp.

If I went more deeply into the details of the analysis I could produce plenty more evidence of Hans's independence of "suggestion"; but I shall break off the discussion of this preliminary objection at this point. I am aware that even with this analysis I shall not succeed in convincing any one who will not let himself be convinced, and I shall proceed with my discussion of the case for the benefit of those readers who are already convinced of the objective reality of unconscious pathogenic material. And I do this with the agreeable assurance that the number of such readers is steadily increasing.

The first trait in little Hans which can be regarded as part of his sexual life was a quite peculiar lively interest in his "widdler"—an organ deriving its name from that one of its two functions which, scarcely the less important of the two, is not to be eluded in the nursery. This interest aroused in him the spirit of enquiry, and he thus discovered that the presence or absence of a widdler made it possible to differentiate between animate and inanimate objects. He assumed that all animate objects were like himself, and possessed this important bodily organ; he observed that it was present in the larger animals, suspected that this was so too in both his parents, and was not deterred by the evidence of his own eyes from authenticating the fact in his newborn sister. One might almost say that it would have been too shattering a blow to his *"Weltanschauung"* if he had had to make up his mind to forgo the presence of this organ in a being similar to him; it would have been as though it were being torn away from himself. It was probably on this account that a threat of his mother's, which was concerned precisely with the loss of his widdler, was hastily dismissed from his thoughts and only succeeded in making its effects apparent at a later period. The reason for his mother's intervention had been that he used to like giving himself feelings of pleasure by touching his member: the little boy had begun to practise the commonest—and most normal—form of auto-erotic sexual activity.

The pleasure which a person takes in his own sexual organ may become associated with scopophilia (or sexual pleasure in looking) in its active and passive forms, in a manner which has been very aptly described by Alfred Adler as "confluence of instincts." So little Hans began to try to get a sight of other people's widdlers; his sexual curiosity developed, and at the same time he liked to exhibit his own widdler. One of his dreams, dating from the beginning of his period of repression, expressed a wish that one of his little girl friends should assist him in widdling, that is, that she should share the spectacle. The dream shows, therefore, that up till then this wish had subsisted unrepressed, and later information confirmed the fact that he had been in the habit of gratifying it. The active side of his sexual scopophilia soon became associated in him with a definite theme. He repeatedly expressed both to his father and his mother his regret that he had never yet seen their widdlers; and it was probably the need *for making a comparison* which impelled him to do this. The ego is always the standard by which one measures the external world; one learns to understand it by means of a constant comparison with oneself. Hans had observed that large animals had widdlers that were correspondingly larger than his; he consequently suspected that the same was true of his parents, and was anxious to make sure of this. His mother, he thought, must certainly have a widdler "like a horse." He was then prepared with the comforting reflection that his widdler would grow with him. It was as though the child's wish to be bigger had been concentrated on his genitals.

Thus in little Hans's sexual constitution the genital zone was from the outset the one among his erotogenic zones which afforded him the most intense pleasure. The only other similar pleasure of which he gave evidence was excretory pleasure, the pleasure attached to the orifices through which micturition and evacuation of the bowels are effected. In his final phantasy of bliss, with which his illness was overcome, he imagined he had children, whom he took to the W.C., whom he made to widdle, whose behinds he wiped—for whom, in short, he did "everything one can do with children"; it therefore seems impossible to avoid the assumption that during the period when he himself had been looked after as an infant these same performances had been the source of pleasurable sensations for him. He had obtained this pleasure from his erotogenic zones with the help of the person who had looked after him—his mother, in fact; and thus the pleasure already pointed the way to object-choice. But it is just possible that at a still earlier date he had been in the habit of giving himself this pleasure auto-erotically—that he had been one of those children who like retaining their excreta till they can derive a voluptuous sensation from their evacuation. I say no more than that it is possible, because the matter was not cleared up in the analysis; the "making a row with the legs" (kicking about), of which he was so much frightened later on, points in that direction. But in any case these sources of pleasure had no particularly striking importance with Hans, as they so often have with other children. He early became clean in his habits, and neither bed-wetting nor diurnal incontinence played any part during his first years; no trace was observed in him of any inclination to play with his excrement, a propensity which is so revolting in adults, and which commonly makes its reappearance at the termination of processes of psychical involution.

At this juncture it is as well to emphasize at once the fact that during his phobia there was an unmistakable repression of these two well-developed components of his sexual activity. He was ashamed of micturating before other people, accused himself of putting his finger to his widdler, made efforts to give up masturbating, and showed disgust at "lumf" and "widdle" and everything that reminded him of them. In his phantasy of looking after his children he undid this latter repression.

A sexual constitution like that of little Hans does not appear to carry with it a predisposition to the development either of perversions or of their negative (we will limit ourselves to a consideration of hysteria). As far as my experience goes (and there is still a real need for speaking with caution on this point) the innate constitution of hysterics—that this is also true of perverts is almost self-evident—is marked by the genital zone being relatively less prominent than the other erotogenic zones. But we must expressly except from this rule one particular ''aberration'' of sexual life. In those who later become homosexuals we meet with the same predominance in infancy of the genital zone (and especially of the penis) as in normal persons.[1] Indeed it is the high esteem felt by the homosexual for the male organ which decides his fate. In his childhood he chooses women as his sexual object, so long as he assumes that they too possess what in his eyes is an indispensable part of the body; when he becomes convinced that women have deceived him in this particular, they cease to be acceptable to him as a sexual object. He cannot forgo a penis in any one who is to attract him to sexual intercourse; and if circumstances are favourable he will fix his libido upon the ''woman with a penis,'' a youth of feminine appearance. Homosexuals, then, are persons who, owing to the erotogenic importance of their own genitals, cannot do without a similar feature in their sexual object. In the course of their development from auto-erotism to object-love, they have remained at a point of fixation between the two.

There is absolutely no justification for distinguishing a special homosexual instinct. What constitutes a homosexual is a peculiarity not in his instinctual life but in his choice of an object. Let me recall what I have said in my *Three Essays* to the effect that we have mistakenly imagined the bond between instinct and object in sexual life as being more intimate than it really is. A homosexual may have normal instincts, but he is unable to disengage them from a class of objects defined by a particular determinant. And in his childhood, since at that period this determinant is taken for granted as being of universal application, he is able to behave like little Hans, who showed his affection to little boys and girls indiscriminately, and once described his friend Fritzl as ''the girl he was fondest of.'' Hans was a homosexual (as all children may very well be), quite consistently with the fact, which must always be kept in mind, that *he was acquainted with only one kind of genital organ*—a genital organ like his own.[2]

In his subsequent development, however, it was not to homosexuality that our young libertine proceeded, but to an energetic masculinity with traits of polygamy; he knew how to vary his behaviour, too, with his varying feminine objects—audaciously aggressive in one case, languishing and bashful in another. His affection had moved from his mother on to other objects of love, but at a time when there was a scarcity of these it returned to her, only to break down in a neurosis. It was not until this happened that it became evident to what a pitch of intensity his love for his mother had developed and through what vicissitudes it had passed. The sexual aim which he pursued with his girl playmates, of sleeping with them, had originated in relation to his mother. It was expressed in words which might be retained in maturity, though they would then bear a richer connotation. The boy had found his way to object-love in the usual manner from the care he had received when he was an infant; and a new pleasure had now become the most important for him—that of sleeping beside his mother. I should like to emphasize the importance of pleasure derived from cutaneous contact

---

[1]As my expectations led me to suppose, and as Sadger's observations have shown, all such people pass through an amphigenic phase in childhood.

[2](*Footnote added* 1923:) I have subsequently (1923) drawn attention to the fact that the period of sexual development which our little patient was passing through is universally characterized by acquaintance with only *one* sort of genital organ, namely, the male one. In contrast to the later period of maturity, this period is marked not by a *genital* primacy but by a primacy of the *phallus*.

as a component in this new aim of Hans's, which, according to the nomenclature (artificial to my mind) of Moll, would have to be described as satisfaction of the instinct of contrectation.

In his attitude towards his father and mother Hans confirms in the most concrete and uncompromising manner what I have said in my *Interpretation of Dreams* (1900) and in my *Three Essays* (1905) with regard to the sexual relations of a child to his parents. Hans really was a little Oedipus who wanted to have his father ''out of the way,'' to get rid of him, so that he might be alone with his beautiful mother and sleep with her. This wish had originated during his summer holidays, when the alternating presence and absence of his father had drawn Hans's attention to the condition upon which depended the intimacy with his mother which he longed for. At that time the form taken by the wish had been merely that his father should ''go away''; and at a later stage it became possible for his fear of being bitten by a white horse to attach itself directly on to this form of the wish, owing to a chance impression which he received at the moment of some one else's departure. But subsequently (probably not until they had moved back to Vienna, where his father's absences were no longer to be reckoned on) the wish had taken the form that his father should be *permanently* away—that he should be ''dead.'' The fear which sprang from this death-wish against his father, and which may thus be said to have had a normal motive, formed the chief obstacle to the analysis until it was removed during the conversation in my consulting-room.[3]

But Hans was not by any means a bad character; he was not even one of those children who at his age still give free play to the propensity towards cruelty and violence which is a constituent of human nature. On the contrary, he had an unusually kindhearted and affectionate disposition; his father reported that the transformation of aggressive tendencies into feelings of pity took place in him at a very early age. Long before the phobia he had become uneasy when he saw the horses in a merry-go-round being beaten; and he was never unmoved if any one wept in his presence. At one stage in the analysis a piece of suppressed sadism made its appearance in a particular context:[4] but it was *suppressed* sadism, and we shall presently have to discover from the context what it stood for and what it was meant to replace. And Hans deeply loved the father against whom he cherished these death-wishes; and while his intellect demurred to such a contradiction, he could not help demonstrating the fact of its existence, by hitting his father and immediately afterwards kissing the place he had hit. We ourselves, too, must guard against making a difficulty of such a contradiction. The emotional life of a man is in general made up of pairs of contraries such as these.[5] Indeed, if it were not so, repressions and neuroses would perhaps never come about. In the adult these pairs of contrary emotions do not as a rule become simultaneously conscious except at the climaxes of passionate love; at other times they usually go on suppressing each other until one of them succeeds in keeping the other altogether out of sight. But in children they can exist peaceably side by side for quite a considerable time.

The most important influence upon the course of Hans's psycho-sexual development

[3]It is quite certain that Hans's two associations, ''raspberry syrup'' and ''a gun for shooting people dead with,'' must have had more than one set of determinants. They probably had just as much to do with his hatred of his father as with his constipation complex. His father, who himself guessed the latter connection, also suggested that ''raspberry syrup'' might be related to ''blood.''

[4]His wanting to beat and tease horses.

[5]Das heisst, ich bin kein ausgeklügelt Buch.
Ich bin ein Mensch mit seinem Widerspruch.
C. F. Meyer, *Huttens letzte Tage*.
(In fact, I am no clever work of fiction;
I am a man, with all his contradiction.)

was the birth of a baby sister when he was three and a half years old. That event accentuated his relations to his parents and gave him some insoluble problems to think about; and later, as he watched the way in which the infant was looked after, the memory-traces of his own earliest experiences of pleasure were revived in him. This influence, too, is a typical one: in an unexpectedly large number of life-histories, normal as well as pathological, we find ourselves obliged to take as our starting-point an outburst of sexual pleasure and sexual curiosity connected, like this one, with the birth of the next child. Hans's behaviour towards the new arrival was just what I have described in *The Interpretation of Dreams* (1900). In his fever a few days later he betrayed how little he liked the addition to the family. Affection for his sister might come later, but his first attitude was hostility. From that time forward fear that yet another baby might arrive found a place among his conscious thoughts. In the neurosis, his hostility, already suppressed, was represented by a special fear—a fear of the bath. In the analysis he gave undisguised expression to his death-wish against his sister, and was not content with allusions which required supplementing by his father. His inner conscience did not consider this wish so wicked as the analogous one against his father; but it is clear that in his unconscious he treated both persons in the same way, because they both took his mummy away from him, and interfered with his being alone with her.

Moreover, this event and the feelings that were revived by it gave a new direction to his wishes: In his triumphant final phantasy he summed up all of his erotic wishes, both those derived from his auto-erotic phase and those connected with his object-love. In that phantasy he was married to his beautiful mother and had innumerable children whom he could look after in his own way.

(II)

One day while Hans was in the street he was seized with an attack of anxiety. He could not yet say what it was he was afraid of; but at the very beginning of this anxiety-state he betrayed to his father his motive for being ill, the advantage he derived from it. He wanted to stay with his mother and to coax with her; his recollection that he had also been separated from her at the time of the baby's birth may also, as his father suggests, have contributed to his longing. It soon became evident that his anxiety was no longer reconvertible into longing; he was afraid even when his mother went with him. In the meantime indications appeared of what it was to which his libido (now changed into anxiety) had become attached. He gave expression to the quite specific fear that a white horse would bite him.

Disorders of this kind are called "phobias," and we might classify Hans's case as an agoraphobia if it were not for the fact that it is a characteristic of that complaint that the locomotion of which the patient is otherwise incapable can always be easily performed when he is accompanied by some specially selected person—in the last resort, by the physician. Hans's phobia did not fulfil this condition; it soon ceased having any relation to the question of locomotion and became more and more clearly concentrated upon horses. In the early days of his illness, when the anxiety was at its highest pitch, he expressed a fear that "the horse'll come into the room," and it was this that helped me so much towards understanding his condition.

In the classificatory system of the neuroses no definite position has hitherto been assigned to "phobias." It seems certain that they should only be regarded as syndromes which may form part of various neuroses and that we need not rank them as an independent pathological process. For phobias of the kind to which little Hans's belongs, and which are in fact the most common, the name of "anxiety-hysteria" seems to me not inappropriate; I suggested the term to Dr. W. Stekel when he was undertaking a description of neurotic anxiety-states, and I hope it will come into general use. It finds its justification in the similarity between the psychological structure of these phobias and that of hysteria—a similarity which is complete except upon a single point. That point, however, is a decisive one and well adapted for purposes of differentiation. For in anxiety-hysteria the libido which has been liberated from the pathogenic material by repression is not *converted* (that is, diverted from the mental sphere into a somatic innervation), but is set free in the shape of *anxiety*. In the clinical cases that we meet with, this "anxiety-hysteria" may be combined with "conversion-hysteria" in any proportion. There exist cases of pure conversion-hysteria without any trace of anxiety, just as there are cases of simple anxiety-hysteria, which exhibit feelings of anxiety and phobias, but have no admixture of conversion. The case of little Hans is one of the latter sort.

Anxiety-hysterias are the most common of all psychoneurotic disorders. But, above all, they are those which make their appearance earliest in life; they are *par excellence* the neuroses of childhood. When a mother uses such phrases as that her child's "nerves" are in a bad state, we can be certain that in nine cases out of ten the child is suffering from some kind of anxiety or from many kinds at once. Unfortunately the finer mechanism of these highly significant disorders has not yet been sufficiently studied. It has not yet been established whether anxiety-hysteria is determined, in contradistinction to conversion-hysteria and other neuroses, solely by constitutional factors or solely by accidental experiences, or by what combination of the two.[6] It seems to me that of all neurotic disorders it is the least dependent upon a special constitutional predisposition and that it is consequently the most easily acquired at any time of life.

One essential characteristic of anxiety-hysterias is very easily pointed out. An anxiety-hysteria tends to develop more and more into a "phobia." In the end the patient may have got rid of all his anxiety, but only at the price of subjecting himself to all kinds of inhibitions and restrictions. From the outset in anxiety-hysteria the mind is constantly at work in the direction of once more psychically binding the anxiety which has become liberated; but this work can neither bring about a retransformation of the anxiety into libido, nor can it establish any contact with the complexes which were the source of the libido. Nothing is left for it but to cut off access to every possible occasion that might lead to the development of anxiety, by erecting mental barriers in the nature of precautions, inhibitions, or prohibitions; and it is these defensive structures that appear to us in the form of phobias and that constitute to our eyes the essence of the disease.

The treatment of anxiety-hysteria may be said hitherto to have been a purely negative one. Experience has shown that it is impossible to effect the cure of a phobia (and even in certain circumstances dangerous to attempt to do so) by violent means, that is, by first depriving the patient of his defences and then putting him in a situation in which he cannot escape the liberation of his anxiety. Consequently, nothing can be done but to leave the patient to look for protection wherever he thinks he may find it; and he is merely regarded with a not very helpful contempt for his "incomprehensible cowardice."

Little Hans's parents were determined from the very beginning of his illness that he was neither to be laughed at nor bullied, but that access must be obtained to his repressed wishes by means of psycho-analysis. The extraordinary pains taken by Hans's father were rewarded

---

[6](*Footnote added* 1923:) The question which is raised here has not been pursued further. But there is no reason to suppose that anxiety-hysteria is an exception to the rule that both predisposition and experience must cooperate in the aetiology of a neurosis. Rank's view of the effects of the trauma of birth seems to throw special light upon the predisposition to anxiety-hysteria which is so strong in childhood.

by success, and his reports will give us an opportunity of penetrating into the fabric of this type of phobia and of following the course of its analysis.

I think it is not unlikely that the extensive and detailed character of the analysis may have made it somewhat obscure to the reader. I shall therefore begin by giving a brief résumé of it, in which I shall omit all distracting side-issues and shall draw attention to the results as they came to light one after the other.

The first thing we learn is that the outbreak of the anxiety-state was by no means so sudden as appeared at first sight. A few days earlier the child had woken from an anxiety-dream to the effect that his mother had gone away, and that now he had no mother to coax with. This dream alone points to the presence of a repressive process of ominous intensity. We cannot explain it, as we can so many other anxiety-dreams, by supposing that the child had in his dream felt anxiety arising from some somatic cause and had made use of the anxiety for the purpose of fulfilling an unconscious wish which would otherwise have been deeply repressed.[7] We must regard it rather as a genuine punishment and repression dream, and, moreover, as a dream which failed in its function, since the child woke from his sleep in a state of anxiety. We can easily reconstruct what actually occurred in the unconscious. The child dreamt of exchanging endearments with his mother and of sleeping with her; but all the pleasure was transformed into anxiety, and all the ideational content into its opposite. Repression had defeated the purpose of the mechanism of dreaming.

But the beginnings of this psychological situation go back further still. During the preceding summer Hans had had similar moods of mingled longing and apprehension, in which he had said similar things; and at that time they had secured him the advantage of being taken by his mother into her bed. We may assume that since then Hans had been in a state of intensified sexual excitement, the object of which was his mother. The intensity of this excitement was shown by his two attempts at seducing his mother (the second of which occurred just before the outbreak of his anxiety); and he found an incidental channel of discharge for it by masturbating every evening and in that way obtaining gratification. Whether the sudden change-over of this excitement into anxiety took place spontaneously, or as a result of his mother's rejection of his advances, or owing to the accidental revival of earlier impressions by the "precipitating cause" of his illness (about which we shall hear presently)—this we cannot decide; and, indeed, it is a matter of indifference, for these three alternative possibilities cannot be regarded as mutually incompatible. The fact remains that his sexual excitement suddenly changed into anxiety.

We have already described the child's behaviour at the beginning of his anxiety, as well as the first content which he assigned to it, namely, that a horse would bite him. It was at this point that the first piece of therapy was interposed. His parents represented to him that his anxiety was the result of masturbation, and encouraged him to break himself of the habit. I took care that when they spoke to him great stress was laid upon his affection for his mother, for that was what he was trying to replace by his fear of horses. This first intervention brought a slight improvement, but the ground was soon lost again during a period of physical illness. Hans's condition remained unchanged. Soon afterwards he traced back his fear of being bitten by a horse to an impression he had received at Gmunden. A father had addressed his child on her departure with these words of warning: "Don't put your finger to the horse; if you do, it'll bite you." The words, "don't put your finger to," which Hans used in reporting this warning, resembled the form of words in which the warning against masturbation had been framed. It

[7]See my *Interpretation of Dreams* (1900).

seemed at first, therefore, as though Hans's parents were right in supposing that what he was frightened of was his own masturbatory indulgence. But the whole nexus remained loose, and it seemed to be merely by chance that horses had become his bugbear.

I had expressed a suspicion that Hans's repressed wish might now be that he wanted at all costs to see his mother's widdler. As his behaviour to a new maid fitted in with this hypothesis, his father gave him his first piece of enlightenment, namely, that women have no widdlers. He reacted to this first effort at helping him by producing a phantasy that he had seen his mother showing her widdler.[8] This phantasy and a remark made by him in conversation, to the effect that his widdler was "fixed in, of course," allow us our first glimpse into the patient's unconscious mental processes. The fact was that the threat of castration made to him by his mother some fifteen months earlier was now having a deferred effect upon him. For his phantasy that his mother was doing the same as he had done (the familiar *tu quoque* repartee of inculpated children) was intended to serve as a piece of self-justification; it was a protective or defensive phantasy. At the same time we must remark that it was Hans's parents who had extracted from the pathogenic material operating in him the particular theme of his interest in widdlers. Hans followed their lead in this matter, but he had not yet taken any line of his own in the analysis. And no therapeutic success was to be observed. The analysis had passed far away from the subject of horses; and the information that women have no widdlers was calculated, if anything, to increase his concern for the preservation of his own.

Therapeutic success, however, is not our primary aim; we endeavour rather to enable the patient to obtain a conscious grasp of his unconscious wishes. And this we can achieve by working upon the basis of the hints he throws out, and so, with the help of our interpretative technique, presenting the unconscious complex to his consciousness *in our own words*. There will be a certain degree of similarity between that which he hears from us and that which he is looking for, and which, in spite of all resistances, is trying to force its way through to consciousness; and it is this similarity that will enable him to discover the unconscious material. The physician is a step in front of him in knowledge; and the patient follows along his own road, until the two meet at the appointed goal. Beginners in psycho-analysis are apt to assimilate these two events, and to suppose that the moment at which one of the patient's unconscious complexes has become known to *them* is also the moment at which the patient himself recognizes it. They are expecting too much when they think that they will cure the patient by informing him of this piece of knowledge; for he can do no more with the information than make use of it to help himself in discovering the unconscious complex *where it is anchored* in his unconscious. A first success of this sort had now been achieved with Hans. Having partly mastered his castration complex, he was now able to communicate his wishes in regard to his mother. He did so, in what was still a distorted form, by means of the *phantasy of the two giraffes,* one of which was calling out in vain because Hans had taken possession of the other. He represented the "taking possession of" pictorially as "sitting down on." His father recognized the phantasy as a reproduction of a bedroom scene which used to take place in the morning between the boy and his parents; and he quickly stripped the underlying wish of the disguise which it still wore. The boy's father and mother were the two giraffes. The reason for the choice of a giraffe-phantasy for the purposes of disguise was fully explained by a visit that the boy had paid to those same large beasts at Schönbrunn a few days earlier, by the giraffe-drawing, belonging to an earlier period, which had been preserved by

---

[8]The context enables us to add: "and touching it." After all, he himself could not show his widdler without touching it.

his father, and also, perhaps, by an unconscious comparison based upon the giraffe's long, stiff neck.[9] It may be remarked that the giraffe, as being a large animal and interesting on account of its widdler, was a possible competitor with the horse for the role of bugbear; moreover, the fact that both his father and his mother appeared as giraffes offered a hint which had not yet been followed up, as regards the interpretation of the anxiety-horses.

Immediately after the giraffe story Hans produced two minor phantasies: one of his forcing his way into a forbidden space at Schönbrunn, and the other of his smashing a railway-carriage window on the Stadtbahn. In each case the punishable nature of the action was emphasized, and in each his father appeared as an accomplice. Unluckily his father failed to interpret either of these phantasies, so that Hans himself gained nothing from telling them. In an analysis, however, a thing which has not been understood inevitably reappears; like an unlaid ghost, it cannot rest until the mystery has been solved and the spell broken.

There are no difficulties in the way of our understanding these two criminal phantasies. They belonged to Hans's complex of taking possession of his mother. Some kind of vague notion was struggling in the child's mind of something that he might do with his mother by means of which his taking possession of her would be consummated; for this elusive thought he found certain pictorial representations, which had in common the qualities of being violent and forbidden, and the content of which strikes us as fitting in most remarkably well with the hidden truth. We can only say that they were symbolic phantasies of intercourse, and it was no irrelevant detail that his father was represented as sharing in his actions: "I should like," he seems to have been saying, "to be doing something with my mother, something forbidden; I do not know what it is, but I do know that you are doing it too."

The giraffe phantasy strengthened a conviction which had already begun to form in my mind when Hans expressed his fear that "the horse'll come into the room'"; and I thought the right moment had now arrived for informing him that he was afraid of his father because he himself nourished jealous and hostile wishes against him—for it was essential to postulate this much with regard to his unconscious impulses. In telling him this, I had partly interpreted his fear of horses for him: the horse must be his father—whom he had good internal reasons for fearing. Certain details of which Hans had shown he was afraid, the black on horses' mouths and the things in front of their eyes (the moustaches and eyeglasses which are the privilege of a grown-up man), seemed to me to have been directly transposed from his father on to the horses.

By enlightening Hans on this subject I had cleared away his most powerful resistance against allowing his unconscious thoughts to be made conscious; for his father was himself acting as his physician. The worst of the attack was now over; there was a plentiful flow of material; the little patient summoned up courage to describe the details of his phobia, and soon began to take an active share in the conduct of the analysis.[10]

It was only then that we learnt what the objects and impressions were of which Hans was afraid. He was not only afraid of horses biting him—he was soon silent upon that point—but also of carts, of furniture-vans, and of buses (their common quality being, as presently became clear, that they were all heavily loaded), of horses that started moving, of horses that looked big and heavy, and of horses that drove quickly. The meaning of these specifications

[9]Hans's admiration of his father's neck later on would fit in with this.

[10]Even in analyses in which the physician and the patient are strangers, fear of the father plays one of the most important parts as a resistance against the reproduction of the unconscious pathogenic material. Resistances are sometimes in the nature of "motifs." But sometimes, as in the present instance, one piece of the unconscious material is capable from its actual *content* of operating as an inhibition against the reproduction of another piece.

was explained by Hans himself: he was afraid of horses *falling down*, and consequently incorporated in his phobia everything that seemed likely to facilitate their falling down.

It not at all infrequently happens that it is only after doing a certain amount of psycho-analytic work with a patient that an analyst can succeed in learning the actual content of a phobia, the precise form of words of an obsessional impulse, and so on. Repression has not only descended upon the unconscious complexes, but it is continually attacking their derivatives as well, and even prevents the patient from becoming aware of the products of the disease itself. The analyst thus finds himself in the position, curious for a doctor, of coming to the help of a disease, and of procuring it its due of attention. But only those who entirely misunderstand the nature of psycho-analysis will lay stress upon this phase of the work and suppose that on its account harm is likely to be done by analysis. The fact is that you must catch your thief before you can hang him, and that it requires some expenditure of labour to get securely hold of the pathological structures at the destruction of which the treatment is aimed.

I have already remarked in the course of my running commentary on the case history that it is most instructive to plunge in this way into the details of a phobia, and thus arrive at a conviction of the secondary nature of the relation between the anxiety and its objects. It is this that accounts for phobias being at once so curiously diffuse and so strictly conditioned. It is evident that the material for the particular disguises which Hans's fear adopted was collected from the impressions to which he was all day long exposed owing to the Head Customs House being situated on the opposite side of the street. In this connection, too, he showed signs of an impulse—though it was now inhibited by his anxiety—to play with the loads on the carts, with the packages, casks and boxes, like the street-boys.

It was at this stage of the analysis that he recalled the event, insignificant in itself, which immediately preceded the outbreak of the illness and may no doubt be regarded as the precipitating cause of its outbreak. He went for a walk with his mother, and saw a bus-horse fall down and kick about with its feet. This made a great impression on him. He was terrified, and thought the horse was dead; and from that time on he thought that all horses would fall down. His father pointed out to him that when he saw the horse fall down he must have thought of him, his father, and have wished that he might fall down in the same way and be dead. Hans did not dispute this interpretation; and a little while later he played a game consisting of biting his father, and so showed that he accepted the theory of his having identified his father with the horse he was afraid of. From that time forward his behaviour to his father was unconstrained and fearless, and in fact a trifle overbearing. Nevertheless his fear of horses persisted; nor was it yet clear through what chain of associations the horse's falling down had stirred up his unconscious wishes.

Let me summarize the results that had so far been reached. Behind the fear to which Hans first gave expression, the fear of a horse biting him, we had discovered a more deeply seated fear, the fear of horses falling down; and both kinds of horses, the biting horse and the falling horse, had been shown to represent his father, who was going to punish him for the evil wishes he was nourishing against him. Meanwhile the analysis had moved away from the subject of his mother.

Quite unexpectedly, and certainly without any prompting from his father, Hans now began to be occupied with the ''lumf'' complex, and to show disgust at things that reminded him of evacuating his bowels. His father, who was reluctant to go with him along that line, pushed on with the analysis through thick and thin in the direction in which he wanted to go. He elicited from Hans the recollection of an event at Gmunden, the impression of which lay concealed behind that of the falling bus-horse. While they were playing at horses, Fritzl, the playmate of whom he was so fond, but at the same time, perhaps, his rival with his many girl friends, had hit his foot against a stone and had fallen down, and his foot had bled. Seeing the bus-horse fall had reminded him of this accident. It deserves to be noticed that Hans, who was at the moment concerned with other things, began by denying that Fritzl had fallen down (though this was the event which formed the connection between the two scenes) and only admitted it at a later stage of the analysis. It is especially interesting, however, to observe the way in which the transformation of Hans's libido into anxiety was projected on to the principal object of his phobia, on to horses. Horses interested him the most of all the large animals; playing at horses was his favourite game with the other children. I had a suspicion—and this was confirmed by Hans's father when I asked him—that the first person who had served Hans as a horse must have been his father; and it was this that had enabled him to regard Fritzl as a substitute for his father when the accident happened at Gmunden. When repression had set in and brought a revulsion of feeling along with it, horses, which had till then been associated with so much pleasure, were necessarily turned into objects of fear.

But, as we have already said, it was owing to the intervention of Hans's father that this last important discovery was made of the way in which the precipitating cause of the illness had operated. Hans himself was occupied with his lumf interests, and thither at last we must follow him. We learn that formerly Hans had been in the habit of insisting upon accompanying his mother to the W. C., and that he had revived this custom with his friend Berta at a time when she was filling his mother's place, until the fact became known and he was forbidden to do so. Pleasure taken in looking on while some one one loves performs the natural functions is once more a "confluence of instincts," of which we have already noticed an instance in Hans. In the end his father went into the lumf symbolism, and recognized that there was an analogy between a heavily loaded cart and a body loaded with faeces, between the way in which a cart drives out through a gateway and the way in which faeces leave the body, and so on.

By this time, however, the position occupied by Hans in the analysis had become very different from what it had been at an earlier stage. Previously, his father had been able to tell him in advance what was coming, while Hans had merely followed his lead and come trotting after; but now it was Hans who was forging ahead, so rapidly and steadily that his father found it difficult to keep up with him. Without any warning, as it were, Hans produced a new phantasy: the plumber unscrewed the bath in which Hans was, and then stuck him in the stomach with his big borer. Henceforward the material brought up in the analysis far outstripped our powers of understanding it. It was not until later that it was possible to guess that this was a remoulding of a *phantasy of procreation,* distorted by anxiety. The big bath of water, in which Hans imagined himself, was his mother's womb; the "borer," which his father had from the first recognized as a penis, owed its mention to its connection with "being born." The interpretation that we are obliged to give to the phantasy will of course sound very curious. "With your big penis you 'bored' me" (i.e., "gave birth to me") "and put me in my mother's womb." For the moment, however, the phantasy eluded interpretation, and merely served Hans as a starting-point from which to continue giving information.

Hans showed fear of being given a bath in the big bath; and this fear was once more a composite one. One part of it escaped us as yet, but the other part could at once be elucidated in connection with his baby sister having her bath. Hans confessed to having wished that his mother might drop the child while she was being given her bath, so that she should die. His own anxiety while he was having his bath was a fear of retribution for this evil wish and of being punished by the same thing happening to him. Hans now left the subject of lumf and passed on directly to that of his baby sister. We may well imagine what this juxtaposition signified: nothing less, in fact, than that little Hanna was a lumf herself—that all babies were lumfs and were born like lumfs. We can now recognize that all furniture-vans and drays and buses were only stork-box carts, and were only of interest to Hans as being symbolic representations of pregnancy; and that when a heavy or heavily loaded horse fell down he can have seen in it only one thing—a childbirth, a delivery. Thus the falling horse was not only his dying father but also his mother in childbirth.

And at this point Hans gave us a surprise, for which we were not in the very least prepared. He had noticed his mother's pregnancy, which had ended with the birth of his little sister when he was three and a half years old, and had, at any rate after the confinement, pieced the facts of the case together—without telling any one, it is true, and perhaps without being able to tell any one. All that could be seen at the time was that immediately after the delivery he had taken up an extremely sceptical attitude towards everything that might be supposed to point to the presence of the stork. *But that—in complete contradiction to his official speeches —he knew in his unconscious where the baby came from and where it had been before,* is proved beyond a shadow of doubt by the present analysis; indeed, this is perhaps its most unassailable feature.

The most cogent evidence of this is furnished by the phantasy (which he persisted in with so much obstinacy, and embellished with such a wealth of detail) of how Hanna had been with them at Gmunden the summer before her birth, of how she had travelled there with them, and of how she had been able to do far more then than she had a year later, after she had been born. The effrontery with which Hans related this phantasy and the countless extravagant lies with which he interwove it were anything but meaningless. All of this was intended as a revenge upon his father, against whom he harboured a grudge for having misled him with the stork fable. It was just as though he had meant to say: "If you really thought I was as stupid as all that, and expected me to believe that the stork brought Hanna, then in return I expect *you* to accept *my* inventions as the truth." This act of revenge on the part of our young enquirer upon his father was succeeded by the clearly correlated phantasy of teasing and beating horses. This phantasy, again, had two constituents. On the one hand, it was based upon the teasing to which he had submitted his father just before; and, on the other hand, it reproduced the obscure sadistic desires directed towards his mother, which had already found expression (though they had not at first been understood) in his phantasies of doing something forbidden. Hans even confessed consciously to a desire to beat his mother.

There are not many more mysteries ahead of us now. An obscure phantasy of missing a train seems to have been a forerunner of the later notion of handing over Hans's father to his grandmother at Lainz, for the phantasy dealt with a visit to Lainz, and his grandmother appeared in it. Another phantasy, in which a boy gave the guard 50,000 florins to let him ride on the truck, almost sounds like a plan of buying his mother from his father, part of whose power, of course, lay in his wealth. At about this time, too, he confessed, with a degree of openness which he had never before reached, that he wished to get rid of his father, and that the reason he wished it was that his father interfered with his own intimacy with his mother. We must not be surprised to find the same wishes constantly reappearing in the course of an analysis. The monotony only attaches to the analyst's interpretations of these wishes. For Hans they were not mere repetitions, but steps in a progressive development from timid hinting to fully conscious, undistorted perspicuity.

What remains are just such confirmations on Hans's part of analytical conclusions which our interpretations had already established. In an entirely unequivocal symptomatic act, which he disguised slightly from the maid but not at all from his father, he showed how he imagined a birth took place; but if we look into it more closely we can see that he showed something else, that he was hinting at something which was not alluded to again in the analysis. He pushed a small penknife which belonged to his mother in through a round hole in the body of an india-rubber doll, and then let it drop out again by tearing apart the doll's legs. The enlightenment which he received from his parents soon afterwards, to the effect that children do in fact grow inside their mother's body and are pushed out of it like a lumf, came too late; it could tell him nothing new. Another symptomatic act, happening as though by accident, involved a confession that he had wished his father dead; for, just at the moment his father was talking of this death-wish, Hans let a horse that he was playing with fall down—knocked it over in fact. Further, he confirmed in so many words the hypothesis that heavily loaded carts represented his mother's pregnancy to him, and the horse's falling down was like having a baby. The most delightful piece of confirmation in this connection—a proof that, in his view, children were "lumfs"—was his inventing the name of "Lodi" for his favourite child. There was some delay in reporting this fact, for it then appeared that he had been playing with this sausage child of his for a long time past.[11]

We have already considered Hans's two concluding phantasies, with which his recovery was rounded off. One of them, that of the plumber giving him a new and, as his father guessed, a bigger widdler, was not merely a repetition of the earlier phantasy concerning the plumber and the bath. The new one was a triumphant, wishful phantasy, and with it he overcame his fear of castration. His other phantasy, which confessed to the wish to be married to his mother and to have many children by her, did not merely exhaust the content of the unconscious complexes which had been stirred up by the sight of the falling horse and which had generated his anxiety. It also corrected that portion of those thoughts which was entirely unacceptable; for, instead of killing his father, it made him innocuous by promoting him to a marriage with Hans's grandmother. With this phantasy both the illness and the analysis came to an appropriate end.

While the analysis of a case is in progress it is impossible to obtain any clear impression of the structure and development of the neurosis. That is the business of a synthetic process which must be performed subsequently. In attempting to carry out such a synthesis of little Hans's phobia we shall take as our basis the account of his mental constitution, of his governing sexual wishes, and of his experiences up to the time of his sister's birth, which we have given in an earlier part of this paper.

The arrival of his sister brought into Hans's life many new elements, which from that time on gave him no rest. In the first place he was obliged to submit to a certain degree of privation: to begin with, a temporary separation from his mother, and later a permanent diminution in the amount of care and attention which he had received from her and which thenceforward he had to grow accustomed to sharing with his sister. In the second place, he experienced a revival of the pleasures he had enjoyed when he was looked after as an infant; for they were called up by all that he saw his mother doing for the baby. As a result of these two influences his erotic needs became intensified, while at the same time they began to obtain insufficient satisfaction. He made up for the loss which his sister's arrival had entailed on him by imagining that he had children of his own; and so long as he was at Gmunden—on his second visit there—and could really play with these children, he found a sufficient outlet for his affections. But after his return to Vienna he was once more alone, and set all his hopes upon his mother. He had meanwhile suffered another privation, having been exiled from his

---

[11]I remember a set of drawings by T. T. Heine in a copy of *Simplicissimus*, in which that brilliant illustrator depicted the fate of the pork-butcher's child, who fell into the sausage machine, and then, in the shape of a small sausage, was mourned over by his parents, received the Church's blessing, and flew up to Heaven. The artist's idea seems a puzzling one at first, but the Lodi episode in this analysis enables us to trace it back to its infantile root.

parents' bedroom at the age of four and a half. His intensified erotic excitability now found expression in phantasies, by which in his loneliness he conjured up his playmates of the past summer, and in regular auto-erotic satisfaction obtained by a masturbatory stimulation of his genitals.

But in the third place his sister's birth stimulated him to an effort of thought which, on the one hand, it was impossible to bring to a conclusion, and which, on the other hand, involved him in emotional conflicts. He was faced with the great riddle of where babies come from, which is perhaps the first problem to engage a child's mental powers, and of which the riddle of the Theban Sphinx is probably no more than a distorted version. He rejected the proffered solution of the stork having brought Hanna. For he had noticed that months before the baby's birth his mother's body had grown big, and then she had gone to bed, and had groaned while the birth was taking place, and that when she got up she was thin again. He therefore inferred that Hanna had been inside his mother's body, and had then come out like a "lumf." He was able to imagine the act of giving birth as a pleasurable one by relating it to his own first feelings of pleasure in passing stool; and he was thus able to find a double motive for wishing to have children of his own: the pleasure of giving birth to them and the pleasure (the compensatory pleasure, as it were) of looking after them. There was nothing in all of this that could have led him into doubts or conflicts.

But there was something else, which could not fail to make him uneasy. His father must have had something to do with little Hanna's birth, for he had declared that Hanna and Hans himself were his children. Yet it was certainly not his father who had brought them into the world, but his mother. This father of his came between him and his mother. When he was there Hans could not sleep with his mother, and when his mother wanted to take Hans into bed with her, his father used to call out. Hans had learnt from experience how well-off he could be in his father's absence, and it was only justifiable that he should wish to get rid of him. And then Hans's hostility had received a fresh reinforcement. His father had told him the lie about the stork and so made it impossible for him to ask for enlightenment upon these things. He not only prevented his being in bed with his mother, but also kept from him the knowledge he was thirsting for. He was putting Hans at a disadvantage in both directions, and was obviously doing so for his own benefit.

But his father, whom he could not help hating as a rival, was the same father whom he had always loved and was bound to go on loving, who had been his model, had been his first playmate, and had looked after him from his earliest infancy: and this it was that gave rise to the first conflict. Nor could this conflict find an immediate solution. For Hans's nature had so developed that for the moment his love could not but keep the upper hand and suppress his hate—though it could not kill it, for his hate was perpetually kept alive by his love for his mother.

But his father not only knew where children came from, he actually performed it—the thing that Hans could only obscurely divine. The widdler must have something to do with it, for his own grew excited whenever he thought of these things—and it must be a big widdler too, bigger than Hans's own. If he listened to these premonitory sensations he could only suppose that it was a question of some act of violence performed upon his mother, of smashing something, of making an opening into something, of forcing a way into an enclosed space—such were the impulses that he felt stirring within him. But although the sensations of his penis had put him on the road to postulating a vagina, yet he could not solve the problem, for within his experience no such thing existed as his widdler required. On the contrary, his conviction that his mother possessed a penis just as he did stood in the way of any solution. His attempt at discovering what it was that had to be done with his mother in order that she might have children sank down into his unconscious; and his two active impulses—the hostile one towards his father and the sadistic-tender one towards his mother—could be put to no use, the first because of the love that existed side by side with the hatred, and the second because of the perplexity in which his infantile sexual theories left him.

This is how, basing my conclusions upon the findings of the analysis, I am obliged to reconstruct the unconscious complexes and wishes, the repression and reawakening of which produced little Hans's phobia. I am aware that in so doing I am attributing a great deal to the mental capacity of a child between four and five years of age; but I have let myself be guided by what we have recently learned, and I do not consider myself bound by the prejudices of our ignorance. It might perhaps have been possible to make use of Hans's fear of the "making a row with the legs" for filling up a few more gaps in our adjudication upon the evidence. Hans, it is true, declared that it reminded him of his kicking about with his legs when he was compelled to leave off playing so as to do lumf; so that this element of the neurosis becomes connected with the problem whether his mother liked having children or was compelled to have them. But I have an impression that this is not the whole explanation of the "making a row with the legs." Hans's father was unable to confirm my suspicion that there was some recollection stirring in the child's mind of having observed a scene of sexual intercourse between his parents in their bedroom. So let us be content with what we have discovered.

It is hard to say what the influence was which, in the situation we have just sketched, led to the sudden change in Hans and to the transformation of his libidinal longing into anxiety —to say from what direction it was the repression set in. The question could probably only be decided by making a comparison between this analysis and a number of similar ones. Whether the scales were turned by the child's *intellectual* inability to solve the difficult problem of the begetting of children and to cope with the aggressive impulses that were liberated by his approaching its solution, or whether the effect was produced by a *somatic* incapacity, a constitutional intolerance of the masturbatory gratification in which he regularly indulged (whether, that is, the mere persistence of sexual excitement at such a high pitch of intensity was bound to bring about a revulsion)—this question must be left open until fresh experience can come to our assistance.

Chronological considerations make it impossible for us to attach any great importance to the actual precipitating cause of the outbreak of Hans's illness, for he had shown signs of apprehensiveness long before he saw the bus-horse fall down in the street.

Nevertheless, the neurosis took its start directly from this chance event and preserved a trace of it in the circumstance of the horse being exalted into the object of his anxiety. In itself the impression of the accident which he happened to witness carried no "traumatic force"; it acquired its great effectiveness only from the fact that horses had formerly been of importance to him as objects of his predilection and interest, from the fact that he associated the event in his mind with an earlier event at Gmunden which had more claim to be regarded as traumatic, namely with Fritzl's falling down while he was playing at horses, and lastly from the fact that there was an easy path of association from Fritzl to his father. Indeed, even these connections would probably not have been sufficient if it had not been that, thanks to the pliability and ambiguity of associative chains, the same event showed itself capable of stirring the second of the complexes that lurked in Hans's unconscious, the complex of his pregnant mother's confinement. From that moment the way was clear for the return of the repressed; and it returned in such a manner that *the pathogenic material was remodelled and transposed on to the horse-complex, while the accompanying effects were uniformly turned into anxiety*.

It deserves to be noticed that the ideational content of Hans's phobia as it then stood had to be submitted to one further process of distortion and substitution before his consciousness took cognizance of it. Hans's first formulation of his anxiety was: "the horse will bite me"; and this was derived from another episode at Gmunden, which was on the one hand related to his hostile wishes towards his father and on the other hand was reminiscent of the warning he had been given against masturbation. Some interfering influence, emanating from his parents perhaps, had made itself felt. I am not certain whether the reports upon Hans were at that time drawn up with sufficient care to enable us to decide whether he expressed his anxiety in this form *before* or not until *after* his mother had taken him to task on the subject of masturbating. I should be inclined to suspect that it was not until afterwards, though this would contradict the account given in the case history. At any rate, it is evident that at every point Hans's hostile complex against his father screened his lustful one about his mother, just as it was the first to be disclosed and dealt with in the analysis.

In other cases of this kind there would be a great deal more to be said upon the structure, the development, and the diffusion of the neurosis. But the history of little Hans's attack was very short; almost as soon as it had begun, its place was taken by the history of its treatment. And although during the treatment the phobia appeared to develop further and to extend over new objects and to lay down new conditions, his father, since he was himself treating the case, naturally had sufficient penetration to see that it was merely a question of the emergence of material that was already in existence, and not of fresh productions for which the treatment might be held responsible. In the treatment of other cases it would not always be possible to count upon so much penetration.

Before I can regard this synthesis as completed I must turn to yet another aspect of the case, which will take us into the very heart of the difficulties that lie in the way of our understanding of neurotic states. We have seen how our little patient was overtaken by a great wave of repression and that it caught precisely those of his sexual components that were dominant.[12] He gave up masturbation, and turned away in disgust from everything that reminded him of excrement and of looking on at other people performing their natural functions. But these were not the components which were stirred up by the precipitating cause of the illness (his seeing the horse fall down) or which provided the material for the symptoms, that is, the content of the phobia.

This allows us, therefore, to make a radical distinction. We shall probably come to understand the case more deeply if we turn to those other components which *do* fulfil the two conditions that have just been mentioned. These other components were tendencies in Hans which had already been suppressed and which, so far as we can tell, had never been able to find uninhibited expression: hostile and jealous feelings towards his father, and sadistic impulses (premonitions, as it were, of copulation) towards his mother. These early suppressions may perhaps have gone to form the predisposition for his subsequent illness. These aggressive propensities of Hans's found no outlet, and as soon as there came a time of privation and of intensified sexual excitement, they tried to break their way out with reinforced strength. It was then that the battle which we call his "phobia" burst out. During the course of it a part of the repressed ideas, in a distorted form and transposed on to another complex, forced their way into consciousness as the content of the phobia. But it was a decidedly paltry success. Victory lay with the forces of repression; *and they made use of the*

---

[12]Hans's father even observed that simultaneously with this repression a certain amount of sublimation set in. From the time of the beginning of his anxiety Hans began to show an increased interest in music and to develop his inherited musical gift.

opportunity to extend their dominion over components other than those that had rebelled. This last circumstance, however, does not in the least alter the fact that the essence of Hans's illness was entirely dependent upon the nature of the instinctual components that had to be repulsed. The content of his phobia was such as to impose a very great measure of restriction upon his freedom of movement, and that was its purpose. It was therefore a powerful reaction against the obscure impulses to movement which were especially directed against his mother. For Hans horses had always typified pleasure in movement (''I'm a young horse,'' he had said as he jumped about); but since this pleasure in movement included the impulse to copulate, the neurosis imposed a restriction on it and exalted the horse into an emblem of terror. Thus it would seem as though all that the repressed instincts got from the neurosis was the honour of providing pretexts for the appearance of the anxiety in consciousness. But however clear may have been the victory in Hans's phobia of the forces that were opposed to sexuality, nevertheless, since such an illness is in its very nature a compromise, this cannot have been all that the repressed instincts obtained. After all, Hans's phobia of horses was an obstacle to his going into the street, and could serve as a means of allowing him to stay at home with his beloved mother. In this way, therefore, his affection for his mother triumphantly achieved its aim. In consequence of his phobia, the lover clung to the object of his love—though, to be sure, steps had been taken to make him innocuous. The true character of a neurotic disorder is exhibited in this twofold result.

Alfred Adler, in a suggestive paper,[13] has recently developed the view that anxiety arises from the suppression of what he calls the ''aggressive instinct,'' and by a very sweeping synthetic process he ascribes to that instinct the chief part in human events, ''in real life and in the neuroses.'' As we have come to the conclusion that in our present case of phobia the anxiety is to be explained as being due to the repression of Hans's aggressive propensities (the hostile ones against his father and the sadistic ones against his mother), we seem to have produced a most striking piece of confirmation of Adler's view. I am nevertheless unable to assent to it, and indeed I regard it as a misleading generalization. I cannot bring myself to assume the existence of a special aggressive instinct alongside of the familiar instincts of self-preservation and of sex, and on an equal footing with them.[14] It appears to me that Adler has mistakenly promoted into a special and self-subsisting instinct what is in reality a universal and indispensable attribute of *all* instincts—their instinctual [*triebhaft*] and ''pressing'' character, what might be described as their capacity for initiating movement. Nothing would then remain of the other instincts but their relation to an aim, for their relation to the means of reaching that aim would have been taken over from them by the ''aggressive instinct.'' In spite of all the uncertainty and obscurity of our theory of instincts I should prefer for the present to adhere to the usual view, which leaves each instinct its own power of becoming aggressive; and I should be inclined to recognize the two instincts which became repressed in Hans as familiar components of the sexual libido.

---

[13]''Der Aggressionsbetrieb im Leben und in der Neurose,'' 1908. This is the same paper from which I have borrowed the term ''confluence of instincts.'' (See above, p. 9.)

[14](*Footnote added* 1923:) The above passage was written at a time when Adler seemed still to be taking his stand upon the ground of psycho-analysis, and before he had put forward the masculine protest and disavowed repression. Since then I have myself been obliged to assert the existence of an ''aggressive instinct,'' but it is different from Adler's. I prefer to call it the ''destructive'' or ''death instinct.'' See *Beyond the Pleasure Principle* (1920) and *The Ego and the Id* (1923). Its opposition to the libidinal instincts finds an expression in the familiar polarity of love and hate. My disagreement with Adler's view, which results in a universal characteristic of instincts in general being reduced to be the property of a single one of them, remains unaltered.

(III)

I shall now proceed to what I hope will be a brief discussion of how far little Hans's phobia offers any contribution of general importance to our views upon the life and upbringing of children. But before doing so I must return to the objection which has so long been held over, and according to which Hans was a neurotic, a "degenerate" with a bad heredity, and not a normal child, knowledge about whom could be applied to other children. I have for some time been thinking with pain of the way in which the adherents of "the normal person" will fall upon poor little Hans as soon as they are told that he can in fact be shown to have had a hereditary taint. His beautiful mother fell ill with neurosis as a result of a conflict during her girlhood. I was able to be of assistance to her at the time, and this had in fact been the beginning of my connection with Hans's parents. It is only with the greatest diffidence that I venture to bring forward one or two considerations in his favour.

In the first place Hans was not what one would understand, strictly speaking, by a degenerate child, condemned by his heredity to be a neurotic. On the contrary, he was well formed physically, and was a cheerful, amiable, active-minded young fellow who might give pleasure to more people than his own father. There can be no question, of course, as to his sexual precocity; but on that point there is very little material upon which a fair comparison can be based. I gather, for instance, from a piece of collective research conducted in America, that it is by no means such a rare thing to find object-choice and feelings of love in boys at a similarly early age; and the same may be learnt from studying the records of the childhood of men who have later come to be recognized as "great." I should therefore be inclined to believe that sexual precocity is a correlate, which is seldom absent, of intellectual precocity, and that it is therefore to be met with in gifted children more often than might be expected.

Furthermore, let me say in Hans's favour (and I frankly admit my partisan attitude) that he is not the only child who has been overtaken by a phobia at some time or other in his childhood. Troubles of that kind are well known to be quite extraordinarily frequent, even in children the strictness of whose upbringing has left nothing to be desired. In later life these children either become neurotic or remain healthy. Their phobias are shouted down in the nursery because they are inaccessible to treatment and are decidedly inconvenient. In the course of months or years they diminish, and the child seems to recover; but no one can tell what psychological changes are necessitated by such a recovery, or what alterations in character are involved in it. When, however, an adult neurotic patient comes to us for psycho-analytic treatment (and let us assume that his illness has only become manifest after he has reached maturity), we find regularly that his neurosis has as its point of departure an infantile anxiety such as we have been discussing, and is in fact a continuation of it; so that, as it were, a continuous and undisturbed threat of psychical activity, taking its start from the conflicts of his childhood, has been spun through his life—irrespective of whether the first symptom of those conflicts has persisted or has retreated under the pressure of circumstances. I think, therefore, that Hans's illness may perhaps have been no more serious than that of many other children who are not branded as "degenerates"; but since he was brought up without being intimidated, and with as much consideration and as little coercion as possible, his anxiety dared to show itself more boldly. With him there was no place for such motives as a bad conscience or a fear of punishment, which with other children must no doubt contribute to making the anxiety less. It seems to me that we concentrate too much upon symptoms and concern ourselves too little with their causes. In bringing up children we aim only at being left in peace and having no difficulties, in short, at training up a model child, and we pay very little attention to whether such a course of development is for the child's good as well. I can therefore quite imagine that it may have been to Hans's advantage to have produced this phobia. For it directed his parents' attention to the unavoidable difficulties by which a child is confronted when in the course of his cultural training he is called upon to overcome the innate instinctual components of his mind; and his trouble brought his father to his assistance. It may be that Hans now enjoys an advantage over other children, in that he no longer carries within him that seed in the shape of repressed complexes which must always be of some significance for a child's later life, and which undoubtedly brings with it a certain degree of deformity of character if not a predisposition to a subsequent neurosis. I am inclined to think that this is so, but I do not know if many others will share my opinion; nor do I know whether experience will prove me right.

But I must now enquire what harm was done to Hans by dragging to light in him complexes such as are not only repressed by children but dreaded by their parents. Did the little boy proceed to take some serious action as regards what he wanted from his mother? Or did his evil intentions against his father give place to evil deeds? Such misgivings will no doubt have occurred to many doctors, who misunderstand the nature of psycho-analysis and think that wicked instincts are strengthened by being made conscious. Wise men like these are being no more than consistent when they implore us for heaven's sake not to meddle with the evil things that lurk behind a neurosis. In so doing they forget, it is true, that they are physicians, and their words bear a fatal resemblance to Dogberry's, when he advised the Watch to avoid all contact with any thieves they might happen to meet: "for such kind of men, the less you meddle or make with them, why, the more is for your honesty."[15]

On the contrary, the only results of the analysis were that Hans recovered, that he ceased to be afraid of horses, and that he got on to rather familiar terms with his father, as the latter reported with some amusement. But whatever his father may have lost in the boy's respect he won back in his confidence: "I thought," said Hans, "you knew everything, as you knew that about the horse." For analysis does not undo the *effects* of repression. The instincts which were formerly suppressed remain suppressed; but the same effect is produced in a different way. Analysis replaces the process of repression, which is an automatic and excessive one, by a temperate and purposeful control on the part of the highest agencies of the mind. In a word, *analysis replaces repression by condemnation.* This seems to bring us the long-looked-for evidence that consciousness has a biological function, and that with its entrance upon the scene an important advantage is secured.[16]

If matters had lain entirely in my hands, I should have ventured to give the child the one remaining piece of enlightenment which his parents withheld from him. I should have confirmed his instinctive premonitions, by telling him of the existence of the vagina and of copulation; thus I should have still further diminished his unsolved residue, and put an end to his stream of questions. I am convinced that this new piece of enlightenment would have made him lose neither his love for his mother nor his own childish nature, and that he would have

---

[15][*Much Ado about Nothing, III, 3.*] At this point I cannot keep back an astonished question. Where do my opponents obtain their knowledge, which they produce with so much confidence, on the question whether the repressed sexual instincts play a part, and if so what part, in the aetiology of the neuroses, if they shut their patients' mouths as soon as they begin to talk about their complexes or their derivatives? For the only alternative source of knowledge remaining open to them are my own writings and those of my adherents.

[16](*Footnote added* 1923:) I am here using the word "consciousness" in a sense which I later avoided, namely, to describe our normal processes of thought—such, that is, as are capable of consciousness. We know that thought processes of this kind may also take place *preconsciously;* and it is wiser to regard their actual "consciousness" from a purely phenomenological standpoint. By this I do not, of course, mean to contradict the expectation that consciousness in this more limited sense of the word must also fulfil some biological function.

understood that his preoccupation with these important, these momentous things must rest for the present—until his wish to be big had been fulfilled. But the educational experiment was not carried so far.

That no sharp line can be drawn between "neurotic" and "normal" people—whether children or adults—that our conception of "disease" is a purely practical one and a question of summation, that predisposition and the eventualities of life must combine before the threshold of this summation is overstepped, and that consequently a number of individuals are constantly passing from the class of healthy people into that of neurotic patients, while a far smaller number also make the journey in the opposite direction,—all of these are things which have been said so often and have met with so much agreement that I am certainly not alone in maintaining their truth. It is, to say the least of it, extremely probable that a child's upbringing can exercise a powerful influence for good or for evil upon the predisposition which we have just mentioned as one of the factors in the occurrence of "disease"; but what that upbringing is to aim at and at what point it is to be brought to bear seem at present to be very doubtful questions. Hitherto education has only set itself the task of controlling, or, it would often be more proper to say, of suppressing, the instincts. The results have been by no means gratifying, and where the process has succeeded it has only been to the advantage of a small number of favoured individuals who have not been required to suppress their instincts. Nor has any one inquired by what means and at what cost the suppression of the inconvenient instincts has been achieved. Supposing now that we substitute another task for this one, and aim instead at making the individual capable of becoming a civilized and useful member of society with the least possible sacrifice of his own activity; in that case the information gained by psycho-analysis, upon the origin of pathogenic complexes and upon the nucleus of every nervous affection, can claim with justice that it deserves to be regarded by educators as an invaluable guide in their conduct towards children. What practical conclusions may follow from this, and how far experience may justify the application of those conclusions within our present social system, are matters which I leave to the examination and decision of others.

I cannot take leave of our small patient's phobia without giving expression to a notion which has made its analysis, leading as it did to a recovery, seem of especial value to me. Strictly speaking, I learnt nothing new from this analysis, nothing that I had not already been able to discover (though often less distinctly and more indirectly) from other patients analysed at a more advanced age. But the neuroses of these other patients could in every instance be traced back to the same infantile complexes that were revealed behind Hans's phobia. I am therefore tempted to claim for this neurosis of childhood the significance of being a type and a model, and to suppose that the multiplicity of the phenomena of repression exhibited by neuroses and the abundance of their pathogenic material do not prevent their being derived from a very limited number of processes concerned with identical ideational complexes.

REFERENCES

Freud, S. The interpretation of dreams. 1900, *4–5.*
Freud, S. Three essays on the theory of sexuality. 1905, *7,* 125.
Freud, S. Beyond the pleasure principle. 1920, *18.*
Freud, S. The ego and the id. 1923a, *19.*
Freud, S. The infantile genital organization of the libido. 1923b, *19.*
Freud, S. The origins of psycho-analysis. 1950, *1.*
All in S. Freud, *The standard edition of the complete psychological works,* J. Strachey (Ed.). London: Hogarth Press, 1953-66.

Calvin Hall and Robert L. Van de Castle
AN EMPIRICAL INVESTIGATION
OF THE CASTRATION COMPLEX

According to the classical theory of the castration complex as it was formulated by Freud (1925; 1931; 1933), the male is afraid of losing his penis (castration anxiety) and the female envies the male for having a penis (penis envy). One consequence of this envy is that she wants to deprive the male of his organ (castration wish).

The empirical work investigating this topic has generally produced results consistent with Freud's formulation. Hattendorf (1932) indicated that the second most frequent question asked of mothers by children in the two- to five-year-old group concerned the physical differences between the sexes. Horney (1932) reported that when a clinic doctor tried to induce boys and girls to insert a finger in a ball that had developed a split, significantly more boys than girls hesitated or refused to accede to this request. Using a doll-play interview, Conn (1940) noted that two-thirds of children who reported that they had seen the genitals of the opposite sex could not recall their attitude or feelings about the initial discovery and over one-third who could recall their attitude definitely felt something was wrong. On the basis of these results the author concludes (Conn, 1940, p. 754), "It appears that the large majority of boys and girls responded to the first sight of genital differences with tranquil, unperturbed acceptance." This conclusion was criticized by Levy (1940) who carried out repeated doll-play interviews with children and concluded (p. 762), "The typical response of the child in our culture, when he becomes aware of the primary difference in sex anatomy, confirms the psychoanalyst's finding, namely, that castration anxiety is aroused in boys and a feeling of envy with destructive impulse toward the penis in girls." In a widely quoted review of psychoanalytic studies by Sears (1943) a few years later he summed up the castration studies with the statement (p. 36), "Freud seriously overestimated the frequency of the castration complex." In a study of problem children, Huschka (1944) reported that 73 per cent of parents dealt with masturbation problems destructively and that the most common threat was that of genital injury. The normal children used by Friedman (1952) completed stories involving castration situations and the author interpreted his data as offering support for the commonness of castration anxiety, particularly in the case of boys.

The remaining studies used college students as Ss. Blum (1949) found significantly more responses to the Blacky Test indicative of castration anxiety among males than females. A method of scoring castration anxiety from TAT scores was developed by Schwartz (1955)

From C. Hall and R. L. Van de Castle, "An Empirical Investigation of the Castration Complex in Dreams," *Journal of Personality*, 1965, *33*, 20–29. Reprinted by permission of the Duke University Press.

who found (1956) that male homosexuals displayed significantly more castration anxiety than normal males and that males obtained higher castration-anxiety scores than females. Using a multiple-choice question about the castration card of the Blacky, Sarnoff and Corwin (1959) reported that males with high castration scores showed a significantly greater increase in fear of death than low-castration males did after being exposed to sexually arousing stimuli.

The foregoing studies indicate that techniques designed to elicit unconscious material are generally successful in demonstrating the manifestations of the castration complex that would be predictable from Freudian theory. It should follow, then, that since dreams have been characterized as "the royal road to the unconscious," manifestations of the castration complex would be clearly discernible in dreams. The present study was undertaken to investigate whether differences in dream contents, presumably related to castration reactions, would appear between adult male and female dreamers.

The specific hypothesis tested in this investigation is that male dreamers will report more dreams expressive of castration anxiety than they will dreams involving castration wishes and penis envy while the pattern will be reversed for females, i.e., they will report more dreams containing expressions of castration wishes and penis envy than they will dreams containing castration anxiety.

METHOD

Subjects

A total of 120 college students divided into three groups of 20 males and 20 females each served as *S*s. Groups 1 and 2 were students in Hall's undergraduate class in personality at Western Reserve University during 1947 and 1948. The recording of nocturnal dreams was described to the students as a class project for which they would be given extra credit if they participated but would not be penalized for not doing so. They were given opportunities to earn extra credit in other ways than recording dreams. Dreams were reported on a standard report form. These dreams have been published in *Primary Records in Psychology* (Barker & Kaplan, 1963) and Groups 1 and 2 consist of the first 40 of the 43 female series and the first 40 of the 44 male series reported therein.

Group 3 were students in Van de Castle's class in abnormal psychology at the University of Denver during 1962 and 1963. They were required to hand in an average of two dreams a week. Standard instructions similar to those on Hall's form were given. Students were allowed to turn in daydreams if they could recall no nocturnal dreams, but only nocturnal dreams were scored in this study.

Scoring for Castration Complex Indicators in Dreams

A scoring manual which sets forth the criteria for castration anxiety (CA), castration wish (CW), and penis envy (PE) in reported dreams was devised. These criteria were selected because either they reflect concern over castration directly or they represent displacements from one part of the body, i.e., the genitals, to another part of the body, e.g., the hand, or they make use of commonly recognized symbols for the male genitals, e.g., guns, knives, and pens. Copies of a revised version of the original manual (Institute of Dream Research, 1964) are available on request to the authors. A summary of the criteria follows.

Criteria for Castration Anxiety

1. Actual or threatened loss, removal, injury to, or pain in a specific part of the dreamer's body; actual or threatened cutting, clawing, biting, or stabbing of the dreamer's body as a whole or to any part of the dreamer's body; defect of a specified part of the dreamer's body; some part of the dreamer's body is infantile, juvenile, or undersized.

2. Actual or threatened injury or damage to, loss of, or defect in an object or animal belonging to the dreamer or one that is in his possession in the dream.

3. Inability or difficulty of the dreamer in using his penis or an object that has phallic characteristics; inability or difficulty of the dreamer in placing an object in a receptacle.

4. A male dreams that he is a woman or changes into a woman, or has or acquires female secondary sex characteristics, or is wearing woman's clothes or accessories.

Criteria for Castration Wish

The criteria for castration wish are the same as those for castration anxiety except that they do not occur to the dreamer but to another person in his dream.

Criteria for Penis Envy

1. Acquisition *within* the dream by the dreamer of an object that has phallic characteristics; acquisition of a better penis or an impressive phallic object.

2. The dreamer envies or admires a man's physical characteristics or performance or possession that has phallic characteristics.

3. A female dreams that she is a man or changes into a man, or has acquired male secondary sex characteristics, or is wearing men's clothing or accessories which are not customarily worn by women.

Each dream was read and scored for each of these criteria. The maximum score was one point for each condition, even if several independent instances of the same condition occurred within the dream. It was possible, however, for the same dream to be scored for more than one condition, e.g., a dream could be given one point for CA and one point for PE.

After the writers had acquired practice in the use of the manual, a reliability study was made. The 119 dreams of eight males and 123 dreams of eight females were scored independently by the writers. The scores were then compared. An agreement was counted if both judges scored the same condition, e.g., castration anxiety, in the same dream or both judges did not score a condition, e.g., penis envy, in the same dream. A disagreement was counted if one judge scored for a condition and the other judge did not score for the same condition in the same dream. The results are presented in Table 1.

Table 1.   Percentage of agreement between two scores

Number dreamers	Number dreams	CA	CW	PE
8 males	119	87	94	96
8 females	123	89	94	93
16	242	88	94	94

RESULTS

The number of dreams containing scorable elements for the three groups of *S*s is shown in Table 2. It will be noted that in every group the number of male dreams exceeds the number of female dreams for castration anxiety, while in every group the number of female dreams is higher than male dreams for both the castration-wish and the penis-envy categories.

Table 2. Number of dreams showing CA, CW, and PE among college students

| Group* | Number of dreams analyzed | | Number of dreams containing | | | | | |
| | M | F | CA | | CW | | PE | |
			M	F	M	F	M	F
1	308	305	40	7	5	8	2	5
2	327	328	54	15	11	21	5	13
3	318	323	57	35	21	32	9	14
Total	953	956	151	57	37	61	16	32
Range (per dreamer)	7–24	10–21	0–8	0–4	0–4	0–6	0–2	0–3

*N = 20 male and 20 female dreamers for each group.

Since the distribution of scores for any category was markedly skewed with zero scores predominating for many individual dreamers, it was felt that the assumptions for any parametric statistic such as *t* could not be met. Statistical evaluation of the hypothesis was therefore made by use of the chi-square technique. The unit of analysis was the *individual dreamer*. The analysis consisted of determining the number of male and female dreamers whose CA score exceeded the combined total of their CW and PE scores and the number of male and female dreamers whose combined CW and PE scores exceeded their CA score. Ties (10 male and 19 female) were evenly divided between these two groupings. The resulting 2 × 2 table is shown in Table 3.

Table 3. Number of male and female dreamers with CA scores higher and lower than CW and PE scores

	CA more than CW and PE	CW and PE more than CA	
Number of male dreamers	48	12	60
Number of female dreamers	21.5	38.5	60
	69.5	50.5	120

chi-square = 23.96

The majority of male dreamers had higher CA scores while the majority of female dreamers had higher CW and PE scores. The hypothesis of this study was thus supported at a high level of statistical significance ($p < .001$).

Do each of the conditions, CW and PE, contribute substantially to the obtained difference? Table 2 reveals that each of these conditions appears in approximately twice as many female dreams as male dreams. To make sure that such a difference was not produced by a few atypical dreamers, a count was made of the number of women whose scores for each of these separate conditions exceeded that of their CA score. It was found that 20 women had CW scores higher than CA scores, whereas only 5 males scored in this direction, and that 12 women had PE scores higher than their CA scores whereas the same was true for only 1 male. The answer to the question raised earlier is that both CW and PE contribute substantially to the obtained difference.

To look at the sex differences from another viewpoint let us examine the relative freedom from castration anxiety in male and female dreamers. Exactly 50 per cent ($N = 30$) of women in the present sample had zero CA scores whereas only 13 per cent ($N = 8$) of males received zero CA scores. These additional analyses concur in supporting the hypothesis of this investigation, namely that manifestations of castration anxiety in dreams are more typical of males and manifestations of both castration wishes and penis envy are more typical of females.

DISCUSSION

Although the differences are clearcut in favor of the hypothesis, nonetheless there are many manifestations of castration wish and penis envy in men's dreams and many manifestations of castration anxiety in women. The male's wish to castrate others and his envy and admiration of another man's physical and sexual equipment are not difficult to understand. In view of the great amount of physical aggression that is expressed in men's dreams (Hall & Domhoff, 1963), and the amount of competition that men engage in during their waking life, perhaps it is not surprising that their dreams should contain castration wishes and penis envy. Moreover, there may be, as psychoanalytic theory claims, an archaic wish in the male to castrate the father which manifests itself in displaced ways in their dreams. But castration anxiety still takes precedence over these other themes in male dreams.

The amount of castration anxiety in female dreams is less easy, perhaps, to comprehend. Why should there be anxiety over losing something they do not have and never have had? The psychoanalytic explanation is that females unconsciously feel they once had the same genital organs as the male and that they were taken from them. The menses are a constant reminder of this fantasied event. Accordingly, we would expect to find in their dreams expressions of this fantasied castration. Men dream of what might happen whereas women dream of what they think has happened. The fact that anxiety is usually stronger for an anticipated future event than for a realized past one would explain why men have more castration anxiety than women do.

It will be observed (Table 2) that more castration anxiety is expressed in the dreams of males (151 occurrences) than castration wish plus penis envy is in the dreams of females (93 occurrences). The explanation of this may be that the female displaces her penis envy in other ways than that of wishing to castrate others. Freud (1917) mentions two such displacements. He writes: "In girls, the discovery of the penis gives rise to envy for it, which later changes into the wish for a man as the possessor of a penis. Even before this the wish for a penis has changed into a wish for a baby" (p. 132).

This suggested to us another testable hypothesis, namely, that more dreams of babies and of getting married should be reported by women than by men. Accordingly, we went through the 1,909 dreams and scored them for the presence of weddings and babies. Females had 60 dreams in which weddings or preparations for weddings occurred; males had only 9 such dreams. Females had 85 dreams in which babies or very young children figured; males had 32 such dreams. These findings appear to confirm the hypothesis, although, of course, other explanations for women dreaming more than men do of weddings and babies may occur to the reader.

The *S*s of this investigation were for the most part in their late teens and early twenties. What happens to manifestations of the castration complex in dreams with age? Relative to this question we would like to mention the findings obtained from analyzing 600 dreams collected from a man between the ages of 37 and 54. The 600 dreams were divided into six sets of 100 dreams each. Each dream was scored for castration anxiety, castration wish, and penis envy. The results are presented in Table 4. The incidence for each of the three categories does not vary to any great extent over the 17 years, nor do the averages differ noticeably from the averages for college men. In this one case, at least, castration anxiety appears to express itself at the same rate in dreams into the fifties.

Table 4.   Manifestations of the castration complex in the dreams of a middle-aged man

| | *Incidence per 100 dreams* | | | | | | | *Average for* |
	I	*II*	*III*	*IV*	*V*	*VI*	*Average*	*college men*
CA	14	18	13	15	10	17	14.5	15.8
CW	4	3	2	5	8	5	4.5	3.9
PE	2	1	2	0	1	2	1.3	1.7

In an earlier investigation by one of the writers (Hall, 1955), it was concluded that the dream of being attacked is not a manifestation of castration anxiety as suggested by the findings of Harris (1948) but represents the feminine attitudes of weakness, passivity, inferiority, and masochism as formulated by Freud. The findings of the present study do not conflict with the earlier one because the criteria used for scoring castration anxiety were different than the criterion used for identifying the dream of being attacked. The dream of being attacked consists, for the most part, of attacks on or threats to the dreamer's *whole* body. In the present study, attacks upon the whole body are categorically excluded except for a small number of cases where the threat is one of cutting, clawing, biting, or stabbing. The damage or threat must be to a *specific part* of the body in order for it to be scored as castration anxiety. Moreover, the criteria used in the present investigation are much more extensive. They include damage to a possession of the dreamer, his difficulty in using phallic objects, and by a male becoming feminized.

Although the hypothesis of this investigation was derived from Freudian theory, and its confirmation therefore supports the theory, the results may be accounted for by other theoretical positions. For example, the greater incidence of injuries and accidents in male dreams may merely reflect the nature of the activities in which they engage in waking life as compared with the activities of women. It is believed that men engage in more dangerous activities and take more risks than women do. If this is the case it might be expected that their dreams would be in accord with their waking life experiences. On the other hand, if they do in fact take more chances and risk physical harm, this raises the question of why they do. It does not suffice, we feel, to say that they have adopted the role which "society" has fashioned for them. Why has "society" created such a role and why do boys acquiesce in being shaped to the role? *Ad hoc* explanations of findings, in any event, are not very satisfying.

SUMMARY

This study was undertaken to investigate whether sex differences would be found in the incidence of manifestations of castration anxiety (CA), castration wish (CW), and penis envy (PE) in dreams. Criteria for each of these three components of the castration complex were formulated, on the basis of which a scoring manual was written.

It was hypothesized that male dreamers will report more dreams expressive of CA than they will dreams involving CW and PE whereas the pattern will be reversed for females, i.e., they will report more dreams containing expressions of CW and PE than they will dreams containing CA. The hypothesis was supported for three different groups of college students evenly divided as to sex, and the combined results for the 120 students were significant beyond the .001 level.

Additional data were also presented to show that many more women than men dream about babies and weddings and that the relative incidence of the various castration components remains quite stable throughout a long dream series spanning 17 years.

Although the results are congruent with Freudian theory, and to that extent add to the construct validity of the castration complex, it was recognized that alternative theoretical positions could be invoked to account for the findings of this investigation.

REFERENCES

Barker, R., & Kaplan, B. (Eds.) *Primary records in psychology*. Publ. No. 2. Lawrence, Kansas: Univer. of Kansas Publ., 1963.

Blum, G. S. A study of the psychoanalytic theory of psychosexual development. *Genet. psychol. Monogr.* 1949, *39*, 3–99.

Conn, J. H. Children's reactions to the discovery of genital differences. *Amer. J. Orthopsychiat.*, 1940, *10*, 747–754.

Freud, S. (1917) On transformations of instinct as exemplified in anal erotism. In *The standard edition*. London: Hogarth Press, 1955. Vol. 17, pp. 127–133.

Freud, S. (1925) Some psychical consequences of the anatomical distinction between the sexes. In *The standard edition*. London: Hogarth Press, 1961. Vol. 19, pp. 248–258.

Freud, S. (1931) Female sexuality. In *The standard edition*. London: Hogarth Press, 1961. Vol. 21, pp. 225–243.

Freud, S. (1933) *A new series of introductory lectures on psychoanalysis*. New York: Norton, 1933. Chap. 5, pp. 153–185.

Friedman, S. M. An empirical study of the castration and Oedipus complexes. *Genet. psychol. Monogr.*, 1952, *46*, 61–130.

Hall, C. S. The significance of the dream of being attacked. *J. Pers.*, 1955, *24*, 168–180.

Hall, C., & Domhoff, B. Aggression in dreams. *Internat. J. Soc. Psychiat.*, 1963, *9*, 259–267.

Harris, I. Observations concerning typical anxiety dreams. *Psychiat.*, 1948, *11*, 301–309.

Hattendorf, K. W. A study of the questions of young children concerning sex. *J. Soc. Psychol.*, 1932, *3*, 37–65.

Horney, Karen. The dread of woman. *Internat. J. Psychoanal.*, 1932, *13*, 348–360.

Huschka, Mabel. The incidence and character of masturbation threats in a group of problem children. In S. S. Tomkins (Ed.), *Contemporary psychopathology*. Cambridge: Harvard Univer. Press, 1944.

Institute of Dream Research. A manual for scoring castration anxiety, castration wishes, and penis envy in dreams. Miami, 1964.

Levy, D. M. "Control-situation" studies of children's responses to the differences in genitalia. *Amer. J. Orthopsychiat.*, 1940, *10*, 755–762.

Sarnoff, I., & Corwin, S. B. Castration anxiety and the fear of death. *J. Pers.*, 1959, *27*, 374–385.

Schwartz, B. J. Measurement of castration anxiety and anxiety over loss of love. *J. Pers.*, 1955, *24*, 204–219.

Schwartz, B. J. An empirical test of two Freudian hypotheses concerning castration anxiety. *J. Pers.*, 1956, *24*, 318–327.

Sears, R. Survey of objective studies of psychoanalytic concepts. *Soc. Sci. Res. Coun.*, 1943, Bull. 51.

Joseph Wolpe and Stanley Rachman
A CRITIQUE OF FREUD'S CASE
OF LITTLE HANS

Beginning with Wohlgemuth's trenchant monograph (1923), the factual and logical bases of psychoanalytic theory have been the subject of a considerable number of criticisms. These have generally been dismissed by psychoanalysts, at least partly on the ground that the critics are oblivious of the ''wealth of detail'' provided by the individual case. One way to examine the soundness of the analysts' position is to study fully-reported cases that they themselves regard as having contributed significantly to their theories. We have undertaken to do this, and have chosen as our subject matter one of Freud's most famous cases, given in such detail that the events of a few months occupy 140 pages of the *Collected Papers*.

In 1909, Freud published ''The Analysis of a Phobia in a Five-year-old Boy'' (1950). This case is commonly referred to as ''The Case of Little Hans.'' Ernest Jones, in his biography of Freud, points out that it was ''the first published account of a child analysis'' (1955, p. 289), and states that ''the brilliant success of child analysis'' since then was ''indeed inaugurated by the study of this very case'' (1955, p. 292). The case also has special significance in the development of psychoanalytic theory because Freud believed himself to have found in it ''a more direct and less round-about proof'' of some fundamental psychoanalytic theorems (1950, p. 150). In particular, he thought that it provided a direct demonstration of the essential role of sexual urges in the development of phobias. He felt his position to have been greatly strengthened by this case and two generations of analysts have referred to the evidence of Little Hans as a basic substantiation of psychoanalytic theories (e.g., Fenichel, 1945; Glover, 1956; Hendrick, 1939). As an example, Glover (1956, p. 76) may be quoted.

> In its time the analysis of Little Hans was a remarkable achievement and the story of the analysis constitutes one of the most valued records in psychoanalytical archives. Our concepts of phobia formation, of the positive Oedipus complex, of ambivalence, castration anxiety and repression, to mention but a few, were greatly reinforced and amplified as the result of this analysis.

In this paper we shall re-examine this case history and assess the evidence presented. We shall show that although there are manifestations of sexual behavior on the part of Hans,

From J. Wolpe and S. Rachman, ''Psychoanalytic 'Evidence': A Critique Based on Freud's Case of Little Hans,'' *Journal of Nervous and Mental Disease*, 1960, *130*, 135–148. Copyright 1960 by The Williams & Wilkins Co., Baltimore, Md., U. S. A. Reprinted by permission of the publisher and the authors.

there is no scientifically acceptable evidence showing any connection between this behavior and the child's phobia for horses; that the assertion of such connection is pure assumption; that the elaborate discussions that follow from it are pure speculation; and that the case affords no factual support for any of the concepts listed by Glover above. Our examination of this case exposes in considerable detail patterns of thinking and attitudes to evidence that are well-nigh universal among psychoanalysts. It suggests the need for more careful scrutiny of the bases of psychoanalytic "discoveries" than has been customary; and we hope it will prompt psychologists to make similar critical examinations of basic psychoanalytic writings.

The case material on which Freud's analysis is based was collected by Little Hans's father, who kept Freud informed of developments by regular written reports. The father also had several consultations with Freud concerning Little Hans's phobia. During the analysis, Freud himself saw the little boy only once.

The following are the most relevant facts noted of Hans's earlier life. At the age of three, he showed "a quite peculiarly lively interest in that portion of his body which he used to describe as his widdler." When he was three and a half, his mother found him with his hand to his penis. She threatened him in these words, "If you do that, I shall send for Dr. A. to cut off your widdler. And then what will you widdle with?" Hans replied, "With my bottom." Numerous further remarks concerning widdlers in animals and humans were made by Hans between the ages of three and four, including questions directed at his mother and father asking them if they also had widdlers. Freud attaches importance to the following exchange between Hans and his mother. Hans was "looking on intently while his mother undressed."

> Mother: "What are you staring like that for?"
> Hans: "I was only looking to see if you'd got a widdler, too."
> Mother: "Of course. Didn't you know that?"
> Hans: "No, I thought you were so big you'd have a widdler like a horse."

When Hans was three and a half his sister was born. The baby was delivered at home and Hans heard his mother "coughing," observed the appearance of the doctor and was called into the bedroom after the birth. Hans was initially "very jealous of the new arrival" but within six months his jealousy faded and was replaced by "brotherly affection." When Hans was four he discovered a seven-year-old girl in the neighborhood and spent many hours awaiting her return from school. The father commented that "the violence with which this 'long-range love' came over him was to be explained by his having no play-fellows of either sex." At this period also, "he was constantly putting his arms round" his visiting boy cousin, aged five, and was once heard saying, "I *am* so fond of you" when giving his cousin "one of these tender embraces." Freud speaks of this as the "first trace of homosexuality."

At the age of four and a half, Hans went with his parents to Gmunden for the summer holidays. On holiday Hans had numerous playmates including Mariedl, a fourteen-year-old girl. One evening Hans said, "I want Mariedl to sleep with me." Freud says that Hans's wish was an expression of his desire to have Mariedl as part of his family. Hans's parents occasionally took him into their bed and Freud claims that, "there can be no doubt that lying beside them had aroused erotic feelings in him;[1] so that his wish to sleep with Mariedl had an erotic sense as well."

Another incident during the summer holidays is given considerable importance by Freud, who refers to it as Hans's attempt to seduce his mother. It must be quoted here in full.

---

[1]This is nothing but surmise—yet Freud asserts "there can be no doubt" about it.

Hans, four and a quarter.[2] This morning Hans was given his usual daily bath by his mother and afterwards dried and powdered. As his mother was powdering round his penis and taking care not to touch it, Hans said, "Why don't you put your finger there?"

Mother: "Because that'd be piggish."
Hans: "What's that? Piggish? Why?"
Mother: "Because it's not proper."
Hans (laughing): "But it's great fun."

Another occurrence prior to the onset of his phobia was that when Hans, aged four and a half, laughed while watching his sister being bathed and was asked why he was laughing, he replied, "I'm laughing at Hanna's widdler." "Why?" "Because her widdler's so lovely." The father's comment is, "Of course his answer was a disingenuous one. In reality her widdler seemed to him funny. Moreover, this is the first time he has recognized in this way the distinction between male and female genitals instead of denying it."

In early January, 1908, the father wrote to Freud that Hans had developed "a nervous disorder." The symptoms he reported were: fear of going into the streets; depression in the evening; and a fear that a horse would bite him in the street. Hans's father suggested that "the ground was prepared by sexual over-excitation due to his mother's tenderness" and that the fear of the horse "seems somehow to be connected with his having been frightened by a large penis." The first signs appeared on January 7th, when Hans was being taken to the park by his nursemaid as usual. He started crying and said he wanted to "coax" (caress) with his mother. At home "he was asked why he had refused to go any further and had cried, but he would not say." The following day, after hesitation and crying, he went out with his mother. Returning home Hans said ("after much internal struggling"), *I was afraid a horse would bite me* (original italics). As on the previous day, Hans showed fear in the evening and asked to be "coaxed." He is also reported as saying, "I know I shall have to go for a walk again tomorrow," and "The horse'll come into the room." On the same day he was asked by his mother if he put his hand to his widdler. He replied in the affirmative. The following day his mother warned him to refrain from doing this.

At this point in the narrative, Freud provided an interpretation of Hans's behavior and consequently arranged with the boy's father "that he should tell the boy that all this nonsense about horses was a piece of nonsense and nothing more. The truth was, his father was to say, that he was very fond of his mother and wanted to be taken into her bed. The reason he was afraid of horses now was that he had taken so much interest in their widdlers." Freud also suggested giving Hans some sexual enlightenment and telling him that females "had no widdler at all."[3]

"After Hans had been enlightened there followed a fairly quiet period." After an attack of influenza which kept him in bed for two weeks, the phobia got worse. He then had his tonsils out and was indoors for a further week. The phobia became "very much worse."

During March, 1908, after his physical illness had been cured, Hans apparently had many talks with his father about the phobia. On March 1, his father again told Hans that horses do not bite. Hans replied that white horses bite and related that while at Gmunden he had heard and seen Lizzi (a playmate) being warned by her father to avoid a white horse lest it bite. The father said to Lizzi, *"Don't put your finger to the white horse"* (original italics). Hans's father's reply to this account given by his son was, "I say, it strikes me it isn't a horse you

---

[2]Earlier his age during the summer holidays is given as four and a half. Unfortunately, there is no direct statement as to the length of the holiday.

[3]Incidentally contradicting what Hans's mother had told him earlier.

mean, but a widdler, that one mustn't put one's hand to.'' Hans answered, ''But a widdler doesn't bite.'' The father: ''Perhaps it does, though.'' Hans then ''went on eagerly to try to prove to me that it was a white horse.'' The following day, in answer to a remark of his father's, Hans said that his phobia was ''so bad because I still put my hand to my widdler every night.'' Freud remarks here that, ''Doctor and patient, father and son, were therefore at one in ascribing the chief share in the pathogenesis of Hans's present condition to his habit of onanism.'' He implies that this unanimity is significant, quite disregarding the father's indoctrination of Hans the previous day.[4]

On March 13, the father told Hans that his fear would disappear if he stopped putting his hand to his widdler. Hans replied, ''But I don't put my hand to my widdler any more.'' Father: ''But you still want to.'' Hans agreed, ''Yes, I do.'' His father suggested that he should sleep in a sack to prevent him from wanting to touch his widdler. Hans accepted this view and on the following day was much less afraid of horses.

Two days later the father again told Hans that girls and women have no widdlers. ''Mummy has none, Hanna has none and so on.'' Hans asked how they managed to widdle and was told ''They don't have widdlers like yours. Haven't you noticed already when Hanna was being given her bath?'' On March 17 Hans reported a phantasy in which he saw his mother naked. On the basis of this phantasy and the conversation related above, Freud concluded that Hans had not accepted the enlightenment given by his father. Freud says, ''He regretted that it should be so, and stuck to his former view in phantasy. He may also perhaps have had his reasons for refusing to believe his father at first.'' Discussing this matter subsequently, Freud says that the ''enlightenment'' given a short time before to the effect that women really do not possess a widdler was bound to have a shattering effect upon his self-confidence and to have aroused his castration complex. For this reason he resisted the information, and for this reason it had no therapeutic effect.[5]

For reasons of space we shall recount the subsequent events in very brief form. On a visit to the Zoo Hans expressed fear of the giraffe, elephant and all large animals. Hans's father said to him, ''Do you know why you're afraid of big animals? Big animals have big widdlers and you're really afraid of big widdlers.'' This was denied by the boy.

The next event of prominence was a dream (or phantasy) reported by Hans. ''In the night there was a big giraffe in the room and a crumpled one; and the big one called out because I took the crumpled one away from it. Then it stopped calling out; and then I sat down on the top of the crumpled one.''

After talking to the boy the father reported to Freud that this dream was ''a matrimonial scene transposed into giraffe life. He was seized in the night with a longing for his mother, for her caresses, for her genital organ, and came into the room for that reason. The whole thing is a continuation of his fear of horses.'' The father infers that the dream is related to Hans's habit of occasionally getting into his parents' bed in the face of his father's disapproval. Freud's addition to ''the father's penetrating observation'' is that sitting down on the crumpled giraffe means taking possession of his mother. Confirmation of this dream interpretation is claimed by reference to an incident which occurred the next day. The father wrote that on leaving the house with Hans he said to his wife, ''Good-bye, big giraffe.'' ''Why giraffe?'' asked Hans.

---

[4]The mere fact that Hans repeats an interpretation he has heard from his father is regarded by Freud as demonstrating the accuracy of the interpretation; even though the child's spontaneous responses noted earlier in the paragraph point clearly in the opposite direction.

[5]It is pertinent at this point to suggest that Hans ''resisted'' this enlightenment because his mother had told him quite the opposite and his observations of his sister's widdler had not been contradicted. When he was four, Hans had observed that his sister's widdler was ''still quite small.'' When he was four and half, again while watching his sister being bathed, he observed that she had ''a lovely widdler.'' On neither occasion was he contradicted.

"Mummy's the big giraffe," replied the father. "Oh, yes," said Hans, "and Hanna's[6] the crumpled giraffe, isn't she?" The father's account continues, "In the train I explained the giraffe phantasy to him, upon which he said 'Yes, that's right.' And when I said to him that I was the big giraffe and that its long neck reminded him of a widdler, he said 'Mummy has a neck like a giraffe too. I saw when she was washing her white neck.' "

On March 30, the boy had a short consultation with Freud who reports that despite all the enlightenment given to Hans, the fear of horses continued undiminished. Hans explained that he was especially bothered "by what horses wear in front of their eyes and the black round their mouths." This latter detail Freud interpreted as meaning a moustache. "I asked him whether he meant a moustache," and then, "disclosed to him that he was afraid of his father precisely because he was so fond of his mother." Freud pointed out that this was a groundless fear. On April 2, the father was able to report "the first real improvement." The next day Hans, in answer to his father's inquiry, explained that he came into his father's bed when he was frightened. In the next few days further details of Hans's fear were elaborated. He told his father that he was most scared of horses with "a thing on their mouths," that he was scared lest the horses fall, and that he was most scared of horse-drawn buses.

> Hans: "I'm most afraid too when a bus comes along."
> Father: "Why? Because it's so big?"
> Hans: "No. Because once a horse in a bus fell."
> Father: "When?"

Hans then recounted such an incident. This was later confirmed by his mother.

> Father: "What did you think when the horse fell down?"
> Hans: "Now it will always be like this. All horses in buses'll fall down."
> Father: "In all buses?"
> Hans: "Yes. And in furniture vans too. Not often in furniture vans."
> Father: "You had your nonsense already at that time?"
> Hans: "*No* (italics added). I only got it then. When the horse in the bus fell down, it gave me such a fright really: That was when I got the nonsense."

The father adds that, "all of this was confirmed by my wife, as well as the fact that *the anxiety broke out immediately afterwards*" (italics added).

Hans's father continued probing for a meaning of the black thing around the horses' mouths. Hans said it looked like a muzzle but his father had never seen such a horse "although Hans asseverates that such horses do exist."[7] He continues, "I suspect that some part of the horse's bridle really reminded him of a moustache and that after I alluded to this the fear disappeared." A day later Hans observing his father stripped to the waist said, "Daddy you are lovely! You're so white."

> Father: "Yes. Like a white horse."
> Hans: "The only black thing's your moustache. Or perhaps it's a black muzzle."[8]

---

[6]Hans's baby sister, *not* his mother. Again, the more spontaneous response directly contradicts Freud's interpretation. Thus Freud's subsequent comment that Hans only confirmed the interpretation of the two giraffes as his father and mother and not the sexual symbolism, transgresses the facts.

[7]Six days later the father reports, "I was at last able to establish the fact that it was a horse with a leather muzzle."

[8]A good example of the success of indoctrination.

Further details about the horse that fell were also elicited from Hans. He said there were actually two horses pulling the bus and that they were both black and "very big and fat." Hans's father again asked about the boy's thoughts when the horse fell.

Father: "When the horse fell down, did you think of your daddy?"[9]
Hans: "Perhaps. Yes. It's possible."

For several days after these talks about horses Hans's interests, as indicated by the father's reports, "centered upon lumf (feces) and widdle, but we cannot tell why." Freud comments that at this point "the analysis began to be obscure and uncertain."
On April 11 Hans related this phantasy.

"I was in the bath[10] and then the plumber came and unscrewed it.[11] Then he took a big borer and stuck it into my stomach." Hans's father translated this phantasy as follows: "I was in bed with Mamma. Then Pappa came and drove me away. With his big penis he pushed me out of my place by Mamma."

The remainder of the case history material, until Hans's recovery from the phobia early in May, is concerned with the lumf theme and Hans's feelings towards his parents and sister. It can be stated immediately that as corroboration for Freud's theories all of this remaining material is unsatisfactory. For the most part it consists of the father expounding theories to a boy who occasionally agrees and occasionally disagrees. The following two examples illustrate the nature of most of this latter information.
Hans and his father were discussing the boy's slight fear of falling when in the big bath.

Father: "But Mamma bathes you in it. Are you afraid of Mamma dropping you in the water?"
Hans: "I am afraid of her letting go and my head going in."
Father: "But you know Mummy's fond of you and won't let you go."
Hans: "I only just thought it."
Father: "Why?"
Hans: "I don't know at all."
Father: "Perhaps it was because you'd been naughty and thought she didn't love you any more?"[12]
Hans: "Yes."
Father: "When you were watching Mummy giving Hanna her bath perhaps you wished she would let go of her so that Hanna should fall in?"[12]
Hans: "Yes."

On the following day the father asks, "Are you fond of Hanna?"

Hans: "Oh, yes, very fond."
Father: "Would you rather that Hanna weren't alive or that she were?"
Hans: "I'd rather she weren't alive."

[9]One of many leading questions, the positive answer to which of course proves nothing. It is worth noticing how the same question, differently phrased, elicits contrasting answers from Hans. When asked earlier what he thought of when the horse fell, Hans replied that he thought it would always happen in future.
[10]"Hans's mother gives him his bath" (Father's note).
[11]"To take it away to be repaired" (Father's note).
[12]Leading question.

In response to close, direct questioning Hans voiced several complaints about his sister. Then his father proceeded again:

> Father: "If you'd rather she weren't alive, you can't be fond of her, at all."
> Hans: (assenting[13]) "Hm, well."
> Father: "That's why you thought when Mummy was giving her her bath if only she'd let go, Hanna would fall in the water. . . ."
> Hans: (taking me up) ". . . and die."
> Father: "and then you'd be alone with Mummy. A good boy doesn't wish that sort of thing, though."

On April 24, the following conversation was recorded.

> Father: "It seems to me that, all the same, you do wish Mummy would have a baby."
> Hans: "But I don't want it to happen."
> Father: "But you wish for it?"
> Hans: "Oh, yes, *wish*."[14]
> Father: "Do you know why you wish for it? It's because you'd like to be Daddy."
> Hans: "Yes. How does it work?"
> Father: "You'd like to be Daddy and married to Mummy; you'd like to be as big as me and have a moustache; and you'd like Mummy to have a baby."
> Hans: "And Daddy, when I'm married I'll have only one if I want to, when I'm married to Mummy, and if I don't want a baby, God won't want it either when I'm married."
> Father: "Would you like to be married to Mummy?"
> Hans: "Oh yes."

THE VALUE OF THE EVIDENCE

Before proceeding to Freud's interpretation of the case, let us examine the value of the evidence presented. First, there is the matter of selection of the material. The greatest attention is naturally paid to material related to psychoanalytic theory and there is a tendency to ignore other facts. The father and mother, we are told by Freud, "were both among my closest adherents." Hans himself was constantly encouraged, directly and indirectly, to relate material of relevance to the psychoanalytic doctrine.

Second, we must assess the value to be placed on the testimony of the father and of Hans. The father's account of Hans's behavior is in several instances suspect. For example, he twice presents his own interpretations of Hans's remarks as observed facts. This is the father's report of a conversation with Hans about the birth of his sister Hanna.

> Father: "What did Hanna look like?"
> Hans: (hypocritically): "All white and lovely. So pretty."

On another occasion, despite several clear statements by Hans of his affection for his sister (and also the voicing of complaints about her screaming), the father said to Hans, "If you'd rather she weren't alive, you can't be fond of her at all." Hans (assenting): "Hm, well." (See above.)

---

[13]A very questionable affirmation.

[14]Original italics suggest a significance that is unwarranted, for the child has been maneuvered into giving an answer contradicting his original one. Note the induced "evidence" as the conversation continues.

The comment in parenthesis in each of these two extracts is presented as observed fact. A third example has also been quoted above. When Hans observes that Hanna's widdler is "so lovely" the father states that this is a "disingenuous" reply and that "in reality her widdler seemed to him funny." Distortions of this kind are common in the father's reports.

Hans's testimony is for many reasons unreliable. Apart from the numerous lies which he told in the last few weeks of his phobia, Hans gave many inconsistent and occasionally conflicting reports. Most important of all, much of what purports to be Hans's views and feelings is simply the father speaking. Freud himself admits this but attempts to gloss over it. He says, "It is true that during the analysis Hans had to be told many things which he could not say himself, that he had to be presented with thoughts which he had so far shown no signs of possessing and that his attention had to be turned in the direction from which his father was expecting something to come. This detracts from the evidential value of the analysis but the procedure is the same in every case. For a psychoanalysis is not an impartial scientific investigation but a therapeutic measure."[15] To sum this matter up, Hans's testimony is subject not only to "mere suggestion" but contains much material that is not his testimony at all!

From the above discussion it is clear that the "facts of the case" need to be treated with considerable caution and in our own interpretation of Hans's behavior we will attempt to make use only of the testimony of direct observation.

FREUD'S INTERPRETATION

Freud's interpretation of Hans's phobia is that the boy's oedipal conflicts formed the basis of the illness which "burst out" when he underwent "a time of privation and the intensified sexual excitement." Freud says, "These were tendencies in Hans which had already been suppressed and which, so far as we can tell, had never been able to find uninhibited expression; hostile and jealous feelings against his father, and sadistic impulses (premonitions, as it were, of copulation) towards his mother. These early suppressions may perhaps have gone to form the predisposition for his subsequent illness. These aggressive propensities of Hans's found no outlet, and as soon as there came a time of privation and of intensified sexual excitement, they tried to break their way out with reinforced strength. It was then that the battle which we call his 'phobia' burst out."

This is the familiar oedipal theory, according to which Hans wished to replace his father "whom he could not help rating as a rival" and then complete the act by "taking possession of his mother." Freud refers for confirmation to the following. "Another symptomatic act, happening as though by accident, involved a confession that he had wished his father dead; for, just at the moment that his father was talking of his death-wish Hans let a horse that he was playing with fall down—knocked it over, in fact." Freud claims that, "Hans was really a little Oedipus who wanted to have his father 'out of the way' to get rid of him, so that he might be alone with his handsome mother and sleep with her." The predisposition to illness provided by the oedipal conflicts is supposed to have formed the basis for "the transformation of his libidinal longing into anxiety." During the summer prior to the onset of the phobia, Hans had experienced "moods of mingled longing and apprehension" and had also been taken into his mother's bed on occasions. Freud says, "We may assume that since then Hans had been in a state of intensified sexual excitement, the object of which was his mother. The intensity of this

[15]Nevertheless, both the theory and practice of psychoanalysis are built on these "not . . . impartial scientific investigations." For Freud to admit this weakness has some merit, but the admission is neither a substitute for evidence nor a good reason for accepting conclusions without evidence.

excitement was shown by his two attempts at seducing his mother (the second of which occurred just before the outbreak of his anxiety); and he found an incidental channel of discharge for it by masturbating. . . . Whether the sudden exchange of this excitement into anxiety took place spontaneously, or as a result of his mother's rejection of his advances, or owing to the accidental revival of earlier impressions by the 'exciting cause' of his illness . . . this we cannot decide. The fact remains that his sexual excitement suddenly changed into anxiety.''[16]

Hans, we are told, ''transposed from his father on to the horses.'' At his sole interview with Hans, Freud told him ''that he was afraid of his father because he himself nourished jealous and hostile wishes against him.'' Freud says of this, ''In telling him this, I had partly interpreted his fear of horses for him: the horse must be his father—whom he had good internal reasons for fearing.'' Freud claims that Hans's fear of the black things on the horses' mouths and the things in front of their eyes was based on moustaches and eye-glasses and had been ''directly transposed from his father on to the horses.''[17] The horses ''had been shown to represent his father.''

Freud interprets the agoraphobic element of Hans's phobia thus. ''The content of his phobia was such as to impose a very great measure of restriction upon his freedom of movement, and that was its purpose. . . . After all, Hans's phobia of horses was an obstacle to his going into the street, and could serve as a means of allowing him to stay at home with his beloved mother.[18] In this way, therefore, his affection for his mother triumphantly achieved its aim.''

Freud interprets the disappearance of the phobia as being due to the resolution by Hans of his oedipal conflicts by ''promoting him (the father) to a marriage with Hans's grandmother . . . instead of killing him.'' This final interpretation is based on the following conversation between Hans and his father.

On April 30, Hans was playing with his imaginary children.

> Father: ''Hullo, are your children still alive? You know quite well a boy can't have any children.''
> Hans: ''I know. I was their Mummy before, *now I'm their Daddy*'' (original italics).
> Father: ''And who's the children's Mummy?''
> Hans: ''Why, Mummy, and you're their *Grandaddy*'' (original italics).
> Father: ''So then you'd like to be as big as me, and be married to Mummy, and then you'd like her to have children.''
> Hans: ''Yes, that's what I'd like, and then my Lainz Grandmamma'' (paternal side) ''will be their Grannie.''

CRITIQUE OF FREUD'S CONCLUSIONS

It is our contention that Freud's view of this case is not supported by the data, either in its particulars or as a whole. The major points that he regards as demonstrated are these: (1) Hans had a sexual desire for his mother, (2) he hated and feared his father and wished to kill him, (3) his sexual excitement and desire for his mother were transformed into anxiety, (4) his fear

---

[16]Thus a theoretical statement, beginning with ''We may assume'' ends up as a ''fact.'' The only fact is that the assumed sexual excitement is assumed to have changed into anxiety.

[17]But in fact the child was thinking of a muzzle (see above).

[18]It should be noted, however, that Hans's horse-phobia and general agoraphobia were present even when he went out with his mother.

of horses was symbolic of his fear of his father, (5) the purpose of the illness was to keep near his mother and finally (6) his phobia disappeared because he resolved his Oedipus complex.

Let us examine each of these points.

(1) That Hans derived satisfaction from his mother and enjoyed her presence we will not even attempt to dispute. But nowhere is there any evidence of his wish to copulate with her. Yet Freud says that, "if matters had lain entirely in my hands . . . I should have confirmed his instinctive premonitions, by telling him of the existence of the vagina and of copulation." The "instinctive premonitions" are referred to as though a matter of fact, though no evidence of their existence is given.

The only seduction incident described (see above) indicates that on *that particular occasion* Hans desired contact of a sexual nature with his mother, albeit a sexual contact of a simple, primitive type. This is not adequate evidence on which to base the claim that Hans had an Oedipus complex which implies a sexual desire for the other, a wish to possess her and to replace the father. The most that can be claimed for this "attempted seduction" is that it provides a small degree of support for the assumption that Hans had a desire for sexual stimulation by some other person (it will be recalled that he often masturbated). Even if it is assumed that stimulation provided by his mother was especially desired, the two other features of an Oedipus complex (a wish to possess the mother and replace the father) are not demonstrated by the facts of the case.

(2) Never having expressed either fear or hatred of his father, Hans was told by Freud that he possessed these emotions. On subsequent occasions Hans denied the existence of these feelings when questioned by his father. Eventually, he said "Yes" to a statement of this kind by his father. This simple affirmative obtained after considerable pressure on the part of the father and Freud is accepted as the true state of affairs and all Hans's denials are ignored. The "symptomatic act" of knocking over the toy horse is taken as further evidence of Hans's aggression towards his father. There are three assumptions underlying this "interpreted fact"—first, that the horse represents Hans's father; second, that the knocking over of the horse is not accidental; and third, that this act indicates a wish for the removal of whatever the horse symbolized.

Hans consistently denied the relationship between the horse and his father. He was, he said, afraid of horses. The mysterious black around the horses' mouths and the things on their eyes were later discovered by the father to be the horses' muzzles and blinkers. This discovery undermines the suggestion (made by Freud) that they were transposed moustaches and eye-glasses. There is no other evidence that the horses represented Hans's father. The assumption that the knocking over of the toy horse was meaningful in that it was prompted by an unconscious motive is, like most similar examples, a moot point. Freud himself (1938) does not state that *all* errors are provoked by unconscious motives and in this sense "deliberate." This is understandable for it is easy to compile numerous instances of errors which can be accounted for in other, simpler terms[19] without recourse to unconscious motivation or indeed motivation of any kind. Despite an examination of the literature we are unable to find a categorical statement regarding the frequency of "deliberate errors." Furthermore, we do not know how to recognize them when they do occur. In the absence of positive criteria the decision that Hans's knocking over of the toy horse was a "deliberate error" is arbitrary.

As there is nothing to sustain the first two assumptions made by Freud in interpreting

---

[19]See for example the experiments on learning and habit interference (McGeoch and Irion, 1952; Woodworth and Schlosberg, 1955).

this "symptomatic act," the third assumption (that this act indicated a wish for his father's death) is untenable; and it must be reiterated that there is no independent evidence that the boy feared or hated his father.

(3) Freud's third claim is that Hans's sexual excitement and desire for his mother were transformed into anxiety. This claim is based on the assertion that "theoretical considerations require that what is today the object of a phobia must at one time in the past have been the source of a high degree of pleasure." Certainly such a transformation is not displayed by the facts presented. As stated above, there is no evidence that Hans sexually desired his mother. There is also no evidence of any change in his attitude to her before the onset of the phobia. Even though there is some evidence that horses were to some extent previously a source of pleasure, in general the view that phobic objects must have been the source of former pleasures is amply contradicted by experimental evidence. Apart from the numerous experiments on phobias in animals which disprove this contention (Gantt, 1944; Liddell, 1944; Woodward, 1959), the demonstrations of Watson and Rayner (1920) and Jones (1924) have clearly shown how phobias may be induced in children by a simple conditioning process. The rat and rabbit used as the conditioned stimuli in these demonstrations can hardly be regarded as sources of "a high degree of pleasure," and the same applies to the generalized stimulus of cotton wool.

(4) The assertion that Hans's horse phobia symbolized a fear of his father has already been criticized. The assumed relationship between the father and the horse is unsupported and appears to have arisen as a result of the father's strange failure to believe that by the "black around their mouths" Hans meant the horses' muzzles.

(5) The fifth claim is that the purpose of Hans's phobia was to keep him near his mother. Aside from the questionable view that neurotic disturbances occur for a purpose, this interpretation fails to account for the fact that Hans experienced anxiety even when he was out walking *with his mother*.

(6) Finally, we are told that the phobia disappeared as a result of Hans's resolution of his oedipal conflicts. As we have attempted to show, there is no adequate evidence that Hans had an Oedipus complex. In addition, the claim that this assumed complex was resolved is based on a single conversation between Hans and his father (see above). This conversation is a blatant example of what Freud himself refers to as Hans having to "be told many things he could not say himself, that he had to be presented with thoughts which he had so far *shown* no signs of possessing, and that his attention had to be turned in the direction that his father was expecting something to come."

There is also no satisfactory evidence that the "insights" that were incessantly brought to the boy's attention had any therapeutic value. Reference to the facts of the case shows only occasional coincidences between interpretations and changes in the child's phobic reactions. For example, "a quiet period" early followed the father's statement that the fear of horses was a "piece of nonsense" and that Hans really wanted to be taken into his mother's bed. But soon afterwards, when Hans became ill, the phobia was worse than ever. Later, having had many talks without effect, the father notes that on March 13 Hans, after agreeing that he still *wanted* to play with his widdler, was "much less afraid of horses." On March 15, however, he was frightened of horses, after the information that females have no widdlers (though he had previously been told the opposite by his mother). Freud asserts that Hans resisted this piece of enlightenment because it aroused castration fears, and therefore no therapeutic success was to be observed. The "first real improvement" of April 2 is attributed to the "moustache enlightenment" of March 30 (later proved erroneous), the boy having been told that he was "afraid of his father precisely because he was so fond of his mother." On April 7, though

Hans was constantly improving, Freud commented that the situation was "decidedly obscure" and that "the analysis was making little progress."[20]

Such sparse and tenuous data do not begin to justify the attribution of Hans's recovery to the bringing to consciousness of various unacceptable unconscious repressed wishes. In fact, Freud bases his conclusions entirely on deductions from his theory. Hans's later improvement appears to have been smooth and gradual and unaffected by the interpretations. In general, Freud infers relationships in a scientifically inadmissible manner: if the enlightenments or interpretations given to Hans are followed by behavioral improvements, then they are automatically accepted as valid. If they are not followed by improvement we are told the patient has not accepted them, and not that they are invalid. Discussing the failure of these early enlightenments, Freud says that in any event therapeutic success is not the primary aim of the analysis,[21] thus sidetracking the issue; and he is not deflected from claiming an improvement to be due to an interpretation even when the latter is erroneous, *e.g.,* the moustache interpretation.

No systematic follow-up of the case is provided. However, fourteen years after the completion of the analysis, Freud interviewed Hans, who "declared that he was perfectly well and suffered from no troubles or inhibitions"(!). He also said that he had successfully undergone the ordeal of his parents' divorce. Hans reported that he could not remember anything about his childhood phobia. Freud remarks that this is "particularly remarkable." The analysis itself "had been overtaken by amnesia!"

AN ALTERNATIVE VIEW OF HANS'S PHOBIA

In case it should be argued that, unsatisfactory as it is, Freud's explanation is the only available one, we shall show how Hans's phobia can be understood in terms of learning theory, in the theoretical framework provided by Wolpe (1958). This approach is largely Hullian in character and the clinical applications are based on experimental findings.

In brief, phobias are regarded as conditioned anxiety (fear) reactions. Any "neutral" stimulus, simple or complex, that happens to make an impact on an individual at about the time that a fear reaction is evoked acquires the ability to evoke fear subsequently. If the fear at the original conditioning situation is of high intensity or if the conditioning is many times repeated, the conditioned fear will show the persistence that is characteristic of *neurotic* fear; and there will be generalization of fear reactions to stimuli resembling the conditioned stimulus.

Hans, we are told, was a sensitive child who "was never unmoved if someone wept in his presence" and long before the phobia developed became "uneasy on seeing the horses in the merry-go-round being beaten." It is our contention that the incident to which Freud refers as merely the exciting cause of Hans's phobia was in fact the cause of the entire disorder. Hans actually says, "No. I only got it [the phobia] then. When the horse in the bus fell down, it gave me such a fright, really! That was when I got the nonsense." The father says, "All of this was confirmed by my wife, as well as the fact that the anxiety broke out immediately afterwards." The evidence obtained in studies on experimental neuroses in animals (*e.g.,* Wolpe, 1958) and the studies by Watson and Rayner (1920), Jones (1924) and Woodward (1959) on phobias in children indicate that it is quite possible for one experience to induce a phobia.

In addition, the father was able to report two other unpleasant incidents which Hans had

---

[20]By Freud's admission Hans was improving despite the absence of progress in the analysis.

[21]But elsewhere he says that a psychoanalysis is a therapeutic measure and not a scientific investigation!

experienced with horses prior to the onset of the phobia. It is likely that these experiences had sensitized Hans to horses or, in other words, he had already been partially conditioned to fear horses. These incidents both occurred at Gmunden. The first was the warning given by the father of Hans's friend to avoid the horse lest it bite, and the second when another of Hans's friends injured himself (and bled) while they were playing horses.

Just as the little boy Albert (in Watson's classic demonstration, 1920) reacted with anxiety not only to the original conditioned stimulus, the white rat, but to other similar stimuli such as furry objects, cotton wool and so on, Hans reacted anxiously to horses, horse-drawn buses, vans and features of horses, such as their blinkers and muzzles. In fact he showed fear of a wide range of generalized stimuli. The accident which provoked the phobia involved two horses drawing a bus and Hans stated that he was more afraid of large carts, vans or buses than small carts. As one would expect, the less close a phobic stimulus was to that of the original incident the less disturbing Hans found it. Furthermore, the last aspect of the phobia to disappear was Hans's fear of large vans or buses. There is ample experimental evidence that when responses to generalized stimuli undergo extinction, responses to other stimuli in the continuum are the less diminished the more closely they resemble the original conditional stimulus.

Hans's recovery from the phobia may be explained on conditioning principles in a number of possible ways, but the actual mechanism that operated cannot be identified, since the child's father was not concerned with the kind of information that would be of interest to us. It is well known that especially in children many phobias decline and disappear over a few weeks or months. The reason for this appears to be that in the ordinary course of life generalized phobic stimuli may evoke anxiety responses weak enough to be inhibited by other emotional responses simultaneously aroused in the individual. Perhaps this process was the true source of Little Hans's recovery. The interpretations may have been irrelevant, or may even have retarded recovery by adding new threats and new fears to those already present. But since Hans does not seem to have been greatly upset by the interpretations, it is perhaps more likely that the therapy was actively helpful, for phobic stimuli were again and again presented to the child in a variety of emotional contexts that may have inhibited the anxiety and in consequence diminished its habit strength. The *gradualness* of Hans's recovery is consonant with an explanation of this kind (Wolpe, 1958).

CONCLUSIONS

The chief conclusion to be derived from our survey of the case of Little Hans is that it does not provide anything resembling direct proof of psychoanalytic theorems. We have combed Freud's account for evidence that would be acceptable in the court of science, and have found none. In attempting to give a balanced summary of the case we have excluded a vast number of interpretations but have tried not to omit any material facts. Such facts, and they alone, could have supported Freud's theories. For example, if it had been observed after Gmunden that Hans had become fearful of his father, and that upon the development of the horse phobia the fear of the father had disappeared, this could reasonably have been regarded as presumptive of a displacement of fear from father to horse. This is quite different from observing a horse phobia and then asserting that it must be a displaced father-fear without ever having obtained any direct evidence of the latter; for then that which needs to be demonstrated is presupposed. To say that the father-fear was repressed is equally no substitute for evidence of it.

Freud fully believed that he had obtained in Little Hans a direct confirmation of his theories, for he speaks towards the end of "the infantile complexes that were revealed behind Hans's phobia." It seems clear that although he wanted to be scientific Freud was surprisingly naive regarding the requirements of scientific evidence. Infantile complexes were not *revealed* (demonstrated) behind Hans's phobia: they were merely hypothesized.

It is remarkable that countless psychoanalysts have paid homage to the case of Little Hans, without being offended by its glaring inadequacies. We shall not here attempt to explain this, except to point to one probable major influence—a tacit belief among analysts that Freud possessed a kind of unerring insight that absolved him from the obligation to obey rules applicable to ordinary men. For example, Glover (1952), speaking of other analysts who arrogate to themselves the right Freud claimed to subject his material to "a touch of revision," says, "No doubt when someone of Freud's calibre appears in our midst he will be freely accorded . . . this privilege." To accord such a privilege to anyone is to violate the spirit of science.

It may of course be argued that some of the conclusions of Little Hans are no longer held and that there is now other evidence for other of the conclusions; but there is no evidence that in general psychoanalytic conclusions are based on any better logic than that used by Freud in respect of Little Hans. Certainly no analyst has ever pointed to the failings of this account or disowned its reasoning, and it has continued to be regarded as one of the foundation stones on which psychoanalytic theory was built.

SUMMARY

The main facts of the case of Little Hans are presented and it is shown that Freud's claim of "a more direct and less roundabout proof" of certain of his theories is not justified by the evidence presented. No confirmation by direct observation is obtained for any psychoanalytic theorem, though psychoanalysts have believed the contrary for 50 years. The demonstrations claimed are really interpretations that are treated as facts. This is a common practice and should be checked, for it has been a great encumbrance to the development of a science of psychiatry.

REFERENCES

Fenichel, O. *The psychoanalytical theory of neurosis.* New York: Norton, 1945.
Freud, S. *Collected papers.* London: Hogarth Press, 1950. Vol. 3.
Freud, S. *Psychopathology of everyday life.* Baltimore: Pelican Books, 1938.
Gantt, W. H. *Experimental basis for neurotic behavior.* New York: Hoeber, 1944.
Glover, E. *On the early development of mind.* New York: International Universities Press, 1956.
Glover, E. Research methods in psychoanalysis. *Int. J. Psychoanal.,* 1952, *33*, 403–409.
Hendrick, I. *Facts and theories of psychoanalysis.* New York: Knopf, 1939.
Jones, E. *Sigmund Freud: Life and work.* London: Hogarth Press, 1955. Vol. 2.
Jones, M. C. Elimination of children's fears. *J. exp. Psychol.,* 1924, *7*, 382–390.
Liddell, H. S. Conditioned reflex method and experimental neurosis. In J. McV. Hunt (Ed.), *Personality and the behavior disorders.* New York: Ronald, 1944.
McGeoch, J., and Irion, A. *The psychology of human learning.* New York: Longmans, 1952.
Watson, J. B., and Rayner, P. Conditioned emotional reactions. *J. exp. Psychol.,* 1920, *3*, 1–14.
Wohlgemuth, A. *A critical examination of psychoanalysis.* London: Allen and Unwin, 1923.
Wolpe, J. *Psychotherapy by reciprocal inhibition.* Stanford, Calif.: Stanford Univ. Press, 1958.
Woodward, J. Emotional disturbances of burned children. *Brit. med. J.,* 1959, *1*, 1009–1013.
Woodworth, R., and Schlosberg, H. *Experimental psychology.* London: Methuen, 1955.

Two
HEINZ HARTMANN

For Freud, a person is a biological organism possessed of instincts that continually strive for gratification. All human behavior can ultimately be traced to the gratification of these instincts, which are animalistic in nature—products of evolution.

Freud constructed his theory of personality in accordance with the biological theory of his day. The problem for Freud was one of translation—translation of the energy concepts of biology into energy concepts suitable for the explanation of mind activity and mental (personality) development. Freud began with the energy concept of instinct. Since one of the characteristics of energy is that it can change from one form into another (the Doctrine of the Conservation of Energy), it seemed reasonable to assert that energy can change in form from physical to mental. For Freud, the *id* is that part of personality that contains the instincts and all of the energy for the running of the mental processes. It is here that physical energy (of the body) is transformed into mental (psychic) energy (of the mind).

At birth, the only structure of the mind that exists is the id. In the course of psychological development, the id becomes differentiated into two other structures—the *ego* and the *superego*. In this regard, it is important to note that psychoanalytic personality theory is essentially a theory of psychic energy—its origin, distribution, and utilization. The activity of psychic energy takes place unconsciously—that is, out of conscious awareness—and thus is totally independent of conscious control.

The id can be conceived of as a kind of dynamo of psychic energy. Because the id contains the instincts, which have the single goal of immediate gratification, and because the id is the primary "organ" of personality, the development of personality structure and function always has as its ultimate purpose instinct gratification. The id is primitive and selfish. As an energy system, it operates solely by the rule of immediate gratification and is never directly influenced by the real world. In this sense, the id is totally irrational.

Obviously, an organism would not survive long (and more important, the species would not survive long) if it acted on all its impulses (instincts) immediately and without regard for the demands of the world in which it lived. It is out of this conflict between the pushing forces of the instincts and the restraining forces of the real world that human personality develops, and it is because of this conflict that the development always involves compromise. The ego develops in order that the instincts may be gratified in ways that will not lead to destruction of the organism (the mechanisms of the ego are called the *defense mechanisms*). According to Freud, the ego is never free of the influence of the id and, in fact, draws its energy exclusively from the id. In this very pessimistic view of human nature, then, all human behavior is a compromise—the result of attempts to both increase the likelihood of instinct gratification and decrease the likelihood of pain.

Since Freud, certain psychoanalytic theorists have suggested alterations in his pessimistic "id psychology"—proposing the concept of the *autonomous ego*. In the forefront of this group of Freudian revisionists is Heinz Hartmann (1894–1970). Hartmann is said to have been one of Freud's favorites among the second-generation analysts and was even invited by Freud to undergo a training analysis with him. His *neo-Freudian* approach goes by the name of *ego psychology*. Hartmann argues that the ego does not emerge out of the id but rather develops independently. In this view, the ego is not wholly dependent on the energies and wishes of the id instincts. At least part of the ego is conflict-free and therefore not directly involved in defensive operations—that is, compromise.

Although this may seem a minor revision in psychoanalytic theory, it is in fact a major departure from classical Freudian thinking regarding human nature and personality development. In ego psychology, one sees a less pessimistic view of human nature—a view that recognizes a biological heritage but that also attributes to people reason and a capacity for social achievement independent of instinctual influence. Ego psychology thus sees people as having constructive tendencies as well as destructive ones; this is indeed a significant departure from Freud.

The first selection in this chapter, by Hartmann, is worth studying for several reasons. One reason is that in it Hartmann describes and explains ego psychology. Second, it offers an excellent summary of the development of psychoanalytic theory. Third, the selection is a good example of an attempt by a psychoanalyst to present psychoanalysis as a scientific theory.

Hartmann makes clear in his article his belief that conflict is the primary motivating force in behavior. Again, if one views psychoanalytic theory as a theory of psychic (mental) energy and thinks of conflict in terms of opposing energy forces, one gets some idea of the dynamic character of mental activity. Energy is always in motion, forces are always moving in some direction, opposition exists between forces, and so on. In Hartmann's view, conflict of forces is inevitable.

But how can conflict be studied, if, as psychoanalytic theory has it, the mental activity that explains human behavior is unconscious? Of course, analysts argue that the best way is through the psychoanalytic interview, and Hartmann discusses this method in his paper. But, as you will read in the third selection in this chapter (by Nagel), from a scientific point of view the psychoanalytic clinical (interview) method leaves much to be desired.

The second article in this chapter, by Lloyd H. Silverman, presents a laboratory method for the experimental testing of hypotheses about unconscious conflict that are generated by psychoanalytic theory. The author claims that his method—"subliminal psychodynamic activation"—allows for the testing of psychoanalytic concepts as well as of alternative theoretical positions within general psychoanalytic theory. In this paper, Silverman reports on the results of a number of experiments that he and his colleagues have carried out over a period of several years, all of them involving the experimental inducement of unconscious conflict and the subsequent effect on "manifest psychopathology." He concludes that his laboratory method is a suitable one for studying unconscious conflict and its causal relationship to psychopathology and should therefore be at least partly acceptable as a test of psychoanalytic theory to such critics of psychoanalytic science as Ernest Nagel.

Nagel, a philosopher, is primarily interested in methodological issues in psychoanalytic theory. In the third selection of this chapter, he addresses himself to problems of the logical structure of the theory as well as to the nature of the evidence in support of psychoanalytic theory. He concludes, as do Wolpe and Rachman in Chapter One, that psychoanalytic theory—whether it be the "classical" psychoanalytic theory of Freud or the ego psychology of Hartmann—falls far short of being an acceptable scientific theory.

SUGGESTIONS FOR FURTHER READING

Hartmann's major work is his book *Ego Psychology and the Problem of Adaptation,* published by International Universities Press in 1958.

Probably the most frequently quoted selection on Hartmann's position is a chapter in a book edited by Anna Freud et al.: *The Psychoanalytic Study of the Child,* Volume 2, published by International Universities Press in 1947. The chapter is written by Heinz Hartmann, E. Kris, and R. M. Loewenstein and appears on pages 11 through 38. In fact, all of the volumes of *The Psychoanalytic Study of the Child* contain articles relevant to the ego-psychology approach in psychoanalytic theory. (Recall that Hartmann describes this approach in his paper in this chapter.) In Volume 1 of this series, there is an excellent presentation of this approach by Hartmann and E. Kris.

Another ego psychologist who has published extensively is David Rapaport. For many years he was associated with the Menninger Clinic in Topeka, Kansas. The Menninger Clinic publishes a journal, called the *Bulletin of the Menninger Clinic,* in which Rapaport has published two important papers on ego autonomy. One is "The Autonomy of the Ego," published in 1951 (Volume 15, pages 113 to 123); the other is entitled "The Theory of Ego Autonomy: A Generalization" and was published in 1958 (Volume 22, pages 13 to 25). Following Rapaport's death in 1960, one of his colleagues, Merton Gill, published a volume of Rapaport's work. This large volume, titled *The Collected Papers of David Rapaport* and published by Basic Books in 1967, is an excellent source for the serious student.

Heinz Hartmann
PSYCHOANALYSIS AS A SCIENTIFIC THEORY

When some forty-five years ago Freud (12) wrote for the first time about the philosophical interests in analysis, his main point was that philosophy could not avoid taking fully into account what he then called "the hypothesis of unconscious mental activities." He also mentioned that philosophers may be interested in the interpretation of philosophical thought in terms of psychoanalysis—adding, though, here as elsewhere, that the fact that a theory or doctrine is determined by psychological processes of many kinds does not necessarily invalidate its scientific truth. Since then, the knowledge of human behavior and motivation we owe to analysis has greatly increased, has become much more comprehensive but also more specific; and this development has certainly influenced not only social science, anthropology, and medicine, but also philosophy in a broad sense. This does not, though, necessarily mean that analysis can "answer" what one usually calls philosophical problems; it usually means that it leads to looking at them from a new angle. Some of its potentialities in this respect have been made use of only rather scantily so far. I am thinking, for example, of its possible contribution toward a better understanding of ethical problems. The interest psychoanalysis may have for philosophers has clearly two aspects: it resides partly in the new psychological findings and theories of analysis, but also in certain questions of methodology raised by Freud's and other psychoanalysts' approach to the study of man.

In speaking of psychoanalysis one often refers to a therapeutic technique. One may also refer to a method of psychological investigation whose main aspects are free association and interpretation; or, finally, to a body of facts and theories (Freud, 13). In this last sense, we would certainly consider as psychoanalytical any knowledge gained directly by Freud's method of investigation; but many of us would today consider analysis to include related procedures such as the application of psychoanalytic insights to data of direct child observation, a field which has grown in importance in the last two decades. Of the three aspects just mentioned, it is the method of exploration that has undergone the least change; it is commonly used in a situation defined by a certain set of rules and referred to as the psychoanalytic situation or the psychoanalytic interview. The therapeutic technique has been repeatedly modified, and psychoanalytic theory has gone through a series of more or less radical modifications, by Freud and by others. I want to emphasize that the interrelations among these three aspects are, in analysis, a central topic—though in the context of this presentation I can refer to them only occasionally.

The theories of psychoanalysis follow principles of systematization, as do theories in

Abridged from "Psychoanalysis as a Scientific Theory," by H. Hartmann. In S. Hook (Ed.), *Psychoanalysis, Scientific Method, and Philosophy*. Copyright 1959 by New York University Press. Reprinted by permission.

other fields. Freud, however, did not speak of analysis as a "system," but rather accentuated its unfinished character, its flexibility, and the tentative nature of a considerable part of it. Actually, adjustments and reformulations of various aspects of theory have repeatedly become necessary. There are chapters such as the psychology of the dream, of libidinal development, of anxiety, and of symptom formation, that have been more systematically worked out than others. Psychoanalysis is obviously far from being a closed system of doctrines, though it has sometimes been represented as such. Also, though some fundamental tenets of psychoanalysis are accepted by all (Freudian) analysts, agreement on all of them is obviously lacking.

There is in analysis a hierarchy of hypotheses as to their closeness to observation, their generality, and the degree to which they have been confirmed. It appears that a neater classification as to these points and a higher degree of systematization (considering the different levels of theorizing) than exist today would not only facilitate my task in discussing psychoanalysis as a scientific theory but also clarify the standing of analysis as a scientific discipline. Promising efforts in this direction have been made and are being made by analysts and also by nonanalysts, but as yet no complete and systematical outline drawn from this angle is available; a recent work by David Rapaport (30), soon to be published, may come close to performing this task. This is probably the reason, or one of the reasons, that in more or less general presentations of psychoanalysis references to its history abound, and the reader will forgive me if they do in this paper too, at least in its first part. I shall mostly refer to the work of Freud, because most of the more general theories of analysis have their origin in it, and because he is in many ways more representative of psychoanalytic thinking than anybody else.

Often historical explanations are substituted for system; an attempt is made to clarify the function of propositions in their relation to others by tracing their place in the development of analysis. Also, without such historical reference it happens over and over again that analytical hypotheses are dealt with on one level, so to say, which belong to different phases of theory formation, and some of which have actually been discarded and replaced by others. Again, because of the comparatively low level of systematization, I think it is true that even today a thorough knowledge of at least some chapters of analytic theory cannot be acquired without knowledge of its history (Hartmann, 16).

From the beginning, explanations of human behavior in terms of propositions about unconscious mental processes have been an essential part and one characteristic feature of psychoanalysis. I may, then, start by introducing Freud's concepts of unconscious processes. He makes a distinction between two forms of unconscious mental activity. The one, called preconscious, functions more or less as conscious activities do. It is not conscious, in a descriptive sense, but can become conscious without having to overcome powerful counter-forces. Where such overcoming of resistances is necessary, as is the case with repressed material, we speak of unconscious processes in the stricter, the dynamic, sense of the word. The dynamic impact of these latter unconscious processes on human behavior—and not only in the case of mental disease—is one main tenet of Freud's theory of unconscious mental activities.

There is rather wide agreement that conscious data are insufficient for the explanation of a considerable part of behavior, and particularly of those aspects that were first studied in analysis. However, its critics have repeatedly claimed that the introduction of unconscious processes is superfluous. The explanation needed could be stated, or should be sought for, in terms of the more reliable data of brain physiology. The question here is not just whether, and why, explanations based on such data would be per se more reliable, nor why psychological hypotheses about mental processes ought not to be introduced in explaining human behavior. We have also to consider the fact that, given the actual state of brain physiology, many and even comparatively simple aspects of behavior of the kind we are dealing with in analysis cannot be explained. To rely on brain physiology alone would mean to renounce explanation of the greatest part of the field that psychoanalysis has set out to explain. Or, if one should insist on attempting an explanation on physiological grounds, the resultant hypotheses would of necessity be considerably more tenuous and more speculative even than psychoanalytic hypotheses are suspected to be by its critics today.

Freud, well trained in the anatomy and physiology of the brain, actually started out by attempting to devise a physiological psychology that could provide him with concepts and hypotheses to account for his clinical insights. But beyond a certain point this approach proved of no use. He was thus led to replace it by a set of psychological hypotheses and constructs; and this step represents probably the most important turning point in the history of psychoanalysis. It was the beginning in analysis of psychological theory, the heuristic value of which he found to be greatly superior—a point that, I think, has been corroborated by its subsequent development.

But it is true that even after this radical turn in his approach Freud held on to the expectation, shared by many analysts, that one day the development of brain physiology would make it possible to base psychoanalysis on its findings and theories. He did not think this would happen during his lifetime, in which he proved to be right. In the meantime certain, though limited, parallels between analytic propositions and discoveries in the physiology of the brain have become apparent. Also, the usefulness of some psychoanalytic hypotheses for their field has been recognized by at least some representatives of brain research (Adrian, 1). As to the psychology of unconscious processes, I think it can be said that Freud in developing that part of analysis was much less interested in the ultimate "nature" or "essence" of such processes—whatever this may mean—than in finding a suitable conceptual framework for the phenomena he had discovered.

While Freud, after the first years of his scientific work, relinquished the attempt to account for his findings in terms of physiology, it is nevertheless characteristic of some of his psychoanalytic theorizing that he used physiological models. He was guided by the trend in German physiology which has been designated as the physicalist school (Bernfeld, 5) whose representatives were, among others, Helmholtz and Bruecke, the latter being one of Freud's teachers. Certain aspects of the psychology of neurosis, for example, led him to introduce into psychoanalysis the concept of regression (to earlier stages of development), which had been used in the physiology of his day; this concept, though, acquired new meaning in the context in which he used it. Also, in making "function" the criterion for defining what he called the mental systems (ego, id, superego), Freud used physiology as a model. But this no longer implies any correlation to any specific physiological organization (Hartmann, Kris, Loewenstein, 21). The value of such borrowings or analogies has, of course, to be determined in every single instance by confronting their application with tested knowledge (data and hypotheses). Physiological models (also occasionally physical models, as is obvious, for instance, in Freud's concept of a "mental apparatus") have been used also by other psychoanalysts (see Kubie in a recent lecture) in order to illustrate certain characteristics of mental phenomena or to suggest a new hypothesis. The use even of metaphors need not of necessity lead into muddled thinking once their place in theory has been clearly delineated. The danger that earlier implications of those model concepts might impair their fruitful use in the new context of psychoanalysis has on the whole been successfully avoided (Hartmann-Kris-Loewenstein).

The broadening of the scope of psychology that came about as the consequence of the inclusion of propositions about unconscious mental processes meant, first of all, that many aspects of a person's life history that had never been explained before—and that, as a matter of fact, one had not even tried to explain—could be accounted for in terms of the individual's experience and dispositions. Causation in the field of personality is traceable only at its fringes without this broadening of theory. Freud was a strict determinist and often stated that to fill that gap in earlier psychological approaches, partly because of which the study of personality had been unsatisfactory, was one of his primary aims in developing analytic theory. More recently it has been said, by the mathematician von Mises (29), that the observations correspond rather to statistical than to causal relations. I may mention at this point that this interest in the causation of mental phenomena included, quite naturally, also the interest in what we call the genetic viewpoint, since Freud's attention had been drawn to many facts of early childhood which had been unknown, and regularities in the relationships between early childhood situations and the behavior of the adult had become apparent. With Freud, the investigation of highly complex series of experience and behavior, extending over long periods of time, soon moved into the center of interest. Developmental research was to become equally important for psychoanalytic theory and practice. It is significant that the reconstructive approach in analysis led not only to the discovery of a great wealth of childhood material in every individual case, but also to the ascertainment of typical sequences of developmental phases. The genetic approach has become so pervasive, not only in psychopathology but also in psychoanalytic psychology in general, that in analysis phenomena are often grouped together, not according to their descriptive similarities but as belonging together if they have a common genetic root (oral character, anal character). It was only much later that this predominance of a genetic conceptualization was counterbalanced by a sharper distinction between genesis and function, to which I shall shortly return in speaking of the structural point of view.

Here I want to add that while I just spoke of the study of the individual's "life history," it would be misleading (though it actually has been done) to classify this aspect of analysis as an historical discipline. This misinterpretation may be traceable to its comparison with archaeology, which Freud occasionally uses. It is true that most analytical knowledge has been gained in the psychoanalytic interview and that the concern with developmental problems refers primarily to the history of individuals. But this should not obfuscate the fact that the aim of these studies is (besides its therapeutic purpose) to develop lawlike propositions which then, of course, transcend individual observations.

At this point I should like briefly to summarize the role of psychoanalysis as a psychology of motivation, bearing in mind that nowadays psychoanalysis takes into consideration the interaction of the individual with his environment, as well as his so-called "inner-psychic" processes. The study of these psychic processes constitutes what, in analysis, we call "metapsychology," a term that signifies not (as it might seem) that which is beyond psychology altogether, but simply those psychological investigations that are not limited to conscious phenomena, and that formulate the most general assumptions of analysis on the most abstract level of theory. Metapsychology is concerned with the substructures of personality, with the ego, the id, and the superego which are defined as units of functions. The id refers to the instinctual aspect, the ego to the reality principle and to the "centralization of functional control" (to borrow a term from brain physiology). The superego has its biological roots in the long dependency on the parents and in the helplessness of the human child; it develops out of identification with the parents; and it accounts for the fact that moral conflict and guilt feelings become a natural and fundamental aspect of human behavior. The theoretical and clinical advantage of the structural formulations, referring to the distinction of ego, id, superego, has several reasons. The most important is probably that the demarcation lines of the three systems, ego, id, superego are geared to the typical conflicts of man: conflicts with the instinctual drives, with moral conscience, and with the outside world. The paramount importance on neurotic *and* normal development of these conflicts, and of the ways to solve them, was one of the earliest discoveries of Freud and has remained central in psychoanalytic practice and theory ever since.

Critics of analysis often tend to underrate the wealth of individual data on which it is built. But on the other hand, it also happens that the theoretical nature of concepts like libido is not fully realized; for example, libido is often identified with sexual experience, or as a mere generalization of some observable connections.

In the beginnings of psychoanalysis (even after the importance of unconscious processes had been realized), Freud still adhered more or less strictly to associationism. But when he found conflict to be a primary motivating force of behavior, and specifically an important etiological agent in neurosis, he gradually developed the concept of mental tendencies and purposive ideas. Psychoanalysis became a psychology of motivation, the motives being partly, but not generally, considered in analogy with those consciously experienced. There originated the idea of wishes, in certain circumstances, warded off by defensive techniques. He discovered the role of repression and later of other defense mechanisms, like projection, isolation, undoing, and so on. The consideration of mental processes from this angle of synergistic or antagonistic motivating forces is what has been known since as the dynamic aspect of psychoanalysis. The systematic and objective study of conflict has remained one of its essential aspects and has proved a necessary and fruitful avenue to the explanation of human behavior. This was a second bold step in the development of psychoanalysis. The importance of "conflict" had, of course, been known in religious and philosophical doctrines and in literature, but scientific psychology before Freud had had no means to approach the subject.

The dynamic factors involved in both sides of a conflict were, for some time, rather poorly defined. It was, then, again primarily data of analytical observation that led to the realization of the dominance of the instinctual drives among the motivating forces. I am referring here to Freud's discovery of infantile sexuality. This discovery was, at the time, considered by many as the product of revolting imagination; today, it can easily be confirmed in every nursery.

Even at the period when instinctual motivation seemed to be pretty much ubiquitous, the basic fact of conflict was not overlooked. Self-preservative instinctual drives were, at the time, thought of as the opponents of sexuality. Besides this, the concept of overdetermination, referring to the multiple motivation of all human behavior, continued also through the phase in which motivation was, on the level of general theory, nearly always considered instinctual.

Again, to fit it to his field of observation Freud has to modify the concept of "instinct" commonly used in other fields. His term, in German, *Trieb,* in English, "instinctual drive," or "drive," is certainly not identical with what one refers to in speaking of the instincts of lower animals. His concept of drives had to prove its usefulness with respect to human psychology. Here, the sources of the drives are of much less importance than their aims and their objects. The lesser rigidity of the human drives, the comparatively easy shift of the aims, the freeing of many activities from a rigid connection with one definite instinctual tendency, the comparative independence from and variety of possible response to outer and inner stimuli have to be taken into account in considering the role of the drives in human psychology. Still, the psychoanalytic theory of instinctual drives is broad enough to show also many impressive parallels with the findings of a modern school of zoologists (ethnologists).

The concept of a continuity of this driving force allows the consideration of a great variety of mental acts from the angle of their investment with drive energy. Also in this way it is possible to understand the close relationship of many mental processes which, looked at from the surface, would appear to be entirely heterogeneous. The capacity for displacement or transformation into various kinds of human activities; also the motivational role traceable through and specific on all levels of man's growth from birth to maturity; their central role in typical conflicts; and the fact that they involve relations to human objects—these are some of the psychologically essential aspects of the psychoanalytic concept of human drives. According to Freud, sexuality and aggression are, among all the drives one could describe, those that come closest to fulfilling the demands psychoanalysis makes on a concept of drives.

The concept of mental energy was then elaborated in the sense that it is the drives that are the main sources of energy in what Freud calls the "mental apparatus." However, a strictly speaking quantifying approach to these energic problems has so far not been developed. Or rather: while it is possible to speak of a greater or lesser degree of, let's say, a resistance (against the uncovering of some hidden material), we have no way of measuring it. To account for the difference in the unconscious and the conscious (and preconscious) processes Freud postulated two forms of energy distribution, conceptualized as, respectively, primary and secondary processes. The primary processes represent a tendency to immediate discharge, while the secondary processes are guided by the consideration of reality. This distinction is again both theoretically significant and clinically quite helpful. The thesis that behavior is to be explained also in terms of its energic cathexis is what we call, in analysis, the economic viewpoint.

The regulation of energies in the mental apparatus is assumed to follow the pleasure principle, the reality principle (derived from the pleasure principle under the influence of ego-development), and a tendency to keep the level of excitation constant or at a minimum. There are parallels to this in hypotheses formulated by others, and again the use of physical and physiological models played a role in the Freudian concepts.

The three aspects of psychoanalytic theory I have mentioned so far—the topographical (conscious-preconscious-unconscious), the dynamic, and the economic (energic)—represent Freud's first approach to what he called "metapsychology." It is postulated that a satisfactory explanation of human behavior includes its consideration in relation to all aspects of metapsychology. The "meta" in this term points to a theory going "beyond" the investigation of conscious phenomena. The word, generally accepted in psychoanalysis, has proved misleading for many outside analysis. Actually, "metapsychology" is nothing but a term for the highest level of abstraction used in analytic psychology.

A fourth aspect of metapsychology, called structural, was explicitly stated considerably later, though it was implicit in earlier theoretical thinking on mental conflicts. The forces opposing the drives in typical conflict formations, warding them off and forcing them to compromise formations (of which the neurotic symptom may serve as an example), are today conceptualized as an essential aspect of what we call the ego. At the core of this concept formation is the recognition of the relevant differences between instinctual tendencies which strive for discharge, and other tendencies that enforce postponement of discharge and are modifiable by the influence of the environment. This means, of course, that the dynamic and economic viewpoints can no longer be limited to the vicissitudes of instinctual drives. The original concept of a defensive ego had to be broadened to include in the ego those nondefensive functions of the mental apparatus that are noninstinctual in character. Many of these are not, or not necessarily, part of the conflictual set-up; we call them today ''the non-conflictual sphere of the ego'' (Hartmann, 15). Here belong (though they too may be involved in conflict, without, however, originating in it) perception, thinking, memory, action, and so on. It is likely that in man not only instinctual factors are in part determined by heredity, but also the apparatus of the ego underlying the functions just mentioned. We speak of the primary autonomous functions of the ego. It is true that analysis is, due to its method, directly dealing with environmental factors and with reactions to them, but this has never implied a denial on principle, of heredity. It is in this sense that we speak of a drive constitution, and today also of constitutional elements in the ego, and of the role of maturational factors in the typical sequence of developmental phases.

To those noninstinctual functions that we attribute to the ego belongs also what one can call the centralized functional control which integrates the different parts of personality with each other and with outer reality. This function (synthetic function or organizing function) is in a way similar to what, since Cannon, we call homeostasis, and may represent one level of it.

The ego is, then, a substructure of personality and is defined by its functions. The instinctual aspect of personality is today conceptualized as the id. Through the development of the ego it becomes possible that the pleasure principle, dominant with the instinctual drives, can be modified to that consideration of reality, in thinking and action, that makes adaptation possible and is termed, as I said before, the reality principle. Through recent work, the relation between adaptation to outer reality and the state of integration of inner reality has become more accessible. This development in psychoanalytic theory has thus led to an improved understanding of man's relations to his environment, and to the most significant part of it, his fellowmen—which is, however, not to say that the socio-cultural aspects of mental functions and development had been overlooked in earlier analysis. Psychoanalysis, in contradistinction to some other schools of psychology, has never considered ''innerpsychic'' processes only, but also, and not only accidentally, includes the consideration of the individual's interactions with the environment. At any rate, the study of object relations in human development has more recently become one of the most fruitful centers of analytic interest (''new environmentalism,'' Kris, 25). Ego psychology represents a more balanced consideration of the biological and the social and cultural aspects of human behavior. We may say that in analysis cultural phenomena are often studied in their biological context and significance and biological phenomena in relation to the socio-cultural environment (Hartmann, 19). But this aspect will be discussed more fully later.

Some of the functions of the ego have, in the course of development, to be wrested from the influence of the drives. Gradually, they then reach, through a change of function, a certain degree of independence from instinctual origins and of resistance against reinvolvement with the drives (secondary autonomy—see Hartmann, 15, 17). A similar concept, though less specific in relation to psychoanalytic propositions, has been introduced by G. Allport (2). This relative independence of the ego is also energically conceptualized, with respect to the sources of energy at the disposal of ego functions. The necessity to distinguish function from genesis more clearly is one of the main implications of the structural viewpoint.

The third unit of functions, considered a substructure of personality, is called the superego. To it we attribute the functions of self-criticism, conscience and the formation of ideals. The acceptance of moral standards is considered a natural step in ontogenesis. Moral conflict, and the guilt feelings that are an expression of it, are, from the time when the superego has been instituted, one fundamental aspect of human behavior. The superego has a biological root in the comparatively long dependency and helplessness of the child of the human species, which also means increased importance of the parents for its development. The superego develops out of identification with them, to which, in subsequent layers of development, identifications with others are added. Also obvious in its genesis is a socio-cultural factor, which accounts for an important segment of tradition formation. The acceptance of certain moral demands, the rejection of others, the degree of severity of the superego and its capacity to enforce its demands can very frequently be traced in clinical investigation.

Structural hypotheses are in many ways more comprehensive, but also, if I may say so, more elegant than earlier formulations of partly the same problems. They have also a considerable value in clinical thinking, because they are particularly fit to account for what has remained dominant in clinical work, that is, the various forms of typical conflict situations. Actually, the demarcation lines of those units of functions, or systems, or substructures of personality are so drawn that they correspond to the main conflicts of man, which we now describe as conflicts between ego and id, superego and ego, and ego and reality. It was in this respect that Freud found the older topographical model, the layer model (conscious-preconscious-unconscious), disappointing, though in other respects it still retains a certain degree of significance. Defenses as well as drives can be unconscious; thus differences between conscious and unconscious processes cannot be used to account for these conflicts.

I thought it advisable to begin by giving a picture of certain fundamentals of psychoanalytic theory, and of the degree of its comprehensiveness, by indicating at least some of its dimensions, and also the relations between different parts of these theories. Its comprehensiveness means also its actual or potential importance in many neighboring fields. My survey shows also at least some of the points at which questions can be raised from the viewpoint of a philosophy of science. There would have been an alternative to the way of presentation I chose. I could have shown how, in the analysis of a symptom or a dream, our observations lead to anticipations, and how the various levels of our conceptual tools are brought to bear on them; also, how in this process theoretical thinking is constantly brought back to the observables. But this alternative would inevitably demand the introduction of a great number of variables and a discussion of the analytic method and the analytic situation much broader than I am able to give here. Of course, a sector of psychoanalytic propositions can be tested outside analysis, and some have been tested in this way; but it is still true that it is, in the field of analysis, extremely difficult to assay the suitability of the hypotheses for the purposes for which they have been primarily devised without the use, in the analytic situation, of the analytic method.

Generally, Freud's views on introspection have not always been clearly appreciated. They are, though, evident already in the kind of psychoanalytic thinking that is comparatively close to observational data, as in Freud's ideas on the psychopathology of everyday life. In a slip of the tongue, for instance, when, in place of a word we consciously intended to use, another one, not consciously intended, appears, we use the behavioral aspect in evaluating the psychological situation—we use it, that is, in taking the word actually spoken as an indication of an unconscious motivation that takes precedence over the conscious one.

The data gathered in the psychoanalytic situation with the help of the psychoanalytic method are primarily behavioral data; and the aim is clearly the exploration of human behavior. The data are mostly the patient's verbal behavior, but include other kinds of action. They include his silences, his postures (Deutsch, 7), and his movements in general, more specifically his expressive movements. While analysis aims at an explanation of human behavior, those data, however, are interpreted in analysis in terms of mental processes, of motivation, of ''meaning''; there is, then, a clear-cut difference between this approach and the one usually called "behavioristic," and this difference is even more marked if we consider the beginnings of behaviorism, rather than its more recent formulations.

As to the data, it is hard to give, outside the analytic process itself, an impression of the wealth of observational data collected in even one single "case." One frequently refers to the comparatively small number of cases studied in analysis and tends to forget the very great number of actual observations on which we base, in every individual case, the interpretations of an aspect of a person's character, symptoms and so on.[1]

By keeping certain variables in the analytic situation, if not constant, as close to constancy as the situation allows, it becomes easier to evaluate the significance of other variables that enter the picture. The best-studied example of this is what is called the "passivity" of the analyst, in contradistinction to the considerably more pronounced activity of the psychotherapist. This is not to claim that psychoanalysis is an experimental discipline. However, there are situations where it comes close to it. At any rate, there is sufficient evidence for the statement that our observations in the psychoanalytic situation, set in the context of psychoanalytic experience and hypotheses, make predictions possible—predictions of various degrees of precision or reliability, but as a rule superior to any others that have been attempted in the psychology of personality. Due to the emphasis on the genetic viewpoint, many predictions are what has been called "predictions of the past," (Hartmann, Kris, 20) that is, reconstructions of the past which can often be confirmed in astonishing detail (Bonaparte, 6). One obvious limitation of our predictive potential is, of course, the great number of factors determining, according to psychoanalytic theory, every single element of behavior—what Freud has termed "overdetermination." Still, our technique is constantly directed by tentative predictions of the patient's reaction. Also, studies in developmental psychology by means of direct child observation, such as have been conducted by E. Kris and other psychoanalysts (M. Kris, 26), are guided by the formulation of expectations and their checking in individual cases. Here I just want to point to one way in which psychoanalytic hypotheses can be used vis-à-vis individual cases and how they may be confirmed in clinical experience. I may mention here that problems of validation of psychoanalytic hypotheses ought not to be equated, as has too often been done, with the problem of therapeutic success.

A further difficulty results from the fact that psychoanalytic theory has also to deal with the relation between observer and observed in the analytic situation. There are personality layers, if you will excuse this term, that in the average case the observed cannot reach without the help of the observer and his method of observation. But the insight of the observer ought not to be confused with the insight of the observed. Some of these problems belong in a theory of psychoanalytic technique. But there is also the problem of the "personal equation" (Hartmann, 18; Kris, 25). The field of observation includes not only the patient, but also the observer who interacts with the former ("participant observation"). The interaction of analyst and analysand are accounted for in the theories of transference and countertransference. As to the potential handicaps of observations traceable to the mental processes of the observer, they are subject to the constant scrutiny of the analyst. Some such handicaps of psychological observation can certainly be eliminated by the personal analysis of the observer, and this is one of the reasons that a didactic analysis is an essential element in the training of our students of analysis. Thus, what I want to say here is not that in the psychology of personality objectivity is impossible. It is rather that psychoanalysis has discovered potential sources of error and found a way to combat them.

---

[1]Thus every single clinical "case" represents, for research, hundreds of data of observed regularities, and in hundreds of respects.

Another aspect of the clinical origins of psychoanalytic theory is the fact that more was found, in the beginning, about pathological than about normal behavior. The etiology of neurosis was studied before the etiology of health, though psychoanalysis has, on principle, always aimed at a comprehensive general psychology. Also, as I mentioned, more became known, in the first attempts to deal with the field, about the instinctual drives, especially about sexuality and its development, than about the forces opposing the drives in the typical ego-id conflicts. This, however, has changed in the last two or three decades, and analysis thus has today come closer to what it always was intended to be, though not every aspect and not every implication of its very comprehensive conceptual frame has so far been actually developed.

In clinical work, one is used to being guided by signs and symptoms in forming an opinion on the presence or absence of a pathological process. But the question of the significance and the use of signs for purposes of explanation is, of course, logically of much wider relevance. Different meanings can be attributed to the terms sign, signal, expressive sign, symbol, and so on, and these differences are important also in psychoanalysis. However, I don't propose to deal with this problem here. Suffice it to say that a considerable part of psychoanalytic work can be described as the use of signs—a series of associations, a dream, an affect vis-à-vis the analyst—as indications of mental processes. In this sense one speaks of the psychoanalytic method as a method of interpretation (Hartmann, 14; Bernfeld, 4; Loewenstein, 28). This has both a cognitive and a therapeutic aspect. They partly coincide, that is, in so far as a therapeutic agent of foremost significance in analysis is making the patient aware of, and capable of integrating, previously unconscious and, through defense, splitoff processes. Some of those signs, for example, some of the symbols we find in dreams, have a rather ubiquitous meaning, while the interpretation of others requires a closer scrutiny of the individual under observation. At any rate, there are many situations in which the relation between a sign and what it signifies becomes easily recognizable, for instance in the associations immediately following the observation of some detail of behavior. In others, various levels of theory have to be introduced to explain the connection. Such sign systems are used today not only in the psychoanalytic situation, but also in the study by analysts, by means of direct observation, of child development. Many childhood situations of incisive significance for the formation of the adult personality have a low probability of direct manifestation. One tries to learn about the sign function of data of child behavior for a recognition of the central, and often unconscious, development that we know from the psychoanalytic interview (Hartmann, 18). At this point it is possible, or even likely, that misunderstanding may occur of what I have said about a low probability of manifestation outside analysis of certain processes investigated in analysis. I want, then, to add explicitly that this was not meant to be a general statement. Many phenomena first studied in the analytic situation could later be studied also in the direct observation of psychotics, in so-called applied psychoanalysis, or in the direct observation of children. What I want to emphasize in this context is that the comparative study of reconstructive data and data of direct observation of children leads, on the one hand, to the confirmation of analytical propositions; on the other hand it leads to the formulation of more specific hypotheses.

The essential importance of constructs for the coherence of the psychoanalytic system (or whatever we choose to call it) can be gathered already from the brief outline I have given in the first part of this discussion. Theories, or hypotheses of a different order, connect them with observational data. That these constructs, which are introduced because of their explanatory value, cannot be directly defined in terms of observational data, but that interferences from the constructs can be tested by observation, has long been known in psychoanalysis (Hartmann, 14). Still, some of these constructs seem particularly suspect to many critics of analysis. An occasional lack of caution in the formulation of its propositions, or Freud's liking for occasional striking metaphors, has led to the accusation against analysis of an anthropomorphization of its concepts. But in all those cases a more careful formulation can be substituted which will dispel this impression.

There is, then, the question whether and in what sense such constructs are considered "real"; and, more specifically, the question has often been asked whether and in what sense Freud considered constructs like libido, the "system unconscious," and the substructures of personality in the sense of structural psychology, as real. He said that the basic concepts of science form rather the roof than the foundation of science and ought to be changed when they no longer seem able to account for experience; also that they have the character of conventions. But he certainly thought that what he meant to cover by these basic concepts had effects which could be observed. He was in no danger of confusing concepts with realities; he was a "realist" in a different sense. He does not seem to have thought that "real" means just "the simplest theoretical presentation of our experiences," but rather that those basic concepts pointed to something real in the ordinary sense of the word.

As to the genetic propositions of analysis, the direct observation of children has not only become a rich source of information, but also given us the possibility to make our hypotheses more specific and to check their validity. A great number of Freud's hypotheses on childhood could be confirmed by direct observation of children. But to validate more completely our genetic propositions, "systematic observations of life histories from birth on" are necessary. "If the longitudinal observation in our own civilization were to be systematized and the study of life histories were to be combined with that of the crucial situations in Freud's sense, many hunches might be formulated as propositions, and others might be discarded" (Hartmann and Kris, 20).

The literature on experimental research, both in animals and in man, devised for the purpose of testing propositions derived from psychoanalysis has become very extensive. It has been repeatedly reviewed (Sears, 31; Kris, 24; Benjamin, 3; Frenkel-Brunswik, 10; and others), and I do not think I should go into it in any detail here. The following remarks are, then, random remarks and do not attempt to be in any way systematic. The classical animal experiments of Hunt, Levy, Miller, Masserman are probably known to many of you. Many of the animal experiments were conducted with considerable insight and great skill. Where the experimental set-up is adequate, the frequency of "confirmation" is impressive. Or, as Halgard (22) states, "It has been possible to parallel many psychoanalytic phenomena in the laboratory. When this is done, the correspondence between predictions according to psychoanalytic theory and what is found is on the whole very satisfactory."

BIBLIOGRAPHY

1. Adrian, E. D., "The Mental and the Physical Origins of Behaviour," *International Journal of Psychoanalysis,* XXVII, 1946.
2. Allport, G., *Personality.* New York: Henry Holt, 1937.
3. Benjamin, J., "Methodological Considerations in the Validation and Elaboration of Psychoanalytical Personality Theory." *American Journal of Orthopsychiatry,* 20, 1950.
4. Bernfeld, S., "Der Begriff der Deutung in der Psychoanalyse," *Zeitschrift für Angewandte Psychologie,* XLII, 1932.
5. ———, "Freud's Earliest Theories and the School of Helmholtz," *Psychoanalytic Quarterly,* XIII, 1944.
6. Bonaparte, M., "Notes on the Analytical Discovery of a Primal Scene," *Psychoanalytic Study of the Child,* I, 1945.

7. Deutsch, F., "Analytic Posturology." *Psychoanalytic Quarterly,* XXI, 1952.

8. Dollard, J. and Miller, N. E., *Personality and Psychotherapy,* New York: McGraw-Hill, 1950.

9. Ellis, A., *An Introduction to the Principles of Scientific Psychoanalysis,* Genetic Psychology Monograph, 41, 1950.

10. Frenkel-Brunswik, E., *Psychoanalysis and the Unity of Science,* Proceedings of the American Academy of Arts and Sciences, 80, 1954.

11. Freud, A., "The Contributions of Psychoanalysis to Genetic Psychology," *American Journal of Orthopsychiatry,* XXI, 1951.

12. Freud, S., *The Claim of Psychoanalysis to Scientific Interest.* London: Hogarth Press, Standard Edition, Vol. XIII.

13. ———, *Psycho-Analysis.* London: Hogarth Press, Standard Edition, Vol. XVIII.

14. Hartmann, H., *Die Grundlagen der Psychoanalyse.* Leipzig, 1927.

15. ———, "Ichpsychologie und Anpassungsproblem," *Internationale Zeitschrift für Psychoanalyse,* XXIV, 1939. Partly translated in: D. Rapaport, *Organization and Pathology of Thought.* New York: Columbia University Press, 1951.

16. ———, "Comments on the Psychoanalytic Theory of Instinctual Drives," *Psychoanalytic Quarterly,* XVII, 1948.

17. ———, "Comments on the Psychoanalytic Theory of the Ego," *Psychoanalytic Study of the Child,* V, 1950.

18. ———, "Psychoanalysis and Developmental Psychology," *Psychoanalytic Study of the Child,* V, 1950.

19. ———, "The Development of the Ego Concept in Freud's Work," *International Journal of Psychoanalysis,* XXXVII, 1956.

20. ——— and Kris, E., "The Genetic Approach in Psychoanalysis," *Psychoanalytic Study of the Child,* I, 1945.

21. ———, Kris, E. and Loewenstein, R., "Comments on the Formation of Psychic Structure," *Psychoanalytic Study of the Child,* II, 1946.

22. Hilgard, E., "Experimental Approaches to Psychoanalysis," in: *Psychoanalysis as Science,* ed. E. Pumpian-Mindlin. Stanford University Press, 1952.

23. Klein, G., "Cognizant Style and Motivation," in: *Assessment of Human Motives,* ed. G. Lindzey. New York: Rinehart, 1958.

24. Kris, E., "The Nature of Psychoanalytic Propositions and their Validation," in: *Freedom and Experience,* ed. S. Hook and M. R. Konvitz, Cornell University Press, 1947.

25. ———, "Notes on the Development and on some Current Problems of Psychoanalytic Child Psychology," *Psychoanalytic Study of the Child,* V, 1950.

26. Kris, M., "The Use of Prediction in a Longitudinal Study," *Psychoanalytic Study of the Child,* XII, 1957.

27. Kubie, L., "Problems and Techniques of Psychoanalytic Validation and Progress," in: *Psychoanalysis as Science,* ed. E. Pumpian-Mindlin. Stanford University Press, 1952.

28. Loewenstein, R., "Some Thoughts on Interpretation in the Theory and Practice of Psychoanalysis," *Psychoanalytic Study of the Child,* XII, 1957.

29. Mises, R. v., *Kleines Lehrbuch des Positivismus.* The Hague, 1939.

30. Rapaport, D., "The Structure of Psychoanalytic Theory (A Systematizing Attempt)," in: *Psychology: A Study of a Science,* ed. S. Koch. New York: McGraw-Hill, 1958, Vol. III.

31. Sears, R., "Survey of Objective Studies of Psychoanalytic Concepts," Social Sciences Research Council *Bulletin,* 1943, 51.

32. Wisdom, J., *Philosophy and Psycho-Analysis.* New York: Philosophical Library, 1953.

Lloyd H. Silverman
AN EXPERIMENTAL METHOD FOR
THE STUDY OF UNCONSCIOUS CONFLICT

A few years ago I reported in this journal (Silverman, 1971) the development of an experimental method that seemed to hold considerable promise for the laboratory study of theoretical propositions that lie at the heart of psychoanalytic theory. The method, which we term "subliminal psychodynamic activation," addresses itself to dynamic propositions in psychoanalysis, i.e. to postulates that relate psychopathology to conflict over unconscious libidinal and aggressive wishes. It involves the tachistoscopic exposure of both "wish-related" and (relatively) neutral pictorial and verbal stimuli to subjects at a subliminal level, then observing the differential effects these stimulations have on manifest psychopathology. In the earlier paper I discussed how the *subliminal* exposure of wish-related stimuli can be expected to influence psychopathology since they stimulate such wishes "silently"— i.e. without allowing them to emerge into consciousness; a condition that according to psychoanalytic theory generally prevails when psychopathology is implicated. In the current paper, after outlining the experimental procedure and briefly reviewing my 1971 communication, I will describe the more recent use of the method by citing the investigations that have been carried out over the past four years.[1]

I

Subjects in all our experiments are seen individually for an experimental session on one day and a control session on another with their order counterbalanced. The first session begins by the experimenter briefly explaining to the subject the purpose of the study in which he is being asked to participate and his cooperation is sought. Then the tasks that will be administered (so that the subject's psychopathology can be assessed) are described and the subject is told that several times during these tasks he will be asked to view flickers of light through an eyepiece of a machine (a tachistoscope). He is further told that at the end of the experiment he will be fully informed about these flickers and the purpose that they serve.

Then the session proper begins with a "baseline" measure obtained of the subject's propensity for whatever pathological manifestations are being studied. This is followed by the subject being asked to look into the tachistoscope and to describe the flickers of light that

Reprinted by permission from the *British Journal of Medical Psychology*, 1975, *48*, pp. 291–298. Copyright 1975 by Cambridge University Press.

[1]Experiments utilizing the subliminal psychodynamic activation method should be distinguished from the more traditional experiments in the "subliminal area" that have aimed at "finding" the tachistoscopically exposed stimulus (in transformed guise) in the subsequent productions of the subject, rather than observing its effects on psychopathology. For a recent exhaustive and detailed review of the traditional experimentation, see Dixon (1971).

appear. There follow four exposures of either a stimulus with content related to libidinal or aggressive wishes (in the experimental session) or one with neutral content (in the control session), each exposure for a 4 msec. duration. Then there is a reassessment of pathology for a determination of how the subject had been affected by the particular stimulus that had been subliminally exposed.

The procedure for the other session is identical with that just described, except that a different stimulus is exposed between the baseline and reassessment task series. Subjects who are exposed to the stimulus with wish-related content in the first session are shown the neutral stimulus in the later session and vice versa. In each session, an assistant inserts the slide with a stimulus on it into the tachistoscope before the experimenter enters the room. Thus the latter who works the tachistoscope and administers the assessment procedures never knows which of the stimuli is being exposed. Since the subject is also unaware of the nature of the stimulus (it being subliminal) the procedure can be described as "double blind" in the same sense as in drug studies where neither the patient nor the person administering the capsule knows whether a drug or a placebo is being ingested. The evaluation of pathological manifestations is carried out "blindly" also.

II

In my earlier communication most of the studies described bore on a particular hypothesis: that "primary process ego pathology"[2] is psychodynamically linked to conflict over aggression. In 14 experiments cited, this dynamic relationship received consistent and substantial support. That is, in each of these experiments the subliminal exposure of stimuli designed to stir aggressive wishes led to intensifications of this kind of pathology which did not appear after the subliminal exposure of neutral stimuli.[3]

The data from these studies allowed the following conclusions to be drawn: (1) Since 12 of the 14 experiments cited involved schizophrenics, the dynamic relationship linking primary process ego pathology with conflict over aggression has clear relevance to persons with this particular diagnosis. (2) From the results of the other two experiments cited, it also could be maintained that certain kinds of *non*-schizophrenics are vulnerable to manifesting such pathology when conflictual aggressive wishes are stimulated; namely persons who are in a state of high aggressive arousal and whose ability to modulate aggressive urges is impaired. (3) The degree of pathology that emerges in schizophrenics in response to the silent triggering

[2]"Primary process ego pathology" has been defined as: (1) thinking that is loose, illogical or unrealistic—in the extreme, the "thought disorder" of the schizophrenic—and (2) overt behaviour that is inappropriate and intrusive.

[3]Various kinds of aggressive and neutral stimuli were used in different experiments. These ranged from pictures of animals (e.g. a lion charging *v.* a bird flying), to pictures of humans (e.g. a snarling man holding a dagger *v.* a man reading a newspaper), to verbal messages (e.g. CANNIBAL EATS PERSON *v.* PEOPLE ARE WALKING). All told, nine different aggressive stimuli have been used and 11 different neutral stimuli and in each pairing, it was always the aggressive stimulus that has produced the increase in ego pathology.

From the point of view of ethical considerations, it should be noted that the intensifications of psychopathology that our experimental method brings about last but for a brief period of time, with the degree of pathology then receding to its baseline level. This becomes understandable when it is borne in mind that this method does no more than many real-life everyday events with which people are constantly confronted. For illustrations and discussion of the real-life analogues to our experimental findings see Silverman (1972).

Finally, let me note that, throughout this paper, all references to wish-related stimuli producing reactions not in evidence after the neutral stimuli imply "statistical significance," i.e. to differences yielding P values of 0.05 or lower.

of aggressive wishes is positively correlated with *(a)* length of hospitalization and *(b)* length of exposure to the noxious aggressive stimulation. (4) It is not just any kind of aggressive wishes that are linked to primary process ego pathology, but rather specifically *oral*-aggressive wishes. (5) While other kinds of ego dysfunction can appear when *libidinal* wishes are stimulated, primary process manifestations—particularly, expressions of primary process *thought,* give evidence of being linked specifically with conflict over (oral) aggression. (6) When persons who are vulnerable to the subliminal presentation of wish-related stimuli are confronted with the same stimuli presented *supraliminally* this typically has *no* pathology-inducing effect. This, we ascribed to the greater possibility of mastery when awareness of threatening stimuli is allowed. (See Silverman, 1972, for a detailed discussion on this latter point.)

III

After carrying out the studies described above on the relationship between aggressive wishes and primary process ego pathology, we turned our attention to a number of other dynamic relationships. These fall under two headings: (1) investigations of conditions that stimulate intensification of other kinds of psychopathology; (2) investigations of a condition that leads to the *reduction* of psychopathology. Let me discuss each of these in turn.

Investigations of pathology intensification. Three series of experiments have been conducted in which the pathology-inducing effects of stimulating conflictual wishes on syndromes other than primary process ego pathology have been studied: depression, homosexuality and stuttering. The most extensive series was on depression. Three experiments have been carried out on very different kinds of depressed populations in which the effects of stimulating aggressive wishes on depressive feelings were studied. One of these involved a population of hospitalized suicidal women (Rutstein & Goldberger, 1973), a second on a non-patient population of college students who manifested both depressive and hypomanic trends (Varga, 1973), and a third on a group of young adults who were prone to depression by virtue of their having lost a parent during childhood (Miller, 1973). Despite the diversity of the populations, the results for each sample were the same. The subliminal presentation of content designed to stimulate aggressive wishes led to an intensification of depressive feelings that was not in evidence after the subliminal presentation of neutral content. These findings thus offer strong support for a cardinal aspect of the psychoanalytic theory of depression: namely that such a symptom involves the turning of unconscious aggressive wishes against the self.[4]

In the investigations of homosexuality (Silverman *et al.,* 1973), two groups of male homosexuals served as subjects. Here in contrast to the studies both of depression and primary process ego pathology where aggressive wishes were assumed to be crucially implicated, the experimental stimulus utilized was intended to stir up conflict over *incestuous* wishes. With both samples of homosexuals the results were the same: after the subliminal incest condition there was an increase in homosexual and a decrease in heterosexual feelings, a constellation which was described as reflecting an intensification of the subject's homosexual orientation.

---

[4]In two of the above studies (Rutstein & Goldberger, 1973; Varga, 1973) the assumption was actually tested that the aggressive urges which were triggered remained *unconscious* while depressive feelings intensified. That is, measures were obtained of hostile as well as depressive feelings and *no change* was found for the former measure after the aggressive condition.

These data thus offer support for a crucial aspect of the psychoanalytic theory of male homosexuality: that this kind of sexual orientation involves (in part) a flight from incest.

In the third line of investigation in which stuttering was studied, two groups of individuals with this speech disturbance served as subjects. Here our interest was in investigating the effects on stuttering of stimulating conflict over *anal* wishes, the conflict that psychoanalytic theory most consistently has linked with this disturbance. Here too the results were consistent. With both samples the subliminal anal condition led to increased stuttering that was not in evidence after the subliminal neutral condition (Silverman *et al.,* 1972).[5]

The results described in the studies of depression, homosexuality and stuttering comprise the first *experimental*[6] evidence for the particular psychoanalytic dynamic formulations cited. Thus these investigations are relevant to the position taken by many academic psychologists and clinicians of non-psychoanalytic theoretical persuasion who have disputed the psychoanalytic view that psychopathology is linked to conflict over unconscious wishes. Experimental data, I believe, are necessary for resolving this theoretical controversy. For as I have detailed elsewhere (Silverman, 1975) clinical material, even in those rare instances when it is recorded verbatim and examined systematically, rigorously and without bias, contains sufficient ambiguity so that adherents of different points of view experience no substantive challenge to their position. Similarly data from *correlational* studies, even at their best, cannot be used as support for *causal relationships* such as that between psychopathology and the arousal of conflictual wishes. Experimental data, on the other hand, do allow for such inferences and are capable of providing objective and relatively unambiguous support for relationships such as those that have been detailed.[7]

The experimental method that has been described, in addition to its utilizability for addressing the issue just mentioned that divides psychoanalytic from non-psychoanalytic points of view, can also be used for addressing questions that are controversial *within* the psychoanalytic community. Our earlier work on the relationship between primary process ego pathology and conflict over aggression comes under this heading and this I have discussed in several prior publications (Silverman, 1967, 1970, 1975). So too are a series of experiments just completed that were intended to follow-up the studies of depression, homosexuality and stuttering referred to above. In these most recent experiments, we asked the question of whether for each of the three syndromes, a wish-related stimulus *different* from the one that intensified the symptom with the original samples studied also would produce symptom intensification. Thus a new group of depressives were given the anal condition as well as the aggressive, a new group of male homosexuals received the aggressive condition as well as the incest, and a new group of stutterers were given the incest condition as well as the anal. While psychoanalytic theory would predict that for each syndrome, the second wish-related condi-

---

[5]With one of the samples of stutterers (Silverman *et al.,* 1972) as well as one of the samples of depressives referred to earlier (Rutstein & Goldberger, 1973), there was also a *supraliminal* conflictual condition in which the same wish-related stimulus which increased pathology when presented subliminally had no effect when the subjects were aware of its content. This offers further support for our assumption that the *subliminal* presentation of wish-related stimuli is the method of choice for studying the effects of unconscious conflict on psychopathology.

[6]The term "experimental" is narrowly defined here as laboratory procedures in which one or more variables is "manipulated" while all other variables are held constant and the effects of this manipulation are contrasted with a "control condition."

[7]The above is not meant to imply that experimental data do not have their own limitations or that they should be viewed in isolation. As I argue in detail elsewhere (Silverman, 1975) such experimental data should be used in conjunction with others kinds of data (including, most importantly, "data" from the clinical situation) so that each source of data can compensate for the limitations of the others.

tion would produce *less* symptom intensification than the original (since the latter had been chosen because it most often had been linked with the symptom in the clinical literature), it is unclear from psychoanalytic theory whether *any* intensification of the symptom should be expected under the second wish-related condition. On the one hand, it could be argued that for anyone with sufficient vulnerability to develop a symptom in the first place, the stirring of any unconscious libidinal or aggressive wish could produce *some* intensification of the symptom; but on the other hand, it could be maintained that the specificity of the psychodynamic relationships psychoanalysis posits would lead one to predict *no* change in the symptom when a different unconscious wish is stimulated.

The findings from these recent experiments were quite consistent (Silverman, Bronstein & Mendelsohn, 1974). While further support was obtained for the original psychodynamic relationships studied, in *no* instance did the second wish-related condition influence the syndrome under consideration. That is, in each case its effect was indistinguishable from that of the neutral-control condition. These results are clearly consonant with the "specificity" hypothesis while contradicting the hypothesis of "generalized vulnerability."

The findings cited above are also important for another reason. They argue rather crucially against attributing the increase in symptoms found in the earlier studies to simply the negative affective tone of the stimuli. For if that was the factor involved, each of the wish-related stimuli would have intensified each of the symptoms and there would not have been the specific relationships found between type of symptom and a particular stimulus content. Rather these differential results lend strong support to the psychoanalytic view that symptoms are rooted in conflict over specifiable unconscious wishes.

IV

Investigations of pathology reduction. Let me turn now from our studies of conditions that *intensify* psychopathology to our investigations of pathology *reduction.* In eight studies completed to date, the subliminal psychodynamic activation method rather than being utilized to *stir up* unconscious conflict, has been used to temporarily *resolve* such conflict by activating a fantasy of symbiotic-gratification. Our work in this area was first stimulated by reports in the clinical literature from a few psychoanalytic workers (Limentani, 1956; Searles, 1965; Freedman *et al.*, 1967) who have worked extensively with schizophrenics. They have reported that at least for some patients with this diagnosis, noteworthy clinical improvement took place when the patients gave evidence of experiencing symbiotic wishes as being gratified in the treatment situation, with the therapist unconsciously perceived as the mother of early infancy. As I have detailed elsewhere (Silverman, 1975), this is a controversial formulation even within the psychoanalytic community; and partly for this reason we have embarked on an extensive experimental study of it. For this, we have utilized a new experimental stimulus to activate a fantasy of symbiotic gratification: the verbal message MOMMY AND I ARE ONE.[8] In studies of six groups of "relatively differentiated" schizophrenics (total $N = 171$), four having been seen in our laboratory (Silverman *et al.*, 1969, 1971; Silverman & Candell, 1970) and two groups seen in replications elsewhere (Leiter, 1972;

---

[8]In our early studies the symbiotic gratification stimulus consisted of this verbal message accompanied by a picture of a male and female merged at the shoulders like Siamese twins. However, in subsequent work we found that the effects that have been obtained can be produced by the verbal message alone and consequently have only employed this in our recent studies.

Kaye, 1975), a consistent finding has emerged. The subliminal presentation of MOMMY AND I ARE ONE (with the subliminal presentation of a neutral message serving as a control) led to *diminished* primary process ego pathology.[9] These results thus lend strong support to the controversial views of the clinicians cited above and have implications for a theoretical understanding of schizophrenic ego pathology (cf. Silverman, 1970, 1975).

V

In our most recent work, the therapeutic impact of the symbiotic-gratification condition just described has been pursued in two directions. In one, we are trying to specify the aspects of the symbiotic fantasy assumed to be triggered by the MOMMY AND I ARE ONE stimulus that is responsible for its therapeutic effects. In one such study (Kaye, 1975), the focus was on determining whether the idea of "oneness" has to be tied specifically to mother in order for it to be therapeutically effective. Three groups of schizophrenics were given a subliminal symbiotic-gratification and control condition. For one group the experimental stimulus was DADDY AND I ARE ONE; and for the third group, MY GIRL AND I ARE ONE.

For the first group the results were the same as they have been in earlier experiments: the MOMMY AND I ARE ONE message reduced primary process ego pathology. For the second group, however, the message DADDY AND I ARE ONE had *no* pathology-diminishing effect, thus making it evident that the fantasy of "oneness," in order to be therapeutic, cannot be associated with anyone—not even with another "significant figure" in the schizophrenic's life. On the other hand, for the third group, MY GIRL AND I ARE ONE *did* produce a therapeutic effect. Moreover, the size of the effect was significantly and substantially greater than the effect both for group 1 in the current study and for all the groups in previous studies that showed diminished pathology after the MOMMY AND I ARE ONE stimulus. The interpretation of this finding was the following: the fantasy of oneness with MY GIRL promises the same gratification that the fantasy of oneness with mother implies *but without the attendant disadvantages.* That is, oneness with mother, while potentially gratifying in certain ways, also can pose such threats as engulfment and incest. The fantasy of oneness with MY GIRL, on the other hand, does not imply these dangers and thus offers a symbiotic experience with an unequivocally gratifying mother substitute.

In two other studies that are under way, we are further investigating the characteristics of the fantasy of symbiotic gratification that allows it to be therapeutic. In these the MOMMY in the message is constant but the rest of the message varies. In one of these studies MOMMY AND I ARE ONE is being compared with MOMMY IS INSIDE ME, MOMMY AND I ARE ALIKE and MOMMY AND I ARE THE SAME to determine if fantasies of introjection, "likeness identification" and "sameness identification" (cf. Schafer, 1968) will have the same therapeutic effect as the fantasy of "oneness." And in the other study, MOMMY AND I ARE ONE is being compared with MOMMY ALWAYS FEEDS ME, MOMMY IS ALWAYS WITH ME and MOMMY CANNOT BE HURT in order to determine if other kinds of reassuring fantasies involving mother will have a therapeutic effect.

---

[9]We have defined "differentiated schizophrenics" as those who show a certain (predesignated) degree of ability to maintain a differentiated image of themselves and their mothers as assessed from a testing procedure that has been described elsewhere (Silverman & Candell, 1970). We have found that such patients comprise between 50 and 80 per cent of the populations of hospitalized schizophrenics. For schizophrenics who are assessed as "undifferentiated" on this procedure, the symbiotic-gratification message is *not* therapeutic, a finding which is discussed elsewhere (Silverman, 1975).

With the completion of these studies, we should be able to specify with much greater precision than is now possible just what it is about symbiotic-gratification fantasies that allow them to be therapeutic for schizophrenics. This illustrates both the general strength of experimental methods in their allowing many variables to be held constant while a particular one is "manipulated"; and the particular strength of the subliminal psychodynamic activation method for eliciting differential reactions to the stirring of different unconscious fantasies even when these fantasies share common elements.

The second way in which we have pursued our findings on the pathology-reducing effects of the symbiotic-gratification condition that has been described is through the study of non-schizophrenics. Here data from two completed investigations have indicated that therapeutic reactions also can occur in individuals who are not schizophrenic. In one study (Silverman *et al.*, 1973) we found that for each of two groups of male homosexuals, the degree of anxiety and defensiveness they manifested diminished after the subliminal exposure of the MOMMY AND I ARE ONE stimulus.

In the second investigation the symbiotic gratification condition was employed in a new way. While in previous studies it was utilized in but a single session and as an isolated intervention, in this study it was repeated many times over a four-day period and used in conjunction with another technique—systematic desensitization. Our interest here was in testing a hypothesis that can be considered a specification of the psychoanalytic postulate of "transference improvement," the concept which has been used by psychoanalysts to explain therapeutic gains that do not result from insight. Our hypothesis was that the marked success systematic desensitization has been shown to have in relieving phobic symptoms resides in it activating an unconscious fantasy of symbiotic gratification. This activation, we thought, is made particularly likely by the tranquility-inducing muscle relaxation procedure, carried out in a darkened room, with the patient in a (regression-encouraging) prone position, and in the presence of the therapist who is unconsciously perceived as "the healing mother." We inferred that with such a fantasy activated, not only does the patient experience himself as broadly rewarded in the way that psychoanalysis has posited underlies all transference improvements (cf. Fenichel, 1945, ch. 23) but, in addition, he can use aspects of the symbiotic experience as a counter to his fears. That is, the sense of protection and omnipotence that can result from feeling merged with "the mother of early infancy" makes what was previously frightening no longer so.

We reasoned that one way of testing this hypothesis would be to substitute for the muscle relaxation procedure in the desensitization paradigm, another procedure which could be viewed as more directly stimulating the symbiotic fantasy referred to above and then observing if this aids desensitization as relaxation has been shown to do. The symbiotic-gratification tachistoscopic intervention that has been described seemed appropriate for this purpose and thus, the following experiment (Silverman, Frank & Dachinger, 1974) was carried out. Twenty women with insect phobias were randomly assigned to either an experimental or control group. Both groups were given a variant of systematic desensitization in which after establishing a hierarchy of feared interactions with insects, they underwent four sessions of desensitization visualizations, but *without* the muscle relaxation procedure. Instead, every time the subject reported a noteworthy degree of anxiety during a visualization, she was asked to look into the tachistoscope and was given subliminal exposures of either MOMMY AND I ARE ONE (experimental group) or PEOPLE WALKING (control group). On measures of both phobic behaviour and anxiety made "blindly" before and after the four intervention sessions, the experimental group was found to have shown improvement not manifested by the control group.

SUMMARY AND CONCLUSION

In this paper I have reviewed the results obtained from experiments that have been carried out on 20 groups of subjects over the past four years in which the method of subliminal psychodynamic activation has been utilized to investigate the relationship between unconscious conflict and psychopathology. Together with the results of earlier experiments with nineteen other groups of subjects (reviewed in Silverman, 1971), they provide ample support for the following conclusions: (1) clear experimental support can be said to exist for a number of psychodynamic propositions that have gained consensus agreement among psychoanalytic clinicians through the years; (2) the validity of other dynamic relationships also has been demonstrated including some that are considered controversial within the psychoanalytic community and others, which while not specifically proposed until now, can be considered extrapolations from recent developments in psychoanalytic thinking. Thus a laboratory method is available which allows for the rigorous experimental study of central aspects of the clinical theory of psychoanalysis.

REFERENCES

Dixon, N. F. (1971). *Subliminal Perception: the Nature of a Controversy*. London: McGraw-Hill.

Fenichel, O. (1945). *The Psychoanalytic Theory of Neurosis*. New York: Norton.

Freedman, N., Cutler, R., Engelhart, D. M. & Margolis, R. (1967). On the modification of paranoid symptomatology. *J. nerv. ment. Dis. 144*, 29–36.

Kaye, M. (1975). The therapeutic value of three merging stimuli for male schizophrenics. (Unpublished doctoral dissertation. Yeshiva University.)

Leiter, E. (1972). A study of the effects of subliminal activation of merging fantasies in differentiated and non-differentiated schizophrenics. (Unpublished doctoral dissertation, New York University.)

Limentani, D. (1956). Symbiotic identification in schizophrenia. *Psychiatry 19*, 231–236.

Miller, J. (1973). The effects of aggressive stimulation upon adults who have experienced the death of a parent during childhood and adolescence. (Unpublished doctoral dissertation, New York University.)

Rutstein, E. H. & Goldberger, L. (1973). The effects of aggressive stimulation on suicidal patients: An experimental study of the psychoanalytic theory of suicide. In B. Rubinstein (ed.), *Psychoanalysis and Contemporary Science*, vol. 2, New York: Macmillan.

Schafer, R. (1968). *Aspects of Internalization*. New York: International Universities Press.

Searles, H. F. (1965). *Collected Papers on Schizophrenia and Related Subjects*. New York: International Universities Press.

Silverman, L. H. (1967). An experimental approach to the study of dynamic propositions in psychoanalysis: The relationship between the aggressive drive and ego regression—initial studies. *J. Am. psychoanal. Ass. 15*, 376–403.

Silverman, L. H. (1970). Further experimental studies of dynamic propositions in psychoanalysis: On the function and meaning of regressive thinking. *J. Am. psychoanal. Ass. 18*, 102–124.

Silverman, L. H. (1971). An experimental technique for the study of unconscious conflict. *Br. J. med. Psychol. 44*, 17–25.

Silverman, L. H. (1972). Drive stimulation and psychopathology: On the conditions under which drive-related external events evoke pathological reactions. In R. R. Holt & E. Peterfreund (eds.), *Psychoanalysis and Contemporary Science*, vol. 1. New York: Macmillan.

Silverman, L. H. (1975). On the role of experimental data in the development of the clinical theory of psychoanalysis. *Int. Rev. Psycho-Anal. 2*, 43–64.

Silverman, L. H., Bronstein, A. & Mendelsohn, E. (1974). The further use of the subliminal psychodynamic activation method for the experimental study of the clinical theory of psychoanalysis: On the specificity of relationships between manifest psychopathology and unconscious conflict. (Unpublished manuscript, New York Veterans Administration Hospital.)

Silverman, L. H. & Candell, P. (1970). On the relationship between aggressive activation, symbiotic merging, intactness of body boundaries and manifest pathology in schizophrenics. *J. nerv. ment. Dis. 150,* 387–399.

Silverman, L. H., Candell, P., Pettit, T. F. & Blum, E. A. (1971). Further data on effects of aggressive activation and symbiotic merging on ego functioning of schizophrenics. *Percept. mot. Skills 32,* 93–94.

Silverman, L. H., Frank, S. G. & Dachinger, P. (1974). A psychoanalytic reinterpretation of the effectiveness of systematic desensitization: Experimental data bearing on the role of merging fantasies. *J. abnorm. Psychol. 83,* 313–318.

Silverman, L. H., Klinger, H., Lustbader, L., Farrell, J. & Martin, A. D. (1972). The effect of subliminal drive stimulation on the speech of stutterers, *J. nerv. ment. Dis. 155,* 14–21.

Silverman, L. H., Spiro, R. H., Weisberg, J. S. & Candell, P. (1969). The effects of aggressive activation and the need to merge on pathological thinking in schizophrenia. *J. nerv. ment. Dis. 148,* 39–51.

Varga, M. (1973). An experimental study of aspects of the psychoanalytic study of elation. (Unpublished doctoral dissertation, New York University.)

Ernest Nagel
METHODOLOGICAL ISSUES
IN PSYCHOANALYTIC THEORY

Dr. Hartmann's comprehensive paper makes amply clear that psychoanalytic theory is intended to be a theory of human behavior in the same sense of "theory" that, for example, the molecular theory of gases is a set of assumptions which systematizes, explains, and predicts certain observable phenomena of gases. Accordingly, he is in effect inviting us to evaluate the merits of Freudian theory by standards of intellectual cogency similar to those we employ in judging theories in other areas of positive science. It would of course be absurdly pedantic to apply to Freudian theory the yardstick of rigor and precision current in mathematical and experimental physics. Proper allowance must certainly be made for the notorious difficulties encountered in all inquiries into distinctively human behavior, and for what is perhaps an inevitable fuzziness of all generalizations about human conduct. Nevertheless, unless I have misconstrued the burden of Dr. Hartmann's paper, no apology is required for raising substantially the same kinds of issues of fact and logic concerning Freudian theory that are pertinent to a general examination of the cognitive worth and standing of a theory in the natural or social sciences.

However, I am not a professional psychologist. I have neither been psychoanalyzed nor am I a profound scholar of psychoanalytic literature, and I am therefore not competent to discuss the detailed observational data upon which Freudian theory supposedly rests. In any event, my interest in Freudian theory is primarily methodological; and my aim in this discussion is to raise two related groups of logical questions concerning which I would very much like to receive instruction. The first group deals with issues relating to the logical structure and empirical content of psychoanalytic theory, and especially of the so-called "metapsychology" to which Dr. Hartmann's paper is so largely devoted. The second group of questions is concerned with the general nature of the evidence that is used to support the theory. The two groups of issues nevertheless do not fall into watertight compartments, so that I have not found it possible in discussing questions in the first set to avoid entirely considerations belonging to the second.

I

Freudian theory maintains, and I think rightly so, that it is not possible to account for most human conduct exclusively in terms either of manifest human traits or of conscious motives and intentions. Accordingly, the theory introduces a number of assumptions contain-

Abridged from "Methodological Issues in Psychoanalytic Theory," by E. Nagel. In S. Hook (Ed), *Psychoanalysis, Scientific Method, and Philosophy.* Copyright 1959 by New York University Press. Reprinted by permission.

ing terms that ostensibly refer to matters neither manifest nor conscious, and that are not explicitly definable by way of what is manifest and conscious. In so far as Freudian theory employs notions of this kind which do not describe anything observable (let me call such notions "theoretical" ones for the sake of brevity), the theory is quite like the molecular theory of gases or the gene theory of heredity. I do not think, therefore, that there is any substance in those criticisms of Freudian theory which object to the theory *merely* on the ground that it uses theoretical notions.

a) My first difficulty with Freudian theory nevertheless is generated by the fact that while it is unobjectionable for a theory to be couched in terms of theoretical notions, the theory does not seem to me to satisfy two requirements which any theory must satisfy if it is to be capable of empirical validation. I must state these requirements briefly. In the first place, it must be possible to deduce determinate consequences from the assumptions of theory, so that one can decide on the basis of logical considerations, and prior to the examination of any empirical data, whether or not an alleged consequence of the theory is indeed implied by the latter. For unless this requirement is fulfilled, the theory has no definite content, and questions as to what the theory asserts cannot be settled except by recourse to some privileged authority or arbitrary caprice. In the second place, even though the theoretical notions are not explicitly defined by way of overt empirical procedures and observable traits of things, nevertheless at least *some* theoretical notions must be *tied down to fairly definite and unambiguously specified* observable materials, by way of rules of procedure variously called "correspondence rules," "coordinating definitions," and "operational definitions." For if this condition is not satisfied, the theory can have no determinate consequences about *empirical* subject matter. An immediate corollary to these requirements is that since a consistent theory cannot imply two incompatible consequences, a credible theory must not only be *confirmed* by observational evidence, but it must also be capable of being *negated* by such evidence. In short, a theory must not be formulated in such a manner that it can always be construed and manipulated so as to explain whatever the actual facts are, no matter whether controlled observation shows one state of affairs to obtain or its opposite. . . .

b) I must now turn to a second difficulty I find in the declared content of Freudian theory. The theory is intended to explain human behavior on the cardinal assumption that all conduct is *motivated* or *wish-fulfilling*. But since most of our conduct is not in fact *consciously* motivated, the theory postulates the complex "mental apparatus" summarized by Dr. Hartmann, which includes under various names what are in some sense *unconscious* motives or wishes. As I understand Freudian theory, and as I think Dr. Hartmann's paper also makes quite plain, these unconscious motives, wishes, drives, urges and intentions must be regarded as "psychic" or "mental processes," as "purposive ideas" which are directed toward definite "aims" or "objects," and not simply as latent somatic dispositions possessing no *specific goals*. Indeed, if these unconscious drives were not strongly analogous to conscious motives and wishes, the claim that psychoanalytic theory explains human conduct in motivational terms would be difficult to make out and would perhaps collapse. On the other hand, these unconscious motives have an enduring character and tenacious attachment to specific objectives that conscious wishes do not exhibit. Indeed, on Freudian theory a thwarted wish of early childhood, directed toward some person, may not completely vanish, but may enjoy a repressed existence in the unconscious, and continue to operate in identical form into the present even though that person has long since died.[1] In consequence, there is an important failure of analogy between conscious motives and unconscious mental processes, so that it is only by a radical shift in the customary meanings of such words as "motive" and "wish" that Freudian theory can be said to offer an explanation of human conduct in terms of motivations and wish-fulfillments.

This comment would perhaps be calling attention only to a relatively verbal matter, were it not for the fact that the unconscious mechanism postulated to account for human conduct is emphatically said to be a *psychical* or *mental* apparatus which is endowed with all the customary attributes of substantiality and causal agency. As is well known, Freud hoped that this mental apparatus would eventually be identified with physiological processes in the body; and he himself observed that the question whether the unconscious processes he postulated are to be conceived as mental or as physical can easily become a war of words.[2] Nevertheless, he not only insisted that the apparatus of metapsychology is *mental,* but also described its parts as if they were things struggling with one another or with the external world. He admitted that the assumption of unconscious mental activity was in a sense an extension of that primitive animism which attributes a consciousness to the things around us, even though he noted that the mental, like the physical, may "in reality" not be what "it appears to us to be."[3] And he repeatedly talked of the id, the ego and the superego as inhabited by drives charged with energies, acting like forces, and in some cases immutably directed toward quite specific objects. *"Psychic reality,"* he once vigorously asserted, "is a special form of existence which must not be confounded with *material* reality."[4] Dr. Hartmann's language is similarly equivocal. He sometimes describes the main theoretical components of the mental apparatus as "units of functions," and suggests that unconscious drives are something like dispositions. But he also declares that these components possess energies and conflict with one another—though without explaining in what sense functions can be charged with energies or dispositions can be engaged in conflicts.

It is certainly tempting to read all this as just metaphorical language, a convenient and dramatically suggestive way of talking about some of the complex but still unknown detailed mechanisms of the body. On this reading of Freudian theory, its assumptions would be formulations of the relations between, and the teleological organization of, various latent capacities and dispositions of the human organism. Accordingly, its "motivational" explanations of human conduct would then not differ in kind, though they would differ in not specifying the detailed mechanisms involved, from teleological explanations of the behavior of such teleologically organized (or "feed-back") systems as an engine provided with a governor or the human body as a self-regulative structure for the maintenance of its internal temperature.

However, such a reading is difficult to carry through if one is to make consistent sense of the theory, in part because of the characterization the theory gives of many drives as immutably fixed to specific objectives, but in larger measure because of the causal powers the theory ascribes to its theoretical entities. If these causal ascriptions are themselves construed figuratively, I cannot make ends meet in understanding the theory as a supposedly "dynamic" account of human personality and conduct. On the other hand, if those ascriptions are taken seriously (i.e., more or less literally), then on the suggested reading of the rest of the theory the latter would in effect be asserting what is to me the unintelligible doctrine that various *modes of organization* of human activities are the *causes* of those activities.

In point of fact, Dr. Hartmann adds to the difficulties of construing the theory in the proposed manner. For he represents Freud as having believed that the theoretical psychic entities have "effects which can be observed" and that the mental apparatus is "real in the ordinary sense of the word." Limitations of time and space prevent me from examining what various things might be meant by the word "real" in this context; and in any event, the whole issue this word of protean meanings raises may not be worth pursuing. But I do want to conclude this part of my discussion with two confessions, even at the risk of being thereby convicted of a failure to understand the actual intent of Freudian theory. The theoretical "mental apparatus" as he apparently conceived it seems to me to reduplicate on an ostensibly "psychic" level the admittedly unknown detailed somatic mechanisms and capacities of the human organism. Accordingly, though psychoanalysis explicitly proclaims the view that human behavior has its roots in the biophysical and biochemical organization of the body, it actually postulates a veritable "ghost in the machine" that does work which a biologically oriented psychology might be expected to assign to the body. Dr. Hartmann denies that the mechanism of metapsychology is anthropomorphic; but I must confess that the theoretical literature of psychoanalysis with which I am acquainted does not seem to me to confirm this denial. And as for the notions of unconscious psychic processes possessing causal efficacies—of unconscious, causally operative motives and wishes that are not somatic dispositions and activities—I will not venture to say that such locutions are inherently nonsense, since a great many people claim to make good sense out of them. But in all candor I must admit that such locutions are just nonsense to me.

II

I come to the second group of questions, those dealing with the nature of the evidence for Freudian theory. There appear to be three major types of such evidence: clinical data, obtained from patients in psychoanalytic interviews; experimental findings in psychological laboratories; and anthropological information gathered by studies of primitive and advanced societies. Since the clinical evidence is regarded by psychoanalysts as by far the most important type, as well as because of limitations of space, I shall devote the remainder of my comments to it. For the sake of the record I think I ought nevertheless to state my conviction, although without supporting reasons, that even when the best face is put on the experimental and anthropological evidence the available data do not uniformly support Freudian theory. Some of this evidence can certainly be construed as being favorable to, or at any rate compatible with, the theory; but some of the evidence is decidedly negative.

The psychoanalytic interview (or method) is the distinctive procedure used by analysts for arriving at psychoanalytic hypotheses, for obtaining evidence for or against such hypotheses, and for effecting therapies. Although Dr. Hartmann has stressed the role of clinical data as the *source* of psychoanalytic hypotheses, this is not a relevant consideration to my present objective. For my concern is not with the origins of such hypotheses, but with the logic of their validation. As everyone knows, the aim of the psychoanalytic interview is to discover the causes of a patient's neurosis or psychosis, on the assumption that his present condition is the manifestation of internal conflicts produced by an unfulfilled but repressed "wish" of early childhood, which is still operative in the unconscious and which is usually sexual in character. Briefly stated, the method of ascertaining such alleged causes consists in having the subject engage in "free association" narration of his conscious thoughts, until the "latent meaning" of his fragmentary recollections of childhood experiences—i.e., the frustrated but suppressed wish that is the source of his present difficulties—is uncovered by the "interpretations" which the analyst places upon what is told him. Accordingly, the crucial issue is how such interpretations are established as valid.

Judging by what analysts themselves say on this question, the grounds for regarding an interpretation as sound are its coherence (or compatibility) with all the things disclosed by the patient in the interview, its acceptance by the patient, and (at least in some cases) the improvement in the condition of the patient when he accepts the interpretation and so recognizes the alleged source of his troubles. Now although the probative worth of such evidence has been frequently challenged, and some of its defects have been acknowledged even by psychoanalysts, I have never come across adequate answers to what seem to me grave criticisms. In the hope of eliciting better answers, permit me therefore to enumerate the difficulties, however familiar they may be, that I regard as important.

a) Only passing mention need be made of the circumstance that although in the interview the analyst is supposedly a "passive" auditor of the "free association" narration by the subject, in point of fact the analyst does direct the course of the narrative. This by itself does not necessarily impair the evidential worth of the outcome, for even in the most meticulously conducted laboratory experiment the experimenter intervenes to obtain the data he is after. There is nevertheless the difficulty that in the nature of the case the full extent of the analyst's intervention is not a matter that is open to public scrutiny, so that by and large one has only his own testimony as to what transpires in the consulting room. It is perhaps unnecessary to say that this is not a question about the personal integrity of psychoanalytic practitioners. The point is the fundamental one that no matter how firmly we may resolve to make explicit our biases, no human being is aware of all of them, and that objectivity in science is achieved through the criticism of publicly accessible material by a community of independent inquirers. It is well to remind ourselves, in this connection, of Stekel's observation that "patients dream in the dialect of whatever physician happens to be treating them. . . . Sadger's patients will dream about urinary eroticism; mine perhaps of the symbolism of death and religion; Adler's of 'top-dogs' and 'underdogs' and of the masculine protest."[5]

Moreover, unless data are obtained under carefully standardized circumstances, or under different circumstances whose dependence on known variables is nevertheless established, even an extensive collection of data is an unreliable basis for inference. To be sure, analysts apparently do attempt to institute standard conditions for the conduct of interviews. But there is not much information available on the extent to which the standardization is actually enforced, or whether it relates to more than what may be superficial matters.

b) The mere coherence of an interpretation with the data supplied by a subject seems to me to carry little weight as evidence for its truth, especially if more than one such coherent interpretation can be given, whether within the general framework of Freudian metapsychology or on the basis of quite different assumptions. I have read enough of the analytic literature to have been impressed by the ingenuity with which the reported data of various cases are made to dovetail into psychoanalytic interpretations. Nevertheless, I am also familiar with the fact that analysts themselves sometimes differ in their diagnoses of the same case; and I have little doubt myself that for every ingenious interpretation of a case, another one no less superficially plausible can be invented.[6] Accordingly, even if we waive the important point to which Dr. Hartmann himself calls attention, that the analyst may base his interpretation not on *all* the information given by the patient, but on an unwittingly biased selection of the data, the question remains whether there is any objective way of deciding between alternative interpretations.

Dr. Hartmann suggests two such ways. One of them is the making of successful predictions, the other is the use of established laws based on experience with various types of patients. I want to consider each of these briefly.

c) What sorts of predictions can be made by an analyst? Dr. Hartmann is not very informative on this point. But apart from therapeutic prognoses, which for the moment I will ignore, the only kinds of predictions I have found mentioned in the relevant literature refer to the reactions of the patient. Thus, Ernst Kris cites as examples of such predictable reactions "the reactions of acknowledgment to any interpretation given, for instance, that of sudden insight combined with the production of confirmatory details or substitute reactions of a variety of kinds," such as the recall by the subject of past experiences which he was previously unable to remember.[7] However, neither the *acceptance* of a given interpretation by a subject, nor his *claim* to a sudden insight into the alleged source of his difficulties, seems to me to constitute, by itself, a critical confirmation of the interpretation. For the interpretation does not, as such, predict either its own acceptance by the subject or the insight claimed by him; and in any event it is pertinent to ask how often an interpretation of a certain kind when proposed to comparable subjects is neither accepted by the subjects nor accompanied by a sense of illumination about themselves. Nor is it clear why the mere say-so of a patient that he now understands the source of his difficulties is competent evidence for the assumption that the alleged source is indeed the actual source. There have been countless numbers of people throughout human history who have believed quite sincerely that their successes or failures could be attributed to various things they did or did not do or that were done to them; nevertheless, most of such beliefs have subsequently been shown to be baseless. Why is not this lesson of human experience relevant for assessing the analogous claims of psychoanalytic subjects?

Moreover, as Kris himself notes, the improvement in recall which sometimes follows the presentation of an interpretation must not be assumed to "produce" the recall: the interpretation can be viewed only as a *help* to better recall. Even with this reservation, however, one is begging the question in supposing that it is the *specific content* of an interpretation, as distinct from the over-all directed prodding of the subject's memory that takes place during the interview, that accounts for the improved recall. More generally, the changes in various symptoms which the patient exhibits as the interview progresses do not constitute critical evidence for an *interpretation,* unless it can be shown that such changes are not produced by some combination of factors for which the interview as a whole is responsible. There is at any rate some ground for the suspicion that the interpretations are frequently imposed on data which are themselves manufactured by the psychoanalytic method. Can an adult who is recalling childhood experiences remember them as he actually experienced them, or does he report them in terms of ideas which carry the burden of much of his later experience, including the experience of a psychoanalytic interview? Is an adult "regressing" to a childish attitude who, in order to recapture a childhood experience, may find it necessary to put himself into a childish frame of mind? I do not pretend to know the answers to such questions. But neither am I convinced that adequate attention has been paid to them by most analysts.

d) Dr. Hartmann is not very explicit about his second suggested way of supplying an objective support for an interpretation, namely, by the use of established laws in developmental psychology. If I understand him correctly, he is saying that different types of neurotic personality can be distinguished, and that each type is in fact associated with a fairly distinctive kind of childhood traumatic experience. Accordingly, once the analyst has determined by way of the interview to which type his patient belongs, his interpretation is supported by an appeal to the corresponding law. Now I agree that such a procedure would make an interpretation prima facie credible, if indeed there are well-established regularities of the kind indicated. Nevertheless, though I am not in the position to question the claim that there are such regularities, I would like to be clearer about their nature. In the first place, do the regularities hold between manifest neurotic symptoms and the *allegations* patients belonging to a certain type make concerning their childhood experiences, or between neurotic symptoms and *actual childhood experiences* whose occurrence has been ascertained independently of the subjects' memories of them? If it is the former, the evidential value of such a regularity for a given interpretation is dubious, for reasons too obvious to need explicit mention.

But in the second place, and on either alternative, the fact that some event or attribute B occurs with a certain relative frequency p when some other event or attribute A occurs, is not sufficient to show that A and B are significantly related—unless there is further evidence that the relative frequency of B in the absence of A, or the relative frequency of the nonoccurrence of B in the presence of A, is markedly different from p. Thus, the fact that many men who have certain kinds of traumatic experiences in childhood develop into neurotic adults does not establish a causal relation between the two, if there is about the same proportion of men who undergo similar childhood experiences but develop into reasonably normal adults. In short, data must be analyzed so as to make possible comparisons on the basis of some *control* group, if they are to constitute cogent evidence for a causal inference. The introduction of such controls is the *minimum* requirement for the reliable interpretation and use of empirical data. I am therefore not impressed by Dr. Hartmann's assertion that psychoanalytic interpretations are based on a great wealth of observations, for it is not the sheer *quantity* of data that is of moment but their probative strength. I am not aware, however, that analysts have in fact subjected their clinical data to systematic and critical statistical scrutiny. I have not read everything that Freud wrote, and I may be doing him an injustice in supposing that he cannot be rightly accused of having made such a scrutiny. But at any rate I have not found in the books of his I have read, in some of which he announced what he regarded as important changes in his theoretical views because of fresh clinical evidence, that these changes were controlled by the elementary logical principle to which I have just been calling attention.

e) This is a convenient place to say a few words about the evidence supplied for Freudian theory by psychoanalytic therapy. I agree with Dr. Hartmann that the adequacy of the theory should not be *equated* with the success of its therapy. Nevertheless, the evidence from the latter is surely not irrelevant to the former. Unfortunately, information about the effectiveness of Freudian therapy is notoriously difficult to obtain, and I am in any case not sufficiently familiar with whatever material is available to have a reasoned opinion about it. However, I would like to mention Dr. P. G. Denker's study of 500 cases of psychoneuroses treated, without psychoanalytic intervention, by general medical practitioners.[8] The study finds that the percentage of improvements was as high as the ratio of improvements sometimes claimed for psychoanalytic therapy. It would certainly be rash to claim that the findings of his study are conclusive on the point at issue. But I think the study does indicate that therapeutic success as supporting evidence for Freudian theory cannot be taken at face value.

f) There is one final point I wish to make. Psychoanalytic interpretations frequently assert that the present difficulties of a patient have their source in an unfulfilled wish of early childhood, which persists in self-identical manner and produces discord in the unconscious stratum of mentality.[9] It is pertinent to ask, therefore, what is the evidence for the tacit assumption that none of the events that have transpired since that early traumatic experience need be considered in accounting for the patient's present neurosis. For even if one grants that such a childhood experience is an indispensable condition for an adult neurosis, the assumption that the repressed wish has continued to operate essentially unmodified in the subject's unconscious, despite the countless number of more proximate happenings in the subject's life, cannot be accepted as a matter of course. If I understand correctly the import of investigations such as those on the impact of thirst on cognition, to which Dr. Hartmann refers, they are not only irrelevant for establishing this assumption, but point in the opposite direction. Indeed, the available evidence on the influence of education and cultural conditioning upon the development of human personality casts serious doubt on that assumption. Without this assumption, however, the clinical data obtained in psychoanalytic interviews do not confirm the typical interpretations that, were they sound, would support Freudian theory.

A possible rejoinder to the difficulties I have been raising is that despite the dubious character of the evidence for Freudian theory, it is the only theory we do possess that explains in a systematic way an extensive domain of important phenomena. To such a comment I can only reply that this is indeed most unfortunate if true, but that nonetheless the imaginative sweep of a set of ideas does not confer factual validity upon them. I do not minimize the importance of having *some* theory, even a dubious one, if it helps to open up fresh areas of investigation and if it is a source of fruitful ideas for the conduct of controlled inquiry. I certainly acknowledge the great service Freud and his school have rendered in directing attention to neglected aspects of human behavior, and in contributing a large number of suggestive notions which have leavened and broadened the scope of psychological, medical and anthropological inquiry. But on the Freudian theory itself, as a body of doctrine for which factual validity can be reasonably claimed, I can only echo the Scottish verdict: Not proven.

NOTES

1. Cf. S. Freud, "The Unconscious," in *Collected Papers* (London: 1956), Vol. IV, pp. 118–19.
2. *Ibid.*, p. 100.
3. *Ibid.*, p. 104.
4. S. Freud, *The Interpretation of Dreams,* in *The Basic Writings of Sigmund Freud,* ed. A. A. Brill (New York: Modern Library, 1938), p. 548.
5. W. Stekel, *The Interpretation of Dreams* (New York: Liveright), I, 14.
6. Freud maintained that absence of agreement among psychoanalysts is sometimes the consequence of insufficient training. He thus declared, for example, that "We shall not be so very greatly surprised if a woman analyst who has not been sufficiently convinced of the intensity of her own desire for a penis also fails to assign an adequate importance to that factor in her patients."—*An Outline of Psychoanalysis,* p. 107.
7. Ernst Kris, "The Nature of Psychoanalytic Propositions and Their Validation," *Freedom and Experience, Essays Presented to Horace M. Kallen,* ed. S. Hook and M. R. Konvitz (Ithaca, N. Y.), p. 246.
8. P. G. Denker, "Results of Treatment of Psychoneuroses by the General Practitioner," *New York State Journal of Medicine,* Vol. XLVI (1946).
9. "In the id there is nothing corresponding to the idea of time, no recognition of the passage of time, and (a thing which is very remarkable and awaits adequate attention in philosophic thought) no alteration of mental processes by the passage of time. Conative impulses which have never got beyond the id, and even impressions which have been pushed down into the id by repression, are virtually immortal and are preserved for whole decades as though they had only recently occurred."—S. Freud, *New Introductory Lectures on Psycho-Analysis* (New York: 1933), p. 104. Cf. also a similar statement in "The Unconscious," *loc. cit.*, p. 119.

Part 2
DEVELOPMENTAL THEORY

Three
ERIK H. ERIKSON

Erik H. Erikson (1902–   ) is one of the most prominent contemporary psychoanalytic theorists. During his long and productive intellectual career, Erikson has made outstanding contributions to the field of child development (see his book *Childhood and Society*) and to the conceptualization of adolescent identity (see *Identity: Youth and Crisis*). He has also figured prominently in a field of inquiry called *psychohistory* with his book *Gandhi's Truth*.

The article by Erikson in this chapter presents his theory of ego-identity development —a theory that accounts for the growth process from birth to maturity. At each stage of growth, individuals are confronted with a particular psychosocial crisis, which they then resolve in one of two ways. Erikson refers to each crisis in terms of its two possible outcomes: trust versus mistrust, autonomy versus shame and doubt, and so on. These stages and their accompanying social realities are embedded in the cultural institutions that are a part of every society. In this paper, Erikson focuses on the psychosocial stage of adolescence, which is characterized by the crisis of identity versus role diffusion. The stage of adolescence is of special theoretical interest to Erikson. At this stage, a sense of self—a coherent self-image—begins to be firmly crystallized. The effective adult personality is a consequence of the resolution of the sexual and interpersonal conflicts that erupt, sometimes violently, during adolescence. Erikson is an interactionist; his interest is in the balance between physiological and psychological patterns of personal growth and the demands of social institutions. A harmonious integration of these elements at the adolescent stage results in a firm sense of identity and the ability to move on confidently to a mature, adult stage of life.

The second selection in this chapter is a paper by N. V. Ciaccio, who describes research she did on some of Erikson's theoretical and clinical speculations about the types of emotional crisis reactions that are typical of various developmental stages. Although Ciaccio studied all five of Erikson's developmental stages, she was particularly interested in Stages II (autonomy versus shame and doubt), III (initiative versus guilt), and IV (industry versus inferiority), because of their special relevance to adolescent emotional conflicts. Children of ages 5, 8, and 11 were chosen as subjects because Erikson would place them at these particular stages. The experimental procedure consisted of giving these children a projective test composed of pictures specially designed to relate to the kinds of emotional issues that children at these stages are thought by Erikson to be coping with. The children were instructed to tell stories in response to these pictures. The stories were later coded by a trained judge in terms of whether or not they expressed the attitudes, behaviors, and conflicts theoretically associated with each particular stage. The data gathered by Ciaccio generally support Erikson's theory—especially his idea that ego development progresses with age. The most interesting finding was that the critical issue at Stage II (autonomy versus shame and doubt) appeared in all of the five stages investigated. Thus, the ability of a child to establish a sense of personal autonomy appears to be a general theme basic to healthy ego development.

The third selection, a review by Kenneth J. Gergen, is a mixture of severe criticism and measured admiration. The review is of Erikson's *Identity: Youth and Crisis*—a collection of essays written over a 21-year period. Gergen criticizes Erikson's Olympian attitude—his giving virtually no recognition or attention to the relevant scientific literature on perception, learning, and child development that has accumulated over the years. Furthermore, Erikson uses as evidence for his theories mostly clinical and literary observations, which meet few of the criteria for rigorous scientific validation. Yet at the same time Gergen appreciates and respects Erikson's insights into adolescent personality development. He recognizes that Erikson's theory regarding the role of social institutions in the development of the self is a major challenge to conventional psychoanalytic thinking about the roots of mental adjustment. Erikson set out boldly in new directions and has been able to offer new perspectives to many social scientists interested in the delicate relationship between personality and social experience.

SUGGESTIONS FOR FURTHER READING

The classic theoretical work by Erikson is *Childhood and Society,* published by Norton Press in 1963. This second edition is in paperback. Two fascinating psychoanalytic studies by Erikson of significant historical figures are *Young Man Luther* and *Gandhi's Truth*, both published by Norton Press in paperback. *Gandhi's Truth* won the 1970 Pulitzer Prize.

Erik H. Erikson
THE PROBLEM OF EGO IDENTITY

INTRODUCTION

In a number of writings I have been using the term *ego identity* to denote certain comprehensive gains which the individual, at the end of adolescence, must have derived from all of his pre-adult experience in order to be ready for the tasks of adulthood. My use of this term reflected the dilemma of a psychoanalyst who was led to a new concept not by theoretical preoccupation but rather through the expansion of his clinical awareness to other fields (social anthropology and comparative education) and through the expectation that such expansion would, in turn, profit clinical work. Recent clinical observations have, I feel, begun to bear out this expectation. I have, therefore, gratefully accepted two opportunities[1] offered me to restate and review the problem of identity. The present paper combines both of these presentations. The question before us is whether the concept of identity is essentially a psychosocial one, or deserves to be considered as a legitimate part of the psychoanalytic theory of the ego.

First a word about the term identity. As far as I know Freud used it only once in a more than incidental way, and then with a psychosocial connotation. It was when he tried to formulate his link to Judaism, that he spoke of an "inner identity"[2] which was not based on race or religion, but on a common readiness to live in opposition, and on a common freedom from prejudices which narrow the use of the intellect. Here, the term identity points to an individual's link with the unique values, fostered by a unique history, of his people. Yet, it also relates to the cornerstone of this individual's unique development: for the importance of the theme of "incorruptible observation at the price of professional isolation" played a central role in Freud's life. It is this identity of something in the individual's core with an essential aspect of a group's inner coherence which is under consideration here: for the young individual must learn to be most himself where he means most to others—those others, to be sure, who have come to mean most to him. The term identity expresses such a mutual relation in that it connotes both a persistent sameness within oneself (self-sameness) and a persistent sharing of some kind of essential character with others.

I can attempt to make the subject matter of identity more explicit only by approaching it from a variety of angles—biographic, pathographic, and theoretical; and by letting the term identity speak for itself in a number of connotations. At one time, then, it will appear to refer

[1]At the 35th Anniversary Institute of the Judge Baker Guidance Center in Boston, May, 1953, and at the Midwinter Meetings of the American Psychoanalytic Association, New York, 1953.

[2]". . . die klare Bewusstheit der inneren Identität."

to a conscious *sense of individual identity;* at another to an unconscious striving for a *continuity of personal character;* at a third, as a criterion for the silent doings of *ego synthesis;* and, finally, as a maintenance of an inner *solidarity* with a group's ideals and identity. In some respects the term will appear to be colloquial and naïve; in another, vaguely related to existing concepts in psychoanalysis and sociology. If, after an attempt at clarifying this relation, the term itself will retain some ambiguity it will, so I hope, nevertheless have helped to delineate a significant problem, and a necessary point of view.

I begin with one extreme aspect of the problem as exemplified in the biography of an outstanding individual—an individual who labored as hard on the creation of a world-wide *public identity* for himself, as he worked on his literary masterpieces.

I.   BIOGRAPHIC: G.B.S. ON GEORGE BERNARD SHAW

When George Bernard Shaw was a famous man of seventy, he was called upon to review and to preface the unsuccessful work of his early twenties, namely, the two volumes of fiction which had never been published. As one would expect, Shaw proceeded to make light of the production of his young adulthood, but not without imposing on the reader a detailed analysis of young Shaw. Were Shaw not so deceptively witty in what he says about his younger years, his observations probably would have been recognized as a major psychological achievement. Yet, it is Shaw's mark of identity that he eases and teases his reader along a path of apparent superficialities and sudden depths. I dare to excerpt him here for my purposes, only in the hope that I will make the reader curious enough to follow him on every step of his exposition.

G.B.S. (for this is the public identity which was one of his masterpieces) describes young Shaw as an "extremely disagreeable and undesirable" young man, "not at all reticent of diabolical opinion," while inwardly "suffering . . . from simple cowardice . . . and horribly ashamed of it." "The truth is," he concludes, "that all men are in a false position in society until they have realized their possibilities and imposed them on their neighbors. They are tormented by a continual shortcoming in themselves; yet they irritate others by a continual overweening. This discord can be resolved by acknowledged success or failure only: everyone is ill at ease until he has found his natural place, whether it be above or below his birthplace." But Shaw must always exempt himself from any universal law which he inadvertently pronounces; so he adds: "This finding of one's place may be made very puzzling by the fact that there is no place in ordinary society for extraordinary individuals."

Shaw proceeds to describe a crisis (of the kind which we will refer to as an *identity crisis*) at the age of twenty. It is to be noted that this crisis was not caused by lack of success or the absence of a defined role but by too much of both: "I made good in spite of myself, and found, to my dismay, that Business, instead of expelling me as the worthless imposter I was, was fastening upon me with no intention of letting me go. Behold me, therefore, in my twentieth year, with a business training, in an occupation which I detested as cordially as any sane person lets himself detest anything he cannot escape from. In March 1876 I broke loose." Breaking loose meant to leave family and friends, business and Ireland, and to avoid the danger of success without identity, of a success unequal to "the enormity of my unconscious ambition." He granted himself a prolongation of the interval between youth and adulthood, which we will call a *psychosocial moratorium.* He writes: ". . . when I left my native city I left this phase behind me, and associated no more with men of my age until, after about eight years of solitude in this respect, I was drawn into the Socialist revival of the early eighties, among Englishmen intensely serious and burning with indignation at very real and very fundamental evils that affected all the world.'' In the meantime, he seemed to avoid opportunities sensing that ''Behind the conviction that they could lead to nothing that I wanted, lay the unspoken fear that they might lead to something I did not want.'' This *occupational* part of the moratorium was reinforced by an *intellectual* one: ''I cannot learn anything that does not interest me. My memory is not indiscriminate; it rejects and selects; and its selections are not academic. . . . I congratulate myself on this; for I am firmly persuaded that every unnatural activity of the brain is as mischievous as any unnatural activity of the body. . . . Civilization is always wrecked by giving the governing classes what is called secondary education. . . .''

Shaw settled down to study and to write as he pleased, and it was then that the extraordinary workings of an extraordinary personality came to the fore. He managed to abandon the *kind* of work he had been doing without relinquishing the work *habit:* ''My office training had left me with a habit of doing something regularly every day as a fundamental condition of industry as distinguished from idleness. I knew I was making no headway unless I was doing this, and that I should never produce a book in any other fashion. I bought supplies of white paper, demy size, by sixpence-worths at a time; folded it in quarto; and condemned myself to fill five pages of it a day, rain or shine, dull or inspired. I had so much of the schoolboy and the clerk still in me that if my five pages ended in the middle of a sentence I did not finish it until the next day. On the other hand, if I missed a day, I made up for it by doing a double task on the morrow. On this plan I produced five novels in five years. It was my professional apprenticeship . . .'' We may add that these five novels were not published for over fifty years; but Shaw had learned to write as he worked, and to wait, as he wrote. How important such initial *ritualization of his worklife* was for the young man's inner defenses may be seen from one of those casual (in fact, parenthetical) remarks with which the great wit almost coyly admits his psychological insight: ''I have risen by sheer gravitation, too industrious by acquired habit to stop working (*I work as my father drank*).''[3] He thus points to that combination of *addictiveness* and *compulsivity* which we see as the basis of much pathology in late adolescence and of some accomplishment in young adulthood.

His father's ''drink neurosis'' Shaw describes in detail, finding in it one of the sources of his biting humor: ''It had to be either a family tragedy or family joke.'' For his father was not ''convivial, nor quarrelsome, nor boastful, but miserable, racked with shame and remorse.'' However, the father had a ''humorous sense of anticlimax which I inherited from him and used with much effect when I became a writer of comedy. His anticlimaxes depended for their effect on our sense of the sacredness (of the subject matter) . . . It seems providential that I was driven to the essentials of religion by the reduction of every factitious or fictitious element in it to the most irreverent absurdity.''

A more unconscious level of Shaw's oedipal tragedy is represented—with dreamlike symbolism—in what looks like a screen memory conveying his father's impotence: ''A boy who has seen 'the governor' with an *imperfectly wrapped-up goose under one arm* and *a ham in the same condition under the other* (both purchased under heaven knows what delusion of festivity) *butting* at the garden wall in the belief that he was *pushing open the gate,* and *transforming his tall hat to a concertina* in the process, and who, instead of being overwhelmed with shame and anxiety at the spectacle, has been so *disabled by merriment* (uproariously shared by the maternal uncle) that he has hardly been able to rush to the rescue of the hat and pilot its wearer to safety, is clearly not a boy who will make tragedies of trifles

[3]My italics.

instead of *making trifles of tragedies*. If you cannot get rid of the family skeleton, you may as well make it dance.'' It is obvious that the analysis of the psychosexual elements in Shaw's identity could find a solid anchor point in this memory.

Shaw explains his father's downfall with a brilliant analysis of the socioeconomic circumstances of his day. For the father was ''second cousin to a baronet, and my mother the daughter of a country gentleman whose rule was, when in difficulties, mortgage. That was my sort of poverty.'' His father was ''the younger son of a younger son of a younger son'' and he was ''a downstart and the son of a downstart.'' Yet, he concludes: ''To say that my father could not afford to give me a university education is like saying he could not afford to drink, or that I could not afford to become an author. Both statements are true; but he drank and I became an author all the same.''

His mother he remembers for the ''one or two rare and delightful occasions when she buttered my bread for me. She buttered it thickly instead of merely wiping a knife on it.'' Most of the time, however, he says significantly, she merely ''accepted me as a natural and customary phenomenon and took it for granted that I should go on occurring in that way.'' There must have been something reassuring in this kind of impersonality, for ''technically speaking, I should say she was the worst mother conceivable, always, however, within the limits of the fact that she was incapable of unkindness to any child, animal, or flower, or indeed to any person or thing whatsoever. . . .'' If this could not be considered either a mother's love or an education, Shaw explains: ''I was badly brought up because my mother was so well brought up. . . . In her righteous reaction against . . . the constraints and tyrannies, the scoldings and browbeatings and punishments she had suffered in her childhood . . . she reached a negative attitude in which having no substitute to propose, she carried domestic anarchy as far as in the nature of things it can be carried.'' All in all, Shaw's mother was ''a thoroughly disgusted and disillusioned woman . . . suffering from a hopelessly disappointing husband and three uninteresting children grown too old to be petted like the animals and the birds she was so fond of, to say nothing of the humiliating inadequacy of my father's income.''

Shaw had really three parents, the third being a man named Lee (''meteoric,'' ''impetuous,'' ''magnetic''), who gave Shaw's mother lessons in singing, not without revamping the whole Shaw household as well as Bernard's ideals: ''Although he supplanted my father as the dominant factor in the household, and appropriated all the activity and interest of my mother, he was so completely absorbed in his musical affairs that there was no friction and hardly any intimate personal contacts between the two men: certainly no unpleasantness. At first his ideas astonished us. He said that people should sleep with their windows open. The daring of this appealed to me; and I have done so ever since. He ate brown bread instead of white: a startling eccentricity.''

Of the many elements of identity formations which ensued from such a perplexing picture, let me single out only three, selected, simplified, and named for this occasion by me.

1. The Snob

''As compared with similar English families, we had a power of derisive dramatization that made the bones of the Shavian skeletons rattle more loudly.'' Shaw recognizes this as ''family snobbery mitigated by the family sense of humor.'' On the other hand, ''though my mother was not consciously a snob, the divinity which hedged an Irish lady of her period was not acceptable to the British suburban parents, all snobs, who were within her reach (as customers for private music lessons).'' Shaw had ''an enormous contempt for family snob-bery,'' until he found that one of his ancestors was an Earl of Fife: ''It was as good as being descended from Shakespeare, whom I had been unconsciously resolved to reincarnate from my cradle.''

2.   The Noisemaker

All through his childhood, Shaw seems to have been exposed to an oceanic assault of music making: the family played trombones and ophicleides, violincellos, harps, and tambourines—and, most of all (or is it worst of all) they sang. Finally, however, he taught himself the piano, and this with dramatic noisiness. ''When I look back on all the banging, whistling, roaring, and growling inflicted on nervous neighbors during this process of education, I am consumed with useless remorse. . . . I used to drive (my mother) nearly crazy by my favorite selections from Wagner's Ring, which to her was 'all recitative,' and horribly discordant at that. She never complained at the time, but confessed it after we separated, and said that she had sometimes gone away to cry. If I had committed a murder I do not think it would trouble my conscience very much; but this I cannot bear to think of.'' That, in fact, he may have learned to get even with his musical tormentors, he does not profess to realize. Instead, he compromised by becoming—a music *critic,* i.e., one who *writes about* the noise made by others. As a critic, he chose the *nom de plume* Corno di Bassetto—actually the name of an instrument which nobody knew and which is so meek in tone that ''not even the devil could make it sparkle.'' Yet Bassetto became a sparkling critic, and more: ''I cannot deny that Bassetto was occasionally vulgar; but that does not matter if he makes you laugh. Vulgarity is a necessary part of a complete author's equipment; and the clown is sometimes the best part of the circus.''

3.   The Diabolical One

How the undoubtedly lonely little boy (whose mother listened only to the musical noisemakers) came to use his imagination to converse with a great imaginary companion, is described thus: ''In my childhood I exercised my literary genius by composing my own prayers . . . they were a literary performance for the entertainment and propitiation of the Almighty.'' In line with his family's irreverence in matters of religion, Shaw's piety had to find and to rely on the rockbottom of religiosity which, in him, early became a mixture of ''intellectual integrity . . . synchronized with the dawning of moral passion.'' At the same time it seems that Shaw was (in some unspecified way) a little devil of a child. At any rate, he did not feel identical with himself when he was good: ''Even when I was a good boy, I was so only theatrically, because, as actors say, I saw myself in the character.'' And indeed, at the completion of his identity struggle, i.e., ''when Nature completed my countenance in 1880 or thereabouts (I had only the tenderest sprouting of hair on my face until I was 24), I found myself equipped with the upgrowing moustaches and eyebrows, and the sarcastic nostrils of the operatic fiend whose airs (by Gounod) I had sung as a child, and whose attitudes I had affected in my boyhood. Later on, as the generations moved past me, I . . . began to perceive that imaginative fiction is to life what the sketch is to the picture or the conception to the statue.''

Thus G.B.S., more or less explicitly, traces his own roots. Yet, it is well worth noting that what he finally *became,* seems to him to have been as *innate,* as the intended reincarnation of Shakespeare referred to above. His teacher, he says, "puzzled me with her attempts to teach me to read; for I can remember no time at which a page of print was not intelligible to me, and can only suppose that I was born literate." However, he thought of a number of professional choices: "As an alternative to being a Michelangelo I had dreams of being a Badeali (note, by the way, that of literature I had no dreams at all, any more than a duck has of swimming)."

He also calls himself "a born Communist" (which, we hasten to say, means a Fabian Socialist), and he explains the peace that comes with the *acceptance of what one seems to be made to be*; the "born Communist . . . knows where he is, and where this society which has so intimidated him is. He is cured of his MAUVAISE HONTE. . . ." Thus "the complete outsider" gradually became his kind of complete insider: "I was," he said, "outside society, outside politics, outside sport, outside the Church"—but this "only within the limits of British barbarism. . . . The moment music, painting, literature, or science came into question the positions were reversed: it was I who was the Insider."

As he traces all of these traits back into childhood, Shaw becomes aware of the fact that only a *tour de force* could have integrated them all: ". . . if I am to be entirely communicative on this subject, I must add that the mere rawness which so soon rubs off was complicated by a deeper strangeness which has made me all my life a sojourner on this planet rather than a native of it. Whether it be that I was born mad or a little too sane, my kingdom was not of this world: I was at home only in the realm of my imagination, and at my ease only with the mighty dead. Therefore, I had to become an actor, and create for myself a fantastic personality fit and apt for dealing with men, and adaptable to the various parts I had to play as author, journalist, orator, politician, committee man, man of the world, and so forth. In this," so Shaw concludes significantly, "I succeeded later on only too well." This statement is singularly illustrative of that faint disgust with which older men at times review the inextricable identity which they had come by in their youth—a disgust which in the lives of some can become mortal despair and inexplicable psychosomatic involvement.

The end of his crisis of younger years, Shaw sums up in these words: "I had the intellectual habit; and my natural combination of critical faculty with literary resource needed only a clear comprehension of life in the light of an intelligible theory: in short, a religion, to set it in triumphant operation." Here the old Cynic has circumscribed in one sentence what the identity formation of any human being must add up to. To translate this into terms more conducive to discussion in ego-psychological and psychosocial terms: Man, to take his place in society must acquire a "conflict-free," habitual use of a dominant *faculty*, to be elaborated in an *occupation;* a limitless *resource,* a feedback, as it were, from the immediate *exercise* of this occupation, from the *companionship* it provides, and from its *tradition;* and finally, an intelligible *theory* of the processes of life which the old atheist, eager to shock to the last, calls a religion. The Fabian Socialism to which he, in fact, turned is rather an *ideology,* to which general term we shall adhere, for reasons which permit elucidation only at the end of this paper.

II.   GENETIC: IDENTIFICATION AND IDENTITY

1

The autobiographies of extraordinary (and extraordinarily self-perceptive) individuals are a suggestive source of insight into the development of identity. In order to find an anchor point for the discussion of the universal genetics of identity, however, it would be well to trace its development through the life histories or through significant life episodes of "ordinary" individuals—individuals whose lives have neither become professional autobiographies (as did Shaw's) nor case histories, such as will be discussed in the next chapter. I will not be able to present such material here; I must, instead, rely on impressions from daily life, from participation in one of the rare "longitudinal" studies of the personality development of children,[4] and from guidance work with mildly disturbed young people.

Adolescence is the last and the concluding stage of childhood. The adolescent process, however, is conclusively complete only when the individual has subordinated his childhood identifications to a new kind of identification, achieved in absorbing sociability and in competitive apprenticeship with and among his age-mates. These new identifications are no longer characterized by the playfulness of childhood and the experimental zest of youth: with dire urgency they force the young individual into choices and decisions which will, with increasing immediacy, lead to a more final self-definition, to irreversible role pattern, and thus to commitments "for life." The task to be performed here by the young person and by his society is formidable; it necessitates, in different individuals and in different societies, great variations in the duration, in the intensity, and in the ritualization of adolescence. Societies offer, as individuals require, more or less sanctioned intermediary periods between childhood and adulthood, institutionalized *psychosocial moratoria,* during which a lasting pattern of "inner identity" is scheduled for relative completion.

In postulating a "latency period" which precedes puberty, psychoanalysis has given recognition to some kind of *psychosexual moratorium* in human development—a period of delay which permits the future mate and parent first to "go to school" (i.e., to undergo whatever schooling is provided for in his technology) and to learn the technical and social rudiments of a work situation. It is not within the confines of the libido theory, however, to give adequate account of a second period of delay, namely, adolescence. Here the sexually matured individual is more or less retarded in his psychosexual capacity for intimacy and in the psychosocial readiness for parenthood. This period can be viewed as a *psychosocial moratorium* during which the individual through free role experimentation may find a niche in some section of his society, a niche which is firmly defined and yet seems to be uniquely made for him. In finding it the young adult gains an assured sense of inner continuity and social sameness which will bridge what he *was* as a child and what he is *about to become,* and will reconcile his *conception of himself* and his *community's recognition* of him.

If, in the following, we speak of the community's response to the young individual's need to be "recognized" by those around him, we mean something beyond a mere recognition of achievement; for it is of great relevance to the young individual's identity formation that he be responded to, and be given function and status as a person whose gradual growth and transformation make sense to those who begin to make sense to him. It has not been sufficiently recognized in psychoanalysis that such recognition provides an entirely indispensable support to the ego in the specific tasks of adolescing, which are: to maintain the most important ego defenses against the vastly growing intensity of impulses (now invested in a matured genital apparatus and a powerful muscle system); to learn to consolidate the most important "conflict-free" achievements in line with work opportunities; and to resynthesize all childhood identifications in some unique way, and yet in concordance with the roles offered by some wider section of society—be that section the neighborhood block, an anticipated occupational field, an association of kindred minds, or, perhaps (as in Shaw's case) the "mighty dead."

[4]Child Guidance Study, Institute of Child Welfare, University of California.

2

Linguistically as well as psychologically, identity and identification have common roots. Is identity, then, the mere sum of earlier identifications, or is it merely an additional set of identifications?

The limited usefulness of the *mechanism of identification* becomes at once obvious if we consider the fact that none of the identifications of childhood (which in our patients stand out in such morbid elaboration and mutual contradiction) could, if merely added up, result in a functioning personality. True, we usually believe that the task of psychotherapy is the replacement of morbid and excessive identifications by more desirable ones. But as every cure attests, "more desirable" identifications, at the same time, tend to be quietly subordinated to a new, a unique Gestalt which is more than the sum of its parts. The fact is that identification as a mechanism is of limited usefulness. Children at different stages of their development identify with those *part aspects* of people by which they themselves are most immediately affected, whether in reality or fantasy. Their identifications with parents, for example, center in certain overvalued and ill-understood body parts, capacities, and role appearances. These part aspects, furthermore, are favored not because of their social acceptability (they often are everything but the parents' most adjusted attributes) but by the nature of infantile fantasy which only gradually gives way to a more realistic anticipation of social reality. The final identity, then, as fixed at the end of adolescence is superordinated to any single identification with individuals of the past: it includes all significant identifications, but it also alters them in order to make a unique and a reasonably coherent whole of them.

If we, roughly speaking, consider introjection-projection, identification, and identity formation to be the steps by which the ego grows in ever more mature interplay with the identities of the child's models, the following psychosocial schedule suggests itself:

The mechanisms of *introjection and projection* which prepare the basis for later identifications, depend for their relative integration on the satisfactory mutuality between the *mothering adult(s) and the mothered child*. Only the experience of such mutuality provides a safe pole of self-feeling from which the child can reach out for the other pole: his first love "objects."

The fate of *childhood identifications,* in turn, depends on the child's satisfactory interaction with a trustworthy and meaningful hierarchy of roles as provided by the generations living together in some form of *family*.

Identity formation, finally, begins where the usefulness of identification ends. It arises from the selective repudiation and mutual assimilation of childhood identifications, and their absorption in a new configuration, which, in turn, is dependent on the process by which a *society* (often through subsocieties) *identifies the young individual,* recognizing him as somebody who had to become the way he is, and who, being the way he is, is taken for granted. The community, often not without some initial mistrust, gives such recognition with a (more or less institutionalized) display of surprise and pleasure in making the acquaintance of a newly emerging individual. For the community, in turn, feels "recognized" by the individual who cares to ask for recognition; it can, by the same token, feel deeply—and vengefully—rejected by the individual who does not seem to care.

3

While the end of adolescence thus is the stage of an overt identity *crisis,* identity *formation* neither begins nor ends with adolescence: it is a lifelong development largely unconscious to the individual and to his society. Its roots go back all the way to the first self-recognition: in the baby's earliest exchange of smiles there is something of a *self-realization coupled with a mutual recognition.*

All through childhood tentative crystallizations take place which make the individual feel and believe (to begin with the most conscious aspect of the matter) as if he approximately knew who he was—only to find that such self-certainty ever again falls prey to the *discontinuities of psychosocial development.* An example would be the discontinuity between the demands made in a given milieu on a little boy and those made on a "big boy" who, in turn, may well wonder why he was first made to believe that to be little is admirable, only to be forced to exchange this effortless status for the special obligations of one who is "big now." Such discontinuities can amount to a crisis and demand a decisive and strategic repatterning of action, and with it, to *compromises* which can be compensated for only by a consistently accruing sense of the social value of such increasing commitment. The cute or ferocious, or good small boy, who becomes a studious, or gentlemanly, or tough big boy must be able—and must be enabled—to combine both sets of values in a recognized identity which permits him, in work and play, and in official and in intimate behavior to be (and to let others be) a big boy *and* a little boy.

The community supports such development to the extent to which it permits the child, at each step, to orient himself toward a complete *"life plan"* with a hierarchical order of roles as represented by individuals of different age grades. Family, neighborhood, and school provide contact and experimental identification with younger and older children and with young and old adults. A child, in the multiplicity of successive and tentative identifications, thus begins early to build up expectations of what it will be like to be older and what it will feel like to have been younger—expectations which become part of an identity as they are, step by step, verified in decisive experiences of psychosocial "fittedness."

4

The *critical phases* of life have been described in psychoanalysis primarily in terms of instincts and defenses, i.e., as "typical danger situations." Psychoanalysis has concerned itself more with the encroachment of psychosexual crises on psychosocial (and other) functions than with the specific crisis created by the maturation of each function. Take for example a child who is learning to speak: he is acquiring one of the prime functions supporting a sense of individual autonomy and one of the prime techniques for expanding the radius of give-and-take. The mere indication of an ability to give intentional sound-signs immediately obligates the child to *"say* what he wants." It may force him to *achieve* by proper verbalization the attention which was afforded him previously in response to mere gestures of needfulness. Speech not only commits him to the kind of voice he has and to the mode of speech he develops; it also *defines him* as one responded to by those around him with changed diction and attention. They, in turn, expect henceforth to be understood by him with fewer explanations or gestures. Furthermore, a spoken word is a *pact:* there is an irrevocably committing aspect to an utterance remembered by others, although the child may have to learn early that certain commitments (adult ones to a child) are subject to change without notice, while others (his) are not. This intrinsic relationship of speech, not only to the world of communicable facts, but also to the social value of verbal commitment and uttered truth is strategic among the experiences which support (or fail to support) a sound ego development. It is this psychosocial aspect of the matter which we must learn to relate to the by now better known *psychosexual* aspects represented, for example, in the autoerotic enjoyment of speech; the use of speech as an erotic "contact"; or in such organ-mode emphases as eliminative or intrusive sounds or uses of speech. Thus the child may come to develop, in the use of voice and word, a particular combination of whining or singing, judging or arguing, as part of a new element of the future identity, namely, the element "one who speaks and is spoken to in such-and-such-a-way." This element, in turn, will be related to other elements of the child's developing identity (he is clever and/or good-looking and/or tough) and will be compared with other people, alive or dead, judged ideal or evil.

It is the ego's function to integrate the psychosexual and psychosocial aspects on a given level of development, and, at the same time, to integrate the relation of newly added identity elements with those already in existence. For earlier crystallizations of identity can become subject to renewed conflict, when changes in the quality and quantity of drive, expansions in mental equipment, and new and often conflicting social demands all make previous adjustments appear insufficient, and, in fact, make previous opportunities and rewards suspect. Yet, such developmental and normative crises differ from imposed, traumatic, and neurotic crises in that the process of growth provides new energy as society offers new and specific opportunities (according to its dominant conception and institutionalization of the phases of life). From a genetic point of view, then, the process of identity formation emerges as an *evolving configuration*—a configuration which is gradually established by successive ego syntheses and resyntheses throughout childhood; it is a configuration gradually integrating *constitutional givens, idiosyncratic libidinal needs, favored capacities, significant identifications, effective defenses, successful sublimations, and consistent roles.*

5

The final assembly of all the converging identity elements at the end of childhood (and the abandonment of the divergent ones)[5] appears to be a formidable task: how can a stage as "abnormal" as adolescence be trusted to accomplish it? Here it is not unnecessary to call to mind again that in spite of the similarity of adolescent "symptoms" and episodes to neurotic and psychotic symptoms and episodes, adolescence is not an affliction, but a *normative crisis,* i.e., a normal phase of increased conflict characterized by a seeming fluctuation in ego strength, and yet also by a high growth potential. Neurotic and psychotic crises are defined by a certain self-perpetuating propensity, by an increasing waste of defensive energy, and by a deepened psychosocial isolation; while normative crises are relatively more reversible, or, better, traversable, and are characterized by an abundance of available energy which, to be sure, revives dormant anxiety and arouses new conflict, but also supports new and expanded ego functions in the searching and playful engagement of new opportunities and associations. What under prejudiced scrutiny may appear to be the onset of a neurosis, often is but an aggravated crisis which might prove to be self-liquidating and, in fact, contributive to the process of identity formation.

It is true, of course, that the adolescent, during the final stage of his identity formation, is apt to suffer more deeply than he ever did before (or ever will again) from a diffusion of roles; and it is also true that such diffusion renders many an adolescent defenseless against the sudden impact of previously latent malignant disturbances. In the meantime, it is important to emphasize that the diffused and vulnerable, aloof and uncommitted, and yet demanding and opinionated personality of the not-too-neurotic adolescent contains many necessary elements of a semideliberate role experimentation of the "I dare you" and "I dare myself" variety. Much of this apparent diffusion thus must be considered *social play* and thus the true genetic

---

[5]William James speaks of an abandonment of "the old alternative ego," and even of "the murdered self."

successor of childhood play. Similarly, the adolescent's ego development demands and permits playful, if daring, experimentation in fantasy and *introspection*. We are apt to be alarmed by the "closeness to consciousness" in the adolescent's perception of dangerous id contents (such as the oedipus complex) and this primarily because of the obvious hazards created in psychotherapy, if and when we, in zealous pursuit of our task of "making conscious," push somebody over the precipice of the unconscious who is already leaning out a little too far. The adolescent's leaning out over any number of precipices is normally an experimentation with experiences which are thus becoming more amenable to ego control, provided they can be somehow communicated to other adolescents in one of those strange codes established for just such experiences—and provided they are not prematurely responded to with fatal seriousness by overeager or neurotic adults. The same must be said of the adolescent's "fluidity of defenses," which so often causes raised eyebrows on the part of the worried clinician. Much of this fluidity is anything but pathological; for adolescence is a crisis in which only fluid defense can overcome a sense of victimization by inner and outer demands, and in which only trial and error can lead to the most felicitous avenues of action and self-expression.

In general, one may say that in regard to the social play of adolescents prejudices similar to those which once concerned the nature of childhood play are not easily overcome. We alternately consider such behavior irrelevant, unnecessary, or irrational, and ascribe to it purely regressive and neurotic meanings. As in the past the study of children's spontaneous games was neglected in favor of that of solitary play,[6] so now the mutual "joinedness" of adolescent clique behavior fails to be properly assessed in our concern for the individual adolescent. Children and adolescents in their pre-societies provide for one another a sanctioned moratorium and joint support for free experimentation with inner and outer dangers (including those emanating from the adult world). Whether or not a given adolescent's newly acquired capacities are drawn back into infantile conflict depends to a significant extent on the quality of the opportunities and rewards available to him in his peer clique, as well as on the more formal ways in which society at large invites a transition from social play to work experimentation, and from rituals of transit to final commitments: all of which must be based on an implicit mutual contract between the individual and society.

6

Is the sense of identity conscious? At times, of course, it seems only too conscious. For between the double prongs of vital inner need and inexorable outer demand, the as yet experimenting individual may become the victim of a transitory extreme *identity consciousness* which is the common core of the many forms of "self-consciousness" typical for youth. Where the processes of identity formation are prolonged (a factor which can bring creative gain) such preoccupation with the "self-image" also prevails. We are thus most aware of our identity when we are just about to gain it and when we (with what motion pictures call "a double take") are somewhat surprised to make its acquaintance; or, again, when we are just about to enter a crisis and feel the encroachment of identity diffusion—a syndrome to be described presently.

An increasing sense of identity, on the other hand, is experienced preconsciously as a sense of psychosocial well-being. Its most obvious concomitants are a feeling of being at home in one's body, a sense of "knowing where one is going," and an inner assuredness of

[6]For a new approach see Anna Freud's and Sophie Dann's report on displaced children.

anticipated recognition from those who count. Such a sense of identity, however, is never gained nor maintained once and for all. Like a "good conscience," it is constantly lost and regained, although more lasting and more economical methods of maintenance and restoration are evolved and fortified in late adolescence.

Like any aspect of well-being or for that matter, of ego synthesis, a sense of identity has a preconscious aspect which is available to awareness; it expresses itself in behavior which is observable with the naked eye; and it has unconscious concomitants which can be fathomed only by psychological tests and by the psychoanalytic procedure. I regret that, at this point, I can bring forward only a general claim which awaits detailed demonstration. The claim advanced here concerns a whole series of criteria of psychosocial health which find their specific elaboration and relative completion in stages of development preceding and following the identity crisis. This is condensed in Figure I.

Identity appears as only one concept within a wider conception of the human life cycle which envisages childhood as a *gradual unfolding of the personality through phase-specific psychosocial crises:* I have, on other occasions, expressed this *epigenetic principle* by taking recourse to a diagram which, with its many empty boxes, at intervals may serve as a check on our attempts at detailing psychosocial development. (Such a diagram, however, can be recommended to the serious attention only of those who can take it *and* leave it.) The diagram (Figure I), at first, contained only the double-lined boxes along the descending diagonal (I,1 — II,2 — III,3 — IV,4 —V,5 — VI,6 — VII,7 — VIII,8) and, for the sake of initial orientation, the reader is requested to ignore all other entries for the moment. The *diagonal* shows the sequence of psychosocial crises. Each of these boxes is shared by a criterion of relative psychosocial health and the corresponding criterion of relative psychosocial ill-health: in "normal" development, the first must persistently outweigh (although it will never completely do away with) the second. The sequence of stages thus represents a successive development of the component parts of the psychosocial personality. Each part exists in some form (verticals) before the time when it becomes "phase-specific," i.e., when "its" psychosocial crisis is precipitated both by the individual's readiness and by society's pressure. But each component comes to ascendance and finds its more or less lasting solution at the conclusion of "its" stage. It is thus *systematically related* to all the others, and all depend on the proper development at the proper *time* of each; although individual make-up and the nature of society determine the rate of development of each of them, and thus the *ratio* of all of them. It is at the end of adolescence, then, that identity becomes phase-specific (V,5), i.e., must find a certain integration as a relatively conflict-free psychosocial arrangement—or remain defective or conflict-laden.

	1.	2.	3.	4.	5.	6.	7.	8.
I. INFANCY	Trust vs. Mistrust				Unipolarity vs. Premature Self-Differentiation			
II. EARLY CHILDHOOD		Autonomy vs. Shame, Doubt			Bipolarity vs. Autism			
III. PLAY AGE			Initiative vs. Guilt		Play Identification vs. (Oedipal) Fantasy Identities			
IV. SCHOOL AGE				Industry vs. Inferiority	Work Identification vs. Identity Foreclosure			
V. ADOLESCENCE	Time Perspective vs. Time Diffusion	Self-Certainty vs. Identity Consciousness	Role Experimentation vs. Negative Identity	Anticipation of Achievement vs. Work Paralysis	Identity vs. Identity Diffusion	Sexual Identity vs. Bisexual Diffusion	Leadership Polarization vs. Authority Diffusion	Ideological Polarization vs. Diffusion of Ideals
VI. YOUNG ADULT					Solidarity vs. Social Isolation	Intimacy vs. Isolation		
VII. ADULTHOOD							Generativity vs. Self-Absorption	
VIII. MATURE AGE								Integrity vs. Disgust, Despair

Figure I

N. V. Ciaccio
A TEST OF ERIKSON'S THEORY
OF EGO EPIGENESIS

The two basic postulates of Erikson's theory of ego epigenesis were tested on a sample of 120 boys (5-, 8-, and 11-year-olds), using a projective instrument designed by Boyd and this author's coding system. Results indicated that the first postulate, ego stage progression with increasing age, found preliminary confirmation; Group I was most concerned with Stages II and III, while Groups 2 and 3 showed peak interest in Stages III and IV, respectively. The validity of the second postulate, that the ego develops as it meets the different crisis elements of the ego stages, was called into question. All three groups showed most conflict for the Stage II crisis—autonomy versus shame and doubt—suggesting that this may be the focal crisis of the first five ego stages.

While Erikson's theory has gained prominence in both clinical and academic settings, research efforts toward testing it have been limited. Most of the references in the literature are descriptive, either pointing to the theoretical importance of his work (e.g., Gill & Klein, 1964; Murphy, Green, Henry, & Friedenberg, 1966) or elaborating on his theory of identity and its clinical or conceptual utility (e.g., Lichtenstein, 1963; Sarlin, 1963). Some authors have inquired into the validity of various isolated aspects of the theory, usually using rating scales or "adjustment measures" based on Erikson's formulations at different points on the developmental continuum (see Arasteh, 1965; Marcia, 1966; Pable, 1965; Pitcher & Prelinger, 1963).

There have been only two attempts to study the course of ego epigenesis per se, represented by the work of Gruen (1964) and Boyd (1961, 1964). Gruen's research was concerned with the adult personality only, and he defined Erikson's eight stages as personality dimensions "each operating within a relatively wide range of behavior" which he then tried to find in the already extant personality; as such, the developmental implications of his work remain unclear.

The first phase of Boyd's (1961) work dealt with the problems involved in devising a quantitive profile which would depict the ego stage development of adults. The second phase (Boyd, 1964) presented a methodology which made it possible to study the problem of ego stage progression. For adults, it consisted of a semistructured interview schedule (a few broad questions are introduced and a nondirective technique used to explore areas of concern) and a coding system based on Eriksonian concepts to evaluate the ego stage status of the responses obtained. He then devised a series of projective pictures for childen, each of which portrays a basic aspect of one of the first five ego stages. The coding system remained the same for both adults and children, however, thus rendering his methodology unclear with respect to

Reprinted by permission from *Developmental Psychology*, 1971, *4*, pp. 306–311. Copyright 1971 by the American Psychological Association.

younger individuals because of the necessity to evaluate their responses from the viewpoint of adult development.

The basic postulate of the theory, derived from general psychoanalytic-psychological propositions, is that the ego develops systematically in stages with increasing age. This postulate actually refers to the orderly development of psychosocial attitudes or strengths (trust, autonomy, initiative, etc.) which emerge—in conjunction with libidinal and maturational processes—as the child interacts in an ever-widening social radius. The second postulate, derived from philosophy and the "behavioral sciences," is that the ego develops as it meets with the psychosocial crises (mistrust, shame and doubt, guilt, etc.) which each new stage affords. Erikson (1963) has lucidly set forth the developmental sequence in a series of hierarchically ordered stages which incorporate both the psychosocial strengths or positive "ego attitudes" and the crisis elements or negative aspects which "are and remain the dynamic part of the 'positive ones' throughout life [Erikson, 1963]."

The purpose of this investigation was to study the validity of these two postulates using Boyd's projective instrument and a coding system appropriate for children. In order to study the question of developmental progression with increasing age through psychosocial crisis, three age levels were represented: 5-, 8-, and 11-year-olds. The hypothesis, combining both postulates, was as follows: The 5-year-olds are expected to be most concerned with the autonomy versus shame and doubt issues of Stage II; the 8-year-olds are expected to be most concerned with the initiative versus guilt issues of Stage III; and the 11-year-olds are hypothesized to show peak interest for the industry versus inferiority issues of Stage IV.

METHOD

Subjects

Four suburban Chicago schools participated (three public and one parochial). The four communities in which these schools were located were either consistent with or above the "average" figures presented by the 1960 Census Bureau statistics with regard to social class status characteristics. The schools provided a cumulative subject pool of 384 white males representing the three age groups used. One hundred and fifty boys were then randomly selected for testing, with 50 in each of the three groups. Since school records were not available to the investigator, IQ range is unknown. However, none of the subjects was drawn from any of the "special education" (educable mentally handicapped or gifted) classes. Testing was conducted from April to May of 1968. The mean age at time of testing for Group I was 5.2 years, 8.6 years for Group II, and 11.7 years for Group III.

Projective Instrument and Coding System

As stated above, the instrument used was designed by Boyd (1964). Responses to these pictures were evaluated by means of a coding system devised by the present investigator, based on a content item analysis of Eirkson's writings concerning the various stages. The major questions throughout the development of the code concerned the attitudes, capacities, behaviors, conflicts, perceptions, and allegiances which were most characteristic of each stage as given by Erikson. All of his published writings, but especially *Childhood and Society* (Erikson, 1963) and *Identity: Youth and Crisis* (Erikson, 1968) were perused for such information and lists were accumulated for each of the five stages. The coding system reflects both the positive (psychosocial strengths) and negative (crisis or conflict) elements of each stage. It thus avoids the pitfalls of being a mere "achievement scale" and retains the inherent dynamic flavor of the theory as Erikson presented it. The code as written is an attempt to cover the full developmental dimensions of the theory rather than only isolated "traits" or "aspirations."

Testing Procedure

Two sessions were devoted to each child from Group I. The first session was a "warm-up" period in which the child was given time to explore the testing room and for the examiner to establish rapport by drawing pictures and playing "Lotto." The actual testing session for all three groups involved introductions and a brief period of conversation. The following instructions were then given to all subjects, regardless of age:

> I'm interested in the kind of stories that children tell. I'm going to show you some pictures and I'd like you to make up a story about them—any kind of story will be okay. Just tell me what has happened in the picture and how it's going to turn out. Okay?

Task set and expectancies were kept at a minimum so that the subjects could respond in a manner most characteristic of them in their own idiom. All sessions were taped in their entirety.

The subjects were given one card, allowed as much time as necessary to complete the story, then given the next card and so on until the series of five cards was completed. Cards were presented in counterbalanced order (the exact order being changed for each subject to correct for sequence and position effects.) To insure uniformity and comparability of method, the only questions directed to the subjects concerning their stories were instances where the examiner was uncertain as to with which character in the card or story the subject identified. This was done only to clarify previous responses so that they could be validly coded.

Coding Procedure

All protocols were taped and then later transcribed by typing exactly what was heard on the tape. Actual coding was not begun until all 150 subjects were tested. In order to minimize scoring bias, the order of protocols was mechanically counterbalanced so that a protocol of one age level was never followed by one of the same age level.

The first part of the actual coding procedure involved the analysis of individual stories comprising a protocol into what are termed "unit utterances." A unit utterance is defined as that group of words which compose the smallest unit of spoken thought dealing with one theme. Each unit utterance was then examined to determine the pertinent coding by referring to the coding system. If the utterance was found to be scorable, the appropriate ego stage number and valence were recorded. All coded utterances received a valence score of either plus (indicating the positive aspects of the stage or the psychosocial strengths) or minus (indicating the negative aspects of the stage or failure to resolve the particular ego stage conflict).

The data originally consisted of a raw number of coded unit utterances which actually amounted to a frequency profile for the individual child. For group comparisons, individual profiles from each of the age groups were converted into grand percentage profiles by finding the total number of coded unit utterances that were contained in each of the five stages; this procedure standardized all individual profiles for differences in the total number of coded unit utterances. These group percentage profiles therefore graphically depicted the ego stage development of a particular age group. Although 150 subjects were tested, only 120 protocols were used in the final analysis of the data. Twenty-one protocols were dismissed because they contained mere descriptions of the physical characteristics of the pictures which rarely yielded scorable material (11 of these were from Group I, 7 from Group II, and 3 from Group II). Four were eliminated because of mechanical difficulties in the recording procedure, and 6 other protocols were incomplete because these subjects were unable to finish the testing session (4 from Group I and 2 from Group II).

Reliability Procedure

Reliability was assessed in three ways: test-retest after a 2-week time intervention between Administrations 1 and 2 (Condition A); "developmental reliability" or test-retest after a 5-month time intervention (Condition B); and intercoder judgments. For Condition A, 15 children (5 from each of the three age levels) who had not been tested previously were selected from the available subject pool. Testing, instructions, and coding procedures were the same for both administrations and these corresponded exactly to the paradigms used in the primary investigation. In Condition B, 15 children (again 5 from each age level) who had participated in the primary investigation were retested after an interval of 5 months.

Eight judges participated in the intercoder reliability study. Three of these had doctorates in clinical psychology with at least 2 years of postdoctoral experience in a child-guidance setting. The remaining five judges were doctoral candidates in clinical psychology; three had already completed formal internships in the clinical child field and two were in the process of such training. Judges received one set of 10 stories to code, along with a copy of the coding system. They were instructed to compute the ego development score (found simply by adding up the ego stage values of each utterance) for each of the stories and then to rank them from 1 to 10. Two independent judges were assigned to each of six story sets, thereby giving three independent series of ranks for each of the story sets: the two coders who worked separately and the investigator's original ranking. This arrangement afforded six three-way analyses of intercoder reliability using the Spearman rank correlation coefficient.

RESULTS

A general summary of the data (recorded as the percentage of coded unit utterances found in each of the five ego stages and the percentage of utterances scored either plus or minus) is given in Table 1. Figure 1 is a representation of these findings in the form of ego stage development profiles (group frequency distributions in terms of coded unit utterances within the ego stages). The following trends emerged from an inspection of these data: for Group I, the majority of responses fell in the Stages II and III categories (46.0% and 41.9% of the total number of coded utterances, respectively); comparatively little concern was shown for the other three stages. Furthermore, 57% of these responses were given a negative valence. Group II scored most heavily in the Stage III category (55.7% of the total); Stages I and V contained few responses, while Stages II and IV had almost equal distributions, each representing about 20% of the total. Twenty percent of the responses were scored as negative. Group III showed the greatest concern for Stage IV (44.3% of the total number of coded utterances); this group also gave many Stage II and Stage III responses (16.1% and 26.1%). Some 8.2% of this group's responses fell into the Stage V category. Only 18% of the total utterances received negative valences.

Table 1.   Percentage of coded units within ego stages for three age groups and valence of total coded units.

Group	Stages					No. units	Valence (percentage)	
	I	*II*	*III*	*IV*	*V*		+	−
I	5.0	46.0	41.9	6.4	.7	480	43	57
II	3.1	20.3	55.7	19.0	1.9	579	80	20
III	5.3	16.1	26.1	44.3	8.2	785	82	18

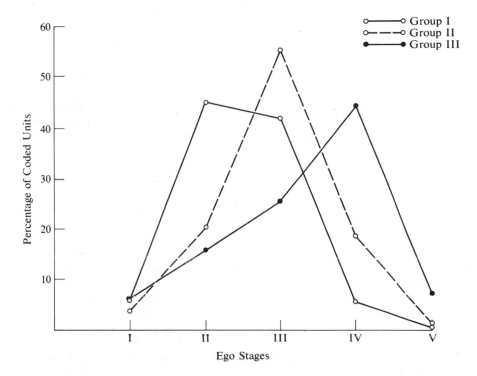

Figure 1. Frequency distributions in terms of percentage of coded units within ego stages for the three age groups.

Tests of significance included the Kolmogorov-Smirnov one-sample test of variance and the Kruskall-Wallis analysis of variance by ranks. In the first procedure, each of the three total distributions of unit utterances was examined by age and stage, providing a vertical check of the null hypothesis that these three samples came from the same population in terms of their unit utterance distribution across the five stages. Incorporating the data given in Table 1 into the formula $F_o(x) - S_{100}(x)$ (Siegel, 1956, pp. 47–52), it was found that the null hypothesis was rejected at the .01 level of significance for all three age groups. The second procedure gave a vertical check of the null hypothesis by stage and age (see Table 2). Here the distributions of unit utterances for each of the age groups were compared for each of the five ego stages; all three groups were compared first for Stage I, then for Stage II and so on. No significant differences emerged for the three Stage I distributions. However, a significant

Table 2.   Results of the Kruskall-Wallis one-way analysis
of variance by ranks for three groups.

Stage	H[a]
I	2.89*
II	67.40***
III	72.70***
IV	83.00***
V	10.00**

[a]H is distributed as chi-square with $K-1$ degrees of freedom.
*$p < .25$.
**$p < .01$.
***$p < .001$.

difference at the .001 level was found when comparing the groups for Stage II, with the 5-year-olds giving the majority of Stage II responses.

Significant differences at the .001 level were found for the Stage III distributions, revealing that the 8-year-olds contributed the most significant percentage of responses here. For Stage IV, a level of significance of .001 was again found, with the 11-year-olds providing the major source of these responses. Analysis of the distributions for Stage V yielded a significant difference at the .01 level, with the 11-year-olds again giving the majority of responses for this stage category.

Reliability Studies

For both test-retest conditions all subjects were first ranked on the percentage of Stage I responses at Time 1 and were then ranked on percentage of Stage I responses at Time 2. The Spearman rank correlation coefficient was then computed for Stage I at both times. This same procedure was used for the remaining four stages; this method provided an assessment of the reliability of the subjects' ego stage responses by stage rather than by card, thereby affording an index of both ego stage stability and change as well as instrument reliability. The average correlation coefficient for Condition A was .78, while the average coefficient for Condition B was .69. Individual distributions were analyzed and it was found that greater response stability was noted for Condition A and that more truly developmental progression was evidenced for Condition B.

Intercoder reliabilities, based on six three-way analyses of coder rank agreement, ranged from a low of .45 to a high of .88 with an average correlation coefficient of .71. None of the eight independent coders received any pretraining or coaching during the coding process, thereby eliminating contaminating factors which could inflate the coefficients.

DISCUSSION

Erikson's first postulate, ego stage progression with increasing age, received support. The 5-year-olds were found to be most concerned with Stages II and III; although it was hypothesized that this group would peak at Stage II, the peak for both stages can be regarded as consistent with theory. This group actually represented a "borderline age group" which could be expected to be struggling with the issues of these two stages simultaneously because of their proximity to both developmental periods. While a more definitive test would demand the inclusion of 2- and 3-year-olds as a separate group, a pilot study proved that such a plan was not feasible. The 8-year-olds met the expectation of peak interest in Stage III. Furthermore, Stage II responses appeared to be "dropping out" of their concern repertoire, while Stage IV responses showed a solid emergent trend. The 11-year-olds were found to be most concerned with Stage IV issues as hypothesized. Their involvement with Stage III, and, to a lesser extent, with Stage II is consistent with Erikson's theoretical predictions with regard to the epigenetic principle which states that although there are "critical periods" for the child to resolve particular crises, "residue" from previous stages is expected, especially during the highly plastic periods of childhood.

It should be emphasized that the unit utterances for Groups II and III were scored largely within the positive valence range—only 29% and 18% of the respective totals were negative—while Group I had 57% of these responses scored negatively. Furthermore, 87% of the negative responses for all three age groups involved issues directly pertinent to the subjects' expressed feelings of lack of autonomy or a sense of shame and doubt. The conflict or crisis elements of the other four ego stages were surprisingly underrepresented. Finding less conflict in the protocols of the older subjects could be interpreted as lending some confirmation to the existence of a latency period, but their continued concern with the conflicts of Stage II rather than with those of Stages III and IV as hypothesized, seriously calls into question the validity of Erikson's second postulate.

The fact that greater conflict was found for the 5-year-olds, particularly with reference to expressions of lack of autonomy or shame and doubt, that the majority of negative responses for the 8- and 11-year-olds also reflected continued concern for these issues, and that much of the "content" of the first five ego stage crises is so easily translated into autonomy terms (Bettleheim, 1967; Ciaccio, 1969) suggests that the establishment of autonomy is the focal crisis of the first five stages. It might be further argued that the first five crises outlined by Erikson are merely different expressions of the focal crisis of autonomy versus shame and doubt, each reflecting different levels or dimensions of the same underlying crisis.

In summary, it appears that the psychosocial strengths or attitudes emerge in the stage sequence postulated by Erikson. The process elements or negative aspects of the ego stages, defined as crises, have not found such confirmation, with the exception of the autonomy versus shame and doubt crisis which the investigator holds to be the focal crisis of the first five stages.

REFERENCES

Arasteh, A. R. *Final integration in the adult personality: A measure for health, social change, and leadership.* Leiden, Netherlands: Brill, 1965.

Bettelheim, B. *The empty fortress.* New York: Free Press of Glencoe, 1967.

Boyd, R. Basic motivations of adults enrolled in non-credit programs. *Journal of Adult Education,* 1961, *11,* 91–96.

Boyd, R. Analysis of the ego-stage development of school-age children. *Journal of Experimental Education,* 1964, *32,* 249–257.

Ciaccio, N. V. Erikson's theory of ego epigenesis: Empirical and theoretical perspectives for child development. Paper presented at the meeting of the American Association of Psychiatric Clinics for Children, Boston, November 1969.

Erikson, E. H. *Childhood and society.* (Rev. ed.) New York: Norton, 1963.

Erikson, E. H. *Identity: Youth and crisis.* New York: Norton, 1968.

Gill, M. M., & Klein, G. S. The structuring of drive and reality: David Rapaport's contributions to psychoanalysis and psychology. *International Journal of Psychoanalysis,* 1964, *45,* 483–498.

Gruen, W. Adult personality: An empirical study of Erikson's theory of ego development. In B. Neugarten (Ed.), *Personality in middle and late life*. New York: Atherton Press, 1964.

Lichtenstein, H. The dilemma of human identity: Notes on self-transformation, self-objectivation and metamorphosis. *Journal of the American Psychoanalytic Association*, 1963, *11*, 173–223.

Marcia, J. E. Development and validation of ego-identity status. *Journal of Personality and Social Psychology*, 1966, *3*, 551–558.

Murphy, L., Green, M., Henry, J., & Friedenberg, E. Eight ages of man. *International Journal of Psychiatry*, 1966, *2*, 281–300.

Pable, M. Some parental determinants of ego identity in adolescent boys. *Dissertation Abstracts*, 1965, *26*, 3480–3481.

Pitcher, E. V., & Prelinger, E. *Children tell stories*. New York: International Universities Press, 1963.

Sarlin, C. N. Feminine identity. *Journal of the American Psychoanalytic Association*, 1963, *11*, 790–816.

Siegel, S. *Nonparametric statistics*. New York: McGraw-Hill, 1956.

Kenneth J. Gergen
FLIGHT FROM THE QUAGMIRE

The profession of psychology is a pleasant one in which to age. The field retains a traditional cast—almost Eastern in its veneration of the elder statesman—and definitely runs counter to the current American grain with its growing adoration of youth. Thus, for those who have fought the major battles, there are always ears to listen. And these ears do not listen in the same way to the boisterous self-avowals of the young. They do not demand strict adherence to the canons of logic; they do not heed only fact, shunning all that smacks of fantasy; nor do they search for significance levels, operational definitions, or any of the other accoutrements of scientism. Rather, when ears are tuned to the voices of time, they are open to the possibility, the dim hope, that out of the sweaty tumult of everyday science might grow wisdom. The elder statesman thus serves as the surrogate for priests, parents, and poets, whose ethics, values, and criteria of merit have long before been drummed out of court because of their incompatibility with the cool logic of scientific premise. For the statesman in psychology, history is purifying as he gains the right to deviate from the strictly cerebral.

Such is the case with Erik H. Erikson's collection of essays in *Identity, Youth and Crisis*. The essays, many previously published, were written over a twenty-one year period and offer little in the way of coolly reasoned dialectic. The reader might wonder as to what machinations would allow a first chapter to be composed of a workshop transcript authored in 1966 and a letter to the Committee on the Year 2000. The second essay is then pieced together from three separate contributions spanning some eight years. And yet, upon delving into the essays, it is soon apparent that few of them form internally coherent wholes, and that indeed, almost any organization of the material would have sufficed as well.

Nor do the arguments within the essays rely on systematically gathered data. To be sure, there is ample use made of materials gathered by Erikson in his encounters with patients, and closely examined biographical writings. (One of these, a case study of Freud, is a classic, wherein events in Freud's daily life as well as his dream life are used to validate Erikson's clearly revisionistic brand of psychoanalytic theory.) But for the great body of empirical literature on self-conception, self-definition, child development, and adolescence, Erikson seems to hold a peculiar disdain. Little direct reference to any of this literature exists in his work. Where indirect references appear, such contributions are dismissed as if superficial products of graceless mechanization. This attitude is ultimately rendered ironic, as a full ten pages of the volume are spent in describing and drawing generalizations from an empirical study carried out by the author himself—a study that meets few of the ordinary requirements of rigor.

Reprinted by permission from *Contemporary Psychology*, 1969, *14*, pp. 49–50. Copyright 1969 by the American Psychological Association.

This propensity to limit his data base almost entirely to what he has encountered in the clinic or non-scientific literature proves highly problematic in other respects as well. Developmentalists, personality theorists, and social psychologists alike have drawn sustenance from Erikson's classic socio-psychoanalytic formulation of the developmental sequence as it appears in *Childhood and Society*. This developmental model receives further elaboration in the present series of essays. Various aspects of identity are linked to each of the developmental stages, the symptoms of extreme identity confusion in adolescence are traced to each of the earlier stages, and social institutions are found to play a supportive role at every stage in the process of identity formation. And yet, so primly and precisely does this entire multi-faceted formulation hold together that one must draw pause. Does the flux of real life truly lend itself to such tidy conceptualizations? Or is it possible that this exquisite superstructure is the result of forces more internal to the theorist? If the theoretical rationale could be supported with data from wide-ranging and methodologically respectable resources, the case would be much more convincing.

Additional problems exist on a semantic level. It is explained at the outset of the volume that a precise meaning of a term such as identity would be a denial of the rich and provocative ways in which the term has been employed over time. This stance does prove to be well chosen, for it allows Erikson to use the term in a variety of highly disparate contexts, weaving together themes and images in unique and interesting ways. And yet, upon completion of the essays, one feels that the term carries such an overload of excess semantic and evaluative baggage that it would be rendered useless in any form of definitive communication. A similar fate befalls such concepts as "inner space," central in Erikson's discussion of feminine psychology, and "autonomy," a term as widely worshiped as it is slippery to grasp.

These comments should not be construed as ruling these essays out of scientific consideration. On the contrary, within the pages of this volume a number of highly challenging arguments are put forward. Investigations of the self-concept, for example, have since the time of Mead and Cooley been concentrated on the impact of the immediate social environment on self-conception. Erikson cogently argues that the span of contributing factors must be viewed far more broadly. Social institutions, for example, may play a crucial role at various stages of self-development; political and ethical ideologies may often funnel the emerging concept of self along particular channels; and a man's grasp of the cultural history in which he is enmeshed may serve at times to sharpen or at times to confuse his present feelings of who he is.

Such themes provide a similar challenge to traditional thinking about mental health—in which the scope is only beginning to expand from an emphasis on biological, familial, and peer group antecedents to include the community. Erikson's analysis would suggest that such thinking has not gone far enough. From his perspective an adequate understanding of mental illness would ultimately take into account social institutions as well as historical context.

And too, the long fermenting field of adolescent psychology may gain much from the special insights that Erikson brings to bear. As an antidote to the simplex thinking about adolescence so often apparent, Erikson probes with great sensitivity a wide array of dimensions and pressures particularly relevant to this possibly crucial stage. Included are discussions of adolescent time perspective, role expectations, bisexual confusion, the role of work and occupation, ideological commitment, identity confusion, autism, and futility. Not only does he make a compelling case for the importance of these various aspects of adolescent experience, but in addition, points to antecedents earlier in the life of the person that would give rise to difficulties in each of these areas.

After confronting Erikson's multiplex analysis of the adolescent state, one also views with some doubt the claims to generality found within much of the current empirical work in social psychology. Out of convenience the vast majority of the research carried out in this tradition utilizes the adolescent as a prime data source. Nowhere does it become more apparent that we are tapping into a syndrome of particulate and peculiar properties. A depressing prospect, but what pass for general laws of behavior in social psychology may ultimately prove to be little more than an elaborate description of a particular personality type.

And yet, in the final analysis, perhaps this entire set of evaluations is misconceived. After all, are Erikson's readers really looking for arguments cast in the mold of diluted physics? Is the fact that so many young readers respond so enthusiastically to his writings based on their appreciation of his rigorous development and test of hypotheses? Assuredly not. Erikson is one of the few psychologists who dare to admit that their work is, after all, welded to an ethical tradition. Most avoid with horror the prospect of revealing the underside, thereby sapping their work of most of its vitality. And many will grimace at Erikson's bold affirmation of love, creativity, marriage, universal ethics, and autonomy—realizing at the same time that while each ideal is an intellectual nightmare, it is not the phantasma that guides their daily behavior.

And Erikson is also a master of the well-turned phrase—the phrase that prompts sudden recognition that borne to lofty flight is a thought previously dwelling only in the quagmire of the preconscious. In speaking of the components of a mature heterosexual relationship we find, "Fidelity without a sense of diversity can become an obsession and a bore; diversity without a sense of fidelity, an empty relativism." And in discussing the impact of totalitarian ideologies, "To have the courage of one's diversity is a sign of wholeness in individuals and in a civilization." Or in discussing race relations, "I came to reformulate the Golden Rule as one that commands us always to act in such a way that the identities of both the actor and the acted upon are enhanced." These are not the types of statements that send one scurrying for his data in defense of theoretical premise; they do, on the other hand, invite a warm and admiring "yes."

Four
JEAN PIAGET

Regarded by many as the world's foremost child psychologist, Jean Piaget (1896–   ) has been writing for the past 50 years about how the mind develops. His unique approach has had a significant impact on the way in which psychologists theorize about the development of mind, or personality. Although Piaget is not, strictly speaking, a personality theorist, we would be remiss if we failed to examine his point of view.

Piaget, a Swiss citizen, was initially trained in biology but has always had major philosophical interests. He calls himself a *genetic epistemologist*, and an appreciation of his work requires an understanding of the philosophical position that this term represents. *Genetic* means developmental, and *epistemology* means the study of the origin and nature of knowledge. In a sense, Piaget's theory is a psychological theory of knowledge. Epistemology—a topic of philosophy, not psychology—defines its problem as one of proving that people's assumptions concerning the external world are valid. How do people know that their beliefs, perceptions, thoughts, judgments, and so on about the real world are accurate? How do they know that what they see in the external world is what others see in the external world? How do they justify the assumption that, when they no longer look at an object, it is still there? What is unique about Piaget's work is the fact that he has examined these problems *empirically*. It is this feature of his approach that makes him a psychologist.

For Piaget, the question concerns *how* the mind works, not *what* it does. The emphasis is on *structure*, not *content*. This approach follows from Piaget's background in the biological sciences. In biology, a question of immense import has to do with how (and why) the function of biological structures changes over time. Many such changes in function seem to be rather intelligent; that is, they have survival value. Here, of course, we are talking about change in an evolutionary sense. And it is in this sense that Piaget approaches the topic of the development of the mind, or personality.

Applying this biological/evolutionary approach to human behavior, Piaget sees mental development as occurring in stages, by age level. He attempts to isolate and describe the psychological processes existing at each stage and to show how they allow adaptation to environmental demands, how they interrelate, how they influence what the environment demands, and, finally, how they result in mental structures allowing the performance of certain cognitive tasks.

The selections presented in this chapter afford the reader the unusual opportunity of following the evolution of an experimental method. The Piaget selection is from his book *The Moral Judgment of the Child* (published in 1932). Here one sees Piaget, the philosopher/empiricist, explaining the evolution of moral judgment in the child by reference to the game of marbles. The method is uniquely Piagetian; some would call it *naturalistic*, others *clinical*. Notice how his method of "interrogation" is structured, yet flexible and capable of being adapted to the particular child. Compare Piaget's method of inquiry with the questioning of Little Hans by his father (Chapter 1). Of these two (clinical) methods of inquiry, which is likely to produce the smaller amount of biased data? How could the method be further refined?

Next note how Piaget takes the mass of information he has gleaned from his interrogations and weaves it into a stage theory of child development. Although here he is considering only the development of moral judgment, this selection is representative of Piaget's approach to theory and research.

The paper by Lawrence Kohlberg presents the results of a contemporary attempt to refine and extend the early work of Piaget on moral development. Kohlberg's refinement is essentially a methodological one; his extension is to a variety of cultures. Beginning with his doctoral dissertation in 1958, Kohlberg has studied the development of moral thinking from childhood through early adulthood in several widely divergent cultures. In this article, he presents the results of his work, carried out over a period of 12 years and in six cultures. (His method—the Moral Judgment Scale—is not described in this article. The third selection in this chapter, by Kurtines and Greif, contains an excellent description of Kohlberg's methodological approach. We suggest that you re-read the Kohlberg article after reading the Kurtines and Greif evaluation of Kohlberg's approach.)

Kohlberg claims that his results confirm Piaget's contention that moral thought, like all thought, develops through several stages and that this development is *invariant*. That is, the development does not skip stages and is always in the same order. Thus, each stage must be passed through, and each stage incorporates and elaborates on the development achieved in the previous stage. Characteristic of this development is a sort of "push" from one stage to the next, a force that moves the development of cognitive structures toward equilibrium. Piaget calls this force *equilibration*, and it is this concept that most clearly reflects Piaget's biological/evolutionary intellectual background. Equilibration is the process by which structures change, always in the direction of better (that is, more adaptive) cognitive organization. Furthermore, Kohlberg contends that cognitive development of this kind is universal—that moral thought develops in the same way in all cultures.

The authors of the third selection in this chapter question the rigor of Kohlberg's methodology. William Kurtines and Esther B. Greif, after a thorough evaluation of the Moral Judgment Scale, conclude that, because of a number of serious problems related to the construction and experimental use of the scale, confirmation of Kohlberg's theory of moral thought has not been demonstrated. As they point out, this is not to say that Kohlberg's theory is not "true." Rather, it means that, because of the methodological inadequacies and conceptual problems inherent in Kohlberg's work, the usefulness of the theory has not been demonstrated.

In studying this selection, pay particular attention to the discussion of the Moral Judgment Scale. Compare Kohlberg's methodology with Piaget's. Notice that Kohlberg's method, although it retains some of the naturalistic (or clinical) flavor of Piaget's work, represents an attempt to measure moral thought in a more scientifically acceptable fashion. The Kurtines and Greif criticism of the Moral Judgment Scale stresses the scale's inability to *reliably and validly measure* moral thought. Remember that, if the method of testing the theory cannot be trusted, neither can the theory.

SUGGESTIONS FOR FURTHER READING

Piaget's major works include *The Language and Thought of the Child* (3rd edition, Humanities Press, 1962), *Judgment and Reasoning in the Child* (Humanities Press, 1962), *The Child's Conception of the World* (Humanities Press, 1960), *The Moral Judgment of the*

Child (Free Press, 1932), and *The Construction of Reality in the Child* (Basic Books, 1954).

A summary of Piaget's work is contained in *The Psychology of the Child*, by Piaget and his long time co-worker, Barbel Inhelder. This book was published by Basic Books in 1969.

Alfred L. Baldwin's textbook, *Theories of Child Development*, published by Wiley in 1967, is an excellent secondary source. In this book, Baldwin devotes five chapters to Piaget.

A fine little paperback on Piaget is *The Origins of Intellect: Piaget's Theory*, by John L. Phillips, Jr., published by W. H. Freeman in 1969.

For the student interested in some of the methodological issues raised in the Kurtines and Greif selection, Lee J. Cronbach's book, *Essentials of Psychological Testing*, 3rd edition (published by Harper & Row in 1970), is strongly recommended.

Jean Piaget
THE MORAL JUDGMENT OF THE CHILD

Children's games constitute the most admirable social institutions. The game of marbles, for instance, as played by boys, contains an extremely complex system of rules, that is to say, a code of laws, a jurisprudence of its own. Only the psychologist, whose profession obliges him to become familiar with this instance of common law, and to get at the implicit morality underlying it, is in a position to estimate the extraordinary wealth of these rules by the difficulty he experiences in mastering their details.

If we wish to gain any understanding of child morality, it is obviously with the analysis of such facts as these that we must begin. All morality consists in a system of rules, and the essence of all morality is to be sought for in the respect which the individual acquires for these rules. The reflective analysis of Kant, the sociology of Durkheim, or the individualistic psychology of Bovet all meet on this point. The doctrines begin to diverge only from the moment that it has to be explained how the mind comes to respect these rules. For our part, it will be in the domain of child psychology that we shall undertake the analysis of this "how."

Now, most of the moral rules which the child learns to respect he receives from adults, which means that he receives them after they have been fully elaborated, and often elaborated, not in relation to him and as they are needed, but once and for all and through an uninterrupted succession of earlier adult generations.

In the case of the very simplest social games, on the contrary, we are in the presence of rules which have been elaborated by the children alone. It is of no moment whether these games strike us as "moral" or not in their contents. As psychologists we must ourselves adopt the point of view, not of the adult conscience, but of child morality. Now, the rules of the game of marbles are handed down, just like so-called moral realities, from one generation to another, and are preserved solely by the respect that is felt for them by individuals. The sole difference is that the relations in this case are only those that exist between children. The little boys who are beginning to play are gradually trained by the older ones in respect for the law; and in any case they aspire from their hearts to the virtue, supremely characteristic of human dignity, which consists in making a correct use of the customary practices of a game. As to the older ones, it is in their power to alter the rules. If this is not "morality," then where does morality begin? At least, it is respect for rules, and it appertains to an enquiry like ours to begin with the study of facts of this order. Of course the phenomena relating to the game of marbles are not among the most primitive. Before playing with his equals, the child is influenced by his parents. He is subjected from his cradle to a multiplicity of regulations, and even before

Reprinted with permission of Macmillan Publishing Co., Inc., and Routledge & Kegan Paul, Ltd., from *The Moral Judgment of the Child*, by Jean Piaget. First Free Press Paperback Edition, 1965. Written with the collaboration of Mme. V. J. Piaget, MM M. Lambercier and L. Martinez.

language he.becomes conscious of certain obligations. These circumstances even exercise, as we shall see, an undeniable influence upon the way in which the rules of games are elaborated. But in the case of play institutions, adult intervention is at any rate reduced to the minimum. We are therefore in the presence here of realities which, if not amongst the most elementary, should be classed nevertheless amongst the most spontaneous and the most instructive.

With regard to game rules there are two phenomena which it is particularly easy to study: first the *practice* of rules, *i.e.,* the way in which children of different ages effectively apply rules: second the *consciousness* of rules, *i.e.,* the idea which children of different ages form of the character of these game rules, whether of something obligatory and sacred or of something subject to their own choice, whether of heteronomy or autonomy.

It is the comparison of these two groups of data which constitutes the real aim of this chapter. For the relations which exist between the practice and the consciousness of rules are those which will best enable us to define the psychological nature of moral realities.

One word more. Before embarking upon an analysis of the practice or of the consciousness of rules, we must first give some account of the actual content of these rules. We must therefore establish the social data of the problem. But we shall confine ourselves only to what is indispensable. We have not attempted to establish the sociology of the game of marbles; this would have meant finding out how this game was played in the past and how it is now played in different parts of the world (it is actually played by Negro children). Even confining ourselves to French Switzerland, we believe it would need several years of research to discover all the local variants of the game and, above all, to outline the history of these variants throughout the last few generations. Such an enquiry, which might be useful to the sociologist, is superfluous for the psychologist. All the latter needs in order to study how rules are learned is a thorough knowledge of a given custom in actual use, just as in order to study child language, all he needs is to know a given dialect, however localized, without troubling to reconstruct all its semantic and phonetic changes is time and space. We shall therefore confine ourselves to a short analysis of the content of the game as it is played in Geneva and Neuchâtel, in the districts where we conducted our work.

§1. THE RULES OF THE GAME OF MARBLES

Three essential facts must be noted if we wish to analyse simultaneously the practice and the consciousness of rules.

The first is that among children of a given generation and in a given locality, however small, there is never one single way of playing marbles, there are quantities of ways. There is the "square game" with which we shall occupy ourselves more especially. A square is drawn on the ground and a number of marbles placed within it; the game consists in aiming at these from a distance and driving them out of the enclosure. There is the game of "courate" where two players aim at each other's marble in indefinite pursuit. There is the game of "troyat" from "trou" (=hole) or "creux" (=hollow), where the marbles are piled into a hole and have to be dislodged by means of a heavier marble, and so on. Every child is familiar with several games, a fact that may help according to his age to reinforce or to weaken his belief in the sacred character of rules.

In the second place, one and the same game, such as the Square game, admits of fairly important variations according to when and where it is played. As we had occasion to verify, the rules of the Square game are not the same in four of the communes of Neuchâtel[1] situated at

---

[1]Neuchâtel, La Coudre, Hauterive and Saint-Blaise.

2–3 kilometres from each other. They are not the same in Geneva and in Neuchâtel. They differ, on certain points, from one district to another, from one school to another in the same town. In addition to this, as through our collaborators' kindness we were able to establish, variations occur from one generation to another. A student of twenty assured us that in his village the game is no longer played as it was "in his days." These variations according to time and place are important, because children are often aware of their existence. A child who has moved from one town, or merely from one school building to another will often explain to us that such and such a rule is in force in one place but not in the other. Very often, too, a child will tell us that his father played differently from him. Last of all, there is the boy of 14 who has given up playing because he is beginning to feel superior to the little ones, and who, according to his temperament, laughs or mourns over the fact that the customs of his generation are going by the board instead of being piously preserved by the rising generation.

Finally, and clearly as a result of the convergence of these local or historical currents, it will happen that one and the same game (like the Square game) played in the playground of one and the same school admits on certain points of several different rules. Children of 11 to 13 are familiar with these variants, and they generally agree before or during the game to choose a given usage to the exclusion of others. These facts must therefore be borne in mind, for they undoubtedly condition the judgment which the child will make on the value of rules.

Having mentioned these points, we shall give a brief exposition of the rules of the Square game, which will serve as a prototype, and we shall begin by fixing the child's language so as to be able to understand the reports of the conversations which will be quoted later on. Besides, as is so often the case in child psychology, some aspects of this language are in themselves highly instructive.

A marble is called "un marbre" in Neuchâtel and "un cœillu" or "un mapis" in Geneva. There are marbles of different value. The cement marble has the place of honour. The "carron" which is smaller and made of the more brittle clay is of less value because it costs less. The marbles that are used for throwing[2] and are not placed inside the square are called according to their consistency "corna" (if in carnelian), "ago," or "agathe," "cassine" (glass ball with coloured veins), "plomb" (large marble containing lead), etc. Each is worth so many marbles or so many "carrons." To throw a marble is to "tirer" (shoot) and to touch another marble with one's own is to "tanner" (hit).

Then comes a set of terms of ritual *consecration*, that is, of expressions which the player uses in order to announce that he is going to perform such-and-such an operation and which thus consecrate it ritually as an accomplished fact. For, once these words have been uttered, the opponent is powerless against his partner's decision; whereas if he takes the initiative by means of the terms of ritual *interdiction*, which we shall examine in a moment, he will in this way prevent the operation which he fears. For example, in order to play first in circumstances when it is possible to do so, the child will say (at Neuchâtel) "prems"—obviously a corruption of the word "premier" (first). If he wants to go back to the line that all the players start from at their first turn and which is called the "coche,"[3] he simply says "coche." If he wishes to advance or retreat to a distance twice as great, he says "deux coches," or if to a distance of one, two, or three hand-breadths he says "one (or two, or three) empans" (spans). If he wishes to place himself in relation to the square at a distance equal to that at which he finds himself at a given moment, but in another direction (so as to avoid the probable attacks of

---

[2]The English technical equivalent is the generic term "shooter" which we shall use in the interrogatories given below. For the rest we have generally retained the French words as one cannot be sure that the English terms mean exactly the same. [Trans.]

[3]English, pitch-line (sometimes). [Trans.]

his opponent) he says "du mien" (mine), and if he wishes to prevent his opponent from doing the same thing he says "du tien" (yours). This applies to Neuchâtel. In Geneva these displacements are expressed by the terms "faire une entasse" or "entorse" (to make a twist). If you wish to give up your turn and be "dead" until your opponent has moved, you say "coup passé" (my turn passed).

As soon as these terms have been uttered in circumstances which of course are carefully regulated by a whole juridical system, the opponent has to submit. But if the opponent wishes to anticipate these operations, it is sufficient for him to pronounce the terms of ritual *interdiction*, which at Neuchâtel are simply the same terms but preceded by the prefix "fan," from "défendu" (forbidden). For example, "fan-du-mien," "fan-du-tien," "fan-coche," "fan-coup-passé," etc. Some children, not having understood this prefix, which does not, after all, correspond with anything in the speech they hear around them, say "femme-du-tien," "femme-coche," etc.

Two more particularly suggestive terms of consecration should be noted, which are current among the little Genevans: "glaine" and "toumiké." When a player places a marble of superior value in the square, thinking that he has put down an ordinary marble (say an "ago" instead of a "cœillu") he is naturally allowed, if he has noticed his mistake, to pick up his "ago" and put an ordinary marble in its place. Only a dishonest opponent would take advantage of his partner's absent-mindedness and pocket this "ago" after having hit it. The children we questioned on this point were unanimous in pronouncing such procedure equivalent to stealing. But if, on the other hand, the opponent spots his partner's mistake in time and utters the word "toumiké" or (by doubling the last syllable) "toumikémik," then the absent-minded player no longer has the right to pick up his "ago"; he must leave it on the ground like a common-or-garden "cœillu," and if one of the players succeeds in hitting it, this player will be allowed in all fairness to take possession of it. This shows us a very interesting example of a word consecrating a mistake and by doing so changing a dishonest action into one that is legitimate and recognized as such by all. We have here for the first time an example of that formalism, which belongs to certain aspects of childish morality, and into whose nature we shall go more deeply in the sequel in connection with objective responsibility.

In the same way, the word "glaine" legitimatizes piracy in certain well-defined conditions. When one of the players has succeeded, either by luck or by skill, in winning all his partners' marbles, it is a point of honour similar to that which sociologists designate with the term "potlatch" that he should offer to play a fresh set and should himself place in the square the necessary marbles, so as to give his less fortunate playmates the chance of recovering a portion of their possessions. If he refuses, of course no law can force him to do this; he has won and there is the end of it. If, however, one of the players pronounces the word "glaine" then the whole gang falls upon the miser, throws him down, empties his pockets and shares the booty. This act of piracy which in normal times is profoundly contrary to morality (since the marbles collected by the winner constitute his lawfully acquired possession) is thus changed into a legitimate act and even into an act of retributive justice approved by the general conscience when the word "glaine" has been pronounced.[4]

At Neuchâtel we noticed neither "glaine" nor "toumiké," but, on the other hand, we found "cougac." When one of the players has won too much (therefore in the situation just

---

[4]This word "glaine" really has a wider sense. According to several children it entitles whoever pronounces it simply to pick up all the marbles that are on the ground when a discussion arises about them, or if a player forgets to take possession of what is his due. It is in this sense that the word is taken, for instance, in Philippe Monnier's, *Le Livre de Blaise* (3rd ed., p. 135).

described) his defeated partner can force him to offer to play another set by uttering the word "cougac" (probably derived from coup-gagné just as "prems" was from premier). If the winner wishes to evade the obligation laid upon him by the fateful word, he has only to anticipate the blow by saying "fan-cougac."

Our reason for emphasizing these linguistic peculiarities is only to show from the first the juridical complexity of game rules. It is obvious that these facts could be analysed more fundamentally from other points of view. One could, for example, work out the whole psychology of consecration and interdiction in connection with the child and, above all, the psychology of social games. But these questions are really outside our scope.[5] Let us therefore return to what is the essential point so far as we are concerned, namely, the rules themselves.

The Square game thus consists, in a word, in putting a few marbles in a square, and in taking possession of them by dislodging them with a special marble, bigger than the rest. But when it comes to details this simple schema contains an indefinite series of complications. Let us take them in order, so as to get some idea of their richness.

First of all, there is the "pose" or outlay. One of the players draws a square and then each places his "pose." If there are two players, each one puts down two, three, or four marbles. If there are three players, each put down two marbles. If there are four or more players, it is customary to put down only one marble each. The main thing is equality: each one puts down what the others do. But in order to reach equality the relative value of the marbles must be taken into account. For an ordinary marble, you must put down eight "carrons." A little "corna" is worth eight "marbres," sixteen "carrons," and so on. The values are carefully regulated and correspond roughly to the price paid at the shop round the corner. But alongside of financial operations proper, there are between children various exchanges in kind which appreciably alter current values.

Then the game begins. A certain distance is agreed upon where the "coche" is drawn; this is the line from which the players start. It is drawn parallel to and generally one or two metres away from one of the sides of the square, and from it each player will fire his first shot. (To "fire" is to throw one's shooter—"agathe" or "cornaline"—into the square.)

All, therefore, start from the coche. In some games you return to the coche at each fresh turn, but it is more usual after the first shot to play from the place that your marble has rolled to. Sometimes this rule is limited by saying that the marble must not be further removed from the square than the coche. Thus if your marble has rolled two metres away from the square in any direction whatsoever, you bring it back to a distance of 1m. 50 if this is the distance at which the coche itself stands.

But before the game begins you must settle who is to play first. For the first player has the advantage of "firing" into a square full of marbles, whereas those who follow are faced only with what is left after the gains of the preceding players. In order to know who is to begin, a series of well-known rites are put in action. Two children walk towards each other stepping heel to toe, and whichever steps on the other's toe has the right to begin. Or else rhymed formulæ or even syllables devoid of any meaning are recited in sacramental order. Each syllable corresponds to a player, and he on whom the last syllable falls is the lucky one. In addition to these customary usages there is a method of procedure peculiar to the game of marbles. Each boy throws his "shooter" in the direction of the coche or of a line specially traced for the purpose. Whoever comes nearest up to the line begins. The others follow in order of their nearness up to the line. The last to play is the boy who has gone beyond the

[5]With regard to social games we are awaiting the publication of R. Cousinet's book which will incorporate all the valuable material which this author has been accumulating for so many years.

coche, and if several have gone beyond it, the last to play will be the boy whose marble has gone furthest.

The order of the players having been settled in this way, the game begins. Each player in turn stands behind the coche and "fires" into the square. There are three ways of throwing one's marble: "Piquette" (Engl., "shooting") which consists in projecting the marble by a jerk of the thumb, the marble being placed against the thumb-nail and kept in place by the first finger; "Roulette" (Engl., "bowling") which consists simply in rolling your marble along the ground, and "Poussette" (Engl., "hunching") which consists in addition in carrying your hand along with it over a sufficient distance to correct the initial direction. Poussette is always banned and may in this connection be compared to the push stroke of a bad billiard player. At Neuchâtel it is customary to say "fan-poussette" or again "femme-poussette." In Geneva, the simpler expression "défendu de trainer" (dragging forbidden) is in use. Roulette ("bowling") is also generally banned ("fan-roulette") but is at times tolerated, in which case everyone will of course have the right to play in this way, and absolute equality before the law will even be agreed upon at the beginning of the game.

The players are therefore throwing in the manner that has been agreed upon. Suppose one of the marbles included in the square has been hit. If it has gone outside the square it becomes the property of the boy who has dislodged it. If it remains inside the enclosure it cannot be taken. If, finally, it remains on the line the case is judged by the partners: a marble which is half outside is regarded as out, not otherwise. Here, naturally, a whole lot of subsidiary rules will establish the procedure in disputed cases. There remains the case of the marble with which one shoots (the shooter, or taw, etc.) remaining in the square or failing to lie beyond one of the lines of the square by at least half of its diameter: its owner is "cuit" (dished), *i.e.*, he cannot play any more. If this marble is projected outside the square by that of another player, it becomes, like the others, the latter's property, except in the case of special conventions generally agreed upon at the beginning of the game. Finally, there are the possible complications arising from cases of rebounding marbles. A marble that bounces out of the square off another is sometimes not held to be won, and *a fortiori* in the case of a marble of value.[6] In other cases, everything that goes outside the enclosure belongs to the player who has expelled it. The particular cases that arise in this way are settled in conformity with principles that are established either before or during the game by mutual agreement between all the participants.

Then comes the question of the number of "shots" to be allowed to each. The player who has succeeded in winning one or more marbles has the right to play again, and so on, for as long as he wins. But sometimes the following reservation is made: for the first round in each game every player plays once in turn, independently of gains or losses. Here again, therefore, it is a matter of previous arrangement.

In addition—and this is an essential rule—everyone has the right not only to "fire" at the marbles in the square, but also to "tanner" (hit) his neighbour's shooter, even outside the enclosure and indeed wherever it may happen to be in the course of the game. And of course the great difficulty is to shoot at the square without placing yourself within reach of your partners. This is why, when a shot would involve too many risks, you are allowed to say "coup-passé" and to remain where you are, provided, of course, that no one has foreseen this decision and said "fan-coup-passé." And this, really, is why you are allowed to change your position provided you place yourself at the same distance from the square as before, and

[6]This is expressed by saying that the "revenette" does not count.

provided you first say "du mien" (mine), unless, once again, your opponent has anticipated your move by saying "du tien" (yours).

Finally, a series of special rules deserves mention, the observance of which depends upon the particular town or school in question. The first player who says "place-pour-moi" (place for me) is not obliged to take up his position at one of the corners of the square. Any player who has succeeded in winning the equivalent of his "pose" (*i.e.*, two marbles if he has placed two in the square, and so on) can say "queue-de-pose" which will allow him to have the first shot from the coche in the next game, and so on.

The game, regulated in this way by an indefinite number of rules, is carried on until the square is empty. The boy who has pocketed the largest number of marbles has won.

§2. THE INTERROGATORY AND ITS GENERAL RESULTS

The rules that we have outlined above constitute a well-marked social reality, "independent of individuals" (in Durkheim's sense) and transmitted, like a language, from one generation to another. This set of customs is obviously more or less plastic. But individual innovations, just as in the case of language, succeed only when they meet a general need and when they are collectively sanctioned as being in conformity with the "spirit of the game." But while fully recognizing the interest attaching to the sociological aspect of the problem, it was from a different standpoint that we raised the questions which we are now going to study. We simply asked ourselves (1) how the individuals adapt themselves to these rules, *i.e.*, how they observe rules at each age and level of mental development; (2) how far they become conscious of rules, in other words, what types of obligation result (always according to the children's ages) from the increasing ascendancy exercised by rules.

The interrogatory is therefore easy to carry out. During the first part, it is sufficient to ask the children (we questioned about 20 boys ranging from 4 to 12-13) how one plays marbles. The experimenter speaks more or less as follows. "Here are some marbles." (The marbles are placed on a large baize-covered table beside a piece of chalk.) "You must show me how to play. When I was little I used to play a lot, but now I've quite forgotten how to. I'd like to play again. Let's play together. You'll teach me the rules and I'll play with you." The child then draws a square, takes half the marbles, puts down his "pose," and the game begins. It is important to bear in mind all possible contingencies of the game and to ask the child about each. This means that you must avoid making any sort of suggestions. All you need do is to appear completely ignorant, and even to make intentional mistakes so that the child may each time point out clearly what the rule is. Naturally, you must take the whole thing very seriously, all through the game. Then you ask who has won and why, and if everything is not quite clear, you begin a new set.

It is of paramount importance during this first half of the interrogatory to play your part in a simple spirit and to let the child feel a certain superiority at the game (while not omitting to show by an occasional good shot that you are not a complete duffer). In this way the child is put at ease, and the information he gives as to how he plays is all the more conclusive. Many of our children become absorbed in the game to the extent of treating me completely as one of them. "You are dished!" cries Ben (10 years) when my marble stops inside the square.

In the case of the little ones, who find difficulty in formulating the rules which they observe in practice, the best way is to make them play in pairs. You begin by playing with one of them in the manner described above, and ask him to tell you all the rules he knows. Then you make the same request of the second boy (the first being no longer present), and finally you bring the two together and ask them to have a game. This control experiment is not needed for older children, except in doubtful cases.

Then comes the second part of the interrogatory, that, namely, which bears upon the consciousness of rules. You begin by asking the child if he could invent a new rule. He generally does this easily enough, but it is advisable to make sure that it really is a new rule and not one of the many existing variants of which this particular child may already have knowledge. "I want a rule that is only by you, a rule that you've made up yourself and that no one else knows—the rule of N——— (the child's name)." Once the new rule has been formulated, you ask the child whether it could give rise to a new game: "Would it be all right to play like that with your pals? Would they want to play that way? etc." The child either agrees to the suggestion or disputes it. If he agrees, you immediately ask him whether the new rule is a "fair" rule, a "real" rule, one "like the others," and try to get at the various motives that enter into the answers. If, on the other hand, the child disagrees with all this, you ask him whether the new rule, could not by being generalized become a real rule. "When you are a big boy, suppose you tell your new rule to a lot of children, then perhaps they'll all play that way and everyone will forget the old rules. Then which rule will be fairest—yours that everyone knows, or the old one that everyone has forgotten?" The formula can naturally be altered in accordance with the turn which the conversation is taking, but the main point is to find out whether one may legitimately alter rules and whether a rule is fair or just because it conforms to general usage (even newly introduced), or because it is endowed with an intrinsic and eternal value.

Having cleared up this point it will be easy enough to ask the two following questions. (1) Have people always played as they do to-day: "Did your daddy play this way when he was little, and your grand-dad, and children in the time of William Tell, Noah, and Adam and Eve, etc., did they all play the way you showed me, or differently?" (2) What is the origin of rules: Are they invented by children or laid down by parents and grown-ups in general?

Sometimes it is best to begin by these last two questions before asking whether rules can be changed; this avoids perseveration, or rather reverses its direction, and so facilitates the interpretation of the answers. All this part of the interrogatory, moreover, requires extremely delicate handling; suggestion is always ready to occur, and the danger of romancing is ever present. But it goes without saying that the main thing is simply to grasp the child's mental orientation. Does he believe in the mystical virtue of rules or in their finality? Does he subscribe to a heteronomy of divine law, or is he conscious of his own autonomy? This is the only question that interests us. The child has naturally got no ready-made beliefs on the origin and endurance of the rules of his games; the ideas which he invents then and there are only indices of his fundamental attitude, and this must be steadily borne in mind throughout the whole of the interrogatory.

The results which we obtained from this double interrogatory and which we shall examine in greater detail later on, are roughly the following.

From the point of view of the practice or application of rules four successive stages can be distinguished.

A first stage of a purely *motor* and *individual* character, during which the child handles the marbles at the dictation of his desires and motor habits. This leads to the formation of more or less ritualized schemas, but since play is still purely individual, one can only talk of motor rules and not of truly collective rules.

The second may be called *egocentric* for the following reasons. This stage begins at the moment when the child receives from outside the example of codified rules, that is to say, some time between the ages of two and five. But though the child imitates this example, he continues to play either by himself without bothering to find play-fellows, or with others, but without trying to win, and therefore without attempting to unify the different ways of playing. In other words, children of this stage, even when they are playing together, play each one "on his own" (everyone can win at once) and without regard for any codification of rules. This dual character, combining imitation of others with a purely individual use of the examples received, we have designated by the term egocentrism.

A third stage appears between 7 and 8, which we shall call the stage of incipient *cooperation*. Each player now tries to win, and all, therefore, begin to concern themselves with the question of mutual control and of unification of the rules. But while a certain agreement may be reached in the course of one game, ideas about the rules in general are still rather vague. In other words, children of 7–8, who belong to the same class at school and are therefore constantly playing with each other, give, when they are questioned separately, disparate and often entirely contradictory accounts of the rules observed in playing marbles.

Finally, between the years of 11 and 12, appears a fourth stage, which is that of the *codification of rules*. Not only is every detail of procedure in the game fixed, but the actual code of rules to be observed is known to the whole society. There is remarkable concordance in the information given by children of 10–12 belonging to the same class at school, when they are questioned on the rules of the game and their possible variations.

These stages must of course be taken only for what they are worth. It is convenient for the purposes of exposition to divide the children up in age-classes or stages, but the facts present themselves as a continuum which cannot be cut up into sections. This continuum, moreover, is not linear in character, and its general direction can only be observed by schematizing the material and ignoring the minor oscillations which render it infinitely complicated in detail. So that ten children chosen at random will perhaps not give the impression of a steady advance which gradually emerges from the interrogatory put to the hundred odd subjects examined by us at Geneva and Neuchâtel.

If, now, we turn to the consciousness of rules we shall find a progression that is even more elusive in detail, but no less clearly marked if taken on a big scale. We may express this by saying that the progression runs through three stages, of which the second begins during the egocentric stage and ends towards the middle of the stage of cooperation (9–10), and of which the third covers the remainder of this co-operating stage and the whole of the stage marked by the codification of rules.

During the first stage rules are not yet coercive in character, either because they are purely motor, or else (at the beginning of the egocentric stage) because they are received, as it were, unconsciously, and as interesting examples rather than as obligatory realities.

During the second stage (apogee of egocentric and first half of cooperating stage) rules are regarded as sacred and untouchable, emanating from adults and lasting forever. Every suggested alteration strikes the child as a transgression.

Finally, during the third stage, a rule is looked upon as a law due to mutual consent, which you must respect if you want to be loyal but which it is permissible to alter on the condition of enlisting general opinion on your side.

The correlation between the three stages in the development of the consciousness of rules and the four stages relating to their practical observance is of course only a statistical correlation and therefore very crude. But broadly speaking the relation seems to us indisputable. The collective rule is at first something external to the individual and consequently sacred to him; then, as he gradually makes it his own, it comes to that extent to be felt as the free product of mutual agreement and an autonomous conscience. And with regard to practical use, it is only natural that a mystical respect for laws should be accompanied by a rudimentary knowledge and application of their contents, while a rational and well-founded respect is accompanied by an effective application of each rule in detail.

There would therefore seem to be two types of respect for rules corresponding to two types of social behaviour. This conclusion deserves to be closely examined, for if it holds good, it should be of the greatest value to the analysis of child morality. One can see at once all that it suggests in regard to the relation between child and adult. Take the insubordination of the child towards its parents and teachers, joined to its sincere respect for the commands it receives and its extraordinary mental docility. Could not this be due to that complex of attitudes which we can observe during the egocentric stage and which combines so paradoxically an unstable practice of the law with a mystical attitude towards it? And will not cooperation between adult and child, in so far as it can be realized and in so far as it is facilitated by co-operation between children themselves, supply the key to the interiorization of commands and to the autonomy of the moral consciousness? Let us therefore not be afraid of devoting a certain amount of time to the patient analysis of the rules of a game, for we are here in possession of a method infinitely more supple, and consequently more sure, than that of merely questioning children about little stories, a method which we shall be obliged to adopt in the latter part of this book.

§3. THE PRACTICE OF RULES.   I. THE FIRST TWO STAGES

We need not dwell at any length upon the first stage, as it is not directly connected with our subject. At the same time, it is important that we should know whether the rules which come into being previous to any collaboration between children are of the same type as collective rules.

Let us give a handful of ten marbles to a child of three years and four months and take note of its reactions:

Jacqueline has the marbles in her hands and looks at them with curiosity (it is the first time she has seen any); then she lets them drop on to the carpet. After this she puts them in the hollow of an arm-chair. *"Aren't they animals?*—Oh, no.—*Are they balls?*—Yes." She puts them back on the carpet and lets them drop from a certain height. She sits on the carpet with her legs apart and throws the marbles a few inches in front of her. She then picks them up and puts them on the arm-chair and in the same hole as before. (The arm-chair is studded with buttons which create depressions in the material.) Then she collects the lot and lets them drop, first all together, then one by one. After this she replaces them in the arm-chair, first in the same place and then in the other holes. Then she piles them up in a pyramid: *"What are marbles?*—What do you think?— . . ." She puts them on the floor, then back on to the arm-chair, in the same holes.—We both go out on to the balcony: she lets the marbles drop from a height to make them bounce.

The following days, Jacqueline again places the marbles on the chairs and arm-chairs, or puts them into her little saucepan to cook dinner. Or else she simply repeats the behaviour described above.

Three points should be noted with regard to facts such as these. In the first place, the lack of continuity and direction in the sequence of behaviour. The child is undoubtedly trying first and foremost to understand the nature of marbles and to adapt its motor schemas to this novel reality. This is why it tries one experiment after another: throwing them, heaping them into pyramids or nests, letting them drop, making them bounce, etc. But once it has got over the first moments of astonishment, the game still remains incoherent, or rather still subject to the whim of the moment. On days when the child plays at cooking dinner, the marbles serve as food to be stewed in a pot. On days when it is interested in classifying and arranging, the marbles are put in heaps in the holes of arm-chairs, and so on. In the general manner in which the game is carried on there are therefore no rules.

The second thing to note is that there are certain regularities of detail, for it is remarkable how quickly certain particular acts in the child's behaviour become schematized and even ritualized. The act of collecting the marbles in the hollow of an arm-chair is at first simply an experiment, but it immediately becomes a motor schema bound up with the perception of the marbles. After a few days it is merely a rite, still performed with interest, but without any fresh effort of adaptation.

In the third place, it is important to note the symbolism[7] that immediately becomes grafted upon the child's motor schemas. These symbols are undoubtedly enacted in play rather than thought out, but they imply a certain amount of imagination: the marbles are food to be cooked, eggs in a nest, etc.

This being so, the rules of games might be thought to derive either from rites analogous to those we have just examined or from a symbolism that has become collective. Let us briefly examine the genesis and ultimate destiny of these modes of behaviour.

Genetically speaking, the explanation both of rites and of symbols would seem to lie in the conditions of preverbal motor intelligence. When it is presented with any new thing, a baby of 5 to 8 months will respond with a dual reaction; it will accommodate itself to the new object and it will assimilate the object to earlier motor schemas. Give the baby a marble, and it will explore its surface and consistency, but will at the same time use it as something to grasp, to suck, to rub against the sides of its cradle, and so on. This assimilation of every fresh object to already existing motor schemas may be conceived of as the starting point of ritual acts and symbols, at any rate from the moment that assimilation becomes stronger than actual accommodation itself. With regard to ritual acts, indeed, one is struck by the fact that from the age of about 8 to 10 months all the child's motor schemas, apart from moments of adaptation in the real sense, give rise to a sort of functioning in the void, in which the child takes pleasure as in a game. Thus, after having contracted the habit of pressing her face against her parents' cheeks, crumpling up her nose and breathing deeply the while, Jacqueline began to perform this rite as a joke, crumpling up her nose and breathing deeply in advance, merely suggesting contact with another person's face, but without, as before, expressing any particular affection by the act. Thus from being actual, and incorporated in an effective adaptation this schema has become ritualized and serves only as a game.[8] Or again, Jacqueline in her bath is engaged in rubbing her hair; she lets go of it to splash the water. Immediately, she repeats the movement, touching her hair and the water alternately, and during the next few days the schema has become ritualized to such an extent that she cannot strike the surface of the water without first outlining the movement of smoothing her hair.[9] In no way automatic, this rite is a game that amuses her by its very regularity. Anyone observing a baby of 10 to 12 months will notice a number of these rites which undoubtedly anticipate the rules of future games.

As for symbols, they appear towards the end of the first year and in consequence of the ritual acts. For the habit of repeating a given gesture ritually, gradually leads to the conscious-

---

[7]We use the term "symbol" in the sense given to it in the linguistic school of Saussure, as the contrary of sign. A sign is arbitrary, a symbol is motivated. It is in this sense, too, that Freud speaks of symbolic thought.

[8]Age: 10 months.

[9]Age: 12 months.

ness of "pretending." The ritual of going to bed, for instance (laying down one's head and arranging the corner of the pillow with the hundred and one complications which every baby invents), is sooner or later utilized "in the void," and the smile of the child as it shuts its eyes in carrying out this rite is enough to show that it is perfectly conscious of "pretending" to go to sleep. Here already we have a symbol, but a "played" symbol. Finally, when language and imagery come to be added to motor intelligence, the symbol becomes an object of thought. The child who pushes a box along saying "tuff-tuff" is assimilating in imagination the box's movement to that of a motor-car: the play symbol has definitely come into being.

This being so, can one seek among rites and symbols for the origin of the actual rules of games? Can the game of marbles, with its infinite complexity both with regard to the actual rules and to all that relates to the verbo-motor system of signs in use—can the game of marbles, then, be conceived simply as the result of an accumulation of individual rites and symbols? We do not think that it can. We believe that the individual rite and the individual symbol constitute the substructure for the development of rules and collective signs, its necessary, but not its sufficient condition. There is something more in the collective rule than in the motor rule or the individual ritual, just as there is something more in the sign than in the symbol.

With regard to motor or ritualistic rules, there can be no doubt that they have something in common with rules in the ordinary sense, namely the consciousness of regularity. When we see the delight taken by a baby of 10 to 12 months or a child of 2–3 in reproducing a given behaviour in all its details, and the scrupulous attention with which it observes the right order in these operations, we cannot help recognizing the *Regelbewusstsein* of which Bühler speaks. But we must distinguish carefully between the behaviour into which there enters only the pleasure of regularity, and that into which there enters an element of obligation. It is this consciousness of obligation which seems to us, as to Durkheim[10] and Bovet,[11] to distinguish a rule in the true sense from mere regularity.

Now this element of obligation, or, to confine ourselves to the question of the practice of rules, this element of obedience intervenes as soon as there is a society, *i.e.,* a relation between at least two individuals. As soon as a ritual is imposed upon a child by adults or seniors for whom he has respect (Bovet), or as soon, we would add, as a ritual comes into being as the result of the collaboration of two children, it acquires in the subject's mind a new character which is precisely that of a rule. This character may vary according to the type of respect which predominates (respect for the senior or mutual respect) but in all cases there enters an element of submission which was not contained in the rite pure and simple.

In actual fact, of course, there is every degree of variety between the simple regularity discovered by the individual and the rule to which a whole social group submits itself. Thus during the egocentric stage we can observe a whole series of cases in which the child will use a rule as a mere rite, to be bent and modified at will, while at the same time he already tries to submit to the common laws. Just as the child very soon acquires the use of language and of the abstract and general concepts while retaining in his attitude to these much that still belongs to egocentric modes of thought and even to the methods peculiar to symbolic and play thought, so, under the rules that are imposed upon him, he will for a long time contrive (in all good faith, needless to say) to maintain his own phantasy in the matter of personal decisions. But this factual continuity between ritual and rule does not exclude a qualitative difference between the two types of behaviour.

---

[10]*L'Education Morale.*

[11]"Les Conditions de l'Obligation de la Conscience," *Année Psychol.,* 1912.

Let us not, however, anticipate what will be said in our analysis of the consciousness of rules, but return to the matter of ritual. The individual rite develops quite naturally, as we have just shown, into a more or less complex symbolism. Can this symbolism be regarded as the starting point of that system of obligatory verbo-motor signs which are connected with the rules of every collective game? As with the previous problem, we believe that the symbol is a necessary, but not a sufficient condition of the appearance of signs. The sign is general and abstract (arbitrary), the symbol is individual and motivated. If the sign is to follow upon the symbol, a group must therefore strip the individual's imagination of all its personal fantasy and then elaborate a common and obligatory imagery which will go hand in hand with the code of rules itself.

Here is an observation showing how far removed are individual rites and symbols from rules and signs, though moving towards these realities in so far as collaboration between children becomes established.

Jacqueline (after the observations given above) is playing with Jacques (2 years, 11 months and 15 days), who sees marbles for the first time. I. Jacques takes the marbles and lets them drop from a height one after another. After which he picks them up and goes away. II. Jacques arranges them on the ground, in a hollow and says, *"I'm making a little nest."* Jacqueline takes one and sticks it in the ground in imitation. III. Jacques also takes one, buries it and makes a mud-pie above it. He digs it up and begins over again. Then he takes 2 at a time which he buries. Then 3, 4, 5 and up to 6 at a time, increasing the number of marbles systematically each time by one. Jacqueline imitates him: she first puts one marble down and makes a mud-pie over it, then two or three at random and without adopting a fixed system of progression. IV. Jacques puts all the marbles on a pile, then he places an india-rubber ball beside them and says: *"That's the Mummy ball and the baby balls."* V. He piles them together again and covers them up with earth which he levels down. Jacqueline imitates him but with only one marble which she covers up without levelling the earth. She adds: *"It's lost,"* then digs it up and begins over again.

This example shows very clearly how all the elements of individual fantasy or symbolism remain uncommunicated; as soon as the game takes on an imaginative turn each child evokes its favourite images without paying any attention to anyone else's. It will also be observed how totally devoid of any general direction are the ritualized schemas successively tried. But as soon as there is reciprocal imitation (end of II and whole of III) we have the beginnings of a rule: each child tries to bury the marbles in the same way as the other, in a common order only more or less successfully adhered to. In bringing out this aspect, the observation leads us to the stage of egocentrism during which the child learns other peoples' rules but practises them in accordance with his own fantasy.

We shall conclude this analysis of the first stage by repeating that before games are played in common, no rules in the proper sense can come into existence. Regularities and ritualized schemas are already there, but these rites, being the work of the individual, cannot call forth that submission to something superior to the self which characterizes the appearance of any rule.

The second stage is the stage of *egocentrism*. In studying the practice of rules we shall make use of a notion which has served on earlier occasions in the descriptions we have given of the child's intellectual behaviour; and, in both cases, indeed, the phenomenon is of exactly the same order. Egocentrism appears to us as a form of behaviour intermediate between purely individual and socialized behaviour. Through imitation and language, as also through the whole content of adult thought which exercises pressure on the child's mind as soon as verbal intercourse has become possible, the child begins, in a sense, to be socialized from the end of its first year. But the very nature of the relations which the child sustains with the adults around him prevents this socialization for the moment from reaching that state of equilibrium which is propitious to the development of reason. We mean, of course, the state of cooperation, in which the individuals, regarding each other as equals, can exercise a mutual control and thus attain to objectivity. In other words, the very nature of the relation between child and adult places the child apart, so that his thought is isolated, and while he believes himself to be sharing the point of view of the world at large he is really still shut up in his own point of view. The social bond itself, by which the child is held, close as it may seem when viewed from outside, thus implies an unconscious intellectual egocentrism which is further promoted by the spontaneous egocentrism peculiar to all primitive mentality.

Similarly, with regard to the rules of games, it is easy to see, and greater authorities than ourselves[12] have already pointed out that the beginnings of children's games are characterized by long periods of egocentrism. The child is dominated on the one hand by a whole set of rules and examples that are imposed upon him from outside. But unable as he is, on the other hand, to place himself on a level of equality with regard to his seniors, he utilizes for his own ends, unaware even of his own isolation, all that he has succeeded in grasping of the social realities that surround him.

To confine ourselves to the game of marbles, the child of 3 to 5 years old will discover, according to what other children he may happen to come across, that in order to play this game one must trace a square, put the marbles inside it, try to expel the marbles from the square by hitting them with another marble, start from a line that has been drawn beforehand, and so on. But though he imitates what he observes, and believes in perfect good faith that he is playing like the others, the child thinks of nothing at first but of utilizing these new acquisitions for himself. He plays in an individualistic manner with material that is social. Such is egocentrism.

Let us analyse the facts of the case.

Mar (6)[13] seizes hold of the marbles we offer him, and without bothering to make a square he heaps them up together and begins to hit the pile. He removes the marbles he has displaced and puts them aside or replaces them immediately without any method. "Do you always play like that?—*In the street you make a square.*—Well, you do the same as they do in the street.—*I'm making a square, I am.*" (He draws the square, places the marbles inside it and begins to play again.) I play with him, imitating each of his movements. "Who has won?—*We've both won.*—But who has won most? . . ."—(Mar does not understand.)

Baum (6½) begins by making a square and puts down three marbles, adding: "*Sometimes you put 4, or 3, or 2.*—Or 5?—*No, not 5, but sometimes 6 or 8.*—Who begins when you play with the boys?—*Sometimes me, sometimes the other one.*—Isn't there a dodge for knowing who is to begin?—*No.*—Do you know what a coche is?—*Rather!*" But the sequel shows that he knows nothing about the coche and thinks of this word as designating another game. "And which of us will begin?—*You.*—Why?—*I want to see how you do it.*"

---

[12]Stern in his *Psychology of Early Childhood* notes the identity of the stages we have established in children's conversations with those he has himself established with regard to play, pp. 177 and 332.

[13]The numbers in brackets give the child's age. The words of the child are in italics, those of the examiner in Roman lettering. Quotation marks indicate the beginning and end of a conversation reported *verbatim*. All the subjects are boys unless the letter G is added, indicating that the subject is a girl.

We play for a while and I ask who has won: *"The one who has hit a mib,*[14] *well, he has won.—Well! who has won?—I have, and then you."* I then arrange things so as to take 4 while he takes 2: "Who has won?—*I have, and then you."* We begin again. He takes two, I none. "Who has won?—*I have.—And I?—You've lost."*

Loeff (6) often pretends to be playing with Mae, of whom we shall speak later. He knows neither how to make a square nor to draw a coche. He immediately begins to "fire" at the marbles assembled in a heap and plays without either stopping or paying any attention to us. "Have you won?—*I don't know. I think I have.—*Why?—*Yes, because I threw the mibs.—*and I?—*Yes, because you threw the mibs."*

Desarz (6): "Do you play often?—*Yes, rather!—*With whom?—*All by myself.—*Do you like playing alone best?—*You don't need two. You can play only one."* He gathers the marbles together without a square and "fires" into the heap.

Let us now see how two children, who have grown accustomed to playing together, set about it when they are left alone. They are two boys of whom one (Mae) is a very representative example of the present stage, while the other (Wid) stands at the border line between the present stage and the next. The analyses of these cases will be all the more conclusive as the children in question are no mere beginners at the game.

Mae (6) and Wid (7) declare that they are always playing together. Mae tells us that they both *"played again, yesterday."* I first examine Mae by himself. He piles his marbles in a corner without counting them and throws his shooter into the pile. He then places 4 marbles close together and puts a fifth on top (in a pyramid). Mae denies that a square is ever drawn. Then he corrects himself and affirms that he always does so: "How do you and Wid know which is to begin?—*One of the two throws his shooter and the other tries to hit it. If he hits it, he begins."* Mae then shows us what the game consists in: he throws his shooter without taking into account the distances or the manner of playing ("piquette"), and when he succeeds in driving a marble out of the square he immediately puts it back. Thus the game has no end. "Does it go on like that all the time?—*You take one away to make a change* (he takes a marble out of the square, but not the one that he has touched). *It'll only be finished when there's only one left* (he 'fires' again twice). *One more shot, and then you take one away."* Then he affirms: *"every third shot you take one away."* He does so. Mae removes a marble every third shot independently of whether he has hit or missed, which is completely irregular and corresponds to nothing in the game as habitually played, or as we have seen it played in Neuchâtel or Geneva. It is therefore a rule which he has invented then and there but which he has the impression of remembering because it presents a vague analogy with what really happens when the player removes the marble he has just "hit" (touched). This game of Mae's is therefore a characteristic game of the second stage, an egocentric game in which "to win" does not mean getting the better of the others, but simply playing on one's own.

Wid, whom I now prepare to question and who has not assisted at Mae's interrogatory, begins by making a square. He places 4 marbles at the 4 corners and one in the middle (the same disposition as Mae's, which was probably a deformation of it). Wid does not know what to do to decide which is to begin, and declares that he understands nothing of the method which Mae had shewn me as being familiar to both of them (trying to hit one's partner's shooter). Wid then throws his shooter in the direction of the square, knocking out one marble which he puts in his pocket. Then I take my turn, but fail to touch anything. He plays again and

---

[14]English equivalent for "marbre." [Trans.]

wins all the marbles, one after the other, keeping them each time. He also declares that when you have knocked a marble out, you have the right to play another shot straight away. After having taken everything he says: *"I've won."* Wid therefore belongs to the third stage if this explanation is taken as a whole, but the sequel will show that he takes no notice of Mae's doings when they are playing together. Wid stands therefore at the boundary line which separates the stage of egocentrism from the stage of cooperation.

I then tell Mae to come into the room and the two children begin to play with each other. Mae draws a square and Wid disposes the marbles in accordance with his habitual schema. Mae begins (he plays "Roulette" whereas Wid most of the time plays "Piquette") and dislodges four marbles. *"I can play four times, now,"* adds Mae. This is contrary to all the rules, but Wid finds the statement quite natural. So one game succeeds another. But the marbles are placed in the square by one child or the other as the spirit moves them (according to the rules each must put his "pose") and the dislodged marbles are sometimes put straight back into the square, sometimes retained by the boy who has won them. Each plays from whatever place he chooses, unchecked by his partner, and each "fires" as many times as he likes (it thus often happens that Mae and Wid are playing at the same time).

I now send Wid out of the room and ask Mae to explain the game to us for a last time. Mae places 16 marbles in the middle of the square. "Why so many as that? *So as to win.*—How many do you put down at home with Wid?—*I put five, but when I'm alone, I put lots.*" Mae then begins to play and dislodges a marble which he puts on one side. I do the same. The game continues in this way, each playing one shot at a time without taking the dislodged marbles into account (which is contrary to what Mae was doing a moment ago). Mae then places five marbles in the square, like Wid. This time I arrange the five marbles as Mae himself had done at the beginning of the interrogatory (four close together and one on top) but Mae seems to have forgotten this way of doing things. In the end Mae plays by taking away a marble every three shots, as before, and says to us: *"It's so that it should stop."*

We have quoted the whole of this example in order to show how little two children from the same class at school, living in the same house, and accustomed to playing with each other, are able to understand each other at this age. Not only do they tell us of totally different rules (this still occurs throughout the third stage), but when they play together they do not watch each other and do not unify their respective rules even for the duration of one game. The fact of the matter is that neither is trying to get the better of the other: each is merely having a game on his own, trying to hit the marbles in the square, *i.e.,* trying to "win" from his point of view.

This shows the characteristics of the stage. The child plays for himself. His interest does not in any way consist in competing with his companions and in binding himself by common rules so as to see who will get the better of the others. His aims are different. They are indeed dual, and it is this mixed behaviour that really defines egocentrism. On the one hand, the child feels very strongly the desire to play like the other boys, and especially like those older than himself; he longs, that is to say, to feel himself a member of the very honorable fraternity of those who know how to play marbles correctly. But quickly persuading himself, on the other hand, that his playing is "right" (he can convince himself as easily on this point as in all his attempts to imitate adult behaviour) the child thinks only of utilizing these acquisitions for himself: his pleasure still consists in the mere development of skill, in carrying out the strokes he sets himself to play. It is, as in the previous stage, essentially a motor pleasure, not a social one. The true "socius" of the player who has reached this stage is not the flesh and blood partner but the ideal and abstract elder whom one inwardly strives to imitate and who sums up all the examples one has ever received.

It little matters, therefore, what one's companion is doing, since one is not trying to contend against him. It little matters what the details of the rules may be, since there is no real contact between the players. This is why the child, as soon as he can schematically copy the big boys' game, believes himself to be in possession of the whole truth. Each for himself, and all in communion with the "Elder": such might be the formula of egocentric play.

It is striking to note the affinity between this attitude of children of 4 to 6 in the game of marbles and the attitude of those same children in their conversations with each other. For alongside of the rare cases of true conversation where there is a genuine interchange of opinions or commands, one can observe in children between 2 and 6 a characteristic type of pseudo-conversation or "collective monologue," during which the children speak only for themselves, although they wish to be in the presence of interlocutors who will serve as a stimulus. Now here again, each feels himself to be in communion with the group because he is inwardly addressing the Adult who knows and understands everything, but here again, each is only concerned with himself, for lack of having disassociated the "ego" from the "socius."

These features of the egocentric stage will not, however, appear in their full light until we come to analyse the consciousness of rules which accompanies this type of conduct.

§4. THE PRACTICE OF RULES.   II. THIRD AND FOURTH STAGES

Towards the age of 7–8 appears the desire for mutual understanding in the sphere of play (as also, indeed, in the conversations between children). This felt need for understanding is what defines the third stage. As a criterion of the appearance of this stage we shall take the moment when by "winning" the child refers to the fact of getting the better of the others, therefore of gaining more marbles than the others, and when he no longer says he has won when he has done no more than to knock a marble out of the square, regardless of what his partners have done. As a matter of fact, no child, even from among the older ones, ever attributes very great importance to the fact of knocking out a few more marbles than his opponents. Mere competition is therefore not what constitutes the affective motive-power of the game. In seeking to win the child is trying above all to contend with his partners *while observing common rules*. The specific pleasure of the game thus ceases to be muscular and egocentric, and becomes social. Henceforth, a game of marbles constitutes the equivalent in action of what takes place in discussion in words: a mutual evaluation of the competing powers which leads, thanks to the observation of common rules, to a conclusion that is accepted by all.

As to the difference between the third and fourth stages, it is only one of degree. The children of about 7 to 10 (third stage) do not yet know the rules in detail. They try to learn them owing to their increasing interest in the game played in common, but when different children of the same class at school are questioned on the subject the discrepancies are still considerable in the information obtained. It is only when they are at play that these same children succeed in understanding each other, either by copying the boy who seems to know most about it, or more frequently, by omitting any usage that might be disputed. In this way they play a sort of simplified game. Children of the fourth stage, on the contrary, have thoroughly mastered their code and even take pleasure in juridical discussions, whether of principle or merely of procedure, which may at times arise out of the points in dispute.

Let us examine some examples of the third stage, and, in order to point more clearly to the differentiating characters of this stage, let us begin by setting side by side the answers of two little boys attending the same class at school and accustomed to playing together. (The children were naturally questioned separately in order to avoid any suggestion between them, but we afterwards compared their answers with one another.)

Ben (10) and Nus (11, backward, one year below the school standard) are both in the fourth year of the lower school and both play marbles a great deal. They agree in regarding the square as necessary. Nus declares that you always place 4 marbles in the square, either at the corners, or else 3 in the center with one on top (in a pyramid). Ben, however, tells us that you place 2 to 10 marbles in the enclosure (not less than 2, not more than 10).

To know who is to begin you draw, according to Nus, a line called the "coche" and everyone tries to get near it: whoever gets nearest plays first, and whoever goes beyond it plays last. Ben, however, knows nothing about the coche: you begin *"as you like.—*Isn't there a dodge for knowing who is to play first?—*No.*—Don't you try with the coche?—*Yes, sometimes.*—What is the coche?— . . . (he cannot explain)." On the other hand, Ben affirms that you "fire" the first shot at a distance of 2 to 3 steps from the square. A single step is not enough, and *"four isn't any good either."* Nus is ignorant of this law and considers the distance to be a matter of convention.

With regard to the manner of "firing," Nus is equally tolerant. According to him you can play "piquette" or "roulette," but *"when you play piquette everyone must play the same. When one boy says that you must play roulette, everyone plays that way."* Nus prefers roulette because *"that is the best way"*: piquette is more difficult. Ben, however, regards piquette as obligatory in all cases. He is ignorant, moreover, of the term roulette and when we show him what it is he says: *"That is bowled piquette!* [Fr., Piquette roulée] *That's cheating!"*

According to Nus everyone must play from the coche, and all through the game. When, after having shot at the square you land anywhere, you must therefore come back to the coche to "fire" the next shot. Ben, on the contrary, who on this point represents the more general usage, is of opinion that only the first shot should be fired from the coche: after that *"you must play from where you are."*

Nus and Ben thus agree in stating that the marbles that have gone out of the square remain in the possession of the boy who dislodged them. This is the only point, this and the actual drawing of the square, on which the children give us results that are in agreement.

When we begin to play, I arrange to stay in the square (to leave my shooter inside the enclosure). *"You are dished* (Fr. cuit), cries Ben, delighted, *you can't play again until I get you out!"* Nus knows nothing of this rule. Again, when I play carelessly and let the shooter drop out of may hand, Ben exclaims *"Fan-coup"* to prevent me from saying "coup-passé" and having another shot. Nus is ignorant of this rule.

At one point Ben succeeds in hitting my shooter. He concludes from this that he can have another shot, just as though he had hit one of the marbles placed in the square. Nus, in the same circumstances does not draw the same conclusions (each must play in turn according to him) but deduces that he will be able to play the first shot in the next game.

In the same way, Ben thinks that everyone plays from the place the last shot has led him to and knows the rule that authorizes the player to change places, saying *"du mien"* or *"un empan,"* whereas Nus, who has certainly heard those words, does not know what they mean.

These two cases, chosen at random out of a class of 10-year-old pupils, show straight away what are the two differential features of the second stage. 1) There is a general will to discover the rules that are fixed and common to all players (cf. the way Nus explains to us that if one of the partners plays piquette *"everyone must play the same"*). 2) In spite of this there is considerable discrepancy in the children's information. Lest the reader should think the above examples exceptional here are, on the same point, the answers of another child from the same class:

Ross (11; I): *"First, every one puts two marbles on the square. You can make the square bigger when there are more playing."* Ross knows the method of the coche for knowing who is to begin. Like Nus, he allows both roulette and piquette. He also allows what is not only contrary to all established usages but also to the sense of the words, a way of playing which he calls "femme-poussette" which consists in carrying one's hand along with the marble as one throws it (push stroke in billiards). Now this is always forbidden, and the very word that Ross has deformed says so—"fan-poussette." According to Ross, you play from the place you have reached with the last shot, and when you have won a marble you have the right to another shot straight away. To change your place you must say "du mien." *If a stone gets in our way, you say 'coup-passé' and have another shot. If it slips* [if the marble slips out of your hand] *you say 'laché'* (Engl. 'gone'). *If you don't say that, you can't have another turn. It's the rules!"* Ross here stands mid-way between Nus and Ben. Finally, Ross knows of a rather peculiar custom which is unknown to Nus and Ben. *"If you stay in the square you can be hit and then he picks up the marbles* [—If your shooter stays inside the square and is touched by your opponent's shooter, he is entitled to all the marbles in the square]. *He* (the opponent) *can have two shots* [to try and hit the shooter in question] *and if he misses the first he can take* [at the second shot] *the shooter from anywhere* [though of course only from the outside of the square] *and make the marbles go out* [=take them]." This rule has generally only been described to us by children of the fourth stage, but the rest of Ross' interrogatory is typically third stage.

Such then is the third stage. The child's chief interest is no longer psycho-motor, it is social. In other words, to dislodge a marble from a square by manual dexterity is no longer an aim in itself. The thing now is not only to fight the other boys but also and primarily to regulate the game with a whole set of systematic rules which will ensure the most complete reciprocity in the methods used. The game has therefore become social. We say "become" because it is only after this stage that any real cooperation exists between the players. Before this, each played for himself. Each sought, it is true, to imitate the play of older boys and of the initiated, but more for the satisfaction, still purely personal, of feeling himself to be a member of a mystical community whose sacred institutions are handed down by the elders out of the remote past, than from any real desire to cooperate with his playmates or with anyone else. If cooperation be regarded as more social than this mixture of egocentrism and respect for one's seniors which characterizes the beginnings of collective life among children, then we may say that it is from the third stage onwards that the game of marbles begins to be a truly social game.

As yet, however, this cooperation exists to a great extent only in intention. Being an honest man is not enough to make one to know the law. It is not even enough to enable us to solve all the problems that may arise in our concrete "moral experience." The child fares in the same way during the present stage, and succeeds, at best, in creating for himself a "provisional morality," putting off till a later date the task of setting up a code of laws and a system of jurisprudence. Nor do boys of 7 to 10 ever succeed in agreeing amongst themselves for longer than the duration of one and the same game; they are still incapable of legislating on all possible cases that may arise, for each still has a purely personal opinion about the rules of the game.

To use an apter comparison, we may say that the child of 7 to 10 plays as he reasons. We have already[15] tried to establish the fact that about the age of 7 or 8, precisely, that is to say, at the moment when our third stage appears, in the very poor districts where we conducted our work,[16] discussion and reflection gain an increasing ascendency over unproved affirmation and intellectual egocentrism. Now, these new habits of thought lead to genuine deductions (as opposed to primitive "transductions") and to deductions in which the child grapples with a given fact of experience, either present or past. But something is still lacking if deduction is to be generalized and made completely rational: the child must be able to reason formally, *i.e.*, he must have a conscious realization of the rules of reasoning which will enable him to apply them to any case whatsoever, including purely hypothetical cases (mere assumptions). In the same way, a child who, with regard to the rules of games, has reached the third stage, will achieve momentary coordinations of a collective order (a well ordered game may be compared on this point to a good discussion), but feels no interest as yet in the actual legislation of the game, in the discussions of principle which alone will give him complete mastery of the game in all its strictness. (From this point of view the juridico-moral discussions of the fourth stage may be compared to formal reasoning in general.)

It is, on an average, towards the age of 11 or 12 that these interests develop. In order to understand what is the practice of rules among children of this fourth stage let us question separately several children from the same class at school, and we shall see how subtle are their answers, and how well they agree with one another.

Rit (12), Gros (13) and Vua (13) often play marbles. We questioned them each separately and took steps to prevent them from communicating to each other during our absence the contents of our interrogatory.

With regard to the square, the "pose," the manner of throwing, and generally speaking all the rules we have already examined, these three children are naturally in full agreement with each other. To know who is to play first, Rit, who has lived in two neighbouring villages before coming to town, tells us that various customs are in usage. You draw a line, the coche, and whoever gets nearest to it plays first. If you go beyond the line, either, according to some, it does not matter, or else *"there is another game: when you go beyond the line, you play last."* Gros and Vua know only of this custom, the only one that is really put into practice by the boys of the neighbourhood.

But there are complications about which the younger boys left us in the dark. *"Whoever,* according to Gros, *says 'queue' plays second. It's easier because he doesn't get 'hit'* [=if a player's shooter lands near the square, it is exposed to hits from the other players]." In the same way, Vua tells us that *"whoever says 'queue de deux' plays last."* And he adds the following rule, also recognized by Gros: *"When you are all at the same distance from the coche whoever cries 'egaux-queue' plays second"* (the problem is therefore to play sufficiently soon still to find marbles in the square, but not first, for fear of being hit).

On the other hand, Gros tells us: *"Whoever takes out two* [two of the marbles placed inside the square, *i.e.*, the equivalent of the player's 'pose'] *can say 'queue-de-pose.' In that way he can play second from the coche in the next game."* And Vua: *"When there are two outside* [when two marbles have been knocked out of the square] *you can dare to say 'queue-de-pose,' and you can play second from the coche again in the second game."* Rit gives us the same information.

This is not all. According to Rit, *"if you say 'deux-coups-de-coche' you can have two*

---

[15]*J. R.,* chap. IV.

[16]We take this opportunity of reminding the reader of what has not been sufficiently emphasized in our earlier books, viz. that most of our research has been carried out on children from the poorer parts of Geneva. In different surroundings the age averages would certainly have been different.

shots from the line. If you say 'deux-coups-d'empan' you play the second shot from where you are. You can only say that when the other [=the opponent] has made up his pose [=has won back as many marbles as he had originally deposited in the square]." This rule is observed in the same way by the other two children.

In addition, there is a whole set of rules, unknown to the younger boys, which bear upon the position of the marbles in the square. According to Gros *"the first boy who says 'place-pour-moi'* [Eng., place-for-me] *does not have to place himself at one of the corners of the square,"* and *"the one who has said 'places-des-marbres'* (Engl., place for the marbles) *can put them down as he likes, in a 'troyat'* (all in a heap) *or at the four corners."* Vua is of the same opinion and adds: *"If you say 'place-pour-toi-pour-tout-le-jeu'* (Engl., your-place-for-the-whole-game) *the other chap* [=the opponent] *must stay at the same place."* Rit, who knows both these rules, adds the further detail that *"you can't say 'place-pour-moi' if you have already said 'place-pour-toi.'* " This gives some idea of the complications of procedure!

Our three legal experts also point the measures of clemency in use for the protection of the weak. According to Vua *"if you knock out three at one shot and there's only one left* [one marble in the square] *the other chap* [the opponent] *has the right to play from half-way* [half-way between the coche and the square] *because the first boy has made more than his 'pose.'* " Also: *"the boy who has been beaten is allowed to begin."* According to Gros, *"if there is one marble left at the end, the boy who has won, instead of taking it, can give it to the other chap."* And again, *"When there's one boy who has won too much, the others say 'coujac,' and he is bound to play another game."*

The number of shots at the disposal of each player also gives rise to a whole series of regulations on which the three boys lay stress, as before, in full agreement with each other. For the sake of brevity we refer the reader on this point to the general rules outlined in Section I.

There is only one point on which we saw our subjects differ. Rit who, it will be remembered, has known the game in three different districts, tells us that the boy whose shooter stays inside the square may generally come out of it. He added, it is true, that in some games the player in such a plight is "dished" (Fr., *brulé*), but this rule does not seem to him obligatory. Vua and Gros, on the contrary, are of opinion that in all cases *"when you stay inside the square you are dished."* We think we may confuse Vua by saying: "Rit didn't say that!—*The fact is,* answers Vua, *that sometimes people play differently. Then you ask each other what you want to do.*—And if you can't agree?—*We scrap for a bit and then we fix things up."*

These answers show what the fourth stage is. Interest seems to have shifted its ground since the last stage. Not only do these children seek to cooperate, to "fix things up," as Vua puts it, rather than to play for themselves alone, but also—and this undoubtedly is something new—they seem to take a peculiar pleasure in anticipating all possible cases and in codifying them. Considering that the square game is only one of the five or ten varieties of the game of marbles, it is almost alarming in face of the complexity of rules and procedure in the square game, to think of what a child of twelve has to store away in his memory. These rules, with their overlapping and their exceptions, are at least as complex as the current rules of spelling. It is somewhat humiliating, in this connection, to see how heavily traditional education sets about the task of making spelling enter into brains that assimilate with such ease the mnemonic contents of the game of marbles. But then, memory is dependent upon activity, and a real activity presupposes interest.

Throughout this fourth stage, then, the dominating interest seems to be interest in the rules themselves. For mere cooperation would not require such subtleties as those attending the disposition of the marbles in the square ("place-pour-moi," "place-des-marbres," "place-pour-toi-pour-tout-le-jeu," etc.). The fact that the child enjoys complicating things at will proves that what he is after is rules for their own sake. We have described elsewhere[17] the extraordinary behavior of eight boys of 10 to 11 who, in order to throw snow-balls at each other, began by wasting a good quarter-of-an-hour in electing a president, fixing the rules of voting, then in dividing themselves into two camps, in deciding upon the distances of the shots, and finally in foreseeing what would be the sanctions to be applied in cases of infringement of these laws. Many other facts analogous to this could be culled from studies that have been made on children's societies.

In conclusion, the acquisition and practice of the rules of a game follow very simple and very natural laws, the stages of which may be defined as follows: 1) Simple individual regularity. 2) Imitation of seniors with egocentrism. 3) Cooperation. 4) Interest in rules for their own sake. Let us now see whether the consciousness of rules describes in its evolution an equally uncomplicated curve.

§5. CONSCIOUSNESS OF RULES.   I. THE FIRST TWO STAGES

As all our results have shown, consciousness of rules cannot be isolated from the moral life of the child as a whole. We might, at the most, study the practical applications of rules without bothering about obedience in general, *i.e.,* about the child's whole social and moral behaviour. But as soon as we try, as in the present case, to analyse a child's feelings and thoughts about rules, we shall find that he assimilates them unconsciously along with the commands to which he is subjected taken as a whole. This comes out particularly clearly in the case of the little ones, for whom the constraint exercised by older children evokes adult authority itself in an attenuated form.

Thus the great difficulty here, even more than with the practice of rules, is to establish the exact significance of the primitive facts. Do the simple individual regularities that precede the rules imposed by a group of players give rise to the consciousness of rules, or do they not? And if they do, is this consciousness directly influenced by the commands of adults? This very delicate point must be settled before we can embark upon the analysis of the more transparent data furnished by the interrogatory of older children. With regard to consciousness of rules, we shall designate as the first stage that which corresponds to the purely individualistic stage studied above. During this stage the child, as we noted, plays at marbles in its own way, seeking merely to satisfy its motor interests or its symbolic fantasy. Only, it very soon contracts habits which constitute individual rules of a sort. This phenomenon, far from being unique, is the counterpart of that sort of ritualization of behaviour which can be observed in any baby before it can speak or have experienced any specifically moral adult pressure. Not only does every act of adaptation extend beyond its content of intellectual effort into a ritual kept up for its own sake, but the baby will often invent such rituals for its own pleasure; hence the primitive reactions of very young children in the presence of marbles.

But in order to know to what consciousness of rules these individual schemas correspond it should be remembered that from its tenderest years everything conspires to impress upon the baby the notion of regularity. Certain physical events (alternation of day and night, sameness of scenery during walks, etc.) are repeated with sufficient accuracy to produce an awareness of "law," or at any rate to favour the appearance of motor schemas of prevision. The parents, moreover, impose upon the baby a certain number of moral obligations, the

[17]*J. R.,* p. 96.

source of further regularities (meals, bed-time, cleanliness, etc.) which are completely (and to the child indissociably) connected with the external regularities. From its earliest months the child is therefore bathed in an atmosphere of rules, so that the task of discerning what comes from itself in the rites that it respects and what results from the pressure of things or the constraint of the social environment is one of extreme difficulty. In the content of each ritual act it is certainly possible to know what has been invented by the child, what discovered in nature, and what imposed by the adult. But in the consciousness of rules, taken as a formal structure, these differentiations are non-existent from the point of view of the subject himself.[18]

An analysis of the rites practised by older children, however, will allow us to introduce a fundamental distinction at this point. On the one hand, certain forms of behaviour are, as it were, ritualized by the child himself (*e.g.,* not to walk on the lines that separate the paving stones from the kerb of the pavement). Now, so long as no other factor intervenes, these motor rules never give rise to the feeling of obligation proper. (This is true even of the example we selected intentionally just now—that of a simple game which only becomes obligatory when it becomes connected later on with a pact, *i.e.,* with a social operation, for the pact with oneself is undoubtedly a derivative of the pact with others.) On the other hand, certain rules—it matters not whether they were previously invented by the child, imitated, or received from outside—are at a given moment sanctioned by the environment, *i.e.,* approved of or enjoined. Only in such a case as this are rules accompanied by a feeling of obligation. Now, although it is always difficult to know to what extent an obligatory rule covers up in the mind of a child of one or two years a motor ritual, it is at any rate obvious that the two things are psychologically distinct. And this distinction should be borne in mind when we come to the study of the rules of the game.

The reader will recognize in the way in which we have stated the problem the striking thesis of M. Bovet on the genesis of the feeling of moral obligation in man's conscience: the feeling of obligation only appears when the child accepts a command emanating from someone whom he respects. All the material analysed in the present work, beginning with the facts relating to consciousness of the rules of the game, confirm this thesis, which is parallel rather than contradictory to Durkheim's doctrine of the social genesis of respect and morality. The only change we wish to effect in Bovet's theory is to extend it and to introduce alongside of the unilateral respect of the younger child for the grown-up, the mutual respect that is entertained among equals. Consequently, a collective rule will appear to us as much the product of the reciprocal approbation of two individuals as of the authority of one individual over another.

What then does consciousness of rules amount to during our first stage? In so far as the child has never seen anyone else play, we can allow that it is engaged here upon purely personal and individual ritual acts. The child, enjoying as it does any form of repetition, gives itself schemas of action, but there is nothing in this that implies an obligatory rule. At the same time, and this is where the analysis becomes so difficult, it is obvious that by the time a child can speak, even if it has never seen marbles before, it is already permeated with rules and regulations due to the environment, and this in the most varied spheres. It knows that some things are allowed and others forbidden. Even in the most modern form of training one cannot avoid imposing certain obligations with regard to sleeping, eating, and even in connection with certain details of no apparent importance (not to touch a pile of plates, daddy's desk, etc.,

---

[18]*e.g.* Heat burns (physical law), it is forbidden to touch the fire (moral law) and the child playing about in the kitchen will amuse himself by touching every piece of furniture except the stove (individual ritual). How can the subject's mind distinguish at first between these three types of regularity?

etc.). It is therefore quite possible that when the child comes across marbles for the first time, it is already convinced that certain rules apply to these new objects. And this is why the origins of consciousness of rules even in so restricted a field as that of the game of marbles are conditioned by the child's moral life as a whole.

This becomes clear in the second stage, the most interesting for our thesis. This second stage sets in from the moment when the child, either through imitation or as the result of verbal exchange, begins to want to play in conformity with certain rules received from outside. What idea does he form of these rules? This is the point that we must now try to establish.

We made use of three groups of questions for the purpose of analysing the consciousness of rules in this second stage. Can rules be changed? Have rules always been the same as they are to-day? How did rules begin? Obviously the first of these questions is the best. It is the least verbal of the three. Instead of making the child think about a problem that has never occurred to him (as do the other two), it confronts the subject with a new fact, a rule invented by himself, and it is relatively easy to note the child's resulting reactions, however clumsy he may be in formulating them. The other two questions, on the contrary, incur all the objections that can be made against questioning pure and simple—the possibility of suggestion, of perseveration, etc. We are of the opinion, nevertheless, that these questions have their use, if only as indices of the respect felt for rules and as complementary to the first.

Now, as soon as the second stage begins, *i.e.,* from the moment that the child begins to imitate the rules of others, no matter how egocentric in practice his play may be, he regards the rules of the game as sacred and untouchable; he refuses to alter these rules and claims that any modification, even if accepted by general opinion, would be wrong.

Actually, it is not until about the age of 6 that this attitude appears quite clearly and explicitly. Children of 4–5 seem, therefore, to form an exception and to take rules rather casually, a feature which, if judged purely externally, recalls the liberalism of older children. In reality, we believe that this analogy is superficial, and that little children, even when they seem not to be so, are always conservative in the matter of rules. If they accept innovations that are proposed to them, it is because they do not realize that there was any innovation.

Let us begin by one of the more difficult cases, the difficulty being all the greater because the child is very young and consequently very much inclined to romance.

Fal (5) is at the second stage with regard to the practice of rules. "Long ago when people were beginning to build the town of Neuchâtel, did little children play at marbles the way you showed me?—*Yes.*—Always that way?—*Yes.*—How did you get to know the rules?—*When I was quite little my brother showed me. My Daddy showed my brother.*—And how did your daddy know?—*My Daddy just knew. No one told him.*—How did he know?—*No one showed him!*" "Am I older than your Daddy?—*No, you're young. My Daddy had been born when we came to Neuchâtel. My Daddy was born before me.*—Tell me some people older than your daddy.—*My grand-dad.*—Did he play marbles?—*Yes.*—Then he played before your daddy?—*Yes, but not with rules!* [said with great conviction].—What do you mean by rules?— . . . [Fal does not know this word, which he has just heard from our lips for the first time. But he realizes that it means an essential property of the game of marbles; that is why he asserts so emphatically that his grand-dad did not play with rules so as to show how superior his daddy is to everyone else in the world.]—Was it a long time ago when people played for the first time?—*Oh, yes.*—How did they find out how to play?—*Well, they took some marbles, and then they made a square, and then they put the marbles inside it . . .* etc. [he enumerates the rules that he knows].—Was it little children who found out or grown-up gentlemen?—*Grown-up gentlemen.*—Tell me who was born first, your daddy or your grand-dad?—*My Daddy was born before my grand-dad.*—Who invented the game of marbles?—*My Daddy did.*—Who is the oldest person in Neuchâtel?—*I dunno.*—Who do you think?—*God.*—Did people know how to play marbles before your daddy?—*Other gentlemen played* [before? at the same time?].—In the same way as your daddy?—*Yes.*—How did they know how to?—*They made it up.*—Where is God?—*In the sky.*—Is he older than your daddy?—*Not so old.''* ''Could one find a new way of playing?—*I can't play any other way.*—Try . . . [Fal does not move]. Couldn't you put them like this [we place the marbles in a circle without a square]?—*Oh, yes.*—Would it be fair?—*Oh, yes.*—As fair as the square?—*Yes.*—Did your daddy use to play that way or not?—*Oh, yes.*—Could one play still other ways?—*Oh, yes.''* We then arrange the marbles in the shape of a T, we put them on a matchbox, etc. Fal says he has never seen this done before, but that it is all quite fair and that you can change things as much as you like. Only his daddy knows all this!

Fal is typical of the cases we were discussing above. He is ready to change all the established rules. A circle, a T., anything will do just as well as the square. It looks, at first, as though Fal were not near those older children who, as we shall see, no longer believe in the sacred character of rules and adopt any convention so long as it is received by all. But in reality this is not the case. However great a romancer Fal may be, the text of which we have quoted the greater part seems to show that he has a great respect for rules. He attributes them to his father, which amounts to saying that he regards them as endowed with divine right. Fal's curious ideas about his father's age are worth noting in this connection; his daddy was born before his grand-dad, and is older than God! These remarks, which fully coincide with those collected by M. Bovet,[19] would seem to indicate that in attributing the rules to his father, Fal makes them more or less contemporaneous with what is for him the beginning of the world. Characteristic, too, is the manner in which the child receives this invention of rules on the part of his father: this gentleman thought of them without having been told or shown anything, but other gentlemen may equally have thought of the same thing. This is not, in our opinion, mere psittacism. One should be careful, of course, not to read into these remarks more logic than they contain: they simply mean that rules are sacred and unchangeable because they partake of paternal authority. But this affective postulate can be translated into a sort of infantile theory of invention, and of the eternity of essences. To the child who attaches no precise meaning to the terms ''before'' and ''after'' and who measures time in terms of his immediate or deeper feelings, to invent means almost the same thing as to discover an eternal and preexisting reality in oneself. Or to put it more simply, the child cannot differentiate as we do between the activity which consists in inventing something new and that which consists in remembering the past. (Hence the mixture of romancing and exact reproduction which characterizes his stories or his memory.) For the child, as for Plato, intellectual creation merges into reminiscence.[20] What, then, is the meaning of Fal's tolerance with regard to the new laws we suggested to him? Simply this, that confident of the unlimited wealth of rules in the game of marbles, he imagines, as soon as he is in possession of a new rule, that he has merely rediscovered a rule that was already in existence.

In order to understand the attitude of the children of the early part of the second stage—they all answer more or less like Fal—we must remember that up till the age of 6–7 the child has great difficulty in knowing what comes from himself and what from others in his own fund of knowledge. This comes primarily from his difficulty in retrospection (see *J. R.*,

---

[19]P. Bovet, *The Child's Religion*, London, 1930.

[20]Cf. *C. W.*, p. 52, the case of Kauf (8; 8): this child believes that the stories she tells were written in her brain by God. *''Before I was born, he put them there.''*

Chap. IV, § 1), and secondly from the lack of organization in memory itself. In this way the child is led to think that he has always known something which in fact he has only just learned. We have often had the experience of telling a child something which immediately afterwards he will imagine himself to have known for months. This indifference to distinctions of before and after, old and new, explains the inability of which we spoke just now to differentiate between invention and reminiscence. The child very often feels that what he makes up, even on the spur of the moment, expresses, in some way, an eternal truth. This being so, one cannot say that very young children have no respect for rules because they allow these to be changed; innovations are not real innovations to them.

Added to this there is a curious attitude which appears throughout the whole of the egocentric stage, and which may be compared to the mental states characteristic of inspiration. The child more or less pleases himself in his application of the rules. At the same time, Fal and others like him will allow any sort of change in the established usage. And yet they one and all insist upon the point that rules have always been the same as they are at present, and that they are due to adult authority, particularly the authority of the father. Is this contradictory? It is so only in appearance. If we call to mind the peculiar mentality of children of this age, for whom society is not so much a successful cooperation between equals as a feeling of continuous communion between the ego and the Word of the Elder or Adult, then the contradiction ceases. Just as the mystic can no longer dissociate his own wishes from the will of his God, so the little child cannot differentiate between the impulses of his personal fancy and the rules imposed on him from above.

Let us now pass on to the typical cases of this stage, *i.e.,* to children who out of respect to rules are hostile to any innovation whatsoever.

We must begin by quoting a child of 5½ years, Leh, whose reaction was among the most spontaneous that we had occasion to note. Leh was telling us about the rules of the game before we had questioned him about consciousness of rules. He had just begun to speak and was showing us how to play from the coche (which was about the only thing in the game that he knew) when the following dialogue took place. We asked Leh quite simply if everyone played from the coche or whether one could not (as is actually done) put the older ones at the coche and let the little ones play closer up. *"No,* answered Leh, *that wouldn't be fair.—Why not?—Because God would make the little boy's shot not reach the marbles and the big boy's shot would reach them."* In other words, divine justice is opposed to any change in the rules of marbles, and if one player, even a very young one were favored in any way, God Himself would prevent him from reaching the square.

Pha (5½): "Do people always play like that—*Yes, always like that.*—Why?—*'Cos you couldn't play any other way.*—Couldn't you play like this [we arrange the marbles in a circle, then in a triangle]?—*Yes, but the others wouldn't want to.*—Why?—*'Cos squares is better.*—Why better?— . . ." We are less successful, however, with regard to the origins of the game: "Did your daddy play at marbles before you were born?—*No, never, because I wasn't there yet!*—But he was a child like you before you were born.—*I was there already when he was like me. He was bigger."* "When did people begin to play marbles?—*When the others began, I began too."* It would be impossible to outdo Pha in placing oneself at the centre of the universe, in time as well as in space! And yet Pha feels very strongly that rules stand above him: they cannot be changed.

Geo (6) tells us that the game of marbles began with *"people, with the Gentlemen of the Commune* [the Town Council whom he has probably heard mentioned in connection with road-mending and the police].—How was that?—*It came into the gentlemen's heads and they made some marbles.*—How did they know how to play?—*In their head. They taught people. Daddies show little boys how to.*—Can one play differently from how you showed me? Can you change the game?—*I think you can, but I don't know how* [Geo is alluding here to the variants already in existence].—Anyhow?—*No there are no games you play anyhow.*—Why?—*Because God didn't teach them* [the Town Council].—Try and change the game.—[Geo then invents an arrangement which he regards as quite new and which consists in marking a big square with three rows of three marbles in each].—Is that one fair, like the other one?—*No, because there are only three lines of three.*—Could people always play that way and stop playing the old way?—*Yes, M'sieu.*—How did you find this game?—*In my head.*—Can we say, then, that the other games don't count and this is the one people must take?—*Yes, M'sieur. There's others too that the Gentlemen of the Commune know.*—Do they know this one that you have made up?—*Yes* [!].—But it was you who found it out. Did you find that game in your head?—*Yes.*—How?—*All of a sudden. God told it to me.*—You know, I have spoken to the gentlemen of the Commune, and I don't think they know your new game.—*Oh!* [Geo is very much taken aback].—But I know some children who don't know how to play yet. Which game shall I teach them, yours, or the other one?—*The one of the Gentlemen of the Commune.*—Why?—*Because it is prettier.''* ''Later on when you are a big man and have got moustaches perhaps there won't be many children left who play the game of the Gentlemen of the Commune. But there may be lots of boys who play at your game. Then which game will be fairest, yours, which will be played most, or the game of the Gentlemen of the Commune, which will be nearly forgotten?—*The game of the Gentlemen of the Commune.''*

The case of Geo comes as a beautiful confirmation of what we said in connection with Fal, viz., that for little children inventing a game comes to the same thing as finding in one's head a game that has already been anticipated and classified by the most competent authorities. Geo attributes the game he has invented to divine inspiration, and supposes it to be already known to the ''Gentlemen of the Commune.'' As soon as we undeceive him he undervalues his own invention and refuses to regard it as right even if ratified by general usage.

Mar (6), whose behaviour in the practice of rules we have already examined in § 3, declares that in the time of his daddy and of Jesus, people played as they do now. He refuses to invent a new game. *''I've never invented games.''* We then suggest a new game which consists of putting marbles on a box and making them fall off by hitting the box: ''Can one play like this?—*Yes* [He does so, and seems to enjoy it].—Could this game ever become a fair game?—*No, because it's not the same.''* Another attempt calls forth the same reaction.

Stor (7) tells us that children played at marbles before Noah's ark: ''How did they play?—*Like we played.*—How did it begin?—*They bought some marbles.*—But how did they learn?—*His daddy taught them.''* Stor invents a new game in the shape of a triangle. He admits that his friends would be glad to play at it, *''but not all of them. Not the big ones, the quite big ones.*—Why?—*Because it isn't a game for the big ones.*—Is it as fair a game as the one you showed me?—*No.*—Why?—*Because it isn't a square.*—And if everyone played that way, even the big ones, would it be fair?—*No.*—Why not?—*Because it isn't a square.''*

With regard to the practical application of rules all these children therefore belong to the stage of egocentrism. The result is clearly paradoxical. Here are children playing more or less as they choose; they are influenced, it is true, by a few examples that have been set before them and observe roughly the general schema of the game; but they do so without troubling to obey in detail the rules they know or could know with a little attention, and without attributing the least importance to the most serious infringements of which they may be guilty. Besides all this, each child plays for himself, he pays no attention to his neighbour, does not seek to control him and is not controlled by him, does not even try to beat him—"to win" simply means to succeed in hitting the marbles one has aimed at. And yet these same children harbour an almost mystical respect for rules: rules are eternal, due to the authority of parents, of the Gentlemen of the Commune, and even of an almighty God. It is forbidden to change them, and even if the whole of general opinion supported such a change, general opinion would be in the wrong: the unanimous consent of all the children would be powerless against the truth of Tradition. As to any apparent changes, these are only complementary additions to the initial Revelation: thus Geo (the most primitive of the above cases, and therefore nearest to those represented by Fal and so confirming what we said about the latter) believes the rule invented by him to be directly due to a divine inspiration analogous to the inspiration of which the Gentlemen of the Commune were the first recipients.

In reality, however, this paradox is general in child behavior and constitutes, as we shall show towards the end of the book, the most significant feature of the morality belonging to the egocentric stage. Childish egocentrism, far from being asocial, always goes hand in hand with adult constraint. It is presocial only in relation to cooperation. In all spheres, two types of social relations must be distinguished: constraint and cooperation. The first implies an element of unilateral respect, of authority and prestige; the second is simply the intercourse between two individuals on an equal footing. Now egocentrism is contradictory only to cooperation, for the latter alone is really able to socialize the individual. Constraint, on the other hand, is always the ally of childish egocentrism. Indeed it is because the child cannot establish a genuinely mutual contact with the adult that he remains shut up in this own ego. The child is, on the one hand, too apt to have the illusion of agreement where actually he is only following his own fantasy; the adult, on the other, takes advantage of his situation instead of seeking equality. With regard to moral rules, the child submits more or less completely in intention to the rules laid down for him, but these, remaining, as it were, external to the subject's conscience, do not really transform his conduct. This is why the child looks upon rules as sacred though he does not really put them into practice.

As far as the game of marbles is concerned, there is therefore no contradiction between the egocentric practice of games and the mystical respect entertained for rules. This respect is the mark of a mentality fashioned, not by free cooperation between equals, but by adult constraint. When the child imitates the rules practised by his older companions he feels that he is submitting to an unalterable law, due, therefore, to his parents themselves. Thus the pressure exercised by older on younger children is assimilated here, as so often, to adult pressure. This action of the older children is still constraint, for cooperation can only arise between equals. Nor does the submission of the younger children to the rules of the older ones lead to any sort of cooperation in action; it simply produces a sort of mysticism, a diffused feeling of collective participation, which, as in the case of many mystics, fits in perfectly well with egocentrism. For we shall see eventually that cooperation between equals not only brings about a gradual change in the child's practical attitude, but that it also does away with the mystical feeling towards authority.

In the meantime let us examine the subjects of the final period of the present stage. We found only three stages with regard to consciousness of rules, whereas there seemed to be four with regard to the practice of the game. In other words, the cooperation that sets in from the age of 7–8 is not sufficient at first to repress the mystical attitude to authority, and the last part of the present stage (in the consciousness of rules) really coincides with the first half of the cooperative stage (in the practice of the game).

Ben (10 yrs.), whose answers we have given with regard to the practice of rules (third stage) is still at the second stage from the point of view that is occupying us just now: "Can one invent new rules?—*Some boys do, so as to win more marbles, but it doesn't always come off. One chap* [quite recently, in his class] *thought of saying 'Deux Empans'* (two spans) *so as to get nearer* [actually this is a rule already known to the older boys]. *It didn't come off.*—And with the little ones?—*Yes, it came off all right with them.*—Invent a rule.—*I couldn't invent one straight away like that.*—Yes you could. I can see that you are cleverer than you make yourself out to be.—*Well, let's say that you're not caught when you are in the square.*—Good. Would that come off with the others?—*Oh, yes, they'd like to do that.*—Then people could play that way?—*Oh, no, because it would be cheating.*—But all your pals would like to, wouldn't they?—*Yes, they all would.*—Then why would it be cheating?—*Because I invented it: it isn't a rule! It's a wrong rule because it's outside of the rules. A fair rule is one that is in the game.*—How does one know if it is fair?—*The good players know it.*—And suppose the good players wanted to play with your rule?—*It wouldn't work. Besides they would say it was cheating.*—And if they all said that the rule was right, would it work?—*Oh, yes, it would. . . . But it's a wrong rule!*—But if they all said it was right how would anyone know that it was wrong?—*Because when you are in the square it's like a garden with a fence, you're shut in* [so that if the shooter stays inside the square, you are 'dished'].—And suppose we draw a square like this [we draw a square with a break in one of the sides like a fence broken by a door]?—*Some boys do that. But it isn't fair. It's just for fun for passing the time.*—Why?—*Because the square ought to be closed.*—But if some boys do it, is it fair or not?—*It's both fair and not fair.*—Why is it fair?—*It is fair for waiting* [for fun].—And why is it not fair?—*Because the square ought to be closed.*—When you are big, suppose everyone plays that way, will it be right or not?—*It will be right then because there will be new children who will learn the rule.*—And for you?—*It will be wrong.*—And what will it be 'really and truly'?—*It will really be wrong.*" Later on, however, Ben admits that his father and grandfather played differently from him, and that rules can therefore be changed by children. But this does not prevent him from sticking to the view that rules contain an intrinsic truth which is independent of usage.

Borderline cases like these are particularly interesting. Ben stands midway between the second and third stages. On the one hand, he has already learned, thanks to cooperation, the existence of possible variations in the use of rules, and he knows, therefore, that the actual rules are recent and have been made by children. But on the other hand, he believes in the absolute and intrinsic truth of rules. Does cooperation, then, impose upon this child a mystical attitude to law similar to the respect felt by little children for the commands given them by adults? Or is Ben's respect for the rules of the game inherited from the constraint that has not yet been eliminated by cooperation? The sequel will show that the latter interpretation is the right one. Older children cease to believe in the intrinsic value of rules, and they do so in the exact measure that they learn to put them into practice. Ben's attitude should therefore be regarded as a survival of the features due to constraint.

Generally speaking, it is a perfectly normal thing that in its beginnings cooperation—on the plane of action—should not immediately abolish the mental states created—on the plane of thought—by the complexus: egocentricity and constraint. Thought always lags behind action and cooperation has to be practised for a very long time before its consequences can be brought fully to light by reflective thought. This is a fresh example of the law of *prise de conscience or* conscious realization formulated by Claparède[21] and of the time-lag[22] or "shifting" which we have observed in so many other spheres (see *J. R.,* Chap. V, § 2 and *C. C.,* 2nd part). A phenomenon such as this is, moreover, well fitted to simplify the problem of egocentrism in general since it explains why intellectual egocentrism is so much more stubborn than egocentrism in action.

§6. CONSCIOUSNESS OF RULES.   II. THIRD STAGE

After the age of 10 on the average, *i.e.,* from the second half of the cooperative stage and during the whole of the stage when the rules are codified, consciousness of rules undergoes a complete transformation. Autonomy follows upon heteronomy: the rule of a game appears to the child no longer as an external law, sacred in so far as it has been laid down by adults; but as the outcome of a free decision and worthy of respect in the measure that it has enlisted mutual consent.

This change can be seen by three concordant symptoms. In the first place, the child allows a change in the rules so long as it enlists the votes of all. Anything is possible, so long as, and to the extent that you undertake to respect the new decisions. Thus democracy follows on theocracy and gerontocracy: there are no more crimes of opinion, but only breaches in procedure. All opinions are tolerated so long as their protagonists urge their acceptance by legal methods. Of course some opinions are more reasonable than others. Among the new rules that may be proposed, there are innovations worthy of acceptance because they will add to the interest of the game (pleasure in risks, art for art's sake, etc.). And there are new rules that are worthless because they give precedence to easy winning as against work and skill. But the child counts on the agreement among the players to eliminate these immoral innovations. He no longer relies, as do the little ones, upon an all-wise tradition. He no longer thinks that everything has been arranged for the best in the past and that the only way of avoiding trouble is by religiously respecting the established order. He believes in the value of experiment in so far as it is sanctioned by collective opinion.

In the second place, the child ceases *ipso facto* to look upon rules as eternal and as having been handed down unchanged from one generation to another. Thirdly and finally, his ideas on the origin of the rules and of the game do not differ from ours: originally, marbles must simply have been rounded pebbles which children threw about to amuse themselves, and rules, far from having been imposed as such by adults, must have become gradually fixed on the initiative of the children themselves.

Here are examples:

Ross (11) belongs to the third stage in regard to the practise of rules. He claims that he often invents new rules with his playmates: *"We make them* [up] *sometimes. We go up to 200. We play about and then hit each other, and then he says to me: 'If you go up to 100 I'll give you a marble.'* Is this new rule fair like the old ones, or not?—*Perhaps it isn't quite fair, because it isn't very hard to take four marbles that way!*—If everyone does it, will it be a real rule, or not?—*If they do it often, it will become a real rule.*—Did your father play the way you showed me, or differently?—*Oh, I don't know. It may have been a different game. It changes.*

[21]This term (Claparède's *prise de conscience*) simply means "coming into consciousness," and has nothing to do with intellectual formulation. [*Trans.*].

[22]This is the term that has been selected by the author for the French *décalage,* a somewhat more complex notion which in previous volumes, cf. *L.T.,* p. 208, ff., has been rendered as a process of "shifting." [*Trans.*].

It still changes quite often.—Have people been playing for long?—*At least fifty years.*—Did people play marbles in the days of the 'Old Swiss'?—*Oh, I don't think so.*—How did it begin?—*Some boys took some motor balls* (ball bearings) *and then they played. And after that there were marbles in shops.*—Why are there rules in the game of marbles?—*So as not to be always quarrelling you must have rules, and then play properly.*—How did these rules begin?—*Some boys came to an agreement amongst themselves and made them.*—Could you invent a new rule?—*Perhaps . . .* [he thinks] *you put three marbles together and you drop another from above on to the middle one.*—Could one play that way?—*Oh, yes.*—Is that a fair rule like the others?—*The chaps might say it wasn't very fair because it's luck. To be a good rule, it has to be skill.*—But if everyone played that way, would it be a fair rule or not?—*Oh, yes, you could play just as well with that rule as with the others."*

Malb (12) belongs to the fourth stage in the practice of rules: "Does everyone play the way you showed me?—*Yes.*—And did they play like that long ago?—*No.*—Why not?—*They used different words.*—And how about the rules?—*They didn't use them either, because my father told me he didn't play that way.*—But long ago did people play with the same rules?—*Not quite the same.*—How about the rule not hitting for one?—*I think that must have come later.*—Did they play marbles when your grandfather was little?—*Yes.*—Like they do now?—*Oh, no, different kinds of games.*—And at the time of the battle of Morat?—*No, I don't think they played then.*—How do you think the game of marbles began?—*At first, children looked for round pebbles.*—And the rules?—*I expect they played from the coche. Later on, boys wanted to play differently and they invented other rules.*—And how did the coche begin?—*I expect they had fun hitting the pebbles. And then they invented the coche.*—Could one change the rules?—*Yes.*—Could you?—*Yes, I could make up another game. We were playing at home one evening and we found out a new one* [he shows it to us].—Are these new rules as fair as the others?—*Yes.*—Which is the fairest, the game you showed me first or the one you invented?—*Both the same.*—If you show this new game to the little ones what will they do?—*Perhaps they will play at it.*—And if they forget the square game and only play this one, which will be the true game, the new one that will be better known, or the old one?—*The best known one will be the fairest."*

Gros (13 yrs. at the fourth stage in the practice of the rules) has shown us the rules as we saw above. "Did your father play that way when he was little?—*No, they had other rules. They didn't play with a square.*—And did the other boys of your father's time play with a square?—*There must have been one who knew, since we know it now.*—And how did that one know about the square?—*They thought they would see if it was nicer than the other game.*—How old was the boy who invented the square?—*I expect thirteen* [his own age].—Did the children of the Swiss who lived at the time of the battle of Morat play at marbles?—*They may have played with a hole, and then later on with a square.*—And in the time of David de Purry [a periwigged gentleman whose statue on one of the public squares of Neuchâtel is known to all]?—*I expect they had a bit of a lark too!*—Have rules changed since the square was invented?—*There may have been little changes.*—And do the rules still change?—*No. You always play the same way.*—Are you allowed to change the rules at all?—*Oh, yes. Some want to, and some don't. If the boys play that way* (changing something) *you have to play like they do.*—Do you think you could invent a new rule?—*Oh, yes . . .* [he thinks]; *you could play with your feet.*—Would it be fair?—*I don't know. It's just my idea.*—And if you showed it to the others would it work?—*It would work all right. Some other boys would want to try. Some wouldn't, by Jove! They would stick to the old rules. They'd think they'd have less of a chance with this new game.*—And if everyone played your way?—*Then it would be a rule like the others.*—Which is the fairest now, yours or the old one?—*The old one.—Why?—Because they can't cheat.* (Note this excellent justification of rules: the old rule is better than the innovation, not yet sanctioned by usage, because only the old rule has the force of a law and can thus prevent cheating.) And if nearly everyone played with their feet, then which would be fairest?—*If nearly everyone played with their feet, then that would be fairest.''*—Finally we ask Gros, ''Suppose there are two games, an easy one where you win often, and a difficult one where you win seldom, which would you like best?—*The most difficult. You end by winning that way.''*

Vua (13), whose answers about the practice of rules we have already examined (4th stage) tells us that his father and his grandfather played differently from him. ''In the days of the 'Three Swiss' did boys play at marbles?—*No. They had to work at home. They played other games.*—Did they play marbles in the days of the battle of Morat?—*Perhaps, after the war.*—Who invented this game?—*Some kids. They saw their parents playing at bowls, and they thought they might do the same thing.*—Could other rules be invented?—*Yes* [he shows us one he has invented and which he calls 'the line' because the marbles are arranged in a row and not in a square].—Which is the real game, yours or the square?—*The square, because it is the one that is always used.*—Which do you like best, an easy game or a difficult one?—*The more difficult, because it is more interesting. The 'Troyat'* (a game that consists in heaping the balls into piles) *is not quite the real game. Some boys invented it. They wanted to win all the marbles.''* On this point Vua seems to be answering like a child of the preceding stage who will invoke the ''real game'' that conforms to tradition as against contemporary innovations. But Vua seems to us rather to be contrasting a demagogic procedure (the ''Troyat,'' which by allowing too great a part to chance gives rise to illicit and immoral gains) with practices that are in keeping with the spirit of the game, whether they are ancient, like the square, or recent like his own game. The proof of this would seem to lie in the following remarks relating to his own playing: ''Is the game you invented as fair as the square, or less fair?—*It is just as fair because the marbles are far apart* (therefore the game is difficult).—If in a few years' time everyone played your line game and only one or two boys played the square game, which would be the fairest, the line or the square?—*The line would be fairest.''*

Blas (12, 4th stage in the practice of rules) thinks that the game of marbles must have begun round about 1500 at the time of the Reformation. *''Children invented the game. They made little balls with earth and water and then they amused themselves by rolling them about. They found it was rather fun making them hit, and then they had the idea of inventing a game, and they said that when you hit anyone else's marble with your own you could have the marble you hit. After that I expect they invented the square, so that you should have to make the marbles go out of the square. They invented the line, so that all the marbles should be at the same distance. They only invented it later. When cement was discovered, marbles were made like they are to-day. The marbles of earth weren't strong enough, so the children asked the manufacturers to make some in cement.''* We ask Blas to make up a new rule, and this is what he thinks of. First there must be a competition, and whoever makes his marbles go furthest can play first. But the rule seems *''bad because you'd have to run too far back to fetch the marbles.''* He then thinks of another which consists in playing in two squares one inside the other. ''Would everyone want to play that way?—*Those who invented it would.*—Later on, if your game is played just as much as the square, which will be the fairest?—*Both the same.''*

The psychological and educational interest of all this stands out very clearly. We are now definitely in the presence of a social reality that has rational and moral organization and is yet peculiar to childhood. Also we can actually put our finger upon the conjunction of cooperation and autonomy, which follows upon the conjunction of egocentrism and constraint.

Up to the present, rules have been imposed upon the younger children by the older ones. As such they had been assimilated by the former to the commands given by adults. They therefore appeared to the child as sacred and untouchable, the guarantee of their truth being precisely this immutability. Actually this conformity, like all conformity, remained external to the individual. In appearance docile, in his own eyes submissive and constantly imbued as it were with the spirit of the Elders or the Gods, the child could in actual fact achieve little more than a simulation of sociality, to say nothing of morality. External constraint does not destroy egocentrism. It covers and conceals when it does not actually strengthen it.

But from henceforward a rule is conceived as the free pronouncement of the actual individual minds themselves. It is no longer external and coercive: it can be modified and adapted to the tendencies of the group. It constitutes no revealed truth whose sacred character derives from its divine origin and historical permanence; it is something that is built up progressively and autonomously. But does this not make it cease to be a real rule? Is it perhaps not a mark of decadence rather than of progress in relation to the earlier stage? That is the problem. The facts, however, seem definitely to authorize the opposite conclusion: it is from the moment that it replaces the rule of constraint that the rule of cooperation becomes an effective moral law.

In the first place, one is struck by the synchronism between the appearance of this new type of consciousness of rules and a genuine observation of the rules. This third stage of rule consciousness appears toward the age of 10–11. And it is at this same age that the simple cooperation characteristic of the third stage in the practice of rules begins to be complicated by a desire for codification and complete application of the law. The two phenomena are therefore related to each other. But is it the consciousness of autonomy that leads to the practical respect for the law, or does this respect for the law lead to the feeling of autonomy? These are simply two aspects of the same reality: when a rule ceases to be external to children and depends only on their free collective will, it becomes incorporated in the mind of each, and individual obedience is henceforth purely spontaneous. True, the difficulty reappears each time that the child, while still remaining faithful to a rule that favours him, is tempted to slur over some article of the law or some point of procedure that favours his opponent. But the peculiar function of cooperation is to lead the child to the practice of reciprocity, hence of moral universality and generosity in his relations with his playmates.

This last point introduces us to yet another sign of the bond between autonomy and true respect for the law. By modifying rules, *i.e.*, by becoming a sovereign and legislator in the democracy which towards the age of 10–11 follows upon the earlier gerontocracy, the child takes cognizance of the *raison d'être* of laws. A rule becomes the necessary condition for agreement. *"So as not to be always quarrelling,"* says Ross, *"you must have rules and then play properly* [=stick to them]." The fairest rule, Gros maintains, is that which unites the opinion of the players, *"because* [then] *they can't cheat."*

Thirdly, what shows most clearly that the autonomy achieved during this stage leads more surely to respect for rules than the heteronomy of the preceding stage is the truly political and democratic way in which children of 12–13 distinguish lawless whims from constitutional innovation. Everything is allowed, every individual proposition is, by rights, worthy of attention. There are no more breaches of opinion, in the sense that to desire to change the laws is no longer to sin against them. Only—and each of our subjects was perfectly clear on this point—no one has the right to introduce an innovation except by legal channels, *i.e.*, by previously persuading the other players and by submitting in advance to the verdict of the majority. There may therefore be breaches but they are of procedure only: procedure alone is obligatory, opinions can always be subjected to discussion. Thus Gros tells us that if a change is proposed *"Some want to and some don't. If boys play that way* [allow an alteration] *you have to play like they do."* As Vua said in connection with the practice of rules (§ 4) *"sometimes people play differently. Then you ask each other what you want to do. . . . We scrap for a bit and then we fix things up."*

In short, law now emanates from the sovereign people and no longer from the tradition laid down by the Elders. And correlatively with this change, the respective values attaching to custom and the rights of reason come to be practically reversed.

In the past, custom had always prevailed over rights. Only, as in all cases where a human being is enslaved to a custom that is not part of his inner life, the child regarded this Custom imposed by his elders as a sort of Decalogue revealed by divine beings (*i.e.,* adults, including God, who is, according to Fal, the oldest gentleman in Neuchâtel after his own father). With the result that, in the eyes of a little child, no alteration of usage will dispense the individual from remaining faithful to the eternal law. Even if people forget the square game, says Ben, and adopt another, this new game *"will really be wrong."* The child therefore distinguishes between a rule that is true in itself and mere custom, present or future. And yet he is all the time enslaved to custom and not to any juridico-moral reason or reality distinct from this custom and superior to it. Nor indeed is this way of thinking very different from that of many conservative adults who delude themselves into thinking that they are assisting the triumph of eternal reason over present fashion, when they are really the slaves of past custom at the expense of the permanent laws of rational cooperation.

But from now on, by the mere fact of tying himself down to certain rules of discussion and collaboration, and thus cooperating with his neighbours in full reciprocity (without any false respect for tradition nor for the will of any one individual) the child will be enabled to dissociate custom from the rational ideal. For it is of the essence of cooperation as opposed to social constraint that, side by side with the body of provisional opinion which exists in fact, it also allows for an ideal of what is right functionally implied in the very mechanism of discussion and reciprocity. The constraint of tradition imposes opinions or customs, and there is an end of it. Cooperation imposes nothing except the actual methods of intellectual or moral interchange (Baldwin's[23] synnomic as opposed to his syndoxic). Consequently we must distinguish alongside of the actual agreement that exists between minds, an ideal agreement defined by the more and more intensive application of the processes of mental interchange.[24] As far as our children are concerned, this simply means that in addition to the rules agreed upon in a given group and at a given moment (constituted morality or rights in the sense in which M. Lalande speaks of "raison constituée")[25] the child has in mind a sort of ideal or spirit of the game which cannot be formulated in terms of rules (constitutive morality or rights in the sense of "raison constituante"). For if there is to be any reciprocity between players in the application of established rules or in the elaboration of new rules, everything must be eliminated that would compromise this reciprocity (inequalities due to chance, excessive individual differences in skill or muscular power, etc.). Thus usages are gradually purified in virtue of an ideal that is superior to custom since it arises from the very functioning of cooperation.

This is why, when innovations are proposed to the child, he regards them as fair or unfair not only according as they are likely or not to rally the majority of players in their favour, but also according as they are in keeping with that spirit of the game itself, which is nothing more or less than the spirit of reciprocity. Ross tells us, for instance, concerning his

---

[23]J. M. Baldwin, *Genetic Theory of Reality.*
[24]See our article, "Logique génétique et sociologie," *Revue Philosophique,* 1928.
[25]Lalande, A., "Raison constituante et raison constituée, *Revue des Cours et des Conférence.*

own proposition, "*Perhaps it isn't quite fair, because it isn't very hard to take four marbles that way,*" and again, "*The chaps might say it wasn't fair because it's luck. To be a good rule, it has to be skill.*" The Troyat, Vua informs us, is less fair than the square (though equally widespread and equally well known to former generations), because it was invented "*to win all the marbles.*" In this way, Vua draws a distinction between demagogy and a sane democracy. In the same way, Gros and Vua prefer difficult games because they are more "interesting": cleverness and skill now matter more than winning. Art for art's sake is far more disinterested than playing for gain.

In a word, as soon as we have cooperation, the rational notions of the just and the unjust become regulative of custom, because they are implied in the actual functioning of social life among equals—a point which will be developed in the third chapter of this book. During the preceding stages, on the contrary, custom overbore the issue of right, precisely in so far as it was deified and remained external to the minds of individuals.

Let us now see what sort of philosophy of history the child will adopt in consequence of having discovered democracy. It is very interesting, in this connection, to note the following synchronism. The moment a child decides that rules can be changed, he ceases to believe in their endless past and in their adult origin. In other words, he regards rules as having constantly changed and as having been invented and modified by children themselves. External events may of course play a certain part in bringing this about. Sooner or later, for example, the child may learn from his father that the game was different for previous generations. But so unmistakable is the correlation (on the average, of course) between the appearance of this new type of consciousness of rules and the disappearance of the belief in the adult origin of the game that the connection must be founded on reality. Is it, then, the loss of belief in the divine or adult origin of rules that allows the child to think of innovations, or is it the consciousness of autonomy that dispels the myth of revelation?

Only someone completely ignorant of the character of childish beliefs could imagine that a change in the child's ideas about the origin of rules could be of a nature to exercise so profound an influence on his social conduct. On the contrary, here as in so many cases, belief merely reflects behaviour. There can be no doubt that children very rarely reflect upon the original institution of the game of marbles. There are even strong reasons for assuming that as far as the children we examined are concerned such a problem never even entered their heads until the day when a psychologist had the ridiculous idea of asking them how marbles were played in the days of the Old Swiss and of the Old Testament. Even if the question of the origin of rules did pass through the minds of some of these children during the spontaneous interrogatories that so often deal with rules in general (*L. T.,* Chap. V, §§ 5 and 10) the answer which the child would give himself would probably be found without very much reflection. In most cases the questions we asked were entirely new to the subject, and the answers were dictated by the feelings which the game had aroused in them in varying intensity. Thus, when the little ones tell us that rules have an adult origin and have never changed, one should beware of taking this as the expression of a systematic belief; all they mean is that the laws of the game must be left alone. And when, conversely, the older ones tell us that rules have varied and were invented by children, this belief is perhaps more thought out since it is held by more developed subjects, but it is still only valuable as an indication: the child simply means that he is free to make the law.

We may well ask ourselves, then, whether it is legitimate to question the child about such verbal beliefs, since these beliefs do not correspond to thought properly so called, and since the child's true thought lies much deeper, somewhere below the level of formulation. But in our opinion these beliefs have their interest because the same phenomena reappear in adult mental life and because the psychological facts lead by a series of intermediate steps to metaphysical systems themselves. What Pareto,[26] basing his relatively simple conclusions on such a wealth of erudition, has called ''derivations'' are really present in germ in our children's remarks about the origin of games. These remarks have no intellectual value, but they contain a very resistant, affective and social element—the ''residuum'' to quote Pareto again. To the residuum peculiar to the conforming attitude of the little ones correspond the derivations ''divine or adult origin'' and ''permanence in history.'' To the residuum peculiar to the more democratic attitude of the older children correspond the derivations ''natural (childish) origin'' and ''progress.''

One more fundamental question must still be discussed. How is it that democratic practice is so developed in the games of marbles played by boys of 11 to 13, whereas it is still so unfamiliar to the adult in many spheres of life? Of course it is easier to agree upon some subjects than on others, and feeling will not run so high on the subject of the rules of the ''Square'' as in an argument about the laws of property or the legitimacy of war. But apart from these questions (and after all, is it so obvious that social questions are more important to us than are the rules of a game to the child of 12?) there are others of greater psychological and sociological interest. For it must not be forgotten that the game of marbles is dropped towards the age of 14–15 at the latest. With regard to this game, therefore, children of 11–13 have no seniors. The following circumstance is important. Since they no longer have to endure the pressure of play-mates who impose their views by virtue of their prestige, the children whose reactions we have been studying are clearly able to become conscious of their autonomy much sooner than if the game of marbles lasted till the age of 18. In the same way, most of the phenomena which characterize adult societies would be quite other than they are if the average length of human life were appreciably different from what it is. Sociologists have tended to overlook this fact, though Auguste Comte pointed out that the pressure of one generation upon the other was the most important phenomenon of social life.

We shall have occasion to see, moreover, that towards the age of 11 the consciousness of autonomy appears in a large number of different spheres. Whether this is the repercussion of collective games on the whole moral life of the child is a question which will be taken up later.

[26]*Traité de Sociologie générale.*

Lawrence Kohlberg
THE CHILD AS A MORAL PHILOSOPHER

How can one study morality? Current trends in the fields of ethics, linguistics, anthropology and cognitive psychology have suggested a new approach which seems to avoid the morass of semantical confusions, value-bias and cultural relativity in which the psychoanalytic and semantic approaches to morality have foundered. New scholarship in all these fields is now focusing upon structures, forms and relationships that seem to be common to all societies and all languages rather than upon the features that make particular languages or cultures different.

For 12 years, my colleagues and I studied the same group of 75 boys, following their development at three-year intervals from early adolescence through young manhood. At the start of the study, the boys were aged 10 to 16. We have now followed them through to ages 22 to 28. In addition, I have explored moral development in other cultures—Great Britain, Canada, Taiwan, Mexico and Turkey.

Inspired by Jean Piaget's pioneering effort to apply a structural approach to moral development, I have gradually elaborated over the years of my study a typological scheme describing general structures and forms of moral thought which can be defined independently of the specific content of particular moral decisions or actions.

The typology contains three distinct levels of moral thinking, and within each of these levels distinguishes two related stages. These levels and stages may be considered separate moral philosophies, distinct views of the socio-moral world.

We can speak of the child as having his own morality or series of moralities. Adults seldom listen to children's moralizing. If a child throws back a few adult cliches and behaves himself, most parents—and many anthropologists and psychologists as well—think that the child has adopted or internalized the appropriate parental standards.

Actually, as soon as we talk with children about morality, we find that they have many ways of making judgments which are not "internalized" from the outside, and which do not come in any direct and obvious way from parents, teachers or even peers.

MORAL LEVELS

The *preconventional* level is the first of three levels of moral thinking; the second level is *conventional,* and the third *postconventional* or autonomous. While the preconventional child is often "well-behaved" and is responsive to cultural labels of good and bad, he interprets these labels in terms of their physical consequences (punishment, reward, exchange of favors) or in terms of the physical power of those who enunciate the rules and labels of good and bad.

This level is usually occupied by children aged four to 10, a fact long known to sensitive observers of children. The capacity of "properly behaved" children of this age to engage in cruel behavior when there are holes in the power structure is sometimes noted as tragic (*Lord of the Flies, High Wind in Jamaica*), sometimes as comic (Lucy in *Peanuts*).

The second or *conventional* level also can be described as conformist, but that is perhaps too smug a term. Maintaining the expectations and rules of the individual's family, group or nation is perceived as valuable in its own right. There is a concern not only with *conforming* to the individual's social order but in *maintaining,* supporting and justifying this order.

The *postconventional* level is characterized by a major thrust toward autonomous moral principles which have validity and application apart from authority of the groups or persons who hold them and apart from the individual's identification with those persons or groups.

MORAL STAGES

Within each of these three levels there are two discernible stages. At the preconventional level we have:

Stage 1: Orientation toward punishment and unquestioning deference to superior power. The physical consequences of action regardless of their human meaning or value determine its goodness or badness.

Stage 2: Right action consists of that which instrumentally satisfies one's own needs and occasionally the needs of others. Human relations are viewed in terms like those of the marketplace. Elements of fairness, of reciprocity and equal sharing are present, but they are always interpreted in a physical, pragmatic way. Reciprocity is a matter of "you scratch my back and I'll scratch yours" not of loyalty, gratitude or justice.

And at the conventional level we have:

Stage 3: Good-boy—good-girl orientation. Good behavior is that which pleases or helps others and is approved by them. There is much conformity to stereotypical images of what is majority or "natural" behavior. Behavior is often judged by intention—"he means well" becomes important for the first time, and is overused, as by Charlie Brown in *Peanuts*. One seeks approval by being "nice."

Stage 4: Orientation toward authority, fixed rules and the maintenance of the social order. Right behavior consists of doing one's duty, showing respect for authority and maintaining the given social order for its own sake. One earns respect by performing dutifully.

At the postconventional level, we have:

Stage 5: A social-contract orientation, generally with legalistic and utilitarian overtones. Right action tends to be defined in terms of general rights and in terms of standards which have been critically examined and agreed upon by the whole society. There is a clear awareness of the relativism of personal values and opinions and a corresponding emphasis upon procedural rules for reaching consensus. Aside from what is constitutionally and democratically agreed upon, right or wrong is a matter of personal "values" and "opinion." The result is an emphasis upon the "legal point of view," but with an emphasis upon the possibility of *changing* law in terms of rational considerations of social utility, rather than freezing it in the terms of Stage 4 "law and order." Outside the legal realm, free agreement and contract are the binding elements of obligation. This is the "official" morality of American government, and finds its ground in the thought of the writers of the Constitution.

Stage 6: Orientation toward the decisions of conscience and toward self-chosen *ethical principles* appealing to logical comprehensiveness, universality and consistency. These principles are abstract and ethical (the Golden Rule, the categorical imperative); they are not concrete moral rules like the Ten Commandments. Instead, they are universal principles of *justice,* of the *reciprocity* and *equality* of human rights, and of respect for the dignity of human beings as *individual persons*.

UP TO NOW

In the past, when psychologists tried to answer the question asked of Socrates by Meno "Is virtue something that can be taught (by rational discussion), or does it come by practice, or is it a natural inborn attitude?" their answers usually have been dictated, not by research findings on children's moral character, but by their general theoretical convictions.

Behavior theorists have said that virtue is behavior acquired according to their favorite general principles of learning. Freudians have claimed that virtue is superego-identification with parents generated by a proper balance of love and authority in family relations.

The American psychologists who have actually studied children's morality have tried to start with a set of labels—the "virtues" and "vices," the "traits" of good and bad character found in ordinary language. The earliest major psychological study of moral character, that of Hugh Hartshorne and Mark May in 1928–1930, focused on a bag of virtues including honesty, service (altruism or generosity), and self-control. To their dismay, they found that there were *no* character traits, psychological dispositions or entities which corresponded to words like honesty, service or self-control.

Regarding honesty, for instance, they found that almost everyone cheats some of the time, and that if a person cheats in one situation, it doesn't mean that he *will* or *won't* in another. In other words, it is not an identifiable character trait, *dis*honesty, that makes a child cheat in a given situation. These early researchers also found that people who cheat express as much or even more moral disapproval of cheating as those who do not cheat.

What Hartshorne and May found out about their bag of virtues is equally upsetting to the somewhat more psychological-sounding names introduced by psychoanalytic psychology: "superego-strength," "resistance to temptation," "strength of conscience," and the like. When recent researchers attempt to measure such traits in individuals, they have been forced to use Hartshorne and May's old tests of honesty and self-control and they get exactly the same results—"superego strength" in one situation predicts little to "superego strength" in another. That is, virtue-words like honesty (or superego-strength) point to certain behaviors with approval, but give us no guide to understanding them.

So far as one can extract some generalized personality factor from children's performance on tests of honesty or resistance to temptation, it is a factor of ego-strength or ego-control, which always involves non-moral capacities like the capacity to maintain attention, intelligent-task performance, and the ability to delay response. "Ego-strength" (called "will" in earlier days) has something to do with moral action, but it does not take us to the core of morality or to the definition of virtue. Obviously enough, many of the greatest evil-doers in history have been men of strong wills, men strongly pursuing immoral goals.

MORAL REASONS

In our research, we have found definite and universal levels of development in moral thought. In our study of 75 American boys from early adolescence on, these youths were presented with hypothetical moral dilemmas, all deliberately philosophical, some of them found in medieval works of casuistry.

On the basis of their reasoning about these dilemmas at a given age, each boy's stage of thought could be determined for each of 25 basic moral concepts or aspects. One such aspect, for instance, is "Motive Given for Rule Obedience or Moral Action." In this instance, the six stages look like this:

1. Obey rules to avoid punishment.
2. Conform to obtain rewards, have favors returned, and so on.
3. Conform to avoid disapproval, dislike by others.
4. Conform to avoid censure by legitimate authorities and resultant guilt.
5. Conform to maintain the respect of the impartial spectator judging in terms of community welfare.
6. Conform to avoid self-condemnation.

In another of these 25 moral aspects, the value of human life, the six stages can be defined thus:

1. The value of a human life is confused with the value of physical objects and is based on the social status or physical attributes of its possessor.
2. The value of a human life is seen as instrumental to the satisfaction of the needs of its possessor or of other persons.
3. The value of a human life is based on the empathy and affection of family members and others toward its possessor.
4. Life is conceived as sacred in terms of its place in a categorical moral or religious order of rights and duties.
5. Life is valued both in terms of its relation to community welfare and in terms of life being a universal human right.
6. Belief in the sacredness of human life as representing a universal human value of respect for the individual.

I have called this scheme a typology. This is because about 50 per cent of most people's thinking will be at a single stage, regardless of the moral dilemma involved. We call our types *stages* because they seem to represent an *invariant developmental sequence*. "True" stages come one at a time and always in the same order.

All movement is forward in sequence, and does not skip steps. Children may move through these stages at varying speeds, of course, and may be found half in and half out of a particular stage. An individual may stop at any given stage and at any age, but if he continues to move, he must move in accord with these steps. Moral reasoning of the conventional or Stage 3-4 kind never occurs before the preconventional Stage-1 and Stage-2 thought has taken place. No adult in Stage 4 has gone through Stage 6, but all Stage-6 adults have gone at least through 4.

While the evidence is not complete, my study strongly suggests that moral change fits the stage pattern just described. (The major uncertainty is whether all Stage 6s go through Stage 5 or whether these are two alternate mature orientations.)

HOW VALUES CHANGE

As a single example of our findings of stage-sequence, take the progress of two boys on the aspect "The Value of Human Life." The first boy Tommy, is asked "Is it better to save the life of one important person or a lot of unimportant people?". At age 10, he answers "all the people that aren't important because one man just has one house, maybe a lot of furniture, but a whole bunch of people have an awful lot of furniture and some of these poor people might have a lot of money and it doesn't look it."

Clearly Tommy is Stage 1: he confuses the value of a human being with the value of the property he possesses. Three years later (age 13) Tommy's conceptions of life's value are most clearly elicited by the question, "Should the doctor 'mercy kill' a fatally ill woman requesting death because of her pain?" He answers, "Maybe it would be good to put her out of her pain, she'd be better off that way. But the husband wouldn't want it, it's not like an animal. If a pet dies you can get along without it—it isn't something you really need. Well, you can get a new wife, but it's not really the same."

Here his answer is Stage 2: the value of the woman's life is partly contingent on its hedonistic value to the wife herself but even more contingent on its instrumental value to her husband, who can't replace her as easily as he can a pet.

Three years later still (age 16) Tommy's conception of life's value is elicited by the same question, to which he replies: "It might be best for her, but her husband—it's a human life—not like an animal; it just doesn't have the same relationship that a human being does to a family. You can become attached to a dog, but nothing like a human you know."

Now Tommy has moved from a Stage 2 instrumental view of the woman's value to a Stage-3 view based on the husband's distinctively human empathy and love for someone in his family. Equally clearly, it lacks any basis for a universal human value of the woman's life, which would hold if she had no husband or if her husband didn't love her. Tommy, then, has moved step by step through three stages during the age 10–16. Tommy, though bright (I.Q. 120), is a slow developer in moral judgment. Let us take another boy, Richard, to show us sequential movement through the remaining three steps.

At age 13, Richard said about the mercy-killing, "If she requests it, it's really up to her. She is in such terrible pain, just the same as people are always putting animals out of their pain," and in general showed a mixture of Stage-2 and Stage-3 responses concerning the value of life. At 16, he said, "I don't know. In one way, it's murder, it's not a right or privilege of man to decide who shall live and who should die. God put life into everybody on earth and you're taking away something from that person that came directly from God, and you're destroying something that is very sacred, it's in a way part of God and it's almost destroying a part of God when you kill a person. There's something of God in everyone."

Here Richard clearly displays a Stage-4 concept of life as sacred in terms of its place in a categorical moral or religious order. The value of human life is universal, it is true for all humans. It is still, however, dependent on something else, upon respect for God and God's authority; it is not an autonomous human value. Presumably if God told Richard to murder, as God commanded Abraham to murder Isaac, he would do so.

At age 20, Richard said to the same question: "There are more and more people in the medical profession who think it is a hardship on everyone, the person, the family, when you know they are going to die. When a person is kept alive by an artificial lung or kidney it's more like being a vegetable than being a human. If it's her own choice, I think there are certain rights and privileges that go along with being a human being. I am a human being and have certain desires for life and I think everybody else does too. You have a world of which you are the center, and everybody else does too and in that sense we're all equal."

Richard's response is clearly Stage 5, in that the value of life is defined in terms of equal and universal human rights in a context of relativity (''You have a world of which you are the center and in that sense we're all equal''), and of conern for utility or welfare consequences.

THE FINAL STEP

At 24, Richard says: ''A human life takes precedence over any other moral or legal value, whoever it is. A human life has inherent value whether or not it is valued by a particular individual. The worth of the individual human being is central where the principles of justice and love are normative for all human relationships.''

This young man is at Stage 6 in seeing the value of human life as absolute in representing a universal and equal respect for the human as an individual. He has moved step by step through a sequence culminating in a definition of human life as centrally valuable rather than derived from or dependent on social or divine authority.

In a genuine and culturally universal sense, these steps lead toward an increased *morality* of value judgment, where morality is considered as a form of judging, as it has been in a philosophic tradition running from the analyses of Kant to those of the modern analytic or ''ordinary language'' philosophers. The person at Stage 6 has disentangled his judgments of—or language about—human life from status and property values (Stage 1), from its uses to others (Stage 2), from interpersonal affection (Stage 3), and so on; he has a means of moral judgment that is universal and impersonal. The Stage-6 person's answers use moral words like ''duty'' or ''morally right,'' and he uses them in a way implying universality, ideals, impersonality: He thinks and speaks in phrases like ''regardless of who it was,'' or ''. . . I would do it in spite of punishment.''

ACROSS CULTURES

When I first decided to explore moral development in other cultures, I was told by anthropologist friends that I would have to throw away my culture-bound moral concepts and stories and start from scratch learning a whole new set of values for each new culture. My first try consisted of a brace of villages, one Atayal (Malaysian aboriginal) and the other Taiwanese.

My guide was a young Chinese ethnographer who had written an account of the moral and religious patterns of the Atayal and Taiwanese villages. Taiwanese boys in the 10–13 age group were asked about a story involving theft of food. A man's wife is starving to death but the store owner won't give the man any food unless he can pay, which he can't. Should he break in and steal some food? Why? Many of the boys said, ''He should steal the food for his wife because if she dies he'll have to pay for her funeral and that costs a lot.''

My guide was amused by these responses, but I was relieved: they were of course ''classic'' Stage-2 responses. In the Atayal village, funerals weren't such a big thing, so the Stage-2 boys would say, ''He should steal the food because he needs his wife to cook for him.''

This means that we need to consult our anthropologists to know what content a Stage-2 child will include in his instrumental exchange calculations, or what a Stage-4 adult will identify as the proper social order. But one certainly doesn't have to start from scratch. What made my guide laugh was the difference in form between the children's Stage-2 thought and his own, a difference definable independently of particular cultures.

Illustrations number 1 and number 2 indicate the cultural universality of the sequence of stages which we have found. Illustration number 1 presents the age trends for middle-class

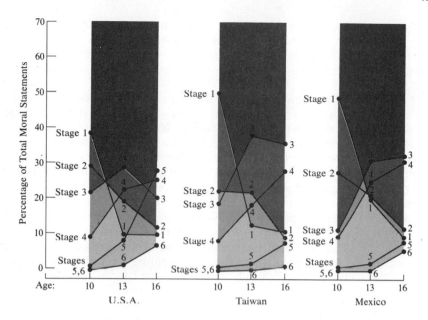

Figure 1. Middle-class urban boys in the U. S., Taiwan and Mexico. At age 10 the stages are used according to difficulty. At age 13, Stage 3 is most used by all three groups. At age 16 U. S. boys have reversed the order of age 10 stages (with the exception of 6). In Taiwan and Mexico, conventional (3–4) stages prevail at age 16, with Stage 5 also little used.

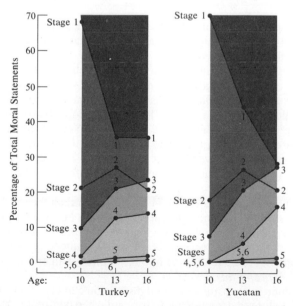

Figure 2. Two isolated villages, one in Turkey, the other in Yucatan, show similar patterns in moral thinking. There is no reversal of order, and preconventional (1–2) thought does not gain a clear ascendancy over conventional stages at age 16.

urban boys in the U. S., Taiwan and Mexico. At age 10 in each country, the order of use of each stage is the same as the order of its difficulty or maturity.

In the United States, by age 16 the order is the reverse, from the highest to the lowest, except that Stage 6 is still little-used. At age 13, the good-boy, middle stage (Stage 3), is not used.

The results in Mexico and Taiwan are the same, except that development is a little slower. The most conspicuous feature is that at the age of 16, Stage-5 thinking is much more salient in the United States than in Mexico or Taiwan. Nevertheless, it *is* present in the other countries, so we know that this is not purely an American democratic construct.

Illustration 2 shows strikingly similar results from two isolated villages, one in Yucatan, one in Turkey. While conventional moral thought increases steadily from ages 10 to 16 it still has not achieved a clear ascendancy over preconventional thought.

Trends for lower-class urban groups are intermediate in the rate of development between those for the middle-class and for the village boys. In the three divergent cultures that I studied, middle-class children were found to be more advanced in moral judgment than matched lower-class children. This was not due to the fact that the middle-class children heavily favored some one type of thought which could be seen as corresponding to the prevailing middle-class pattern. Instead, middle-class and working-class children move through the same sequences, but the middle-class children move faster and farther.

This sequence is not dependent upon a particular religion, or any religion at all in the usual sense. I found no important differences in the development of moral thinking among Catholics, Protestants, Jews, Buddhists, Moslems and atheists. Religious values seem to go through the same stages as all other values.

TRADING UP

In summary, the nature of our sequence is not significantly affected by widely varying social, cultural or religious conditions. The only thing that is affected is the *rate* at which individuals progress through this sequence.

Why should there be such a universal invariant sequence of development? In answering this question, we need first to analyze these developing social concepts in terms of their internal logical structure. At each stage, the same basic moral concept or aspect is defined, but at each higher stage this definition is more differentiated, more integrated and more general or universal. When one's concept of human life moves from Stage 1 to Stage 2 the value of life becomes more differentiated from the value of property, more integrated (the value of life enters an organizational hierarchy where it is "higher" than property so that one steals property in order to save life) and more universalized (the life of any sentient being is valuable regardless of status or property). The same advance is true at each stage in the hierarchy. Each step of development then is a better cognitive organization than the one before it, one which takes account of everything present in the previous stage, but making new distinctions and organizing them into a more comprehensive or more equilibrated structure. The fact that this is the case has been demonstrated by a series of studies indicating that children and adolescents comprehend all stages up to their own, but not more than one stage beyond their own. And importantly, *they prefer this next stage.*

We have conducted experimental moral discussion classes which show that the child at an earlier stage of development tends to move forward when confronted by the views of a child one stage further along. In an argument between a Stage-3 and Stage-4 child, the child in the third stage tends to move toward or into Stage 4, while the Stage-4 child understands but does not accept the arguments of the Stage-3 child.

Moral thought, then, seems to behave like all other kinds of thought. Progress through the moral levels and stages is characterized by increasing differentiation and increasing integration, and hence is the same kind of progress that scientific theory represents. Like acceptable scientific theory—or like *any* theory or structure of knowledge—moral thought may be considered partially to generate its own data as it goes along, or at least to expand so as to contain in a balanced, self-consistent way a wider and wider experiential field. The raw data in the case of our ethical philosophies may be considered as conflicts between roles, or values, or as the social order in which men live.

THE ROLE OF SOCIETY

The social worlds of all men seem to contain the same basic structures. All the societies we have studied have the same basic institutions—family, economy, law, government. In addition, however, all societies are alike because they *are* societies—systems of defined complementary roles. In order to *play* a social role in the family, school or society, the child must implicitly take the role of others toward himself and toward others in the group. These role-taking tendencies form the basis of all social institutions. They represent various patternings of shared or complementary expectations.

In the preconventional and conventional levels (Stages 1–4), moral content or value is largely accidental or culture-bound. Anything from "honesty" to "courage in battle" can be the central value. But in the higher postconventional levels, Socrates, Lincoln, Thoreau and Martin Luther King tend to speak without confusion of tongues, as it were. This is because the ideal principles of any social structure are basically alike, if only because there simply aren't that many principles which are articulate, comprehensive and integrated enough to be satisfying to the human intellect. And most of these principles have gone by the name of justice.

Behavioristic psychology and psychoanalysis have always upheld the Philistine view that fine moral words are one thing and moral deeds another. Morally mature reasoning is quite a different matter, and does not really depend on "fine words." The man who understands justice is more likely to practice it.

In our studies, we have found that youths who understand justice act more justly, and the man who understands justice helps create a moral climate which goes far beyond his immediate and personal acts. The universal society is the beneficiary.

William Kurtines and Esther B. Greif
AN EVALUATION OF KOHLBERG'S THEORY

Piaget's (1932) classic study, *The Moral Judgment of the Child,* provided the basis for much of the current psychological research in the area of moral judgment. His cognitive-developmental approach supplied a conceptual framework for the study of the growth of moral thought, and his "clinical method" furnished a widely used technique for assessing moral reasoning (e.g., Boehm, 1962; Haan, Smith, & Block, 1968; Kohlberg, 1969; MacRae, 1954; Rest, 1973; Turiel, 1966).

Perhaps the most influential and systematic extension of Piaget's theory and method can be found in the work of Kohlberg (1958, 1963a, 1963b, 1964, 1966a, 1966b, 1969). He has been instrumental in reviving and legitimizing the empirical study of moral development and has developed a major model of the growth of moral reasoning. Since its appearance in 1958, Kohlberg's paradigm has generated a great deal of research. Despite its demonstrated heuristic value, however, Kohlberg's model, like all theoretical systems, must ultimately be evaluated empirically. It is therefore timely and appropriate that some attempt be made to determine how well this model has stood the test of time. Before discussing the model in detail, it is useful to review the basic assumptions of Kohlberg's system.

KOHLBERG'S APPROACH

Kohlberg's theory of moral development has its historical roots in the developmental theories of Baldwin (1906) and Mead (1934). As previously noted, however, its more immediate conceptual foundations lie in the cognitive-developmental theory of Piaget (1932). For Piaget, intellectual development consists of the successive transformation of cognitive structures in response to both internal and external pressures. The sequence of this development is set by the structure of the mind. Since the evolution of moral reasoning is assumed to reflect cognitive development, the order of moral development is also preset. This sequence involves a shift from heteronomous reasoning, in which adult rules are viewed as sacred and immutable, to autonomous reasoning, in which rules are viewed as human products.

For Kohlberg, as for Piaget, the development of moral reasoning proceeds through an invariant sequence of stages. Kohlberg, however, defined *six* different steps, each characterized by a separate type of moral reasoning. Moral reasoning becomes more sophisticated as

From "The Development of Moral Thought: Review and Evaluation of Kohlberg's Approach," by W. Kurtines and E. B. Greif, *Psychological Bulletin,* 1974, *81,* pp. 453–470. Copyright 1974 by the American Psychological Association. Reprinted by permission.

The authors wish to thank Doris Entwisle, Robert Hogan, Constance Holstein, and Julian Stanley for their critical comments on an earlier version of this article.

development proceeds in a stepwise fashion through the stages. Ideally, the individual continues to develop until he is capable of reasoning and making judgments on the highest level (Stage 6). Kohlberg, like Piaget, viewed each stage as qualitatively different from the previous one. Each new stage is "a differentiation and integration of a set of functional contents present at the prior state [Kohlberg & Kramer, 1969, p. 99]."

Piaget's and Kohlberg's systems also differ on certain points. The primary differences lie in the number of stages of moral reasoning and the end point of development. Kohlberg's system is more highly differentiated; that is, it is based on six distinct stages rather than two general ones. The six developmental types are grouped into three moral levels and are shown in Table 1. Additionally, whereas for Piaget moral maturity is attained when an individual is capable of autonomous reasoning (for most people, around age 12), for Kohlberg moral maturity, defined as the capacity for principled (Stage 6) reasoning, is reached by very few people. Individuals who attain this level of moral reasoning do so in their late teens.

Table 1. Levels and stages of moral development

Level	*Stage*
I. Premoral level	1. Punishment and obedience orientation
	2. Naive instrumental hedonism
II. Morality of conventional role conformity	3. Good-boy morality of maintaining good relations, approval of others
	4. Authority-maintaining morality
III. Morality of self-accepted moral principles	5. Morality of contract and of democratically accepted law
	6. Morality of individual principles of conscience

Note. Data from Kohlberg (1963a, pp. 13–14).

The primary source for Kohlberg's derivation of his stages of moral reasoning was his doctoral dissertation (Kohlberg, 1958). To identify his stages of moral development, Kohlberg administered a variety of moral dilemmas to 72 middle-class and lower-class boys (ages 10, 13, and 16) in suburban Chicago. The dilemmas were designed to present "a conflict between habitual conformity to a rule or authority as against a utilitarian or 'greatest good' response to situational values and social value objects [1958, p. 77]. From examination of the boys' responses to these situations, Kohlberg "isolated" six developmental types of value orientations: (1) obedience and punishment, (2) naively egoistic, (3) good boy, (4) authority and social-order maintaining, (5) contractual legalistic, (6) conscience or principles (cf. Kohlberg, 1969). These types provided the basis for the six stages of reasoning previously discussed. As Kohlberg (1958) himself noted, however, "The number of types we came out with was eventually rather arbitrary, and undoubtedly determined by the limits of variation of our particular population [p. 89]."

THE MORAL JUDGMENT SCALE

Only one method has been used to assess Kohlberg's stages—the Moral Judgment Scale. The purpose of the scale is to determine an individual's stage of moral development by examining his moral judgments and moral reasoning. Additionally, because of the hierarchical nature of the stages, the Moral Judgment Scale defines the individual's level of moral maturity.

The only relatively complete description of this scale and its contents is Kohlberg's dissertation (1958). The Moral Judgment Scale is a structured projective test consisting of nine hypothetical dilemmas either invented by Kohlberg or adapted from other sources. These same dilemmas apparently were used to derive the stages which the scale measures. Since research using the scale seems to be affected by some of its characteristics (e.g., lack of standardized administration procedures, a variable scoring system, and other features), we examine each in turn.

Administration of the Scale

To use the Moral Judgment Scale, an interviewer presents a subject with one dilemma at a time and the person must make a judgment about the situation and then justify his choice. The following is a frequently used example:

> In Europe, a woman was near death from cancer. One drug might save her, a form of radium that a druggist in the same town had recently discovered. The druggist was charging $2,000, ten times what the drug cost him to make. The sick woman's husband, Heinz, went to everyone he knew to borrow the money, but he could only get together about half of what it cost. He told the druggist that his wife was dying and asked him to sell it cheaper or let him pay later. But the druggist said, ''No.'' The husband got desperate and broke into the man's store to steal the drug for his wife. Should the husband have done that? Why? [Kohlberg, 1969, p. 379].

The interviewer encourages the subject to respond freely and asks probing questions to elicit additional responses, all of which are recorded. Since these probing questions vary in accordance with the subject's original judgment, each person receives a different set of questions. Further, because administration of all nine dilemmas is time consuming (taking approximately two hours), few researchers use them all. In fact, in eight of the published studies covered in this review, the mean number of dilemmas administered was 6.1 (see Table 2). Moreover, these researchers rarely reported which of the nine dilemmas they used, thereby raising the possibility that different studies used different situations. This lack of a standardized scale content contributes further to the difficulty of evaluating research results because not all of the situations are equally effective for assessing moral reasoning (cf. Kohlberg, 1958, p. 91).

The administration of the Moral Judgment Scale, then, is time consuming and variable. Not only do interview questions differ across subjects, but the number and content of dilemmas presented also vary across studies. As a consequence, generalizability of research results is problematical.

Several researchers (e.g., Haan et al., 1968) have used a five-item written version of the scale. This shorter form would, if properly standardized, eliminate some of the administration problems associated with the longer interview procedure (e.g., lack of generalizability). However, no published information concerning this scale is available.

Scoring of the Moral Judgment Scale

Scoring of the Moral Judgment Scale is based not on a subject's specific judgment to each moral dilemma, but rather on the reasoning which he gives in support of his judgment. The scale is complex and difficult to score. Precise scoring instructions are available only from Kohlberg personally, and extensive training is necessary in order to score protocols correctly. Although published descriptions of the scoring procedures are discrepant (see Table 2 for a list of the various scoring systems cited in the literature), examination of the literature reveals two main methods for scoring the protocols: a global system and a detailed system.

For global scoring, a subject receives a stage rating for each dilemma. "These ratings are based on intuitive weighting by the rater of the various elements included [in the response] and imply some feel for the types as a whole and some experience of the range of possible responses [Kohlberg, 1958, p. 91]." Scores based on these ratings can be reported in two ways: One can report a score for each stage (thereby giving a profile of percentage usage of stages), or one can report the dominant stage alone.

The detailed scoring system is more complex. Here scores are assigned to each "thought-content" unit, defined as "all of a subject's utterances which, taken together, seems to express a single moral idea [Fodor, 1972, p. 258]." These responses are assigned scores in accordance with an elaborate coding scheme devised by Kohlberg (1958). The system is based on 30 "general aspects of morality" (Kohlberg, 1963a), each defined by a six-level scale. After all thought-content units are assigned to stages, percentages of responses at each stage are computed. Results are then reported in at least one of three ways. In some studies, profiles of responses are used for analyses (e.g., 40% Stage 1, 30% Stage 2, 20% Stage 3, 10% Stage 4, and 0% Stages 5 and 6; cf. Kohlberg, 1968). In other cases, a single total score is obtained by multiplying the percentage usage by weights assigned to each stage (e.g., $(0 \times 40) + (1 \times 30) + (2 \times 20) + (3 \times 10) + (4 \times 0) + (5 \times 0) + (6 \times 0) = 100$; cf. Fodor, 1972). This score is called a moral maturity score. Finally, in some studies analyses are based on only the dominant (modal) stage (e.g., Turiel, 1966) or on a mixed score (major and minor stages). From the detailed coding scheme, then, there appears to be three methods of reporting results. Combining these methods with the two possible ways for reporting results from the global scoring technique, one arrives at five possible combinations of scoring and reporting scores for the Moral Judgment Scale.

The variability and complexity of the scoring schemes for the Moral Judgment Scale have three major consequences for the evaluation of research conducted with the scale. First, the judgmental nature of the coding procedures introduces a potential for scorer bias. Standardized and objective scoring procedures would reduce the possibility of scores reflecting biases of individual judges. Second, the variability of scoring and reporting procedures confounds the interpretation of results. With both administration and scoring of the scale varying from study to study, it is difficult to estimate from the literature the extent to which results actually reflect differences among people. Finally, the intricate and often ambiguous nature of the scoring scheme almost surely discourages independent research, thereby preventing confirmation or disconfirmation of Kohlberg's model.

Other Features of the Scale

There are other features of the scale which may confound research results. First, the main characters in the dilemmas are male. Recognition of differential role expectations for males and females suggests that sex of the main character may influence an individual's judgments (cf. Magowan & Lee, 1970). It is not surprising then that, as defined by Kohlberg's scale, females appear to be less morally mature than males (Holstein, 1972; Kohlberg & Kramer, 1969).[1]

[1]C. B. Holstein. Moral Judgment Change in Early Adolescence and Middle Age: A Longitudinal Study. Paper presented at the biannual meeting of the Society for Research in Child Development, Philadelphia, March 1973.

Second, not all of the dilemmas are independent in content; some are continuations of previous stories. For example, after the situation in which Heinz steals the drug for his wife, there occurs a sequence in which we learn that the drug did not cure her and, with only a few months to live, she is in agonizing pain. The subject must make a judgment about the justification for mercy killing. Because the purpose of the Moral Judgment Scale is to assess underlying reasoning rather than responses to specific situations, the lack of independence of the dilemmas necessarily reduces the range of responses it can elicit.

In addition to these content considerations, the Moral Judgment Scale is subject to problems common to all projective measures. For example, there is considerable evidence that scores on projective tests are influenced by IQ, social class, and verbal facility (cf. Entwisle, 1972; Jensen, 1959; Magowan & Lee, 1970). Also, both the age and the sex of the interviewer could influence a subject's responses (cf. Masling, 1960). Children may respond differently to younger and older, or male and female interviewers. Moreover, the examiner's freedom to ask probing questions adds an additional opportunity for the operation of experimenter bias. As Kohlberg (1958) explained,

> [a child might] change and revise his decision . . . in response to what [he] . . . would see as "hints" in the probing as to what might be the answer preferred by the examiner. If one probes the reasons for a choice sufficiently, almost inevitably this probing is seen as implying that the choice is inadequate [pp. 118-119].

RELIABILITY

Reliability refers generally to accuracy of measurement. Ideally, a reliable instrument assesses a certain trait or characteristic in a consistent and stable manner. Because of chance error in measurement, however, perfect reliability is virtually impossible to obtain. Consequently, reliability estimates are necessary in order to make reasonable interpretations of the scale scores (cf. Anastasi, 1968; Stanley, 1971).

Measurement theory bases reliability of scores on the distinction between true variation and error variation: The larger the ratio of true to error (or total) variance, the greater the reliability of a measure. Because many factors contribute to test variances, "their allocation to true and error variance could rightly be considered to be dependent upon the conditions and purposes of testing [Stanley, 1971, p. 363]." Thus determination of reliability involves not only use of statistical procedures but also a consideration of the functions of the test.

There are two major categories of scale reliability—estimates of temporal stability and estimates of internal consistency. Both deal with interindividual accuracy of measurement. The first is concerned with the stability of scores over time and the second, with homogeneity of measurement. In addition to scale reliability, it is also necessary to estimate the accuracy of individual scores and (in the case of subjective scoring) interscorer agreement. Intraindividual accuracy is usually assessed by estimating the standard error of measurement of a scale, and interrater reliability is commonly estimated by measuring agreement among independent scorers.

Temporal Stability

An estimate of the stability with which the Moral Judgment Scale measures a given individual's stage of moral reasoning would indicate the degree to which such scores reflect actual characteristics of the individual rather than random fluctuations resulting from the testing session. Because accurate assessment of stages is crucial for testing the assumptions of Kohlberg's model (e.g., invariance of sequence, reorganization of stages), an estimate of temporal stability is important.

Both test–retest and parallel form reliability measure stability of scores across time. Thus, an estimate of the temporal stability of the Moral Judgment Scale would indicate the degree to which an individual whose judgments fell at Stage 4 at Time 1 would also score at Stage 4 at Time 2. In all the published studies employing the Moral Judgment Scale, there are no reported estimates of temporal stability.

Consistency

Other forms of reliability concern homogeneity of test items. Applied to the Moral Judgment Scale, a consistency measure would estimate the degree to which dilemmas assess a similar dimension (viz., maturity of moral reasoning). While empirically keyed tests need not be homogeneous, a rationally devised test such as the Moral Judgment Scale should have considerable item homogeneity. If each dilemma taps a unique dimension, adding scores across dilemmas would be meaningless. For a total score to make sense, then, covariation among items must be positive and appreciable.

Several methods are available for assessing this type of reliability. The Kuder–Richardson coefficient, for example, estimates interitem consistency on the basis of intercorrelations among items. Split-half reliability involves a correlation between two comparable halves of a test. Although these procedures are applicable to the Moral Judgment Scale, there are no estimates of internal consistency to be found anywhere in the research literature.

Standard Error of Measurement

The most common way to assess the accuracy of an individual's test score is with the standard error of measurement, that is, the standard deviation of an individual's score. Suppose, for example, that a subject's score on the Moral Judgment Scale falls at Stage 3. Without an estimate of the standard error of measurement, one does not know whether this is $3 \pm .2$, 3 ± 1.2, or even 3 ± 3.0. Knowledge of the standard error of measurement not only clarifies the meaning of individual scores, it also facilitates the comparison of scores among individuals. Further, it is particularly important for the Moral Judgment Scale because a majority of an individual's responses are rarely at his modal stage. For example, a subject whose modal stage is 5 may have 45% of his responses at this stage, with 35% of his responses at Stage 4 and 20% at Stage 6. There are no reported estimates of this form of reliability in the published research literature.

Interrater Reliability

Interrater reliability indicates the degree to which independent raters agree concerning the nature of an individual's responses to a test item. Thus, it focuses on the scoring of a scale rather than the scale itself. This type of reliability, appropriate for subjectively scored instruments, has been reported for the Moral Judgment Scale.

The first estimates of interscorer reliability for the Moral Judgment Scale were reported by Kohlberg (1958). Product-moment correlations for global ratings for two of the nine dilemmas (2 and 7), using two raters (one of whom was Kohlberg), were .64 ($n = 44$) and .79 ($n = 36$). According to Kohlberg, differences in reliability between the situations are probably not random; rather, ''This may be due to the differential values of the questions in representing the typology [p. 91].'' If this is in fact the case, then reliability information for all dilemmas would help to determine which are the more scorable. Kohlberg did not compute reliability estimates for the detailed scoring system because ''The coding operation, as opposed to the ratings, appeared to be concrete and objective enough to obviate assessing reliabilities [p. 92].''

Table 2 summarizes the studies reporting interscorer reliabilities for the Moral Judgment Scale.

Many other studies using the Moral Judgment Scale report no new interrater reliability, relying instead on previous estimates; these studies do not appear in Table 2. The correlations indicate an acceptable degree of reliability. A measure of actual agreement would be helpful for interpreting the scoring procedures, since the use of the product-moment correlation coefficient does not necessarily indicate absolute agreement between judges. For example, if Judge 1 rated Dilemmas 1 to 4 as representative of Stages 2, 3, 2, and 2, respectively; and Judge 2 rated the same dilemmas as representative of Stages 4, 5, 4, and 4, the product-

Table 2. Summary of published interscorer reliability estimates for the Moral Judgment Scale

Study	Number of response protocols used	Number of dilemmas	Scoring procedure	Reliability estimate[a]
Product-moment correlations				
Fodor (1969)	10	9	detailed	.85
Fodor (1972)	10	9	detailed	.85[b]
Haan, Smith, & Block (1968)[c]	957	5	detailed	.82
Keasey (1971)	20	5	detailed	.87
Ruma & Mosher (1967)	10	6	not stated	.84
Turiel (1966)	48	9	detailed for one scorer; global for one scorer	.78
Interscorer agreement				
Haan, Smith, & Block (1968)	not given	5	detailed	85%
Rest, Turiel, & Kohlberg (1969)	not given	2	detailed	71%[d]
Saltzstein, Diamond, & Belenky (1972)	not given[e]	4	global	86%

[a]All estimates are based on correlations between two raters unless otherwise noted.
[b]Represents the mean correlation based on scoring by four raters.
[c]This study used the written version of the Moral Judgment Scale.
[d]Method of computation was not reported.
[e]The authors stated that agreement was based on 166 comparisons.

moment correlation would be 1.0, but the judges would not be in agreement on any of their ratings. There are some such estimates for certain subsets of items in the literature.

Haan et al. (1968), for example, provided such an estimate for five situations. By defining agreement as "either complete (both major and minor), major code only, or reversals of major and minor designations [p. 187]," they found that agreement between the two judges was 85%. Other studies report agreement of 71% and 86% (Rest, Turiel, & Kohlberg, 1969; Saltzstein, Diamond, and Belenky, 1972). Thus, these findings suggest that scoring for some dilemmas can be replicated. Evidence for the interscorer reliability of the entire coding and scoring procedure, however, would facilitate research in the area.

VALIDITY

Validity, in its most general sense, requires that a measure perform as would be expected on the basis of its underlying concepts. There are several methods for estimating validity (cf. Cronbach, 1971), two of which are particularly salient for this review. The first, predictive validity, concerns the effectiveness of a scale in predicting an external criterion. The second, construct validity, concerns the relationship between a scale and the theory from which it is derived. While the first form of validity can often be assessed more or less directly, construct validation is an inferential process which closely resembles the more general phenomenon of theory construction. Thus, a measure must be embedded in a "nomothetic" net, a matrix of empirical and logical relationships which provide its meaning (cf. Cronbach & Meehl, 1955).

Predictive Validity

Kohlberg's framework does not require a relationship between moral reasoning and moral action. Theoretically, individuals at different stages can exhibit the same behaviors using different types of reasoning, whereas individuals at the same stage can exhibit different behaviors using the same type of reasoning. However, Kohlberg (1969) himself suggested that there should be some relationship between moral reasoning and moral action, and several studies contain information bearing on this relationship. In order to justify six distinct stages, each stage should contribute to the prediction of nontest criteria, that is, all six stages should make better predictions than any subset of stages. The following review is neither detailed nor exhaustive; however, it does illustrate both the variety of procedures employed to validate the Moral Judgment Scale and the model of moral development, and the actual predictive utility of the six stages of moral reasoning.

The first study, by Haan et al. (1968), constitutes perhaps the major application of Kohlberg's technique to real world data. Among other things, the study attempted to identify differences in political and social activism associated with Kohlberg's stages. The study used two samples of college students and a group of Peace Corps volunteers. Level of moral reasoning was determined from a self-administered, five-dilemma version of the Moral Judgment Scale. Using the detailed scoring technique, three judges trained by Kohlberg rated the protocols. Because only individuals "who could be assigned to one or another of five 'pure' moral types according to their responses to the Moral Judgment Scale [1968, p. 184]" were retained, 46% of the responding sample was excluded from the data analysis.

The most interesting behavioral findings concerned the activism–nonactivism criterion. Activism and nonactivism were defined as participation, or nonparticipation, in a free speech movement sit-in at Berkeley. For males, 75% of Stage 6 individuals were activists, 41% of Stage 5, 6% of Stage 4, and 18% of Stage 3 people were activists. However, the most striking finding of the study was the activism of Stage 2 males: 60% of them participated in the sit-in, the second highest percentage of the sample. The authors account for this unexpected finding with a distinction:

> Principled arrestees [Stage 6] were more concerned with the basic issues of civil liberties and rights and the relationship of students as citizens within a university community. The IRs' [Stage 2] reasons were more often concerned with their individual rights in a conflict of power [p. 198].

The results, however, indicate that actual behavior of Stage 2 and Stage 6 males was similar, which raises questions about the discriminant and predictive validity of the stages.

Schwartz, Feldman, Brown, and Heingartner (1969), using a sample of college students, examined differences among Kohlberg's stages of moral development along two dimensions of moral conduct (cheating and helpfulness). Cheating was defined as using prohibited information on a vocabulary test, and helpfulness was defined as a willingness to aid a confederate in an experiment in which such help entailed a loss on the subject's part. Level of moral thought was determined from responses to four situations from Kohlberg's scale. The protocols were scored by Kohlberg using a detailed method. After the level of development was determined, those subjects who scored above the median for the group were classified as "high in level of moral thought" and the others were classified as "low." Of the two dependent variables, only cheating was related to the moral types: Highs cheated significantly less than lows. This result does support a distinction between the high and low end of Kohlberg's scale; however, it provides no evidence for the predictive validity of the individual stages.

Ruma and Mosher (1967) examined the relationship between several measures of guilt and Kohlberg's stages of development. Using a sample of 36 delinquent boys, they measured guilt with four separate indexes (e.g., the Mosher Guilt Scale) and assessed level of moral reasoning with six of Kohlberg's dilemmas. Ruma, who was trained by Kohlberg, scored the situations using the global method. Scores for level of moral reasoning were then intercorrelated with the measures of guilt. Three of the four measures were significantly related to level of moral reasoning, that is, higher moral reasoning was associated with higher measured guilt. Since, however, all but one of the subjects were at Stage 3 or below, the study provides no evidence for the validity of Stages 4, 5, and 6.

Fodor (1972) examined the relationship between delinquency and level of moral development. Using matched groups of delinquents and nondelinquents, he administered nine dilemmas from the Moral Judgment Scale. Protocols were analyzed using the detailed coding system and scores were computed by "weighing percentage usage by each stage by the score assigned that stage: i.e., from 0 to 5 [p. 258]." A comparison of mean scores for both groups revealed that delinquents received significantly lower scores than nondelinquents, thereby providing some validational support for the stages. However, Fodor also noted that mean scores for both groups fell at Stage 3, indicating that dominant stage does not distinguish between delinquents and nondelinquents. It is also worth noting that this study, like the one by Ruma and Mosher (1967), had few, if any, subjects above Stage 4.

Finally, an article by Saltzstein et al. (1972) dealt with the relationship between conformance in an Asch-type situation (cf. Asch, 1951) and levels of moral reasoning. The sample consisted of 63 seventh-grade boys and girls. Conformity was assessed under two conditions: In the first, goal attainment was dependent upon group cooperation; in the second, it was dependent upon individual effort. Level of moral reasoning was determined with four situations using the interview technique. Protocols were scored by two of the authors and by

Kohlberg using both the detailed and global methods. Saltzstein et al. found that Stage 3 subjects conformed most, Stages 2 and 1 next, and Stages 4, 5, and 6 least. These results provide only ambiguous evidence for a systematic relationship between measured level of moral reasoning and conformity. For example, while it is clear that Stage 3 types are conformers, there are no reported differences in the conformance of persons at Stages 4, 5, and 6.

Although this brief review is not exhaustive, it is representative and serves to illustrate several points. First, while Kohlberg's stages are moderately effective in discriminating between unsophisticated and sophisticated reasoning, there seems to be no evidence that each of the six stages by itself has discriminant validity or predictive utility. Second, it is hard to distinguish among the final three stages on the basis of existing evidence. Moreover, few published studies have included any sizable number of Stage 5 and Stage 6 types. In the study by Haan et al. (1968) in which these stages are represented, the results indicate that Stage 2 males are similar to Stage 6 males in their behavior. Finally, although the scale scores seem to have some behavioral correlates, it is not clear, for example, how Stage 3 delinquents (Fodor, 1972) differ from Stage 3 conformers (Saltzstein et al., 1972) or from Stage 2 political demonstrators (Haan et al., 1968); or why Haan et al. (1968) found such a high percentage of Stage 2 subjects among college students, while Schwartz et al. (1969), using a college sample, found none.

Construct Validity

Several lines of evidence are used to support two major assumptions of Kohlberg's model, namely, the invariant sequence and qualitative nature of the six stages of development. This is a problem in construct validation.

Rest, Turiel, and Kohlberg (1969) defined an invariant sequence as one

> in which attainment of an advanced stage is dependent on the attainment of each of the preceding stages. It is further assumed that a more advanced stage is not simply an addition to a less advanced stage, but represents a reorganization of less advanced levels [p. 226].

In this article, Rest et al. stated that there are four major forms of evidence for the propositions of invariance and reorganization:

> age trends in various cultures and social classes supporting the ordering of the stages (Kohlberg, 1968); a Guttman "quasi-simplex" pattern in the correlations between the stages (Kohlberg, 1963[a]); and longitudinal studies of individual development (Kohlberg, 1970). Experimental evidence comes from a study by Turiel (1966), which is the point of departure for the present research [p. 226].

Two issues are at stake here (i.e., invariance and reorganization of stages) and each of the four forms of evidence is not necessarily relevant to both propositions. This evidence constitutes the primary construct validity for both Kohlberg's measure of moral judgment and his theory of moral development; consequently, we examine each form of evidence in detail.

The first type of support for the notion of an invariant development sequence in the stages of moral judgment comes from cross-cultural trends. To demonstrate age trends in the development of moral reasoning, Kohlberg (1968) presented some data from an apparently unpublished study of moral reasoning in children in America, Taiwan, Mexico, Turkey, and

Yucatan. Quantitative information concerning any of the samples is missing from the article (e.g., sample size is unspecified, characteristics of subjects are omitted, actual percentage scores are absent, range and standard deviation of scores are not reported). Further, there is no description of the method used to determine stage of moral reasoning in the various groups of cultures. The only usable information comes from five graphs (one for each country) which contain the mean percentage of children's responses at each of the six stages of moral reasoning for three different age levels (10, 13, and 16 years).

The pattern of percentages of judgments on the graphs seem to lend moderate support for age trends across the first three stages. For example, the percentage of Stage 1 judgments does appear to decrease with increasing age (e.g., age 10 = 40%, age 13 = 10%, age 16 = 10%, for the American sample). However, because information concerning the actual number of children tested, the number of responses involved, the method of scoring, and the standard deviation of scores were all unreported, the actual size and significance of this decrease remains unclear. In view of the unknown reliability of the Moral Judgment Scale, this deficiency is an important one. Conclusions concerning the invariance of the first three stages, therefore, are at best tentative and ambiguous.

Evidence to support the invariance of the final three stages is less convincing. Further inspection of the graphs presented by Kohlberg (1968) reveals that, while approximately 7% of the 16-year-olds in America and Mexico used moral reasoning at Stage 6, 1% or less of the 16-year-olds in Taiwan reasoned at this stage. Moreover, *none* of the children in either Turkey or Yucatan were able to reach even Stage 5. Thus, Stage 5 reasoning is missing in two of the five samples, and Stage 6 reasoning is absent in three of the samples. Age trends in Stages 5 and 6 are clearly present only in the United States sample—the same group Kohlberg (1958) used to derive the stages.

In a 1967 study, Kohlberg reported this cross-cultural data in support of invariant age trends in the stages of development. This report presents only two of the original five samples. With regard to the absence of Stage 6 reasoning in the Taiwan sample, Kohlberg observed,

> In general, the cross-cultural studies suggest a similar sequence of development in all cultures, although they suggest that the last two stages of thought do not develop clearly in preliterate village or tribal communities [p. 170].

In addition to being an inaccurate description of Taiwanese society, the absence of individuals in the final stages provides no evidence for age trends in these stages. Further, these data provide no support for the claim that the stages are universal.

The presence of response shifts in young children lends some support to the notion of age trends in moral reasoning in general. It does not, however, provide support for either the assumption of the sequential invariance of the stages or the qualitative nature of the stages. Kohlberg (1963a) has acknowledged that age trends themselves are not adequate evidence for his sequence of stages. As he observed,

> While the age trends indicate that some modes of thought are generally more difficult or advanced than other modes of thought, they do not demonstrate that attainment of each mode of thought is prerequisite to the attainment of the next higher in a hypothetical sequence [pp. 15–16].

Thus, cross-cultural evidence for age trends, even if it were well documented, would provide no support for an invariant sequence of development.

"If our stages of moral thinking are to be taken as supporting the developmental view of moralization," said Kohlberg (1963a), "evidence . . . of sequentiality is required [p. 15]."

The second major form of evidence for the invariant sequence comes from a Guttman "quasi-simplex" pattern of correlations among the stages (Kohlberg, 1958, 1963a). Kohlberg (1958) explained that Guttman's simplex is not an appropriate procedure because the stages in his model are not cumulative, but rather each new stage involves a restructuring of a previous stage. Therefore, he adopted the quasi-simplex procedure.

Using the original sample of 72 boys (ages 10 to 16), a single correlation matrix was derived from the intercorrelations of percentages of moral judgments made at each stage. If development proceeds sequentially, then adjacent stages should correlate more highly with each other than with more distant stages. Examination of the correlations in the matrix indicates that the general pattern is in the expected direction: In most cases, correlations decrease as one moves horizontally or vertically from the diagonal in the matrix (see Table 3).

Closer examination reveals, however, that the quasi-simplex provides no direct support

Table 3. Quasi-simplex correlation matrix

Type of moral judgment	(Level I)		(Level II)		(Level III)	
	1	2	3	4	5	6
1	—					
2	.55	—				
3	−.41	−.19	—			
4	−.52	−.41	.18	—		
5	−.52	−.58	.09	.00	—	
6	−.37	−.43	−.29	−.07	.23	—

Note. Data from Kohlberg (1958).

for the invariance of the six stages. The correlations were computed for the stages in order, 1 through 6. Suppose, however, that one reversed the order of pairs of stages in each of the three levels (instead of 1, 2; 3, 4; 5, and 6 make the order 2, 1; 4, 3; 6, and 5), how would the pattern of correlations change? Table 4 contains an appropriately revised version of the matrix. As can be seen, the pattern of correlations is similar to that found in the first matrix; thus, each matrix seems to provide support for an invariant sequence of stages.

An even more serious criticism of this form of evidence centers on the sample used. Specifically, the correlations are based on moral reasoning responses of Kohlberg's (1958) original sample. Thus, the same responses used to derive the stage sequence are also used to

Table 4. Revised quasi-simplex correlation matrix

Type of moral judgment	(Level I)		(Level II)		(Level III)	
	2	1	4	3	6	5
2	—					
1	.55	—				
4	−.41	−.52	—			
3	−.19	−.41	.18	—		
6	−.43	−.37	−.07	−.29	—	
5	−.58	−.52	.00	.09	.23	—

provide evidence for the sequentiality of the stages. This is analogous to validating a test on the same sample from which it was derived. The lack of independence in the matrix greatly reduces the credibility of the quasi-simplex analysis.

The third form of evidence offered in support of the invariant sequence of Kohlberg's six stages of moral thought comes, according to Rest et al. (1969), from longitudinal studies of individual development. The only relevant published longitudinal data are contained in a study by Kohlberg and Kramer (1969). Based on Kramer's dissertation, the study is a follow-up of Kohlberg's original (1958) sample. Moral judgment scores were obtained for middle-class and lower-class men. Within the middle-class sample, 29 subjects were 16 years old, 16 were 20 years old, and 13 were 24 years old. In the lower-class sample, 35 subjects were 16 years old, 18 were 20 years old, and 8 were 24 years old. Moral reasoning was determined using the global method. No information is presented concerning the number of dilemmas used, the number of raters, or the interrater reliability.

To demonstrate the developmental invariance of the six stages, Kohlberg and Kramer presented two graphs (for middle-class and lower-class boys) of moral judgment profiles at three ages. There were few significant changes in the moral judgment profiles of the samples over time, indicating that development (as Kohlberg defined it) is virtually complete by age 16. In both samples, at ages 16, 20, and 24, Stage 4 responses were more frequent than any other type, suggesting (as do several other studies) that the baseline response for most people is Stage 4. Not only do few people reach Stages 5 and 6, but there is no evidence in the study to show that (a) people who reach Stage 4 have gone through Stages 1, 2, and 3, and (b) people pass through these stages in a specified order. One can equally conclude that individuals skip from stage to stage in a random fashion. Finally, college students actually had lower stage scores than high school students. Although interpreted as a regression, the downward shift seems to indicate that the stage sequence is flexible. Thus, this longitudinal study provides no clear evidence for either the invariant developmental sequence or the reorganization of stages as postulated by Kohlberg.

The final important source of evidence for an invariant sequence comes from a series of experimental studies (Rest, 1973; Rest et al., 1969; Turiel, 1966). Overall, these studies provide some support for both sequential and hierarchical organization of the earlier stages of development. However, they fail to support the sequence for the last three stages. In the first study, Turiel (1966) attempted experimentally to induce changes in the stages of moral reasoning. The second two studies (Rest, 1973; Rest et al., 1969) were attempts to assess preference and comprehension for the type of reasoning that characterizes each of Kohlberg's stages.

Turiel's study used 44 middle-class boys ranging in age from 12 years 0 months to 13 years 7 months. The experimental procedure was designed to test two main hypotheses: (a) The six stages of moral judgment form an invariant sequence, and (b) each stage represents a reorganization and displacement of the preceding stages. From these hypotheses, Turiel predicted that (a) because the sequence of development is fixed, subjects will be influenced more by reasoning one stage above their dominant stage than by reasoning further above, and (b) because the stages are progressively reorganized, subjects will reject reasoning at lower stages.

The design involved a pretest, to determine a subject's dominant moral stage; an experimental session, to expose subjects to moral reasoning different from their own; and a posttest interview, to assess the influence of the experimental procedure. The addition of a control group made the design a simple pretest-posttest control group design. While this procedure is unusually robust, allowing for the simultaneous control of a multitude of rival hypotheses (cf. Campbell & Stanley, 1966), a close examination of the study reveals that results were analyzed incorrectly and that the only meaningful comparisons produced negligible results. Because this study is frequently cited as major evidence for the invariant sequence of development, it must be examined in detail.

Initially, six dilemmas from the Moral Judgment Scale were administered to 69 males. Dominant stage of moral reasoning was determined by using both the global rating procedure and the detailed coding method. Because of difficulty in the classification of some people, 25 subjects were dropped from the sample leaving a total of 44 subjects. These subjects were assigned randomly to one of three treatment groups or to a control group ($n = 11$ per cell). After a two-week interval, subjects in the three experimental groups returned for the experimental procedures. During this phase, boys in each group were exposed to moral reasoning one stage below (-1 condition), one stage above ($+1$ condition), or two stages above ($+2$ condition) their own level of moral reasoning. The control group did nothing.

The final step of the experiment (the posttest) was conducted one week after the experimental manipulation when the experimental groups were retested using all nine situations (the same six used in the pretest plus the same three used in the experimental manipulation). The control group was retested with all nine situations three weeks after the pretest.

The obtained results were analyzed in two parts; both analyses are complex and difficult to understand. In the first and more confounded analysis, posttest responses to the same three situations used in the treatment conditions were examined. These scores were called the "direct scores" because "the experimental subjects were directly influenced on those three situations [Turiel, 1966, p. 614]." Direct scores were represented in terms of the average percentage of stage usage. For each of the three treatment groups and for the control group, responses were reported as -1, 0, $+1$, or $+2$ relative to the initial dominant stage of the subjects. Of all possible comparisons, two have direct relevance for the hypotheses of invariance and reorganization: (a) comparisons of the number of $+1$ scores in the $+1$ treatment group with the number of -1 scores of the -1 treatment group and the number of $+2$ scores of the $+2$ treatment group and (b) comparison of the number of $+1$ scores of the $+1$ treatment group with $+1$ scores of all other groups. That is, according to the hypotheses of invariance and reorganization, people in the $+1$ treatment group should show a larger treatment effect than people in either the -1 treatment group or the $+2$ treatment group. For the first comparisons, control group scores were subtracted out, although the justification for this procedure is unexplained. A one-tailed t test between the corrected mean scores of the $+2$ treatment group and $+1$ treatment group did reach significance ($t = 3.55$, $p < .005$), suggesting that the $+1$ treatment was more effective than the $+2$ treatment. However, the one-tailed t test between the corrected mean scores of the -1 treatment group and the $+1$ treatment group was not significant ($t = 1.43$, $p < .10$). Thus, there appears to be no significant difference between the $+1$ and -1 treatments; both seem equally effective. (Turiel claimed that his hypothesis was supported because the results reached a "borderline level of significance"; this, however, is not true by usual standards.)

Additional support would be provided for the hypotheses of invariance and reorganization if it could be shown that the $+1$ treatment was generally more effective than the -1 treatment. Turiel (1966) claimed that the number of $+1$ scores of the $+1$ treatment group was higher than the number of $+1$ scores of any other treatment group. This claim is at best ambiguous, however, since the actual ts are unreported. Further, Turiel claimed that the number of -1 scores of the -1 treatment group was not significantly higher than the -1 scores of any other treatment group. For support, he noted that the difference between the -1 scores of both the -1 treatment group and the control group "did not reach significance"

($t = 1.66$, $p < .10$). This difference, however, is larger than the borderline level of significance ($t = 1.43$) offered in support of the major comparison ($+1$ and -1 scores). Thus, this secondary analysis provides only inconclusive support for the hypotheses of invariance and reorganization.

Even if the results were clear-cut, this entire analysis would still lack credibility because it is also confounded by a memory effect. During the experimental conditions, subjects were told possible responses to three moral dilemmas; in the posttest, they were asked to provide responses to the same dilemmas. Thus, rather than demonstrating the effects of the treatments, results obtained from subjects' responses may merely reflect the effects of memory, learning, and suggestion.

Turiel's second and only valid analysis compared pretest and posttest change scores. Each subject's scores on the six-item pretest were subtracted from his posttest scores for the same six items. This change score, called the "indirect score," reflected the effect of the experimental procedures. That is, pretest-posttest changes in an individual's moral reasoning were considered to reflect the exposure to reasoning different from his own.

Mean indirect scores were presented in a table according to treatment (-1, $+1$, $+2$, control) and stage level relative to pretest dominant stage (-1, 0, $+1$, $+2$). No variability measures were presented. There are three important points to note about the table. First, it is impressive in terms of the small effect due to the treatments. The mean change for all groups (disregarding signs) was 2.2%; the modal change was zero. It is little wonder, then, that Turiel reported "The evidence is only suggestive since significant findings were minimal [1966, p. 616]."

The second point to note in this table is that the mean change scores of the control group illustrate the probable unreliability of the Moral Judgment Scale. As noted above, none of the treatments produced any clear-cut effects. Thus, it is interesting to examine the change scores of the control group. In the interval between the pretest and the posttest, the dominant stage scores of the control group decreased by 6.1%. This change was the largest obtained in the study. Furthermore, the largest change for any treatment group was a 5.7% move by the -1 group to the -1 stage, indicating that if there were any differences, the -1 treatment was more effective than $+1$ treatment. The second largest treatment change was a 4.5% increase in the $+1$ scores of the $+1$ treatment group. Over the same period of times, however, the -1 scores of the control group also increased by 4.5%. This suggests that the control group spontaneously regressed in its moral judgments as far as the critical treatment group progressed. Thus, the low reliability of the dependent variable may have confounded the obtained results. Consequently, the instability of the moral judgment scores leaves open to question any interpretation of the observed changes in the treatment groups.

Third, the only comparisons that seem directly relevant to the hypothesis that the stages form an invariant sequence are those between the $+1$ change scores of the $+1$ treatment group and the -1 and $+2$ change scores of the comparable treatment groups. Once again, according to the hypotheses of invariance and reorganization, the $+1$ treatment should show a larger effect than either the -1 treatment group or the $+2$ treatment group.

The one-tailed t test indicated that the corrected mean[2] $+2$ change score of the $+2$ treatment group was statistically smaller than the $+1$ change score of the $+1$ treatment group ($t = 2.70$, $p < .025$). A second one-tailed t test between the corrected mean -1 change

---

[2]Corrected mean change scores were obtained by subtracting control group mean change scores from treatment group mean change scores.

score of the -1 treatment group and the $+1$ change score of the $+1$ treatment group was not significant, although Turiel claimed that it reached a "borderline level of significance $(t = 1.46, p < .10)$ [1966, p. 616]." Thus, the evidence for invariance of sequence or reorganization of stages is unconvincing.

Overall, Turiel's study provides only minimal support for the hypotheses of invariance and reorganization in the development of moral judgment. The results are qualified by several considerations. First, his article presented only two t tests directly relevant to the hypotheses of invariance and reorganization, and the actual differences obtained for these crucial comparisons were not significant. Second, treatment effects were quite small. While not necessarily problematic in itself, when interpreted in light of the possible unreliability of the dependent variable (the control group scores changed as much as the treatment group scores), the obtained significance levels become suspect. Additionally, the -1 treatment was at least as effective in eliciting change as was the $+1$ treatment. Third, due to constraints of the experimental design, none of Turiel's subjects were at the Stage 5 or 6 levels (since the subjects were presented with reasoning two stages above their present stage, no subject could be higher than Stage 4). This leaves entirely untested the question of the invariance of the final three stages. Finally, other studies (using similar designs) indicate that it is possible to induce significant changes in moral judgment that run counter to developmental expectations (e.g., Bandura & McDonald, 1963). Thus, although Turiel's study is often cited as providing support for an invariant sequence in the development of moral judgment, in fact it does not.

The final two studies (Rest, 1973; Rest et al., 1969) attempt to show that the sequence of the stages of development form a hierarchical organization. The hierarchy is conceived of as one of complexity; each higher stage is viewed as logically more complex than the lower ones. The implication is that moral development concerns the capacity for making increasingly more sophisticated moral judgments. Both studies provide some evidence that the stages, as defined by Kohlberg, constitute a hierarchy of logical complexity. That is, the higher stages do seem to be more logically complex than the lower ones. However, the evidence does not demonstrate that actual development follows these six stages.

Both studies are similar in design and attempt to assess preference and comprehension for the types of reasoning characteristic of each of the stages in Kohlberg's model. The first study (Rest, 1973) contained 45 fifth- and eighth-grade children; the second (Rest et al., 1969) used 47 twelfth-grade students. The subjects were first administered a subset of dilemmas from the Moral Judgment Scale and their dominant stages were determined. They were then grouped by stage and administered a booklet containing two of the remaining dilemmas. After reading the situations, the subjects read the "advice" of six friends. The advice of each friend was a pro and con argument for the solution to the dilemma. Each of the three sets of arguments was characteristic of the reasoning of stages below the subject's dominant stage (-1), directly above the subject's dominant stage $(+1)$, and two above the subject's dominant stage $(+2)$. Thus, the reasoning formed a continuum of simple-to-complex moral reasoning. After reading these arguments, subjects were asked to state which advice they thought best (preference) and to recapitulate the advice of each friend (comprehension).

Preference was consistently greater for moral reasoning higher than the subject's dominant stage. Comprehension was greater for the lower stages and decreased with higher stages. Thus, while the data do suggest that there is some shift in preference and comprehension (the subjects prefer stages above their own and comprehend those below), they do not show that the normal course of development (either within the individual or among groups) follows the six stages as defined by Kohlberg.

Counter Evidence

Few researchers employing Kohlberg's cognitive-developmental framework have reported findings which contradict the model. How can this relative absence of negative findings be explained? First, independent validation is made difficult by the nature of the scale itself. It has never been published and there is no readily available source of information describing its administration and scoring. Further, the methods and procedures concerning its use have changed continuously, although these modifications have not been publicly reported. The latest method of scoring is available only from Kohlberg himself. Second, the dearth of negative evidence may reflect the nature of the American research enterprise. As Entwisle (1972) remarked,

> Even a complete survey of the literature can be misleading . . . because of the often remarked tendency of American authors to publish only positive findings, with lesser findings never reaching an editor's desk or even being rejected there [p. 385].

There are several considerations which suggest that the evolution of moral reasoning may not be as Kohlberg described it. First, one can question Kohlberg's (1963a) statement that the various stages of moral reasoning

> represent structures emerging from the interaction of the child with his social environment, rather than directly reflecting external structures given by the child's culture [p. 30].

Several experimental studies (e.g., Bandura & McDonald, 1963; Cowan, Langer, Heaven-rich, & Nathanson, 1969; Prentice, 1972) have argued that moral judgments are directly affected by social influence. These studies all demonstrate that it is possible to induce changes in moral judgments that run counter to cognitive-developmental predictions. Bandura and McDonald, for example, found that "children's judgmental responses are readily modifiable, particularly through the utilization of adult modeling cues [1963, p. 280]." While interpretations of the meaning of these results have been variable (cf. Cowan et al., 1969), the implications of the data are clear—modes of moral thought are subject to social influence; consequently, one would not necessarily expect them to follow a preset order.

A second line of evidence suggesting that Kohlberg's six stages do not form an invariant sequence comes from cross-sectional and longitudinal data (Holstein, 1972, see also Footnote 1). Over a three-year period, Holstein administered a written version of the Moral Judgment Scale (five dilemmas) to 53 families (children ages 13 to 16 and parents). Protocols were scored by an experienced coder (trained by Kohlberg).

Holstein's (1972, see Footnote 1) research is important for two reasons: It provides a detailed look at some cross-sectional and longitudinal data on moral reasoning, and it offers a systematic study of sex differences using the Moral Judgment Scale. In general, neither the cross-sectional, longitudinal nor sex-difference data support the notion of an invariant developmental sequence. For example, Holstein's data provide no direct evidence that development over the three-year period proceeded in a stepwise fashion; they suggest that there was considerable skipping of stages and much regression among the final stages for both sexes. Furthermore, cross-sectional sex differences in modal response did not support the notion of an invariant sequence. For both the 16-year-old sample and the adult samples, the modal response for males was Stage 4, while at the same age the modal response for females was Stage 3. Kohlberg and Kramer (1969) noted this in their longitudinal study:

> while girls are moving from high school or college to motherhood, sizeable proportions of them

are remaining at Stage 3, while their male age mates are dropping Stage 3 in favor of the stages above it. Stage 3 personal concordance morality is a functional morality for housewives and mothers; it is not for businessmen and professionals [p. 108].

The obvious implication, according to the stage model, is that females are less developed in their moral reasoning than males.

The absence of support for a six-stage model does not imply that there are no trends in moral development. It simply indicates that Kohlberg's six specific stages may not be useful. There is some evidence to suggest that the reasoning which characterizes Kohlberg's final two stages can be viewed as alternative, but equally valid, forms of moral thought. For example, Hogan (1970) developed a 35-item scale designed to measure the disposition to adopt an instrumental or utilitarian attitude toward the law, as opposed to a disposition to invoke intuitive principles (Stages 5 and 6). The scale discriminates strongly between persons whose vocational choices reflect a belief in law and established procedures (e.g., policemen, ROTC seniors, etc.) and persons who believe in civil disobedience as a means for promoting social change. In addition, there are clear-cut personality differences between individuals characterized by both types of reasoning. Persons who invoke intuitive principles tend to be independent, innovative, and form creating; however, they also tend to be impulsive, opportunistic, and irresponsible. Persons who adopt utilitarian attitudes toward law are seen as reasonable, helpful, and dependable; on the other hand, they are also conventional and resistant to change. On the whole, the more mature individuals tend to cluster in the center of this dimension.

We have reviewed several sources of evidence which conflict with Kohlberg's model of moral development. These include results from experimental, cross-sectional, longitudinal, and personological research. Although most of this review concerned the absence of evidence for the invariance of Kohlberg's six stages of moral thought, there is also evidence indicating that the stages may not be invariant.

DISCUSSION

Research in the area of moral development has important implications for the understanding and explanation of human conduct. A great deal of work has been done using a cognitive model of moral development proposed by Kohlberg. As we have tried to show, however, the research done within this framework is beset with a multitude of problems which detract from the model's usefulness.

We divided these problems into four main areas. First, the intuitive derivation of the six stages of moral reasoning, which provide a foundation for this approach, resulted in an arbitrary set of stages whose general meaningfulness is not yet clear. Further, the scale developed to measure these stages of moral reasoning lacks standardization of both administration and scoring. Because the number of dilemmas used differs across studies, the actual content of the Moral Judgment Scale is constantly changing. This raises questions about the basis for comparison of results across studies; in effect, each study employs a unique scale. In the absence of evidence demonstrating that each dilemma taps the same cognitive dimension, there is no basis for making comparisons among studies using the Moral Judgment Scale. In addition to this limitation, meaningfulness is further attenuated by the absence of a standard scoring procedure. Until (a) a relationship between the global and detailed scoring schemes is established, (b) the reasons for using the five different schemes are elucidated, and (c) some general norms are published, interpretations of results obtained with the Moral Judgment Scale are tenuous. Finally and perhaps most importantly, the general unavailability of the scale discourages independent research. Since the Moral Judgment Scale is the only means of assessing Kohlberg's stages, the absence of a complete and systematic published exposition of the scale's derivation, content, and psychometric properties is inexplicable.

Second, the reliability of the scale needs to be demonstrated. After 15 years of research with the Moral Judgment Scale, there are *no* reported reliability estimates for the scale itself. Further, evidence from experimental studies indicates that scores on the scale fluctuate greatly even over short periods of time. The only reported estimates are for the scoring scheme and most studies fail to report independent estimates. Uncertainty about the accuracy of measurement limits the utility of the measure.

A third problem concerns the predictive validity of the model. The validities of both the Moral Judgment Scale and Kohlberg's conceptual model rest on the assumption that moral development follows a six-stage invariant sequence and that the Moral Judgment Scale can assess these six stages. We have reviewed several studies representative of attempts to relate scores on the Moral Judgment Scale to nontest criteria. Despite some evidence suggesting that general trends in development are related to behavior, there is no clearly demonstrated connection between moral judgment, as measured by the Moral Judgment Scale, and moral action. Overall, predictive validity is minimal. There is no evidence to indicate that the six distinct stages, and particularly the final three stages, add predictive power to the scale or model beyond that which would be obtained with a simple dichotomous classification of high–low or mature–immature. This would not be particularly troublesome if there were no theoretical reason to expect a relationship between moral reasoning and moral behavior. However, the relationship, if any, between moral reasoning and moral behavior has not been clarified.

Finally, there seems to be little actual construct validation for the scale or model. A careful examination of the four types of evidence offered in support of the invariant sequence (viz., cross-cultural, statistical, longitudinal, and experimental) revealed that in actuality results do not support clearly the major assumptions of the developmental model. General cross-cultural age trends in early development provide no support for qualitative differences between stages or their sequential invariance. While the pattern of correlations in the quasi-simplex provided some support for the sequence, order of the stages within levels does not seem immutable. Longitudinal data demonstrated only that most males are at Stage 4 morality. Not only did the data fail to show that people go through the stages in a preset order, but it also failed to demonstrate that people go through each of the distinct stages at all. Furthermore, there is no support for the view that each new stage is a reintegration of the previous one and therefore qualitatively different.

Not only is there no clear-cut evidence supporting the assumptions of invariance of stages and their hierarchical nature, but there is also evidence suggesting that these assumptions may be incorrect. Several researchers have demonstrated that different types of moral reasoning may be learned. Further, the cross-sectional and longitudinal data from Holstein's study provide evidence suggesting that people do not develop through the stages of moral reasoning in the order set by Kohlberg. Finally, there is some evidence questioning the order of the final stages. Hogan (1970), for example, maintained that contractual legalistic (positive law) and principled conscience (higher law) moralities are both equally defensible moral postures. He also provided evidence that personality differences are important determinants of an individual's style of moral reasoning. Several lines of evidence, then, seem to suggest that moral development may not proceed in the fashion described by Kohlberg's model.

In view of these many problems, it is difficult to make a definitive statement about the utility of Kohlberg's cognitive-developmental model of moral development. After 15 years of research, the general lack of evidence for the model is suggestive. The possibility remains that the stages do reflect actual development and that the general lack of evidence reflects the inadequacy of the measuring device used to assess the stages of moral reasoning. However, without additional information on the scale or an alternative way to assess stages of reasoning, we cannot know whether it is the scale, the model, or both that is problematic. Thus, we can only conclude that the value of the model remains to be demonstrated.

REFERENCES

Anastasi, A. *Psychological testing.* (3rd ed.) New York: Macmillan, 1968.

Asch, S. E. Effects of group pressure upon the modification and distortion of judgments. In H. Guetzkow (Ed.), *Groups, leadership and men.* Pittsburgh: Carnegie Press, 1951.

Baldwin, J. M. *Social and ethical interpretations in mental development.* New York: Macmillan, 1906.

Bandura, A., & McDonald, F. J. Influence of social reinforcement and the behavior of models in shaping children's moral judgments. *Journal of Abnormal and Social Psychology,* 1963, *67,* 274–281.

Boehm, L. The development of conscience: A comparison of students in Catholic parochial schools and in public schools. *Child Development,* 1962, *33,* 591–602.

Campbell, D. T., & Stanley, J. C. *Experimental and quasi-experimental designs for research.* Chicago: Rand McNally, 1966.

Cowan, P. A., Langer, J., Heavenrich, J., & Nathanson, M. Social learning and Piaget's cognitive theory of moral development. *Jounal of Personality and Social Psychology,* 1969, *11,* 261–274.

Cronbach, L. J. Test validation. In R. L. Thorndike (Ed.), *Educational measurement.* (2nd ed.) Washington, D. C.: American Council on Education, 1971.

Cronbach, L. J., & Meehl, P. E. Construct validity in psychological tests. *Psychological Bulletin,* 1955, *52,* 281–302.

Entwisle, D. R. To dispel fantasies about fantasy-based measures of achievement motivation. *Psychological Bulletin,* 1972, *77,* 377–391.

Fodor, E. M. Moral judgment in Negro and white adolescents. *Journal of Social Psychology,* 1969, *79,* 289–291.

Fodor, E. M. Delinquency and susceptibility to social influence among adolescents as a function of moral development. *Journal of Social Psychology,* 1972, *86,* 257–260.

Jensen, A. R. The reliability of projective techniques: Review of the literature. *Acta Psychologica,* 1959, *16,* 108–136.

Haan, N., Smith, M. B., & Block, J. Moral reasoning of young adults: Political-social behavior, family background, and personality correlates. *Journal of Personality and Social Psychology,* 1968, *10,* 183–201.

Hogan, R. A dimension of moral judgment. *Journal of Consulting and Clinical Psychology,* 1970, *35,* 205–212.

Holstein, C. B. The relation of children's moral judgment level to that of their parents and to communications patterns in the family. In R. C. Smart & M. S. Smart (Eds.), *Reading in child development and relationships.* New York: Macmillan, 1972.

Keasey, C. B. Social participation as a factor in the moral development of preadolescents. *Developmental Psychology,* 1971, *5,* 216–220.

Kohlberg, L. The development of modes of moral thinking and choice in the years ten to sixteen. Unpublished doctoral dissertation, University of Chicago, 1958.

Kohlberg, L. The development of children's orientations toward a moral order: I. Sequence in the development of moral thought. *Vita Humana,* 1963, *6,* 11–33. (a)

Kohlberg, L. Moral development and identification. In H. W. Stevenson (Ed.), *Child psychology, 62nd yearbook of the National Society for the Study of Education.* Chicago: University of Chicago Press, 1963. (b)

Kohlberg, L. Development of moral character and moral ideology. In M. L. Hoffman & L. W. Hoffman (Eds.), *Review of child development research*. Vol. 1. New York: Russell Sage Foundation, 1964.

Kohlberg, L. Cognitive stages and preschool education. *Human Development*, 1966, *9*, 5–17. (a)

Kohlberg, L. Moral education in the schools: A developmental view. *The School Review*, 1966, *74*, 1–30. (b)

Kohlberg, L. Moral and religious education and the public schools: A developmental view. In T. R. Sizer (Ed.), *The role of religion in public education*. Boston: Houghton Mifflin, 1967.

Kohlberg, L. The child as a moral philosopher. *Psychology Today*, 1968, *2*, 25–30.

Kohlberg, L. Stage and sequence: The cognitive-developmental approach to socialization. In D. A. Goslin (Ed.), *Handbook of socialization theory and research*. Chicago: Rand McNally, 1969.

Kohlberg, L., & Kramer, R. Continuities and discontinuities in childhood and adult moral development. *Human Development*, 1969, *12*, 93–120.

MacRae, D., Jr. A test of Piaget's theories of moral development. *Journal of Abnormal and Social Psychology*, 1954, *49*, 14–18.

Magowan, S. A., & Lee, T. Some sources of error in the use of the projective method for the measurement of moral judgment. *British Journal of Psychology*, 1970, *61*, 535–543.

Masling, J. The influence of situational and interpersonal variables in projective testing. *Psychological Bulletin*, 1960, *57*, 65–85.

Mead, G. H. *Mind, self, and society*. Chicago: University of Chicago Press, 1934.

Piaget, J. *The moral judgment of the child*. London: Routledge & Kegan Paul, 1932.

Prentice, N. M. The influence of live and symbolic modeling on promoting moral judgment of adolescent delinquents. *Journal of Abnormal Psychology*, 1972, *80*, 157–161.

Rest, J. R. The hierarchical nature of moral judgment: A study of patterns of comprehension and preference of moral stages. *Journal of Personality*, 1973, *41*, 86–109.

Rest, J., Turiel, E., & Kohlberg, L. Level of moral development as a determinant of preference and comprehension of moral judgments made by others. *Journal of Personality*, 1969, *37*, 225–252.

Ruma, E. H., & Mosher, D. L. Relationship between moral judgment and guilt in delinquent boys. *Journal of Abnormal Psychology*, 1967, *72*, 122–127.

Saltzstein, H. D., Diamond, R. M. & Belenky, M. Moral judgment level and conformity behavior. *Developmental Psychology*, 1972, *7*, 327–336.

Schwartz, S. H., Feldman, K. A., Brown, M. E., & Heingartner, A. Some personality correlates of conduct in two situations of moral conflict. *Journal of Personality*, 1969, *37*, 41–57.

Stanley, J. C. Reliability. In R. L. Thorndike (Ed.), *Educational measurement*. (2nd ed.) Washington, D. C.: American Council on Education, 1971.

Turiel, E. An experimental test of the sequentiality of developmental stages in the child's moral judgments. *Journal of Personality and Social Psychology*, 1966, *3*, 611–618.

Part 3
LEARNING THEORY

Five
B. F. SKINNER

Typical personality theorists observe people—in natural, therapeutic, and laboratory settings—and create theories on the basis of these observations. In contrast, learning theorists have traditionally used animals as the subjects of their investigations, confined their observations to laboratory experimentation, and extrapolated from the apparent regularities in animal behavior to the realm of human behavior. In the terms of this latter definition, B. F. Skinner (1904–   ), one of the most important contemporary learning theorists, is a typical learning theorist. His work provides a theoretical and applied science of behavior designed to account not only for animal behavior but also for the intricate patterns of human behavior.

Skinner's interest is in the identification and manipulation of the environmental variables that create the conditions for the development, maintenance, and change of overt behavior. He is widely known for his theory and research concerning *operant conditioning*. An *operant* is, according to Skinner's definition, any behavior that is controlled by its environmental consequences, or reinforcements. A major empirical principle that guides his theoretical and experimental work is that *behavior that is reinforced tends to recur,* whereas behavior that has no positive environmental consequence has a low probability of recurrence. It is Skinner's contention that all of the "voluntary" and "purposive" actions of the organism are operant behaviors. Operant conditioning is thus intended to modify behavior that already exists in the organism's behavioral repertoire.

Insofar as the concept of personality is concerned, Skinner generally dismisses the popular theoretical approaches, on the grounds that they perpetuate a vague and unscientific attitude toward the study of human behavior. Mentalistic concepts such as "the ego" and "the id" hold no appeal for Skinner because they are seldom tied to any observable behavior. The proper goal of a behavioral analysis, Skinner says, is to establish the connections between behavior and the environmental context in which it is emitted and then to use this understanding to further behavioral control. Skinner argues that, in order for the study of human behavior to be a science, its subject must be capable of being observed and measured, and its data must be capable of being reproduced. Yet, despite his scientific rigor and commitment to experimental evidence, Skinner is not reluctant to boldly extend the principles of his system to the idea of the establishment of a utopian community, as he does in his novel, *Walden Two*. He has also speculated on social behavior, language, psychotherapy, and other complex human functions in his book *Science and Human Behavior*.

The theory paper by Skinner that is included here is on the process of self-control. In it, Skinner analyzes the variables that influence the way in which persons go about regulating their own behavior. According to Skinner, the learning principles that govern this regulation are really no different from those that govern other situations in which control of some sort is required. However, in this instance, persons are controlling their own behavior, by arranging for the manipulation of variables of which their own behavior is a function.

The research paper by Frederick H. Kanfer and David A. Goldfoot examines the varieties of self-control methods that subjects use in order to better tolerate pain. The authors start with the assumption that people do try to control themselves in stressful situations. Their research goal was to determine which of the several experimental self-control options presented to the subjects was the most successful. Subjects were randomly assigned in equal numbers to five experimental groups. Each group was instructed to cope with the pain stimulus (the *independent variable*) in a certain way. The *dependent variable*—that is, the subject's response to the effects of the independent variable—was the amount of time for which the subject tolerated the pain stimulus. The subjects were also asked to rate the efficiency of the self-control mechanism they had used. In analyzing these data, Kanfer and Goldfoot discovered that external stimulation (such as projected slides or a clock) was significantly more effective as a distraction than self-control mechanisms generated without external stimulation. Two important points illustrated by this research are (1) that all people naturally employ previously learned self-control devices and (2) that self-control can be enhanced through relevant training procedures.

Carl R. Rogers's critique is a vigorous commentary on the social and philosophical implications of Skinner's position on the control of human behavior. Skinner argues that behavioral control is a historical reality and that, in the course of history, this control has been used improperly, exploitatively, and unproductively. However, Skinner says, with advances in their knowledge, behavioral scientists have within their grasp the ability to design, create, and control the social conditions that would be instrumental in the creation of an ideal environment for human beings. This strategy emphasizes the use of positive reinforcement, in contrast to the use of punishment and aversive methods that is frequently made in the attempt to control behavior.

Rogers and Skinner agree that the behavioral sciences are acquiring an enormous potential for behavioral control and that the dangers inherent in this potential ought not to be underestimated or ignored. But, to Rogers, Skinner's idea of a good society created by means of a benevolent science is unappetizing. Unlike Skinner, Rogers feels that, if science begins with a set of goals that cannot be modified along the way, it will become locked into its own rigid design. Once this has happened, individual freedom will become a mere appendage of science. For Rogers, free choice and humanistic values are the foundations of a humane science.

SUGGESTIONS FOR FURTHER READING

The most comprehensive view of Skinner's thinking on personality, psychotherapy, and social institutions is found in *Science and Human Behavior,* published by Macmillan in 1953. Skinner's *Walden Two* is a visionary utopian fantasy that has aroused tremendous controversy since its publication by Macmillan in 1948. Since that time, several Walden communities, based to a large extent on Skinner's behavioral principles, have sprung up around the country. An article titled "Walden Two, Three, Many More" in the New York Times Magazine, March 15, 1970, provides a detailed picture of some of these communities.

In 1971 Skinner published his most exciting and controversial statement to date: *Beyond Freedom and Dignity.* This work, perhaps more than any other, introduced the ideas of B. F. Skinner to academic and lay circles outside of psychology. A fascinating group of critical evaluations of *Beyond Freedom and Dignity* is found in *Beyond the Punitive Society,* edited by Harvey Wheeler. Published in 1973 by Freeman Press, this book is an intellectual delight.

B. F. Skinner
SELF-CONTROL

THE "SELF-DETERMINATION" OF CONDUCT

Implicit in a functional analysis is the notion of control. When we discover an independent variable which can be controlled, we discover a means of controlling the behavior which is a function of it. This fact is important for theoretical purposes. Proving the validity of a functional relation by an actual demonstration of the effect of one variable upon another is the heart of experimental science. The practice enables us to dispense with many troublesome statistical techniques in testing the importance of variables.

The practical implications are probably even greater. An analysis of the techniques through which behavior may be manipulated shows the kind of technology which is emerging as the science advances, and it points up the considerable degree of control which is currently exerted. The problems raised by the control of human behavior obviously can no longer be avoided by refusing to recognize the possibility of control. Later sections of this book will consider these practical implications in more detail. In Section IV, for example, in an analysis of what is generally called social behavior, we shall see how one organism utilizes the basic processes of behavior to control another. The result is particularly impressive when the individual is under the concerted control of a group. Our basic processes are responsible for the procedures through which the ethical group controls the behavior of each of its members. An even more effective control is exerted by such well-defined agencies as government, religion, psychotherapy, economics, and education; certain key questions concerning such control will be considered in Section V. The general issue of control in human affairs will be summarized in Section VI.

First, however, we must consider the possibility that the individual may control his own behavior. A common objection to a picture of the behaving organism such as we have so far presented runs somewhat as follows. In emphasizing the controlling power of external variables, we have left the organism itself in a peculiarly helpless position. Its behavior appears to be simply a "repertoire"—a vocabulary of action, each item of which becomes more or less probable as the environment changes. It is true that variables may be arranged in complex patterns; but this fact does not appreciably modify the picture, for the emphasis is still upon behavior, not upon the behaver. Yet to a considerable extent an individual does appear to shape his own destiny. He is often able to do something about the variables affecting him. Some degree of "self-determination" of conduct is usually recognized in the creative behavior of the artist and scientist, in the self-exploratory behavior of the writer, and in the self-discipline of the ascetic. Humbler versions of self-determination are more familiar. The individual "chooses" between alternative courses of action, "thinks through" a problem while isolated from the relevant environment and guards his health or his position in society through the exercise of "self-control."

Any comprehensive account of human behavior must, of course, embrace the facts referred to in statements of this sort. But we can achieve this without abandoning our program. When a man controls himself, chooses a course of action, thinks out the solution to a problem, or strives toward an increase in self-knowledge, he is *behaving*. He controls himself precisely as he would control the behavior of anyone else—through the manipulation of variables of which behavior is a function. His behavior in so doing is a proper object of analysis, and eventually it must be accounted for with variables lying outside the individual himself.

It is the purpose of Section III to analyze how the individual acts to alter the variables of which other parts of his behavior are functions, to distinguish among the various cases which arise in terms of the processes involved, and to account for the behavior which achieves control just as we account for behavior of any other kind. The present chapter concerns the processes involved in *self-control,* taking that term in close to its traditional sense, while Chapter XVI concerns behavior which would traditionally be described as *creative thinking*. The two sets of techniques are different because in self-control the individual can identify the behavior to be controlled while in creative thinking he cannot. The variables which the individual utilizes in manipulating his behavior in this way are not always accessible to others, and this has led to great misunderstanding. It has often been concluded, for example, that self-discipline and thinking take place in a nonphysical inner world and that neither activity is properly described as behavior at all. We may simplify the analysis by considering examples of self-control and thinking in which the individual manipulates *external* variables, but we shall need to complete the picture by discussing the status of private events in a science of behavior (Chapter XVII). A purely private event would have no place in a study of behavior, or perhaps in any science; but events which are, for the moment at least, accessible only to the individual himself often occur as links in chains of otherwise public events and they must then be considered. In self-control and creative thinking, where the individual is largely engaged in manipulating his own behavior, this is likely to be the case.

When we say that a man controls himself, we must specify who is controlling whom. When we say that he knows himself, we must also distinguish between the subject and object of the verb. Evidently selves are multiple and hence not to be identified with the biological organism. But if this is so, what are they? What are their dimensions in a science of behavior? To what extent is a self an integrated personality or organism? How can one self act upon another? The interlocking systems of responses which account for self-control and thinking make it possible to answer questions of this sort satisfactorily, as we shall see in Chapter XVIII. We can do this more conveniently, however, when the principal data are at hand. Meanwhile, the term "self" will be used in a less rigorous way.

"SELF-CONTROL"

The individual often comes to control part of his own behavior when a response has conflicting consequences—when it leads to both positive and negative reinforcement. Drinking alcoholic beverages, for example, is often followed by a condition of unusual confidence in which one is more successful socially and in which one forgets responsibilities, anxieties, and other troubles. Since this is positively reinforcing, it increases the likelihood that drinking will take place on future occasions. But there are other consequences—the physical illness of the "hang-over" and the possibly disastrous effects of over-confident or irresponsible behavior—which are negatively reinforcing and, when contingent upon behavior, represent a form of punishment. If punishment were simply the reverse of reinforcement, the two might combine to produce an intermediate tendency to drink, but we have seen that this is not the case. When a similar occasion arises, the same or an increased tendency to drink will prevail; but the occasion as well as the early stages of drinking will generate conditioned aversive stimuli and emotional responses to them which we speak of as shame or guilt. The emotional responses may have some deterrent effect in weakening behavior—as by "spoiling the mood." A more important effect, however, is that any behavior which weakens the behavior of drinking is automatically reinforced by the resulting reduction in aversive stimulation. We have discussed the behavior of simply "doing something else," which is reinforced because it displaces punishable behavior, but there are other possibilities. The organism may make the punished response less probable by altering the variables of which it is a function. Any behavior which succeeds in doing this will automatically be reinforced. We call such behavior self-control.

The positive and negative consequences generate two responses which are related to each other in a special way: one response, the *controlling response,* affects variables in such a way as to change the probability of the other, the *controlled response.* The controlling response may manipulate any of the variables of which the controlled response is a function; hence there are a good many different forms of self-control. In general it is possible to point to parallels in which the same techniques are employed in controlling the behavior of others. A fairly exhaustive survey at this point will illustrate the process of self-control and at the same time serve to summarize the kind of control to be emphasized in the chapters which follow.

TECHNIQUES OF CONTROL

Physical Restraint and Physical Aid

We commonly control behavior through physical restraint. With locked doors, fences, and jails, we limit the space in which people move. With strait-jackets, gags, and arm braces, we limit the movement of parts of their bodies. The individual controls his own behavior in the same way. He claps his hand over his mouth to keep himself from laughing or coughing or to stifle a verbal response which is seen at the last moment to be a "bad break." A child psychologist has suggested that a mother who wishes to keep from nagging her child should seal her own lips with adhesive tape. The individual may jam his hands into his pockets to prevent fidgeting or nail-biting or hood his nose to keep from breathing when under water. He may present himself at the door of an institution for incarceration to control his own criminal or psychotic behavior. He may cut his right hand off lest it offend him.

In each of these examples we identify a controlling response, which imposes some degree of physical restraint upon a response to be controlled. To explain the existence and strength of the controlling behavior we point to the reinforcing circumstances which arise when the response has been controlled. Clapping the hand over the mouth is reinforced and will occur again under similar circumstances because it reduces the aversive stimulation generated by the cough or the incipient bad break. In the sense of Chapter XII, the controlling response *avoids* the negatively reinforcing consequences of the controlled response. The aversive consequences of a bad break are supplied by a social environment; the aversive consequences of breathing under water do not require the mediation of others.

Another form of control through physical restraint is simply to move out of the situation in which the behavior to be controlled may take place. The parent avoids trouble by taking an aggressive child away from other children, and the adult controls himself in the same way. Unable to control his anger, he simply walks away. This may not control the whole emotional pattern, but it does restrain those features which are likely to have serious consequences.

Suicide is another form of self-control. Obviously a man does not kill himself because he has previously escaped from an aversive situation by doing so. As we have already seen, suicide is not a form of behavior to which the notion of frequency of response can be applied. If it occurs, the components of the behavior must have been strengthened separately. Unless this happens under circumstances in which frequency is an available datum, we cannot say meaningfully that a man is "likely or unlikely to kill himself"—nor can the individual say this of himself (Chapter XVII). Some instances of suicide, but by no means all, follow the pattern of cutting off one's right hand that it may not offend one; the military agent taken by the enemy may use this method to keep himself from divulging secrets of state.

A variation on this mode of control consists of removing the situation, so to speak, rather than the individual. A government stops inflationary spending by heavy taxation—by removing the money or credit which is a condition for the purchase of goods. A man arranges to control the behavior of his spendthrift heir by setting up a trust fund. Non-coeducational institutions attempt to control certain kinds of sexual behavior by making the opposite sex inaccessible. The individual may use the same techniques in controlling himself. He may leave most of his pocket money at home to avoid spending it, or he may drop coins into a piggy bank from which it is difficult to withdraw them. He may put his own money in trust for himself. H. G. Wells's Mr. Polly used a similar procedure to distribute his funds over a walking trip. He would mail all but a pound note to himself at a village some distance along his route. Arriving at the village, he would call at the post office, remove a pound note, and readdress the balance to himself at a later point.

In a converse technique we increase the probability of a desirable form of behavior by supplying physical *aid*. We facilitate human behavior, make it possible, or expand and amplify its consequences with various sorts of equipment, tools, and machines. When the problem of self-control is to generate a given response, we alter our own behavior in the same way by obtaining favorable equipment, making funds readily available, and so on.

Changing the Stimulus

Insofar as the preceding techniques operate through physical aid or restraint, they are not based upon a behavioral process. There are associated processes, however, which may be analyzed more accurately in terms of stimulation. Aside from making a response possible or impossible, we may create or eliminate the occasion for it. To do so, we manipulate either an eliciting or a discriminative stimulus. When a drug manufacturer reduces the probability that a nauseous medicine will be regurgitated by enclosing it in tasteless capsules—or by "sugar-coating the pill"—he is simply removing a stimulus which elicits unwanted responses. The same procedure is available in the control of one's own reflexes. We swallow a medicine quickly and "chase" it with a glass of water to reduce comparable stimuli.

We remove *discriminative* stimuli when we turn away from a stimulus which induces aversive action. We may forcibly look away from a wallpaper design which evokes the compulsive behavior of tracing geometrical patterns. We may close doors or draw curtains to eliminate distracting stimuli or achieve the same effect by closing our eyes or putting our fingers in our ears. We may put a box of candy out of sight to avoid overeating. This sort of self-control is described as "avoiding temptation," especially when the aversive consequences have been arranged by society. It is the principle of "Get thee behind me, Satan."

We also *present* stimuli because of the responses they elicit or make more probable in our own behavior. We rid ourselves of poisonous or indigestible food with an emetic—a substance which generates stimuli which elicit vomiting. We facilitate stimulation when we wear eyeglasses or hearing aids. We arrange a discriminative stimulus to encourage our own behavior at a later date when we tie a string on our finger or make an entry in a date book to serve as the occasion for action at an appropriate time. Sometimes we present stimuli because the resulting behavior displaces behavior to be controlled—we "distract" ourselves just as we distract others from a situation which generates undesirable behavior. We amplify stimuli generated by our own behavior when we use a mirror to acquire good carriage or to master a difficult dance step, or study moving pictures of our own behavior to improve our skill in a sport, or listen to phonograph recordings of our own speech to improve pronunciation or delivery.

Conditioning and extinction provide other ways of changing the effectiveness of stimuli. We arrange for the future effect of a stimulus upon ourselves by pairing it with other stimuli, and we extinguish reflexes by exposing ourselves to conditioned stimuli when they are not accompanied by reinforcement. If we blush, sweat, or exhibit some other emotional response under certain circumstances because of an unfortunate episode, we may expose ourselves to these circumstances under more favorable conditions in order that extinction may take place.

Depriving and Satiating

An impecunious person may make the most of an invitation to dinner by skipping lunch and thus creating a high state of deprivation in which he will eat a great deal. Conversely, he may partially satiate himself with a light lunch before going to dinner in order to make the strength of his ingestive behavior less conspicuous. When a guest prepares himself for an assiduous host by drinking a large amount of water before going to a cocktail party, he uses self-satiation as a measure of control.

Another use is less obvious. In *Women in Love,* D. H. Lawrence describes a practice of self-control as follows:

> A very great doctor . . . told me that to cure oneself of a bad habit, one should force oneself to do it, when one would not do it;—make oneself do it—and then the habit would disappear. . . .
> If you bite your nails, for example, then when you don't want to bite your nails, bite them, make yourself bite them. And you would find the habit was broken.

This practice falls within the present class if we regard the behavior of "deliberately" biting one's finger nails, or biting a piece of celluloid or similar material, as automatically satiating. The practice obviously extends beyond what are usually called "bad habits." For example, if we are unable to work at our desk because of a conflicting tendency to go for a walk, a brisk walk may solve the problem—through satiation.

A variation on this practice is to satiate one form of behavior by engaging in a somewhat similar form. Heavy exercise is often recommended in the control of sexual behavior on the assumption that exercise has enough in common with sexual behavior to produce a sort of transferred satiation. (The effect is presumed to be due to topographical overlap rather than sheer exhaustion.) A similar overlap may account for a sort of transferred deprivation. The practice of leaving the table while still hungry has been recommended as a way of generating good work habits. Presumably for the same reason the vegetarian may be especially alert and highly efficient because he is, in a sense, always hungry. Self-deprivation in the field of sex has been asserted to have valuable consequences in distantly related fields—for example, in encouraging literary or artistic achievements. Possibly the evidence is weak; if the effect does not occur, we have so much the less to explain.

Manipulating Emotional Conditions

We induce emotional changes in ourselves for purposes of control. Sometimes this means simply presenting or removing stimuli. For example, we reduce or eliminate unwanted emotional reactions by going away for a "change of scene"—that is, by removing stimuli which have acquired the power to evoke emotional reactions because of events which have occurred in connection with them. We sometimes prevent emotional behavior by eliciting incompatible reponses with appropriate stimuli, as when we bite our tongue to keep from laughing on a solemn occasion.

We also control the *predispositions* which must be distinguished from emotional *responses* (Chapter X). A master of ceremonies on a television program predisposes his studio audience toward laughter before going on the air—possibly by telling jokes which are not permissible on the air. The same procedure is available in self-control. We get ourselves into a "good mood" before a dull or trying appointment to increase the probability that we shall behave in a socially acceptable fashion. Before asking the boss for a raise, we screw our courage to the sticking place by rehearsing a history of injustice. We reread an insulting letter just before answering it in order to generate the emotional behavior which will make the answer more easily written and more effective. We also engender strong emotional states in which undesirable behavior is unlikely or impossible. A case in point is the practice described vulgarly as "scaring the hell out of someone." This refers almost literally to a method of controlling strongly punished behavior by reinstating stimuli which have accompanied punishment. We use the same technique when we suppress our own behavior by rehearsing past punishments or by repeating proverbs which warn of the wages of sin.

We reduce the extent of an emotional reaction by delaying it—for example, by "counting ten" before acting in anger. We get the same effect through the process of adaptation, described in Chapter X, when we gradually bring ourselves into contact with disturbing stimuli. We may learn to handle snakes without fear by beginning with dead or drugged snakes of the least disturbing sort and gradually moving on to livelier and more frightening kinds.

Using Aversive Stimulation

When we set an alarm clock, we arrange for a strongly aversive stimulus from which we can escape only by arousing ourselves. By putting the clock across the room, we make certain that the behavior of escape will fully awaken us. We *condition* aversive reactions in ourselves by pairing stimuli in appropriate ways—for example, by using the "cures" for the tobacco and alcohol habits already described. We also control ourselves by creating verbal stimuli which have an effect upon us because of past aversive consequences paired with them by other people. A simple command is an aversive stimulus—a threat—specifying the action which will bring escape. In getting out of bed on a cold morning, the simple repetition of the command "Get up" may, surprisingly, lead to action. The verbal response is easier than getting up and easily takes precedence over it, but the reinforcing contingencies established by the verbal community may prevail. In a sense the individual "obeys himself." Continued use of this tendency may lead to a finer discrimination between commands issued by oneself and by others, which may interfere with the result.

We prepare aversive stimuli which will control our own future behavior when we make a resolution. This is essentially a prediction concerning our own behavior. By making it in the presence of people who supply aversive stimulation when a prediction is not fulfilled, we arrange consequences which are likely to strengthen the behavior resolved upon. Only by behaving as predicted can we escape the aversive consequences of breaking our resolution. As we shall see later, the aversive stimulation which leads us to keep the resolution may eventually be supplied automatically by our own behavior. The resolution may then be effective even in the absence of other people.

Drugs

We use drugs which simulate the effect of other variables in self-control. Through the use of anesthetics, analgesics, and soporifics we reduce painful or distracting stimuli which cannot otherwise be altered easily. Appetizers and aphrodisiacs are sometimes used in the belief that they duplicate the effects of deprivation in the fields of hunger and sex, respectively. Other drugs are used for the opposite effects. The conditioned aversive stimuli in "guilt" are counteracted more or less effectively with alcohol. Typical patterns of euphoric behavior are generated by morphine and related drugs, and to a lesser extent by caffeine and nicotine.

Operant Conditioning

The place of operant reinforcement in self-control is not clear. In one sense, all reinforcements are self-administered since a response may be regarded as "producing" its reinforcement, but "reinforcing one's own behavior" is more than this. It is also more than simply generating circumstances under which a given type of behavior is characteristically reinforced—for example, by associating with friends who reinforce only "good" behavior. This is simply a chain of responses, an early member of which (associating with a particular friend) is strong because it leads to the reinforcement of a later member (the "good" behavior).

Self-reinforcement of operant behavior presupposes that the individual has it in his power to obtain reinforcement but does not do so until a particular response has been emitted. This might be the case if a man denied himself all social contacts until he had finished a particular job. Something of this sort unquestionably happens, but is it operant reinforcement? It is certainly roughly parallel to the procedure in conditioning the behavior of another person. But it must be remembered that the individual may at any moment drop the work in hand and obtain the reinforcement. We have to account for his not doing so. It may be that such indulgent behavior has been punished—say, with disapproval—except when a piece of work has just been completed. The indulgent behavior will therefore generate strong aversive stimulation except at such a time. The individual finishes the work in order to indulge himself free of guilt (Chapter XII). The ultimate question is whether the consequence has any strengthening effect upon the behavior which precedes it. Is the individual more likely to do a similar piece of work in the future? It would not be surprising if he were *not,* although we must agree that he has arranged a sequence of events in which certain behavior has been followed by a reinforcing event.

A similar question arises as to whether one can extinguish one's own behavior. Simply emitting a response which is not reinforced is not self-control, nor is behavior which simply brings the individual into circumstances under which a particular form of behavior will go unreinforced. Self-extinction seems to mean that a controlling response must arrange the lack of consequence; the individual must step in to break the connection between response and reinforcement. This appears to be done when, for example, a television set is put out of order so that the response of turning the switch is extinguished. But the extinction here is trivial; the primary effect is the removal of a source of stimulation.

Punishment

Self-punishment raises the same question. An individual may stimulate himself aversively, as in self-flagellation. But punishment is not merely aversive stimulation; it is aversive stimulation which is contingent upon a given response. Can the individual arrange this contingency? It is not self-punishment simply to engage in behavior which is punished, or to seek out circumstances in which certain behavior is punished. The individual appears to punish himself when, having recently engaged in a given sort of behavior, he injures himself. Behavior of this sort has been said to show a "need for punishment." But we can account for it in another way if in stimulating himself aversively, the individual escapes from an even more aversive condition of guilt (Chapter XII).

There are other variations in the use of aversive self-stimulation. A man concerned with reducing his weight may draw his belt up to a given notch and allow it to stay there in spite of a strong aversive effect. This may directly increase the conditioned and unconditioned aversive stimuli generated in the act of overeating and may provide for an automatic reinforcement for eating with restraint. But we must not overlook the fact that a very simple response— loosening the belt—will bring escape from the same aversive stimulation. If this behavior is not forthcoming, it is because it has been followed by even more aversive consequences arranged by society or by a physician—a sense of guilt or a fear of illness or death. The ultimate question of aversive self-stimulation is whether a practice of this sort shows the effect which would be generated by the same stimulation arranged by others.

"Doing Something Else"

One technique of self-control which has no parallel in the control of others is based upon the principle of prepotency. The individual may keep himself from engaging in behavior which leads to punishment by energetically engaging in something else. A simple example is avoiding flinching by a violent response of holding still. Holding still is not simply "not-flinching." It is a response which, if executed strongly enough, is prepotent over the flinching response. This is close to the control exercised by others when they generate incompatible behavior. But where another person can do this only by arranging external variables, the individual appears to generate the behavior, so to speak, simply by executing it. A familiar example is talking about something else in order to avoid a particular topic. Escape from the aversive stimulation generated by the topic appears to be responsible for the strength of the verbal behavior which displaces it (Chapter XXIV).

In the field of emotion a more specific form of "doing something else" may be especially effective. Emotions tend to fall into pairs—fear and anger, love and hate—according to the direction of the behavior which is strengthened. We may modify a man's behavior in fear by making him angry. His behavior is not simply doing something else; it is in a sense doing the opposite. The result is not prepotency but algebraic summation. The effect is exemplified in self-control when we alter an emotional predisposition by practicing the opposite emotion—reducing the behavioral pattern in fear of practicing anger or nonchalance, or avoiding the ravages of hatred by "loving our enemies."

THE ULTIMATE SOURCE OF CONTROL

A mere survey of the techniques of self-control does not explain why the individual puts them into effect. This shortcoming is all too apparent when we undertake to engender self-control. It is easy to tell an alcoholic that he can keep himself from drinking by throwing away available supplies of alcohol; the principal problem is to get him to do it. We make this controlling behavior more probable by arranging special contingencies of reinforcement. By punishing drinking—perhaps merely with "disapproval"—we arrange for the automatic reinforcement of behavior which controls drinking because such behavior then reduces conditioned aversive stimulation. Some of these additional consequences are supplied by nature, but in general they are arranged by the community. This is indeed the whole point of ethical training (Chapter XXI). It appears, therefore, that society is responsible for the larger part of the behavior of self-control. If this is correct, little ultimate control remains with the individual. A man may spend a great deal of time designing his own life—he may choose the circumstances in which he is to live with great care, and he may manipulate his daily environment on an extensive scale. Such activity appears to exemplify a high order of self-determination. But it is also behavior, and we account for it in terms of other variables in the environment and history of the individual. It is these variables which provide the ultimate control.

This view is, of course, in conflict with traditional treatments of the subject, which are especially likely to cite self-control as an important example of the operation of personal responsibility. But an analysis which appeals to external variables makes the assumption of an inner originating and determining agent unnecessary. The scientific advantages of such an analysis are many, but the practical advantages may well be even more important. The traditional conception of what is happening when an individual controls himself has never been successful as an educational device. It is of little help to tell a man to use his "will power" or his "self-control." Such an exhortation may make self-control slightly more probable by establishing additional aversive consequences of failure to control, but it does not help anyone to understand the actual processes. An alternative analysis of the *behavior* of control should make it possible to teach relevant techniques as easily as any other technical repertoire. It should also improve the procedures through which society maintains self-controlling behavior in strength. As a science of behavior reveals more clearly the variables of which behavior is a function, these possibilities should be greatly increased.

It must be remembered that formulae expressed in terms of personal responsibility underlie many of our present techniques of control and cannot be abruptly dropped. To arrange a smooth transition is in itself a major problem. But the point has been reached where a sweeping revision of the concept of responsibility is required, not only in a theoretical analysis of behavior, but for its practical consequences as well.

Frederick H. Kanfer and David A. Goldfoot
SELF-CONTROL AND
TOLERANCE OF NOXIOUS STIMULATION

Summary.—This study investigated the effects of several behaviors as potential self-controlling devices in the tolerance of a noxious stimulus. In a cold-pressor test, experimental groups were instructed: (1) to expect severe pain; (2) to verbalize aloud their momentary experiences; (3) to use a clock for setting a goal for tolerance; or (4) to view and describe slides, in order to enhance tolerance of the ice water. Duration of tolerance differed significantly, with a descending order of mean tolerance in groups (4), (3), (1), control, (2). Post-test questionnaires revealed varying use of other self-controlling mechanisms in the groups. The utility of Skinner's paradigm for the study of self-control was discussed.

Tolerance of pain can be modified by changing the stimulational input to an *S*, or by physiological and pharmacological agents which change the threshold for pain stimulus. When continuing exposure to a pain stimulus is under *S*'s *own* control, the event can be classified under the general paradigm provided by Skinner (1953) for the operation of self-controlling mechanisms. Skinner defines self-control as a process in which a person makes a response that alters the probability of the occurrence of another response. The first of these may be called a controlling response and the second the controlled response. The self-control paradigm characteristically involves either of two types of conflict situations. In the first, *S* has available the means for terminating a noxious stimulus at any time, but continuation of exposure to the noxious stimulus is also associated with reinforcement of high magnitude. In the second, *S* can make a response which leads to immediate reinforcement, but the behavior also has ultimate aversive consequences which tend to inhibit the occurrence of the instrumental response, or to strengthen antagonistic responses.[1]

The present study utilized the first type of situation. The purpose of this study was to examine the effectiveness of several different behaviors as self-controlling responses which might alter tolerance of a noxious stimulus.

All *S*s were given the cold-pressor test and asked to keep a hand in ice water as long as possible. For two experimental groups the potential self-controlling responses were verbal and related in content to the noxious stimulus. In a *Negative Set* group, emphasis on the aversive aspects of the stimulus was intended to shorten tolerance by increasing *S*'s attention to the ice water effects and arousing a repertoire of motor responses associated with pain

From F. H. Kanfer and D. A. Goldfoot, "Self-Control and Tolerance of Noxious Stimulation," *Psychological Reports*, 1966, *18*, 79–85. Reprinted by permission of the publisher and the authors.

[1]The first of these conflict situations is illustrated by such widely known dilemmas as that of a brave boy's pain endurance in the presence of peers, or the silence of a military prisoner in the face of physical assaults. The second type is encountered in "resistance to temptation" situations, such as those faced by the alcoholic or the obese excessive eater.

stimuli. In a *Talk* group, the availability of competing verbal responses was intended to facilitate pain tolerance. In the remaining two experimental groups, the self-controlling responses involved *ad lib* use by *S* of environmental objects (a timing clock or a slide projector) not directly related to the pain stimulus. These external stimuli represented potential sources of distraction for *S*.

METHOD

Subjects

*S*s were 60 female undergraduates in business and psychology courses who volunteered and were paid for their participation. Three additional *S*s began the experiment but terminated after discovering the nature of the task. All *S*s were naive about the purpose of the experiment. *S*s were randomly assigned to five equal groups of 12 *S*s.

The Noxious Stimulus

It is known that phasic vasoconstriction and vasodilatation (Lewis effect) occur during the course of hand immersion in ice water (Lewis, 1929). Various *E*s (Carlson, 1962; Krog, *et al.*, 1960; Kunckle, 1949; Teichner, 1965) have demonstrated that this phasic phenomenon is associated with the perception of pain. Kunckle (1949) hypothesizes that cyclic pain is associated with the Lewis effect. Although this hypothesis has not been thoroughly studied, it is apparent that *S*s not manifesting the Lewis effect find the ice water task exceedingly uncomfortable (Teichner, 1965). In addition, Teichner (1965) has shown that the absence of phasic vasodilatation is in part a function of *S*'s emotional state.

Marked individual differences can be expected in this stimulus situation, then, due to both the physiological and psychological state of *S*. Since the majority of *S*s who experience the Lewis effect do so within 4½ min. (Teichner, 1965), and since Kunckle (1949), and Wolff and Hardy (1941) reported an increasing numbness for *S*s between 4 and 7 min., it was decided to expose *S*s for a maximum of 5 min. to ice water kept at a constant temperature of 1°C.

Design and Procedure

The experiment was conducted in a bare, soundproof room, softly illuminated and containing only *S*'s chair and a low table for holding the ice water pan. Precautions were taken to eliminate any distracting visual or auditory stimuli in the room, since pilot work had shown that the amount of environmental stimulation is a relevant variable in the present experimental procedure.

Each *S* was seated in the experimental room and asked to remove her rings, bracelet and watch. These items were collected and kept in the adjoining room from which *E* monitored the experimental procedure. *S*s in all groups were then told: "We are interested in measuring some physical changes that occur in people under various circumstances. For the first part of this experiment I would like you to wear these electrodes around your arm. They will measure the electrical activity in your skin. Now, when I tell you to, please place your hand in this cold water, and keep it there as long as you can." *S*'s dominant hand was placed in the water and a signal button, activated by *S*'s other hand, was used to permit *S* to make a definite decision and to provide a clear-cut response for terminating the task. In order to increase the plausibility of the stated purpose of the study, *E* excused himself at this point "to take a reading in the adjoining room." He then returned and continued with the instructions appropriate for each *S*'s particular group. Since the instructions describe the experimental treatments of the groups, they are reproduced verbatim:

> *Group I* (Control).—You might find this experience uncomfortable. Keep your hand in the water as long as you can. Be sure to let me know when you take your hand out of the water by pushing this button.
> *Group II (Verbal,* Negative set).—You will find this water very uncomfortable. Most people experience severe pain and cramping, especially in the area of the back of the hand, the palm, and in the joints of the fingers. The pain is quite severe. Keep your hand in the water as long as you can. Be sure to let me know when you take your hand out of the water by pushing this button.
> *Group III (Verbal,* Talk).—You might find this experience uncomfortable. To help you keep your hand in the water, please describe aloud your moment-to-moment sensations. Be careful to observe and to verbalize all sensations and thoughts you have pertaining to this situation. This microphone will record what you say. Try to verbalize every thought. Keep your hand in the water as long as you can. Be sure to let me know when you take your hand out of the water by pushing this button.
> *Group IV (External distraction,* Clock).—You might find this experience uncomfortable. To help you keep your hand in the water, you may use this clock. It will be useful for you to know how long you have kept your hand in the water. Most people use the clock to set goals for themselves to continue for another *X* amount of time. Please use the clock to help you keep your hand in the water as long as you can. Be sure to let me know when you take your hand out of the water by pushing this button.
> *Group V (External distraction,* Slide).—You might find this experience uncomfortable. To help you keep your hand in the water, you may use this slide projector. Please describe aloud each slide which you look at. Press this button with your (nondominant) hand to change slides. You may change slides as often as you wish. Please use the slide projector to help you keep your hand in the water as long as you can. Be sure to let me know when you take your hand out of the water by pushing this button.

For the *Clock* group only, a large wall clock was mounted at *S*'s eye level. For the *Slide* group, a Sawyer 700 projector with remote control was arranged to project a picture in front of *S* at eye level. The projector was loaded with 100 slides of Europe. Slides varied, containing pictures of landscapes, buildings, landmarks, and people. The slides were arranged in random order and started at different points for each *S*.

The electrodes were non-functional, terminating in wires clearly leading to *E*'s monitoring room. A one-way observation screen permitted *E* to observe *S* in the soundproof room. *S* was asked to submerge her hand into the water up to her wrist, palm down, under the floating ice. *E* determined proper positioning of *S*'s hand, began timing, and left the soundproof room.

Each *S* was stopped when her hand had been in the ice water for 5 min. After completion of the cold-pressor test, *S* was asked to complete a post-test questionnaire. On this questionnaire, *S* was asked: (1) to rate the discomfort of the water on a scale from 1 (mildly unpleasant) to 8 (absolutely intolerable); (2) to describe what she was thinking about while her hand was in the water; (3) to indicate any mechanisms or tricks which she might have used; (4) to indicate whether she had ever used these tricks before; (5) to predict whether she could have done better if something else were available to help her keep her hand in the water; (6) to indicate whether and how the particular self-controlling response used in her group affected her performance; (7) to rate her everyday sensitivity to pain on a scale from 1 (intolerant) to 5 (very tolerant); (8) to state what made her want to keep her hand in the water; and (9) to estimate the total duration of having kept her hand in the water.

RESULTS

The main measure of the effectiveness of the self-controlling devices was the time Ss kept their hands in the standard ice water preparation. The mean numbers of seconds for the groups were: *Control*, 174.2; *Negative* set, 178.2; *Talk*, 129.0; *Clock*, 196.5; *Slide*, 271.3. An F test for the total number of seconds of toleration (Table 1) indicates a significant difference between groups at $p < .05$. The significant F value indicates that the various controlling devices differed in their effectiveness in prolonging pain tolerance. The *Slide* group showed the longest tolerance, with least tolerance by the *Talk* group.

Table 1. Analysis of variance of toleration time (in sec.) for all groups

Source	df	MS	F	p
Between	4	32266.0	2.97	.05
Within	55	10869.4		
Total	59			

A Neuman-Keuls test was carried out to examine further the differences among groups. The greatest difference, significant at $p < .05$, was obtained between the *Slide* group and the *Talk* group. The order of means suggests the superiority of those groups using environmental distraction responses (*Slide* and *Clock* groups) over those using verbal mechanisms, and over the *Control* group.

Several post-test questionnaire data gave frequency distributions and limited ranges which precluded use of statistical comparisons. Therefore, only descriptive statistics are given. Average water discomfort ratings were as follows: *Control*, 4.3; *Negative*, 5.2; *Talk*, 4.1; *Clock*, 4.7; *Slide*, 4.3. Similarly, when Ss rated their tolerance of pain in everyday life, their average ratings ranged from 2.8 to 3.5, and appeared to be similar in the groups.

All Ss were asked whether the self-control mechanism they were instructed to use affected their tolerance time. Table 2 summarizes the findings. In addition, Ss were asked to indicate whether any further external aid would have helped them. Fifty percent of the Ss in the *Negative, Talk,* and *Clock* groups responded in the affirmative, whereas 58.0% of the *Control* group and only 16.6% of the *Slide* group responded in the affirmative. From these data and from Table 2, it appears that the subjective appraisal of the utility of the self-controlling devices closely paralleled the toleration time data. The *Slide* group indicated the greatest satisfaction with the provided self-control mechanism and also performed better than the other groups.

Ss also reported the mechanisms which they actually employed during the task, in

Table 2. Responses to the question, "Did (the self-control mechanism) affect your performance?"

Response	Negative set	Talk	Clock	Slide
Hindrance	2	3	0	0
Help	4	5	9	12
No effect	6	4	3	0

addition to those which they were instructed to use. While 9 *S*s in the *Slide* group and 7 *S*s in the *Clock* group reported that they used no additional mechanisms, 10 *S*s in the *Negative* group, and 6 *S*s in *Control* and *Talk* groups used other self-controlling behaviors. The *Negative* group reported the greatest use of motor mechanisms. Eight *S*s said that they tried "squirming," fist clenching, etc., to reduce their discomfort and increase tolerance. The questionnaire replies suggest that, when the self-control mechanism supplied by *E* was effective, no additional mechanisms were employed by *S*.

The results indicate that *S*s in all groups significantly underestimated the length of time they tolerated the ice water. Thirty-five *S*s underestimated this period of time, as opposed to 4 correct estimations and 9 overestimations. The *Clock* group, for obvious reasons, was not included in this analysis. A product-moment correlation between actual time and estimated time of toleration was computed, with $r = .57$ $(p < .005, 47\ df)$.

DISCUSSION

The results of this study support the hypothesis that tolerance of an aversive stimulus can be affected by providing *S* with controlling responses which he can utilize at his own discretion, without further intervention by *E*. The findings further suggest that self-control behaviors which provide some external stimulation, e.g., a clock or slides, effect greater facilitation than verbal devices. Particular parameters of the environmental distraction procedure, e.g., modality of presentation, stimulus complexity, *S*'s interest in the task, etc., remain to be investigated. Since it appears that those cues which compete with the response-produced cues associated with noxious events may further prolong toleration, it would be of interest to explore further effects of direct reduction of the pain-associated cues by self-controlling devices. For instance, if increased muscle tension or irregular breathing characterized response to the cold-pressor test, then behaviors which result in normal breathing and reduced muscle tension may be effective responses to be utilized in self-control.

The low tolerance in the *Talk* group is of interest because clinicians often ascribe beneficial "cathartic" effects to verbalized reports of subjective experiences. Under the conditions of the present study, it is more plausible to hypothesize that attention to a noxious stimulus and the labelling of its aversive effects enhanced the tendency toward hand withdrawal because, in *S*'s past history, these additional responses have probably been followed by an escape response from the stimuli which are described or experienced as aversive. In the *Negative Set* group the instructions also may have resulted in increased attention to the aversive stimulus. In addition, anticipation of severe pain would be expected to arouse anticipatory motor responses designed to reduce pain. Further, *S*s indicated on the post-experimental questionnaire that the instructions in this group led them to set a tolerance goal toward longer exposure. These conflicting response tendencies produced by the instructions in the *Negative Set* group could have acted to yield the results for this group. Isolation of the contribution of each of these factors would have to be carried out in a separate experiment.

An inherent problem in research on self-control lies in the fact that most *S*s come to the experiment with well-learned self-controlling mechanisms. If a noxious stimulus must be tolerated in an experiment, and no further instructions are given, *S*s use the particular devices which they had found helpful in their past experience. In the *Control* group, for example, *S*s reported the use of many self-controlling devices including thinking of something else, counting, teeth clenching, and others. Consequently, the experimental groups in this study differed from the *Control* group mainly because *E* provided the same method for control of the tolerance response to all *S*s, or because the controlling response involved some external stimulation. With adult Ss it would be difficult to eliminate completely the occurrence of self-instructed devices in the study of self-control. The results therefore represent only the relative increase in effectiveness of experimental mechanisms as compared to the uncontrolled and variable effects of pre-experimentally learned self-controlling responses.

The behavioral analysis of self-control reveals yet another set of variables which influence the behavioral outcome. Since the controlled response is usually an element in an approach-avoidance conflict situation, conflict theory suggests that manipulations of any of the variables which change the approach or avoidance tendency in S could serve as self-controlling devices. Thus, the probability of occurrence of those approach or avoidance responses could be altered by varying responses on which they are contingent. The present study has served mainly the methodological purpose of testing the utility of the Skinnerian self-control paradigm rather than establishment of substantive knowledge about different forms of self-control. The main advantage of the present approach over the traditional concept of self-control as a "voluntary" act lies in its potential for application of training methods for this behavior. It suggests that a person may learn to manipulate and control his own behavior and that the manner in which he does so is subject to learning as a function of the very same variables which affect other behaviors not commonly considered to be under S's "voluntary" control.

REFERENCES

Carlson, L. D. Temperature. *Annu. Rev. Physiol.*, 1962, *24*, 85–101.

Krog, J., Folkow, B., Fox, R. H., & Andersen, K. L. Hand circulation in the cold of Lapps and North Norwegian fishermen, *J. appl. Physiol.*, 1960, *15*, 654–658.

Kunckle, E. C. Phasic pains induced by cold. *J. appl. Physiol.*, 1949, *1*, 811–824.

Lewis, T. Observations upon the reaction of the vessels of the human skin to cold. *Heart*, 1929, *15*, 177–189.

Skinner, B. F. *Science and human behavior*. New York: Macmillan, 1953.

Teichner, W. H. Delayed cold-induced vasodilation and behavior, *J. exp. Psychol.*, 1965, *69*, 426–432.

Wolff, S., & Hardy, J. D. Studies on pain: observations on pain due to local cooling and factors involved in the cold pressor response, *J. clin. Invest.*, 1941, *20*, 521–533.

Carl R. Rogers
THE PLACE OF THE INDIVIDUAL IN
THE NEW WORLD
OF THE BEHAVIORAL SCIENCES

In the preceding lecture I endeavored to point out, in a very sketchy manner, the advances of the behavioral sciences in their ability to predict and control behavior. I tried to suggest the new world into which we will be advancing at an evermore headlong pace. Today I want to consider the question of how we—as individuals, as groups, as a culture—will live in, will respond to, will adapt to, this brave new world. What stance will we take in the face of these new developments?

I am going to describe two answers which have been given to this question, and then I wish to suggest some considerations which may lead to a third answer.

DENY AND IGNORE

One attitude which we can take is to deny that these scientific advances are taking place, and simply take the view that there can be no study of human behavior which is truly scientific. We can hold that the human animal cannot possibly take an objective attitude toward himself, and that therefore no real science of behavior can exist. We can say that man is always a free agent, in some sense that makes scientific study of his behavior impossible. Not long ago, at a conference on the social sciences, curiously enough, I heard a well known economist take just this view. And one of this country's most noted theologians writes, "In any event, no scientific investigation of past behavior can become the basis of predictions of future behavior." (3, p. 47)

The attitude of the general public is somewhat similar. Without necessarily denying the possibility of a behavioral science, the man in the street simply ignores the developments which are taking place. To be sure he becomes excited for a time when he hears it said that the Communists have attempted to change the soldiers they have captured, by means of "brainwashing." He may show a mild reaction of annoyance to the revelations of a book such as Whyte's (13) which shows how heavily, and in what manipulative fashion, the findings of the behavioral sciences are used by modern industrial corporations. But by and large he sees nothing in all this to be concerned about, any more than he did in the first theoretical statements that the atom could be split.

We may, if we wish, join him in ignoring the problem. We may go further, like the older intellectuals I have cited, and looking at the behavioral sciences may declare that "there ain't no such animal." But since these reactions do not seem particularly intelligent I shall leave them to describe a much more sophisticated and much more prevalent point of view.

THE FORMULATION OF HUMAN LIFE IN TERMS OF SCIENCE

Among behavioral scientists it seems to be largely taken for granted that the findings of such science will be used in the prediction and control of human behavior. Yet most psychologists and other scientists have given little thought to what this would mean. An exception to this general tendency is Dr. B. F. Skinner of Harvard who has been quite explicit in urging psychologists to use the powers of control which they have in the interest of creating a better world. In an attempt to show what he means Dr. Skinner wrote a book some years ago entitled *Walden Two* (12), in which he gives a fictional account of what he regards as a Utopian community in which the learnings of the behavioral sciences are fully utilized in all aspects of life—marriage, child rearing, ethical conduct, work, play, and artistic endeavor. I shall quote from his writings several times.

There are also some writers of fiction who have seen the significance of the coming influence of the behavioral sciences. Aldous Huxley, in his *Brave New World* (1), has given a horrifying picture of saccharine happiness in a scientifically managed world, against which man eventually revolts. George Orwell, in *1984* (5), has drawn a picture of the world created by dictatorial power, in which the behavioral sciences are used as instruments of absolute control of individuals so that not behavior alone but even thought is controlled.

The writers of science fiction have also played a role in visualizing for us some of the possible developments in a world where behavior and personality are as much the subject of science as chemical compounds or electrical impulses.

I should like to try to present, as well as I can, a simplified picture of the cultural pattern which emerges if we endeavor to shape human life in terms of the behavioral sciences.

There is first of all the recognition, almost the assumption, that scientific knowledge is the power to manipulate. Dr. Skinner says: ''We must accept the fact that some kind of control of human affairs is inevitable. We cannot use good sense in human affairs unless someone engages in the design and construction of environmental conditions which affect the behavior of men. Environmental changes have always been the condition for the improvement of cultural patterns, and we can hardly use the more effective methods of science without making changes on a grander scale. . . . Science has turned up dangerous processes and materials before. To use the facts and techniques of a science of man to the fullest extent without making some monstrous mistake will be difficult and obviously perilous. It is no time for self-deception, emotional indulgence, or the assumption of attitudes which are no longer useful.'' (10, pp. 56–57)

The next assumption is that such power to control is to be used. Skinner sees it as being used benevolently, though he recognizes the danger of its being misused. Huxley sees it as being used with benevolent intent, but actually creating a nightmare. Orwell describes the results if such power is used malignantly, to enhance the degree of regulation exercised by a dictatorial government.

STEPS IN THE PROCESS

Let us look at some of the elements which are involved in the concept of the control of human behavior as mediated by the behavioral sciences. What would be the steps in the process by which a society might organize itself so as to formulate human life in terms of the science of man?

First would come the selection of goals. In a recent paper Dr. Skinner suggests that one possible goal to be assigned to the behavioral technology is this: ''Let man be happy, informed, skillful, well-behaved, and productive'' (10, p. 47). In his *Walden Two,* where he can use the guise of fiction to express his views, he becomes more expansive. His hero says, ''Well, what do you say to the design of personalities? Would that interest you? The control of temperament? Give me the specifications, and I'll give you the man! What do you say to the control of motivation, building the interests which will make men most productive and most successful? Does that seem to you fantastic? Yet some of the techniques are available, and more can be worked out experimentally. Think of the possibilities! . . . Let us control the lives of our children and see what we can make of them.'' (12, p. 243)

What Skinner is essentially saying here is that the current knowledge in the behavioral sciences plus that which the future will bring, will enable us to specify, to a degree which today would seem incredible, the kind of behavioral and personality results which we wish to achieve. This is obviously both an opportunity and a very heavy burden.

The second element in this process would be one which is familiar to every scientist who has worked in the field of applied science. Given the purpose, the goal, we proceed by the method of science—by controlled experimentation—to discover the means to these ends. If for example our present knowledge of the conditions which cause men to be productive is limited, further investigation and experimentation would surely lead us to new knowledge in this field. And still further work will provide us with the knowledge of even more effective means. The method of science is self-correcting in thus arriving at increasingly effective ways of achieving the purpose we have selected.

The third element in the control of human behavior through the behavioral sciences involves the question of power. As the conditions or methods are discovered by which to achieve our goal, some person or group obtains the power to establish those conditions or use those methods. There has been too little recognition of the problem involved in this. To hope that the power being made available by the behavioral sciences will be exercised by the scientists, or by a benevolent group, seems to me a hope little supported by either recent or distant history. It seems far more likely that behavioral scientists, holding their present attitudes, will be in the position of the German rocket scientists specializing in guided missiles. First they worked devotedly for Hitler to destroy Russia and the United States. Now, depending on who captured them, they work devotedly for Russia in the interest of destroying the United States, or devotedly for the United States in the interest of destroying Russia. If behavioral scientists are concerned solely with advancing their science, it seems most probable that they will serve the purposes of whatever individual or group has the power.

But this is, in a sense, a digression. The main point of this view is that some person or group will have and use the power to put into effect the methods which have been discovered for achieving the desired goal.

The fourth step in this process whereby a society might formulate its life in terms of the behavioral sciences is the exposure of individuals to the methods and conditions mentioned. As individuals are exposed to the prescribed conditions this leads, with a high degree of probability, to the behavior which has been desired. Men then become productive, if that has been the goal, or submissive, or whatever it has been decided to make them.

To give something of the flavor of this aspect of the process as seen by one of its advocates, let me again quote the hero of *Walden Two.* ''Now that we *know* how positive reinforcement works, and why negative doesn't,'' he says, commenting on the method he is advocating, ''we can be more deliberate and hence more successful, in our cultural design. We can achieve a sort of control under which the controlled, though they are following a code much more scrupulously than was ever the case under the old system, nevertheless *feel free*. They are doing what they want to do, not what they are forced to do. That's the source of the tremendous power of positive reinforcement—there's no restraint and no revolt. By a careful design, we control not the final behavior, but the *inclination* to behave—the motives, the desires, the wishes. The curious thing is that in that case *the question of freedom never arises.''* (12, p. 218)

THE PICTURE AND ITS IMPLICATIONS

Let me see if I can sum up very briefly the picture of the impact of the behavioral sciences upon the individual and upon society, as this impact is explicitly seen by Dr. Skinner, and implied in the attitudes and work of many, perhaps most, behavioral scientists. Behavioral science is clearly moving forward; the increasing power for control which it gives will be held by some one or some group; such an individual or group will surely choose the purposes or goals to be achieved; and most of us will then be increasingly controlled by means so subtle we will not even be aware of them as controls. Thus whether a council of wise psychologists (if this is not a contradiction in terms) or a Stalin or a Big Brother has the power, and whether the goal is happiness, or productivity, or resolution of the Oedipus complex, or submission, or love of Big Brother, we will inevitably find ourselves moving toward the chosen goal, and probably thinking that we ourselves desire it. Thus if this line of reasoning is correct, it appears that some form of completely controlled society—a *Walden Two* or a *1984*—is coming. The fact that it would surely arrive piecemeal rather than all at once, does not greatly change the fundamental issues. Man and his behavior would become a planned product of a scientific society.

You may well ask, ''But what about individual freedom? What about the democratic concepts of the rights of the individual?'' Here too Dr. Skinner is quite specific. He says quite bluntly, ''The hypothesis that man is not free is essential to the application of scientific method to the study of human behavior. The free inner man who is held responsible for the behavior of the external biological organism is only a pre-scientific substitute for the kinds of causes which are discovered in the course of a scientific analysis. All these alternative causes lie *outside* the individual.'' (11, p. 447)

In another source he explains this at somewhat more length. ''As the use of science increases, we are forced to accept the theoretical structure with which science represents its facts. The difficulty is that this structure is clearly at odds with the traditional democratic conception of man. Every discovery of an event which has a part in shaping a man's behavior seems to leave so much the less to be credited to the man himself; and as such explanations become more and more comprehensive, the contribution which may be claimed by the individual himself appears to approach zero. Man's vaunted creative powers, his original accomplishments in art, science and morals, his capacity to choose and our right to hold him responsible for the consequences of his choice—none of these is conspicuous in this new self-portrait. Man, we once believed, was free to express himself in art, music and literature, to inquire into nature, to seek salvation in his own way. He could initiate action and make spontaneous and capricious changes of course. Under the most extreme duress some sort of choice remained to him. He could resist any effort to control him, though it might cost him his life. But science insists that action is initiated by forces impinging upon the individual, and that caprice is only another name for behavior for which we have not yet found a cause.'' (10, pp. 52-53)

The democratic philosophy of human nature and government is seen by Skinner as having served a useful purpose at one time. ''In rallying men against tyranny it was necessary that the individual be strengthened, that he be taught that he had rights and could govern himself. To give the common man a new conception of his worth, his dignity, and his power to save himself, both here and hereafter, was often the only resource of the revolutionist.'' (10, p. 53) He regards this philosophy as being now out of date and indeed an obstacle ''if it prevents us from applying to human affairs the science of man.'' (10, p. 54)

A PERSONAL REACTION

I have endeavored, up to this point, to give an objective picture of some of the developments in the behavioral sciences, and an objective picture of the kind of society which might emerge out of these developments. I do however have strong personal reactions to the kind of world I have been describing, a world which Skinner explicitly (and many other scientists implicitly) expect and hope for in the future. To me this kind of world would destroy the human person as I have come to know him in the deepest moments of psychotherapy. In such moments I am in relationship with a person who is spontaneous, who is responsibly free, that is, aware of this freedom to choose who he will be, and aware also of the consequences of his choice. To believe, as Skinner holds, that all this is an illusion, and that spontaneity, freedom, responsibility, and choice have no real existence, would be impossible for me.

I feel that to the limit of my ability I have played my part in advancing the behavioral sciences, but if the result of my efforts and those of others is that man becomes a robot, created and controlled by a science of his own making, then I am very unhappy indeed. If the good life of the future consists in so conditioning individuals through the control of their environment, and through the control of the rewards they receive, that they will be inexorably productive, well-behaved, happy or whatever, then I want none of it. To me this is a pseudo-form of the good life which includes everything save that which makes it good.

And so I ask myself, is there any flaw in the logic of this development? Is there any alternative view as to what the behavioral sciences might mean to the individual and to society? It seems to me that I perceive such a flaw, and that I can conceive of an alternative view. These I would like to set before you.

ENDS AND VALUES IN RELATION TO SCIENCE

It seems to me that the view I have presented rests upon a faulty perception of the relationship of goals and values to the enterprise of science. The significance of the *purpose* of a scientific undertaking is, I believe, grossly underestimated. I would like to state a two-pronged thesis which in my estimation deserves consideration. Then I will elaborate the meaning of these two points.

1. In any scientific endeavor—whether ''pure'' or applied science—there is a prior personal subjective choice of the purpose or value which that scientific work is perceived as serving.

2. This subjective value choice which brings the scientific endeavor into being must always lie outside of that endeavor, and can never become a part of the science involved in that endeavor.

Let me illustrate the first point from Dr. Skinner's writings. When he suggests that the task for the behavioral sciences is to make man ''productive,'' ''well-behaved,'' etc., it is obvious that he is making a choice. He might have chosen to make men submissive, dependent, and gregarious, for example. Yet by his own statement in another context man's ''capacity to choose,'' his freedom to select his course and to initiate action—these powers do not exist in the scientific picture of man. Here is, I believe, the deep-seated contradiction, or paradox. Let me spell it out as clearly as I can.

Science, to be sure, rests on the assumption that behavior is caused—that a specified event is followed by a consequent event. Hence all is determined, nothing is free, choice is impossible. But we must recall that science itself, and each specific scientific endeavor, each change of course in a scientific research, each interpretation of the meaning of a scientific finding and each decision as to how the finding shall be applied, rests upon a personal subjective choice. Thus science in general exists in the same paradoxical situation as does Dr. Skinner. A personal subjective choice made by man sets in motion the operations of science, which in time proclaims that there can be no such thing as a personal subjective choice. I shall make some comments about this continuing paradox at a later point.

I stressed the fact that each of these choices initiating or furthering the scientific venture, is a value choice. The scientist investigates this rather than that, because he feels the first investigation has more value for him. He chooses one method for his study rather than another because he values it more highly. He interprets his findings in one way rather than another because he believes the first way is closer to the truth, or more valid—in other words that it is closer to a criterion which he values. Now these value choices are never a part of the scientific venture itself. The value choices connected with a particular scientific enterprise always and necessarily lie outside of that enterprise.

I wish to make it clear that I am not saying that values cannot be included as a subject of science. It is not true that science deals only with certain classes of "facts" and that these classes do not include values. It is a bit more complex than that, as a simple illustration or two may make clear.

If I value knowledge of the "three R's" as a goal of education, the methods of science can give me increasingly accurate information as to how this goal may be achieved. If I value problem-solving ability as a goal of education, the scientific method can give me the same kind of help.

Now if I wish to determine whether problem-solving ability is "better" than knowledge of the three R's, then scientific method can also study those two values, but *only*—and this is very important—only in terms of some other value which I have subjectively chosen. I may value college success. Then I can determine whether problem-solving ability or knowledge of the three R's is most closely associated with that value. I may value personal integration or vocational success or responsible citizenship. I can determine whether problem-solving ability or knowledge of the three R's is "better" for achieving any one of these values. But the value or purpose which gives meaning to a particular scientific endeavor must always lie outside of that endeavor.

Though our concern in these lectures is largely with applied science what I have been saying seems equally true of so-called pure science. In pure science the usual prior subjective value choice is the discovery of truth. But this is a subjective choice, and science can never say whether it is the best choice, save in the light of some other value. Geneticists in Russia, for example, had to make a subjective choice of whether it was better to pursue truth, or to discover facts which upheld a governmental dogma. Which choice is "better"? We could make a scientific investigation of those alternatives, but only in the light of some other subjectively chosen value. If, for example, we value the survival of a culture then we could begin to investigate with the methods of science the question as to whether pursuit of truth or support of governmental dogma is most closely associated with cultural survival.

My point then is that any scientific endeavor, pure or applied, is carried on in the pursuit of a purpose or value which is subjectively chosen by persons. It is important that this choice be made explicit, since the particular value which is being sought can never be tested or evaluated, confirmed or denied, by the scientific endeavor to which it gives birth and meaning. The initial purpose or value always and necessarily lies outside the scope of the scientific effort which it sets in motion.

Among other things this means that if we choose some particular goal or series of goals for human beings, and then set out on a large scale to control human behavior to the end of achieving those goals, we are locked in the rigidity of our initial choice, because such a scientific endeavor can never transcend itself to select new goals. Only subjective human persons can do that. Thus if we choose as our goal the state of happiness for human beings (a goal deservedly ridiculed by Aldous Huxley in *Brave New World*), and if we involved all of society in a successful scientific program by which people became happy, we would be locked in a colossal rigidity in which no one would be free to question this goal, because our scientific operations could not transcend themselves to question their guiding purposes. And without laboring this point, I would remark that colossal rigidity, whether in dinosaurs or dictatorships, has a very poor record of evolutionary survival.

If, however, a part of our scheme is to set free some "planners" who do not have to be happy, who are not controlled, and who are therefore free to choose other values, this has several meanings. It means that the purpose we have chosen as our goal is not a sufficient and satisfying one for human beings, but must be supplemented. It also means that if it is necessary to set up an elite group which is free, then this shows all too clearly that the great majority are only the slaves—no matter by what high-sounding name we call them—of those who select the goals.

Perhaps, however, the thought is that a continuing scientific endeavor will evolve its own goals; that the initial findings will alter the directions, and subsequent findings will alter them still further and that the science somehow develops its own purpose. This seems to be a view implicitly held by many scientists. It is surely a reasonable description, but it overlooks one element in this continuing development, which is that subjective personal choice enters in at every point at which the direction changes. The findings of a science, the results of an experiment, do not and never can tell us what next scientific purpose to pursue. Even in the purest of science, the scientist must decide what the findings mean, and must subjectively choose what next step will be most profitable in the pursuit of his purpose. And if we are speaking of the application of scientific knowledge, then it is distressingly clear that the increasing scientific knowledge of the structure of the atom carries with it no necessary choice as to the purpose to which this knowledge will be put. This is a subjective personal choice which must be made by many individuals.

Thus I return to the proposition with which I began this section of my remarks—and which I now repeat in different words. Science has its meaning as the objective pursuit of a purpose which has been subjectively chosen by a person or persons. This purpose or value can never be investigated by the particular scientific experiment or investigation to which it has given birth and meaning. Consequently, any discussion of the control of human beings by the behavioral sciences must first and most deeply concern itself with the subjectively chosen purposes which such an application of science is intended to implement.

AN ALTERNATIVE SET OF VALUES

If the line of reasoning I have been presenting is valid, then it opens new doors to us. If we frankly face the fact that science takes off from a subjectively chosen set of values, then we are free to select the values we wish to pursue. We are not limited to such stultifying goals as producing a controlled state of happiness, productivity, and the like. I would like to suggest a radically different alternative.

Suppose we start with a set of ends, values, purposes, quite different from the type of goals we have been considering. Suppose we do this quite openly, setting them forth as a possible value choice to be accepted or rejected. Suppose we select a set of values which focuses on fluid elements of process, rather than static attributes. We might then value:

Man as a process of becoming; as a process of achieving worth and dignity through the development of his potentialities;

The individual human being as a self-actualizing process, moving on to more challenging and enriching experiences;

The process by which the individual creatively adapts to an ever-new and changing world;

The process by which knowledge transcends itself, as for example the theory of relativity transcended Newtonian physics, itself to be transcended in some future day by a new perception.

If we select values such as these we turn to our science and technology of behavior with a very different set of questions. We will want to know such things as these:

Can science aid us in the discovery of new modes of richly rewarding living? More meaningful and satisfying modes of interpersonal relationships?

Can science inform us as to how the human race can become a more intelligent participant in its own evolution—its physical, psychological and social evolution?

Can science inform us as to ways of releasing the creative capacity of individuals, which seem so necessary if we are to survive in this fantastically expanding atomic age? Dr. Oppenheimer has pointed out (4) that knowledge, which used to double in millennia or centuries, now doubles in a generation or a decade. It appears that we will need to discover the utmost in release of creativity if we are to be able to adapt effectively.

In short, can science discover the methods by which man can most readily become a continually developing and self-transcending process in his behavior, his thinking, his knowledge? Can science predict and release an essentially "unpredictable" freedom?

It is one of the virtues of science as a method that it is as able to advance and implement goals and purposes of this sort as it is to serve static values such as states of being well-informed, happy, obedient. Indeed we have some evidence of this.

A SMALL EXAMPLE

I will perhaps be forgiven if I document some of the possibilities along this line by turning to psychotherapy, the field I know best.

Psychotherapy, as Meerloo (2) and others have pointed out, can be one of the most subtle tools for the control of one person by another. The therapist can subtly mold individuals in imitation of himself. He can cause an individual to become a submissive and conforming being. When certain therapeutic principles are used in extreme fashion, we call it brainwashing, an instance of the disintegration of the personality and a reformulation of the person along lines desired by the controlling individual. So the principles of therapy can be used as a most effective means of external control of human personality and behavior. Can psychotherapy be anything else?

Here I find the developments going on in client-centered psychotherapy (8) an exciting hint of what a behavioral science can do in achieving the kinds of values I have stated. Quite aside from being a somewhat new orientation in psychotherapy, this development has important implications regarding the relation of a behavioral science to the control of human behavior. Let me describe our experience as it relates to the issues of the present discussion.

In client-centered therapy, we are deeply engaged in the prediction and influencing of behavior. As therapists we institute certain attitudinal conditions, and the client has relatively little voice in the establishment of these conditions. Very briefly we have found that the therapist is most effective if he is: (a) genuine, integrated, transparently real in the relationship; (b) acceptant of the client as a separate, different, person, and acceptant of each fluctuating aspect of the client as it comes to expression; and (c) sensitively empathic in his understanding, seeing the world through the client's eyes. Our research permits us to predict that if these attitudinal conditions are instituted or established, certain behavioral consequences will ensue. Putting it this way sounds as if we are again back in the familiar groove of being able to predict behavior, and hence able to control it. But precisely here exists a sharp difference.

The conditions we have chosen to establish predict such behavioral consequences as these: that the client will become more self-directing, less rigid, more open to the evidence of his senses, better organized and integrated, more similar to the ideal which he has chosen for himself. In other words we have established, by external control, conditions which we predict will be followed by internal control by the individual, in pursuit of internally chosen goals. We have set the conditions which predict various classes of behaviors—self-directing behaviors, sensitivity to realities within and without, flexible adaptiveness—which are by their very nature *unpredictable* in their specifics. The conditions we have established predict behavior which is essentially "free." Our recent research (9) indicates that our predictions are to a significant degree corroborated, and our commitment to the scientific method causes us to believe that more effective means of achieving these goals may be realized.

Research exists in other fields—industry, education, group dynamics—which seems to support our own findings. I believe it may be conservatively stated that scientific progress has been made in identifying those conditions in an interpersonal relationship which, if they exist in B, are followed in A by greater maturity in behavior, less dependence upon others, an increase in expressiveness as a person, an increase in variability, flexibility and effectiveness of adaptation, an increase in self-responsibility and self-direction. And quite in contrast to the concern expressed by some we do not find that the creatively adaptive behavior which results from such self-directed variability of expression is too chaotic or too fluid. Rather, the individual who is open to his experience, and self-directing, is harmonious, not chaotic, ingenious rather than random, as he orders his responses imaginatively toward the achievement of his own purposes. His creative actions are no more a chaotic accident than was Einstein's development of the theory of relativity.

Thus we find ourselves in fundamental agreement with John Dewey's statement: "Science has made its way by releasing, not by suppressing, the elements of variation, of invention and innovation, of novel creation in individuals." (7, p. 359) We have come to believe that progress in personal life and in group living is made in the same way, by releasing variation, freedom, creativity.

A POSSIBLE CONCEPT OF THE CONTROL OF HUMAN BEHAVIOR

It is quite clear that the point of view I am expressing is in sharp contrast to the usual conception of the relationship of the behavioral sciences to the control of human behavior, previously mentioned. In order to make this contrast even more blunt, I will state this possibility in a form parallel to the steps which I described before.

1. It is possible for us to choose to value man as a self-actualizing process of becoming; to value creativity, and the process by which knowledge becomes self-transcending.

2. We can proceed, by the methods of science, to discover the conditions which necessarily precede these processes, and through continuing experimentation, to discover better means of achieving these purposes.

3. It is possible for individuals or groups to set these conditions, with a minimum of power or control. According to present knowledge, the only authority necessary is the authority to establish certain qualities of interpersonal relationship.

4. Exposed to these conditions, present knowledge suggests that individuals become more self-responsible, make progress in self-actualization, become more flexible, more unique and varied, more creatively adaptive.

5. Thus such an initial choice would inaugurate the beginnings of a social system or subsystem in which values, knowledge, adaptive skills, and even the concept of science would be continually changing and self-transcending. The emphasis would be upon man as a process of becoming.

I believe it is clear that such a view as I have been describing does not lead to any definable Utopia. It would be impossible to predict its final outcome. It involves a step by step development, based upon a continuing subjective choice of purposes, which are implemented by the behavioral sciences. It is in the direction of the "open society," as that term has been defined by Popper (6), where individuals carry responsibility for personal decisions. It is at the opposite pole from his concept of the closed society, of which *Walden Two* would be an example.

I trust it is also evident that the whole emphasis is upon process, not upon end states of being. I am suggesting that it is by choosing to value certain qualitative elements of the process of becoming, that we can find a pathway toward the open society.

THE CHOICE

It is my hope that I have helped to clarify the range of choice which will lie before us and our children in regard to the behavioral sciences. We can choose to use our growing knowledge to enslave people in ways never dreamed of before, depersonalizing them, controlling them by means so carefully selected that they will perhaps never be aware of their loss of personhood. We can choose to utilize our scientific knowledge to make men necessarily happy, well-behaved, and productive, as Dr. Skinner suggests. We can, if we wish, choose to make men submissive, conforming, docile. Or at the other end of the spectrum of choice we can choose to use the behavioral sciences in ways which will free, not control; which will bring about constructive variability, not conformity; which will develop creativity, not contentment; which will facilitate each person in his self-directed process of becoming; which will aid individuals, groups, and even the concept of science, to become self-transcending in freshly adaptive ways of meeting life and its problems. The choice is up to us, and the human race being what it is, we are likely to stumble about, making at times some nearly disastrous value choices, and at other times highly constructive ones.

If we choose to utilize our scientific knowledge to free men, then it will demand that we live openly and frankly with the great paradox of the behavioral sciences. We will recognize that behavior, when examined scientifically, is surely best understood as determined by prior causation. This is the great fact of science. But responsible personal choice, which is the most essential element in being a person, which is the core experience in psychotherapy, which exists prior to any scientific endeavor, is an equally prominent fact in our lives. We will have to live with the realization that to deny the reality of the experience of responsible personal choice is as stultifying, as closed-minded, as to deny the possibility of a behavioral science. That these two important elements of our experience appear to be in contradiction has perhaps the same significance as the contradiction between the wave theory and the corpuscular theory of light, both of which can be shown to be true, even though incompatible. We cannot profitably deny our subjective life, any more than we can deny the objective description of that life.

In conclusion then, it is my contention that science cannot come into being without a personal choice of the values we wish to achieve. And these values we choose to implement will forever lie outside of the science which implements them; the goals we select, the purposes we wish to follow, must always be outside of the science which achieves them. To me this has the encouraging meaning that the human person, with his capacity of subjective choice, can and will always exist, separate from and prior to any of his scientific undertakings. Unless as individuals and groups we choose to relinquish our capacity of subjective choice, we will always remain free persons, not simply pawns of a self-created behavioral science.

REFERENCES

1. Huxley, A. *Brave New World*. New York and London: Harper and Bros., 1946.
2. Meerloo, J. A. M. Medication into submission: the danger of therapeutic coercion. *J. Nerv. Ment. Dis.*, 1955, *122*, 353–360.
3. Niebuhr, R. *The Self and the Dramas of History*. New York: Scribner, 1955.
4. Oppenheimer, R. Science and our times. *Roosevelt University Occasional Papers*. 1956, *2*, Chicago, Illinois.
5. Orwell, G. *1984*. New York: Harcourt, Brace, 1949; New American Library, 1953.
6. Popper, K. R. *The Open Society and Its Enemies*. London: Routledge and Kegan Paul, 1945.
7. Ratner, J. (Ed.). *Intelligence in the Modern World: John Dewey's Philosophy*. New York: Modern Library, 1939.
8. Rogers, C. R. *Client-Centered Therapy*. Boston: Houghton Mifflin, 1951.
9. Rogers, C. R. and Rosalind Dymond (Eds.). *Psychotherapy and Personality Change*. University of Chicago Press, 1954.
10. Skinner, B. F. Freedom and the control of men. *Amer. Scholar*, Winter, 1955-56, *25*, 47–65.
11. Skinner, B. F. *Science and Human Behavior*. New York: Macmillan, 1953. Quotation by permission of The Macmillan Co.
12. Skinner, B. F. *Walden Two*. New York: Macmillan, 1948. Quotations by permission of The Macmillan Co.
13. Whyte, W. H. *The Organization Man*. New York: Simon & Schuster, 1956.

Six
ALBERT BANDURA

In 1942, an outstanding attempt to describe in theoretical terms the operation of higher mental processes in the solving of emotional problems was presented by Neal Miller and John Dollard in their book *Social Learning and Imitation*. The authors elaborated on their theory sometime later in their classic work, *Personality and Psychotherapy*. In their discussion, Dollard and Miller distinguished between automatic and reflexive behavior and responses mediated by higher mental processes. They theorized that mental phenomena such as language, thinking, and images mediate between stimuli and responses and serve as cues, instigating complex social behavior. The patterning of these mediating responses and the inherent flexibility of symbolic behavior allow people to solve a wide variety of intellectual and emotional problems. These mediators, labeled by Miller and Dollard *cue-producing responses,* provide human beings with a unique advantage over other organisms on the evolutionary ladder and account for the enormous strides that people are capable of making in many areas of living. The pioneering efforts of Dollard and Miller are the precursors of the recent advances made by Bandura and other social learning theorists.

Albert Bandura (1925–   ) is most widely known for his work on modeling, vicarious learning, self-reinforcement, and, most recently, self-control. Bandura leans toward a formulation that emphasizes symbolic mental activity as a special human phenomenon that cannot be adequately studied through research using animals as subjects. For Bandura, a complex human response such as self-reinforcement lies in the realm of symbolic behavior, mediated by language, imagery, and thinking. Therefore, he believes that learning models that rely strictly on animal data are inadequate as explanations of complex human behavior. In Bandura's view, human beings have the unique capacity to think, to delay immediate gratification in favor of long-term gain, to learn complicated skills by observing models performing sequences of emotional and motor behavior, and to use information-processing capabilities to anticipate the best ways of solving problems.

The paper by Bandura in this chapter is his presidential address to the American Psychological Association. In it he reviews current trends in social learning theory, emphasizing the recent research in observational learning and self-reinforcement and discussing the broader issues of determinism and the limits of human freedom. Bandura stresses the role of the person in the selection of behavior. Although he acknowledges that the environment helps to shape behavior, he contends that each individual plays a large part in the creation of his or her own environmental conditions.

One of the most provocative issues in current personality theory and research is that of consistency versus specificity in personality functioning. It is a topic that sharply separates psychodynamic and behavioral approaches to personality, and in the past few years it has generated a substantial amount of empirical research and heated discussion. The questions raised in this dispute have far-reaching implications for a conceptual understanding of human behavior and bear a striking resemblance to the issues debated in the nature-versus-nurture controversy of earlier years. Put quite simply, the question is whether a person will function in pretty much the same way no matter what environmental conditions are present or whether situations or environments always demand and receive from a person behavior that is appropriate to the situation. If it is assumed that personality is mainly consistent, then a person should demonstrate relatively similar behavior across situations. If personality is mainly specific to the situation, then there should be greater behavioral variability across situations. Of course, none of the scientists involved in this debate naïvely assume that either the individual or the environment is independent of the other. There is always some interaction. Rather, the issue is whether a person's individuality accounts for most of his or her behavioral predictability. . The psychodynamic approach assumes that inner direction predominates, whereas the behavioral approach emphasizes outer direction.

The research recorded in the paper by Walter Mischel, Ebbe B. Ebbesen, and Antonette R. Zeiss was designed to study the effects of situational experience (success or failure) on the performance of subjects defined as repressors or sensitizers. On the basis of previous research it was hypothesized that repressors and sensitizers would behave in predictably different ways when situational conditions were relatively neutral. Here, the stable personality orientation would be the strongest factor influencing behavior. However, it was also predicted that, when powerful situational expectancies were introduced via the success and failure experiences, there would be more similarities within each situational condition than within the personality groups. Both of these hypotheses were supported. The authors feel that these data support the social learning theory of personality, which emphasizes the impact of situational experience on behavior.

The paper by Paul L. Wachtel is a powerful defense of the psychodynamic position and a critique of social learning theory as outlined by Bandura and Mischel. Wachtel argues that, even if people seem to behave differently in various situations, this apparent inconsistency does not necessarily contradict the idea that personality is in reality consistent. Wachtel believes that beneath the seemingly diverse reactions there is an underlying organization of personality that provides a basic consistency to our behavior. Wachtel goes on to clarify the nature of contemporary psychoanalytic theory. He feels that Bandura and others are misconstruing psychoanalysis when they say that it focuses exclusively on inner motivation. In fact, the interpersonal orientation of innovative analysts such as Harry Stack Sullivan, the work of Heinz Hartmann on ego adaptation to reality, and the important theoretical work by Erik H. Erikson on social influences on personality development highlight the tremendous range of psychoanalytic thought. Wachtel protests that the rigid characterization of psychoanalysis that behavior theorists perpetuate is simply inaccurate.

SUGGESTIONS FOR FURTHER READING

Bandura has published many books and research papers. One of his most important books is *Social Learning and Personality Development,* written with Richard Walters in 1963 and published by Holt, Rinehart & Winston. *Principles of Behavior Modification,* published in 1969 by Holt, Rinehart & Winston, contains a large and impressive summary of research on behavioral treatment, as well as original thinking on the subject. Bandura's most recent book is *Social Learning Theory*, Prentice-Hall, 1977. An excellent, concise statement of the principles of social learning theory is available in a General Learning Press module (pamphlet) written by Bandura and called "Social Learning Theory."

Albert Bandura
BEHAVIOR THEORY
AND THE MODELS OF MAN

The views about the nature of man conveyed by behavior theory require critical examination on conceptual and social grounds. What we believe man to be affects which aspects of human functioning we study most thoroughly and which we disregard. Premises thus delimit research and are, in turn, shaped by it. As knowledge gained through study is put into practice, the images of man on which social technologies rest have even vaster implications. This is nowhere better illustrated than in growing public concern over manipulation and control by psychological methods. Some of these fears arise from expectations that improved means of influence will inevitably be misused. Other apprehensions are aroused by exaggerated claims of psychological power couched in the language of manipulation and authoritarian control. But most fears stem from views of behaviorism, articulated by popular writers and by theorists themselves, that are disputed by the empirical facts of human behavior.

In the minds of the general public, and of many within our own discipline, behavior theory is equated with "conditioning." Over the years, the terms *behaviorism* and *conditioning* have come to be associated with odious imagery, including salivating dogs, puppetry, and animalistic manipulation. As a result, those who wish to disparage ideas or practices they hold in disfavor need only to label them as behavioristic or as Pavlovian precursors of a totalitarian state.

Contrary to popular belief, the fabled reflexive conditioning in humans is largely a myth. *Conditioning* is simply a descriptive term for learning through paired experiences, not an explanation of how the changes come about. Originally, conditioning was assumed to occur automatically. On closer examination it turned out to be cognitively mediated. People do not learn despite repetitive paired experiences unless they recognize that events are correlated (Dawson & Furedy, 1974; Grings, 1973). So-called conditioned reactions are largely self-activated on the basis of learned expectations rather than automatically evoked. The critical factor, therefore, is not that events occur together in time, but that people learn to predict them and to summon up appropriate anticipatory reactions.

The capacity to learn from correlated experiences reflects sensitivity, but because Pavlov first demonstrated the phenomenon with a dog, it has come to be regarded as a base animalistic process. Had he chosen to study physiological hyperactivity in humans to cues associated with stress, or the development of empathetic reactions to expressions of suffering, conditioning would have been treated in a more enlightened way. To expect people to remain unaffected by events that are frightening, humiliating, disgusting, sad, or pleasurable is to require that they be less than human. Although negative effects such as fears and dislikes

Reprinted by permission from the *American Psychologist*, 1974, *29*, pp. 859–869. Copyright 1974 by the American Psychological Association.

can arise from paired experiences of a direct or vicarious sort, so do some of the ennobling qualities of man. The pejorative accounts of learning principles, which appear with regularity in professional and lay publications, degrade both the science of psychology and the audiences that the offensive rhetoric is designed to sway.

It is well documented that behavior is influenced by its consequences much of the time. The image of man that this principle connotes depends on the types of consequences that are acknowledged and on an understanding of how they operate. In theories that recognize only the role of proximate external consequences and contend they shape behavior automatically, people appear as mechanical pawns of environmental forces. But external consequences, influential as they often are, are not the sole determinants of human behavior, nor do they operate automatically.

Response consequences serve several functions. First, they impart information. By observing the effects of their actions individuals eventually discern which behaviors are appropriate in which settings. The acquired information then serves as a guide for action. Contrary to the mechanistic metaphors, outcomes change behavior in humans through the intervening influence of thought.

Consequences motivate, through their incentive value, as well as inform. By representing foreseeable outcomes symbolically, future consequences can be converted into current motivators of behavior. Many of the things we do are designed to gain anticipated benefits and to avert future trouble. Our choices of action are largely under anticipatory control. The widely accepted dictum that man is ruled by response consequences thus fares better for anticipated than for actual consequences. Consider behavior on a fixed-ratio schedule (say, 50:1) in which only every fiftieth response is reinforced. Since 96% of the outcomes are extinctive and only 4% are reinforcing, behavior is maintained despite its dissuading consequences. As people are exposed to variations in frequency and predictability of reinforcement, they behave on the basis of the outcomes they expect to prevail on future occasions. When belief differs from actuality, which is not uncommon, behavior is weakly controlled by its actual consequences until repeated experience instills realistic expectations (Bandura, 1971b; Kaufman, Baron, & Kopp, 1966).

Had humans been ruled solely by instant consequences, they would have long become museum pieces among the extinct species. Not that our future is unquestionably secure. The immediate rewards of consumptive life-styles vigorously promoted for short-term profit jeopardize man's long-term chances of survival. But immediate consequences, unless unusually powerful, do not necessarily outweigh deferred ones (Mischel, 1974). Our descendants shall continue to have a future only because those who foresee the aversive long-term consequences of current practices mobilize public support for contingencies that favor survival behavior. Hazardous pesticides, for example, are usually banned before populations suffer maladies from toxic residues. The information-processing capacities with which humans are endowed provide the basis for insightful behavior. Their capacity to bring remote consequences to bear on current behavior by anticipatory thought supports foresightful action.

Explanations of reinforcement originally assumed that consequences increase behavior without conscious involvement. The still prevalent notion that reinforcers can operate insidiously arouses fears that improved techniques of reinforcement will enable authorities to manipulate people without their knowledge or consent. Although the empirical issue is not yet completely resolved, there is little evidence that rewards function as automatic strengtheners of human conduct. Behavior is not much affected by its consequences without awareness of what is being reinforced (Bandura, 1969; Dulany, 1968). After individuals discern the instrumental relation between action and outcome, contingent rewards may produce accommodating or oppositional behavior depending on how they value the incentives, the influencers and the behavior itself, and how others respond. Thus reinforcement, as it has become better understood, has changed from a mechanical strengthener of conduct to an informative and motivating influence.

People do not function in isolation. As social beings, they observe the conduct of others and the occasions on which it is rewarded, disregarded, or punished. They can therefore profit from observed consequences as well as from their own direct experiences (Bandura, 1971c). Acknowledgment of vicarious reinforcement introduces another human dimension—namely, evaluative capacities—into the operation of reinforcement influences. People weigh consequences to themselves against those accruing to others for similar behavior. The same outcome can thus become a reward or a punishment depending upon the referents used for social comparison.

Human conduct is better explained by the relational influence of observed and direct consequences than by either factor alone. However, behavior is not fully predictable from a relational coefficient because social justifications alter the impact of outcome disparities. Inequitable reinforcement is willingly accepted when people are graded by custom into social ranks and rewarded according to position rather than by performance. Arbitrary inequities are also likely to be tolerated if the underrewarded are led to believe they possess attributes that make them less deserving of equal treatment. Persuasively justified inequities have more detrimental personal effects than acknowledged unfairness because they foster self-devaluation in the maltreated. Negative reactions to inequitable reinforcement, which is acknowledged to be unwarranted, can likewise be diminished by temporizing. If people are led to expect that unfair treatment will be corrected within the foreseeable future, it becomes less aversive to them.

Theories that explain human behavior as the product of external rewards and punishments present a truncated image of man because people partly regulate their actions by self-produced consequences (Bandura, 1971c; Thoresen & Mahoney, 1973). Example and precept impart standards of conduct that serve as the basis for self-reinforcing reactions. The development of self-reactive functions gives humans a capacity for self-direction. They do things that give rise to self-satisfaction and self-worth, and they refrain from behaving in ways that evoke self-punishment.

After self-reinforcing functions are acquired, a given act produces two sets of consequences: self-evaluative reactions and external outcomes. Personal and external sources of reinforcement may operate as supplementary or as opposing influences on behavior. Thus, for example, individuals commonly experience conflicts when rewarded for conduct they personally devalue. When self-condemning consequences outweigh rewarding inducements, external influences are relatively ineffective. On the other hand, if certain courses of action produce stronger rewards than self-censure, the result is cheerless compliance. Losses in self-respect for devalued conduct can be abated, however, by self-exonerating justifications. I shall return to this issue shortly.

Another type of conflict between external and self-produced consequences arises when individuals are punished for behavior they regard highly. Principled dissenters and nonconformists often find themselves in this predicament. Personally valued conduct is expressed provided its costs are not too high. Should the threatened consequences be severe, one inhibits self-praiseworthy acts under high risk of penalty but readily performs them when the chances of punishment are reduced. There are individuals, however, whose sense of self-worth is so strongly invested in certain convictions that they will submit to prolonged maltreatment rather than accede to what they regard as unjust or immoral.

External consequences exert greatest influence on behavior when they are compatible with those that are self-produced. These conditions obtain when rewardable acts are a source of self-pride and punishable ones are self-censured. To enhance compatibility between personal' and social influences, people select associates who share similar standards of conduct and thus ensure social support for their own system of self-reinforcement.

Individualistic theories of moral action assume that internalization of behavioral standards creates a permanent control mechanism within the person. Restraints of conscience thereafter operate as enduring controls over reprehensible conduct. The testimony of human behavior, however, contradicts this view. Much human maltreatment and suffering are, in fact, inflicted by otherwise decent moral people. And some of the most striking changes in moral conduct, as evidenced, for example, in political and military violence, are achieved without altering personality structures or moral standards. Personal control is clearly more complex and flexible than the theorizing implies.

Although self-reinforcing influences serve as regulators of conduct, they can be dissociated from censurable deeds by self-exonerating practices (Bandura, 1973). One device is to make inhumane behavior personally and socially acceptable by defining it in terms of high moral principle. People do not act in ways they ordinarily consider evil or destructive until such activities are construed as serving moral purposes. Over the years, much cruelty has been perpetrated in the name of religious principles, righteous ideologies, and regulatory sanctions. In the transactions of everyday life, euphemistic labeling serves as a handy linguistic device for masking reprehensible activities or according them a respectable status. Self-deplored conduct can also be made benign by contrasting it with more flagrant inhumanities. Moral justifications and palliative comparisons are especially effective because they not only eliminate self-generated deterrents but engage self-reward in the service of reprehensible conduct. What was morally unacceptable becomes a source of self-pride.

A common dissociative practice is to obscure or distort the relationship between one's actions and the effects they cause. People will perform behavior they normally repudiate if a legitimate authority sanctions it and acknowledges responsibility for its consequences. By displacing responsibility elsewhere, participants do not hold themselves accountable for what they do and are thus spared self-prohibiting reactions. Exemption from self-censure can be facilitated additionally by diffusing responsibility for culpable behavior. Through division of labor, division of decision making, and collective action, people can contribute to detrimental practices without feeling personal responsibility or self-disapproval.

Attribution of blame to the victim is still another exonerative expedient. Victims are faulted for bringing maltreatment on themselves, or extraordinary circumstances are invoked as justifications for questionable conduct. One need not engage in self-reproof for committing acts prescribed by circumstances. A further means of weakening self-punishment is to dehumanize the victim. Inflicting harm upon people who are regarded as subhuman or debased is less likely to arouse self-reproof than if they are looked upon as human beings with sensitivities.

There are other self-disinhibiting maneuvers that operate by misrepresenting the consequences of actions. As long as detrimental effects are ignored or minimized, there is little reason for self-censure. If consequences are not easily distortable, distress over conduct that conflicts with self-evaluative standards can be reduced by selectively remembering the benefits and forgetting the harm of one's acts.

Given the variety of self-disinhibiting devices, a society cannot rely on control by conscience to ensure moral and ethical conduct. Though personal control ordinarily serves as a self-directive force, it can be nullified by social sanctions conducive to destructiveness.

Indoctrination and social justifications give meaning to events and create anticipations that determine one's actions. Control through information, which is rooted in cognitive processes, is more pervasive and powerful than conditioning through contiguity of events. Cultivation of humaneness therefore requires, in addition to benevolent personal codes, safeguards built into social systems that counteract detrimental sanctioning practices and uphold compassionate behavior.

A conceptual orientation not only prescribes what facets of man will be studied in depth but also how one goes about changing human behavior. Early applications of reinforcement principles, for example, were guided by the then prevalent belief that consequences alter behavior automatically and unconsciously. Since the process supposedly operated mechanically, the reinforcers had to occur instantly to be effective. Participants in change programs were, therefore, uninformed about why they were being reinforced, and, in an effort to ensure immediacy of effects, reinforcers were presented intrusively as soon as the requisite responses were emitted. The net effect was a tedious shaping process that produced, at best, mediocre results in an ethically questionable manner. In many public and professional circles, reinforcement still connotes furtive control even though reinforcement theory and practices have progressed well beyond this level.

Realization that reinforcement is an unarticulated way of designating appropriate conduct prompted the use of cognitive factors in the modification of behavior. Not surprisingly, people change more rapidly if told what behaviors are rewardable and punishable than if they have to discover it from observing the consequences of their actions. Competencies that are not already within their repertoires can be developed with greater ease through the aid of instruction and modeling than by relying solely on the successes and failures of unguided performance.

As further research revealed that reinforcers function as motivators, consequences were recognized as sources of motivation that depend heavily for their effectiveness upon the incentive preferences of those undergoing change. Hence, people do not indiscriminately absorb the influences that impinge upon them. Outcomes resulting from actions need not necessarily occur instantly. Humans can cognitively bridge delays between behavior and subsequent reinforcers without impairing the efficacy of incentive operations.

At this second evolutionary stage, reinforcement practices changed from unilateral control to social contracting. Positive arrangements affirm that if individuals do certain things they are entitled to certain rewards and privileges. In the case of negative sanctions, reprehensible conduct carries punishment costs. The process is portrayed in reinforcement terms, but the practice is that of social exchange. Most social interactions are, of course, governed by conditional agreements, though they usually are not couched in the language of reinforcement. Describing them differently does not change their nature, however.

Contingencies vary in the human qualities they embody and in the voice individuals have in decisions concerning the social arrangements that affect their lives. Reflecting the salient values of our society, reinforcement practices have traditionally favored utilitarian forms of behavior. But conditions are changing. With growing reservations about materialistic life-styles, reinforcement practices are being increasingly used to cultivate personal potentialities and humanistic qualities. These emerging changes in value commitments will probably accelerate as people devote fewer hours to working for income and have more leisure time for self-development.

Another change of some consequence is the renewed concern for individual rights. People are seeking a collaborative role in the development of societal contingencies that affect the course and quality of their lives. As part of this social trend, even the actions taken in the name of psychotherapy are being examined for their ethics and social purposes. These concerns have provided the impetus for prescripts to ensure that reinforcement techniques are used in the service of human betterment rather than as instruments of social control.

A closely related issue is the relative attention devoted to changing individuals or to altering the institutions of society to enrich life. If psychologists are to have a significant impact on common problems of life, they must apply their corrective measures to detrimental societal practices rather than limit themselves to treating the casualties of these practices. This, of course, is easier said than done. Practitioners, whatever their specialty, are reinforced more powerfully for using their knowledge and skills in the service of existing operations than for changing them. Socially oriented efforts are hard to sustain under inadequate reinforcement supports.

The methods of change discussed thus far draw heavily upon external consequences of action. Evidence that people can exercise some control over their own behavior provided the impetus for further changes in reinforcement practices. Interest began to shift from managing conduct to developing skills in self-regulation. In the latter approach, control is vested to a large extent in the hands of individuals themselves: They arrange the environmental inducements for desired behavior; they evaluate their own performances; and they serve as their own reinforcing agents (Goldfried & Merbaum, 1973; Mahoney & Thoresen, 1974). To be sure, the self-reinforcing functions are created and occasionally supported by external influences. Having external origins, however, does not refute the fact that, once established, self-influence partly determines what actions one performs. Citing historical determinants of a generalizable function cannot substitute for contemporaneous influences arising through exercise of that function.

The recognition of self-directing capacities represents a substantial departure from exclusive reliance upon environmental control. But the emerging self-influence practices are still closely rooted in physical transactions   the self-administered consequences are, for the most part, material. Eventually changes in form, as well as source, of reinforcement will appear as the insufficiency of material outcomes is acknowledged. Most people value their self-respect above commodities. They rely extensively on their own self-demands and self-approval as guides for conduct. To ignore the influential role of covert self-reinforcement in the regulation of behavior is to disavow a uniquely human capacity of man.

Proponents who recognize only external consequences restrict their research and practice to such influences and thus generate evidence that reinforces their conceptions. Those who acknowledge personal influences as well tend to select methods that reveal and promote self-directing capabilities in man. The view of man embodied in behavioral technologies is therefore more than a philosophical issue. It affects which human potentialities will be cultivated and which will be underdeveloped.

The preceding remarks addressed the need to broaden the scope of research into the reinforcement processes regulating human behavior. Much the same might be said for the ways in which human learning is conceptualized and investigated. Our theories have been incredibly slow in acknowledging that man can learn by observation as well as by direct experience. This is another example of how steadfast adherence to orthodox paradigms makes it difficult to transcend the confines of conceptual commitment. Having renounced cognitive determinants, early proponents of behaviorism advanced the doctrine that learning can occur only by performing responses and experiencing their effects. This legacy is still very much with us. The rudimentary form of learning based on direct experience has been exhaustively studied, whereas the more pervasive and powerful mode of learning by observation is largely ignored. A shift of emphasis is needed.

The capacity to represent modeled activities symbolically enables man to acquire new patterns of behavior observationally without reinforced enactment. From observing others, one forms an idea of how certain behavior is performed, and on later occasions the coded information serves as a guide for action. Indeed, research conducted within the framework of social learning theory shows that virtually all learning phenomena resulting from direct experience can occur on a vicarious basis by observing other people's behavior and its consequences for them (Bandura, 1969). The abbreviation of the acquisition process through observational learning is, of course, vital for both development and survival. Modeling reduces the burden of time-consuming performance of inappropriate responses. Since errors can produce costly, if not fatal, consequences, the prospects of survival would be slim indeed if people had to rely solely on the effects of their actions to inform them about what to do.

In many instances the behavior being modeled must be learned in essentially the same form. Driving automobiles, skiing, and performing surgery, for example, permit little, if any, departure from essential practices. In addition to transmitting particular response patterns, however, modeling influences can create generative and innovative behavior. In the latter process, observers abstract common features from seemingly diverse responses and formulate generative rules of behavior that enable them to go beyond what they have seen or heard. By synthesizing features of different models into new amalgams, observers can achieve through modeling novel styles of thought and conduct. Once initiated, experiences with the new forms create further evolutionary changes. A partial departure from tradition eventually becomes a new direction.

Some of the limitations commonly ascribed to behavior theory are based on the mistaken belief that modeling can produce at best mimicry of specific acts. This view is disputed by growing evidence that abstract modeling is a highly effective means of inducing rule-governed cognitive behavior (Bandura, 1971a; Zimmerman & Rosenthal, 1974). On the basis of observationally derived rules, people alter their judgmental orientations, conceptual schemes, linguistic styles, information-processing strategies, as well as other forms of cognitive functioning. Nevertheless, faulty evaluations continue to be mistaken for weaknesses inherent in theory.

Observational learning has recently come to be accepted more widely, but some theorists are willing to grant it full scientific respectability only if it is reduced to performance terms. As a result, enactment paradigms are used which are rooted in the traditional assumption that responses must be performed before they can be learned. Instant reproduction of modeled responses is favored, thereby minimizing dependence upon cognitive functions which play an especially influential role when retention over time is required. The issue of whether reinforcement enhances modeling is pursued to the neglect of the more interesting question of whether one can keep people from learning what they have seen.

When learning is investigated through observational paradigms, a broader range of determinants and intervening mechanisms gains prominence. Learning by observation is governed by four component processes: *(a)* attentional functions regulate sensory input and perception of modeled actions; *(b)* through coding and symbolic rehearsal, transitory experiences are transformed for memory representation into enduring performance guides; *(c)* motor reproduction processes govern the integration of constituent acts into new response patterns; and *(d)* incentive or motivational processes determine whether observationally acquired responses will be performed. Studied from this perspective, observational learning emerges as an actively judgmental and constructive, rather than a mechanical copying, process.

Because observational learning entails several subfunctions that evolve with maturation and experience, it obviously depends upon prior development. Differences in theoretical perspectives prescribe different methodologies for studying how the capacity for observational learning itself is acquired. When modeling is conceptualized in terms of formation of stimulus–response linkages, efforts are aimed at increasing the probability of imitative responses through reinforcement. Modeling can be increased by rewarding matching behavior, but such demonstrations are not of much help in identifying what exactly is being acquired during the process, or in explaining imitation failures under favorable conditions of reinforcement. From a social learning view, the capability for observational learning is developed by acquiring skill in discriminative observation, in memory encoding, in coordinating ideomotor and sensorimotor systems, and in judging probable consequences for matching behavior. Understanding how people learn to imitate becomes a matter of understanding how the requisite subfunctions develop and operate. Capacity for observational learning is restricted by deficits, and expanded by improvements, in its component functions.

Over the years, proponents of the more radical forms of behaviorism not only disclaimed interest in mentation but also marshaled numerous reasons why cognitive events are inadmissible in causal analyses. It was, and still is, argued that cognitions are inaccessible except through untrustworthy self-reports, they are inferences from effects, they are epiphenomenal, or they are simply fictional. Advances in experimental analysis of behavior, it was claimed, would eventually show them to be unnecessary. Empirical evidence, however, has shown the opposite to be true. A large body of research now exists in which cognition is activated instructionally with impressive results. People learn and retain much better by using cognitive aids that they generate than by repetitive reinforced performance (Anderson & Bower, 1973; Bandura, 1971a). With growing evidence that cognition has causal influence in behavior, the arguments against cognitive determinants are losing their force.

These recent developments have shifted emphasis from the study of response learning to analyses of memory and cognition. From this effort we have gained a better understanding of the mechanisms whereby information is acquired, stored, and retrieved. There is more to learning, however, than the acquisition and retention of information. Behavioristic theories addressed themselves to performance but deemphasized internal determinants, whereas the cognitive approaches remain immersed in thought but divorced from conduct. In a complete account of human behavior, internal processes must eventually be tied to action. Hence, explanations of how information eventuates in skilled performance must additionally be concerned with the organization and regulation of behavior. Social learning includes within its framework both the processes internal to the organism as well as performance-related determinants.

Speculations about man's nature inevitably raise the fundamental issues of determinism and human freedom. In examining these questions it is essential to distinguish between the metaphysical and the social aspects of freedom. Many of the heated disputes on this topic arise as much, if not more, from confusion over the dimensions of freedom being discussed as from disagreements over the doctrine of determinism.

Let us first consider freedom in the social sense. Whether freedom is an illusion, as some writers maintain, or a social reality of considerable importance depends upon the meaning given to it. Within the social learning framework, freedom is defined in terms of the number of options available to people and the right to exercise them. The more behavioral alternatives and social prerogatives people have, the greater is their freedom of action.

Personal freedom can be limited in many different ways. Behavioral deficits restrict possible choices and otherwise curtail opportunities to realize one's preferences. Freedom can therefore be expanded by cultivating competencies. Self-restraints arising from unwarranted fears and stringent self-censure restrict the effective range of activities that individuals can engage in or even contemplate. Here freedom is restored by eliminating dysfunctional self-restraints.

In maximizing freedom a society must place some limits on conduct because complete license for any individual is likely to encroach on the freedom of others. Societal prohibitions against behavior that is socially injurious create additional curbs on conduct. Conflicts often arise over behavioral restrictions when many members of society question conventional customs and when legal sanctions are used more to enforce a particular brand of morality than to prohibit socially detrimental conduct.

The issue of whether individuals should be allowed to engage in activities that are self-injurious but not detrimental to society has been debated vigorously over the years. Prohibitionists argue that it is difficult for a person, other than a recluse, to impair himself without inflicting secondary harm on others. Should self-injury produce incapacities, society usually ends up bearing the treatment and subsistence costs. Libertarians do not find such arguments sufficiently convincing to justify a specific prohibition because some of the self-injurious activities that society approves may be as bad or worse than those it outlaws. Normative changes over time regarding private conduct tend to favor an individualistic ethic. Consequently, many activities that were formerly prohibited by law have been exempted from legal sanctions.

Some groups have their freedom curtailed by socially condoned discrimination. Here, the alternatives available to a person are limited by skin color, sex, religion, ethnic background, or social class, regardless of capabilities. When self-determination is prejudicially restricted, those who are subordinated remove inequities by altering practices that compromise or temporize the professed values of society.

Freedom deals with rights as well as options and behavioral restraints. Man's struggle for freedom is principally aimed at structuring societal contingencies so that certain forms of behavior are exempted from aversive control. After protective laws are built into the system, there are certain things that a society may not do to an individual, however much it might like to. Legal prohibitions on societal control create freedoms that are realities, not simply feelings or states of mind. Societies differ in their institutions of freedom and in the number and types of behaviors that are officially exempted from punitive control. Social systems that protect journalists from punitive control, for example, are freer than those that allow authoritative power to be used to silence critics or their vehicles of expression. Societies that possess an independent judiciary ensure greater social freedom than those that do not.

In philosophical discourses, freedom is often considered antithetical to determinism. When defined in terms of options and rights, there is no incompatibility of freedom and determinism. From this perspective, freedom is not conceived negatively as the absence of influences or simply the lack of external constraints. Rather, it is defined positively in terms of the skills at one's command and the exercise of self-influence upon which choice of action depends.

Psychological analyses of freedom eventually lead to discourses on the metaphysics of determinism. Are people partial determiners of their own behavior, or are they ruled exclusively by forces beyond their control? The long-standing debate over this issue has been enlivened by Skinner's (1971) contention that, apart from genetic contributions, human behavior is controlled solely by environmental contingencies, for example, "A person does not act upon the world, the world acts upon him" (p. 211). A major problem with this type of analysis is that it depicts the environment as an autonomous force that automatically shapes and controls behavior. Environments have causes as do behaviors. For the most part, the environment is only a potentiality until actualized and fashioned by appropriate actions. Books do not influence people unless someone writes them and others select and read them. Rewards and punishments remain in abeyance until prompted by appropriate performances.

·It is true that behavior is regulated by its contingencies, but the contingencies are partly of a person's own making. By their actions, people play an active role in producing the reinforcing contingencies that impinge upon them. Thus, behavior partly creates the environment, and the environment influences the behavior in a reciprocal fashion. To the oft-repeated dictum, change contingencies and you change behavior, should be added the reciprocal side, change behavior and you change the contingencies.

The image of man's efficacy that emerges from psychological research depends upon which aspect of the reciprocal control system one selects for analysis. In the paradigm favoring environmental control, investigators analyze how environmental contingencies change behavior $[B = f(E)]$. The personal control paradigm, on the other hand, examines how behavior determines the environment $[E = f(B)]$. Behavior is the effect in the former case, and the cause in the latter. Although the reciprocal sources of influence are separable for experimental purposes, in everyday life two-way control operates concurrently. In ongoing interchanges, one and the same event can thus be a stimulus, a response, or an environmental reinforcer depending upon the place in the sequence at which the analysis arbitrarily begins

A survey of the literature on reinforcement confirms the extent to which we have become captives of a one-sided paradigm to map a bidirectional process. Environmental control is overstudied, whereas personal control has been relatively neglected. To cite but one example, there exist countless demonstrations of how behavior varies under different schedules of reinforcement, but one looks in vain for studies of how people, either individually or by collective action, succeed in fashioning reinforcement schedules to their own liking. The dearth of research on personal control is not because people exert no influence on their environment or because such efforts are without effect. Quite the contrary. Behavior is one of the more influential determinants of future contingencies. As analyses of sequential interchanges reveal, aggressive individuals actualize through their conduct a hostile environment, whereas those who display friendly responsiveness produce an amicable social milieu within the same setting (Rausch, 1965). We are all acquainted with problem-prone individuals who, through their aversive conduct, predictably breed negative social climates wherever they go.

It should be noted that some of the doctrines ascribing preeminent control to the environment are ultimately qualified by acknowledgment that man can exercise some measure of countercontrol (Skinner, 1971). The notion of reciprocal interaction, however, goes considerably beyond the concept of countercontrol. Countercontrol portrays the environment as an instigating force to which individuals react. As we have already seen, people activate and create environments as well as rebut them.

People may be considered partially free insofar as they can influence future conditions by managing their own behavior. Granted that selection of particular courses of action from available alternatives is itself determined, individuals can nevertheless exert some control over the factors that govern their choices. In philosophical analyses all events can be submitted to an infinite regression of causes. Such discussions usually emphasize how man's actions are determined by prior conditions but neglect the reciprocal part of the process showing that the conditions themselves are partly determined by man's prior actions. Applications of self-control practices demonstrate that people are able to regulate their own behavior in preferred directions by arranging environmental conditions most likely to elicit it and administering self-reinforcing consequences to sustain it. They may be told how to do it and initially be given some external support for their efforts, but self-produced influences contribute significantly to future goal attainment.

To contend, as environmental determinists often do, that people are controlled by external forces and then to advocate that they redesign their society by applying behavioral technology undermines the basic premise of the argument. If humans were in fact incapable of influencing their own actions, they could describe and predict environmental events but hardly exercise any intentional control over them. When it comes to advocacy of social change, however, thoroughgoing environmental determinists become ardent exponents of man's power to transform environments in pursuit of a better life.

In backward causal analyses, conditions are usually portrayed as ruling man, whereas forward deterministic analyses of goal setting and attainment reveal how people can shape conditions for their purposes. Some are better at it than others. The greater their foresight, proficiency, and self-influence, all of which are acquirable skills, the greater the progress toward their goals. Because of the capacity for reciprocal influence, people are at least partial architects of their own destinies. It is not determinism that is in dispute, but whether it is treated as a one-way or a two-way control process. Considering the interdependence of behavior and environmental conditions, determinism does not imply the fatalistic view that man is but a pawn of external influences.

Psychological perspectives on determinism, like other aspects of theorizing, influence the nature and scope of social practice. Environmental determinists are apt to use their methods primarily in the service of institutionally prescribed patterns of behavior. Personal determinists are more inclined to cultivate self-directing potentialities in man. The latter behavioral approach and humanism have much in common. Behavioral theorists, however, recognize that "self-actualization" is by no means confined to human virtues. People have numerous potentialities that can be actualized for good or ill. Over the years, man has suffered considerably at the hands of self-actualized tyrants. A self-centered ethic of self-realization must therefore be tempered by concern for the social consequences of one's conduct. Behaviorists generally emphasize environmental sources of control, whereas humanists tend to restrict their interest to personal control. Social learning encompasses both aspects of the bidirectional influence process.

When the environment is regarded as an autonomous rather than as an influenceable determinant of behavior, valuation of dignifying human qualities and accomplishments is diminished. If inventiveness emanates from external circumstances, it is environments that should be credited for people's achievements and chastised for their failings or inhumanities. Contrary to the unilateral view, human accomplishments result from reciprocal interaction of external circumstances with a host of personal determinants including endowed potentialities, acquired competencies, reflective thought, and a high level of self-initiative.

Musical composers, for example, help to shape tastes by their creative efforts, and the public in turn supports their performances until advocates of new styles generate new public preferences. Each succeeding form of artistry results from a similar two-way influence process for which neither artisans nor circumstances deserve sole credit.

Superior accomplishments, whatever the field, require considerable self-disciplined application. After individuals adopt evaluative standards, they expend large amounts of time, on their own, improving their performances to the point of self-satisfaction. At this level of functioning, persistence in an endeavor is extensively under self-reinforcement control. Skills are perfected as much, or more, to please oneself as to please the public.

Without self-generated influences most innovative efforts would be difficult to sustain. This is because the unconventional is initially resisted and gradually accepted only as it proves functionally valuable or wins prestigious advocates. As a result, the early efforts of innovators bring rebuffs rather than rewards or recognition. In the history of creative endeavors, it is not uncommon for artists or composers to be scorned when they depart markedly from convention. Some gain recognition later in their careers. Others are sufficiently convinced of the worth of their work that they labor indefatigably even though their productions are negatively received during their lifetimes. Ideological and, to a lesser extent, technological advances follow similar courses. Most innovative endeavors receive occasional social support in early phases, but environmental conditions alone are not especially conducive to unconventional developments.

The operation of reciprocal influence also has bearing on the public concern that advances in psychological knowledge will produce an increase in human manipulation and control. A common response to such apprehensions is that all behavior is inevitably controlled. Social influence, therefore, is not a question of imposing controls where none existed before. This type of argument is valid in the sense that every act has a cause. But it is not the principle of causality that worries people. At the societal level, their misgivings center on the distribution of controlling power, the means and purposes for which it is used, and the availability of mechanisms for exercising reciprocal control over institutional practices. At the individual level, they are uneasy about the implications of psychotechnology in programming human relations.

Possible remedies for exploitative use of psychological techniques are usually discussed in terms of individual safeguards. Increased knowledge about modes of influence is prescribed as the best defense against manipulation. When people are informed about how behavior can be controlled, they tend to resist evident attempts at influence, thus making manipulation more difficult. Awareness alone, however, is a weak countervalence.

Exploitation was successfully thwarted long before there existed a discipline of psychology to formulate principles and practices of behavior change. The most reliable source of opposition to manipulative control resides in the reciprocal consequences of human interactions. People resist being taken advantage of, and will continue to do so in the future, because compliant behavior produces unfavorable consequences for them. Sophisticated efforts at influence in no way reduce the aversiveness of yielding that is personally disadvantageous. Because of reciprocal consequences, no one is able to manipulate others at will, and everyone experiences some feeling of powerlessness in getting what they want. This is true at all levels of functioning, individual and collective. Parents cannot get their children to follow all their wishes, while children feel constrained by their parents from doing what they desire. At universities, the administrators, faculty, students, and alumni all feel that the other constituencies are unduly influential in promoting their self-interests but that one's own group is granted insufficient power to alter the institutional practices. In the political arena, Congress feels that the executive branch possesses excessive power, and conversely the executive branch feels thwarted in implementing its policies by congressional counteraction.

If protection against exploitation relied solely upon individual safeguards, people would be continually subjected to coercive pressures. Accordingly, they create institutional sanctions which set limits on the control of human behavior. The integrity of individuals is largely secured by societal safeguards that place constraints on improper means and foster reciprocity through balancing of interests.

Because individuals are conversant with psychological techniques does not grant them license to impose them on others. Industrialists, for example, know full well that productivity is higher when payment is made for amount of work completed rather than for length of time at work. Nevertheless, they cannot use the reinforcement system most advantageous to them. When industrialists commanded exclusive power, they paid workers at a piece-rate basis and hired and fired them at will. Reductions in power disparity between employers and employees resulted in a gradual weakening of performance requirements. As labor gained economic coercive strength through collective action, it was able to negotiate guaranteed wages on a daily, weekly, monthly, and eventually on an annual basis. At periodic intervals new contractual contingencies are adopted that are mutually acceptable. In the course of time, as better means of joint action are developed, other constituents will use their influence to modify arrangements that benefit certain segments of labor and industry but adversely affect the quality of life for other sectors of society.

As the previous example illustrates, improved knowledge of how to influence behavior does not necessarily raise the level of social control. If anything, the recent years have witnessed a diffusion of power, creating increased opportunities for reciprocal influence. This has enabled people to challenge social inequities, to effect changes in institutional practices, to counteract infringements on their rights, and to extend grievance procedures and due process of law to activities in social contexts that hitherto operated under unilateral control. The fact that more people wield power does not in and of itself ensure a humane society. In the final analysis, the important consideration is the purposes that power serves, however it might be distributed. Nor does knowledgeability about means of influence necessarily produce mechanical responsiveness in personal relations. Whatever their orientations, people model, expound, and reinforce what they value. Behavior arising out of purpose and commitment is no less genuine than improvised action.

The cliché of *1984*, and its more recent kin, diverts public attention from regulative influences that pose continual threats to human welfare. Most societies have instituted reciprocal systems that are protected by legal and social codes to prevent imperious control of human behavior. Although abuses of institutional power arise from time to time, it is not totalitarian rule that constitutes the impending peril. The hazards lie more in the intentional pursuit of personal gain, whether material or otherwise, than in control by coercion. Detrimental social practices arise and resist change, even within an open society, when many people benefit from them. To take a prevalent example, inequitable treatment of disadvantaged groups for private gain enjoys public support without requiring despotic rule.

Man, of course, has more to contend with than inhumanities toward one another. When the aversive consequences of otherwise rewarding life-styles are delayed and imperceptibly cumulative, people become willful agents of their own self-destruction. Thus, if enough people benefit from activities that progressively degrade their environment, then, barring contravening influences, they will eventually destroy their environment. Although individuals contribute differentially to the problem, the harmful consequences are borne by all. With growing populations and spread of lavish life-styles taxing finite resources, people will have to learn to cope with new realities of human existence.

Psychology cannot tell people how they ought to live their lives. It can, however, provide them with the means for effecting personal and social change. And it can aid them in making value choices by assessing the consequences of alternative life-styles and institutional arrangements. As a science concerned about the social consequences of its applications, psychology must also fulfill a broader obligation to society by bringing influence to bear on public policies to ensure that its findings are used in the service of human betterment.

REFERENCES

Anderson, J. R., & Bower, G. H. *Human associative memory*. New York: Wiley, 1973.

Bandura, A. *Principles of behavior modification*. New York: Holt, Rinehart & Winston, 1969.

Bandura, A. (Ed.) *Psychological modeling: Conflicting theories*. Chicago: Aldine-Atherton, 1971. (a)

Bandura, A. *Social learning theory.* New York: General Learning Press, 1971. (b)

Bandura, A. Vicarious and self-reinforcement processes. In R. Glaser (Ed.), *The nature of reinforcement.* New York: Academic Press, 1971. (c)

Bandura, A. *Aggression: A social learning analysis.* Englewood Cliffs, N.J.: Prentice-Hall, 1973.

Dawson, M. E., & Furedy, J. J. The role of relational awareness in human autonomic discrimination classical conditioning. Unpublished manuscript, University of Toronto, 1974.

Dulany, D. E. Awareness, rules, and propositional control: A confrontation with S-R behavior theory. In T. R. Dixon & D. L. Horton (Eds.), *Verbal behavior and general behavior theory.* Englewood Cliffs, N. J.: Prentice-Hall, 1968.

Goldfried, M. R., & Merbaum, M. (Eds.) *Behavior change through self-control.* New York: Holt, Rinehart & Winston, 1973.

Grings, W. W. The role of consciousness and cognition in autonomic behavior change. In F. J. McGuigan & R. Schoonover (Eds.), *The psychophysiology of thinking.* New York: Academic Press, 1973.

Kaufman, A., Baron, A., & Kopp, R. E. Some effects of instructions on human operant behavior. *Psychonomic Monograph Supplements,* 1966, *1,* 243–250.

Mahoney, M. J., & Thoresen, C. E. *Self-control: Power to the person.* Monterey, Calif.: Brooks/Cole, 1974.

Mischel, W. Processes in delay of gratification. In L. Berkowitz (Ed.), *Advances in experimental social psychology.* Vol. 7. New York: Academic Press, 1974.

Rausch, H. L. Interaction sequences. *Journal of Personality and Social Psychology,* 1965, *2,* 487–499.

Skinner, B. F. *Beyond freedom and dignity.* New York: Knopf, 1971.

Thoresen, C. E., & Mahoney, M. J. *Behavioral self-control.* New York: Holt, Rinehart & Winston, 1973.

Zimmerman, B. J., & Rosenthal, T. L. Observational learning of rule-governed behavior by children. *Psychological Bulletin,* 1974, *81,* 29–42.

Walter Mischel, Ebbe B. Ebbesen, and Antonette R. Zeiss
SELECTIVE ATTENTION TO THE SELF: SITUATIONAL AND DISPOSITIONAL DETERMINANTS

A paradigm was developed to investigate the influence of success and failure experiences on subsequent selective attention to information about the self. College students were assigned to success, failure, or control experiences on an achievement task ostensibly testing intellectual ability. Half also expected further testing, and half expected no further testing. Immediately after the achievement task subjects had available positive and negative personality information about themselves as well as information about the task. They could choose to attend, or not attend, to any of the information in any order for 10 minutes. Successful subjects attended more to their personality assets, and less to liabilities, than did subjects who failed or had a control experience. The latter two groups did not differ. These effects were strongest when there was no expectancy for further testing. The discussion analyzed the theoretical bases for the effects of positive experiences (e.g., success) on subsequent self-regulatory patterns. In addition, main effects and interactions with individual differences on the Repression–Sensitization Scale indicated that sensitizers were more likely to attend to their liabilities and repressors were more likely to attend to their assets; these effects of individual differences were strongest in control conditions, and were nullified when treatment effects were powerful, in accord with theoretical expectations.

It has become increasingly obvious during the last decade that an adequate approach to personality must illuminate the individual's self-regulatory and self-monitoring processes (e.g., Bandura, 1969; Mischel, 1968). Recent research has already begun to explore some of the many variables that determine an individual's decision to self-administer or withhold rewards and punishments for his own behavior. But self-regulatory processes are not limited to the individual's self-administration of such outcomes as the tokens, "prizes," or verbal approval and disapproval that have been favored in most previous studies of self-reinforcement (e.g., Bandura, 1969; Kanfer & Phillips, 1970; Mischel, Coates, & Raskoff, 1968). An especially pervasive but thus far neglected feature of self-regulation is the person's selective exposure to different types of positive and negative information about himself.

Almost limitless "good" and "bad" information about the self is potentially available (e.g., in the form of memories), depending on where one looks and how one searches. An individual can seek, and usually find, information to support his positive or negative attributes, his successes or failures, almost boundlessly. He can focus cognitively, for example, on his past, present, and expected assets or liabilities and attend either to his strengths or to his weaknesses by ideating about selective aspects of his perceived personality and behavior. Affective self-reactions, as in the enhancement of one's own self-esteem and, in common sense terms, the individual's positive and negative feelings about himself,

Reprinted by permission from the *Journal of Personality and Social Psychology*, 1973, 27, pp. 129–142. Copyright 1973 by the American Psychological Association.

presumably hinge on selective attentional processes through which the individual exposes himself only to particular types of information from the enormous array potentially available to him. By means of such selective attention the individual presumably can make himself feel either good or bad, can privately congratulate or condemn himself and, in the extreme, can generate emotions from euphoria to depression. Given that every person perceives himself as having *both* some positive and some negative qualities, what determines his attention to one or the other type of attribute? The present experiment was one in a program of research designed to study the interactions between situational and dispositional variables that guide this process of selective attention to information of different affective value for the person.

In the present study, success and failure was one of the variables whose impact on the self-regulation of affective states was explored. Although the psychological experiences of success and failure have received an enormous amount of research attention (e.g., Feather, 1966; Rotter, 1954; Weiner, 1966; Weiner, Frieze, Kukla, Reed, Rest, & Rosenbaum, 1971), the exact role of such experiences in the individual's self-regulatory processes remains far from clear. If a person receives feedback indicating that he is doing well on a task, he rewards his performance on it more generously than when he thinks that his performance is less deserving (e.g., Kanfer & Marston, 1963). Thus, success on a task increases self-reward on it, and failure tends to lower self-reward for one's performance. But it is much less evident how such success and failure experiences might influence later *noncontingent* self-gratification in a context which is objectively irrelevant to the initial task on which success or failure was obtained. Success and failure experiences could influence later noncontingent self-gratification in a new domain in two opposite ways. For example, after failing at a job assignment one might continue to berate himself later at home and engage in self-punitive deprivations of freely available pleasures. Alternatively, the individual might react to the initial failure on his job by self-therapeutically indulging himself at home. Similarly, after success a person might become more self-indulgent and noncontingently benign, "glowing" with the pleasure of success and hence more generous toward himself. But after success he also might have less need for gratification and greater "frustration tolerance" (as "ego strength" theories would suggest) and therefore might indulge himself less rather than more.

A directly relevant earlier study (Mischel et al., 1968) investigated exactly this problem with grade school children. The question was how success or failure experiences (on a bowling game) would affect the children's self-gratification later, in a new situation, in which they were free to indulge themselves noncontingently with reinforcers in the form of valuable tokens. These tokens deliberately were made independent of the child's earlier performance. The findings showed that the children who had failed initially did not later indulge themselves excessively, providing no support for a defensive compensation or "self-therapy" hypothesis. Instead, the successful children became more noncontingently generous toward themselves, gratifying themselves with more tokens than did those who had failed and those who had obtained no feedback regarding their performance. Moreover, the failure group did not differ significantly from the no-feedback control. The overall results were interpreted to mean that, feeling strongly positive and "glowing with success," the children celebrated by taking more of the noncontingent, freely available reinforcers, thus becoming more self-indulgent.

The delivery of valuable goodies to oneself is only one of the ways in which an individual might celebrate his successes. One aim of the present study was to clarify how experimentally induced success and failure experiences influence the self-delivery of positive and negative information about the other aspects of oneself. The results should permit us to see if the effects of success and failure obtained by Mischel et al. (1968) with "tokens" self-administered by children aged 7–10 also hold in a different paradigm when the subjects are adults and when the outcomes available for self-administration are data about one's personal assets and liabilities. If the same pattern of results found previously occurs again under such extremely different conditions, there would be substantial support for the hypothesis that the positive state induced by success experiences leads to subsequent noncontingent positive self-reactions across diverse types of subject populations, success–failure experiences, and modes of self-reactions.

In addition to investigating the effects of prior success–failure, the present study also explored how the subject's expectancies influence his selective attention. The manner in which a subject uses positive and negative information about himself is likely to depend not only on his prior experiences but also on what he expects will happen to him in the immediate future. If a subject believes that the performance situation is terminated, the "glow" of his recent success (Isen, 1970) may lead him to increase his attention to his positive attributes just as it leads to greater self-gratification (Mischel et al., 1968). On the other hand, if the testing situation is to continue in the near future, the effects of the subject's prior success or failure on self-regulation of his affective state may be considerably diminished. The subject's attention may shift away from his attributes to more task-oriented information, such as effective strategies for improving his future performance. In other words, an expectancy for further testing may direct the subject's attention toward problem solving and away from the feelings generated by his prior success or failure experience.

To explore these possibilities a paradigm was developed in which subjects obtained success, failure, and control experiences with regard to their performance on an ostensible test of their intellectual ability. Thereafter, some subjects in each condition were led to believe that they would soon have to experience more testing of the same type, whereas the remaining subjects were not given any expectancy for further testing. We anticipated that subjects who expected further testing would selectively attend to information that could enhance their future performance, whereas subjects without this expectancy would focus selectively on their positive or negative personal qualities. In the "no-expectancy" condition, moreover, we anticipated in accord with the earlier findings on noncontingent self-reinforcement after success and failure (Mischel et al., 1968) that success would increase positive self-reactions (attention to positive information about the self) when compared to both failure and control experiences.

Selective attention to positive and negative information about the self is also likely to depend in part on dispositional variables. Perhaps the most theoretically relevant personality variable is "repression–sensitization" (e.g., Byrne, 1961). Prior research with this dimension suggests that "repressors" (subjects with low repression–sensitization scores on the Repression–Sensitization Scale [R–S]) tend to use denial and avoidance in response to threatening stimuli. In contrast, "sensitizers" (subjects with high repression–sensitization scores on the R–S Scale) supposedly use response patterns such as intellectualization and approach. A considerable body of research has helped to elaborate this distinction between repressors and sensitizers (e.g., Axtell & Cole, 1971; Byrne, 1964; Markowitz, 1969; Merbaum & Badia, 1967; Tempone, 1964). In accord with this literature, it was hypothesized that sensitizers would attend more to their liabilities and less to their assets when compared to repressors. Furthermore, consistent with recent theorizing about the role of situational and dispositional variables in behavior (Mischel, 1968, 1971), it was expected that repression–sensitization scores would account for more of the individual difference variance when situational constraints were ambiguous or absent (i.e., the control groups) than when the situation exerted powerful control over self-regulatory processes.

METHOD

Overview of Design

All subjects were exposed to a test of intellectual attainment which supposedly would differentiate among above-average people on one aspect of higher intelligence, namely conceptual ability. Subjects in the "success" condition were given feedback which indicated they had performed very well; subjects in the "failure" condition were told they had done very poorly. In both cases the performance level was judged in comparison to other people who had purportedly taken the same test. Subjects in the control condition were merely shown how the test operated but did not take it. Half of the subjects in each condition were given the expectancy that there would be further testing of the same kind and half were not given any expectancy for further testing. Thus a 3×2 factorial design was used: Success, Failure, Control $\times$ Expectancy, No Expectancy. The dependent variable was assessed after these manipulations by observing each subject's behavior while in a room containing three kinds of information. The information consisted of positive and negative feedback which the subjects believed was from a personality test, which they had taken earlier, and some strategies of performance on intelligence tests. In addition repression–sensitization scores were obtained in a preexperimental session so that the associations between repression–sensitization and responses to the treatments could be assessed.

Subjects and Experimenters

Sixty Stanford University undergraduates from introductory psychology courses were the subjects. They were randomly assigned in equal numbers to each of the six conditions, yielding 10 subjects per cell, 5 male and 5 female. Two male and 2 female experimenters conducted the study. For each subject, one experimenter gave instructions to the subject and operated the test apparatus. Another experimenter, who was unaware of the subject's experimental condition, was the observer and scorer of the subject's behavior on the dependent measures.

Preexperimental Session and Repression–Sensitization Groups

Personality tests were administered to the introductory psychology courses at the beginning of each quarter. Students were given the opportunity to take the personality tests and were advised they would obtain feedback later during the quarter. They also were informed that research on other aspects of assessment would be conducted later in the quarter in which they could participate for experimental credit (required in the introductory psychology course). The personality tests were the Byrne (1961) Repression–Sensitization (R–S) Scale (based on the Minnesota Multiphasic Personality Inventory) and various self-ratings and self-predictions.

The R–S Scale is scored so that higher scores indicate greater sensitization. Byrne's (1964) standardizing sample had a mean of 42, a standard deviation of 20, and a range from 0 to 109. The present sample had a mean of 36, a standard deviation of 17, and a range from 9 to 100. Although most past research on repression–sensitization has preselected subjects at the extremes of the repression–sensitization distribution (e.g., top and bottom quartiles), in the present study the analysis was more conservative and all subjects were included in the analysis. Therefore repression–sensitization scores were divided at the median (34.0) to form one group of sensitizers (with scores above the median) and one group of repressors (scores below the median). There were five scores at the median, and no scores were available for four subjects who failed to complete their repression–sensitization forms. These subjects (who were evenly distributed among the experimental conditions) were randomly designated repressors or sensitizers. The median split resulted in a total of 29 sensitizers and 31 repressors.

General Procedure

The individual experimental sessions began a week after the preexperimental personality testing. The room was arranged to give the overall impression of an area designed especially for the testing of both personality and intelligence. The experimenters attempted to convey, in dress and manner, a cordial but efficient and "professional" atmosphere. A complicated looking "concept-learning" apparatus rested on a desk. This apparatus consisted of two stimulus light arrays, three response bars, one reinforcement light, and a buzzer signal. The apparatus was perpendicular to a wall on which there was a one-way mirror, permitting observation from the adjoining room.

At the beginning of the experimental session, subjects in all groups received instructions about the operation and purpose of the concept-learning intelligence test. They also were given instructions regarding the feed-back from the personality tests and the use of the "computer-generated strategies" (described in a later section). After completing these instructions, the experimenter directed the subject's attention to the concept-learning apparatus, saying that they now could proceed to the main intelligence testing portion of the study. The experimenter added that later in the session there would be about 10 minutes free time while he reset and adjusted the apparatus: During that time the subject could look at the computer strategies, the personality feedback, or anything else that he wanted.

Success–Failure Experience

Each subject was told that the intelligence test which he was about to take had been designed to differentiate between people with above average IQs. To assure plausibility, the instructions emphasized that the test was being developed especially to differentiate between people who were all at the upper levels of the IQ distribution (e.g., college students) and focused on only one aspect of intellectual activity: "speed of concept identification and accuracy of concept learning." The subject was given a lengthy description of the concept-display panel and was informed that he would have five test subtasks; in each, *one* concept would be tested. He was given examples of concepts, instructed in detail on how to operate the apparatus, and shown how the reinforcement light would indicate correct responses.

After it was clear that the subject understood the concept-learning task, he was told how to interpret the feedback that he would receive from the feedback lights which ostensibly would reflect the speed and accuracy of his performance. A set of norm tables informed the subject how his feedback light scores compared to those of other students taking the test, and each subject wrote down his score and his percentile rank from the norm tables. After each of the five subtasks, the subject was given feedback. The entire concept-learning and feedback procedure took a total of 15–20 minutes, depending upon the subject's response rate.

The success subjects received feedback which places them in the upper 99th percentile on the first two and last two subtasks and the 90th percentile on the third of the five subtasks. In addition to receiving high feedback, the success subjects were given relatively easy concepts. This ensured that subjective feelings of task success would not be discrepant with the manipulated feedback information.

The failure subjects received feedback which put them in the lower 1st percentile on the first two and last two subtasks and the 20th percentile on the third of the five subtasks. The concept-learning tasks in these conditions were designed to be almost impossible to learn in the presented number of trials for each subtask, so that the negative feedback would be subjectively plausible.

In the control groups, before the instructions regarding the purpose of the experiment were read to them, subjects were told that tests of intelligence, as well as the apparatus and procedure, were being developed. They were also told, however, that before anyone was actually tested, the clarity and time requirements of the procedure had to be checked. Subjects in the control groups heard the standard instructions but were told they would not be asked to solve any tasks. Instead, they were asked to check how long it took to present all the arrays; they checked also that the apparatus functioned smoothly by matching each stimulus light presentation against a stack of cards showing the order in which the lights should be presented by the machine.

Expectancy Manipulation

At this point in the procedure, the experimenter repeated the instructions with regard to the 10 minutes free time which the subjects would have after the intelligence test. Then the experimenter looked at an index card which indicated whether the particular subject was to be in the no-expectancy or the expectancy condition. If the card indicated an expectancy condition, the experimenter added to the instructions that, after the apparatus was reset, the subject later would be given another set of five subtasks very similar to the first series of five. In the no-expectancy conditions the experimenter said that when the subject finished the five subtasks he would be finished with the testing phase of the study. All subjects were reminded at this point that they would have about 10 minutes of free time during which the experimenter would have to reset the apparatus; during that time they would have a chance to look at the personality information, the computer strategies, or anything else they wanted, as had been explained previously.

After completing these instructions the experimenter left the room and consulted a prearranged random schedule which determined the feedback and tests the subject was to receive. In this way the experimenter was blind to the success–failure manipulation during his interactions with the subject. Because the feedback conditions required that different initial instructions be given than those used in the control conditions, the experimenter was not blind with regard to control subjects. Finally, the experimenter was also blind to the expectancy conditions until shortly before he left the room.

All feedback regarding the subject's performance on the concept apparatus was given while the subject was alone in the experimental room. The experimenter operated the concept board and watched the subject perform from an adjacent room by means of the one-way mirror.

Assessing Selective Attention to the Self

At the start of the experimental session the personality information was introduced. It was explained to subjects that the 12 trait dimensions on which they showed the greatest personality strengths and *positive* resources (assets) and, on the other extreme, the 12 dimensions on which they showed the greatest personality weaknesses and *negative* qualities (liabilities) had been selected actuarially on the basis of their personality tests (administered in the preexperimental session). To interpret their own position on these positive and negative scales, and to help them understand the meaning of the data, they would have access to several types of information. The information was located on the opposite wall from the concept-learning apparatus on a shelf 4 feet from the floor. On this shelf were boxes of punched IBM cards and on each side of these boxes there was a black loose-leaf notebook. One notebook was titled, "Actuarial Norm Tables, Negative Liabilities" and the other, "Actuarial Norm Tables, Positive Assets." The IBM card boxes were also labeled either "Positive Assets" or "Negative Liabilities."

First, the subject was shown a sample deck of IBM cards. It was pointed out that he would get two decks, one for the positive and one for the negative feedback. Each deck would contain a list of the 12 scales on which he had scored most extreme. Once the subject had looked up his "corrected score" for each scale, he could look in the black books (the actuarial norm tables) to determine just where he fell relative to other people on a particular scale of the test. It was also stressed that the subject should check each norm table for the correct sex-related code number.

The last information to be introduced consisted of booklets containing paragraph descriptions of the assets and liabilities about which subjects had so far received only statistical information. Subjects were told that personality profiles would name the scale and describe the traits being measured, thus providing a synopsis, or thumbnail sketch, of their assets and liabilities.

During the instructions, the experimenter paused and asked the subject for his code number (which the subject had been given when he had taken the personality tests) by which the personality tests and feedback were presumably identified. After supposedly finding out the code number for the first time, the experimenter walked over to a filing cabinet and after some shuffling look out two brown loose-leaf folders. One was labeled "Positive Assets," and the other "Negative Liabilities" in large block letters. The front page of each folder had been arranged previously to have the subject's code number conspicuously written on it after the words "Subject code no. . . . ." The notebooks contained paragraph descriptions of the extreme forms of the personality characteristics supposedly tapped by each scale. One example of the extreme of the characteristics measured by a positive scale follows:

Affiliation (Af)

Capable of cooperating and reciprocating deeply in relations with others. Can be wholeheartedly affectionate, although these attributes are displayed only when he feels that they will be appreciatively received. Does not force himself on others, but is willing to share possessions or time and knowledge with friends. Remains loyal to friends and is willing to use energies to aid them, if and when they are placed in situations which overwhelm them. Knows how to develop meaningful, sincere relationships with a few really close people, and can get much beyond surface facades in these intimate friendships.

In addition to Affiliation, positive scales included such traits as Surgency ("interested, knowledgeable, and genuinely engaged . . .") and Autonomous ("desires independence and freedom to act according to own fundamental ideals . . ."). Negative traits included such traits as Dominance ("manipulative persuasion or self-seeking commands . . ."), Nonperseverative ("procrastination and distractability . . . resultant failures lead to greater and greater apathy''), and Ego Weakness (''indecisiveness, brittle defenses, flat emotional affect . . .'').

In the final arrangement of materials, the experimenter placed all the negative information on one side of the shelf and all the positive information on the opposite side of the shelf. Subjects thus could attend to IBM cards indicating their scores on positive and negative scales, norm tables showing score distributions for each scale, and paragraph personality descriptions for their assets and, separately, their liabilities. The personality information and the procedures for interpreting it seemed to be accepted as valid and compelling by all subjects, and most subjects appeared highly enthusiastic and totally involved with the data about themselves. In fact, all subjects, of course, saw the same personality descriptions, had the same scores on the IBM cards, and used the same norm tables.

Computer Strategies

On a small table near the previously mentioned shelf was another loose-leaf folder labeled ''Computer Generated Strategies–Concept Learning Task.'' This loose-leaf folder consisted of a series of probability tables and a few verbal statements describing what the best response (left or right bar) would be, given various stimulus arrays. Subjects were told that these strategies suggested the most efficient methods of using individual aptitude for solving concept-learning problems. This task-relevant information was included in an exploratory effort to see whether the experimental manipulations would have any systematic effect on subjects' interest in task information as opposed to personality information.

Final Instructions

After completing all instructions regarding the personality feedback and computer strategies, the experimenter directed the subject's attention to the concept-learning task, saying that they could proceed to the main intelligence testing portion of the study. The experimenter then added that the time was structured so that the subject would have about 10 minutes free time, to be signaled by all of the lights on the concept apparatus coming on. During that time the subject could look at the computer strategies and the personality feedback.

Scoring the Dependent Measure

The dependent variable was recorded by an observer blind to the subject's experimental condition. From behind the one-way mirror, the observer recorded on prearranged data sheets where the subject spent his time in the room during every 10-second block in the subsequent 10-minute period. Whenever a person was standing in front of the positive or negative information, he was scored as attending to it. The third location was the ''computer-generated strategies.'' Whenever the subject was not standing in one of the first three locations, he was scored as doing ''nothing.'' He might be reading a book of his own, looking out the window, sitting by the concept apparatus, or anything else not involving the computer strategies or personality information.

After the 10-minute interval, the experimenter returned to the room and conducted an elaborate and carefully planned debriefing session. He explained in detail the purpose of the study, the standardized nature of both the concept-learning and the personality feed-back, and the purpose of the research which was being conducted. All subjects seemed to leave quite satisfied with this description and committed not to talk about the experiment.

RESULTS

The data of main interest consisted of the effects of conditions on the length of time which subjects attended to their assets and liabilities and the task-relevant information within the 10-minute time period. To begin with, subjects spent an average of only 7% of the total time on activities other than the personality information and computer strategies (i.e., the "nothing" scoring category), and there were no differences between any conditions on this measure. Furthermore, attention to the computer strategies accounted for an average of only 15% of the total time, and again, unexpectedly, there were no differences between conditions on this measure. The overwhelming majority of the time was spent attending to personality information: Attention to assets and liabilities combined accounted for 78% of the total time. When the time on assets and liabilities was combined, no differences between groups were found. In addition, time on assets, while significantly correlated with time on liabilities ($r = -.48$, $p < .01$), still left over 70% of the variance in time on liabilities unaccounted for.

Thus the main results were analyzed separately for the time spent on assets and the time spent on liabilities. Specifically, $3 \times 2 \times 2$ analyses of variance for the effects of success, failure, or control experience, expectancy or no expectancy for further testing, and repression–sensitization (median split) were computed on the time spent attending to assets and, separately, the time spent attending to liabilities.

The success–failure experience significantly affected selective attention to positive information about the self, as indicated by the significant main effect of experience shown in Table 1. This main effect resulted from the fact that successful subjects spent much more time ($M = 259$ seconds) on their assets than did those in the failure and control groups ($M = 150$ and 114 seconds, respectively). A contrast to test this comparison was highly significant ($F = 12.35$, $df = 1/48$, $p < .01$). Subjects in the failure and control conditions did not differ from each other in the amount of time spent on their assets ($F < 1$). On the measure of amount of time spent on liabilities, neither the success–failure experience nor the expectancy variable yielded a significant main effect.

Table 1. Effects of success–failure experience, expectancy, and
repression–sensitization on attention to assets and liabilities:
Summary of analyses of variance

Source	df	Assets MS	Assets F	Liabilities MS	Liabilities F
Experience (A)	2	123,040	6.23**	14,433	<1
Expectancy (B)	1	2,147	<1	40,549	1.57
Repression–sensitization (C)	1	85,214	4.32*	245,952	9.49**
A × B	2	93,246	4.72*	98,962	3.82*
A × C	2	47,957	2.43	71,097	2.74
B × C	1	82,055	4.16*	24,526	<1
A × B × C	2	20,977	1.06	15,943	<1
Error	48	19,737		25,910	

*$p < .05$.
**$p < .01$.

As Table 1 indicates, there was a significant interaction between experience and expectancy on the time that subjects spent attending to assets and to liabilities. The relevant means are shown in Table 2. These interactions for assets and for liabilities were essentially identical and complementary in direction. Specifically, when subjects expected further testing there were no significant effects of the success–failure experience. These subjects neither spent differential amounts of time on their assets ($F = 2.30, df = 1/48, p < .20$) nor on their liabilities ($F = 1.53$) as a function of the success–failure experience. However, when the subjects did not expect further testing, those who experienced success attended to their assets more and to their liabilities less than did those who had experienced failure or control treatments. With regard to assets, a contrast comparing the success with the failure and control groups was highly significant ($F = 18.79, df = 1/48, p < .001$). In the case of liabilities, the same contrast was also significant ($F = 7.01, df = 1/48, p < .05$). In neither case was there a difference between the failure and control conditions ($F < 1$ for assets; $F = 1.53$ for liabilities).

Table 2. Mean time spent on assets and liabilities in each success–failure and expectancy condition

	Assets		Liabilities	
Condition	Expectancy	No expectancy	Expectancy	No expectancy
Success	188	329	330	239
Failure	209	91	221	367
Control	103	125	273	327

In sum, after success, when subjects did not expect further testing, they attended more to their assets and less to their liabilities (as compared to failure and control groups). These effects were wiped out when subjects expected further testing.

In addition to the effects of situational variables, the dispositional variable of repression–sensitization significantly affected the amount of time subjects attended both to their assets and to their liabilities (Table 1). Overall, sensitizers spent much more time on their liabilities ($M = 350$ seconds) than did repressors ($M = 239$ seconds); sensitizers also spent less time on their assets ($M = 144$ seconds) than did repressors ($M = 202$ seconds).

Although the interactions between repression–sensitization and the success–failure experience did not reach statistical significance, it is informative to examine the differences in the selective attention patterns displayed by repressors and sensitizers in response to each experience. Figure 1 depicts the mean attention to assets by sensitizers and repressors following success, failure, and control experiences. As Figure 1 suggests, after success, sensitizers spent much more time (283 seconds) attending to their assets than they did after failure (81 seconds) or control (45 seconds) experiences. A selected contrast comparing success versus failure and control was highly significant ($F = 16.21, df = 1/48, p < .001$). Repressors, on the other hand, did not pay significantly more attention to their assets after success than they did after failure and control experiences ($F < 1$). Thus the sensitizers, rather than the repressors, appear to have made the major contribution to the overall finding that success leads to more attention to positive information about the self than does failure or the control experience.

Figure 2 shows the mean attention to liabilities by sensitizers and repressors after success, failure, and no experience. The results for liabilities reflected those for assets. That

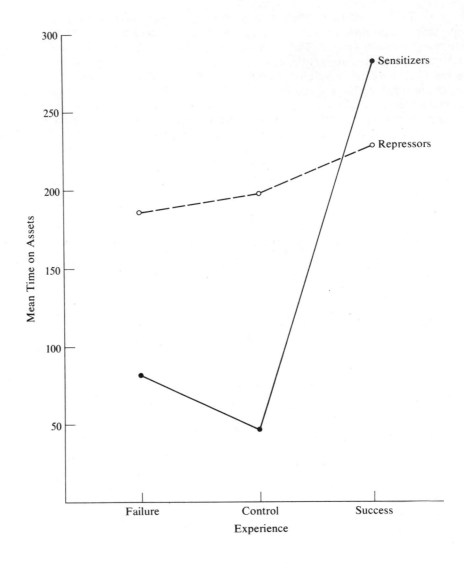

Figure 1. Mean amount of time (in seconds) spent on assets by sensitizers and by repressors in each experience condition.

is, sensitizers spent significantly less time attending to their liabilities after success than they did after failure and control experiences ($F = 4.27$, $df = 1/48$, $p < .05$), while for repressors the contrast was again not significant ($F = 1.18$).

The effect of repression–sensitization on the subjects' attention to their assets was moderated by the expectancy conditions. Specifically, the significant interaction between repression–sensitization and expectancy (see Figure 3) indicated that the greater attention by repressors to assets occurred only when they had no expectancy for further testing: When they expected further testing, repressors and sensitizers did not differ appreciably. However, the

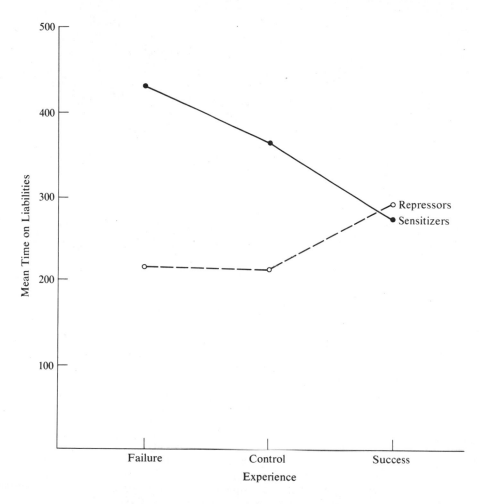

Figure 2. Mean amount of time (in seconds) spent on liabilities by sensitizers and by repressors in each experience condition.

effect of repression–sensitization on attention to liabilities did not interact significantly with expectancy (see Figure 4 and Table 1).

To further elucidate the role of repression–sensitization, correlational analyses were performed with the repression–sensitization scores and the attention data for assets and liabilities separately. These correlations were computed for each experience condition (success, failure, and control). Expectancy and no-expectancy groups were combined to avoid excessively small Ns, after t tests confirmed that repression–sensitization mean differences between groups were nonsignificant and of trivial size. The correlations, presented in Table 3, support the results from the analyses of variance, as well as adding some new information. Overall, the correlations indicated that the higher a person's sensitization score was, the more likely he was to attend to his liabilities rather than to his assets; conversely,

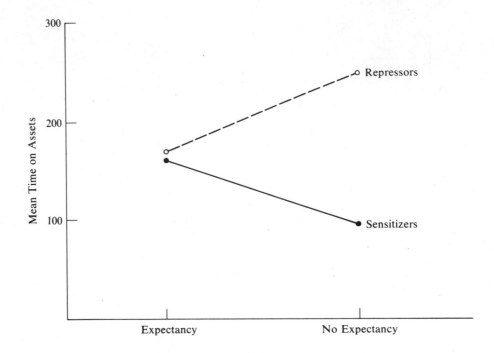

Figure 3. Mean amount of time (in seconds) spent on assets by sensitizers and by repressors in each expectancy condition.

repressors on the repression–sensitization scale were more likely to attend to their assets rather than to their liabilities.[1] It can be seen that the associations between repression–sensitization and selective attention were especially strong in the control conditions. In the failure conditions the correlations were similar, but smaller and of only borderline statistical significance. For success conditions there were no significant correlations between attentional measures and the personality variable.

Table 3. Correlations between repression–sensitization and attention to assets and liabilities in each experience condition

Condition	N	Assets	Liabilities
Success	18	.117	.007
Failure	20	−.353	.399
Control	18	−.510*	.610**
Total sample	56	−.247	.384**

Note. Expectancy and no-expectancy groups combined.
  * $p < .05$.
  ** $p < .01$.

[1]Note that high scores on the R–S Scale indicate "sensitization" and low scores "repression."

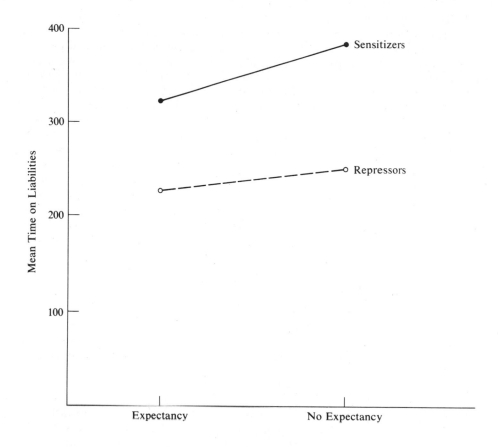

Figure 4.   Mean amount of time (in seconds) spent on liabilities by sensitizers and by repressors in each expectancy condition.

Tests also were conducted to assess the significance of any differences between the repression–sensitization correlations in the various conditions. These tests revealed two significantly different correlations: The correlations in the control group were significantly larger than those in the success condition for both assets ($z = 1.87$, $p < .05$) and liabilities ($z = 1.92$, $p < .05$).

DISCUSSION

The results indicated that, as expected, selective attention to information about the self was significantly influenced by prior success–failure experiences. In general, after a success experience, subjects spent more than twice as much time attending to information about their personal assets than they did after failure or control experiences. This effect was entirely congruent with the previous finding that after success children became more non-contingently benign toward themselves and self-administered more tokens (on a new, unrelated task) than did youngsters who either had failed or had been in a control group (in the "sequential condition" of Mischel et al., 1968).

In the present study there were no differences on any measure between subjects who failed and subjects in the control condition. This also replicates earlier findings in the study by Mischel et al. (1968). Thus the pattern of results in the present study is remarkably similar to that of the Mischel et al. experiment: In both studies failure and control groups did not differ from each other but jointly showed less noncontingent self-gratification than did successful subjects. This similarity seems especially impressive because of the great differences between the subject populations, procedures, and measures employed in the two investigations. In the earlier experiment, children from the second through the fourth grades of school served as the subjects, and success–failure experiences were manipulated on a bowling game. Most important, the dependent measure was the amount of noncontingent self-gratification in the form of tokens taken in a new, unrelated nonachievement situation (maze designs). In sharp contrast, in the present study the subjects were college students, success–failure occurred for performance on an intelligence test, and the dependent measure was the amount of time spent attending to positive information about the self rather than the number of self-administered tokens.

The finding that the effects of failure did not differ from those of the control experience may have been due to the use of an ineffective failure manipulation. That interpretation, however, is undermined by the fact that the same pattern of results was found in the present study and in the earlier one which used such different tasks, failure criteria, and subject populations. An alternative interpretation for the strong effects of success but not of failure (when compared to control experiences) suggests that the results instead may reflect in part a tendency of subjects to attribute the failure outcome to external factors rather than to their own performance. Several researchers have demonstrated that, in general, subjects tend to attribute their success to internal causes, such as their own ability, but their failure to external causes, such as the difficulty of the task (Epstein & Komorita, 1971; Fitch, 1970; Frieze & Weiner, 1971). Moreover, college students, using a concept-learning task very similar to the one in the current study, indicated success on it was a result of their own ability, and failure was less of a reflection of their true ability (Ebbesen, 1971). These findings help to clarify why subjects who failed in the present study and in the cited earlier work acted as if they had received a control experience; after all, the failure was not their fault, and hence its impact could be neutralized.

The present results are also relevant to recent research on the role of positive affect, induced by success and failure experiences, on subsequent altruistic behavior. Success not only increases noncontingent positive reactions toward oneself; it also seems to facilitate benign reactions toward other people. Isen (1970) found that after a success experience, adult subjects (school teachers) became more helpful to others. Similarly, Berkowitz and Connor (1966) found that after success college students became more altruistic. Isen, as well as Berkowitz and Connor, interpreted their results as due to the "warm glow" produced by success. Additional studies corroborate that success experiences also lead to greater generosity in children as well as in adults (Isen, Horn, & Rosenhan, 1971).

The present data, taken collectively with the results of previous research, thus strongly support the conclusion that success leads to more benign reactions to the self as well as to others. The manifestations of this positive glow are diverse indeed; they include increased noncontingent self-reward, increased attention to the positive aspects of the self and, in one's interactions with others, more charitable behavior and a variety of helpful acts.

While the pervasive consequences of the warm glow for enhancing generosity both toward the self and toward others are becoming increasingly well established, the mechanisms responsible for these phenomena are less evident. The tendency for people to become non-contingently more benign—in their noncontingent self-reward, in their selective attention to positive information about themselves, and in their helpfulness toward others—might be specific to the experience of success. For example, the effects might be mediated by changes in self-esteem and perceived competence produced by successful performance. Alternatively, this benign tendency might be the result of any increment in positive affect, regardless of how it is generated and regardless of specific changes in self-esteem. At present we favor the hypothesis that the increments in noncontingent positive self-reactions and altruism obtained in this study and in the other cited investigations are not unique to successful performance achievements; we expect that the same effects could be obtained by the induction of strongly positive moods from other sources (e.g., from a "windfall" or other intense "good luck" experiences that would generate positive affect).

A recent study (Isen & Levin, 1972) supports these speculations. Positive affective states were induced in adult subjects (e.g., by letting them find a dime in the coin return of a public telephone while making a call). After subjects were thus made to "feel good" they became more helpful than did subjects in control conditions. In a similar vein, on the basis of a field study, Berkowitz and Macaulay (1971) reported that women shoppers were more likely to grant a college student's request for 40 cents for a bus ticket after they had been put in a good mood by receiving approval during a prior interview.

To test the hypothesis that generosity toward the *self* also would be increased by a more positive mood produced by events unrelated to one's abilities, a follow-up to the present study was conducted.[2] The same methods and procedures were used as in the no-expectancy conditions of the present main experiment, with two exceptions. The computer-strategies measure was omitted and a manipulation designed to produce positive or negative affective states was substituted for the success–failure experience. Specifically, affective states were induced by exposing 36 college subjects to tape recordings and asking them to create vivid mental images of the scenes presented verbally on the tapes. Positive affect included such scenes as skin diving in the Caribbean and driving down the coast on a warm day in a convertible. Scenes to induce negative affect included being lost in the mountains with a storm coming and feeling spiders crawling on oneself in the dark. The neutral tape asked subjects to imagine a normal day in their lives—not an especially good or bad one, just the activities of an ordinary day. The dependent variable was time spent on negative and positive personality information. Since no other activities were available, all of the 10 minutes were spent on personality information. Thus analyses were done on time spent on assets; time on liabilities was the remainder of the 10 minutes and would show exactly inverse results if analyzed. The results of mood ratings before and after exposure to the tapes suggested that the affective manipulation was relatively weak. Nevertheless, the overall findings supported the present hypothesis. Time on assets was first windsorized to eliminate extreme cases (this procedure removes the highest and lowest score in *every* group). After listening to the affectively positive tape recording, subjects spent more time ($M = 6$ minutes) attending to their personal assets than they did after the negative tape ($M = 3$ minutes), with neutral subjects spending a moderate amount of time ($M = 4.5$ minutes). A linear contrast was significant ($F = 4.25$, $df = 1/27$, $p < .05$ with the residual $F < 1$).

On the basis of the available data, we suggest that when a person is in a strongly positive affective state he is more likely to engage in *any* behaviors that might perpetuate his good

[2]The authors wish to express their gratitude to Susan Hoffman for conducting the follow-up experiment.

mood and avoid behaviors that might terminate it. Note that the hypothesized tendency to engage in behaviors that maintain an affective state applies only to positive emotional experiences; under most conditions of social learning there would be little basis for subjects to behave in ways that would maintain negative affective states (although exceptions would be encountered when "feeling bad" has been widely reinforced, as in masochistic behavior).

These speculations about a learned tendency for perpetuating positive affect are consistent with the finding that when both children and adults experience the warm glow presumably induced by success they become more likely to engage in such behaviors as greater noncontingent self-reward, selective attention to positive qualities of the self, and more positive (altruistic) behavior toward others. All of these activities would function to maintain the warm glow, whereas the alternative behaviors would quickly dispel it. These speculations are also consistent with the finding that people tend to be less likely to cheat after they receive positive feedback regarding their scores on a personality test (Aronson & Mettee, 1968) since cheating would spoil the subject's happy mood and hence is avoided.

The impact of affective states in general and of success in particular, of course, is not situation free. Just as with other variables throughout the field of personality, the effects are moderated by numerous interactions with other situational and dispositional variables (e.g., Mischel, 1968, 1973). This fact is reflected in the present finding that the expectancy conditions interacted significantly with the success–failure experience. While successful subjects who did not expect further testing spent more time on their assets than did those who failed, successful subjects who did expect to undergo further testing attended to their assets no longer than did those who had failed.

Thus the presence of the expectancy variable nullified any main effect of the success–failure experience. In interpreting this finding, it must be noted that the expectancy manipulation was quite general and did not specify precisely the degree or quality of similarity between the future tests and those the subject had just completed. The subjects were therefore free to generate their own specific expectations. After a success experience a subject, rather than expecting to succeed again, might be worried that he would not do as well the next time; rather than glowing from his previous achievement the subject might be concerned about the possibility of his future failure. Similarly, after failure, subjects might have been expecting to recuperate from a momentary setback. Whether or not such effects did in fact occur is, of course, mere speculation. It would be necessary to manipulate the specific nature of the expectancy (success versus failure) before one could discern the exact effects of expectancy on self-regulation.

It had been anticipated originally that when subjects expected further testing they would become more goal oriented and attend more to the task than to information about themselves. While the expectancy manipulation did nullify the main effects of success–failure, there were no differences in time spent attending to the task-relevant information in any conditions. It should be noted that the small overall proportion of time spent on the measure of attention to the task (less than 15%) reduced the possibility of obtaining any effects on it. Apparently most subjects found the personality information too interesting to ignore and were unwilling to leave it for long, since time spent on task-relevant information would mean that the subject could not examine his personality feedback extensively (because of the total time restriction).

Individual differences in repression–sensitization had the expected effects on selective attention. Overall, sensitizers spent much more time on their liabilities and much less time on their assets when compared to repressors. These effects were especially strong on the measure of time that subjects spent attending to their liabilities (Table 1). The present data are consistent with the earlier findings concerning the relations between repression–sensitization and selective attention. For example, sensitizers more readily admitted faults (negative self-descriptions) than repressors (Byrne, 1961). Moreover, after failure on a test, repressors were slower than sensitizers to recognize words associated with the test; after success the differences between repressors and sensitizers in word recognition thresholds were not significant (Tempone, 1964). The present strong findings seem especially impressive since they were based on a median-split dichotomization of repression–sensitization scores, rather than selecting merely the highest and lowest individuals on the dimension (as has been the customary practice in most previous studies of repression–sensitization).

While extensive correlations exist between repression–sensitization and a host of other measures (e.g., Byrne, 1964), the meaning of the repression–sensitization dimension is far from clear (e.g., Sarason & Smith, 1971). The present finding that repressors attended less to their liabilities and more to their assets (when compared to sensitizers) suggests that repression–sensitization scores may reflect individual differences in selective attention rather than in unconscious defense mechanisms. Rather than defensively repressing negative information about the self, repressors may simply avoid attending to it and instead focus on their positive features; sensitizers, in contrast, show the opposite attentional patterns. These differences in attention in turn seem consistent with the repressors' strong tendency to describe themselves in more positive, socially desirable terms than do sensitizers. For example, Joy (1963) reported a correlation of $-.91$ ($N = 35$ college students) between repression–sensitization and the tendency to emphasize socially desirable characteristics on the Edwards Social Desirability Scale (Edwards, 1957). Also congruent with this interpretation is the high negative correlation ($r = -.81$) between repression–sensitization and self-reported self-esteem found by Ebbesen (1971) in a sample of Stanford college students ($N = 40$): Repressors described themselves more positively than sensitizers and hence emerged with higher self-esteem scores. This configuration of results, coupled with the lack of clear experimental evidence for the existence of an unconscious repression mechanism (Eriksen, 1960; Mischel, 1971), suggests that the R–S Scale may be better understood as a measure of a subject's tendency to attend to and focus on his positive qualities and to present himself in a favorable light than as a sign of his tendency to employ an unconscious mechanism of repression. Most simply, repressors (low repression–sensitization scores) tend to emphasize their positive characteristics and minimize their negative qualities more than do sensitizers; the present data indicate that they also attended more to their positive characteristics and less to their negative attributes even under ostensibly private conditions.

In accord with previous theorizing (Mischel, 1968), it was anticipated that the effects of individual differences (on the repression–sensitization dimension) would be greatest when the impact of the experimental conditions was absent or minimal (i.e., the control condition); conversely, it was anticipated that the role of individual differences would be least important when the experimental treatment was most potent (i.e., the success condition). The data strongly supported these expectations. While repressors generally spent more time on assets than did sensitizers, the differences were greatest in the failure and control conditions and were eliminated after the success experience. Thus sensitizers responded strongly to the impact of the experimental manipulation and attended much more to their assets after success than after failure and control experiences. Indeed, the impact of success on sensitizers was so powerful that they spent slightly *more* time on their assets after success than did repressors.

In sum, individual differences exerted their expected impact when treatment effects were minimal (the control conditions) but were nullified when the situational manipulations were powerful (the success condition). Specifically, after a success experience subjects attended more to positive information about themselves than after failure or control experiences, regardless of individual differences in repression–sensitization.

REFERENCES

Aronson, E., & Mettee, D. Dishonest behavior as a function of differential levels of induced self-esteem. *Journal of Personality and Social Psychology*, 1968, *9*, 121–127.

Axtell, B., & Cole, C. W. Repression–sensitization response mode and verbal avoidance. *Journal of Personality and Social Psychology*, 1971, *18*, 133–137.

Bandura, A. *Principles of behavior modification*. New York: Holt, Rinehart & Winston, 1969.

Berkowitz, L., & Connor, W. H. Success, failure and social responsibility. *Journal of Personality and Social Psychology*, 1966, *4*, 664–669.

Berkowitz, L., & Macaulay, J. R. Ideals, ideas and feelings in help-giving. Unpublished manuscript, University of Wisconsin, 1971.

Byrne, D. The repression–sensitization scale: Rationale, reliability, and validity. *Journal of Personality*, 1961, *29*, 334–349.

Byrne, D. Repression–sensitization as a dimension of personality. In B. A. Maher (Ed.), *Progress in experimental personality research*. New York: Academic Press, 1964.

Ebbesen, E. B. The effects of levels of success–failure on selective memory for and self-adoption of positive and negative information about oneself. Unpublished doctoral dissertation, Stanford University, 1971.

Edwards, A. L. *The social desirability variable in personality assessment and research*. New York: Dryden, 1957.

Epstein, R., & Komorita, S. S. Self-esteem, success–failure, and locus of control in Negro children. *Developmental Psychology*, 1971, *4*, 2–8.

Eriksen, C. W. Discrimination and learning without awareness: A methodological survey and evaluation. *Psychological Review*, 1960, *67*, 279–300.

Feather, N. T. Effects of prior success and failure on expectations of success and subsequent performance. *Journal of Personality and Social Psychology*, 1966, *3*, 287–298.

Fitch, G. Effects of self-esteem, perceived performance, and choice on causal attributions. *Journal of Personality and Social Psychology*, 1970, *16*, 311–315.

Frieze, I., & Weiner, B. Cue utilization and attributional judgments for success and failure. *Journal of Personality*, 1971, *39*, 591–605.

Isen, A. M. Success, failure, attention, and reaction to others: The warm glow of success. *Journal of Personality and Social Psychology*, 1970, *15*, 294–301.

Isen, A. M., Horn, N., & Rosenhan, D. R. Effects of success and failure on children's generosity. Unpublished manuscript, Franklin and Marshall College, 1971.

Isen, A. M., & Levin, P. F. The effect of feeling good on helping: Cookies and kindness. *Journal of Personality and Social Psychology*, 1972, *21*, 384–388.

Joy, V. L. Repression–sensitization and interpersonal behavior. Paper presented at the meeting of the American Psychological Association, Philadelphia, August 1963.

Kanfer, F. H., & Marston, A. R. Conditioning of self-reinforcing responses: An analogue to self-confidence training. *Psychological Reports*, 1963, *13*, 63–70.

Kanfer, F. H., & Phillips, J. S. *Learning foundations of behavior therapy*. New York: Wiley, 1970.

Markowitz, A. Influence of the repression–sensitization dimension, affect value, and ego threat on incidental learning. *Journal of Personality and Social Psychology*, 1969, *11*, 374–380.

Merbaum, M., & Badia, P. Tolerance of repressors and sensitizers to noxious stimulation. *Journal of Abnormal Psychology*, 1967, *72*, 349–353.

Mischel, W. *Personality and assessment*. New York: Wiley, 1968.

Mischel, W. *Introduction to personality*. New York: Holt, Rinehart & Winston, 1971.

Mischel, W. Toward a cognitive social learning reconceptualization of personality. *Psychological Review,* 1973, *80,* in press.

Mischel, W., Coates, B., & Raskoff, A. Effects of success and failure on self-gratification. *Journal of Personality and Social Psychology,* 1968, *10,* 381–390.

Rotter, J. B. *Social learning and clinical psychology.* Englewood Cliffs, N. J.: Prentice-Hall, 1954.

Sarason, I. G., & Smith, R. E. Personality. In P. Mussen & M. Rosenzweig (Eds.), *Annual review of psychology.* Vol. 22. Palo Alto: Annual Reviews, 1971.

Tempone, V. J. Extension of the repression–sensitization hypothesis to success and failure experience. *Psychological Reports,* 1964, *15,* 39–45.

Weiner, B. The role of success and failure in the learning of easy and complex tasks. *Journal of Personality and Social Psychology,* 1966, *3,* 339–348.

Weiner, B., Frieze, I., Kukla, A., Reed, L., Rest, S., & Rosenbaum, R. M. *Perceiving the causes of success and failure.* Morristown, N. J.: General Learning Press, 1971.

Paul L. Wachtel

PSYCHODYNAMICS, BEHAVIOR THERAPY, AND THE IMPLACABLE EXPERIMENTER

Possible integrations of dynamic and behavioral approaches to theory and therapy have been obscured by polemics. One area of confusion concerns the degree of generality of specificity in personality. Variability in behavior from situation to situation has been misleadingly construed by some behavioral critics as casting doubt upon psychodynamic theories. This view is refuted, and a number of factors that account for the differing viewpoints of psychodynamic and behaviorally oriented approaches are considered. Among these are differences in subjects from which original ideas were generated, differences in phenomena of central interest (with special focus on the implications of psychodynamic concern with ambiguous affective phenomena), and the consequences of an experimental strategy (the "implacable experimenter") which limits the ways in which the subject may structure the environment in which he behaves.

One of the central points of contention between behavior therapists and those theorists and clinicians with a psychodynamic viewpoint is the degree of consistency and generality evident in personality functioning. Dynamic therapists tend to view personality as an organized system. Many diverse events are viewed as functionally related, and the person's individuality is expected to show itself in a wide variety of situations. Even where seemingly inconsistent behaviors appear, the viewpoint of most psychodynamic thinkers points toward a search for underlying organizational principles that can account for the phenotypic behavioral differences in terms of a genotypic description of that person's psychic structure.

Such a characterization of psychodynamic approaches as seeking coherence in people's behavior may at first glance seem inconsistent with the strong emphasis of psychodynamicists on conflict. But an examination of the explanatory role of conflict in most psychodynamic theories reveals that often *conflict itself* is the organizing principle providing coherence in the seeming diversity of everyday behavior. For example, excessive timidity in one context and extreme aggressiveness in another may both be seen as manifestations of a strong conflict over aggression. Both kinds of behavior may be seen as bearing the stamp of the person who is readily aroused to act hostilely and who is also afraid of this tendency in himself. Such divergent extremes are viewed from a psychodynamic perspective, especially one that emphasizes the analysis of character, with an eye toward finding underlying unities, though these unities lie in the organizing role of conflict or apparent *dis*unity.

In contrast, the theoretical underpinnings of behavior therapy have tended to stress

Reprinted by permission from the *Journal of Abnormal Psychology*, 1973, 82, pp. 324–334. Copyright 1973 by the American Psychological Association.

Much of the work on this paper was accomplished while the author was at the Research Center for Mental Health at New York University and was supported by Grants 5-P01-MH17545 from the National Institute of Mental Health.

specificity in behavior and the relative independence of an individual's various response dispositions. Little emphasis is placed on the relation among the responses made by a person in different situations or between these responses and any organizing personality structure. As Mischel (1968) pointed out, low response-response correlations are expected by social behavior theory, and the focus of investigation by workers in this framework is on how particular behaviors are independently related to particular stimulus situations. Mischel's influential brief for a social behaviorist approach to personality assessment and therapy begins with and is largely based upon a critical examination of the research on consistency of personality. The meager yield of efforts to demonstrate consistency is one of the central issues in Mischel's argument against the psychodynamic approach.

Mischel's arguments are cogent and his analysis thoughtful and perceptive. But before psychodynamic concepts are forever consigned to that scientific Valhalla flowing bountifully with phlogiston, ether, and the four humors, it may be of value to take another look both at the kind of consistency in fact predicted by psychodynamic theories and the kind of studies that have supported the case for specificity. The present paper argues (*a*) that modern psychodynamic theories are far more able to deal with the facts of man's responsiveness to variations in stimulus conditions than the model of psychoanalysis typically described by proponents of behavior therapy; and (*b*) that the particular way of framing questions in much experimental personality research tends to underestimate the degree of consistency that does exist in the everyday behavior of individuals. Consequently, there is far more possibility of convergence between the theories and techniques of behavior therapists and dynamic therapists than is generally recognized. The worker from either perspective who dismisses the work of the "opposing" approach risks diminishing his efficacy in aiding men of flesh and blood for the pleasures of slaying men of straw.

VARIETIES OF PYSCHODYNAMIC APPROACHES

Typically, when proponents of behavioral approaches discuss psychodynamic theories, it is Freudian psychoanalysis of the early twentieth century that is their focus. Little attention is paid to the later developments in Freud's own work, much less to those contributions of later writers within the psychoanalytic and interpersonal traditions. For example, Bandura and Walters (1963) stated:

> the psychodynamic "disease" model thus leads one to seek determinants of deviant behavior in terms of relatively autonomous internal agents and processes in the form of "unconscious psychic forces," "dammed-up energies," "cathexes," "countercathexes," "defenses," "complexes," and other hypothetical conditions or states having only a tenuous relationship to the social stimuli that precede them or even to the behavioral "symptoms" or "symbols" that they supposedly explain [p. 30].

In a later volume, Bandura (1969) again suggested that psychodynamic theories posit "an organism that is impelled from within but is relatively insensitive to environmental stimuli or to the immediate consequences of its actions [p. 19]."

Were such characterizations written before World War I, they might have been cogent and important. For a variety of reasons, discussed elsewhere, Freud did for a time emphasize internal, "instinctual" processes almost to the exclusion of environmental and learning factors. Even in his later writings, despite the introduction of important conceptual changes pointing toward concern with environmental events (e.g., Freud, orig. publ. 1923, 1926),

Freud's theorizing showed an imbalance in favor of the inner and automatic. And it is unfortunately the case that many psychodynamic thinkers continue to operate on the basis of this inadequate early model.

But more sophisticated modern varieties of psychodynamic thinking are quite different from this early model. An important example of the development in psychodynamic models is provided by recent psychoanalytic discussions of the energy concepts in psychoanalysis. Critics of psychoanalysis have often, with considerable cogency, pointed particularly to the circular and pseudoscientific way in which terms and concepts such as cathexis, counter-cathexis, and dammed-up libido are used. Within the psychoanalytic community as well, such criticisms were at times voiced (e.g., Kubie, 1947), and Erikson (1950), in his highly influential *Childhood and Society,* commented that Freud's use of the thermodynamic language of his day, with its emphasis on the conservation and transformation of energy, was an analogy or working hypothesis that "appeared to be making concrete claims which neither observation nor experiment could even attempt to substantiate [p. 59]." But despite Erikson's clear illustration by example that the important insights of psychoanalysis could be expressed more clearly without resort to the confusing and vulnerable energy formulations, such "metapsychological" theorizing continued to abound in psychoanalytic writing.

Within the past few years, however, a number of authors writing from a perspective within the psychoanalytic point of view have provided not only serious criticism of the energy constructs but demonstrations that *such constructs are not at all essential to the main points of psychoanalysis* (e.g., Holt, 1967; Klein, 1966, 1969; Loevinger, 1966; Schafer, 1970; Wachtel, 1969). Thus criticisms of psychoanalysis as positing a closed energy system within which blind energies build up and discharge, oblivious to the world outside, address themselves to an outmoded and inessential feature of the psychoanalytic approach.

Other developments in psychoanalytic theory in recent years also distinguish it from the model usually discussed by behavior therapists, and render it more able to handle the data indicative of behavioral specificity. Although earlier versions of psychoanalytic theory paid inadequate attention to adaptation and response to real situations, the psychoanalytic ego psychology that has developed from the work of Hartmann (1939), Erikson (1950), and others has led to a far greater concern with how the developing human being learns to adapt to the real demands, opportunities, and dangers that his ever-widening world presents to him. To be sure, psychoanalytic workers do attribute greater organization and consistency to personality than stimulus-response theorists, and posit greater residual influence of psychic structures formed by the early interaction of biological givens with environmental contingencies. But these integrating structures are not independent entities driving people to predetermined behaviors regardless of the stimulus conditions that prevail. They are, rather, persistent proclivities to perceive particular classes of stimulus configurations in particular idiosyncratic fashion, and to behave in accordance with these perceptions.

Accordingly, selectivity of perception has become a central concern of modern psychoanalytic researchers, who, far from being indifferent to how stimuli influence and guide our behavior, have intensively studied precisely how we do register, interpret, and respond to environmental stimulation. Thus psychoanalytically oriented researchers have in recent years been studying processes of selective attention and inattention (Luborsky, Blinder, & Schimek, 1965; Shapiro, 1965; Wachtel, 1967), styles of perceiving and thinking (e.g., Gardner, Holzman, Klein, Linton, & Spence, 1959), the effects of weak or ambiguous stimuli (Pine, 1964), and the effects of the *absence* of environmental stimulation (e.g., Goldberger, 1966; Holt, 1965). Psychoanalytic thinkers guided by such models would hardly be embarrassed by observations of different behavior in different situations.

Even more explicitly attentive to situational influences and the occurrence of different behavior in different situations is the interpersonal school of psychodynamic thought (e.g., Sullivan, 1953). Sullivan has in fact questioned the very concept of a "personality" as an entity independent of the interpersonal situations in which a person exists. In place of the older, more static model of the analyst as a blank screen upon which the patient's transference distortions are projected, Sullivan emphasized the analyst's role as a *participant* observer. The blank screen model did stem largely from a conception of personality that paid little attention to stimulus determinants of a person's thoughts, feelings, and actions. The underlying structure was sought in a way that implied it could be described independently of the situations in which the person found himself. In the absence of external distractions, the true personality was expected to be revealed. In contrast, the model of the participant observer implies not only that the analyst cannot be a blank screen (after all, a person upon whom one is relying for relief from suffering, who does not permit himself to be looked at, rarely answers questions, and requests a good portion of one's income is hardly a "neutral" stimulus) but also that to even attempt to observe the "personality" free from the "distorting" effects of one's own influence upon the person's behavior is to seek after an illusion. For the person is always responding to some situation, and a silent, unresponsive analyst is no less "real" a stimulus than a warm, energetic, or humorous one.[1]

The contrast between the "blank screen" and "participant observer" models raises a number of therapeutic issues that cannot be discussed in detail in this presentation. Among them are: (*a*) the importance of the therapist knowing clearly what kind of stimulus he in fact is (the "myth of therapist homogeneity" is apparent not only in outcome research, where Kiesler [1966] first labeled it, but also in much theoretical writing on technique in the psychoanalytic literature); (*b*) the advisability of the therapist *intentionally* being a different stimulus at different times (cf. Alexander, 1956; Wolf, 1966); (*c*) the role of group therapy in eliciting a wider range of the patient's responses to various interpersonal situations; and (*d*) the relation between interpersonal assessments and behavioral assessments as ways of sampling response to a variety of situations (cf. below and Goldfried & Kent, 1972).

It may also be noted that in some sense experimenters are now going through a reorientation similar to that which occurred in psychoanalysis. The work of writers such as Rosenthal (1966) and Orne (1962) points to the limits of a "blank screen" conception of the experimenter, and the importance of recognizing that the experimenter too is a *participant* observer. Parts of the discussion below suggest that, rather than being merely a nuisance to be corrected for, the experimenter's influence as a participating human other may be an untapped source of richer knowledge of personality functioning.

FRAMING OF QUESTIONS BY ANALYSTS AND EXPERIMENTERS

It should now be clear that the picture of psychodynamic theories as necessarily describing people as moved solely by inner urges and as inattentive to environmental demands is a portrait in straw. The mere fact that behavior varies from situation to situation is in no way a refutation of the psychodynamic approach. Equally fallacious is the view, held by many dynamic thinkers, that all behavior therapists are unaware of individual differences, blind to the role of language and cognition, and uninterested in how a person's history has led to

---

[1]It should be clear, however, that when the therapist does not reveal his reactions to the patient's behavior, he makes more likely the observation of hidden assumptions and strivings which might not emerge were clearer clues as to "expected" or "appropriate" behavior to homogenize patient response. Stone (1961) and Greenson (1967) have presented sophisticated discussions of these issues from a Freudian point of view. The present author's differences from their view center on the degree to which psychodynamic descriptions can and should consider evoking situations.

idiosyncratic patterns of equating situations and developing preferences (see, e.g., Mischel, 1968, or Bandura, 1969). Tenable theories converge as their range of inquiry begins to expand and overlap. Nonetheless, it hardly needs to be pointed out that Mischel's conclusions from the data he cited do differ considerably from the view of man evident in the writings of even modern pyschodynamic thinkers. This article now considers how in some respects both views may be seen as correct, as a step toward guidelines for theoretical integration and practical innovation.

"Neurotics" and "Normals"

Psychodynamic theories developed originally to account for primarily maladaptive behavior. Learning theories, in contrast, have tended to start with observations of successful alteration of behavior in response to situational demands. (Learning curves are typically monotonically increasing.) Though both broad theoretical perspectives have subsequently developed to encompass detailed consideration of both adaptive and maladaptive behavior, each still bears the stamp of its origin. Learning theorists prefer to examine how even behavior that is troublesome is in some way in tune with current environmental contingencies. Dynamically oriented thinkers, on the other hand, frequently are most interested in how a person's behavior is *out of touch* with the current situation, how he *fails* to adapt to changing situations.

In a sense, the defining property of neurotic behavior is its rigidity, its inflexibility in the face of changed conditions. Psychodynamic theories, which originated as theories of neurosis, heavily emphasize concepts that account for lack of change and are particularly designed to describe the persistence of past patterns into the present. Among the most prominent of these concepts is that of transference, the tendency to react to persons in the present as though they were important figures from one's past.[2] Transference is viewed by psychodynamic thinkers as a phenomenon evident in all people, but one whose influence may be expected to be greater in more severely neurotic persons than in the general population. When one considers the difference between the population of severe neurotics who constitute the observational base for psychodynamic theories, and the less psychologically handicapped groups who form the population for most of the studies Mischel cited as evidence for specificity, at least some of the difference in theoretical perspective becomes understandable.[3] It is likely that the neurotic patients seen by psychoanalysts are considerably less able to alter their behavior appropriately from situation to situation and person to person than a typical group of children or adults. That inability is a major reason why the former are in therapy.

Ambiguity and Affect

Mischel noted in passing, but did not emphasize, that when stimulus conditions are ambiguous, individual differences arising from past history are more noticeable. Here lies another important source of difference in the observations and theorizing of analysts

---

[2]Here again it should be clear that transference need not be viewed as a completely autonomous inner disposition but rather as a particular way of organizing new stimulus input, biased but not completely unresponsive to the actual situation (cf. Alexander, 1956; Sullivan, 1953; Wolf, 1966).

[3]Alker (1972) has made a similar point in an important recent paper that may be seen as complementing the present contribution. Several sections which appeared in earlier drafts of this paper have been shortened or omitted because they are excellently dealt with by Alker.

and social behaviorist researchers. In addition to focusing their efforts on somewhat different populations, workers from these differing orientations also concentrate on different phenomena.

The data generated and examined by most behaviorally oriented students of normal and abnormal behavior involve changes in clearly denotable behaviors in response to clear, unambiguous changes in environmental events. The subject, or the model in some studies, is given money or has it taken away, he is shocked or he escapes from shock, he is allowed privileges or they are denied him, etc. Under such circumstances, a kind of lawfulness tends to emerge in which the complicated formulations of psychodynamic theorists seem very much beside the point. Behavior varies closely with changes in environmental events. The individual's "learning history with similar stimuli" is, of course, relevant, but one hardly needs to conceptualize complex personality structures with considerable cross-situational application. Change the situation and you change the behavior.

To the analyst, however, such studies are likely to seem irrelevant to the phenomena of interest to him. The data he observes consist largely of statements such as: "I feel angry at my girlfriend because she smiled in a condescending way. She said it was a warm smile, but it didn't feel that way to me." Or, "My boss criticized me for being so insistent with him, but I could tell from his tone of voice he was really proud of my assertiveness, and I had a good feeling that he supports me." Or, "It seemed to me you were more silent this hour. I felt you were angry with me because I complained about the fee, and I was afraid you'd say we should stop therapy. I know you'll think *I'm* the angry one, and *I* want to stop, but I think you're wrong, and I resent your distortion of my feelings."

Such reports do describe behavior in response to environmental events. In principle, a girlfriend's smile, a boss' tone of voice, or an analyst's silence are events that can be observed just as the administration of a food pellet to a rat or a token to a back-ward patient. But whereas the latter two events are specifically chosen to be clear and unequivocal, the interpersonal events scrutinized by the analyst are often exceedingly ambiguous. The experimenter, no less than the subject, must judge on largely idiosyncratic grounds whether a smile is warm or condescending, and observer reliability regarding a tone of voice is unlikely to be impressive. Views may and do differ as to whether it is a wise *strategy* to study such ambiguous events at this point in the development of our discipline, but it must be acknowledged that we all spend a good portion of each day responding more or less adequately to just such ambiguous "stimuli."

The events focused on by analysts, then, tend to be those in which their patients' ability to discriminate is most challenged. Finely articulated alteration of response with stimulus changes, evident in studies where environmental events are readily discriminable, is not so evident where affective, interpersonal events are concerned. In the latter realm, early global and generalized predispositions may less readily become differentiated, and assumptions and reaction tendencies may apply to a wider range of situations. In Piagetian terms, analysts are likely observing phenomena where difficulties in perceptual discrimination make assimilation predominant, whereas Mischel's emphasis on specificity applies to situations where a greater degree of accommodation and differentiation is possible.

It should also be noted that in the examples of psychoanalytic data noted above, the patient's *response* is complicated and ambiguous, as well as the situation to which the response is made. The man who claimed his analyst was more silent during the hour stressed that he (the patient) was not angry, that it was the analyst who was angry at him. But he ended up saying he *resented* the analyst's distortion, and he earlier *complained* about the fee. One may well wonder whether this man was in fact angry, or framed differently, at what point in the session he first became angry, or from a slightly different perspective, which situations evoke in him a tendency to attack or hurt and which to experience and label his response as ''anger.'' However one wishes to frame the question, it would seem that how best to conceptualize and describe his affective response to the situation he perceives is exceedingly difficult, and that a great deal of interpretation and inference is necessary to decide fully just how he did respond.

Many researchers, faced with such ambiguity, have decided it is best to study simply the overt behaviors that can be reliably and consistently identified and that to worry about whether or not the patient is really ''angry'' is a fruitless endeavor. Such a strategy does yield clearer curves and a greater sense of having discerned a repeatable pattern. But it must also be noted that the dilemma faced by the researcher is also faced by each of us in our everyday lives. We are all frequently faced with the task of understanding and identifying our own affective responses to the events of our lives, and as Dollard and Miller (1950) have pointed out, failure to label accurately one's own drive states has very serious consequences. Further, the personal experience of feeling and wishing, no matter how difficult to study, remains an exceedingly important psychological phenomenon, and changes in experienced feeling states are often the implicit hidden criteria of avowedly behavioral programs of therapy (Locke, 1971).

The difficulty in accurately identifying ambiguous affective and motivational phenomena renders perception of these events, whether one's own feelings and wishes or those of others, peculiarly susceptible to the distorting effects of anxiety; hence the particular emphasis on anxiety and defense by psychoanalytic authors. In attempting to study defensive processes experimentally, researchers have frequently focused on distortions of perception of *external* stimuli and have been forced to introduce ambiguity through artificial means, such as tachistoscopic presentation. Such procedures correctly take into account that the concept of defensive distortion depends on ambiguity and does not imply an arbitrary and unchecked intrusion upon perception of clearly discriminable events. The study of defense via perceptual experiments has, however, typically involved a number of other difficulties (Wachtel, 1972; Wolitzky & Wachtel, 1972). Psychodynamic concepts of defense are concerned primarily with phenomena of *self*-perception, particularly perception of one's own affective and motivational states. As with other aspects of psychoanalytic thinking, defensive phenomena too are now seen as responsive to environmental, as well as organismic, events, but their relation to environmental occurrences is seen as far more complex than is the case with the behavioral phenomena typically studied in social learning experiments (see Silverman, 1972, for an interesting and lucid discussion of clinical and experimental data bearing on the psychoanalytic conceptualization of this relationship).

The preference of behaviorally oriented investigators for seeking simple stimulus-response relationships, and for focusing on clearly discernible events, may lead to an underestimation of the importance of complex anxiety-distorted mediating processes. In turn, the particularly strong interest of psychoanalytic investigators in the murky subtleties of wish and feeling has likely led to an underestimation of how directly their patients might respond to environmental contingencies when they are up off the couch and taking clearly visible steps. Results of efforts to alter directly psychotic behaviors (e.g., Ayllon & Azrin, 1968; Ullmann & Krasner, 1966) or particular behavioral deficits in children (e.g., Allen, Hart, Buell, Harris, & Wolf, 1964) suggest that this may be the case. As Davison (1969) has pointed out, however, such alterations of overt behavior do not necessarily imply an alteration of the ideas and feelings that accompany them.

The "Implacable Experimenter"

Still another way in which differing strategies of investigation may lead dynamic and behavioral investigators to differing conclusions is illuminated by an interpersonal perspective on human behavior. If each person's behavior is largely a function of the interpersonal situation in which he is engaged, then when two or more people interact, they are each not only influenced by the behavior of the other (in the familiar sense of a response to a stimulus); each also influences the behavior of the other, by virtue of the stimulus properties of his own behavior. Person A responds to the stimulus properties of Person B, but Person B in turn is responsive to the behavior of Person A which he has in part determined. Further, these are both continuous adaptations, not simply sequential. From such a systems orientation, the understanding of any one person's behavior in an interpersonal situation solely in terms of the stimuli *presented to* him gives only a partial and misleading picture. For to a very large extent, these stimuli are *created by* him. They are responses to his own behaviors, events he has played a role in bringing about, rather than occurrences independent of who he is and over which he has no control. The seductive, hysterical woman who is annoyed at having to face the aggressive amorous advances of numbers of men has much to learn about the origin of the stimuli she complains she must cope with. So too does the man who complains about the problems in dealing with his wife's nagging, but fails to understand how this situation, which presents itself to him, derives in turn from his own procrastinating, unresponsible behavior.

From the above considerations we may see that the postulation of consistency of personality need not be incompatible with the view that people may be acutely sensitive to changes in the stimulus situation. For consistency need not be the result of a static structure that moves from situation to situation and pays no heed to stimuli. Much of the rigidity and persistence of human behavior can be accounted for without conceiving of an id, cut off from the perceiving, adapting aspect of the personality; and the striking tendency, observed by Freud and many others, for human beings to persist in beating their heads against countless proverbial walls does not require the postulation of a repetition compulsion (Freud, orig. publ. 1920). Rather, one can in many cases view consistency as a result of being in particular situations frequently, but situations largely of one's own making and themselves describable as a characteristic of one's personality.[4]

These considerations suggest that the finding in many experiments of rather minimal consistency in behavior from situation to situation (Mischel, 1968) may be in part an artifact of the conceptual model and research strategy that has typically guided American personality research. Mischel noted the discrepancy between these research findings and the persistent impression that people are characterizable by their typical way of acting. He attributed the discrepancy largely to a documented tendency for observers to *falsely* construe consistency when diversity is the fact. But genuine consistency may also occur in most life situations and yet not be evident in the laboratory. For the typical experiment, with its emphasis on standardized independent variables as antecedents of the behavior to be studied, may short-circuit the mutual influence process described above, which is importantly involved in the generation of consistency.

In most experiments, some stimulus event is designated as the independent variable, and every effort is made to assure that this independent variable is presented to each subject in

---

[4]Millon (1969, Ch. 5) has also pointed to ways in which the principles of social learning theory may be consistent with the expectation of considerable generality in important aspects of personality.

the same fashion. Research assistants are trained to behave similarly with each subject, and if they do vary their behavior in response to some feature of the subject's interpersonal style, this is generally viewed as a failure of the experimental method; the "independent variable" is supposed to be standardized. Such a model of research, with the behavior of the experimenter preprogrammed to occur independently of the myriad interpersonal cues of the subject may be designated as the model of the "implacable experimenter."[5]

Such a model is well suited for testing the isolated effect of a particular independent variable, for it assures, if proper controls are included, that that variable is what accounts for the differing behaviors in the various experimental groups. Mischel's survey suggests that in experiments conducted in this fashion, the behavior of individuals will vary considerably when the "independent variable" is varied (subject, of course, to the limiting parameters discussed above, e.g., degree of psychopathology and ambiguity of the situation encountered).

, But let us note what such a research procedure does *not* examine. Although the highly practiced and routinized behavior of the experimenter does not rule out all opportunity for observing individual differences in the subjects of the study—differences in perception or interpretation of events, or in response to the same situation, may be noted—it does effectively prevent the subject from recreating familiar stimulus situations by evoking typical complementary behavior by the experimenter in response to the subject's behavior. In most life situations, whether someone is nice to us or nasty, attentive or bored, seductive or straight-laced, is in good part a function of our own behavior. But in the typical experiment the subject has little control over the interpersonal situation he encounters. It has been determined even before he enters the room. Borrowing the language of the existentialists, such experiments reveal a person in his "thrownness," but do not make clear his responsibility for his situation.

Mischel (1968) suggested that the impression of identity or constancy in personality may be reinforced by regularities in the environmental contexts in which a person is observed. Mischel's focus is on the occasions when the regularity is a function of the conditions of observation rather than of the person's life, as when we only see someone in a particular context, though he in fact operates in a wide variety of situations. But what if the person is *usually* in a particular situation? In such a case it may be true that his behavior is describable as a function of his situation, and perhaps also that he could act differently if the situation were different. But then we must ask why for some people the situation is so rarely different. How do we understand the man who is constantly in the presence of overbearing women, or constantly immersed in his work, or constantly with weaker men who are cowed by him but offer little honest feedback? Further, how do we understand the man who seems to bring out the bitchy side of *whatever* woman he encounters, or ends up turning almost all social encounters into work sessions, or intimidates even men who usually are honest and direct?

Certainly we need a good deal more data before we are sure just how general such phenomena are, how characterizable people are by the situations they "just happen" to run into. What should be clear, however, is that piecemeal observation of "stimuli" and "responses" or "independent" and "dependent" variables, divorced from the temporal context of mutually influencing events, can shed little light on these questions. If experiments

---

[5]Of course, some behavior of the experimenter may be *contingent* on the subject's behavior, but it should be clear that this is a far cry from the kind of interpersonal processes discussed in this section (see Carson [1969] for descriptions of research that comes closer to the model discussed here; see also Laing, Phillipson, & Lee, 1966).

in the implacable experimenter model are the central source of data for one's view of man, it is understandable that conceptions of man as constructing his life or his world, or of personality as a self-maintaining system, would have little appeal.

Bem (1972), in a recent defense of Mischel's critique, has argued that the burden of proof lies with those who would posit considerable consistency in personality to demonstrate it empirically. But empirical studies may get different answers depending on how they ask their questions. A conceptual understanding of the limits of the implacable experimenter model, as well as of the other issues discussed above, may prevent a premature judgment of failure.

CONCLUDING COMMENTS

To ask whether behavior is best describable in terms of global traits or as responses to particular situations is to misleadingly dichotomize a very complex and important question. We have seen that modern psychodynamic thinkers do indeed consider how an individual responds to the situations he encounters. The difference between psychodynamic and social behaviorist positions lies not in whether the role of environmental events is considered, but rather in the nature of the relationship between environmental and behavioral events. To the psychodynamic theorist, this relationship is more complex and less direct than it tends to be in social learning accounts. Psychodynamic investigators have been particularly impressed with the complicating effects of anxiety and efforts learned to avoid it. The protracted helplessness of the human young, his need to rely on seemingly all-powerful giants for many years, and his almost inevitable fear of displeasing these enigmatic authorities are seen by psychodynamic thinkers as making anxiety and defense a regularly important feature in the development of personality and psychopathology.

It follows from the considerations advanced in this article that recent efforts to invalidate the psychodynamic viewpoint on the basis of currently available data on specificity and generality are based on misconceptions both of what modern psychodynamic theories are like and of the bearing of most research studies on the critical issues addressed by psychodynamic thinkers. The present arguments do not imply, however, that this is a time for psychodynamic workers to breathe easy and conduct business as usual. Mischel, for example, has based his case against psychodynamic theories not only on the observations of behavioral variability considered above but also on what he views as a failure of psychodynamic clinicians to demonstrate the utility of their judgments. In his more recent writings (e.g., Mischel, 1971) this issue has become the central focus of Mischel's critique of the psychodynamic approach, and his earlier work (Mischel, 1968), like that of Meehl (1954), Sawyer (1966), and others, reviews considerable evidence that may be construed as casting doubt on the utility of psychodynamically derived assessment methods. Holt's (1970) recent paper is in many respects a cogent and effective reply to such critiques; but it is consistent with the arguments of the present paper, and with Holt's paper as well, to suggest that psychodynamic theories might well benefit from further consideration of specificity in human behavior, and to consider as well ways in which clinical assessment methods may have lagged behind the theoretical developments in psychodynamic theory discussed earlier.

Psychodynamic theories are still based largely on a body of clinical observation. Work such as that of Chapman and Chapman (1967), which illustrates the pitfalls in such observational methods, presents another serious challenge to psychodynamic workers. Whether psychodynamic ideas can or should be examined by strictly experimental methods is a controversial question.[6] Although a great many experiments have been inspired by psychoanalytic concepts, the bearing of experimental findings on psychoanalytic theory is far from clear (cf. Hilgard, 1968; Horwitz, 1963; Rapaport, 1959). The present discussion has pointed to ways in which current experimental studies tend to focus on different phenomena than those traditionally of central interest to psychoanalytic investigators. Unless experiments can be devised that adequately deal with the problem of man's behavior as both chosen and caused (Wachtel, 1969), with disavowed intentionality (Schafer, in press), with freedom and inhibition of affective experience, and with the perpetuation of old patterns and expectations by the evocation of "countertransferential" behavior (cf. Laing et al., 1966; Wolf, 1966), some form of naturalistic clinical observation will probably continue to be an important means of exploring key psychological questions. The need for such efforts to be more systematic (e.g., by examination of tape-recorded clinical data, open to alternative interpretations and checks of reliability) is obvious. Some of the work reviewed by Luborsky and Spence (1971, especially pp. 423–430) represents important steps in this direction. It is likely that some of Freud's more baroque formulations will prove casualties of such refined observation. But the conviction of many social behaviorist writers that almost all of psychodynamic thought will prove to be merely a time-wasting detour on the road to a purely situational theory (see Bowers, in press) seems to this writer to be a product of the failure to recognize that psychodynamic theories have developed from observations of phenomena that experimentally derived theories have hardly considered.

Developments in behavior therapy are likely to prove a corrective to the zealots of both dynamic and behavioral persuasion. Already, the impressive results reported by behavior therapists are forcing psychodynamic thinkers to reconsider a number of their basic premises and their limitations. On the other hand, contact with the more complex problems of neurosis and "real life" joy and suffering is likely to bring more to the fore the phenomena that until now behavioral theories have dealt with only by analogy. In observations of behavior therapists at work, the present author has noted a good deal more interviewing and efforts to grasp ambiguous occurrences interpretively than one would expect from the literature (see also Klein, Dittman, Parloff, & Gill, 1969). Recent writings by practicing behavior therapists (e.g., Lazarus, 1971) have stressed the primacy of careful clinical observation over strict adherence to a stimulus-response faith. In future communications, guidelines for the integration of dynamic and behavioral approaches will be examined in detail. It is hoped that the present contribution will aid in diminishing the resistance to such efforts.

REFERENCES

Alexander, F. *Psychoanalysis and psychotherapy*. New York: Norton, 1956.

Alker, H. A. Is personality situationally specific or intrapsychically consistent? *Journal of Personality*, 1972, *40*, 1–16.

Allen E. K., Hart, B. M., Buell, J. S., Harris, F. R., & Wolf, M. M. Effects of social reinforcement on isolate behavior of a nursery school child. *Child Development*, 1964, *34*, 511–518.

Ayllon, T., & Azrin, N. *The token economy*. New York: Appleton-Century-Crofts, 1968.

Bandura, A. *Principles of behavior modification*. New York: Holt, Rinehart & Winston, 1969.

Bandura, A., & Walters, R. *Social learning and personality development*. New York: Holt, Rinehart & Winston, 1963.

---

[6]The too ready assumption by many psychologists that the experimental method is the only path to truth has been critically examined by Bowers (in press) in a valuable paper that is in many respects complementary to the present one.

Bem, D., Constructing cross-situational consistencies in behavior: Some thoughts on Alker's critique of Mischel. *Journal of Personality,* 1972, *40,* 17–26.

Bowers, K. S. Situationism in psychology: An analysis and a critique. *Psychological Review,* 1973, *80,* 307–336.

Carson, R. C. *Interaction concepts of personality.* Chicago: Aldine, 1969.

Chapman, L. J., & Chapman, J. Genesis of popular but erroneous psychodiagnostic observations. *Journal of Abnormal Psychology,* 1967, *72,* 193–204.

Davison, G. C. Appraisal of behavior modification techniques with adults in institutional settings. In C. Franks (Ed.), *Behavior therapy: Appraisal and status.* New York: McGraw-Hill, 1969.

Dollard, J., & Miller, N. E. *Personality and psychotherapy.* New York: McGraw-Hill, 1950.

Erikson, E. H. *Childhood and society.* New York: Norton, 1950.

Freud, S. Beyond the pleasure principle. In J. Strachey (Ed.), *The standard edition of the complete psychological works of Sigmund Freud.* Vol. 18. London: Hogarth, 1955. (Originally published: 1920).

Freud, S. The ego and the id. In J. Strachey (Ed.), *The standard edition of the complete psychological works of Sigmund Freud.* Vol. 19. London: Hogarth, 1961. (Originally published: 1923).

Freud, S. Inhibitions, symptoms and anxiety. In J. Strachey (Ed.), *The standard edition of the complete psychological works of Sigmund Freud.* Vol. 20. London: Hogarth, 1959. (Originally published: 1926).

Gardner, R. W., Holzman, P. S., Klein, G. S., Linton, H. B., & Spence, D. P. Cognitive control: A study of individual consistencies in cognitive behavior. *Psychological Issues,* 1959, *1* (4), 1–185.

Goldberger, L. Experimental isolation: An overview. *American Journal of Psychiatry,* 1966, *122,* 774–782.

Goldfried, M. R., & Kent, R. N. Traditional versus behavioral personality assessment: A comparison of methodological and theoretical assumptions. *Psychological Bulletin,* 1972, *77,* 409–420.

Greenson, R. *The technique and practice of psychoanalysis.* New York: International Universities Press, 1967.

Hartmann, H. *Ego psychology and the problem of adaptation.* New York: International Universities Press, 1958. (Orig. publ. 1939).

Hilgard, E. R. Psychoanalysis: Experimental studies. In D. L. Sills (Ed.), *International encyclopedia of the social sciences.* Vol. 13. New York: Macmillan, 1968.

Holt, R. R. Ego autonomy re-evaluated. *International Journal of Psychoanalysis,* 1965, *56,* 151–167.

Holt, R. R. Beyond vitalism and mechanism: Freud's concept of psychic energy. In J. Masserman (Ed.), *Science and psychoanalysis.* Vol. 11. New York: Grune and Stratton, 1967.

Holt, R. R. Yet another look at clinical and statistical prediction: Or, is clinical psychology worthwhile? *American Psychologist,* 1970, *25,* 337–349.

Horwitz, L. Theory construction and validation in psychoanalysis. In M. H. Marx (Ed.), *Theories in contemporary psychology.* New York: Macmillan, 1963.

Kiesler, D. J. Some myths of psychotherapy research and the search for a paradigm. *Psychological Bulletin,* 1966, *65,* 110–136.

Klein, G. S. Two theories or one? Perspectives to change in psychoanalytic theory. Paper presented at the Conference of Psychoanalysts of the Southwest, Galveston, Texas, March 1966.

Klein, G. S. Freud's two theories of sexuality. In L. Breger (Ed.), *Clinical-cognitive psychology.* Englewood Cliffs, N. J.: Prentice-Hall, 1969.

Klein, M. H., Dittman, A. T., Parloff, M. B., & Gill, M. M. Behavior therapy: Observations and reflections. *Journal of Consulting and Clinical Psychology,* 1969, *33,* 259–269.

Kubie, L. S. The fallacious use of quantitative concepts in dynamic psychology. *Psychoanalytic Quarterly,* 1947, *16,* 507–518.

Laing, R. D., Phillipson, H., & Lee, A. R. *Interpersonal perception.* New York: Springer, 1966.

Lazarus, A. A. *Behavior therapy and beyond.* New York: McGraw-Hill, 1971.

Locke, E. A. Is "behavior therapy" behavioristic? (An analysis of Wolpe's psychotherapeutic methods). *Psychological Bulletin,* 1971, *76,* 318–327.

Loevinger, J. Three principles for a psychoanalytic psychology. *Journal of Abnormal Psychology,* 1966, *71,* 432–443.

Luborsky, L., Blinder, B., & Schimek, J. G. Looking, recalling, and GSR as a function of defense. *Journal of Abnormal Psychology,* 1965, *70,* 270–280.

‧ Luborsky, L., & Spence, D. P. Quantitative research on psychoanalytic therapy. In A. Bergin & S. Garfield (Eds.), *Handbook of psychotherapy and behavior change.* New York: Wiley, 1971.

Meehl, P. E. *Clinical versus statistical prediction: A theoretical analysis and a review of the evidence.* Minneapolis: University of Minnesota Press, 1954.

Millon, T. *Psychopathology.* Philadelphia: Saunders, 1969.

Mischel, W. *Personality and assessment.* New York: Wiley, 1968.

Mischel, W. Specificity theory and the construction of personality. Paper presented at the annual meeting of the American Psychological Association, Washington, D. C., September 3, 1971.

Orne, M. T. On the social psychology of the psychological experiment: With particular reference to demand characteristics and their implications. *American Psychologist,* 1962, *17,* 776–783.

Pine, F. The bearing of psychoanalytic theory on selected issues in research on marginal stimuli. *Journal of Nervous and Mental Disease,* 1964, *13,* 205–222.

Rapaport, D. The structure of psychoanalytic theory: A systematizing attempt. In S. Koch (Ed.), *Psychology: A study of a science.* Vol. 3. New York: McGraw-Hill, 1959.

Rosenthal, R. *Experimenter effects in behavioral research.* New York: Appleton-Century-Crofts, 1966.

Sawyer, J. Measurement *and* prediction, clinical *and* statistical. *Psychological Bulletin,* 1966, *66,* 178–200.

Schafer, R. An overview of Heinz Hartmann's contributions to psychoanalysis. *International Journal of Psychoanalysis,* 1970, *51,* 425–446.

Schafer, R. Action: Its place in psychoanalytic interpretation and theory. *The Annual of Psychoanalysis,* Vol. 1, in press.

Shapiro, D. *Neurotic styles.* New York: Basic Books, 1965.

Silverman, L. H. Drive stimulation and psychopathology: On the conditions under which drive related external events trigger pathological reactions. *Psychoanalysis and contemporary science.* Vol. 1, New York: International Universities Press, 1972.

Stone, L. *The psychoanalytic situation.* New York: International Universities Press, 1961.

Sullivan, H. S. *The interpersonal theory of psychiatry.* New York: Norton, 1953.

Ullmann, L. P., & Krasner, L. *Case studies in behavior modification.* New York: Holt, Rinehart & Winston, 1966.

Wachtel, P. L. Conceptions of broad and narrow attention. *Psychological Bulletin,* 1967, *68,* 417–429.

Wachtel, P. L. Psychology, metapsychology, and psychoanalysis. *Journal of Abnormal Psychology,* 1969, *74,* 651–660.

Wachtel, P. L. Cognitive style and style of adaptation. *Perceptual and Motor Skills,* 1972, *35,* 779–785.

Wolf, E. Learning theory and psychoanalysis. *British Journal of Medical Psychology,* 1966, *39,* 1–10.

Wolitzky, D. L., & Wachtel, P. L. Personality and perception. In B. Wolman (Ed.), *Handbook of general psychology.* Englewood Cliffs, N. J.: Prentice-Hall, 1972.

Seven
JULIAN B. ROTTER

Social learning theory, as defined by Julian B. Rotter (1916–   ), is a creative synthesis of *reinforcement* and *cognitive,* or *field,* theories of human behavior. Social learning theory postulates the interaction of four major elements: behavior potential, expectancy, reinforcement value, and the psychological situation. *Behavior potential* is the probability of occurrence of a behavior in a situation; it is dependent on the type and amount of reinforcement available for this behavior. *Expectancy* refers to a prediction made by the person that a particular behavior expressed in a given situation will receive reinforcement. *Reinforcement value* is the value that an individual places on a particular kind of reinforcer. There are cultural as well as individual regularities in the assignment of value to reinforcers. Finally, all persons are continually reacting to both internal and external stimulation; hence, the impact of a stimulus event is often different for each person who experiences the event. The *psychological situation* is the situation as uniquely experienced by the individual. Induction into the army, for instance, although a common stimulus event, constitutes a different psychological situation for each person who experiences it.

Rotter believes that, when these four variables are known, they can be combined into a formula that should be capable of predicting how a person will behave under specified conditions. Rotter is basically an interactionist in his analysis of clinical and real-life phenomena. That is, in his explanation of learning, he gives individual differences and environmental events equal weight. Like most theorists who take a learning-theory approach to personality development, Rotter assumes that people are vitally concerned with the consequences of their behavior and are therefore predisposed to learn responses that will allow them to achieve the greatest possible amount of satisfaction or reinforcement in their lives.

The paper in this chapter by Rotter is a concise restatement of social learning theory and a clarification of some misconceptions about the theory. The concept that is most strongly associated with Rotter—internal–external locus of control—is the focus of the paper. An early project of Rotter's was the development of a scale capable of differentiating between a person oriented toward internal control of reinforcement and a person oriented toward external control of reinforcement. "Internals" have a tendency to attribute reinforcement to their own efforts and thus to assume responsibility for the creation of conditions of reinforcement. "Externals," on the other hand, are more likely to feel and believe that other people or events determine their fate and the availability of reinforcements. Rotter's paper is devoted to a clarification of the use of the I–E scale, including discussions of the psychometric properties of the scale, test-situation variables that must be considered in the evaluation of scores, and cautions about the validation of the concept of internal and external locus of control.

The research paper by E. Jerry Phares, D. Elaine Ritchie, and William L. Davis describes a study in which the authors examined hypotheses about how subjects defined as internals and externals would respond to positive and negative information about their personality. It was predicted, for example, that externals would respond with less anxiety than internals to threatening (negative) material about the self.

The research data revealed some interesting differences and similarities between internals and externals. The major finding, contrary to predictions, was that there were no differences between the two groups in defensiveness or anxiety responses to threat. However, the internals appeared to be more willing than the externals to confront emotional problems and challenges by taking positive action.

There are a number of ways in which arguments about the inadequacy of a theoretical position may be presented. One strategy is to demonstrate, by force of logic, the contradictory and inconsistent aspects of the theoretical structure. The critic may also refer to empirical evidence that, according to his or her view, negates the central argument of the theoretical position. For an example of the latter style of criticism, refer to Nagel's criticism of psychoanalysis in the Hartmann chapter in this volume. Another method of criticism involves experimental testing of alternative theoretical approaches to the same problem. The final paper in this chapter provides an example of this last type of criticism.

Bernard Weiner, Richard Nierenberg, and Mark Goldstein describe how attribution theory and social learning theory were compared in an experiment designed to test which theory could more convincingly account for a particular phenomenon: expectancy change. This experimental design is known as a *crucial-experiment design*. In the crucial-experiment design, it is imperative that the experimental procedures not favor either of the theories being tested and that the researchers define the theoretical issues impartially. It is up to you to judge whether the authors satisfied these conditions. Researchers who run "crucial experiments" usually favor one theoretical position over the other. Weiner, Nierenberg, and Goldstein, advocates of attribution theory, believe that attribution theory accounts for their empirical data better than social learning theory does.

SUGGESTIONS FOR FURTHER READING

Rotter's first major book appeared in 1954 and was titled *Social Learning and Clinical Psychology*. It was published by Prentice-Hall. "Generalized Expectancies for Internal versus External Control of Reinforcement," in *Psychological Monographs*, 1966, *80*(1, Whole No. 609), is a major research effort by Rotter to define the construct of internal versus external locus of control.

A book published in 1972 by Holt, Rinehart & Winston and written by J. B. Chance and E. J. Phares—*Applications of a Social Learning Theory of Personality*—contains a summary statement of social learning theory and describes a group of important research studies investigating various aspects of Rotter's theory. Recently, E. J. Phares has written *Locus of Control in Personality*. This work was published by General Learning Press.

Julian B. Rotter
SOME PROBLEMS RELATED TO THE CONSTRUCT OF INTERNAL VERSUS EXTERNAL CONTROL OF REINFORCEMENT

Research involving perceived internal versus external control of reinforcement as a personality variable has been expanding at a rapid rate. It seems clear that for some investigators there are problems associated with understanding the conceptualization of this construct as well as understanding the nature and limitations of methods of measurement. This article attempts to discuss in detail (a) the place of this construct within the framework of social learning theory, (b) misconceptions and problems of a theoretical nature, and (c) misuses and limitations associated with measurement. Problems of generality specificity and unidimensionality–multidimensionality are discussed as well as the logic of predictions from test scores.

Estimates of the number of published articles dealing with some aspect of internal versus external control of reinforcement (sometimes referred to as "locus of control") vary, but it is clear that there are well over 600 studies. The number of unpublished investigations, master's theses, and doctoral dissertations dealing with this topic are impossible to estimate. Most of these studies have been published in the last 15 years, and there seems to be still an active, if not increasing, interest in the topic. The concept deals both with situational parameters and individual differences, although the bulk of the studies have been concerned with the latter.

One can only speculate on the surprising popularity of this concept as a subject for psychological investigations. Interest in this concept surely must be related to some persistent social problems, which in turn are related to the tremendous growth in population, increasing complexity of society, and the subsequent feeling of powerlessness that seems to permeate all levels of society, at least in Western culture. The research referred to above has produced some important and some well-replicated findings. It has also produced a series of studies that appear to reflect a basic misunderstanding of the nature of the variables and measurement devices used to assess individual differences. It is hoped that this article will help to clarify some of the theoretical problems, so as to enhance either the practical or theoretical contribution of future research. It may also be helpful to try to specify some of the limitations both of the predictive power of the concept as well as of the devices used for measuring individual differences. This article is not intended to review the locus of control research. A number of reviews and bibliographies are available (Joe, 1971; Lefcourt, 1966, 1972; Phares, 1973, in press; Rotter, 1966; Throop & McDonald, 1971). The most comprehensive and recent review and analysis of the locus of control literature is in a book recently completed by Phares (in press).

The concept of internal versus external control of reinforcement developed out of social learning theory (Rotter, 1954; Rotter, Chance, & Phares, 1972). It seems to be referred to by some investigators as the major or central concept in social learning theory. It is not. Our interest in this variable developed because of the persistent observation that increments and decrements in expectancies following reinforcement appeared to vary systematically, depending on the nature of the situation and also as a consistent characteristic of the particular person who was being reinforced. We were interested, in other words, in a variable that might correct or help us to refine our prediction of how reinforcements change expectancies. The nature of the reinforcement itself, whether positive or negative; the past history, sequence, and patterning of such reinforcements; and the *value* attached to the reinforcement are obviously important and probably more crucial determinants of behavior. This concept is defined as follows:

> When a reinforcement is perceived by the subject as following some action of his own but not being entirely contingent upon his action, then, in our culture, it is typically perceived as the result of luck, chance, fate, as under the control of powerful others, or as unpredictable because of the great complexity of the forces surrounding him. When the event is interpreted in this way by an individual, we have labeled this a belief in *external control*. If the person perceives that the event is contingent upon his own behavior or his own relatively permanent characteristics, we have termed this a belief in *internal control* (Rotter, 1966, p. 1).

As a situational variable, those situations in a particular culture that produced the belief that the reinforcement was under outside control would be called external control situations, and those that produced a belief that reinforcement was under the subject's own control could be called internal control situations. Most of the research dealing with situational parameters has used chance and skill situations; such situations, though clearly external and internal, are not identical with the concept of internal and external control of reinforcement, but rather they represent an important class of internal and external situations. In neither the case of situational differences nor individual differences were we hypothesizing a typology or a bimodal distribution. Rather, we assumed that with internal–external control something approximating a normal curve described the populations that we were interested in.

INTERNAL–EXTERNAL CONTROL AND SOCIAL LEARNING THEORY

Social learning theory is a molar theory of personality that attempts to integrate two diverse but significant trends in American psychology—the stimulus–response, or reinforcement, theories on the one hand and the cognitive, or field, theories on the other. It is a theory that attempts to deal with the complexity of human behavior without yielding the goal of utilizing operationally definable constructs and empirically testable hypotheses.

There are four classes of variables in social learning theory: behaviors, expectancies, reinforcements, and psychological situations. In its most basic form, the general formula for behavior is that the potential for a behavior to occur in any specific psychological situation is a function of the expectancy that the behavior will lead to a particular reinforcement in that situation and the value of that reinforcement.

It is hypothesized in social learning theory that when an organism perceives two situations as similar, then his expectancies for a particular kind of reinforcement, or a class of reinforcements, will generalize from one situation to another. This does not mean that the expectancies will be the same in the two similar situations, but the changes in the expectancies in one situation will have some small effect in changing expectancies in the other. *Expectancies in each situation are determined not only by specific experiences in that situation but also, to some varying extent, by experiences in other situations that the individual perceives as similar.* One of the determinants of the relative importance of generalized expectancies versus specific expectancies developed in the same situation is the amount of experience in the particular specific situation. These relationships are expressed in the formula below (Rotter, 1954, p. 166):

$$E_{s_1} = f\left(E'_{s_1} \, \& \, \frac{GE}{N_{s_1}}\right).$$

In this formula s_1 represents the specific situation and N represents the amount of previous experience the individual has had in that situation. E represents expectancy; E' represents a specific expectancy; and GE represents generalized expectancy. Clearly, if the formula is correct, and there is considerable empirical evidence to support it, then the relative importance of generalized expectancy goes up as the situation is more novel or ambiguous and goes down as the individual's experience in that situation increases. The point is important in understanding under what conditions one might expect clear prediction from an accurate measure of a generalized expectancy.

In social learning theory we have described two kinds of generalized expectancies. One of these that is involved in the formula for need potential involves expectancies for a particular kind of reinforcement, such as achievement, dependency, conformity, social approval, etc. Perceived similarity has to do with the nature of the reinforcement. The second kind of generalized expectancy deals with expectancies that generalize from other aspects of a series of situations involving some decision or problem solving where the nature of the reinforcements themselves may vary. For example, in situations involving different kinds of reinforcements, we may be asking ourselves if we can trust this individual to tell the truth or we may ask ourselves how we are going to find the solution when our previous plan was blocked. The first kind of generalized expectancy we designate with the subscript r for reinforcement (GE_r); the second kind is designated as a problem-solving generalized expectancy (GE_{ps}). In considering the expectancy for some reinforcement to follow some behavior in a given situation, not only would a generalized expectancy reinforcement be involved, but very possibly one or more problem-solving generalized expectancies would be involved. The above discussion can be represented in the following formula (Rotter et al., 1972, p. 41):

$$E_{s_1} = f\left(E' \, \& \, \frac{GE_r \, \& \, GE_{ps_1} \, \& \, GE_{ps_2} \cdots GE_{ps_n}}{f(N_{s_1})}\right).$$

If we could accurately calculate all of the relevant variables in determining an expectancy, we would still be a long way from the prediction of a specific behavior. Expectancy is only one of the three major determinants of a behavior potential in social learning theory. The second is the value of the reinforcement. If we want to predict a specific behavior, such as studying for an exam, voting in an election, taking part in a student protest, etc., we would have to know something about the values of the available reinforcement to a particular person before anything like an accurate prediction could be made.

The third major variable is the psychological situation. Psychological situations determine both expectancies and reinforcement values; consequently, they affect behavior potential. In addition, in social learning theory, the predictions of the potential of a particular behavior occurring in some situations must involve assessment of the alternative behaviors available in the same situation. For example, it is not sufficient if we would want to predict students' participation in some all-day protest to determine whether they are internals or externals according to some test; we would also need to know something about what alternative behaviors (such as reading in the library, attending classes, or even playing tennis) are available.

It is necessary to consider one further complication before one can thoroughly understand how subjective expectancy operates in the prediction of a behavior. The generalized expectancy that one might wish to use in a predictive formula, or rely upon as a basis for prediction, is arbitrary in the breadth of situations it might include. For example, if we want to predict a particular behavior involving studying for a psychology exam, and we wish to take into account some generalized expectancy that studying would lead to a better grade, we could assess this as a generalized expectancy for studying based on the person's previous experience in psychology courses. We may wish to use an even broader expectancy including not only studying but all other forms of increased effort as a technique of obtaining achievement satisfactions. A theorist may choose to use a construct of any breadth that he wishes, as long as it meets the criterion of functionality. That is, the referents that are included within the construct have a greater than chance correlation. Not every referent must correlate greater than chance with every other, but any referent must on the *average* correlate better than chance with all of the others. This is the same criteria that should be used in developing a measure of the same construct; namely, that each item should correlate significantly with the sum of the other items, with that item removed.

Clearly, we would expect that the more narrowly we define our generalized expectancy, the higher the prediction that results. It can also be seen that the distinction between specific expectancy and generalized expectancy is also arbitrary and is only a means of clarifying the problem of arriving at an accurate estimate. If we could obtain an exact expectancy measurement, regardless of how much of it was generalized and how much was specific, we would not have to look at separate components. However, generalized expectancies are interesting in their own right, since they may be thought of (a) as important personality characteristics, (b) as defining dimensions of generalization, and (c) as allowing broad predictions from limited data. They do, however, have their limitations, since they represent only one of many variables that enter into the prediction of behavior, and their relative importance is a function of the novelty and/or ambiguity of the situation.

The implication of the above statement is that some measure of a very broad generalized expectancy allows prediction in a large number of different situations, but at a low level. A narrower or more specific generalized expectancy should allow greater prediction for a situation of the same subclass but poorer prediction for other kinds of situations that are nevertheless to some degree similar. That is, some measure of a generalized expectancy that studying leads to higher grades in psychology might produce a better predictor of studying behavior for a particular psychology exam (the same subclass) but a poor one for a prediction of how much time someone may spend studying in order to improve their grades in mathematics (similar, but a different subclass). A very broad generalized expectancy might give a significant, but lower, prediction of the studying behavior in psychology and also a significant and low prediction for studying for a mathematics exam. What kind of measure an investigator might prefer and the kind of data available to him depends on his purpose. Since development of any adequate measure includes careful test construction and discriminant validity studies, constructing a different measure for every specific purpose would be a very expensive undertaking. Nevertheless, it would be worth developing such a specific measure if one's interest is in a limited area and particularly if one is seeking some practical application where every increment in prediction is important. A very broad measure has the advantage that it can be used to explore a large variety of possible theoretical and practical problems without necessitating the years of research necessary to develop the more specific instrument for every purpose. Such a measure, however, is necessarily limited to a lower level of prediction.

With this background in mind, it should now be possible to explore a number of misconceptions or misuses of the concept of a generalized expectancy for internal versus external control of reinforcement, at least as this concept was developed and measuring devices were constructed.

INTERNAL–EXTERNAL CONTROL PROBLEMS

Problems Associated with Conceptualization

Without doubt, the most frequent conceptual problem on the part of a number of investigators is the failure to treat reinforcement value as a separate variable. To make a locus of control prediction, one must either control reinforcement value or measure it, and systematically take it into account. The problem arises particularly in studies of social action, social protest, independence, conformity, etc. As we mentioned earlier, an internal person may *not* protest, be a member of a protest group, or sign a petition, simply because he does not believe in the cause; he may feel that his best interests lie in some other kind of activity, or he may merely feel that the particular action involved is bad strategy. On the other hand, a very external person may be a member of a protest group because he likes the other people who are members of the group, because it is less boring than studying, because it will upset his parents if they find out, because it is the conforming thing to do, etc. In some of the early studies of locus of control differences (e.g., the tubercular patients of Seeman and Evans, 1962, who differed in their efforts to find out about their disease and do something about it, or the Southern blacks in the early days of the civil rights movement, Gore & Rotter, 1963, who differed in their willingness to take part in civil rights activities), there is a strong reason to assume high motivation for all subjects toward the same goals. The same cannot be said about many recent studies attempting to evaluate the relationship between internal and external control and social action. In fact, it may very well be, and there is some evidence to support the notion, that people engage in violent demonstrations rather than take part in some kind of planned activity leading to a constructive end, because they feel unable to cope with their frustrations.

A second problem area is that of specificity–generality. This seems to be a particular problem for those people concerned with predicting achievement behavior or performance in achievement situations. There seems to be a persistent effort to obtain highly accurate and reliable predictions of achievement behavior by the use of a generalized expectancy for internal versus external control. While this appears, on the face of it, to be reasonable, it becomes *less* reasonable the more structured, the more familiar, and the more unambiguous a particular situation is. There seems to be some successful prediction, with ability controlled, of achievement in early grades as a function of attitudes toward internal versus external control. But as the child becomes older and enters college, the relationship between locus of control and grades or college entrance scores is no longer apparent. On the other hand, some studies do show relationships between locus of control scores and study habits, that is, study habits as described in questionnaires by the subject. If it is true that internals study more, then according to the myths of our society, they ought to get higher grades. Why don't they?

Probably because what differs is the self-reports about studying rather than their actual studying behavior. It may well be that when two students are faced with the prospect of having to guess what to study in order to pass an exam, then such generalized expectancies as internal versus external control may play some role in their behavior. However, by the time the student is in college, he knows pretty well what the relationship is for him between effort, studying, etc., and grades. What will differentiate his behavior from that of another student with the same ability is apparently level of motivation or the value placed upon academic achievement reinforcements versus other reinforcements that are competing. A great many achievement situations may be relatively novel or ambiguous for most subjects. The ones that are least ambiguous are academic achievement situations and tasks involving motor coordination or motor skills. Unfortunately, it is the latter two kinds of achievement situations that have been used most often in investigations attempting to demonstrate the predictive utility of individual differences in internal versus external control.

It is also true that some subjects may verbally express external attitudes on locus of control measures as a defense or rationalization for expected failure but act in an internal fashion in competitive situations. These individuals have been designated as defensive externals, and the problem of identifying them is discussed in the next section.

The third problem in conceptualization is the intrusion of the "good guy–bad guy" dichotomy. In spite of fears, and even warnings to the contrary, some psychologists quickly assume that it is good to be internal and bad to be external. Of course, in some senses, this may be true, but the problem then lies in assuming that all good things are characteristic of internals and all bad things are characteristic of externals. Internals should be more liberal, more socially skilled, better adjusted, more efficient, etc. Our early studies showed no relationship between locus of control and political liberalness–conservatism. I do not think that the situation has changed, although there may be some greater tendency recently for the endorsement of some external items by people who identify themselves as political radicals. But aside from the peculiarities of one test or another, there is no logical basis to assume any relationship.

The problem of the relationship between such a generalized expectancy such as locus of control and adjustment is indeed complicated. Adjustment, after all, is only a value concept, and any relationship must depend upon the definition of adjustment. It seems clear that self-report locus of control scales correlate with self-report scales of anxiety, adjustment, or scales involving self-description of symptoms. However, there are several studies (Efran, 1963; Lipp, Kolstoe, James, & Randall, 1968; Phares, 1968) that suggest that it is typical of internals to repress (forget?) failures and unpleasant experiences. Consequently, they may report (or admit) less anxiety, fewer symptoms, etc., and thereby create a positive relationship between internality and adjustment. Of course, we do not know whether people who repress a great deal are happier or better off than those who do not. Neither the Freudian hypothesis nor its opposite has been demonstrated. And what is the relationship between internality and guilt? Can one feel guilty without first feeling some responsibility for one's actions?

It may be better for people who are in obvious difficulties, who are trying to cope with failing abilities, such as the aged and those who have become victims of addictions, to have a greater feeling that they can, in fact, control what happens to them. But there must also be a limit on personal control. Many people may already feel that they have more control than is warranted by reality, and they may be subject in the future (or may have already been subjected) to strong trauma when they discover that they cannot control such things as automobile accidents, corporate failures, diseases, etc. Our early hypothesis that locus of control would have a curvilinear relationship to adjustment has not been borne out, but the fault may be in the methods of measurement of the adjustment variable. There are many interesting problems that can be investigated here, some practical and some theoretical. It would help in such investigations if the researcher had not already predetermined that internals are always "good guys" and externals are always "bad guys."

Problems Associated with the Measurement of Individual Differences

The preceding section deals with some of the limitations of prediction from a conceptual point of view. The following section deals with limitations related to the measurement problem. In discussing problems arising in the measurement of locus of control, we are concerned primarily with the adult Internal–External Locus of Control (I–E) Scale. Most of the comments, however, are appropriate for all of the children's and adults' scales that have been developed to date.

In the development of the I–E scale, it was intended to build an easily administered instrument with a low, but not zero, correlation with a social desirability scale that could be used to investigate the potential operation of the variable in a broad array of specific situations. In the process of development, various scales were built, tried out, and discarded. The Likert format, which has certain advantages, was discarded in favor of a forced-choice instrument in order to reduce correlations with the Marlowe-Crowne Social Desirability Scale. Tests of 100 items and 60 items, each including a number of subscales, were built and discarded, usually because the subscale intercorrelations were almost as high as the subscale internal reliabilities. Finally, only those items were included in the measure (a) that correlated with at least one of two criteria, (b) that had low correlations with the Marlowe-Crowne Social Desirability Scale, (c) for which both alternatives were selected by college students at least 15% of the time, and (d) that correlated with the total of the other items with that item removed. The two criterion behaviors were expectancy statements in a laboratory task (Rotter, Liverant, & Crowne, 1961) and the behavior of tubercular patients in actively trying to improve their condition (Seeman & Evans, 1962). While the criterion behaviors used were both drawn logically from the population of locus of control referents, they were obviously quite different from each other.

Many items dealing with academic achievement had to be dropped because of high correlations with social desirability. However, some items concerned with the basis for grades produced sufficient endorsement of the external alternative to be retained.

The final scale that is referred to in the literature as the Rotter I–E scale was based on the contributions of many people, including E. Jerry Phares, William James, Shepherd Liverant, Douglas Crowne, and Melvin Seeman. The late Shepherd Liverant, particularly, contributed to the development of the final forced-choice scale.

The final test used was developed on college students. It consisted of 23 items and 6 filler items that sampled widely from different life situations where locus of control attitudes might be relevant to behavior. Each item was given equal weight, and it was hoped that the content of the various items would provide an adequate sampling of situations in which internal–external attitudes might be expected to affect behavior. In other words, it was developed as a broad gauge instrument—not as an instrument to allow for very high prediction in some specific situation, such as achievement or political behavior, but rather to allow for a low degree of prediction of behavior across a wide range of potential situations.

Because additive scales (Rotter, Chance, & Phares, 1972, p. 326) such as this one sample widely from a variety of different situations, they cannot be expected to have as high internal consistency as a power scale that samples different strengths of response in a narrow area. While they may also be expected to provide some significant prediction in comparing groups, the level of that prediction in any specific situation is theoretically limited, and individual prediction for practical purposes using such a scale would not be warranted.

Even though the forced-choice method allows some control over social desirability, it is well-known that such measures change in their relationship to social desirability under different testing conditions. It may be equally socially desirable to select either alternative to a question that asks the subject to choose between the statements (a) ''Success in business is a matter of luck'' and (b) ''Success in business is a matter of hard work and skill,'' when they are college students. It is obviously not equally socially desirable to choose either alternative when applying for a job. Responses to questionnaires may be consciously or unconsciously distorted regardless of format. *All questionnaires are subject to error under particular testing conditions.* They are also limited by their dependence on conscious awareness. For example, studies have shown that alcoholics (Goss & Morosko, 1970) are more internal in their test response scores than college students. It is possible that this is an accurate portrayal of alcoholics and that their alcoholism is related to their guilt over failure. However, it is more likely that they have been told so many times and by so many people that their cure is ''up to them'' that they have fully recognized that this is the attitude they are supposed to present to the staff when they are trying to appear cooperative in a treatment program, either in an institution or as an outpatient. Very similar statements can be made for delinquents and drug addicts. Clearly, if one wished to determine which of the two explanations described above is more applicable to these groups, a more subtle form of testing would be necessary.

A last point should be made regarding test characteristics. When the I–E scale was first developed, most of the research used a median split to obtain groups called ''internals'' and ''externals.'' Since that time the mean for college students has risen from a score of 8 (*SD* = approximately 4.0) to somewhere between 10 and 12, depending upon the sample (the test is scored in the external direction). In early samples and in current samples, the distribution of scores tends to be normal. There is nothing to suggest a typology. In addition, it is clear that if median scores are now used, subjects who were considered externals in the early samples would now be considered internals. In other words, there is absolutely no justification for thinking in terms of a typology.

In summary, the I–E scale is subject, as are all personality measures, to the conditions of testing and the known or suspected purposes or nature of the examinee. For many studies, questionnaires to measure internal–external control are simply not appropriate, and either more subtle or unobtrusive behavioral measures are called for. Adams-Webber (1969) and Dies (1968) have developed projective measures of internal–external control with a reasonable correlation with the questionnaire measure.

The second important problem involves the question of unidimensionality versus multidimensionality: whether or not there are important subscales within the I–E scale or whether the concept itself should be broken down into more specific subconcepts. This issue has often been approached in an either/or manner. Either it is a unidimensional construct, or it is a multidimensional construct. Such thinking is contrary to a social learning approach to the nature of stable behavior.

The kinds of differentiation that appear among a group of items may vary from one sex to the other, or from one population to the other, and in effect, that is what is being found by a number of investigators. Since the availability of computer programs for factor analyses, a large number of such analyses have been done, and they have produced considerable variations (MacDonald, in press; Phares, in press). If the scale had been built in some other way, or had included 40 items instead of 23, the nature of the factor analyses might well be different from the ones now obtained. In other words, such factor analyses do not reveal "the true structure of the construct"; they only reveal the kinds of similarities perceived by a particular group of subjects for a particular selection of items.

In the early development of the I–E scale, two factor analyses were done (Franklin, 1963; Rotter, 1966), both of which showed that most of the variance was accounted for by one general factor. But some factors with only a few items with significant loadings did account for a small but significant variance. Since that time there has been strong reason to feel that there has been an increased differentiation in attitudes, so that some separate factors are emerging, although these still vary from population to population and between the sexes (Gurin, Gurin, Lao, & Beattie, 1969; Mirels, 1970). It is still true, however, that each of the items correlates with the total of the other items with that item removed, and that usually when factor analyses are done and applied to a different population, the factor scores, based on specific items that load most heavily on a particular factor, intercorrelate significantly.

The point of the preceding discussion is not to discourage factor analyses, the use of subscales, or conceptualizing in terms of subconcepts. It is only to discourage the notion that the factor analysis of any particular scale reveals the "true structure of a concept." Such factor analyses are not interesting in themselves, but they may be important as a first step toward the building of new instruments. They may be useful if it can be demonstrated that reliable and logical predictions can be made from the subscales to specific behaviors and that a particular subscale score produces a *significantly higher relationship than that of the score of the total test*. It is possible, as was done in one such factor analysis, to develop subscales that do not intercorrelate by throwing out those items that load highly on more than one factor. But whether or not the resulting factors are usable can only be demonstrated by showing that they have a logical and significant prediction to a *set* of criteria.

A third problem in interpreting locus of control scores has to do with the meaning of externality on the I–E scale. It would seem that if a person felt that what happens to him is the result of forces outside his own control, then he would tend to be relatively passive, unambitious, and noncompetitive. In our early studies involving expectancy stating in laboratory motor skill tasks we found that some externals showed patterns of behavior much like the behavior of ambitious, aggressive, and competitive subjects previously identified in studies of level of aspiration. It was also surprising, but true, that externals showed a wide spread of scores on college entrance tests and with grades, often including a number of subjects with very high scores. Stated another way, particularly in competitive achievement skill situations, there were a number of externals who acted much as we expected internals to act and others who acted much as we expected externals to act. That we were not dealing with simple absence of validity of the concept but rather with two different groups was suggested by the high variability of the external as compared to internal subjects—a fact later strikingly confirmed by Hersch and Scheibe (1967).

In these early samples our competitive externals tended to show up more in male samples. Although the correlations of college entrance scores and the I–E scale are uniformly low, with large samples it is true that the correlation for males was positive (i.e., externals were slightly higher on college aptitude scores) and negative for females. While neither correlation differed from zero significantly, they differed significantly from each other. We attributed this difference to a greater number of these competitive externals among our male subjects.

It also became apparent that psychologists interpreted the meaning of the external alternatives differently (presumably depending on their own locus of control attitudes). Some felt that when an individual endorses an item which states that success is primarily a matter of luck, he is rationalizing, or that when he agrees that powerful others control his life, he is blame projecting. In other words, the nature of externality was essentially defensive. Other psychologists regarded endorsement of external statements much more literally and assumed that passivity was the only logically expected outcome of external attitudes. Such passive attitudes result from direct teaching or learning, although it is contrary to the middle-class "Protestant ethic," which supposedly, but does not necessarily, typify American society. Such passive-external attitudes would clearly be the norm in more fatalistic cultures, such as Hindu and Moslem. This latter observation has been substantiated in studies involving translated versions of the I–E scale (Parsons & Schneider, 1974). In other words, it is clearly possible that we could have two kinds of "externals" in our society.

Using the more versus less ambitious patterns of expectancy statements, we tried to differentiate our two groups of externals (which we tentatively called "defensive externals" and "passive externals") on the basis of the items they endorsed. We tried two methods: one involving the content of items and the other involving the question of whether or not they endorsed internal items when dealing with success and external items when dealing with failure. Both attempts resulted in failure. We found that if rationalization was the basis for saying that luck was important, it was also a basis for saying that powerful others and fate were important. Item content did not differentiate our groups. We also found, at least among our college students, that if the subject said luck was important for failure, he remained consistent and said luck was also important for success. More recently, Levenson (1973, in press) has developed separate scales for belief in powerful others and chance. It is still true, however, that these scales have a relatively high intercorrelation in most samples that she studies.

Using the adult I–E scale, an investigation by Hamsher, Geller, and Rotter (1968) produced some unexpected results which suggested that a differentiation between defensive and passive externals might be made by the use of the Interpersonal Trust Scale (Rotter, 1967). This notion has been followed up by Hochreich (1968, in press; Note 2) in a series of studies and in a recent dissertation by Bander (Note 1). The rationale for using trust as a moderator variable is aptly described by Hochreich (in press). In substance, these studies demonstrate that the trust scale can help select these two different kinds of externals and that differential predictions can be made regarding their behavior in a variety of situations. Phares and his students (Davis, 1970) have also used other kinds of questionnaire data to make this differentiation with some success. They used the terms "defensive" and "congruent" for the two groups. It is possible that Levenson's distinction of belief in powerful others versus belief in chance overlaps that of defensive and passive externals.

Our own early attempt to pick up defensiveness by endorsement of failure versus success items did not work for college adults who apparently felt the necessity for some consistency in their responses. However, this differentiation does appear to work for children, as demonstrated by Crandall, Katkovsky, and Crandall (1965) and later by Mischel, Zeiss, and Zeiss (1974). It may be the case that younger children are less influenced by social desirability factors, particularly in the area of academic achievement. Long experiences in our school system must increase the social desirability of internal attitudes. There is, however, some evidence that internal attitudes are seen as more socially desirable even in the early grades. The direct prediction of school achievement by locus of control scales has been consistently more successful with children than with college students (Coleman, Campbell, Hobson, McPartland, Mood, Weinfeld, & York, 1966; Crandall, Katkovsky, & Preston, 1960; Nowicki & Strickland, 1973). It may well be that this is partly a function of the fact that only those who have achieved at a consistently high level appear in the college population, and the children samples involve a much broader range of abilities, or the difference may be related to an increased tendency toward defensive externality with increased age and time in the school system.

If it is true that those people whose achievement behavior is affected by external attitudes are less likely to go on to college, while we continue to have many college students agreeing to external items on adult scales, then it may be true that defensive externals represent a higher proportion of the college population than the population at large. However, no tests of this hypothesis have been made.

It should be mentioned here that in talking about defensive versus congruent externals we are not talking about types. For subjects who may score above the median on externality, both of these reasons for endorsing external items may exist to varying proportions in varying individuals.

The importance of this distinction between two bases for endorsing external items lies in the prediction of specific criteria. It seems clear from our present data that there is a group of defensive externals who are competitive, striving, and ambitious when placed in competitive achievement situations, although the same individuals may avoid competition when it is possible to do so without apparent loss of status. In other words, depending upon the criteria, sometimes defensive externals and congruent externals act in opposing fashions (e.g., in expectancy stating on a competitive skill task), sometimes they may act in the same fashion for different reasons, and in some instances predictions are borne out because one group of externals behaves in a manner consistent with some hypothesis and the other group behaves in a manner neutral to the hypothesis. For example, in the latter case, studies showing that externals are more maladjusted or defensive may depend mainly on the presence of defensive externals within the external group (Hochreich, in press). In order to understand or make predictions regarding the relationship of internal–external test behavior and some other criteria, it is important to make a careful theoretical analysis of the criterion behavior and its possible relationship to defensive versus congruent externality, and it may be important to use one of the methods already developed or a new method to differentiate between the two groups.

CONCLUSION

The preceding discussion permits no simple, general conclusion. It is offered in the hope that new studies involving the construct of internal versus external control of reinforcement will be carried out, taking into account the underlying theory and recognizing the limitations of this construct and its measurement so that the data obtained can be integrated into a meaningful body of knowledge. Particularly, one must guard against the assumption that expectancy regarding control of reinforcement is a behavioral trait and that the prediction of behavior can ignore the value of the reinforcement that is the expected outcome of the behavior being studied.

New methods of measurement and new scales, general or more specific, may be justified and needed, but the mere development of instruments without theoretical or practical justification based on the factor structure of old ones does not seem promising.

REFERENCE NOTES

1. K. Bander. The relationship of internal–external control and academic choice behavior. Doctoral dissertation, University of Connecticut, in preparation.
2. Also a recent study by D. J. Hochreich. Defensive externality and blame projection following failure. Unpublished manuscript, University of Connecticut, 1974.

REFERENCES

Adams-Webber, J. R. Generalized expectancies concerning the locus of control of reinforcements and the perception of moral sanctions. *British Journal of Clinical Psychology*, 1969, *8*, 340–343.

Coleman, J. S., Campbell, E. Q., Hobson, C. J., McPartland, J., Mood, A. M., Weinfeld, F. D., & York, R. L. *Equality of educational opportunity*. (Superintendent of Documents Catalog No. FS 5.238: 38001) Washington, D. C.: U. S. Government Printing Office, 1966.

Crandall, V. C., Katkovsky, W., & Crandall, V. J. Children's beliefs in their own control of reinforcement in intellectual-academic achievement situations. *Child Development*, 1965, *36*, 91–109.

Davis, D. E. *Internal–external control and defensiveness*. Unpublished doctoral dissertation, Kansas State University, 1970.

Dies, R. R. Development of a projective measure of perceived locus of control. *Journal of Projective Techniques and Personality Assessment*, 1968, *32*, 487–490.

Efran, J. *Some personality determinants of memory for success and failure*. Unpublished doctoral dissertation, Ohio State University, 1963.

Franklin, R. D. *Youth's expectancies about internal versus external control of reinforcement related to N variables*. Unpublished doctoral dissertation, Purdue University, 1963.

Gore, P. M., & Rotter, J. B. A personality correlate of social action. *Journal of Personality*, 1963, *31*, 58–64.

Goss, A., & Morosco, T. E. Relation between a dimension of internal–external control and the MMPI with an alcoholic population. *Journal of Consulting and Clinical Psychology*, 1970, *34*, 189–192.

Gurin, P., Gurin, G., Lao, R. C., & Beattie, M. Internal–external control in the motivational dynamics of Negro youth. *Journal of Social Issues*, 1969, *25*, 29–53.

Hamsher, J. H., Geller, J. D., and Rotter, J. B. Interpersonal trust, internal–external control, and the Warren Commission Report. *Journal of Personality and Social Psychology*, 1968, *9*, 210–215.

Hersch, P. D., & Scheibe, K. E. Reliability and validity of internal–external control as a personality dimension. *Journal of Consulting Psychology*, 1967, *31*, 609–613.

Hochreich, D. J. *Refined analysis of internal–external control and behavior in a laboratory situation*. Unpublished doctoral dissertation, University of Connecticut, 1968.

Hochreich, D. J. Defensive externality and attribution of responsibility. *Journal of Personality*, in press.

Joe, V. C. Review of the internal–external control construct as a personality variable. *Psychological Reports*, 1971, *28*, 619–640.

Lefcourt, H. M. Internal versus external control of reinforcement: A review. *Psychological Bulletin*, 1966, *65*, 206–220.

Lefcourt, H. M. Recent developments in the study of locus of control. In B. A. Maher (Ed.), *Progress in experimental personality research*. Vol. 6. New York: Academic Press, 1972.

Levenson, H. Multidimensional locus of control in psychiatric patients. *Journal of Consulting and Clinical Psychology*, 1973, *41*, 397–404.

Levenson, H. Activism and powerful others: Distinctions within the concept of internal–external control. *Journal of Personality Assessment*, in press.

Lipp, L., Kolstoe, R., James, W., & Randall, H. Denial of disability and internal control of reinforcement: A study using a perceptual defense paradigm. *Journal of Consulting and Clinical Psychology*, 1968, *32*, 72–75.

MacDonald, A. P. Measures of internal–external control. In J. P. Robinson & P. R. Shaver (Eds.), *Measures of social psychological attitudes* (rev. ed.) Ann Arbor: Institute for Social Research, University of Michigan, in press.

Mirels, H. L. Dimensions of internal versus external control. *Journal of Consulting and Clinical Psychology*, 1970, *34*, 226–228.

Mischel, W., Zeiss, R., & Zeiss, A. Internal–external control and persistence: Validation and implications of the Stanford Preschool Internal–External Scale. *Journal of Personality and Social Psychology*, 1974, *29*, 265–278.

Nowicki, S., & Strickland, B. R. A locus of control scale for children. *Journal of Consulting and Clinical Psychology,* 1973, *40,* 148–154.

Parsons, A., & Schneider, J. M. Locus of control in university students from eastern and western societies. *Journal of Consulting and Clinical Psychology,* 1974, *42,* 456–461.

Phares, E. J. *Locus of control: A personality determinant of behavior.* (A modular publication). Morristown, N. J.: General Learning Press, 1973.

Phares, E. J. *Locus of control in personality.* Morristown, N. J.: General Learning Press, in press.

Phares, E. J., Ritchie, D. E., & Davis, W. L. Internal–external control and reaction to threat. *Journal of Personality and Social Psychology,* 1968, *10,* 402–405.

Rotter, J. B. *Social learning and clinical psychology.* Englewood Cliffs, N. J.: Prentice-Hall, 1954.

Rotter, J. B. Generalized expectancies for internal versus external control of reinforcement. *Psychological Monographs,* 1966, *80*(1, Whole No. 609).

Rotter, J. B. A new scale for the measurement of interpersonal trust. *Journal of Personality,* 1967, *35,* 651–665.

Rotter, J. B., Chance, J., & Phares, E. J. (Eds.). *Applications of a social learning theory of personality.* New York: Holt, Rinehart & Winston, 1972.

Rotter, J. B., Liverant, S., & Crowne, D. P. The growth and extinction of expectancies in chance controlled and skilled tasks. *Journal of Psychology,* 1961, *52,* 161–177.

Seeman, M., & Evans, J. W. Alienation and learning in a hospital setting. *American Sociological Review,* 1962, *27,* 772–783.

Throop, W. F., & MacDonald, A. P. Internal–external locus of control: A bibliography. *Psychological Reports,* 1971, *28,* 175–190.

E. Jerry Phares, D. Elaine Ritchie, and William L. Davis
INTERNAL–EXTERNAL CONTROL AND REACTION TO THREAT

Groups of internally and externally controlled Ss were administered personality tests and then subsequently provided individualized reports containing both positive and negative information about their personality. Contrary to prediction, there were no differences in anxiety between internals and externals following their reading of the threatening material. However, as predicted, externals recalled significantly more of the negative material than did internals. They also were superior in recall of total material. Internals showed a significantly greater willingness to engage in remedial behaviors to confront their problems. Various alternative explanations of the data are also explored.

Internal versus external control of reinforcement (I–E) refers to the extent to which an individual feels that he has control over the reinforcements that occur relative to his behavior (Rotter, 1966). Internals tend to feel they are the effective agents in determining the occurrence of rewards. Externals, however, tend to believe that forces beyond their control determine the occurrence of reinforcements (fate, chance, powerful others, the complexity of the world, etc.). I–E represents a continuum of individual differences that cuts across specific need areas. It is a generalized expectancy relating behavior to reinforcement in a variety of situations.

In terms of the definition of I–E, a relationship to psychopathological phenomena is suggested. That is, to believe that one has little control over the occurrence of reinforcements seems similar to what might be called "rationalization." An external belief could thus be construed as a means of escaping punishment by attributing control of reinforcement to external agents. It could be a method of evading the responsibility for anticipated negative reinforcements.

Regardless of the origin of one's I–E orientation (whether based on veridical evidence or representing a means of reducing punishment), the possibility remains that internal and external orientations permit one to cope with threatening situations in different ways. For example, internals show a greater tendency to attend to and recall material immediately present in the environment (Seeman, 1963; Seeman & Evans, 1962). Davis and Phares (1967) found that internals are superior to externals in *actively* seeking information relevant to problem solution. Phares (1968) demonstrated that internals better utilize information in solving problems. Gore and Rotter (1963) suggested that internals are more likely to take overt action to effect social change than are externals. Together, such research suggests a

Reprinted by permission from the *Journal of Personality and Social Psychology*, 1968, *10*, pp. 402–405. Copyright 1968 by the American Psychological Association.

pattern wherein internals are more likely to engage in behaviors that will confront a problem directly than are externals.

Efran (1963) found that the tendency to forget failures was significantly related to internal scores. This could mean that an external has less need to avoid the unpleasant thought of failure since his external orientation already provides him with a less threatening explanation of his failure—forces outside himself are responsible. Internals, on the other hand, accepting responsibility for the failure, tend to resort to forgetting in the situation as an avoidant technique.

Lipp, Kolstoe, and Randall (1967) reported an interesting finding. Contrary to their expectations (but consistent with the present authors' thesis), they found that pictures of physically handicapped persons, when exposed tachistoscopically, resulted in lower recognition thresholds by handicapped externals than by handicapped internals. In short, there appeared to be less denial on the part of externals.

The relationship between anxiety and I–E is not clear but correlations are generally low (Efran, 1963; Rotter, 1966; Watson, 1967). There may be a greater tendency on the part of externals to admit to the common referents for anxiety; or it may be that the external's tendency to handle anxiety material by resorting to an external orientation is not completely effective, while the internal's greater tendency toward action-oriented solutions results in greater success and, ultimately, less anxiety.

Rotter (1966) reported that studies of I–E and maladjustment have generally not found linear relationships and while some curvilinear relationships have been significant, they are not U-shaped distributions and cannot be explained simply. Of course, "maladjustment" is not a highly specific term.

In view of the preceding, several hypotheses can be stated. First, when confronted by threatening material which presents a challenge to one's views of himself, an external will react with less anxiety than will an internal. For example, if adverse information regarding the results of a personality test is presented to an external, he will behave less anxiously than the internal because he can attribute the event to forces outside himself. Secondly, for similar reasons, it can be predicted that when both adverse and positive material is presented, the external will forget less of the adverse material than will the internal, while there will be no differences between the two groups as regards the retention of the positive material.

The third hypothesis is that when presented an opportunity to take overt remedial action as regards personal shortcomings, internals will show a greater tendency to do so than will externals. Again, internals having the generalized expectancy that they control the nature of behavior-reinforcement sequences will attempt to correct such deficiencies. Externals, however, will not to the same degree feel that such action will alter things. Such reasoning represents an application of the Gore and Rotter (1963) finding concerning social action-taking. Thus, the interference engendered by anxiety will not enable the internal to recall as much specific adverse material as the external. Nonetheless, he will be more disposed to engage actively in behaviors calculated to improve his status.

METHOD

The I–E scale (Rotter, 1966) was administered to 225 students in several summer school classes at Kansas State University. The mean was 14.56 scored in the internal direction. Subjects were drawn from the upper 27% and lower 26% of the distribution. From these extremes, subjects participated as paid volunteers. There were 19 externals and 21 internals. In the former group there were 14 females and 5 males; in the latter, 13 females and 8 males. No sex differences appeared in any of the subsequent measures.

The creation of a condition of threat was achieved by informing the subjects that they would take a series of personality tests which would be individually interpreted by trained clinical psychologists.[1] The procedure was presented to them as a study of psychotherapy to find out what kinds of interpretations are most effective. Confidentiality was assured. Subjects were administered parts of the Rorschach, the Thematic Apperception Test (TAT), the Wechsler Adult Intelligence Scale (WAIS), and the Repression–Sensitization (R–S) scale (Byrne, 1961).

Subjects were initially tested in groups of three to six. Two days later subjects returned and each was presented an individually typed personality analysis consisting of 19 brief two- and three-line interpretations. Eight were positive and 11 were of a threatening nature. Unknown to the subjects, of course, everyone received identical interpretations. Two examples of these are:

1. She is warm and is able to maintain very positive interpersonal relationships.
2. At times, sexual thoughts become a problem and make her doubt her maturity.

When the subjects returned, they were allowed approximately 5 minutes to examine the interpretations. After this, they were instructed to circle the number of each interpretation that made them at least slightly uncomfortable. Next, subjects were given Rating Scale A which required them to check each interpretation on a 7-point scale indicating how comfortable-uncomfortable the interpretation made them. Rating Scale B was then administered and required them to check, on a 7-point scale, for each interpretation, how true-untrue the interpretation was. Finally, Rating Scale C was given which, again, on a 7-point scale, required that they indicate how well or poorly each interpretation was worded.

The succeeding step in this questionnaire procedure requested that subjects check any or all of the items on the following five-step questionnaire:

I would be interested in:
A. Receiving a copy of a brochure listing several sources of library material dealing with techniques of achieving better mental health.
B. Attending a lecture by a psychiatrist on techniques of achieving better mental health.
C. Attending a small group discussion to talk about common problems of college students in dealing with the stresses of college life.
D. Making an appointment with a clinical psychologist to discuss in greater depth the meaning and implication of my test results.
E. I would not be interested in any of the foregoing.

At the conclusion of this, all the interpretation sheets were collected and subjects were then asked to write on a blank piece of paper all the interpretations they could recall within 10 minutes. Following this, Rating Scale D was administered on which subjects were instructed to rate (on a 7-point scale) how useful they felt the overall experiment was in shedding light on the process of psychotherapy.

This concluded the experimental procedure whereupon the experimenter carefully explained the purpose of the experiment and the necessity for deception.

---

[1] A fuller account of the experimental instructions and procedure may be obtained by writing the senior author.

RESULTS AND DISCUSSION

None of the rating scales produced any differences approaching significance. Internals checked a mean of 5.81 interpretations which made them uncomfortable, while for externals the mean was 6.37. In terms of amount of discomfort elicited by each interpretation, similar results were obtained from both groups indicating a moderate degree of discomfort (means clustered around 4). The rating scales for truth or falsity and adequacy of wording likewise produced no differential results and indicated both groups felt the interpretations to be moderately true and worded slightly better than average. Similarly, both groups thought the experiment was useful. Nothing in these results, therefore, is supportive of differential defensiveness on the part of internals and externals.

For the recall data, two independent judges counted the number of interpretations recalled by a random selection of 20 subjects. The resultant coefficient was .88. Table 1 presents the recall data. A repeated-measures analysis of variance indicated that I–E was a significant source of variation ($F = 4.50$, $df = 1/38$, $p = < .05$). Thus externals recalled a greater number of interpretations (including both positive plus negative items) than did internals. However, although the trend of the means is in the expected direction, the predicted interaction between I–E and type of interpretation (positive versus negative) failed to reach significance ($F = 1.14$, $df = 1/38$, $p > .20$).

Table 1. Recall of interpretation data for internals and externals

Group	n	Negative (11 items)		Positive (8 items)		Total (19 items)	
		M	*SD*	*M*	*SD*	*M*	*SD*
Internals	21	6,67	2.17	4.19	1.25	10.86	2.89
Externals	19	7.89	1.66	4.84	1.26	12.74	2.70

The third hypothesis involved differential action-taking. For scoring purposes, each questionnaire item was assigned a numerical value. It was assumed that Alternatives A through D represented an increasing degree of personal commitment to deal with problems suggested in the interpretations. Therefore, Alternative A was scored 2, Alternative D, 5, etc. Alternative E was assigned a value of 1. Each subject received a score which represented the sum of the values of all items checked. The internal mean was 8.57 ($SD = 4.01$) and the external mean, 5.95 ($SD = 3.52$). This yielded a *t* of 2.19, which is significant at the .025 level (one-tailed test) in the expected direction.

These results, then, would appear supportive of the hypothesis that internals will agree to engage in what might be called more confronting behavior than will external subjects.

As a check against social desirability, R–S scale scores were correlated with the anxiety, retention, and action-taking measures. None of these correlations approached significance, nor were there differences between internals and externals on the scale.

Contrary to the predictions, internals did not report greater anxiety in response to threat than externals. Both groups expressed a moderate degree of discomfort. Several interpretations are possible. For example, one could argue that the questionnaire method utilized was not sensitive enough to detect differences in anxiety. Another possibility is that anxiety dissipates at differential rates in internals and externals. It may be that the two groups do not immediately differ in their anxiety reactions to threat as is suggested by the present data. However, after an unspecified period, the external becomes less anxious as his external orientation engages the threat. Differential levels of anxiety in internals and externals may then have the effect of interfering with the recall of material associated with threat.

It is interesting that past work on I–E reports superior retention on the part of internals. Seeman and Evans (1962) and Seeman (1963) both reported greater retention of material by internals. Phares (1968) also reported *trends* for better retention on the part of internals even when degree of initial learning is controlled and the task is a problem-solving one. The present study, along with Efran's (1963), is about the only one to report data that indicates superior recall of material by externals. The fact that this occurred in the context of threat, while previous studies were of a nonthreatening nature, suggests the role of anxiety or threat.

Another major finding was that internals indicated a greater willingness to engage in action-taking behaviors to confront problems suggested by the interpretations. These results are consonant with findings by Gore and Rotter (1963) which were obtained in a context of social change.

It is possible, of course, that if internals subsequently became more anxious about the interpretations than externals, then differential anxiety levels could be utilized to explain the differences in willingness to engage in action-taking behavior. Therefore, in future research it would be desirable to equate groups for anxiety levels and then note whether one group is more action oriented than the other. This should more definitively explicate the role of anxiety and expectancies. Further research in this area, coupled with a greater understanding of the origins of I–E, should go a long way toward creating an understanding of the role of I–E in the economy of the individual.

REFERENCES

Byrne, D. The Repression–Sensitization scale: Rationale, reliability, and validity. *Journal of Personality*, 1961, *29*, 334–349.

Davis, W. L., & Phares, E. J. Internal–external control as a determinant of information-seeking in a social influence situation. *Journal of Personality*, 1967, *35*, 547–561.

Efran, J. Some personality determinants of memory for success and failure. Unpublished doctoral dissertation, Ohio State University, 1963.

Gore, P. M., & Rotter, J. B. A personality correlate of social action. *Journal of Personality*, 1963, *31*, 58–64.

Lipp, L., Kolstoe, R., & Randall, H. Denial of disability and internal control of reinforcement: A study utilizing a perceptual defense paradigm. Paper presented at the meeting of Midwestern Psychological Association, Chicago, 1967.

Phares, E. J. Differential utilization of information as a function of internal–external control. *Journal of Personality*, 1968, in press.

Rotter, J. B. Generalized expectancies for internal versus external control of reinforcement. *Psychological Monographs*, 1966, *80*(1, Whole No. 609).

Seeman, M. Alienation and social learning in a reformatory. *American Journal of Sociology*, 1963, *69*, 270–284.

Seeman, M., & Evans, J. W. Alienation and learning in a hospital setting. *American Sociological Review*, 1962, *27*, 772–783.

Watson, D. Relationship between locus of control and anxiety. *Journal of Personality and Social Psychology*, 1967, *6*, 91–92.

Bernard Weiner, Richard Nierenberg, and Mark Goldstein
SOCIAL LEARNING VERSUS ATTRIBUTIONAL INTERPRETATIONS OF EXPECTANCY OF SUCCESS

Social learning theory (Rotter, 1954) and attribution theory (Heider, 1958) have distinctive origins and idiosyncratic "ranges of convenience." On the one hand, social learning theory makes use of concepts from reinforcement theory to furnish an explanation of clinical phenomena. In contrast, attribution theory utilizes concepts that evolved from "everyday life" to provide an analysis of social perception. It is therefore surprising that these conceptions are commensurable with respect to a given phenomenon: expectancy shifts following attainment or nonattainment of a goal. Furthermore, the two theories make disparate predictions about expectancy change. Hence, it is possible to perform a series of "crucial" experiments and compare the validities of the theories with respect to this phenomenon.

SOCIAL LEARNING THEORY

Social learning theory is quite explicit concerning the determinants of expectancy shifts and, in turn, behavioral potential (or strength of motivation). Rotter (1966) states: "If a person perceives a reinforcement as contingent upon his own behavior, then the occurrence of either a positive or a negative reinforcement will strengthen or weaken potential for that behavior to recur in the same or similar situation. If he sees the reinforcement as being outside his own control or not contingent, that is, depending upon chance, fate, powerful others, or unpredictable, then the preceding behavior is less likely to be strengthened or weakened" (p. 5).

More specifically, social learning theorists contend: "It is a matter of common sense that most individuals who would find a $5 bill on a given street would not return and walk up and down the street many times to find more $5 bills because they consider the event that occurred to be a matter of chance. On the other hand, should someone take up ping pong and be told that he plays an excellent game for someone just learning, he is quite likely to increase the number of times he plays ping pong. In the first case, the reinforcement appears to be a matter of chance . . . and in the second instance, the reinforcement appears to be dependent on some characteristic or quality of the person which he can label as skill" (Rotter, Seeman, & Liverant, 1962, p. 474).

In sum, the magnitude of expectancy change and behavioral potential following a

Reprinted by permission from the *Journal of Personality*, 1976, *44*, pp. 52–68. Copyright 1976 by Duke University Press.

success or a failure is influenced by the perceived locus of control of the event, with internal or personal control producing greater shifts than external or environmental control.[1]

To test this general supposition, locus of control is either experimentally manipulated or assessed with an individual difference measure. Success and/or failure are then induced and expectancy shifts are related to locus of control. Phares (1957) was among the first to vary locus of control experimentally. He instructed one-half of his subjects that performance at a matching task was only a matter of luck (external control), while subjects in a second experimental condition received information that performance was determined by skill (internal control). Subjective probability of success was assessed prior to each trial, with a fixed order of partial reinforcement given in both experimental conditions. The data revealed that typical expectancy shifts (an increment in the expectancy of success after a success and a decrement in the expectancy of success after a failure) were more frequent and of greater magnitude in the skill than in the chance condition. That is, as predicted by social learning theorists, the preceding outcome was believed more likely to recur given internal (skill) rather than external (luck) perceptions of control. Phares (1957) also found that atypical shifts (decrements in the expectancy of success following a success and increments after a failure) were more evident in the chance than in the skill condition.

The differential frequency and/or magnitude of typical expectancy shifts in skill- as opposed to chance-related situations has been replicated in other investigations (James, 1957; Rotter, Liverant, & Crowne, 1961). In addition, atypical shifts are well documented in the literature pertaining to games of chance (e.g., Jarvik, 1951; Skinner, 1942). Such shifts have been labeled the "gambler's fallacy," connoting the misconception that in games of chance the events are not perceived as independent and the same outcome is believed unlikely to recur on successive occasions (the "negative recency" effect). Furthermore, in chance tasks the conviction that the future outcome will differ from the prior results increases as a function of the number of consecutive occurrences of the past event (Jarvik, 1951; Lepley, 1963). This finding is in marked opposition to data in skill situations, for with increasing success (or failure) at a skill-related task, there is increasing certainty that success (or failure) again will be experienced. That is, a "positive recency" effect is displayed (see, for example, Diggory, Riley, & Blumenfeld, 1960; Zajonc & Brickman, 1969).

Correlational studies in which locus of control is assessed rather than manipulated have been far less successful in substantiating the hypothesized relationship between locus of control and expectancy shifts. Partially confirmatory data have been reported in only two investigations (Battle & Rotter, 1963; James, 1957). One suspects that the lack of published investigations in this area may be an indication of research failures. But, even if the existence of unreliability is assumed, the social learning hypothesis would not necessarily be invalidated. In laboratory studies the experimental task generally is a simply binary-choice game. But the measure of individual differences, most often the Rotter (1966) locus of control scale, includes questions that concern life philosophy, social recognition, and so on. It is well known that the more closely related the items on a measurement instrument are to the behavior being predicted, the more likely it is that the test will prove "valid." Thus, the absence of published confirmatory results in the correlational studies may merely indicate shortcomings in the assessment instrument, particularly its lack of situational specificity (see, for example, Mischel, Zeiss, & Zeiss, 1974).

---

[1]Related issues, such as the contribution of generalized expectancy to a stated expectancy (e.g., Schwartz, 1969), and the interaction of reinforcement schedules with locus of control (e.g., James & Rotter, 1958), are ignored here.

In sum, investigations manipulating perceptions of control strongly support the social learning theory hypothesis regarding expectancy shifts. Indeed, the differential shifting of probabilities given luck versus skill perceptions of control can be accepted as an empirical truth. On the other hand, correlational studies in which perceptions of control are assessed rather than manipulated at best only weakly support the contention of social learning theorists. However, the experimental investigations provide much better tests of the locus of control-expectancy shift linkage than do the correlational studies.

ATTRIBUTION THEORY

Attribution theorists postulate that future behavior is in part determined by the perceived causes of past events. In achievement-related contexts, success and failure are perceived as chiefly caused by ability, effort, the difficulty of the task, and luck (Frieze, 1973; Heider, 1958; Weiner, Frieze, Kukla, Reed, Rest, & Rosenbaum, 1971). There are, of course, numerous other perceived causes of success and failure, such as mood, illness, fatigue, bias, and so on. In this paper, however, the discussion primarily is restricted to the four main causes enumerated above.

The perceived causes of achievement outcomes can be subsumed within a few basic causal dimensions. These dimensions are imposed by attribution theorists upon the causal concepts actually used in "everyday life"; hence, the dimensions may be considered "second order concepts" (Schütz, 1967, p. 59). One such dimension already introduced is the locus of control: causes are either internal to the person (e.g., ability, effort, mood) or are external (e.g., task difficulty, luck, bias). A second causal dimension has been labeled "stability" or "relative endurance." Some causes, such as ability, task difficulty, and bias are perceived as relatively stable, whereas other causes, such as effort, luck, and mood are subject to moment-to-moment or periodic fluctuations. Thus, considering the causes and the causal dimensions outlined here, ability is an internal, stable cause; effort and mood are internal but unstable; task difficulty and bias are generally perceived as external and stable; and luck is an external, unstable cause of success and failure.

It has been argued that the stability of a cause, rather than its locus of control, determines expectancy shifts (Weiner et al., 1971; Weiner, 1972, 1974). That is, if conditions (the presence or absence of causes) are expected to remain the same (such as one's level of ability, the difficulty of the task, or the bias of the teacher), then the outcome experienced on past occasions will be expected to recur (see Mischel, Jeffery, & Patterson, 1974). A success should therefore produce relatively large increments in the anticipation of future success, and a failure should strengthen the belief that there will be subsequent failures. On the other hand, if the causal conditions are perceived as likely to change (such as the amount of effort expended, the encountered luck, or one's mood state), then the present outcome may not be expected to repeat itself in the future. A success therefore should yield relatively small increments or perhaps even decrements (atypical shifts) in the expectancy of subsequent success, while a failure need not necessarily intensify the belief that there will be future failures.[2]

The attributional analysis of expectancy shifts is consistent with the data reported by

---

[2]The dimensional categorization of a particular causal element is not invariant. For example, one may be considered "lazy" or "lucky." In these instances effort and luck are internal and stable. The predictions regarding expectancy change refer to a linkage with a causal dimension. Nonetheless, there is a general agreement regarding the dimensional placement of specific causes.

James (1957), Phares (1957), Rotter et al. (1961) and others. In these prior investigations expectancy shifts are compared between skill and luck experimental conditions. Skill (ability) is an internal, stable cause, whereas luck is an external, unstable cause. Hence, two dimensions of causality are linked. The differential expectancy shifts displayed in these prior investigations therefore can be logically imputed to either the locus of control or the stability dimension of causality.

What is required, then, is a series of "crucial" experiments that separate the two causal dimensions and relate expectancy shifts to both locus of control and causal stability. Such experiments have been conducted; they unequivocally support the attributional, rather than the social learning theory, hypothesis. These studies have been published quite recently and a detailed review is fitting here (see Table 1).[3]

Table 1. Summary of past and present research studies

Experimenter	Subjects	Design	Task	Attributions
Fontaine (1974)	Australian; college males	Experimental	Unspecified "tasks"	Manipulated
McMahan (1973)	American; grammar, high school, and college students	Correlational; repeated-measure	Anagrams	Paired-comparison
Meyer (1973)	German; high school students	Correlational; repeated-measure	Digit-symbol substitution	Percentage rating
Rosenbaum (1972)	American; college students	Experimental; simulation	Unspecified "project"	Manipulated
Valle (1974)	American; college students	Experimental and correlational; simulation	Sales	Manipulated and rating scale
Present study	American; college males	Correlational; between-subjects	Block design	Within-dimension rating scale

Table 1 alphabetically outlines five experiments that examine the effects of causal stability as well as locus of control on expectancy and expectancy shifts. Fontaine (1974) gave his subjects information about a variety of "tasks" which they believed would be performed at a later time. The information included whether a similar reference group ("psychology students from this University") previously succeeded or failed, as well as the outcome attributions of the reference group (ability, effort, task difficulty, or luck). The subjects were then asked to estimate their own expected score on the tasks. The data revealed: "Highest expectancies were associated with comparison group success and attribution to stable factors (ability and task difficulty), while the lowest expectancies were associated with attributions to stable factors and comparison group failure. Expectancies following attribution to variable factors (effort and luck) were intermediate and not so affected by outcome information" (Fontaine, 1974, p. 492). Furthermore, in direct opposition to social learning theory, "internal attributions resulted in higher expected performance than external attribution after

[3]Another investigation supporting attribution theory has recently been reported by Pancer and Eiser (1975).

comparison group failure, while there were no differences after success" (Fontaine, 1974, p. 494).

McMahan (1973) gave sixth-grade, tenth-grade, and college students five trials of repeated success or repeated failure at an anagrams task. Prior to each trial the subjects stated their future expectancy of success as well as their causal ascriptions for the past success or failure. Attributions were determined by means of sets of six paired-comparison questions. The comparisons represented all possible pairings of the ability, effort, task difficulty, and luck causal factors (e.g., "Did you succeed because you tried hard or because you were lucky?"). McMahan (1973) reports: "The relationships between ability and task attributions and subsequent expectancy tend to be positive following success [high attributions, high expectancy of success] and negative following failure [high attributions, low expectancy of success]; the relationships between effort and luck attributions and subsequent expectancy tend to be negative following success and positive following failure. . . . Rotter's (1966) . . . statement suggests that the relationship between attributions to effort (an internal factor) and subsequent expectancy would be positive following success and negative following failure, while [the relationship] between attributions to task (an external factor) and subsequent expectancy would be negative following success and positive following failure. . . . The obtained correlations tend to be in the opposite direction" (p. 112).

The study by Meyer (1973) reported, in part, in Weiner, Heckhausen, Meyer, and Cook (1972) was the first to sever experimentally the locus of control and stability dimensions of causality. In a manner similar to the subsequent research by McMahan (1973), Meyer conducted a correlational study in which repeated success or failure was induced. Causal ascriptions as well as future expectancy of success were ascertained after each of five trials at a digit-symbol substitution task. Attributions were described in percentage figures ("The outcome was ___% dependent upon ability") and were required to total 100 percent. In the failure condition Meyer found that "Expectancy of success following failure was greater given high than low ascriptions to effort and luck. . . . Ascriptions to ability and task difficulty reverse this relationship: Low rather than high attributions to these stable elements are associated with greater goal expectancies. . . . Comparing expectancy shifts of subjects high versus low in . . . internal factors, or in . . . external factors . . . virtually eliminates between-group probability differences" (Weiner et al., 1972, pp. 244–245). The reported results in the success condition were less definitive. High attributions to ability and low ascriptions to luck were associated with a heightened expectancy of success, as predicted by both social learning and attribution theory. But neither effort nor task difficulty ascriptions were significantly related to expectancy of success.

Rosenbaum (1972) conducted two simulation experiments in which the subjects were asked to imagine that they worked with another person on a "project." The project was described as a success or a failure, and the causes of the outcome were specified. The causes were either stable (e.g., usually tries hard at these projects; has the ability to do well) or unstable (e.g., tried hard at that project; was unusually tired). In addition, the causes described either the actor or his partner. Again the findings strongly supported the hypothesis that attributions to stable factors augment expectancies following success and dampen expectancies after failure. Locus of control did not influence expectancy.

Finally, Valle (1974) conducted four simulation experiments that described the sales performance of male and female employees. Both success and failure were manipulated, with the causes of the performance manipulated in two of the experiments and assessed in the remaining two studies. In addition to including both stable and unstable descriptions of effort in one of her experimental manipulation studies, Valle was able to characterize task difficulty as either stable or unstable by stipulating that the sales person would or would not be transferred to a different sales district. Valle (1974) reported systematic and reliable relationships between future performance and the perceived causes of success and failure in the direction hypothesized by attribution theory.

In sum, the results of these studies decidedly support the attributional conception and contradict the predictions from social learning theory. The stability of causal attributions, rather than their locus of control, is related to expectancy of success. The investigations demonstrating this relationship used group and individual testing procedures, manipulated success and/or failure, were within- and between-subject experimental designs, employed a wide variety of experimental tasks, were both correlational designs assessing causal attributions and experimental designs manipulating causal ascriptions, and the causal ascriptions were measured in diverse ways.

In spite of all this convincing empirical support, it was decided to conduct one additional study pertinent to expectancy estimates. The present experiment incorporates certain positive features of the prior research and introduces some methodological advances. First, the experiment was "real" rather than simulation, with subjects tested individually to maximize the effectiveness of the outcome manipulation. Furthermore, repeated success was induced, but a between-subjects experimental design was employed with different subjects receiving varied amounts of success experience. Finally, and of most importance, a new measure of attributions was employed that allowed the causal judgments to be made within a single causal dimension while holding constant the remaining dimension of causality.

METHOD

Subjects

Subjects were 126 male undergraduates at the University of California, Los Angeles. The subjects participated as part of a course requirement in introductory psychology.

Achievement Task

A task fulfilling several criteria was needed for the study. The task had to be sufficiently ambiguous regarding the determinants of performance to yield variations in the perceived reasons for success. Further, the outcome had to be under experimental control. Finally, a task having some importance for the participants was desired.

The task chosen was a modification of the block design test on the WAIS. The subjects were required to match a design shown by the experimenter. Five new designs were conceived that pilot subjects were able to solve within a reasonable period of time. Success was induced by apparently timing each subject, waiting for him to solve the puzzle, and then stating that he had succeeded by completing the design within the allotted time period. In contrast to some of the prior research in this area (e.g., McMahan, 1973), no subject had to be excluded from the analysis because of failure to complete the designs.

Procedure

The block design test was explained to the subject and one practice trial was given. If the subject had trouble with the practice trial, a second design was presented prior to the test series. Subjects ($N = 21$ in each condition) were randomly assigned to one of six conditions

(0, 1, 2, 3, 4, or 5 successes). Twenty-one subjects were not given any success to obtain baseline expectancy data. These subjects stated their expectancy of success prior to any task performance. In the remaining five conditions the expectancy of future success and attributions for the prior outcome(s) were ascertained following the achievement test(s).

Expectancy of future success was determined by having subjects indicate "how many of the next ten similar designs he believed that he would successfully complete." To assess perceptions of causality a new attributional self-report questionnaire was developed. Subjects were required to mark four rating scales that were identical with respect to either the stability or locus of control dimensional anchors, but which differed along the remaining dimension. For example, one attribution question was "Did you succeed on this task because you are always good at these kinds of tasks or because you tried especially hard on this particular task?" "Always good" and "tried hard," the anchors on this scale, are identical on the locus of control dimension (internal), but they differ in perceived stability, with ability a stable attribute and effort an unstable cause. In a similar manner, judgments were made between "lucky" and "tried hard" (unstable causes differing in locus of control), "these tasks are always easy" and "lucky" (external causes differing in stability), and "always good" versus "always easy" (stable causes differing in locus of control). Thus, the judgments were made within a single causal dimension. This separation permitted a direct test of the locus of control versus stability hypotheses. For scoring purposes the scales were divided into fifteen equal intervals.

Following the questionnaire a complete explanation of the experiment was given to the subjects. Because the theories under consideration do not make differential predictions regarding success versus failure outcomes, only the success condition was included in this study. This avoided ethical problems at times associated with the induction of failure.

RESULTS

Table 2 shows the correlations between the scores on the four attributional questions. The correlations are low, but have greater than chance probabilities. The meaning of the correlations is ambiguous. Some are due to the inclusion of the identical variable in the two dependent measures; others may be ascribed to response bias, causal preferences for internal or stable attributions, or avoidance of a particular cause that is represented on both a stability and a locus scale.

Within each of the success conditions the subjects were classified as high (above the

Table 2. Correlations between the four attributional measures

Variable	Variable no.			
	1	*2*	*3*	*4*
1. Stability within internal control[a]				
2. Locus of control within instability[b]	.20*			
3. Stability within external control[c]	.31**	.34**		
4. Locus of control within stability[d]	.37**	.31**	.26**	

[a]Always good vs. tried hard.
[b]Tried hard vs. lucky.
[c]Easy tasks vs. lucky.
[d]Always good vs. easy task.
*$p < .05$.
**$p < .005$.

median) or low (below the median) in perceived causal stability and perceived locus of control. Two analyses were performed; the first added the two judgments within each dimension to yield an overall dimensional score, while the second analysis considered each of the four attributional questions separately.

Table 3 shows the mean expectancy of success scores in the combined analysis as a function of the number of success experiences. As anticipated on the basis of the skill research literature, expectancy of success increases as a function of the number of prior successes, $F(5,113) = 5.41, p < .001$. The magnitude of this effect may have been somewhat attenuated because of the prevailing high subjective expectancies. In addition, Table 3 reveals that expectancy of future success is directly related to the stability of the perceived cause of the prior positive outcome(s), $F(1, 95) = 11.51, p < .001$. The Stability × Number of Successes interaction does not approach significance, $F(4, 95) = 1.20, p > .25$. Analysis of Table 3 also reveals that perceptions of control are not significantly related to the stated expectancies of success, either as a main effect, $F(1, 95) = 1.24, p > .25$, or in interaction with Number of Successes ($F < 1$).

Table 3. Mean expectancy scores for subjects classified as high (above the median) or low (below the median) in stability and locus of control as a function of number of success trials

				Trials			
Causal dimensions	*0*	*1*	*2*	*3*	*4*	*5*	*M*
Stability							
High		8.18[a]	8.18	8.82	9.00	8.91	8.63
Low		6.90	6.60	8.00	8.20	9.00	7.74
	M 7.09[b]	7.57	7.43	8.43	8.62	8.95	8.20
Locus of control (internal)							
High		7.91	7.73	8.70	8.60	8.82	8.35
Low		7.20	7.10	8.18	8.64	9.10	8.08
	M 7.09	7.57	7.43	8.43	8.62	8.95	8.20

[a]$N = 10$ or 11 in each cell.
[b]$N = 21$.

Expectancy estimates were next examined separately for each of the two stability and two locus of control ascriptions. Figure 1 shows the relationship between stability and expectancy judgments within internal control (ability versus effort ascriptions), while Figure 2 depicts this relationship within external locus of control (task difficulty versus luck ascriptions). Figures 1 and 2 show that both within internal control and within external control expectancy increments are positively associated with the stability of the ascriptions; respectively, $F(1, 95) = 7.27, p < .01; F(1, 95) = 4.81, p < .05$. It also may be observed that the findings are in the expected direction in all five of the independent comparisons within each of the two figures. The Stability × Number of Successes interaction does not approach significance in these analyses ($F < 1$). Comparing locus of control differences within either the stable or the unstable ascriptions reveals that the high versus low groups do not differ in expectancy of success ($F < 1$).

DISCUSSION

The results of the study definitively support the attributional conception and contradict the predictions from social learning theory. The stability of causal attributions, and not their locus of control, is related to expectancy of success and expectancy shifts. We now consider

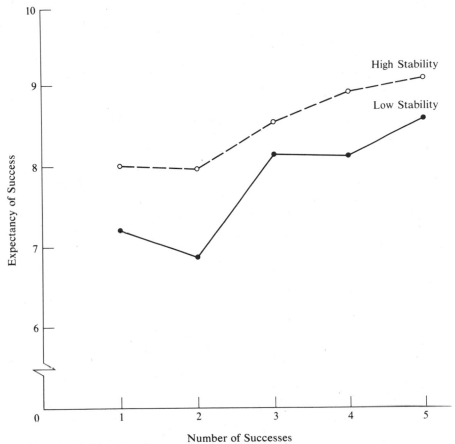

Figure 1. Mean expectancy of success as a function of the number of successes for subjects classified according to stability ascription, within internal locus of control (ability versus effort attribution).

this relationship to be proven. It is unfortunate from our point of view that psychologists continue to discuss locus of control in relation to expectancy of success and continue to confound the internal aspects of perceived control with the volitional and stable dimensions of causality.

Locus of Control Theory

The implications of this research for attribution theory and, more specifically, attributional approaches to motivation, have been recently examined in detail (Weiner, 1974). But the significance of the expectancy research and attribution theory for social learning theory and the general locus of control area has been slighted. Thus, some evaluation and speculation are warranted.

First, locus of control refers to a causal belief and represents one particular dimension associated with the encoding of the causal structure of one's world. Thus, internal–external

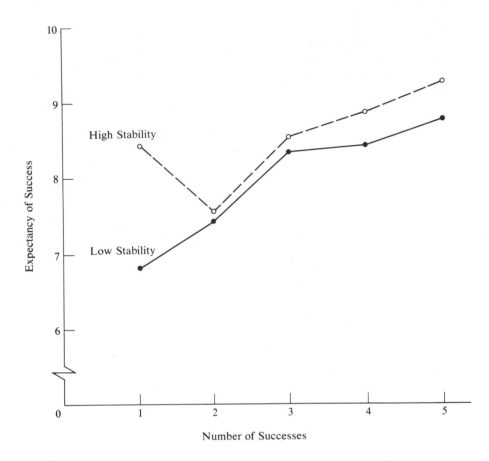

Figure 2.   Mean expectancy of success as a function of the number of successes for subjects classified according to stability ascription, within external locus of control (task difficulty versus luck attribution).

locus of control should perhaps be dislodged from the conceptual foundation of social learning theory and expectancy of reinforcement, which it does not predict, and be placed within a broader cognitive framework.

Further, it is evident from the research summarized in Table 1 and the present study that there are dimensions of causality in addition to locus of control. The concentration of research upon any single causal dimension, to the exclusion of other dimensions, constrains both empirical and theoretical growth.

Finally, there are a wide array of internal determinants of behavior in addition to skill, and an equally far-reaching variety of external determinants of behavior in addition to luck. There are important differences between, for example, ability and effort, or luck and powerful others, although these dissimilarities have not been distinguished in locus of control theory and research. These distinctions will have to be taken into consideration in future investigations and theorizing.

Locus of Control Research

There is an interesting paradox in the research concerned with perceptions of control. Many studies by social learning theorists that manipulate perceived control have focused attention upon the expectancy of success and/or expectancy shifts. As already indicated, reliable empirical findings that appeared to support their conception were generated. But the experimental manipulation studies have systematically examined little else. Conversely, investigations that assess rather than manipulate locus of control have probed almost everything, with systematic data emerging in a few areas, such as information seeking and information utilization (e.g., DuCette and Wolk, 1973). But the great bulk of this voluminous literature falls well beyond the network of social learning theory. Thus, there is an imbalance between experimental manipulation-theoretically relevant-constricted range investigations and a grouping characterized as correlational-theoretically irrelevant-extended range studies.

There is a rapidly growing literature originating outside of social learning that manipulates perceptions of control and examines a number of psychological reactions and states, such as affect (Weiner, 1974), feelings of helplessness and persistence in the face of failure (Dweck and Reppucci, 1973), reactance (Brehm, 1966), and so on (also see Lefcourt, 1973). These empirical findings may provide the foundation for new and more comprehensive conceptions that also combine individual differences with the study of psychological processes. At the same time, individual difference research that is more restrictive in range and theoretically germane must be undertaken.

SUMMARY

Social learning theory and attribution theory make contrasting predictions regarding the influence of causal factors on the expectancy of success. Social learning theory specifies that expectancy is influenced by the locus of control of causal factors, while attribution theory specifies that expectancy is influenced by the stability of causal factors. An investigation manipulating the number of success experiences and assessing causal attributions and expectancy of success was conducted. In contrast to prior research, a between-subjects experimental design was used and a new method of assessing attributions was devised that separated the locus of control and the stability dimensions of causality. The results strongly supported the attributional position, while contradicting social learning theory. The significance of this investigation and attribution theory for empirical research and theorizing in the locus of control area was discussed.

REFERENCES

Battle, E. S., & Rotter, J. B. Children's feelings of personal control as related to social class and ethnic group. *Journal of Personality*, 1963, *31*, 482–490.

Brehm, J. W. *A theory of psychological reactance*. New York: Academic Press, 1966.

Diggory, J. C., Riley, E. J., & Blumenfeld, R. Estimated probability of success for a fixed goal. *American Journal of Psychology*, 1960, *73*, 41–55.

DuCette, J., & Wolk, S. Cognitive and motivational correlates of generalized expectancies for control. *Journal of Personality and Social Psychology*, 1973, *26*, 420–426.

Dweck, C. S., & Reppucci, N. D. Learned helplessness and reinforcement responsibility in children. *Journal of Personality and Social Psychology*, 1973, *25*, 109–116.

Fontaine, G. Social comparison and some determinants of expected personal control and expected performance in a novel task situation. *Journal of Personality and Social Psychology*, 1974, *29*, 487–496.

Frieze, I. Studies of information processing and the attributional process in achievement-related contexts. Unpublished doctoral dissertation, University of California, Los Angeles, 1973.

Heider, F. *The psychology of interpersonal relations*. New York: Wiley, 1958.

James, W. H. Internal vs. external control of reinforcement as a basic variable in learning theory. Unpublished doctoral dissertation, Ohio State University, 1957.

James, W. H., & Rotter, J. B. Partial and 100% reinforcement under chance and skill conditions. *Journal of Experimental Psychology, 1958, 55,* 397–403.

Jarvik, M. E. Negative recency effect in probability learning. *Journal of Experimental Psychology, 1951, 41,* 291–297.

Lefcourt, H. M. The function of the illusions of control and freedom. *American Psychologist, 1973, 28,* 417–425.

Lepley, W. M. The maturity of the chances: A gambler's fallacy. *Journal of Psychology, 1963, 56,* 69–72.

McMahan, I. D. Relationships between causal attributions and expectancy of success. *Journal of Personality and Social Psychology, 1973, 28,* 108–115.

Meyer, W. U. *Leistungsmotiv und Ursachenerklärung von Erfolg und Misserfolg.* Stuttgart: Ernst Klett, 1973.

Mischel, W., Jeffery, K. M., & Patterson, C. J. The layman's use of trait and behavioral information to predict behavior. *Journal of Research in Personality, 1974, 8,* 231–242.

Mischel, W., Zeiss, R., & Zeiss, A. Internal–external control and persistence: Validation and implications of the Stanford Preschool Internal–External Scale. *Journal of Personality and Social Psychology, 1974, 29,* 265–278.

Pancer, S. M., & Eiser, J. R. Expectations, aspirations, and evaluations as influenced by another's attributions for success and failure. Paper presented at the meeting of the American Psychological Association, Chicago, September, 1975.

Phares, E. J. Expectancy changes in skill and chance situations. *Journal of Abnormal and Social Psychology, 1957, 54,* 339–342.

Rosenbaum, R. M. A dimensional analysis of the perceived causes of success and failure. Unpublished doctoral dissertation, University of California, Los Angeles, 1972.

Rotter, J. B. *Social learning and clinical psychology.* Englewood Cliffs, N. J.: Prentice-Hall, 1954.

Rotter, J. B. Generalized expectancies for internal versus external control of reinforcement. *Psychological Monographs*, 1966, *80*(1, Whole No. 609), 1–28.

Rotter, J. B., Liverant, S., & Crowne, D. P. The growth and extinction of expectancies in chance controlled and skilled tasks. *Journal of Psychology*, 1961, *52*, 161–177.

Rotter, J. B., Seeman, M., & Liverant, S. Internal versus external control of reinforcement: A major variable in behavior theory. In N. F. Washburne (Ed.), *Decisions, values, and groups*, Vol. 2. London: Pergamon Press, 1962.

Schütz, A. *Collected papers. 1. The problem of social reality.* The Hague: Martinus Nijhoff, 1967.

Schwartz, J. C. Contributions of generalized expectancy to stated expectancy under conditions of success and failure. *Journal of Personality and Social Psychology*, 1969, *11*, 157–164.

Skinner, B. F. The process involved in the repeated guessing of alternatives. *Journal of Experimental Psychology*, 1942, *30*, 495–503.

Valle, V. A. Attributions of stability as a mediator in the changing of expectations. Unpublished doctoral dissertation, University of Pittsburgh, 1974.

Weiner, B. *Theories of motivation: From mechanism to cognition.* Chicago: Rand McNally, 1972.

Weiner, B. (Ed.). *Achievement motivation and attribution theory.* Morristown, N. J.: General Learning Press, 1974.

Weiner, B., Frieze, I., Kukla, A., Reed, L., Rest, S., & Rosenbaum, R. M. *Perceiving the causes of success and failure.* Morristown, N. J.: General Learning Press, 1971.

Weiner, B., Heckhausen, H., Meyer, W. U., & Cook, R. E. Causal ascriptions and achievement behavior: A conceptual analysis of effort and reanalysis of locus of control. *Journal of Personality and Social Psychology*, 1972, *21*, 239–248.

Zajonc, R. B., & Brickman, P. Expectancy and feedback as independent factors in task performance. *Journal of Personality and Social Psychology*, 1969, *11*, 148–156.

Part 4
HUMANISTIC THEORY

Eight
CARL R. ROGERS

Carl R. Rogers (1902–   ) is perhaps best known for his development of a psychotherapeutic approach—client-centered therapy—that is rivaled in popularity only by psychoanalysis. Rogers's interest isn't limited to the problems of abnormal psychology, however; he has, throughout his career, been a champion of the view that the psychotherapeutic situation offers psychology a valuable laboratory for the development and testing of hypotheses that are relevant to the more general area of personality theory. In this role, he has been concerned mainly with personality change and growth and with the factors that bring about these phenomena. Perhaps Rogers's unique contribution to the psychology of personality and psychotherapy has been his success in subjecting a psychology of inner experience to the rigors of scientific objectivism. His humanism and deep respect for the value of the person have certainly influenced the basic assumptions that his theory makes about human nature, while at the same time his insistence on using the scientific method and empirical research to test hypotheses has placed his theory squarely in the arena of psychological science.

The first of the following papers is illustrative of Rogers's ability to study people in an objective, scientific way without stripping them of their humanness. Rogers is able to achieve this by assuming a *phenomenological* stance. For the phenomenologist, all behavior is determined by immediate, individual perceptual events (experience), and the focus of psychological study should be on these events. Note in this paper the fact that Rogers attempts to abstract from his own phenomenal experience certain theoretical principles that can be subjected to scientific scrutiny.

Rogers first lists the conditions that he feels are necessary and sufficient to bring about constructive personality change. Although these conditions are initially stated in brief (and untestable) form, Rogers, in his characteristic style, goes on to *operationally define* each of these conditions in such a way that he is able to generate hypotheses amenable to empirical test.

In recent years, Rogers has actively involved himself in the *encounter movement*—an extension of his theory and practice perfectly in accord with his humanistic position. Rogers sees the encounter movement as the most important social development of this century. For him, an encounter group is a group of people who have come together to experience living. Experiencing living involves experiencing oneself and others in an atmosphere of acceptance, genuineness, and openness. The encounter group is a kind of "mini-community," offering Rogers the opportunity to test his theory in a situation much more like the real world than the one-to-one psychotherapeutic situation is.

The second selection in this chapter, by Betty D. Meador, is an empirical study of the process of change that took place in eight individuals who participated in an intensive weekend encounter group conducted by Carl Rogers and his associate Richard Farson. The entire proceeding (which consisted of five sessions) was recorded on film.

Meador was able to empirically measure the growth of each of the individual participants through the five sessions of the weekend encounter experience. She did this by randomly selecting early and late film segments from each of the five sessions for each of the participants. Thus, for each of the eight participants, there were 10 segments, which were then spliced together in random order. These films were then observed by judges who had been trained to identify stages of "process" (growth), as defined by Rogers's *Process Scale*. (The scale describes seven stages of growth, or *movement*, ranging from Stage 1, in which the individual communicates about things external to self, through Stage 7, in which the individual communicates self and is comfortable with his or her own experiencing. Meador describes the scale in some detail in her article.)

The results indicate that, even in the short span of a 16-hour weekend encounter experience, significant growth (as defined by Rogers) takes place. Also, Meador's results support Rogers's theory and lend further validity to his Process Scale.

In the final article in this chapter, you can again observe, as you did in the Weiner, Nierenberg, and Goldstein paper in Chapter Seven, the collation, in a single experiment, of two opposing theoretical positions. In this paper, Charles B. Truax describes an experiment in which he tested a prediction generated by Rogers's theory against an alternative prediction derived from the theory of B. F. Skinner. The primary difference between Rogers and Skinner, in terms of what they believe allows psychotherapy to produce personality change, stems from their basic philosophical positions on the issue of *control* (see Chapter Five). Rogers's contention is that it is the therapist's noncontrolling attitude in the therapeutic relationship that results in successful psychotherapy. This nondirective attitude is reflected in the therapist's nonselective responding to the client; the therapist neither approves nor disapproves of what the client says or does. Skinner, on the other hand, insists that behavior is controlled by its consequences and that therefore the successful therapist modifies the client's behavior by the systematic, selective use of reinforcement techniques.

Using the transcript of a successful therapy case in which Rogers was the therapist, Truax is able to analyze his data in such a way that the results will support only one of the alternative predictions. Thus, if the results show that the therapist responds to the client in an unsystematic, nonselective manner, Rogers's theory will have been supported. If, however, it is demonstrated that there is a systematic relationship between the therapist's behavior and that of the client, and if it is also evident that client behaviors followed by therapist responses significantly increase during therapy, whereas client behaviors not followed by therapist responses show no change during therapy, then the results of the experiment will have supported Skinner's position.

The results were overwhelmingly in support of the Skinnerian position.

SUGGESTIONS FOR FURTHER READING

The development of Rogers's thinking can be discerned in three books published from 1942 through 1961. In *Counseling and Psychotherapy*, published in 1942, appears the first systematic statement of what Rogers then called "nondirective therapy." In 1951, while at the University of Chicago, Rogers published *Client-Centered Therapy*. A book called *On Becoming a Person* was published in 1961; it is a collection of his papers. All three books are published by Houghton Mifflin and are highly readable.

For a formalized statement of Rogers's theory, read Rogers's chapter in Volume 3 of

Psychology: A Study of a Science—a seven-volume treatment of contemporary psychology edited by Sigmund Koch and published by McGraw-Hill. The chapter is titled "A Theory of Therapy, Personality, and Interpersonal Relationships, As Developed in the Client-Centered Framework."

Rogers's autobiography appears in Volume 5 of *A History of Psychology in Autobiography*, published by Appleton-Century-Crofts in 1967.

For a thorough presentation of Rogers's research on client-centered therapy, the volume edited by him and Rosalind F. Dymond, titled *Psychotherapy and Personality Change* and published by the University of Chicago Press in 1954, should be consulted. A critique of Rogers and Dymond's book is contained in a book edited by Hans J. Eysenck titled *Handbook of Abnormal Psychology*. This critique by Eysenck has also been reprinted as a little book called *The Effects of Psychotherapy*, published by The International Science Press in 1966.

For the student interested in the encounter movement, an interesting source is the book *Encounter*, edited by Arthur Burton and published by Jossey-Bass in 1969.

Rogers's own statement on the topic of encounter appears as a chapter titled "The Process of the Basic Encounter Group" in the book *Challenge of Humanistic Psychology*, edited by J. F. T. Bugental and published by McGraw-Hill in 1967.

Carl R. Rogers
THE NECESSARY AND SUFFICIENT
CONDITIONS OF THERAPEUTIC
PERSONALITY CHANGE

For many years I have been engaged in psychotherapy with individuals in distress. In recent years I have found myself increasingly concerned with the process of abstracting from that experience the general principles which appear to be involved in it. I have endeavored to discover any orderliness, any unity which seems to inhere in the subtle, complex tissue of interpersonal relationship in which I have so constantly been immersed in therapeutic work. One of the current products of this concern is an attempt to state, in formal terms, a theory of psychotherapy, of personality, and of interpersonal relationships which will encompass and contain the phenomena of my experience. What I wish to do in this paper is to take one very small segment of that theory, spell it out more completely, and explore its meaning and usefulness.

THE PROBLEM

The question to which I wish to address myself is this: Is it possible to state, in terms which are clearly definable and measurable, the psychological conditions which are both necessary and sufficient to bring about constructive personality change? Do we, in other words, know with any precision those elements which are essential if psychotherapeutic change is to ensue?

Before proceeding to the major task let me dispose very briefly of the second portion of the question. What is meant by such phrases as "psychotherapeutic change," "constructive personality change"? This problem also deserves deep and serious consideration, but for the moment let me suggest a common-sense type of meaning upon which we can perhaps agree for purposes of this paper. By these phrases is meant: change in the personality structure of the individual, at both surface and deeper levels, in a direction which clinicians would agree means greater integration, less internal conflict, more energy utilizable for effective living; change in behavior away from behaviors generally regarded as immature and toward behaviors regarded as mature. This brief description may suffice to indicate the kind of change for which we are considering the preconditions. It may also suggest the ways in which this criterion of change may be determined.[1]

From C. R. Rogers, "The Necessary and Sufficient Conditions of Therapeutic Personality Change," *Journal of Consulting Psychology*, 1957, *21*, 95–103. Reprinted by permission of the American Psychological Association.
[1]That this is a measurable and determinable criterion has been shown in research already completed. See (7), especially chapters 8, 13, and 17.

THE CONDITIONS

As I have considered my own clinical experience and that of my colleagues, together with the pertinent research which is available, I have drawn out several conditions which seem to me to be *necessary* to initiate constructive personality change, and which, taken together, appear to be *sufficient* to inaugurate that process. As I have worked on this problem I have found myself surprised at the simplicity of what has emerged. The statement which follows is not offered with any assurance as to its correctness, but with the expectation that it will have the value of any theory, namely that it states or implies a series of hypotheses which are open to proof or disproof, thereby clarifying and extending our knowledge of the field.

Since I am not, in this paper, trying to achieve suspense, I will state at once, in severely rigorous and summarized terms, the six conditions which I have come to feel are basic to the process of personality change. The meaning of a number of the terms is not immediately evident, but will be clarified in the explanatory sections which follow. It is hoped that this brief statement will have much more significance to the reader when he has completed the paper. Without further introduction let me state the basic theoretical position.

For constructive personality change to occur, it is necessary that these conditions exist and continue over a period of time:

1. Two persons are in psychological contact.
2. The first, whom we shall term the client, is in a state of incongruence, being vulnerable or anxious.
3. The second person, whom we shall term the therapist, is congruent or integrated in the relationship.
4. The therapist experiences unconditional positive regard for the client.
5. The therapist experiences an empathic understanding of the client's internal frame of reference and endeavors to communicate this experience to the client.
6. The communication to the client of the therapist's empathic understanding and unconditional positive regard is to a minimal degree achieved.

No other conditions are necessary. If these six conditions exist, and continue over a period of time, this is sufficient. The process of constructive personality change will follow.

A Relationship

The first condition specifies that a minimal relationship, a psychological contact, must exist. I am hypothesizing that significant positive personality change does not occur except in a relationship. This is of course an hypothesis, and it may be disproved.

Conditions 2 through 6 define the characteristics of the relationship which are regarded as essential by defining the necessary characteristics of each person in the relationship. All that is intended by this first condition is to specify that the two people are to some degree in contact, that each makes some perceived difference in the experiential field of the other. Probably it is sufficient if each makes some "subceived" difference, even though the individual may not be consciously aware of this impact. Thus it might be difficult to know whether a catatonic patient perceives a therapist's presence as making a difference to him— a difference of any kind—but it is almost certain that at some organic level he does sense this difference.

Except in such a difficult borderline situation as that just mentioned, it would be relatively easy to define this condition in operational terms and thus determine, from a hard-boiled research point of view, whether the condition does, or does not, exist. The simplest method of determination involves simply the awareness of both client and therapist. If each is aware of being in personal or psychological contact with the other, then this condition is met.

This first condition of therapeutic change is such a simple one that perhaps it should be labeled an assumption or a precondition in order to set it apart from those that follow. Without it, however, the remaining items would have no meaning, and that is the reason for including it.

The State of the Client

It was specified that it is necessary that the client be "in a state of incongruence, being vulnerable or anxious." What is the meaning of these terms?

Incongruence is a basic construct in the theory we have been developing. It refers to a discrepancy between the actual experience of the organism and the self picture of the individual insofar as it represents that experience. Thus a student may experience, at a total or organismic level, a fear of the university and of examinations which are given on the third floor of a certain building, since these may demonstrate a fundamental inadequacy in him. Since such a fear of his inadequacy is decidedly at odds with his concept of himself, this experience is represented (distortedly) in his awareness as an unreasonable fear of climbing stairs in this building, or any building, and soon an unreasonable fear of crossing the open campus. Thus there is a fundamental discrepancy between the experienced meaning of the situation as it registers in his organism and the symbolic representation of that experience in awareness in such a way that it does not conflict with the picture he has of himself. In this case to admit a fear of inadequacy would contradict the picture he holds of himself; to admit incomprehensible fears does not contradict his self concept.

Another instance would be the mother who develops vague illnesses whenever her only son makes plans to leave home. The actual desire is to hold on to her only source of satisfaction. To perceive this in awareness would be inconsistent with the picture she holds of herself as a good mother. Illness, however, is consistent with her self concept, and the experience is symbolized in this distorted fashion. Thus again there is a basic incongruence between the self as perceived (in this case as an ill mother needing attention) and the actual experience (in this case the desire to hold on to her son).

When the individual has no awareness of such incongruence in himself, then he is merely vulnerable to the possibility of anxiety and disorganization. Some experience might occur so suddenly or so obviously that the incongruence could not be denied. Therefore, the person is vulnerable to such a possibility.

If the individual dimly perceives such an incongruence in himself, then a tension state occurs which is known as anxiety. The incongruence need not be sharply perceived. It is enough that it is subceived—that is, discriminated as threatening to the self without any awareness of the content of that threat. Such anxiety is often seen in therapy as the individual approaches awareness of some element of his experience which is in sharp contradiction to his self concept.

It is not easy to give precise operational definition to this second of the six conditions, yet to some degree this has been achieved. Several research workers have defined the self concept by means of a *Q* sort by the individual of a list of self-referent items. This gives us an operational picture of the self. The total experiencing of the individual is more difficult to capture. Chodorkoff (2) has defined it as a *Q* sort made by a clinician who sorts the same self-referent items independently, basing his sorting on the picture he has obtained of the individual from projective tests. His sort thus includes unconscious as well as conscious elements of the individual's experience, thus representing (in an admittedly imperfect way) the totality of the client's experience. The correlation between these two sortings gives a crude operational measure of incongruence between self and experience, low or negative correlation representing of course a high degree of incongruence.

The Therapist's Genuineness in the Relationship

The third condition is that the therapist should be, within the confines of this relationship, a congruent, genuine, integrated person. It means that within the relationship he is freely and deeply himself, with his actual experience accurately represented by his awareness of himself. It is the opposite of presenting a facade, either knowingly or unknowingly.

It is not necessary (nor is it possible) that the therapist be a paragon who exhibits this degree of integration, of wholeness, in every aspect of his life. It is sufficient that he is accurately himself in this hour of this relationship, that in this basic sense he is what he actually is, in this moment of time.

It should be clear that this includes being himself even in ways which are not regarded as ideal for psychotherapy. His experience may be ''I am afraid of this client'' or ''My attention is so focused on my own problems that I can scarcely listen to him.'' If the therapist is not denying these feelings to awareness, but is able freely to be them (as well as being his other feelings), then the condition we have stated is met.

It would take us too far afield to consider the puzzling matter as to the degree to which the therapist overtly communicates this reality in himself to the client. Certainly the aim is not for the therapist to express or talk out his own feelings, but primarily that he should not be deceiving the client as to himself. At times he may need to talk out some of his own feelings (either to the client, or to a colleague or supervisor) if they are standing in the way of the two following conditions.

It is not too difficult to suggest an operational definition for this third condition. We resort again to *Q* technique. If the therapist sorts a series of items relevant to the relationship (using a list similar to the ones developed by Fiedler [3, 4] and Bown [1]), this will give his perception of his experience in the relationship. If several judges who have observed the interview or listened to a recording of it (or observed a sound movie of it) now sort the same items to represent *their* perception of the relationship, this second sorting should catch those elements of the therapist's behavior and inferred attitudes of which he is unaware, as well as those of which he is aware. Thus a high correlation between the therapist's sort and the observer's sort would represent in crude form an operational definition of the therapist's congruence or integration in the relationship; and a low correlation, the opposite.

Unconditional Positive Regard

To the extent that the therapist finds himself experiencing a warm acceptance of each aspect of the client's experience as being a part of that client, he is experiencing unconditional positive regard. This concept has been developed by Standal (8). It means that there are no *conditions* of acceptance, no feeling of ''I like you only *if* you are thus and so.'' It means a ''prizing'' of the person, as Dewey has used that term. It is at the opposite pole from a selective evaluating attitude—"You are bad in these ways, good in those." It involves as much feeling of acceptance for the client's expression of negative, "bad," painful, fearful, defensive, abnormal feelings as for his expression of "good," positive, mature, confident, social feelings, as much acceptance of ways in which he is inconsistent as of ways in which he is consistent. It means a caring for the client, but not in a possessive way or in such a way as simply to satisfy the therapist's own needs. It means a caring for the client as a *separate* person, with permission to have his own feelings, his own experiences. One client describes the therapist as "fostering my possession of my own experience . . . that [this] is *my* experience and that I am actually having it: thinking what I think, feeling what I feel, wanting what I want, fearing what I fear: no 'ifs,' 'buts,' or 'not reallys.'" This is the type of acceptance which is hypothesized as being necessary if personality change is to occur.

Like the two previous conditions, this fourth condition is a matter of degree,[2] as immediately becomes apparent if we attempt to define it in terms of specific research operations. One such method of giving it definition would be to consider the Q sort for the relationship as described under Condition 3. To the extent that items expressive of unconditional positive regard are sorted as characteristic of the relationship by both the therapist and the observers, unconditional positive regard might be said to exist. Such items might include statements of this order: "I feel no revulsion at anything the client says"; "I feel neither approval nor disapproval of the client and his statements—simply acceptance"; "I feel warmly toward the client—toward his weaknesses and problems as well as his potentialities"; "I am not inclined to pass judgment on what the client tells me"; "I like the client." To the extent that both therapist and observers perceive these items as characteristic, or their opposites as uncharacteristic, Condition 4 might be said to be met.

Empathy

The fifth condition is that the therapist is experiencing an accurate, empathic understanding of the client's awareness of his own experience. To sense the client's private world as if it were your own, but without ever losing the "as if" quality—this is empathy, and this seems essential to therapy. To sense the client's anger, fear, or confusion as if it were your own, yet without your own anger, fear, or confusion getting bound up in it, is the condition we are endeavoring to describe. When the client's world is this clear to the therapist, and he moves about in it freely, then he can both communicate his understanding of what is clearly known to the client and can also voice meanings in the client's experience of which the client is scarcely aware. As one client described this second aspect: "Every now and again, with me in a tangle of thought and feeling, screwed up in a web of mutually divergent lines of movement, with impulses from different parts of me, and me feeling the feeling of its being all too much and suchlike—then whomp, just like a sunbeam thrusting its way through cloudbanks and tangles of foliage to spread a circle of light on a tangle of forest paths, came some comment from you. [It was] clarity, even disentanglement, an additional twist to the picture, a putting in place. Then the consequence—the sense of moving on, the relaxation. These were

---

[2]The phrase "unconditional positive regard" may be an unfortunate one, since it sounds like an absolute, an all or nothing dispositional concept. It is probably evident from the description that completely unconditional positive regard would never exist except in theory. From a clinical and experiential point of view I believe the most accurate statement is that the effective therapist experiences unconditional positive regard for the client during many moments of his contact with him, yet from time to time he experiences only a conditional positive regard—and perhaps at times a negative regard, though this is not likely in effective therapy. It is in this sense that unconditional positive regard exists as a matter of degree in any relationship.

sunbeams.'' That such penetrating empathy is important for therapy is indicated by Fiedler's research (3) in which items such as the following placed high in the description of relationships created by experienced therapists:

> The therapist is well able to understand the patient's feelings.
> The therapist is never in any doubt about what the patient means.
> The therapist's remarks fit in just right with the patient's mood and content. ·
> The therapist's tone of voice conveys the complete ability to share the patient's feelings.

An operational definition of the therapist's empathy could be provided in different ways. Use might be made of the *Q* sort described under Condition 3. To the degree that items descriptive of accurate empathy were sorted as characteristic by both the therapist and the observers, this condition would be regarded as existing.

Another way of defining this condition would be for both client and therapist to sort a list of items descriptive of client feelings. Each would sort independently, the task being to represent the feelings which the client had experienced during a just completed interview. If the correlation between client and therapist sortings were high, accurate empathy would be said to exist, a low correlation indicating the opposite conclusion.

Still another way of measuring empathy would be for trained judges to rate the depth and accuracy of the therapist's empathy on the basis of listening to recorded interviews.

The Client's Perception of the Therapist

The final condition as stated is that the client perceives, to a minimal degree, the acceptance and empathy which the therapist experiences for him. Unless some communication of these attitudes has been achieved, then such attitudes do not exist in the relationship as far as the client is concerned, and the therapeutic process could not, by our hypothesis, be initiated.

Since attitudes cannot be directly perceived, it might be somewhat more accurate to state that therapist behaviors and words are perceived by the client as meaning that to some degree the therapist accepts and understands him.

An operational definition of this condition would not be difficult. The client might, after an interview, sort a *Q*-sort list of items referring to qualities representing the relationship between himself and the therapist. (The same list could be used as for Condition 3.) If several items descriptive of acceptance and empathy are sorted by the client as characteristic of the relationship, then this condition could be regarded as met. In the present state of our knowledge the meaning of ''to a minimal degree'' would have to be arbitrary.

Some Comments

Up to this point the effort has been made to present, briefly and factually, the conditions which I have come to regard as essential for psychotherapeutic change. I have not tried to give the theoretical context of these conditions nor to explain what seem to me to be the dynamics of their effectiveness. Such explanatory material is available in my chapter in volume 3 of *Psychology: A Study of a Science*, edited by Sigmund Koch and published by McGraw-Hill.

I have, however, given at least one means of defining, in operational terms, each of the conditions mentioned. I have done this in order to stress the fact that I am not speaking of vague qualities which ideally should be present if some other vague result is to occur. I am presenting conditions which are crudely measurable even in the present state of our technology, and have suggested specific operations in each instance even though I am sure that more adequate methods of measurement could be devised by a serious investigator.

My purpose has been to stress the notion that in my opinion we are dealing with an if-then phenomenon in which knowledge of the dynamics is not essential to testing the hypotheses. Thus, to illustrate from another field: if one substance, shown by a series of operations to be the substance known as hydrochloric acid, is mixed with another substance, shown by another series of operations to be sodium hydroxide, then salt and water will be products of this mixture. This is true whether one regards the results as due to magic, or whether one explains it in the most adequate terms of modern chemical theory. In the same way it is being postulated here that certain definable conditions precede certain definable changes and that this fact exists independently of our efforts to account for it.

THE RESULTING HYPOTHESES

The major value of stating any theory in unequivocal terms is that specific hypotheses may be drawn from it which are capable of proof or disproof. Thus, even if the conditions which have been postulated as necessary and sufficient conditions are more incorrect than correct (which I hope they are not), they could still advance science in this field by providing a base of operations from which fact could be winnowed out from error.

The hypotheses which would follow from the theory given would be of this order:

If these six conditions (as operationally defined) exist, then constructive personality change (as defined) will occur in the client.

If one or more of these conditions is not present, constructive personality change will not occur.

These hypotheses hold in any situation whether it is or is not labeled "psychotherapy."

Only Condition 1 is dichotomous (it either is present or is not), and the remaining five occur in varying degree, each on its continuum. Since this is true, another hypothesis follows, and it is likely that this would be the simplest to test:

If all six conditions are present, then the greater the degree to which Conditions 2 to 6 exist, the more marked will be the constructive personality change in the client.

At the present time the above hypothesis can only be stated in this general form—which implies that all of the conditions have equal weight. Empirical studies will no doubt make possible much more refinement of this hypothesis. It may be, for example, that if anxiety is high in the client, then the other conditions are less important. Or if unconditional positive regard is high (as in a mother's love for her child), then perhaps a modest degree of empathy is sufficient. But at the moment we can only speculate on such possibilities.

SOME IMPLICATIONS

Significant Omissions

If there is any startling feature in the formulation which has been given as to the necessary conditions for therapy, it probably lies in the elements which are omitted. In present-day clinical practice, therapists operate as though there were many other conditions in addition to those described, which are essential for psychotherapy. To point this up it may be well to mention a few of the conditions which, after thoughtful consideration of our research and our experience, are not included.

For example, it is *not* stated that these conditions apply to one type of client, and that other conditions are necessary to bring about psychotherapeutic change with other types of clients. Probably no idea is so prevalent in clinical work today as that one works with neurotics in one way, with psychotics in another; that certain therapeutic conditions must be provided for compulsives, others for homosexuals, etc. Because of this heavy weight of clinical opinion to the contrary, it is with some "fear and trembling" that I advance the concept that the essential conditions of psychotherapy exist in a single configuration, even though the client or patient may use them very differently.[3]

It is *not* stated that these six conditions are the essential conditions for client-centered therapy, and that other conditions are essential for other types of psychotherapy. I certainly am heavily influenced by my own experience, and that experience has led me to a viewpoint which is termed "client centered." Nevertheless my aim in stating this theory is to state the conditions which apply to *any* situation in which constructive personality change occurs, whether we are thinking of classical psychoanalysis, or any of its modern offshoots, or Adlerian psychotherapy, or any other. It will be obvious then that in my judgment much of what is considered to be essential would not be found, empirically, to be essential. Testing of some of the stated hypotheses would throw light on this perplexing issue. We may of course find that various therapies produce various types of personality change, and that for each psychotherapy a separate set of conditions is necessary. Until and unless this is demonstrated, I am hypothesizing that effective psychotherapy of any sort produces similar changes in personality and behavior, and that a single set of preconditions is necessary.

It is *not* stated that psychotherapy is a special kind of relationship, different in kind from all others which occur in everyday life. It will be evident instead that for brief moments, at least, many good friendships fulfill the six conditions. Usually this is only momentarily, however, and then empathy falters, the positive regard becomes conditional, or the congruence of the "therapist" friend becomes overlaid by some degree of facade or defensiveness. Thus the therapeutic relationship is seen as a heightening of the constructive qualities which often exist in part in other relationships, and an extension through time of qualities which in other relationships tend at best to be momentary.

It is *not* stated that special intellectual professional knowledge—psychological, psychiatric, medical, or religious—is required of the therapist. Conditions 3, 4, and 5, which apply especially to the therapist, are qualities of experience, not intellectual information. If they are to be acquired, they must, in my opinion, be acquired through an experiential training—which may be, but usually is not, a part of professional training. It troubles me to hold such a radical point of view, but I can draw no other conclusion from my experience. Intellectual training and the acquiring of information have, I believe, many valuable results—but becoming a therapist is not one of those results.

---

[3]I cling to this statement of my hypothesis even though it is challenged by a just completed study by Kirtner (5). Kirtner has found, in a group of 26 cases from the Counseling Center at the University of Chicago, that there are sharp differences in the client's mode of approach to the resolution of life difficulties, and that these differences are related to success in psychotherapy. Briefly, the client who sees his problem as involving his relationships, and who feels that he contributes to this problem and wants to change it, is likely to be successful. The client who externalizes his problem, feeling little self-responsibility, is much more likely to be a failure. Thus the implication is that some other conditions need to be provided for psychotherapy with this group. For the present, however, I will stand by my hypothesis as given, until Kirtner's study is confirmed, and until we know an alternative hypothesis to take its place.

It is *not* stated that it is necessary for psychotherapy that the therapist have an accurate psychological diagnosis of the client. Here too it troubles me to hold a viewpoint so at variance with my clinical colleagues. When one thinks of the vast proportion of time spent in any psychological, psychiatric, or mental hygiene center on the exhaustive psychological evaluation of the client or patient, it seems as though this *must* serve a useful purpose insofar as psychotherapy is concerned. Yet the more I have observed therapists, and the more closely I have studied research such as that done by Fiedler and others (4), the more I am forced to the conclusion that such diagnostic knowledge is not essential to psychotherapy.[4] It may even be that its defense as a necessary prelude to psychotherapy is simply a protective alternative to the admission that it is, for the most part, a colossal waste of time. There is only one useful purpose I have been able to observe which relates to psychotherapy. Some therapists cannot feel secure in the relationship with the client unless they possess such diagnostic knowledge. Without it they feel fearful of him, unable to be empathic, unable to experience unconditional regard, finding it necessary to put up a pretense in the relationship. If they know in *advance* of suicidal impulses they can somehow be more acceptant of them. Thus, for some therapists, the security they perceive in diagnostic information may be a basis for permitting themselves to be integrated in the relationship, and to experience empathy and full acceptance. In these instances a psychological diagnosis would certainly be justified as adding to the comfort and hence the effectiveness of the therapist. But even here it does not appear to be a basic precondition for psychotherapy.[5]

Perhaps I have given enough illustrations to indicate that the conditions I have hypothesized as necessary and sufficient for psychotherapy are striking and unusual primarily by virtue of what they omit. If we were to determine, by a survey of the behaviors of therapists, those hypotheses which they appear to regard as necessary to psychotherapy, the list would be a great deal longer and more complex.

Is This Theoretical Formulation Useful?

Aside from the personal satisfaction it gives as a venture in abstraction and generalization, what is the value of a theoretical statement such as has been offered in this paper? I should like to spell out more fully the usefulness which I believe it may have.

In the field of research it may give both direction and impetus to investigation. Since it sees the conditions of constructive personality change as general, it greatly broadens the opportunities for study. Psychotherapy is not the only situation aimed at constructive personality change. Programs of training for leadership in industry and programs of training for military leadership often aim at such change. Educational institutions or programs frequently aim at development of character and personality as well as of intellectual skills. Community agencies aim at personality and behavioral change in delinquents and criminals. Such programs would provide an opportunity for the broad testing of the hypotheses offered. If it is found that constructive personality change occurs in such programs when the hypothesized conditions are not fulfilled, then the theory would have to be revised. If however the

---

[4]There is no intent here to maintain that diagnostic evaluation is useless. We have ourselves made heavy use of such methods in our research studies of change in personality. It is its usefulness as a precondition to psychotherapy which is questioned.

[5]In a facetious moment I have suggested that such therapists might be made equally comfortable by being given the diagnosis of some other individual, not of this patient or client. The fact that the diagnosis proved inaccurate as psychotherapy continued would not be particularly disturbing, because one always expects to find inaccuracies in the diagnosis as one works with the individual.

hypotheses are upheld, then the results, both for the planning of such programs and for our knowledge of hyman dynamics, would be significant. In the field of psychotherapy itself, the application of consistent hypotheses to the work of various schools of therapists may prove highly profitable. Again the disproof of the hypotheses offered would be as important as their confirmation, either result adding significantly to our knowledge.

For the practice of psychotherapy the theory also offers significant problems for consideration. One of its implications is that the techniques of the various therapies are relatively unimportant except to the extent that they serve as channels for fulfilling one of the conditions. In client-centered therapy, for example, the technique of "reflecting feelings" has been described and commented on (6, pp. 26–36). In terms of the theory here being presented, this technique is by no means an essential condition of therapy. To the extent, however, that it provides a channel by which the therapist communicates a sensitive empathy and an unconditional positive regard, then it may serve as a technical channel by which the essential conditions of therapy are fulfilled. In the same way, the theory I have presented would see no essential value to therapy of such techniques as interpretation of personality dynamics, free association, analysis of dreams, analysis of the transference, hypnosis, interpretation of life style, suggestion, and the like. Each of these techniques may, however, become a channel for communicating the essential conditions which have been formulated. An interpretation may be given in a way which communicates the unconditional positive regard of the therapist. A stream of free association may be listened to in a way which communicates an empathy which the therapist is experiencing. In the handling of the transference an effective therapist often communicates his own wholeness and congruence in the relationship. Similarly for the other techniques. But just as these techniques *may* communicate the elements which are essential for therapy, so any one of them may communicate attitudes and experiences sharply contradictory to the hypothesized conditions of therapy. Feeling may be "reflected" in a way which communicates the therapist's lack of empathy. Interpretations may be rendered in a way which indicates the highly conditional regard of the therapist. Any of the techniques may communicate the fact that the therapist is expressing one attitude at a surface level, and another contradictory attitude which is denied to his own awareness. Thus one value of such a theoretical formulation as we have offered is that it may assist therapists to think more critically about those elements of their experience, attitudes, and behaviors which are essential to psychotherapy, and those which are nonessential or even deleterious to psychotherapy.

Finally, in those programs—educational, correctional, military, or industrial—which aim toward constructive changes in the personality structure and behavior of the individual, this formulation may serve as a very tentative criterion against which to measure the program. Until it is much further tested by research, it cannot be thought of as a valid criterion, but, as in the field of psychotherapy, it may help to stimulate critical analysis and the formulation of alternative conditions and alternative hypotheses.

SUMMARY

Drawing from a larger theoretical context, six conditions are postulated as necessary and sufficient conditions for the initiation of a process of constructive personality change. A brief explanation is given of each condition, and suggestions are made as to how each may be operationally defined for research purposes. The implications of this theory for research, for psychotherapy, and for educational and training programs aimed at constructive personality change, are indicated. It is pointed out that many of the conditions which are commonly regarded as necessary to psychotherapy are, in terms of this theory, nonessential.

REFERENCES

Bown, O. H. An investigation of therapeutic relationship in client-centered therapy. Unpublished doctor's dissertation, Univer. of Chicago, 1954. (1)

Chodorkoff, B. Self-perception, perceptual defense, and adjustment. *J. abnorm. soc. Psychol.*, 1954, *49*, 508–512. (2)

Fiedler, F. E. A comparison of therapeutic relationships in psychoanalytic, non-directive and Adlerian therapy. *J. consult. Psychol.*, 1950, *14*, 436–445. (3)

Fiedler, F. E. Quantitative studies on the role of therapists' feelings toward their patients. In O. H. Mowrer (Ed.), *Psychotherapy: Theory and research*. New York: Ronald, 1953. (4)

Kirtner, W. L. Success and failure in client-centered therapy as a function of personality variables. Unpublished master's thesis, Univer. of Chicago, 1955. (5)

Rogers, C. R. *Client-centered therapy*. Boston: Houghton Mifflin, 1951. (6)

Rogers, C. R., & Dymond, Rosalind F. (Eds.), *Psychotherapy and personality change*. Chicago: Univer. of Chicago Press, 1954. (7)

Standal, S. The need for positive regard: A contribution to client-centered theory. Unpublished doctor's dissertation, Univer. of Chicago, 1954. (8)

Betty D. Meador
INDIVIDUAL PROCESS IN AN ENCOUNTER GROUP

The intensive small group experience, variously known as sensitivity training, T group, or basic encounter group, is a social invention of the behavioral sciences to facilitate individual change (Bradford, Gibb, & Benne, 1964; Rogers, 1967a). Few would disagree with Carl Rogers' (1967b) assessment that participation in a group can be a "highly potent experience [p. 276]," but current judgments of the value of this experience range from zealous enthusiasm to grave mistrust. The increasing availability of such experiences adds to the need for research into what happens to individuals who participate in them.

This study sought to observe the process of change in individuals within the group experience such as suggested by Barrett-Lennard (1967): "Identification of such change occurring *within* the intensive group situation would appear to be of critical importance in predicting and understanding the results of outcome analysis [p. 12]." Rogers' process theory was chosen for the present research as a framework through which individuals could be observed during a basic encounter group experience.

Rogers' theory posits that an individual, in a relationship whose climate is characterized by acceptance, genuine personal response, and accurate understanding, will quite naturally, that is, as a part of his organismic nature, move toward openness to his own experiencing and positive acceptance of himself, toward a more fluid, self-trusting behavior (Rogers, 1958, 1961, 1967c).

Aspects of Rogers' process theory have been the basis of two studies of T groups. These two studies were of T groups which met once a week for a designated period of time. The first T group study (Clark & Culbert, 1965) found that gain in self-awareness of the participants was related to the number of mutually perceived therapeutic relationships formed between group members. This study supports Rogers' contention that growth along the process continuum is related to the perception of the climate of the relationship on the part of the client. In the second T group study (Culbert, 1968), self-awareness among the group members was related to the degree of self-disclosure of the trainer or leader of the group, the greater participant self-awareness occurring in association with a more self-disclosing trainer. This

Reprinted by permission from the *Journal of Counseling Psychology*, 1971, *18*, pp. 70–76. Copyright 1971 by the American Psychological Association.

Based on the author's dissertation at the Graduate School of Education, United States International University, in partial fulfillment of the requirements for the PhD degree.

The author wishes to express appreciation to Carl R. Rogers who supervised the research; to Clifford Weedman for his valuable assistance with the statistical aspects of the study; and to the staff members of the Western Behavioral Sciences Institute for the use of the group film and for their assistance and support of this research. A brief version of this paper was presented at the Sixteenth Annual Convention of the Southwestern Psychological Association, Austin, Texas, April 1969.

finding supports the Rogerian theory that genuine personal response or congruence perceived by a client in his therapist is a prior condition of the client's growthful change.

In both T group studies some of the participants made significant positive movement along Rogers' (1958) process continuum. It seemed possible that in a weekend encounter group with the consequent building of intensity which the long sequential sessions afford, all the participants might achieve significant movement on the process continuum. In addition, the T group studies cited above measured self-awareness changes on the Problem Expression Scale, a scale which represents one of the seven behavior strands identified by Rogers in his process continuum. It was postulated that consideration of all seven strands, using the global Process Scale which Rogers and Rablen (1958) developed, would more readily enable the judges to rate randomly selected segments of behavior from the group.

Thus, the hypothesis formulated for the present study was that positive process movement along the strands of Rogers' process continuum will be apparent for each of the individuals in a basic encounter group.

METHOD

Subjects

Subjects were the eight participants in a weekend basic encounter group whose proceedings were recorded on film. The participants, all of whom volunteered, were four men and four women—three businessmen, a minister, two housewives, a teacher, and a school principal—along with two male facilitators,[1] both client-centered psychologists. The group met for a total of 16 hours in five separate sessions: Friday evening, Saturday morning, Saturday evening, Sunday morning, and Sunday afternoon. Each session lasted from 2½ to 4 hours.

Instruments

Individual process movement was measured on the Process Scale. The seven-stage scale represents a continuum of psychological activity ranging from rigidity to flow in the categories of feelings and personal meanings, manner of experiencing, degree of incongruence, communication of self, construing of experience, relationship to problems, and manner of relating. Brief and partial descriptions of each of these different stages of process are as follows:

First stage. Communication is about externals. There is an unwillingness to communicate self. Feelings and personal meanings are neither recognized as such nor owned. Constructs are extremely rigid. Close relationships are construed as dangerous.

Second stage. Feelings are sometimes *described* but as unowned past objects external to self. The individual is remote from his subjective experiencing. He may voice contradictory statements about himself somewhat freely on nonself topics. He may show some recognition that he has problems or conflicts but they are perceived as external to the self.

Third stage. There is much *description* of feelings and personal meanings which are not now present. These distant feelings are often pictured as unacceptable or bad. The *experiencing* of situations is largely described as having occurred in the past or is cast in terms

---

[1]The facilitators were Carl R. Rogers and Richard E. Farson, both formerly of the Western Behavioral Sciences Institute, under the sponsorship of which the film was made.

of the past. There is a freer flow of expression about self as an *object*. There may be communication about self as a reflected object, existing primarily in others. Personal constructs are rigid but may at times be thought of as constructs, with occasionally a questioning of their validity. There is a beginning recognition that any problems that exist are inside the individual rather than external.

Fourth stage. Feelings and personal meanings are freely described as present objects owned by the self. Feelings of an intense sort are still described as not now present. There is a dim recognition that feelings denied to awareness may break through in the present, but this is a frightening possibility. There is an unwilling, fearful recognition that one is *experiencing* things. Contradictions in experience are clearly realized and a definite concern over them is experienced. There is a beginning loosening of personal constructs. It is sometimes discovered that experience has been *construed* as having a certain meaning but this meaning is not inherent nor absolute. There is some expression of self-responsibility for problems. The individual is occasionally willing to risk relating himself to others on a feeling basis.

Fifth stage. Many feelings are freely expressed in the moment of their occurrence and are thus experienced in the immediate present. These feelings are owned or accepted. Feelings previously denied now tend to bubble through into awareness though there is fear of this occurrence. There is some recognition that experiencing with immediacy is a referent and possible guide for the individual. Contradictions are recognized as attitudes existing in different aspects of the personality as indicated by statements such as, "My mind tells me this is so but *I* don't seem to believe it." There is a desire to be the self-related feelings, "To be the real me." There is a questioning of the validity of many personal constructs. The person feels that he has a definite responsibility for the problems which exist in him.

Sixth stage. Feelings previously denied are now experienced both with immediacy and *acceptance*. Such feelings are not something to be denied, feared, or struggled against. This experiencing is often vivid, dramatic, and releasing for the individual. There is full acceptance now of experiencing as providing a clear and usable referent for getting at the implicit meanings of the individual's encounter with himself and with life. There is also the recognition that the self is now becoming this process of experiencing. There is no longer much awareness of the self as an object. The individual often feels somewhat "shaky" as his solid constructs are recognized as construings taking place within him. The individual risks being himself in process in the relationship to others. He takes the risk of being the flow that is himself and trusting another person to accept him as he is in this flow (Carl Rogers, personal communication, 1970).

Seventh stage. The individual lives comfortably in the flowing process of his experiencing. New feelings are experienced with richness and immediacy, and this inner experiencing is a clear referent for behavior. Incongruence is minimal and temporary. The self is a confident awareness of this process of experiencing. The meaning of experiencing is held loosely and constantly checked and rechecked against further experiencing (Rogers & Rablen, 1958).

Procedure

One segment of verbal interaction, approximately 2 minutes in length, was selected at random for each of the eight group participants from the first and second halves of each of the five sessions (early–late within-session measures), yielding 10 segments for each individual. These filmed segments were then spliced together in random order resulting in one 10-segment reel of film for each participant.

Thirteen clinically naive judges, all graduate students in education, made independent ratings of the 80 filmed segments using the Process Scale. Prior to the actual rating, three training sessions allowed the judges to identify key behaviors of the seven stages of the scale and made practice ratings of individuals in an entirely different, but also filmed, encounter group. In addition, the judges, themselves, participated in two weekend encounter groups during the training period.

Actual ratings were completed in two sessions. Each judge was provided with a typed script of the film he was to rate and made non-time-limited ratings after seeing a given film segment twice. The judges were divided into two groups, and the order in which the reels were played for rating was reversed for the second group. The judges were instructed not to discuss the films until all ratings were completed.

RESULTS

A four-factor analysis of variance computer program was written to analyze the data, following the computational scheme spelled out in Winer (1962, p. 162). Factors were Judges, Target Individuals, Sessions, and Early–Late Within-Session Measures. The summary of this analysis is presented in Table 1.

Table 1. Analysis of variance

Source	SS	df	MS	F
Judges (A)	4490.0	12	374.17	4.65**
Target Individuals (B)	13999.6	7	1999.94	248.69**
Sessions (C)	34198.8	4	8549.70	106.31**
Early-Late Within-Session Measures (D)	471.2	1	471.20	5.86*
A × C	5607.4	48	116.82	1.45*
B × C	13832.0	28	494.00	6.14**
Error	75516.0	939	80.42	
Total		1039		

$*p < .05.$
$**p < .01.$

Judges

A detailed analysis was performed on the judges' ratings to determine an index of reliability. First, a matrix was developed (see Table 2) of each judge's mean score of each half-session summing across target individuals. Interreliability of these mean scores ranges from .69 to .99. Second, an intraclass correlation measure (Hays, 1966) was computed for the judges' raw ratings of individuals in each half-session, shown in Table 3. The RI (estimated reliability of individual ratings) measure of internal consistency reliability (Veldman, 1967) ranges from .13 to .67. The RA (estimated reliability of averaged ratings) coefficient, a reliability estimate of hypothetical composite scores combining all raters, ranges from .66 to .96.

Table 2. Interreliability of mean scores of half sessions

Judge	2	3	4	5	6	7	8	9	10	11	12	13
1	.93	.91	.95	.88	.91	.80	.93	.89	.96	.90	.90	.92
2		.83	.84	.95	.80	.88	.95	.95	.96	.94	.89	.94
3			.85	.72	.81	.72	.83	.72	.83	.72	.69	.82
4				.83	.96	.76	.87	.86	.90	.90	.91	.87
5					.83	.91	.96	.99	.96	.97	.95	.95
6						.71	.88	.86	.88	.88	.89	.89
7							.89	.90	.83	.90	.82	.87
8								.94	.94	.94	.95	.93
9									.95	.98	.95	.97
10										.94	.93	.95
11											.97	.93
12												.88

Table 3. Intraclass correlation of judges' ratings of half sessions

Sessions	RI	RA
1	.13	.66
1½	.59	.95
2	.25	.81
2½	.37	.89
3	.32	.86
3½	.41	.90
4	.38	.89
4½	.30	.85
5	.67	.96
5½	.35	.88

Target Individuals

The summary finding of the study is that each of the eight individuals made significant positive process movement over the sessions ($p < .01$), supporting the hypothesis of this study. A detailed representation of process movement of the eight individuals is shown in Figure 1, the eight lines of the figure plotting the mean process ratings for the individuals in the five sessions. Generally, Figure 1 shows that the higher process levels occur in the later sessions, although some exceptions to this are apparent.

Sessions

The differences among the means for each session (see Table 4) were found to be statistically significant ($p < .01$). These means indicate a significant positive increase in process level over the sessions.

A detailed picture of the judges' mean ratings of the five sessions is presented in Figure 2. The function best describing the Session 4 and 5 ratings (ratings at Process Stage 4 and above) is different from that function which would best describe the Sessions 1, 2, and 3 ratings (ratings at Stage 4 and below). This difference contributes to the significance of the interaction of judges' ratings by sessions (Judges × Sessions interaction, Table 1).

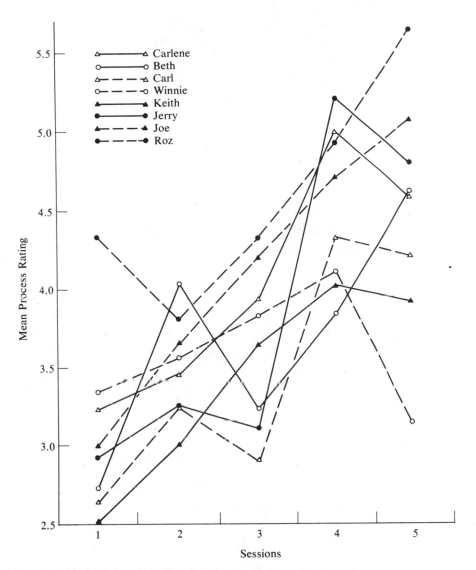

Figure 1. Individual mean process ratings in sessions.

Early–Late Within-Session Measures

The differences between the early and the late within-session measures when summed across judges, target individuals, and sessions was found to be statistically significant ($p < .05$). The mean rating for the early portion of each session was 3.89 compared to a mean of 3.75 for the late portion of each session. This significant difference can be attributed to the individual within-session decreases in process levels as follows: three in session one; five in session two; three in session three; six in session four; and four in session five.

Table 4. Mean process rating of sessions

Session	M	SD
1	3.0	5.4
2	3.5	3.1
3	3.6	4.8
4	4.5	4.8
5	4.5	6.9

Note.—$N = 8$.

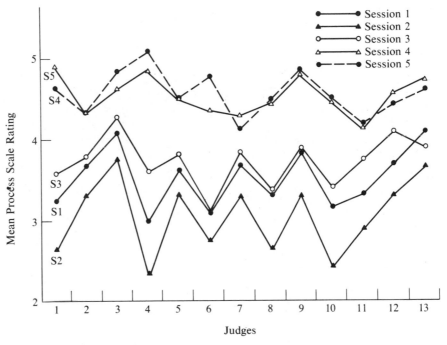

Figure 2.   Judges' mean ratings of sessions.

DISCUSSION

The results show that individuals can make significant gains in their process levels in a weekend basic encounter group. Movement among the participants was generally from a minimum of Stages 2.5 to 3.5 to a maximum of Stages 4.0 to 5.5. In terms of the description of the stages on the scale the individuals moved from a distancing of feelings, rigidity, and past orientation of Stages 2 and 3 to allowing feelings to be expressed in the present, risking relating on a feeling basis, experiencing the inner-self as a referent for behavior of Stages 4 and 5. The group as a whole moved across what Rogers (1958) calls "an important threshold in psychotherapeutic process [p. 26]," Stage 4, beyond which they began to relate to each other in terms of present feelings and experiencing. Each person moved through at least two of the process stages; one moved through three, and one moved through four stages. Rogers (1967c) points out that "movement, whatever its magnitude and location on this continuum, is theoretically meaningful [p. 151]," and positive movement on the continuum is in the direction of what Rogers terms the fully functioning person.

This research suggests that the amount of positive process movement is related to the weekend format, since significant positive process movement was not apparent for all the participants in studies of groups which met once a week (Culbert, 1968; Clark & Culbert, 1965). This indication needs further research controlling for other variables such as the facilitator.

Although generalizations are difficult with the small N, this study indicates a relationship between initial process level and process movement. Three of the four individuals who had the highest mean rating in the first session were among the four who made the most total movement. Similarly, three individuals of the four with lower mean ratings in Session 1 were among the four who made the least total movement. One of the two exceptions to this trend, Jerry, received the lowest mean rating of all the group in a half session (1.7), and made the most total process movement, four stages. As Rogers (1958) has said, Stage 5 (Jerry's highest rating was 5.7) "is several hundred psychological miles from the first stage described [p. 145]." Thus, while those who entered this group at higher process levels tended to make the most total process movement, this exception suggests that even persons operating at low process levels can make dramatic changes in quite a short time.

The finding of the negative trend of the early–late within-session process level was unexpected. Replication of the study could determine whether or not this is a recurring tendency and could unfold possible causes.

The Process Scale, which was developed from a description of sequential changes observed in persons in individual therapy (Rogers, 1958), was able to reflect change in the individuals in the group with adequate reliability. However, certain dimensions of group interaction, such as giving "feedback," are virtually unratable on the present scale. The scale could be revised for group situations.

The interesting change in the relationship of the judges in their ratings of Process Stages 1 to 3 and 4 to 7 (Figure 2) raises the question whether or not there are in fact two scales involved. One scale would describe process levels of persons talking about the past, and one would describe process levels of persons relating in the immediacy of the present.

This study demonstrates that the weekend basic encounter group is an efficient structure in which individuals can experience and observe what Carkhuff (1969) calls high-level functioning, a finding which is relevant to trainers and practitioners in the helping professions. The study also supports Rogers' process theory in terms of the positive direction of movement under the stated conditions and in terms of the kinds of changes individuals make.

REFERENCES

Barrett-Lennard, G. T. Experiential living in small groups: The basic encounter process. *Proceedings of the Canadian Association of University Student Personnel Services,* 1967, 3–12.

Bradford, L. P., Gibb, J. R., & Benne, K. D. (Eds.). *T-group theory and laboratory method: Innovation in reeducation.* New York: Wiley, 1964.

Carkhuff, R. R. Critical variables in effective counselor training. *Journal of Counseling Psychology,* 1969, *16,* 238–245.

Clark, J. V., & Culbert, S. A. Mutually therapeutic perception and self-awareness in a T group. *Journal of Applied Behavioral Science,* 1965, *4,* 47–73.

Culbert, S. A. Trainer self-disclosure and member growth in two T-groups. *Journal of Applied Behavioral Science,* 1968, *4,* 47–73.

Hays, W. L. *Statistics for psychologists.* New York: Holt, Rinehart, & Winston, 1966.

Rogers, C. R. A process conception of psychotherapy. *American Psychologist,* 1958, *13,* 142–149.

Rogers, C. R. The process equation of psychotherapy. *American Journal of Psychotherapy,* 1961, *15,* 27–45.

Rogers, C. R. A plan for self-directed change in an educational system. *Educational Leadership,* 1967, *24,* 717–731. (a)

Rogers, C. R. The process of the basic encounter group. In J. F. T. Bugental (Ed.), *Challenges of humanistic psychology.* New York: McGraw-Hill, 1967. (b)

Rogers, C. R. *The therapeutic relationship and its impact: A study of psychotherapy with schizophrenics.* With Gendlin, E. T., Kiesler, D. J., and Truax, C. Madison: University of Wisconsin Press, 1967. (c)

Rogers, C. R., & Rablen, R. A. A scale of process in psychotherapy. Unpublished manuscript, University of Wisconsin, 1958.

Veldman, D. J. Edstat-V: Basic statistical computer programs (1st rev., mimeo). Personality Research Center, R and D Center for Teacher Education, The University of Texas at Austin, 1967.

Winer, B. J. *Statistical principles in experimental design.* New York: McGraw-Hill, 1962.

Charles B. Truax
REINFORCEMENT VS. NONREINFORCEMENT
IN CLIENT-CENTERED PSYCHOTHERAPY

The present study is aimed at exploring the possibility that important reinforcement effects occur within the transactions of nondirective therapy.[1]

Client-centered theorists have specified the "therapeutic conditions" of empathic understanding and acceptance or unconditional positive regard as two main antecedents to constructive behavioral or personality change in the client (Dymond, 1949; Hobbs, 1962; Jourard, 1959; Rogers, 1951, 1957; Rogers & Truax, 1965; Truax, 1961; Truax & Carkhuff, 1963). Rogers, as the leading exponent of this viewpoint, holds that these "conditions" are primarily attitudinal in nature and are offered in a nonselective fashion to the patient: they are specifically not contingent upon the patients' verbalizations or behaviors. This viewpoint, in pure form, is incompatible with the behavioristic view of therapy and was one basis for the Rogers-Skinner debates (1956).

The basic difference between the views exemplified by Rogers and Skinner is that the latter holds that an effective therapist attempts to alter the patient's behavior while Rogers holds otherwise. Differential reinforcement is one of the procedures used in operant research *positions*. Thus, whether or not Rogers as a therapist uses differential reinforcement, thereby altering patient behavior, is a central question in the basic issue of control which philosophically differentiates the two positions.

The growing body of evidence indicates that the therapist's accurate empathy and unconditional positive regard are significant antecedents to therapeutic change (Rogers, 1962; Rogers, Kiesler, Gendlin & Truax, 1965). This evidence has been used both as support of Rogers's view and as an argument against the behavioristic views of psychotherapy typified by such theorists as Krasner (1962), Wolpe (1958), Eysenck (1952, 1960), and Bandura (1961). The evidence does suggest that when patients receive high levels of empathy and warmth there is significantly more constructive personality and behavioral change than when the patients receive relatively lower levels (Barrett-Lennard, 1962; Bergin & Solomon, 1963; Cartwright & Lerner, 1963; Dickenson & Truax, 1965; Halkides, 1958; Lesser, 1961; Rogers, 1962; Strupp, 1960; Truax, 1961a, 1961b, 1963; Truax & Carkhuff, 1964; Truax, Carkhuff & Kodman, in press; Truax, Wargo, & Silber, 1965; Wargo, 1962; and Whitehorn

From C. B. Truax, "Reinforcement and Nonreinforcement in Rogerian Psychotherapy," *Journal of Abnormal Psychology*, 1966, *71*, 1–9. Reprinted by permission of the American Psychological Association.

[1]Appreciation is gratefully extended to Carl R. Rogers for his freely given consent to the use of the completed successful counseling case recorded at the University of Chicago Counseling Center in 1955. This particular case is perhaps of special significance since it was heavily used by Rogers and others in the development of the "process conception of psychotherapy" and the "Process Scale" developed in 1957. Thanks are also due to James C. Baxter and Leon D. Silber for their critical comments. This work was supported in part by a grant from the Vocational Rehabilitation Administration, No. RD-906-PM.

& Betz, 1954). None of the research just cited, however, *necessarily* argues against a behavioristic view of psychotherapy.

If, in contrast to Rogers's contention, the therapist does respond differentially to different patient behaviors (i.e., more accepting of and empathic to, some patient behaviors but less accepting of and more directive in response to other patient behaviors) then a reinforcement view would not be inconsistent with the findings. It could be argued that if empathic understanding, warmth (and nondirectiveness) are therapeutic, then it may also be argued that these therapeutic conditions are reinforcing, rewarding, or somehow encouraging, and that the types of patient behavior (presumably more adaptive ones) that are followed by high levels of these therapeutic conditions will consequently increase during the course of therapy. For example, it may be that the "high conditions" therapist offers more intense levels of accurate empathy and unconditional warmth or acceptance on both a nonselective random basis at, say, a 40% rate of reinforcement for all behaviors and, say, an 85% rate for exploration of material relevant to the private self. By contrast the "low conditions" therapist may offer less intense levels of empathy and warmth, with only a 20% rate of reinforcement for all behavior emitted and only a 40% rate of reinforcement for the patient's explorations of private material.

Support for the position exemplified by Rogers, viewed from the findings on empathy and warmth, rests upon the assumption that the therapist offers levels of conditions that do not systematically covary with the verbalizations or behavior emitted by the patient. If this were true (if, say, the level of therapist empathy or warmth did not systematically covary with patient response classes) then differential reinforcement could not account for the research findings of relationships between therapist behavior and patient outcome. On the other hand, if the therapist, in this case Rogers, does systematically vary his level of empathy depending on the behavior, then Rogers's position would not be supported.

In an attempt to add clarity to this theoretic controversy, an exploratory analysis of a single successful case handled by Rogers was aimed at determining whether or not important reinforcing effects are imbedded in the transactions of client-centered therapy.

Three qualities of the therapist's behavior were studied as potential reinforcers: (*a*) empathic understanding, (*b*) acceptance or unconditional positive regard, and (*c*) directiveness (a negative reinforcer). These therapist behaviors were examined in relation to nine classes of patient behavior in order to determine the presence or absence of differential therapist responding and any consequent changes in the patient behaviors.[2] The patient behaviors studied which might theoretically be of significance were: (*a*) degree of discrimination learnings by the patient, (*b*) ambiguity of patient's statements, (*c*) degree of insight development by the patient, (*d*) degree of similarity of patient's style of expression to that of the therapist, (*e*) problem orientation of the patient, (*f*) degree of patient catharsis, (*g*) degree of patient blocking, (*h*) degree of patient anxiety, and (*i*) degree of patient negative versus positive feeling expression.

CASE ANALYSIS PROCEDURE

Five clinical psychologists rated an unbiased sample of 40 typewritten interaction units consisting of (*a*) a therapist statement, (*b*) a succeeding patient statement,(*c*) the succeeding therapist statement. These interaction units (TPT, Therapist-Patient-Therapist) were desig-

---

[2]Thanks are due to Israel Goldiamond for critical and helpful questions which served as the stimulus for the analysis of change in patient behaviors over time.

nated by code numbers prior to the ratings, and were then assigned in random order to the five clinical psychologists who served as judges. Each judge rated separately each of the nine patient scales and the three therapist scales in different order, so as to minimize rating biases. The ratings were then decoded, and the ratings of the three classes of "reinforcers" were simply correlated separately with the nine classes of patient behavior under examination. The presence of significant correlations would then be positive evidence to indicate systematic, nonrandom use of these reinforcers with particular classes of patient behavior. Thus the question became, for example, "Does the therapist's degree of acceptance significantly covary with the patient's degree of discrimination learning?" If a positive correlation was found, this would indicate that the therapist systematically was most accepting and unconditionally warm when the patient was engaged in discrimination learning, and was least accepting and warm when the patient was engaged in very little discrimination learning.

The interaction unit sample. The TPT interaction units were selected from the following interviews out of a total of 85 therapy sessions for the complete case, 1, 3, 5, 7, 10, 15, 20, 25, 30, 35, 40, 45, 50, 55, 60, 65, 70, 75, 80, and 85. Two intersection units were taken from each of the above 20 interviews for a total of 40 interaction units. Interviews from which the samples were drawn, with the exception of Numbers 3 and 7, which were added to give more weight to the earlier stages of therapy, were evenly spaced and should constitute an unbiased sample of interviews throughout the therapy case. The two interaction units from each interview were obtained by starting the playback of the recordings at approximately the end of the first and second one-third of the hour-long tape and then listening until the therapist made a statement. Transcriptions started at the therapist's first words and included the ensuing TPT interaction unit. As a result of this sampling procedure, the length of the therapist and the patient statements varied considerably. When measured to the nearest one-tenth of an 80-character type line the range was from 0.4 to 14.0 lines.

The clinical psychologists as raters. Of the five raters, none was trained in client-centered psychotherapy. One was trained in analytic therapy, while the remaining four clinicians described themselves as eclectic in orientation. All five judges had a minimum of 100 hours of supervised training as therapists, and 1,000 hours of experience as therapists. All post-doctoral clinical psychologists, the judges did not know the hypothesis being investigated. Further, they wrongly assumed that some of the more "nondirective" and "directive" statements could not have come from the same therapist.

The rating scales. A set of graphic rating scales was prepared for each of the three therapist behaviors and nine patient behaviors, each having a brief statement of the variable to be rated and horizontal lines 170 millimeters long on which the rating was marked. The rating was made by simply placing an X along the line labeled "most," "very much," to "least," and "very little." The scales for each therapist and patient behavior class stated a bipolarity of the variable. The bipolar definitions for the three reinforcer variables were taken from Rogers's (1951) theoretic descriptions.

Although the actual therapy samples did not contain extreme examples of the scale values, examples from the present case should add meaning to the present study. Two examples of TPT samples, rated high on each of the three reinforcer variables, are presented below.

Therapist acceptance of unconditional positive regard. The first example illustrates relatively high acceptance of the patient as he is feeling disappointed in the early results of therapy. This sample was rated relatively low on both empathy and directiveness:

T: There is nothing that I can do, but I can and do hope that the person will "lift" or something.

P: Yeh, but, well, for something to happen, or things to change, or me to change . . . inside, or . . . things to change outside, so I can change inside or something. Talking about it . . . doesn't really . . . seem to help, this kind of feeling. I mean, well . . . well, I don't know what I mean. I mean, I guess we're just talking about it. Well I don't know what I'm doing (he has been thumping on something—beating on the desk?—long, long pause) . . . I feel so tremendously self-conscious. I don't know, maybe it was the therapy session yesterday, and the other thing that happened yesterday, that has just thrown, so much on me, myself again. And dangerous, I don't know, not dangerous but . . . I feel so un-free today. So . . . Hmm . . . (long pause) . . . Yeh, boy I really am self-conscious . . . sure tensed up inside.

T: I can't get the feel of what you mean by "self-conscious." It's very much aware of yourself? Or something, or generally embarrassed?

The second example illustrates relatively high acceptance of the patient's feelings of inadequacy and dependency. This sample was rated slightly above average on empathy but below average on directiveness:

T: I guess you're saying "I just can't trust those weak, and helpless and inadequate parts of me. I have to have someone to . . ."

P: To really be me. (T, Mmm, mmm) Someone else, you know . . . that's so absurd . . . that would never work. It's the same thing as, as this, uh . . . being afraid of people. It ties in with being afraid. It's like . . . well, you can use any one of a number of examples. If you really want to be someone genuinely . . . or express something genuinely . . . then, all you have to do is feel the slightest tinge of fear and you won't be able to—really. And it's like that with myself . . . It's kind of . . . when I am myself, it kind of echoes on me and makes me afraid. I suddenly hear myself saying that, and then know, "careful" (T: Mmm, mmm) . . . like that. (T: Mmm, mmm) "You won't be allowed to live if you do that." (T: Mmm, mmm) "You won't be allowed to . . . *anything*" . . . just, "You'll be blown to smithereens if you try that kind of thing."

T: Mmmm, So that if you sense yourself . . . being yourself . . . then my (P: I become afraid) Gosh! Lookout! You don't know what you're getting into—you'll be destroyed.

Therapist directiveness. The first example shows the therapist making a direct request to change the topic of discussion. This sample was rated slightly below average in empathy and low in acceptance:

T: Let's talk about something closer to you than that.

P: Or closer to you. I don't understand this at all, because I was really looking forward to this all the time, and now I just don't feel very good . . . about having harmed you.

T: You anticipated coming in, and now . . . today.

A second example of directiveness involves a more subtle "leading" of the patient. This sample was rated as average in empathy but above average in acceptance or unconditional positive regard:

T: It frightens you to even start to put it into words.

P: I guess I'll have to find it with someone else . . . first.

T: You feel that what would be demanded would be . . . put it in terms of "me" and, "you" . . . uh . . . make this the sort of thing you can sort of dimly visualize. I would need to want to really relate to that fine part of you, and find that so personally rewarding that, that in an attempt I would just . . . keep after it, or something. (P interjects: Yeh) One, one phrase that I . . . I'm bringing in my feelings rather than yours, but . . . ever read the poem "The Hound of Heaven"? It's kinda a weird thing, but, uh, the kind of persistent love of God is the whole theme, that, that won't let the person go . . . and, and, I think that's sort of what you're talking about.

Therapist empathy. The first example illustrates an excerpt in which the therapist attempts to verbalize what he senses is the client's uncertainty; this sample received an average rating on acceptance and a slightly above average rating on directiveness:

> T: I've been trying to soak up that tone, uh, I'm not sure I'm right, but does it have some meaning like this, "What is it you want with me? I'm possibly willing to, to meet that, but I don't know what you want." Does that kinda describe it?
> P: Yes, I'm sympathetic, I'll try and do what I can. "Don't be this, and this, and this way to me." What is it? Yeh, that's it.
> T: "So if you want me to get in with whatever it is you expect of me, just let me know."

The second example involves a moment when the therapist attempts to reflect the client's feelings and move one step beyond. This sample was rated average on directiveness and acceptance:

> T: Seems as though all the dark things—hurting, and being hurt—and . . . decay, and corruption, ugliness, uhmmm, Death. It's all of those that (P: frightening) that you're afraid of.
> P: Yeh . . . stink and corruption and . . . pus, and . . . There's just as . . . It's something dark that ties them all together (T: Mmm, uhuh). Something putrid and (T: Mmm, mmm) . . . there are 10 times the words (T: Mmm, mmm) for it . . . (laughs) it scares me.
> T: Just to wander into that field verbally, and . . . and even name all these things that have to do with it . . . this dark side of hurting and rottenness . . . that's hurting in itself.

The patient scales measuring the degree of insight developed, the degree of similarity of the patient's style of expression to that of the therapist, the degree of problem orientation, the degree of catharsis, the degree of blocking in thought and feeling, the degree of anxiety present, and the degree of positive- versus negative-feeling expression were defined by the trained clinical psychologists who served as judges. Degree of ambiguity of the patient's statement was defined in terms of its clarity of meaning. The judges were asked to disregard speech disturbances and length of statement in rating ambiguity. Discrimination learning was defined as making new distinctions between old feelings or experiences, and thus included both cognitive and emotional discrimination learning.[3]

FINDINGS AND DISCUSSION

Qualitative Aspects

There are three qualitative aspects exemplified in this case which perhaps are worth noting. The first concerns the style of expression by the therapist: it was characteristic of the therapist to express, restate, or interpret what the patient has been saying by "quoting" what the patient *might well have said* in the first person singular—"In a sense I feel. . . ." Out of

[3]Available from the author.

the 40 sampled interaction units, 23 involved first person singular quotes while an additional five (for a total of 28 out of 40) involved impersonal quotes of the type: "In a sense it's like feeling. . . ." A second characteristic of this particular case was the almost total absence of psychological jargon. Few even semitechnical terms such as "anxious" or "hostile" were used by the therapist. Instead, the therapist relied heavily on everyday language that conveys effect. Thus instead of saying "depressed" the therapist says "hopeless badness." The third qualitative characteristic of this case is the tentative character of therapist statements. There is almost universal use of such prefacing remarks as "in a sense," "I guess," and "maybe." This tentative approach might tend to elicit less resistance from the patient so that actual confrontation might sound much like an attempt to agree with the patient.

The Question of Selective Responding

The reliability of each scale, which is given in parentheses under the scale label in Table 1, was estimated by the variance formula presented by Ebel (1951) for the intraclass correlation. As can be seen in Table 1, reliabilities range from .26 to .64 for the classes of patient behavior, and from .48 to .68 for levels of "reinforcement" offered by the therapist.

The low reliabilities obtained on certain classes of patient behavior would make it difficult to detect any but the strongest of relationships. For the present hypothesis of selective reinforcement the absence of particular relationships is not critical. Rather, the *presence* of selective responding (as indicated by some significant relationship between therapist and patient classes of behavior) would be evidence in support of the hypothesis.

Table 1. Interrelationships between the level of therapist reinforcement and levels of patient behaviors

Classes of patient behavior	*Therapist empathy* (r = .48)	Reinforcers Therapist acceptance UPR (r = .59)	*Therapist directiveness* (r = .68)
Patient learning of discriminations (r = .59)	.47	.37	*ns*
Patient ambiguity (r = .35)	−.35	−.38	.33
Patient insight (r = .32)	.46	.37	*ns*
Similarity of patient style of expression to that of the therapist (r = .57)	.48	.32	−.31
Problem orientation (r = .64)	*ns*	.35	*ns*
Catharsis (r = .44)	*ns*	*ns*	*ns*
Blocking (r = .54)	*ns*	*ns*	*ns*
Anxiety (r = .26)	*ns*	*ns*	*ns*
Patient negative feeling expression (r = .29)	*ns*	*ns*	*ns*

The obtained average intercorrelations between the levels of therapist reinforcements and the levels of the selected patient behaviors are presented in Table 1. These average intercorrelations were obtained in the following manner. First a matrix of intercorrelations was generated for each of the five raters separately. The matrices were then inspected separately for correlations which were significant at or beyond the .05 level of significance. Average correlations for the five raters combined were then obtained for those intercorrelations that were significant in three out of five individual rater matrices. All other correlations were recorded as nonsignificant in the present study so that the reported correlations tend to minimize rather than maximize the possibility of obtaining significant relationships.

The significant intercorrelations presented in Table 1 show a quite different pattern than would be expected if therapist responses were not highly selective in client-centered psychotherapy. If there was no systematic selective use of empathy, acceptance, or directiveness, then all correlations would be nonsignificant and would approach zero. Such is not the case. The therapist significantly tended to respond selectively with differential levels of empathy, warmth, or directiveness to high and low levels of the following classes of patient behavior: (*a*) learning of discriminations about self and feelings, (*b*) a lack of patient ambiguity (patient clarity), (*c*) patient expressions of insight, (*d*) patient verbal expressions that were similar in style to the therapist's way of expressing himself, and (*e*) problem orientation of the patient. Thus, when the patient expressed himself in a style similar to that of the therapist, the therapist was more empathic, more warm and accepting, and less directive. When the patient expressed himself in a style quite different from that of the therapist, the therapist tended to show significantly less empathy, less acceptance or warmth, and more directiveness.

No significant relationships were obtained between the therapist's use of empathy, acceptance, or directiveness, and patient behaviors described as blocking, anxiety, negative-versus positive-feeling expression, or catharsis. While it may be that the absence of these relationships might, in part, be accounted for by the relatively low reliabilities of measurement, it also seems likely that Rogers as a therapist does not tend to respond differentially to these classes of patient behavior. In particular, as a theoretician and therapist, Rogers (1957, 1961) has felt it important for the therapist *not* to respond selectively to negative- versus positive-feeling expression.

The Further Question of Reinforcement

The above findings are consistent with, but not direct evidence for, the view that the therapist, in this case Rogers, is consciously or unconsciously using empathy, acceptance, and directiveness as reinforcers. The basic property of a reinforcer is that its use with specific classes of behavior leads to consequent changes in the probability of occurrence of these classes of behavior.

From Table 1, the nine classes of patient behavior can be ranked according to the degree of contingency between therapist "reinforcer" responses and patient responses. Now, if the therapist's systematic selective responding has the properties of reinforcement it would be predicted that, other things being equal, the five patient classes of behavior that were selectively "reinforced" would show increases over time in therapy, while the four classes of patient behavior not reinforced would show no such increase over time. Thus, for example, one would expect an increase over time in therapy of the "Similarity of the Patient's Style of Expression to that of the Therapist" and of "Patient-Learning Discriminations," and no such increase (or decrease) in patient "Blocking" or "Negative Feeling Expression."

To evaluate this the ratings of the 40 samples for each class of patient behavior were grouped into five blocks across time-in-therapy (five raters for eight samples per block or 40 ratings per block) and the Grant Orthogonal Polynomial Trend Test Analysis of Variance (Grant, 1956) was used to test for the significance of components of trend. Further, *t* tests were used to test for significance of differences between early and late in therapy on all nine patient behavior classes. These data are presented in Table 2.

Table 2. Analysis of changes over time in patient response classes

Patient response classes	Highest single correlation with therapist "reinforcer"	Grant orthogonal polynomial analysis of variance for trend			*t*Test between first and all later blocks
		F Linear trend	F Quadratic trend	F Cubic trend	
Similarity of patient style of expression to that of the therapist	.48	7.89***	1.20	.85	2.84***
Patient learning of discriminations	.47	3.10	.79	1.05	2.94***
Patient insight	.46	4.73**	1.70	0.75	2.73***
Patient ambiguity	−.38	3.04	1.50	0.91	1.35
Problem orientation	.35	3.28*	1.61	2.10	1.76**
Catharsis	ns	6.10**	2.13	1.20	2.03**
Blocking	ns	1.50	6.01**	1.50	1.29
Anxiety	ns	2.00	0.98	1.70	0.93
Patient negative-feeling expression	ns	1.17	0.65	0.89	0.75

* $p \leq .07$ for 1/39 *df* for trend.
** $p \leq .05$ for 1/39 *df* for trend or for 38 *df* for *t*.
*** $p \leq .01$ for 1/39 *df* for trend or for 38 *df* for *t*.

Of the classes of patient behavior to which the therapist selectively responded (i.e., reinforced), four out of five showed changes in patient behavior over time-in-therapy. Thus the data agree with the predictions in seven out of the nine classes of patient behaviors (78% correct prediction).

Considering the probability that the therapist also used other types of rewards or reinforcers and also rewarded other related patient behavior classes, considering the unknown differential complexity levels of the patient response classes, and considering the crudity of measurement, the findings strongly suggest that important reinforcement effects do indeed occur even in client-centered therapy.

Toward Evaluating the Validity of the Findings

There are, of course, some difficulties in interpreting the intercorrelation matrix. One might argue that these are simply interrelationships in the "heads" of the raters, as the raters might have known what the "X" value was when they rated a sample on "Y." However, each of the 12 variables was rated separately and they were rated in different orders. One would think it difficult to recall the X value of a given unit when the rating of the other units intervened between the X value and its corresponding Y value (an average of 240 ratings intervening between corresponding X and Y values). It could be argued that some of this bias is removed by the procedure for averaging the five different raters, since the raters were unaware of the actual hypothesis under study.

Beyond the above considerations, tabulation of one well-known characteristic of the therapist's behavior also suggests selective differential responding. The use of "uh huh" or "Mmm mmm" verbalizations has become, perhaps unfortunately, the hallmark of Rogerian psychotherapy. In the samples used in the present analysis, Mmm mmm's or Uh huh's occurred 23 times in a total of 12 of the 40 samples (in 30% of the samples). The Mmm mmm occurred in 9 of the 12 samples (75% of its occurrence) during high expression of negative feeling by the patient (all above the mean of ratings), while 0% occurred during low "patient negative feeling expression." In the remaining three samples, they occurred during the patient's direct restatement of what the therapist had just said. This tabulation alone suggests conscious or unconscious selective responding by the therapist, and is consistent with the obtained findings based upon relationships between rated therapist and patient classes of behavior.[4]

Finally, and most importantly, the obtained data dealing with changes in patient-in-therapy behavior were consistent with the obtained findings based upon prediction from a reinforcement view. Since the raters had no knowledge of whether a given sample came from early- or late-in-therapy, those findings of a tendency for significant linear increases to occur over time in reinforced patient behaviors and not to occur in nonreinforced patient behaviors, would also argue strongly against the notion that the obtained intercorrelations were simply "in the heads" of the raters.

IMPLICATIONS

The present findings point to the presence of significant differential reinforcement effects imbedded in the transactions of client-centered psychotherapy. Since differential reinforcement is one of the procedures used in operant research to alter (or control) behavior, the findings suggest that the therapist, in this case Rogers, implicitly alters (or controls) the patient's behavior in the therapeutic setting. To this extent, then, the evidence weighs in favor of the view proposed by Skinner rather than that of Rogers. The present findings are not consistent with Rogers' view that relatively *uniform conditions* which are globally "facilitative of personal growth and integration," are offered to patients in a manner not contingent upon the patient's behavior.

The present data, by demonstrating the role of empathy and warmth as positive reinforcers, suggest that the available evidence relating levels of these therapeutic conditions to patient outcome in therapy does not argue against a reinforcement interpretation of psychotherapy. On the contrary, the finding that empathy and warmth act as reinforcers suggests that the evidence relating empathy and warmth to patient outcome is open to a behavioristic interpretation, based in part on the therapist's use of differential reinforcement.

Recent studies have suggested that such humanistic qualities as empathy and warmth are antecedents to patient personality or behavioral change. In attempting to understand *how* such therapist qualities operate in producing therapeutic change, the present data suggest the potential value of studies utilizing behavioristic models. Since the available evidence relating

---

[4]It should be noted that the therapist's use of the "Uh huh reinforcer" is relatively ineffective since there is no increase over time in "patient negative feeling expression."

empathy and warmth to patient outcome deals primarily with differences in *intensity levels* contaminated by differences in *rates* between therapists, it seems likely that additional and more precise understanding of the role of empathy (and hence more effective practice) might grow out of studies carried out from a reinforcement frame of reference. Considering only empathy as the type of reinforcer used in psychotherapy, it would be expected that successful and nonsuccessful therapists might differ in: (*a*) the particular patient behaviors chosen for differential reinforcement (say, self-concept statements versus historical-genetic statements); (*b*) the differential rate of reinforcement (say, 25% versus 75% for a specific class of patient behavior); (*c*) the intensity levels of the reinforcer used (say, the depth of empathy); and even the (*d*) scheduling of reinforcement (say, fixed ratio versus variable ratio).

Research aimed at identifying which patient behaviors, if reinforced at what intensity levels etc., lead to positive therapeutic outcomes would provide more specific knowledge of how such positive human qualities as empathy and warmth operate to produce personality or behavioral change in the patient.

Such an approach aims toward more specific knowledge, but not at all toward more mechanical therapy. As the communication of any "reinforcing machine" qualities would by definition mean a low level of empathy and warmth, the present viewpoint is in full agreement with Schonbar's (1964) statement that "as a therapist I am no more a 'reinforcing machine' than my patient is a 'talking pigeon.'"

REFERENCES

Bandura, A. Psychotherapy as a learning process. *Psychological Bulletin,* 1961, *58,* 143–159.

Barrett-Lennard, G. T. Dimensions of therapist response as causal factors in therapeutic change. *Psychological Monographs,* 1962, *76*(43, Whole No. 562).

Bergin, A. E., & Solomon, S. Personality and performance correlates of empathic understanding in psychotherapy. Paper read at American Psychological Association, Philadelphia, September 1963.

Cartwright, R. D., & Lerner, B. Empathy: Need to change and improvement with psychotherapy. *Journal of Consulting Psychology,* 1963, *27,* 138–144.

Dickenson, W. A., & Truax, C. B. Group counseling with college underachievers: Comparisons with a control group and relationship to empathy, warmth, and genuineness. University of Kentucky and Kentucky Mental Health Institute, 1965.

Dymond, R. A scale for the measurement of empathic ability. *Journal of Consulting Psychology,* 1949, *13,* 127–133.

Ebel, R. L. Estimation of the reliability of ratings. *Psychometrika,* 1951, *16,* 407–424.

Eysenck, H. J. The effects of psychotherapy: An evaluation. *Journal of Consulting Psychology,* 1952, *16,* 319–324.

Eysenck, H. J. The effects of psychotherapy. In H. J. Eysenck (Ed.), *Handbook of abnormal psychology.* New York: Basic Books, 1960. Pp. 697–725.

Grant, David A. Analysis of variance tests in the analysis and comparison of curves. *Psychological Bulletin,* 1956, *53,* 141–154.

Halkides, G. An investigation of therapeutic success as a function of four variables. Unpublished doctoral dissertation, University of Chicago, 1958.

Hobbs, N. Sources of gain in psychotherapy. *American Psychologist,* 1962, *17,* 741–747.

Jourard, S. I-thou relationship versus manipulation in counseling and psychotherapy. *Journal of Individual Psychology,* 1959, *15,* 174–179.

Krasner, L. The therapist as a social reinforcement machine. In H. H. Strupp & L. Luborsky (Eds.), *Research in psychotherapy.* Vol. II. Washington, D. C.: American Psychological Association, 1962.

Lesser, W. M. The relationship between counseling progress and empathic understanding. *Journal of Counseling Psychology,* 1961, *8,* 330–336.

Rogers, C. R. *Client-centered therapy.* Cambridge, Mass.: Riverside Press, 1951. Pp. 73–74.

Rogers, C. R. The necessary and sufficient conditions of therapeutic personality change. *Journal of Consulting Psychology,* 1957, *21,* 95–103.

Rogers, C. R. *On becoming a person.* Cambridge, Mass.: Riverside Press, 1961.

Rogers, C. R. The interpersonal relationship: The core of guidance. *Harvard Educational Review,* 1962, *32,* 416–429.

Rogers, C. R., Kiesler, D., Gendlin, E. T., & Truax, C. B. *The therapeutic relationship and its impact: A study of psychotherapy with schizophrenics.* Madison: Univer. Wisconsin Press, 1965.

Rogers, C. R., & Skinner, B. F. Some issues concerning the control of human behavior. *Science,* 1956, *124,* 1057–1066.

Rogers, C. R., & Truax, C. B. The therapeutic conditions antecedent to change: A theoretical view. Chapter in, *The therapeutic relationship and its impact: A study of psychotherapy with schizophrenics.* Univer. Wisconsin Press, 1965.

Schonbar, R. A. A practitioner's critique of psychotherapy research. Paper read at American Psychological Association, Los Angeles, September 1964.

Strupp, H. H. Nature of psychotherapists' contribution to the treatment process. *Archives of General Psychiatry,* 1960, *3,* 219–231.

Truax, C. B. Clinical implementation of therapeutic conditions. In Carl R. Rogers (Chm.), Therapeutic and research progress in a program of psychotherapy research with hospitalized schizophrenics. Symposium presented at the American Psychological Association, New York, September 1961.(a)

Truax, C. B. The process of group psychotherapy. *Psychological Monographs,* 1961, *75*(7, Whole No. 511). (b)

Truax, C. B. Effective ingredients in psychotherapy: An approach to unraveling the patient-therapist interaction. *Journal of Counseling Psychology,* 1963, *10,* 256–263.

Truax, C. B., & Carkhuff, R. R. For better or for worse. The process of psychotherapeutic personality change. Chapter in, *Recent advances in the study of behavioral change.* Montreal: McGill Univer. Press, 1963. Pp. 118–163.

Truax, C. B., & Carkhuff, R. R. Significant developments in psychotherapy research. In Abt & Riess (Eds.), *Progress in clinical psychology.* New York: Grune & Stratton, 1964. Pp. 124–155.

Truax, C. B., Carkhuff, R. R., & Kodman, F., Jr. Relationships between therapist-offered conditions and patient change in group psychotherapy. *Journal of Clinical Psychology.*

Truax, C. B., Wargo, D. G., & Silber, L. D. Effects of high conditions group psychotherapy with female juvenile delinquents. University of Kentucky and Kentucky Mental Health Institute, 1965.

Wargo, D. G. The Barron Ego Strength and LH[4] scales as predictors and indicators of change in psychotherapy. *Brief Research Reports,* 1962, *21.* (University of Wisconsin, Wisconsin Psychiatric Institute.)

Whitehorn, J. C., & Betz, B. J. A study of psychotherapeutic relationships between physicians and schizophrenic patients. *American Journal of Psychiatry,* 1954, *3,* 321–331.

Wolpe, J. *Psychotherapy by reciprocal inhibition.* Stanford: Stanford Univer. Press, 1958.

Nine
ABRAHAM H. MASLOW

Perhaps the most widely respected personality theorist representing the "third force" in contemporary psychology is Abraham H. Maslow (1908–1970). The third force is a movement comprising a variety of psychological and philosophical viewpoints and including an assortment of Adlerian, Jungian, gestalt, ego psychoanalytic, and existential theorists. Although differing on many substantive issues, the members of this movement are united in a reaction against what they consider to be the sterile provincialism of classical psychoanalysis and experimental behaviorism, which have dominated 20th-century psychology. Their alternative is a rejection of orthodoxy in science and a redirection of scientific inquiry toward such intimate human concerns as creativity, beauty, love, and value. Maslow's theoretical posture is fully consistent with this attitude.

The theory paper by Maslow that appears in this chapter gives a broad outline of his philosophical and theoretical views on human nature. The central core of his position is that people are continually striving toward the realization of their basic biological and psychological potentials. The human organism is motivated by needs both for survival and for self-actualization, but, once the survival motive has been satisfied, the individual is free to choose a productive course of psychological growth. This growth can be stunted, however, if the individual's "inner nature" is frustrated by circumstance or by emotional defeats suffered in the struggle for maturity. Unlike many theorists, Maslow has constructed a model of the person that is essentially optimistic. His contribution to the understanding of psychological health, maturity, and self-fulfillment is a significant achievement.

The research project reported on in the paper by Rosemary Rizzo and Edgar Vinacke was an attempt to discover various aspects of human experience that might be associated with the process of self-actualization. The authors reasoned that, if there is validity to Maslow's conception of a hierarchy of needs, one might predict that healthy persons who have progressed toward self-actualization will be more likely than persons who have not so progressed to regard as important those personal experiences reflecting a high level of need. Thus, self-actualized persons should be found to emphasize more than people who are not self-actualized experiences that offer truth, beauty, goodness, and so on, the striving for which is characteristic of high levels of need definition. The researchers studied 65 subjects from various age groups and socioeconomic backgrounds. The major assessment tools were written reports by the subjects about critical life experiences and the subjects' responses to a questionnaire called the *Personal Orientation Inventory (POI)*. The POI is a personality inventory constructed specifically to assess qualities of self-actualization as described by Maslow and Rogers.

The results of the research suggested that there continues to be some confusion about what the POI actually measures. However, it appeared clear that people who report more personally satisfying experiences score higher than people who report fewer satisfying experiences on qualities of self-actualization, as measured by the POI. Thus, it seems that happy and self-satisfied people have achieved higher levels of self-actualization than have people who are not so happy.

The critique paper by M. Brewster Smith contains a brief review of Maslow's main concepts, including self-actualization, the growth process, and critical experiences in self-actualization. Smith then analyzes the way in which Maslow compiled the research data to support his theories. Smith is sharply critical of Maslow's approach. In particular, Smith argues that the creative persons Maslow selected as models of self-actualization constituted a biased sample. The group included such famous individuals as Lincoln, Jefferson, Eleanor Roosevelt, and Einstein. Maslow felt that they typified the category of highly creative self-actualizers. Smith wonders why Maslow chose only creative people who seem to have been free of gross psychopathology. What about the Dostoevskys and Van Goghs, who suffered pain and anguish throughout their lives yet produced literature and art of the highest order? Were these greats not self-actualized in their own ways? Can Maslow's theory account for their greatness? Is self-actualization a phenomenon that progresses smoothly from one level to the next, or is the process jagged and unpredictable? Smith feels that one might evidence the quality of self-actualization at one phase in life and then decline in another epoch of life. There is no reason to believe, Smith says, that the trait of self actualization is so stable that once it is achieved it can never be lost.

Smith presents a generally friendly, although pointedly critical, survey of some aspects of Maslow's work. A final disagreement he discusses has to do with Maslow's tendency to ignore the impact of social conditions and, instead, to hypothesize a kind of biological determinism. For Maslow, self-actualization is an ultimate reflection of people's basic biological potential for self-improvement. Smith remains thoroughly unconvinced of the validity of this undercurrent in Maslow's thinking.

SUGGESTIONS FOR FURTHER READING

An excellent collection of Maslow's papers can be found in *Toward a Psychology of Being,* an Insight Book published by Van Nostrand in 1962. A recent theoretical paper and a personal interview are both contained in the July 1969 issue of the magazine *Psychology Today.*

The latest statement by Maslow of his personality theory, completed just prior to his death, is *Motivation and Personality,* 2nd edition, published by Harper & Row in 1970.

Abraham Maslow
SOME BASIC PROPOSITIONS OF A GROWTH AND SELF-ACTUALIZATION PSYCHOLOGY

When the philosophy of man (his nature, his goals, his potentialities, his fulfillment) changes, then everything changes, not only the philosophy of politics, of economics, of ethics and values, of interpersonal relations and of history itself, but also the philosophy of education, the theory of how to help men become what they can and deeply need to become.

We are now in the middle of such a change in the conception of man's capacities, potentialities and goals. A new vision is emerging of the possibilities of man and of his destiny, and its implications are many, not only for our conceptions of education, but also for science, politics, literature, economics, religion, and even our conceptions of the non-human world.

I think it is now possible to begin to delineate this view of human nature as a total, single, comprehensive system of psychology even though much of it has arisen as a reaction *against* the limitations (as philosophies of human nature) of the two most comprehensive psychologies now available—behaviorism (or associationism) and classical, Freudian psychoanalysis. Finding a single label for it is still a difficult task, perhaps a premature one. In the past I have called it the "holistic-dynamic" psychology to express my conviction about its major roots. Some have called it "organismic" following Goldstein. Sutich and others are calling it the Self-psychology or Humanistic psychology. We shall see. My own guess is that, in a few decades, if it remains suitably eclectic and comprehensive, it will be called simply "psychology."

I think I can be of most service by speaking primarily for myself and out of my own work rather than as an "official" delegate of this large group of thinkers, even though I am sure that the areas of agreement among them are very large. . . . Because of the limited space I have, I will present here only some of the major propositions of this point of view, especially those of importance to the educator. I should warn you that at many points I am way out ahead of the data. Some of these propositions are more based on private conviction than on publicly demonstrated facts. However, they are all in principle confirmable or disconfirmable.

1. We have, each one of us, an essential inner nature which is instinctoid, intrinsic, given, "natural," i.e., with an appreciable hereditary determinant, and which tends strongly to persist.

It makes sense to speak here of the hereditary, constitutional and very early acquired roots of the *individual* self, even though this biological determination of self is only partial, and far too complex to describe simply. In any case, this is "raw material" rather than

From A. Maslow, *Toward a Psychology of Being* (Princeton, N. J.: Van Nostrand, 1962), pp. 177–200. Reprinted by permission of Van Nostrand-Reinhold, a division of Litton Industries.

finished product, to be reacted to by the person, by his significant others, by his environment, etc.

I include in this essential inner nature instinctoid basic needs, capacities, talents, anatomical equipment, physiological or temperamental balances, prenatal and natal injuries, and traumata to the neonate. This inner core shows itself as natural inclinations, propensities or inner bent. Whether defense and coping mechanisms, "style of life," and other characterological traits, all shaped in the first few years of life, should be included is still a matter for discussion. This raw material very quickly starts growing into a self as it meets the world outside and begins to have transaction with it.

2. These are potentialities, not final actualizations. Therefore they have a life history and must be seen developmentally. They are actualized, shaped or stifled mostly (but not altogether) by extra-psychic determinants (culture, family, environment, learning, etc.). Very early in life these goalless urges and tendencies become attached to objects ("sentiments") by canalization but also by arbitrarily learned associations.

3. This inner core, even though it is biologically based and "instinctoid," is weak in certain senses rather than strong. It is easily overcome, suppressed or repressed. It may even be killed off permanently. Humans no longer have instincts in the animal sense, powerful, unmistakable inner voices which tell them unequivocally what to do, when, where, how and with whom. All that we have left are instinct-remnants. And furthermore, these are weak, subtle and delicate, very easily drowned out by learning, by cultural expectations, by fear, by disapproval, etc. They are *hard* to know, rather than easy. Authentic selfhood can be defined in part as being able to hear these impulse-voices within oneself, i.e., to know what one really wants or doesn't want, what one is fit for and what one is *not* fit for, etc. It appears that there are wide individual differences in the strength of these impulse-voices.

4. Each person's inner nature has some characteristics which all other selves have (species-wide) and some which are unique to the person (idiosyncratic). The need for love characterizes every human being that is born (although it can disappear later under certain circumstances). Musical genius however is given to very few, and these differ markedly from each other in style, e.g., Mozart and Debussy.

5. It is possible to study this inner nature scientifically and objectively (that is, with the right kind of "science") and to discover what it is like (*discover*—not invent or construct). It is also possible to do this subjectively, by inner search and by psychotherapy, and the two enterprises supplement and support each other.

6. Many aspects of this inner, deeper nature are either (a) actively repressed, as Freud has described, because they are feared or disapproved of or are ego-alien, or (b) "forgotten" (neglected, unused, overlooked, unverbalized or suppressed), as Schachtel has described. Much of the inner, deeper nature is therefore unconscious. This can be true not only for impulses (drives, instincts, needs) as Freud has stressed, but also for capacities, emotions, judgments, attitudes, definitions, perceptions, etc. Active repression takes effort and uses up energy. There are many specific techniques of maintaining active unconsciousness, such as denial, projection, reaction-formation, etc. However, repression does not kill what is repressed. The repressed remains as one active determinant of thought and behavior.

Both active and passive repressions seem to begin early in life, mostly as a response to parental and cultural disapprovals.

However, there is some clinical evidence that repression may arise also from intra-psychic, extra-cultural sources in the young child, or at puberty, i.e., out of fear of being overwhelmed by its own impulses, of becoming disintegrated, of "falling apart," exploding, etc. It is theoretically possible that the child may spontaneously form attitudes of fear and disapproval toward its own impulses and may then defend himself against them in various ways. Society need not be the only repressing force, if this is true. There may also be ·intra-psychic repressing and controlling forces. These we may call ''intrinsic counter-cathexes.''

It is best to distinguish unconscious drives and needs from unconscious ways of cognizing because the latter are often easier to bring to consciousness and therefore to modify. Primary process cognition (Freud) or archaic thinking (Jung) is more recoverable by, e.g., creative art education, dance education, and other non-verbal educational techniques.

7. Even though ''weak,'' this inner nature rarely disappears or dies, in the usual person, in the U.S. (such disappearance or dying is possible early in the life history, however). It persists underground, unconsciously, even though denied and repressed. Like the voice of the intellect (which is part of it), it speaks softly but it *will* be heard, even if in a distorted form. That is, it has a dynamic force of its own, pressing always for open, uninhibited expression. Effort must be used in its suppression or repression from which fatigue can result. This force is one main aspect of the ''will to health,'' the urge to grow, the pressure to self-actualization, the quest for one's identity. It is this that makes psychotherapy, education and self-improvement possible in principle.

8. However, this inner core, or self, grows into adulthood only partly by (objective or subjective) discovery, uncovering, and acceptance of what is ''there'' beforehand. Partly it is also a creation of the person himself. Life is a continual series of choices for the individual in which a main determinant of choice is the person as he already is (including his goals for himself, his courage or fear, his feeling of responsibility, his ego-strength or ''will power,'' etc.). We can no longer think of the person as ''fully determined'' where this phase implies ''determined only by forces external to the person.'' The person, insofar as he *is* a real person, is his own main determinant. Every person is, in part, ''his own project'' and makes himself.

9. If this essential core (inner nature) of the person is frustrated, denied or suppressed, sickness results, sometimes in obvious forms, sometimes in subtle and devious forms, sometimes immediately, sometimes later. These psychological illnesses include many more than those listed by the American Psychiatric Association. For instance, the character disorders and disturbances are now seen as far more important for the fate of the world than the classical neuroses or even the psychoses. From this new point of view, new kinds of illness are most dangerous, e.g., ''the diminished or stunted person,'' i.e., the loss of any of the defining characteristics of humanness, or personhood, the failure to grow to one's potential, valueless-ness, etc.

That is, general-illness of the personality is seen as any falling short of growth, or of self-actualization, or of full-humanness. And the main source of illness (although not the only one) is seen as frustrations (of the basic needs, of the B-values, of idiosyncratic potentials, of expression of the self, and of the tendency of the person to grow in his own style and at his own pace) especially in the early years of life. That is, frustration of the basic needs is not the only source of illness or of human diminution.

10. This inner nature, as much as we know of it so far, is definitely not ''evil,'' but is either what we adults in our culture call ''good,'' or else it is neutral. The most accurate way to express this is to say that it is ''prior to good and evil.'' There is little question about this if we speak of the inner nature of the infant and child. The statement is much more complex if we speak of the ''infant'' as he still exists in the adult. And it gets still more complex if the individual is seen from the point of view of B-psychology rather than D-psychology.

This conclusion is supported by all the truth-revealing and uncovering techniques that have anything to do with human nature: psychotherapy, objective science, subjective science, education and art. For instance, in the long run, uncovering therapy lessens hostility, fear, greed, etc., and increases love, courage, creativeness, kindness, altruism, etc., leading us to the conclusion that the latter are "deeper," more natural, and more basic than the former, i.e., that what we call "bad" behavior is learned or removed by uncovering, while what we call "good" behavior is strengthened and fostered by uncovering.

11. We must differentiate the Freudian type of superego from intrinsic conscience and intrinsic guilt. The former is in principle a taking into the self of the disapprovals and approvals of persons other than the person himself, fathers, mothers, teachers, etc. Guilt then is recognition of disapproval by others.

Intrinsic guilt is the consequence of betrayal of one's own inner nature or self, a turning off the path to self-actualization, and is essentially justified self-disapproval. It is therefore not as culturally relative as is Freudian guilt. It is "true" or "deserved" or "right and just" or "correct" because it is a discrepancy from something profoundly real within the person rather than from accidental, arbitrary or purely relative localisms. Seen in this way it is good, even *necessary,* for a person's development to have intrinsic guilt when he deserves to. It is not just a symptom to be avoided at any cost but is rather an inner guide for growth toward actualization of the real self, and of its potentialities.

12. "Evil" behavior has mostly referred to unwarranted hostility, cruelty, destructiveness, "mean" aggressiveness. This we do not know enough about. To the degree that this quality of hostility is instinctoid, mankind has one kind of future. To the degree that it is reactive (a response to bad treatment), mankind has a very different kind of future. My opinion is that the weight of the evidence so far indicates that indiscriminately *destructive* hostility is reactive, because uncovering therapy reduces it, and changes its quality into "healthy" self-affirmation, forcefulness, selective hostility, self-defense, righteous indignation, etc. In any case, the *ability* to be aggressive and angry is found in all self-actualizing people, who are able to let it flow forth freely when the external situation "calls for" it.

The situation in children is far more complex. At the very least, we know that the healthy child is also able to be justifiably angry, self-protecting and self-affirming, i.e., reactive aggression. Presumably, then, a child should learn not only how to control his anger, but also how and when to express it.

Behavior that our culture calls evil can also come from ignorance and from childish misinterpretations and beliefs (whether in the child or in the repressed or "forgotten" child-in-the-adult). For instance, sibling rivalry is traceable to the child's wish for the exclusive love of his parents. Only as he matures is he in principle capable of learning that his mother's love for a sibling is compatible with her continued love for him. Thus out of a childish version of love, not in itself reprehensible, can come unloving behavior.

The commonly seen hatred or resentment of or jealousy of goodness, truth, beauty, health or intelligence, ("counter-values") is largely (though not altogether) determined by threat of loss of self-esteem, as the liar is threatened by the honest man, the homely girl by the beautiful girl, or the coward by the hero. Every superior person confronts us with our own shortcomings.

Still deeper than this, however, is the ultimate existential question of the fairness and justice of fate. The person with a disease may be jealous of the healthy man who is more deserving than he.

Evil behaviors seem to most psychologists to be reactive as in these examples, rather than instinctive. This implies that though "bad" behavior is very deeply rooted in human nature and can never be abolished altogether, it may yet be expected to lessen as the personality matures and as the society improves.

13. Many people still think of "the unconscious," of regression, and of primary process cognition as necessarily unhealthy, or dangerous or bad. Psychotherapeutic experience is slowly teaching us otherwise. Our depths can also be good, or beautiful or desirable. This is also becoming clear from the general findings from investigations of the sources of love, creativeness, play, humor, art, etc. Their roots are deep in the inner, deeper self, i.e., in the unconscious. To recover them and to be able to enjoy and use them we must be able to "regress."

14. No psychological health is possible unless this essential core of the person is fundamentally accepted, loved and respected by others and by himself (the converse is not necessarily true, i.e., that if the core is respected, etc., then psychological health must result, since other prerequisite conditions must also be satisfied).

The psychological health of the chronologically immature is called healthy growth. The psychological health of the adult is called variously, self-fulfillment, emotional maturity, individuation, productiveness, self-actualization, authenticity, full-humanness, etc.

Healthy growth is conceptually subordinate, for it is usually defined now as "growth toward self-actualization," etc. Some psychologists speak simply in terms of one overarching goal or end, or tendency of human development, considering all immature growth phenomena to be only steps along the path to self-actualization (Goldstein, Rogers).

Self-actualization is defined in various ways but a solid core of agreement is perceptible. All definitions accept or imply, (a) acceptance and expression of the inner core or self, i.e., actualization of these latent capacities, and potentialities, "full functioning," availability of the human and personal essence. (b) They all imply minimal presence of ill health, neurosis, psychosis, of loss or diminution of the basic human and personal capacities.

15. For all these reasons, it is at this time best to bring out and encourage, or at the very least, to recognize this inner nature, rather than to suppress or repress it. Pure spontaneity consists of free, uninhibited, uncontrolled, trusting, unpremeditated expression of the self, i.e., of the psychic forces, with minimal interference by consciousness. Control, will, caution, self-criticism, measure, deliberateness are the brakes upon this expression made intrinsically necessary by the laws of the social and natural worlds outside the psychic world, and secondarily, made necessary by fear of the psyche itself (intrinsic counter-cathexis). Speaking in a very broad way, controls upon the psyche which come from *fear of the psyche* are largely neurotic or *psychotic*, or not intrinsically or theoretically necessary. (The healthy psyche is not terrible or horrible and therefore doesn't have to be feared, as it has been for thousands of years. Of course, the *unhealthy* psyche is another story.) This kind of control is usually lessened by psychological health, by deep psychotherapy, or by any *deeper* self-knowledge and self-acceptance. There are also, however, controls upon the psyche which do not come out of fear, but out of the necessities for keeping it integrated, organized and unified (intrinsic counter-cathexes). And there are also "controls," probably in another sense, which are necessary as capacities are actualized, and as higher forms of expression are sought for, e.g., acquisition of skills through hard work by the artist, the intellectual, the athlete. But these controls are eventually transcended and become aspects of spontaneity, as they become self.

The balance between spontaneity and control varies, then, as the health of the psyche and the health of the world vary. Pure spontaneity is not long possible because we live in a world which runs by its own, non-psychic laws. It *is* possible in dreams, fantasies, love, imagination, sex, the first stages of creativity, artistic work, intellectual play, free association, etc. Pure control is not permanently possible, for then the psyche dies. Education must be directed then *both* toward cultivation of controls and cultivation of spontaneity and expression. In our culture and at this point in history, it is necessary to redress the balance in favor of spontaneity, the ability to be expressive, passive, unwilled, trusting in processes other than will and control, unpremeditated, creative, etc. But it must be recognized that there have been and will be other cultures and other areas in which the balance was or will be in the other direction.

16. In the normal development of the normal child, it is now known that, *most* of the time, if he is given a really free choice, he will choose what is good for his growth. This he does because it tastes good, feels good, gives pleasure or *delight*. This implies that *he* "knows" better than anyone else what is good for him. A permissive regime means not that adults gratify his needs directly but make it possible for *him* to gratify his needs, and make his own choices, i.e., let him *be*. It is necessary in order for children to grow well that adults have enough trust in them and in the natural processes of growth, i.e., not interfere too much, not *make* them grow, or force them into predetermined designs, but rather *let* them grow and *help* them grow in a Taoistic rather than an authoritarian way.

17. Coordinated with this "acceptance" of the self, of fate, of one's call, is the conclusion that the main path to health and self-fulfillment for the masses is via basic need gratification rather than via frustration. This contrasts with the suppressive regime, the mistrust, the control, the policing that is necessarily implied by the belief in basic, instinctive evil in the human depths. Intrauterine life is completely gratifying and non-frustrating and it is now generally accepted that the first year or so of life had better also be primarily gratifying and non-frustrating. Asceticism, self-denial, deliberate rejection of the demands of the organism, at least in the West, tend to produce a diminished, stunted or crippled organism, and even in the East, bring self-actualization to only a very few, exceptionally strong individuals.

18. But we know also that the *complete absence* of frustration is dangerous. To be strong, a person must acquire frustration-tolerance, the ability to perceive physical reality as essentially indifferent to human wishes, the ability to love others and to enjoy their need-gratification as well as one's own (not to use other people only as means). The child with a good basis of safety, love and respect-need-gratification, is able to profit from nicely graded frustrations and become stronger thereby. If they are more than he can bear, if they overwhelm him, we call them traumatic, and consider them dangerous rather than profitable.

It is via the frustrating unyieldingness of physical reality and of animals and of other people that we learn about *their* nature, and thereby learn to differentiate wishes from facts (which things wishing makes come true, and which things proceed in complete disregard of our wishes), and are thereby enabled to live in the world and adapt to it as necessary.

We learn also about our own strengths and limits and extend them by overcoming difficulties, by straining ourselves to the utmost, by meeting challenge and hardship, even by failing. There can be great enjoyment in a great struggle and this can displace fear.

Overprotection implies that the child's needs are gratified *for* him by his parents, without effort of his own. This tends to infantilize him, to prevent development of his own strength, will and self-assertion. In one of its forms it may teach him to use other people rather than to respect them. In another form it implies a lack of trust and respect for the child's own powers and choices, i.e., it is essentially condescending and insulting, and can help to make a child feel worthless.

19. To make growth and self-actualization possible, it is necessary to understand that

capacities, organs and organ systems press to function and express themselves and to be used and exercised, and that such use is satisfying, and disuse irritating. The muscular person likes to use his muscles, indeed, *has* to use them in order to "feel good" and to achieve the subjective feeling of harmonious, successful, uninhibited functioning (spontaneity) which is so important an aspect of good growth and psychological health. So also for intelligence, for the uterus, the eyes, the capacity to love. Capacities clamor to be used, and cease their clamor only when they *are* well used. That is, capacities are also needs. Not only is it fun to use our capacities, but it is also necessary for growth. The unused skill or capacity or organ can become a disease center or else atrophy or disappear, thus diminishing the person.

20. The psychologist proceeds on the assumption that for his purposes there are two kinds of worlds, two kinds of reality, the natural world and the psychic world, the world of unyielding facts and the world of wishes, hopes, fears, emotions, the world which runs by non-psychic rules and the world which runs by psychic laws. This differentiation is not very clear except at its extremes, where there is no doubt that delusions, dreams and free associations are lawful and yet utterly different from the lawfulness of logic and from the lawfulness of the world which would remain if the human species died out. This assumption does not deny that these worlds are related and may even fuse.

I may say that this assumption is acted upon by *many* or *most* psychologists, even though they are perfectly willing to admit that it is an insoluble philosophical problem. Any therapist *must* assume it or give up his functioning. This is typical of the way in which psychologists bypass philosophical difficulties and act "as if" certain assumptions were true even though unprovable, e.g., the universal assumption of "responsibility," "will power," etc. One aspect of health is the ability to live in both of these worlds.

21. Immaturity can be contrasted with maturity from the motivational point of view, as the process of gratifying the deficiency-needs in their proper order. Maturity, or self-actualization, from this point of view, means to transcend the deficiency-needs. This state can be described then as metamotivated, or unmotivated (if deficiencies are seen as the only motivations). It can also be described as self-actualizing, Being, expressing, rather than coping. This state of Being, rather than of striving, is suspected to be synonymous with selfhood, with being "authentic," with being a person, with being fully human. The process of growth *is* the process of *becoming* a person. *Being* a person is different.

22. Immaturity can also be differentiated from maturity in terms of the cognitive capacities (and also in terms of the emotional capacities). Immature and mature cognition have been best described by Werner and Piaget. We can now add another differentiation, that between D-cognition and B-cognition (D = Deficiency, B = Being). D-cognition can be defined as the cognitions which are organized from the point of view of basic needs or deficiency-needs and their gratification and frustration. That is, D-cognition could be called selfish cognition, in which the world is organized into gratifiers and frustrators of our own needs, with other characteristics being ignored or slurred. The cognition of the object, in its own right and its own Being, without reference to its need-gratifying or need-frustrating qualities, that is, without primary reference to its value for the observer or its effects upon him, can be called B-cognition (or self-transcending, or unselfish, or objective cognition). The parallel with maturity is by no means perfect (children can also cognize in a selfless way), but in general, it is mostly true that with increasing selfhood or firmness of personal identity (or acceptance of one's own inner nature) B-cognition becomes easier and more frequent. (This is true even though D-cognition remains for *all* human beings, including the mature ones, the main tool for living-in-the-world.)

To the extent that perception is desire-less and fear-less, to that extent is it more veridical, in the sense of perceiving the true,'or essential or intrinsic whole nature of the object (without splitting it up by abstraction). Thus the goal of objective and true description of any reality is fostered by psychological health. Neurosis, psychosis, stunting of growth—all are, from this point of view, cognitive diseases as well, contaminating perception, learning, remembering, attending and thinking.

23. A by-product of this aspect of cognition is a better understanding of the higher and lower levels of love. D-love can be differentiated from B-love on approximately the same basis as D-cognition and B-cognition, or D-motivation and B-motivation. No ideally good relation to another human being, especially a child, is possible without B-love. Especially is it necessary for teaching, along with the Taoistic, trusting attitude that it implies. This is also true for our relations with the natural world, i.e., we can treat it in its own right, or we can treat it as if it were there only for our purposes.

24. Though, in principle, self-actualization is easy, in practice it rarely happens (by my criteria, certainly in less than 1% of the adult population). For this, there are many, many reasons at various levels of discourse, including all the determinants of psychopathology that we now know. We have already mentioned one main cultural reason, i.e., the conviction that man's intrinsic nature is evil or dangerous, and one biological determinant for the difficulty of achieving a mature self, namely that humans no longer have strong instincts which tell them unequivocally what to do, when, where and how.

There is a subtle but extremely important difference between regarding psychopathology as blocking or evasion or fear of growth toward self-actualization, and thinking of it in a medical fashion, as skin to invasion from without by tumors, poisons or bacteria, which have no relationship to the personality being invaded. Human diminution (the loss of human potentialities and capacities) is a more useful concept than ''illness'' for our theoretical purposes.

25. Growth has not only rewards and pleasures but also many intrinsic pains and always will have. Each step forward is a step into the unfamiliar and is possibly dangerous. It also means giving up something familiar and good and satisfying. It frequently means a parting and a separation, even a kind of death prior to rebirth, with consequent nostalgia, fear, loneliness and mourning. It also often means giving up a simpler and easier and less effortful life, in exchange for a more demanding, more responsible, more difficult life. Growth forward *is in spite* of these losses and therefore requires courage, will, choice, and strength in the individual, as well as protection, permission and encouragement from the environment, especially for the child.

26. It is therefore useful to think of growth or lack of it as the resultant of a dialectic between growth-fostering forces and growth-discouraging forces (regression, fear, pains of growth, ignorance, etc.). Growth has both advantages and disadvantages. Not-growing has not only disadvantages, but also advantages. The future pulls, but so also does the past. There is not only courage but also fear. The total way of growing healthily is, in principle, to enhance all the advantages of forward growth and all the disadvantages of not-growing, and to diminish all the disadvantages of growth forward and all the advantages of not-growing.

Homeostatic tendencies, ''need-reduction'' tendencies, and Freudian defense mechanisms are not growth-tendencies but are often defensive, pain-reducing postures of the organism. But they are quite necessary and not always pathological. They are generally prepotent over growth-tendencies.

27. All this implies a naturalistic system of values, a by-product of the empirical description of the deepest tendencies of the human species and of specific individuals. The study of the human being by science or by self-search can discover where he is heading, what

is his purpose in life, what is good for him and what is bad for him, what will make him feel virtuous and what will make him feel guilty, why choosing the good is often difficult for him, ·what the attractions of evil are. (Observe that the word ''ought'' need not be used. Also such knowledge of man is relative to man only and does not purport to be ''absolute.'')

28. A neurosis is not part of the inner core but rather a defense against or an evasion of it, as well as a distorted expression of it (under the aegis of fear). It is ordinarily a compromise between the effort to seek basic need gratifications in a covert or disguised or self-defeating way, and the fear of these needs, gratifications and motivated behaviors. To express neurotic needs, emotions, attitudes, definitions, action, etc., means *not* to express the inner core or real self fully. If the sadist or exploiter or pervert says, ''Why shouldn't *I* express myself?'' (e.g., by killing), or, ''Why shouldn't *I* actualize myself?'' the answer to them is that such expression is a denial of, and not an expression of, instinctoid tendencies (or inner core).

Each neuroticized need, or emotion or action is a *loss of capacity* to the person, something that he cannot do or *dare* not do except in a sneaky and unsatisfying way. In addition, he has usually lost his subjective well-being, his will, and his feeling of self-control, his capacity for pleasure, his self-esteem, etc. He is diminished as a human being.

29. The state of being without a system of values is psychopathogenic, we are learning. The human being needs a framework of values, philosophy of life, a religion or religion-surrogate to live by and understand by, in about the same sense that he needs sunlight, calcium or love. This I have called the ''cognitive need to understand.'' The value-illnesses which result from valuelessness are called variously anhedonia, anomie, apathy, amorality, hopelessness, cynicism, etc., and can become somatic illness as well. Historically, we are in a value interregnum in which all externally given value systems have proven to be failures (political, economic, religious, etc.) e.g., nothing is worth dying for. What man needs but doesn't have, he seeks for unceasingly, and he becomes dangerously ready to jump at *any* hope, good or bad. The cure for this disease is obvious. We need a validated, usable system of human values that we can believe in and devote ourselves to (be willing to die for), because they are true rather than because we are exhorted to ''believe and have faith.'' Such an empirically based Weltanschauung seems now to be a real possibility, at least in theoretical outline.

Much disturbance in children and adolescents can be understood as a consequence of the uncertainty of adults about their values. As a consequence, many youngsters in the United States live not by adult values but by adolescent values, which of course are immature, ignorant and heavily determined by confused adolescent needs. An excellent projection of these adolescent values is the cowboy, ''Western'' movie, or the delinquent gang.

30. At the level of self-actualizing, many dichotomies become resolved, opposites are seen to be unities and the whole dichotomous way of thinking is recognized to be immature. For self-actualizing people, there is a strong tendency for selfishness and unselfishness to fuse into a higher, superordinate unity. Work tends to be the same as play; vocation and avocation become the same thing. When duty is pleasant and pleasure is fulfillment of duty, then they lose their separateness and oppositeness. The highest maturity is discovered to include a childlike quality, and we discover healthy children to have some of the qualities of mature self-actualization. The inner-outer split, between self and all else, gets fuzzy and much less sharp, and they are seen to be permeable to each other at the highest levels of personality development. Dichotomizing seems now to be characteristic of a lower level of personality development and of psychological functioning; it is both a cause and an effect of psychopathology.

31. One especially important finding in self-actualizing people is that they tend to

integrate the Freudian dichotomies and trichotomies, i.e., the conscious, preconscious and the unconscious (as well as id, ego, superego). The Freudian "instincts" and the defenses are less sharply set off against each other. The impulses are more expressed and less controlled; the controls are less rigid, inflexible, anxiety-determined. The superego is less harsh and punishing and less set off against the ego. The primary and secondary cognitive processes are more equally available and more equally valued (instead of the primary processes being stigmatized as pathological). Indeed, in the "peak-experience" the walls between them tend to fall together.

This is in sharp contrast with the early Freudian position in which these various forces were sharply dichotomized as (a) mutually exclusive, (b) with antagonistic interests, i.e., as antagonistic forces rather than as complementary or collaborating ones, and (c) one "better" than the other.

Again we imply here (sometimes) a healthy unconscious, and desirable regression. Furthermore, we imply also an integration of rationality and irrationality with the consequence that irrationality may, in its place, also be considered healthy, desirable or even necessary.

32. Healthy people are more integrated in another way. In them the conative, the cognitive, the affective and the motor are less separated from each other, and are more synergic, i.e., working collaboratively without conflict to the same ends. The conclusions of rational, careful thinking are apt to come to the same conclusions as those of the blind appetites. What such a person wants and enjoys is apt to be just what is good for him. His spontaneous reactions are as capable, efficient and right as if they had been thought out in advance. His sensory and motor reactions are more closely correlated. His sensory modalities are more connected with each other (physiognomical perception). Furthermore, we have learned the difficulties and dangers of those age-old rationalistic systems in which the capacities were thought to be arranged dichotomously-hierarchically, with rationality at the top, rather than in an integration.

33. This development toward the concept of a healthy unconscious, and of a healthy irrationality, sharpens our awareness of the limitations of purely abstract thinking, of verbal thinking and of analytic thinking. If our hope is to describe the world fully, a place is necessary for preverbal, ineffable, metaphorical, primary process, concrete-experience, intuitive and esthetic types of cognition, for there are certain aspects of reality which can be cognized in no other way. Even in science this is true, now that we know (a) that creativity has its roots in the nonrational, (2) that language is and must always be inadequate to describe total reality, (3) that any abstract concept leaves out much of reality, and (4) that what we call "knowledge" (which is usually highly abstract and verbal and sharply defined) often serves to blind us to those portions of reality not covered by the abstraction. That is, it makes us more able to see some things, but *less* able to see other things. Abstract knowledge has its dangers as well as its uses.

Science and education, being too exclusively abstract, verbal and bookish, don't have enough place for raw, concrete, esthetic experience, especially of the subjective happenings inside oneself. For instance, organismic psychologists would certainly agree on the desirability of more creative education in perceiving and creating art, in dancing, in (Greek style) athletics and in phenomenological observation.

The ultimate of abstract, analytical thinking, is the greatest simplification possible, i.e., the formula, the diagram, the map, the blueprint, the schema, the cartoon, and certain types of abstract paintings. Our mastery of the world is enhanced thereby, but its richness may be lost as a forfeit, *unless* we learn to value B-cognitions, perception-with-love-and-care, free-floating attention, all of which enrich the experience instead of impoverishing it. There is no reason why ''science'' should not be expanded to include both kinds of knowing.

34. This ability of healthier people to dip into the unconscious and preconscious, to use and value their primary processes instead of fearing them, to accept their impulses instead of always controlling them, to be able to regress voluntarily without fear, turns out to be one of the main conditions of creativity. We can then understand why psychological health is so closely tied up with certain universal forms of creativeness (aside from special talent), as to lead some writers to make them almost synonymous.

This same tie between health and integration of rational and irrational forces (conscious and unconscious, primary and secondary processes) also permits us to understand why psychologically healthy people are more able to enjoy, to love, to laugh, to have fun, to be humorous, to be silly, to be whimsical and fantastic, to be pleasantly ''crazy,'' and in general to permit and value and enjoy emotional experiences in general and peak-experiences in particular and to have them more often. And it leads us to the strong suspicion that learning *ad hoc* to be able to do all these things may help the child move toward health.

35. Esthetic perceiving and creating and esthetic peak-experiences are seen to be a central aspect of human life and of psychology and education rather than a peripheral one. This is true for several reasons. (1) All the peak-experiences are (among other characteristics) integrative of the splits within the person, between persons, within the world, and between the person and the world. Since one aspect of health is integration, the peak-experiences are moves toward health and are themselves momentary healths. (2) These experiences are life-validating, i.e., they make life worthwhile. These are certainly an important part of the answer to the question, ''Why don't we all commit suicide?'' (3) They are worthwhile in themselves, etc.

36. Self-actualization does not mean a transcendence of all human problems. Conflict, anxiety, frustration, sadness, hurt, and guilt can all be found in healthy human beings. In general, the movement, with increasing maturity, is from neurotic pseudoproblems to the real, unavoidable, existential problems, inherent in the nature of man (even at his best) living in a particular kind of world. Even though he is not neurotic he may be troubled by real, desirable and necessary guilt rather than neurotic guilt (which isn't desirable or necessary), by an intrinsic conscience (rather than the Freudian superego). Even though he has transcended the problems of Becoming, there remain the problems of Being. To be untroubled when one *should* be troubled can be a sign of sickness. Sometimes, smug people have to be scared ''*into* their wits.''

37. Self-actualization is not altogether general. It takes place via femaleness *or* maleness, which are prepotent to general-humanness. That is, one must first be a healthy, femaleness-fulfilled woman or maleness-fulfilled man before general-human self-actualization becomes possible.

There is also a little evidence that different constitutional types actualize themselves in somewhat different ways (because they have different inner selves to actualize).

38. Another crucial aspect of healthy growth of selfhood and full-humanness is dropping away the techniques used by the child, in his weakness and smallness, for adapting himself to the strong, large, all-powerful, omniscient, godlike adults. He must replace these with the techniques of being strong and independent and of being a parent himself. This involves especially giving up the child's desperate wish for the exclusive, total love of his parents while learning to love others. He must learn to gratify his own needs and wishes, rather than the needs of his parents, and he must learn to gratify them himself, rather than depending upon the parents to do this for him. He must give up being good out of fear and in

order to keep their love, and must be good because *he* wishes to be. He must discover his own conscience and give up his internalized parents as a sole ethical guide. All these techniques by which weakness adapts itself to strength are necessary for the child but immature and stunting in the adult. He must replace fear with courage.

39. From this point of view, a society or a culture can be either growth-fostering or growth-inhibiting. The sources of growth and of humanness are essentially within the human person and are not created or invented by society, which can only help or hinder the development of humanness, just as a gardener can help or hinder the growth of a rose-bush, but cannot determine that it shall be an oak tree. This is true even though we know that a culture is a *sine qua non* for the actualization of humanness itself, e.g., language, abstract thought, ability to love; but these exist as potentialities in human germ plasm prior to culture.

This makes theoretically possible a comparative sociology, transcending and including cultural relativity. The "better" culture gratifies all basic human needs and permits self-actualization. The "poorer" cultures do not. The same is true for education. To the extent that it fosters growth toward self-actualization, it is "good" education.

As soon as we speak of "good" or "bad" cultures, and take them as means rather than as ends, the concept of "adjustment" comes into question. We must ask, "What kind of culture or subculture is the 'Well adjusted' person well adjusted *to?*" Adjustment is, very definitely, *not* necessarily synonymous with psychological health.

40. The achievement of self-actualization (in the sense of autonomy) paradoxically makes *more* possible the transcendence of self, and of self-consciousness and of selfishness. It makes it *easier* for the person to be homonomous, i.e., to merge himself as a part in a larger whole than himself. The condition of the fullest homonomy is full autonomy, and to some extent, vice versa, one can attain to autonomy only via successful homonomous experiences (child dependence, B-love, care for others, etc.). It is necessary to speak of levels of homonomy (more and more mature), and to differentiate a "low homonomy" (of fear, weakness, and regression) from a "high homonomy" (of courage and full, self-confident autonomy), a "low Nirvana" from a "high Nirvana," union downward from union upward.

41. An important existential problem is posed by the fact that self-actualizing persons (and *all* people in their peak-experiences) occasionally live out-of-time and out-of-the-world (atemporal and aspatial) even though mostly they *must* live in the outer world. Living in the inner psychic world (which is ruled by psychic laws and not by the laws of outer-reality), i.e., the world of experience, of emotion, of wishes and fears and hopes, of love, of poetry, art, and fantasy, is different from living in and adapting to the non-psychic reality which runs by laws he never made and which are not essential to his nature even though he has to live by them. (He *could*, after all, live in other kinds of worlds, as any science fiction fan knows.) The person who is not afraid of this inner, psychic world, can enjoy it to such an extent that it may be called Heaven by contrast with the more effortful, fatiguing, externally responsible world of "reality," of striving and coping, of right and wrong, of truth and falsehood. This is true even though the healthier person can also adapt more easily and enjoyably to the "real" world, and has better "reality testing," i.e., doesn't confuse it with his inner psychic world.

It seems clear now that confusing these inner and outer realities, or having either closed off from experience, is highly pathological. The healthy person is able to integrate them both into his life and therefore has to give up neither, being able to go back and forth voluntarily. The difference is the same as the one between the person who can *visit* the slums and the one who is forced to live there always. (*Either* world is a slum if one can't leave it.) Then, paradoxically, that which was sick and pathological and the "lowest" becomes part of the healthiest and "highest" aspect of human nature. Slipping into "craziness" is frightening only for those who are not fully confident of their sanity. Education must help the person to live in both worlds.

42. The foregoing propositions generate a different understanding of the role of action in psychology. Goal-directed, motivated, coping, striving, purposeful action is an aspect or by-product of the necessary transactions between a psychic and a non-psychic world.

(a) The D-need gratifications come from the world outside the person, not from within. Therefore adaptation to this world is made necessary, e.g., reality-testing, knowing the nature of this world, learning to differentiate this world from the inner world, learning the nature of people and of society, learning to delay gratification, learning to conceal what would be dangerous, learning which portions of the world are gratifying and which dangerous, or useless for need-gratification, learning the approved and permitted cultural paths to gratification and techniques of gratification.

(b) The world is in itself interesting, beautiful and fascinating. Exploring it, manipulating it, playing with it, contemplating it, enjoying it are all motivated kinds of action (cognitive, motor, and esthetic needs).

But there is also action which has little or nothing to do with the world, at any rate at first. Sheer expression of the nature or state or powers (Funktionslust) of the organism is an expression of Being rather than of striving. And the contemplation and enjoyment of the inner life not only is a kind of "action" in itself but is also antithetical to action in the world, i.e., it produces stillness and cessation of muscular activity. The ability to wait is a special case of being able to suspend action.

43. From Freud we learned that the past exists *now* in the person. Now we must learn, from growth theory and self-actualization theory, that the future also *now* exists in the person in the form of ideals, hopes, duties, tasks, plans, goals, unrealized potentials, mission, fate, destiny, etc. One for whom no future exists is reduced to the concrete, to hopelessness, to emptiness. For him, time must be endlessly "filled." Striving, the usual organizer of most activity, when lost, leaves the person unorganized and unintegrated.

Of course, being in a state of Being needs no future, because it is already *there*. Then Becoming ceases for the moment and its promissory notes are cashed in the form of the ultimate rewards, i.e., the peak-experiences, in which time disappears and hopes are fulfilled.

Rosemary Rizzo and Edgar Vinacke
SELF-ACTUALIZATION AND
THE MEANING OF CRITICAL EXPERIENCE

In recent years we have seen a remarkable movement in psychology toward the study of cognitive processes. In experimental psychology, for example, we can point to an outburst of interest in conceptual behavior and in mediation as it affects verbal learning. The investigation of imagery (Klinger, 1971) and dreams (Foulkes, 1966) has become a well-developed enterprise. In clinical psychology, cognitive theories like those of Adler (Ansbacher & Ansbacher, 1956) and Kelly (1955) among others, are receiving more attention. Perhaps, too, we shall in the future witness a greater effort to examine the implications of Jungian theory for an understanding of cognition (Hall & Lindzey, 1970). Piaget's theories of cognitive development have also become a dominant force in developmental psychology. Since humanistic psychologists are a major force in emphasizing intrinsic states as a proper field of study, their principles must sooner or later be brought within the scope of systematic investigation. Both Rogers (1961) and Maslow (1967) have seen their theoretical statements in this light.

Can there be a better way to examine cognitive events than to look as directly as possible at the character of human experience? Such an approach is familiar enough in clinical psychology, where, through interviews and personal reporting, a person supplies information that can then be interpreted. However, we are more likely to reach an understanding of a single individual rather than of human experience in general. If one seeks to look across the personal reports of a large sample of people, methodological issues arise that defy ready solution.

Our study is a modest attempt to find out something about important personal experiences. Humanistic writers emphasize that self-actualization is a continuous process of growth toward fuller fulfillment of one's potentials and that healthy persons achieve both a better understanding of themselves and of the world. They also increasingly move toward levels of existence that transcend lower basic needs (toward the realization of values of "being," such as truth, goodness, beauty, unity, perfection, and self-sufficiency; see Maslow, 1967). We ought to see, therefore, such trends reflected in the kinds of experiences people regard as important. Furthermore, Frankl (1959) has movingly described the significance of personal experiences in discovering the meaning of life, which he regards as the fundamental trend in human growth. From these perspectives, we ought to see the differences between persons lower and higher in self-actualization in the meanings they derive from their experiences. In addition, because we are concerned with personal growth, we might expect to see differences between younger and older persons in the effects of experiences.

Reprinted by permission from the *Journal of Humanistic Psychology*, 1975, *15*, 9–20.

METHOD

The 65 subjects for this study fall into three age groups, 41 college students (18–25 years; 22 male, 19 female), 9 mature adults (35–55 years; 2 male, 7 female), and 15 old persons (70–80 years; 7 male, 8 female). The students were recruited from undergraduate classes. To obtain the mature adult subjects one of the experimenters made house-to-house calls, explaining the character of the study and inviting whoever answered the door to participate. Since we included the middle group primarily to provide an anchorage point for interpreting the results—and since, in fact, the findings seem quite clear—we are not overly concerned about the small number obtained. Nevertheless, the small size of this subsample must be kept in mind. The old people were all volunteers secured by the help of professional personnel in three residences.[1]

Measure of Self-Actualization

The Personal Orientation Inventory (POI) was administered to all subjects. This test was developed by Shostrom (1966) to assess the characteristics of self-actualization, as described mainly by Maslow and Rogers. Many studies have been devoted to checking the POI's reliability and validity. The POI compares favorably in reliability to other personality tests (e.g., Ilardi & May, 1968; Klavetter & Mogar, 1967). Although "fakeable" by subjects schooled in concepts of self-actualization (Braun, 1966), it is apparently quite difficult for the average person who lacks knowledge of self-actualizing theory to represent himself favorably in that respect (Foulds & Warehime, 1971). Validity, as always, presents greater problems. Shostrom (1966) cites various studies that demonstrate significant differences between groups clinically judged to be higher and lower in self-actualization. Several studies suggest that sensitivity training may result in improved test scores (Culbert, Clark, & Bobele, 1968, for example, found one group changed, another did not), that POI scores correlate with "positive mental health" (Leib & Snyder, 1968), and that campus demonstrators score higher on most of the scales than do nondemonstrators (Freeman & Brubaker, 1971). Finally, high and low scorers differ significantly on a number of other test variables, such as some of the Edwards Personal Preference Schedule scales (Grossack, Armstrong, & Lussier, 1966; LeMay & Damm, 1969), the neurotic scale of the Eysenck Personality Inventory (Knapp, 1965), and the Rotter Internal-External Control Scale (Wall, 1970).

The POI consists of the following scales: Time Competence (Tc), Inner-Direction (I), Self-Actualizing Values (SAV), Existentiality (Ex), Feeling Reactivity (FR), Spontaneity (S), Self-Regard (SR), Self-Acceptance (SA), Nature of Man (Na), Synergy (Sy), Acceptance of Aggression (A), and Capacity for Intimate Contact (C).

Reports of Important Experiences

The subjects were given the following instruction sheet, along with additional sheets of paper:

[1]Our thanks in this regard go to Otto Popper and Dorothy Gawranski of the Rosa Coplon Jewish Home and Infirmary, Ann Wayland and Priscilla Armstrong of the Presbyterian Homes of Western New York, and Cathy Dirschedl of the St. Francis Home.

Critical Experiences

Everyone has personal experiences during his life that are especially significant. They may be all kinds of different things, happy or unhappy, a single event or a longer episode, or private or involving others, and so forth. All kinds of different experiences are important to different people. Spend some time carefully thinking back over your life and the kinds of experiences you have had.

Which experiences seem most critical for your life? As most important and significant to you, please describe each event briefly. Tell what they were; when they occurred; where they happened; who else, if anyone, was involved; and describe your feelings and thoughts. Also, explain what consequences they had for your life. Evaluate what the experiences personally meant to you—that is, what was the meaning you derived from them?

Please write each experience on a different sheet of paper and after you have finished, rate them according to importance—for example: No. 1 for most important, No. 2 for the next important, etc.

All information is strictly confidential, and no names will be needed.

A second set of materials came from a questionnaire intended to supplement the written report. Items concerned such points as why the event was important, feelings about and understanding of the experience, whether the event (if tragic) might have had some beneficial consequences or (if happy) it might have had some unfortunate effects, and whether the subject could think of other experiences, not previously mentioned, about which he wished to talk.

A wide variety of significant experiences were reported. Especially frequent were death or illness of the subject or a loved one, love affairs, marriage, and personal accomplishment. The college group often described social and family problems as critical. The older subjects usually cited events that occurred during their mature adult years, rather than earlier years, and childhood incidents were rare at all age levels. Unhappy and tragic experiences were reported about twice as often as happy ones.

The present study utilizes as data only the experience rated as most important. Since the subjects produced different numbers of experiences, this decision obviated the necessity to devise some method of weighting or averaging. The experience rated as most important was reported most fully and appeared to offer the most information for our purposes.

We used the following categories to dimensionalize the experiences:

1. *Happy vs. unhappy*: whether the subject generally felt that the event was personally satisfying;

2. *Self or others vs. life-in-general*: whether the subject interpreted the experience as teaching him something important about himself or other people[2] or about the character or meaning of life;

3. *Positive or mixed vs. negative*: whether the emotions at the time the event occurred were positive, such as happiness, pride, and love, or negative, such as anger, fear, anxiety, or guilt;

4. *Same vs. different*: whether the subject felt now that he had not been changed by the experience or had been basically altered by it; and

5. *Better vs. worse*: the degree to which, in general, the subject felt that he had significantly benefited from the experience—even, for example, in the case of losing a loved

[2]Originally these aspects were treated as separate categories, but a low incidence of "others" made us decide to combine them.

one, a person may come to appreciate better the good qualities of the lost person, or acquire increased compassion for the suffering of others, or could see nothing but bad consequences.

One of the authors served as a primary judge in making ratings of these dimensions, with the other author checking on them and helping to resolve ambiguities. In treating the data, each subsample was divided at the median on each dimension.

Procedure

Since the three age groups posed different problems in data collection, we adapted the procedure to each one. The college subjects were given a packet of materials to take with them. Sealed and numbered envelopes contained the POI, the report-of-experience form, and the questionnaire. Instructions asked the subject to open the three envelopes in specified order. For one-half, the POI was placed in envelope number 1, for the other half it was placed in envelope number 3. The questionnaire always followed the report envelope. The instructions required the subject to return the material to its proper envelope and then to reseal it, before proceeding to the next one. A similar method was employed for the mature adults, except that the materials were given to them at home, with the experimenter returning at a later date to pick them up. Since we wanted the subjects to work in privacy and to have an opportunity to think about the assignment, the aged people were also given the report and POI packets (numbered to control for order) at home. Recruitment was, therefore, limited by the subject's reading and writing skills. In place of the questionnaire, each old subject was personally interviewed to cover these items.

Design for Analysis of Variance

The data were treated with three independent variables, age, sex, and experience-category, with POI scales as dependent measures ($3 \times 2 \times 2$ design). The analysis of interactions involving sex and age is, however, incomplete, because the male-mature adult cell contains only two cases. An analysis was run for each experience dimension for each POI scale.[3]

RESULTS

There was no main effect for sex on any of the POI scales, indicating that males and females are, on the average, very much alike in these self-actualizing variables. Age differences on the POI, however, are very striking, as shown in Table 1. In general, the college students and mature adults are much alike, with the old subjects scoring markedly lower. However, differences are not significant for Time Competence, Self-Actualizing Values, Self-Regard, Nature of Man, and Synergy. In addition, the mature adults tend to fall in between the other groups. These results are certainly very provocative. It appears that many of the POI scales reflect the attitudes, feelings, or roles of the young person, a point important to consider in the general theory of self-actualization. Scales that seem most explicitly to fit the theory display nonsignificant age differences (e.g., SAV, Na, Sy). Especially to be noted are the almost identical means across age groups for self-regard. Evidently, whatever the differences with age, there is retained a level of perceived self-worth quite comparable to that of the young adult; older subjects are significantly lower in Self-Acceptance, however.

---

[3]We wish to thank Steven Lewis for his assistance in planning and conducting the computer analyses.

Finally, the very large differences in Existentiality, Capacity for Intimate Contact, and other scales suggest that older persons (at least those who live in residence homes) display a decrement in personal functioning itself, rather than in areas of valuing.

The "Same-Different" and "Self-Life" dimensions rated showed very little relation to POI scores. The experience categories of "Happy-Unhappy," "Positive-Negative" and "Better-Worse" yielded numerous significant differences, showing a clear trend in the direction of higher POI scores for subjects whose experiences were judged to be *"Happy,"* *"Positive,"* and *"Better"* (see Tables 1 and 2). Table 2 and Figure 1 show that people who perceived their most significant past experience as *bettering their lives* scored higher on the POI scales regardless of their age group. (There are only five exceptions.) This finding holds for the older subjects even though they score significantly lower on almost all POI scales.

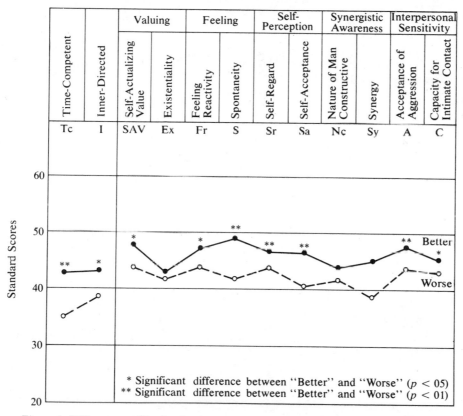

Figure 1. POI mean profiles for *S*s whose experiences fell into "Better" (*N* = 31) and "Worse" (*N* = 34) categories.

Interactions

Several significant interactions were found. With respect to Feeling Reactivity, the Age × Positive-Negative interaction showed that the old subjects did not differ, but the college students who reported positive experiences scored higher with the opposite effect for the

Table 1. POI means by age and experience category

Scale	Age					Experience							
	Col-lege[a]	Mature adult[b]	Old[c]	F	p<	Posi-tive	Nega-tive	F	p<	Happy	Un-happy	F	p<
Tc	15.4	16.2	13.4	1.75	ns	15.5	14.6	2.67	ns	15.7	14.6	3.30	ns
I	80.4	76.9	63.9	7.22	.002	77.1	75.3	5.47	.02	77.0	75.5	4.42	.04
SAV	19.2	19.1	17.3	1.78	ns	19.1	18.5	2.64	ns	19.3	18.4	3.79	ns
Ex	20.3	17.4	12.1	21.81	.001	17.3	18.7	2.12	ns	17.2	18.6	1.69	ns
FR	15.4	14.8	10.5	13.40	.001	14.0	14.4	3.26	ns	13.8	14.5	1.65	ns
S	11.3	10.6	8.3	6.51	.01	10.9	10.2	7.58	.01	10.8	10.3	5.84	.02
SR	11.1	11.4	11.5	.28	ns	12.1	10.6	6.16	.02	12.2	10.7	5.88	.02
SA	15.2	15.8	12.3	3.97	.03	14.7	14.4	1.91	ns	14.8	14.4	1.92	ns
Na	11.4	11.3	10.3	1.15	ns	11.5	10.9	2.97	ns	11.5	10.9	3.23	ns
Sy	6.7	6.3	5.8	1.49	ns	6.6	6.3	3.14	ns	6.7	6.2	4.29	.05
A	16.0	16.9	11.9	10.62	.001	15.0	15.4	1.33	ns	14.8	15.5	.64	ns
C	18.1	14.9	12.9	10.13	.001	16.0	16.8	1.32	ns	15.9	16.8	.70	ns

Note.—Analysis of variance with $df = 2,54$ for age and $df = 1,54$ for experience categories.
[a]N = 41.
[b]N = 9.
[c]N = 15.

Table 2. POI means by age and "Better" or "Worse" past experience

Scale	Experience	Age College	Adult	Old	Combined	F[a]	$p<$
Tc	Better	16.2	17.5	14.4	15.9	6.84	.01
	Worse	14.5	13.7	9.3	13.8		
I	Better	84.2	78.7	65.1	77.7	4.34	.04
	Worse	76.1	73.3	59.0	73.7		
SAV	Better	19.9	20.2	17.4	19.2	4.10	.05
	Worse	18.4	17.0	17.0	18.0		
Ex	Better	21.4	17.2	12.7	18.1	3.47	ns
	Worse	19.1	18.0	10.0	17.9		
FR	Better	16.6	14.5	15.3	14.5	6.42	.02
	Worse	14.0	10.5	10.3	13.7		
S	Better	12.9	10.8	8.6	11.3	21.66	.001
	Worse	9.5	10.0	7.0	9.2		
SR	Better	12.1	11.8	11.7	11.9	7.30	.01
	Worse	10.0	10.7	11.0	10.2		
SA	Better	16.6	16.7	12.6	15.4	10.78	.01
	Worse	13.4	14.0	11.0	13.2		
Na	Better	11.6	12.2	10.5	11.4	1.58	ns
	Worse	11.2	9.7	9.7	10.8		
Sy	Better	7.0	7.0	5.8	6.7	3.36	ns
	Worse	6.3	5.0	5.7	6.1		
A	Better	17.6	16.8	11.7	15.7	9.52	.01
	Worse	14.2	17.0	12.7	14.4		
C	Better	19.4	14.2	13.8	16.9	6.16	.02
	Worse	16.6	16.3	9.3	15.7		

[a]Analysis of variance for combined means; $df = 1,54$.

mature adults ($F_{2,54} = 3.90, p < .03$). The interaction between Sex and the Positive-Negative dimension showed that females who reported negative experiences scored higher on Existentiality, but with little difference for males ($F_{1,54} = 4.48, p < .04$). This effect suggests that females are *more* flexible than males in learning from negative experiences, a point that deserves further investigation.

DISCUSSION

Two features of these data require careful interpretation; namely, their contribution to an understanding of the self-actualizing process and to clarifying the properties of the POI.

On the first point, the results very strongly and consistently show that persons who differ in the effects of their experiences also differ in the variables measured by the POI. Those persons, at all ages, who score higher on self-actualizing characteristics report generally more positive and personally satisfying ("happy") experiences, and quite strikingly interpret them as having beneficial effects on them. There is, to this extent, confirmation of Frankl's contention that actualization is associated with abilities to derive positive and meaningful interpretations from experience. Even a casual perusal of the reports reveals this difference quite clearly. For example, the individuals who score lower frequently say that the reported experience left them with distrust, hostility, profound disillusionment, a sense of loss, and so on, whereas high scorers emphasize such effects as appreeiation of the good qualities in others, increased independence or self-control or self-knowledge, and greater faith in human capacities for solving problems of existence.

The other point concerns what the POI actually measures. The general tenor of the results accords with the logic that underlies the test. However, the distinctive pattern of age differences poses some interesting questions. In the first place, we must consider the possibility that this test, like others, may not be equally appropriate for old and young subjects. No doubt it was constructed primarily for use with the latter, so that some unknown number of items may be biased in that direction. In addition, the special test-taking attitudes of aged persons may be a factor in their tendency to score lower. Until there is greater attention to the test-taking behavior of old persons, we cannot tell whether their POI scores actually reflect age-related differences.

But the fact that significant differences did not occur for certain scales indicates that it is the POI that needs to be reexamined as it bears on self-actualization. Many of the low scores of the aged subjects seem to reflect a decline in intellectual or behavioral efficiency, rather than in values, sense of fulfillment, or the understanding and appreciation of life. After all, what does the concept of self-actualization signify? It is hard to believe that the typical old person is *less* self-actualized than the younger individual. (And he or she certainly seems to be just as well-developed in self-regard and in values.) The interpretation is justified, then, that many of the POI scales are better indicators of the attitudes, feelings, and self-concepts of that period in life which we generally regard as most productive in work, interpersonal, social, and community activities. Thus, to some extent, high scores on the POI may stereotype the normal, socially approved mature adult. Probably, then, some of the scales are not really sensitive to the valuing, understanding, integrative, and transcending implications of self-actualization theory.

REFERENCES

Ansbacher, H. L., & Ansbacher, R. R. *The individual psychology of Alfred Adler*. New York: Basic Books, 1956.

Braun, J. R. Effects of "typical neurotic" and "after therapy" sets on Personal Orientation Inventory scores. *Psychological Reports,* 1966, *19,* 1282.

Culbert, S. A., Clark, J. V., & Bobclc, H. K. Measures of change toward self-actualization in two sensitivity training groups. *Journal of Counseling Psychology,* 1968, *15,* 53–57.

Foulds, M. L., & Warehime, R. G. Effects of a "fake good" response set on a measure of self-actualization. *Journal of Counseling Psychology,* 1971, *18,* 279–280.

Foulkes, D. *The psychology of sleep*. New York: Scribner's, 1966.

Frankl, V. E. *Man's search for meaning: An introduction to logotherapy*. New York: Simon & Schuster, 1959.

Freeman, H. R., & Brubaker, P. Personality characteristics of campus demonstrators compared to nondemonstrators. *Journal of Counseling Psychology,* 1971, *18,* 462–464.

Grossack, M. M., Armstrong, T., & Lussier, G. Correlates of self-actualization. *Journal of Humanistic Psychology,* 1966, *6,* 87–88.

Hall, C. S., & Lindzey, G. *Theories of personality*. (2nd ed.) New York: Wiley, 1970.

Ilardi, R. L., & May, W. T. A reliability study of Shostrom's Personal Orientation Inventory. *Journal of Humanistic Psychology,* 1968, *8,* 68–72.

Kelly, G. A. *The psychology of personal constructs*. Vol. I. *A theory of personality*. New York: Norton, 1955.

Klavetter, R. E., & Mogar, R. E. Stability and internal consistency of a measure of self-actualization. *Psychological Reports,* 1967, *21,* 422–424.

Klinger, E. *Structure and functions of fantasy.* New York: Wiley-Interscience, 1971.

Knapp, R. R. Relationship of a measure of self-actualization to neuroticism and extraversion. *Journal of Consulting Psychology,* 1965, *29,* 168–172.

Leib, J. W., & Snyder, W. U. Achievement and positive mental health. *Journal of Counseling Psychology,* 1968, *15,* 388–389.

LeMay, M. L., & Damm, V. J. Relationship of the Personal Orientation Inventory to the Edwards Personal Preference Schedule. *Psychological Reports,* 1969, *24,* 834.

Maslow, A. H. A theory of metamotivation: The biological rooting of the value-life. *Journal of Humanistic Psychology,* 1967, *7,* 93–127.

Rogers, C. R. *On becoming a person; A therapist's view of psychotherapy.* Boston: Houghton Mifflin, 1961.

Shostrom, E. L. *Manual: Personal Orientation Inventory.* San Diego, Calif.: Educational and Testing Service, 1966.

Wall, J. B. Relationships of locus of control to self-actualization. *Psychological Reports,* 1970, *27,* 282.

M. Brewster Smith
AN EXAMINATION OF A FOCAL THEME
IN MASLOW'S PSYCHOLOGY

Somewhere Abe Maslow observed that self-actualizing people manage to transcend their ambivalences. Over many years—essentially the full course of my life as a psychologist thus far—I have been profoundly ambivalent about Maslow's contributions. There is much in his writings that appeals to me strongly. There is much else that sets my intellectual teeth on edge and makes me squirm in discomfort or withdraw in impatience or disagreement. When I am most annoyed I typically find that if I read on, in his great tolerance for ambiguity—indeed, his evident delight in the intellectually inchoate and disordered—Abe has anticipated my objections and said something sensible to mollify me (though usually not to put in order the problems that bothered me). My personal relationship with Abe was small but delightful; my intellectual relationship with his writings has been ambivalent to the core.

This essay is an attempt to penetrate and transcend my ambivalence by focusing on a theme that is recurrent and central in Maslow's writings, that is, self-actualization. It is a theme that he shares with other spokesmen of humanistic psychology (e.g., Rogers, 1961), and it is central to the rationale of the personal growth movement (see Back, 1972) of Esalen-style centers and encounter groups with which humanistic psychology is linked. I have to come to terms with it, if I am to make further headway with my private agenda (Smith, 1969a, 1972b), to advance a psychology that is both *humanistic* (germane to man's experience and distinctive concerns) and *scientific* in a sense that is more self-critical, more abstractive, and hence, I believe, more potentially self-corrective and cumulative than Maslow's "Taoistic" version of science (Maslow, 1966; Smith, 1966). The time is ripe for me to face the problem head-on—and a difficult, weighty problem it is. As Maslow (1971) has noted, "the notion of self-actualization gets to be almost like a Rorschach inkblot [p. 41]"—a test of a psychologist's fundamental conceptions of human nature.

SOME PERSONAL AGENDA

I have been worrying about aspects of the problem ever since I wrote a sophomoric paper in college on "Nietzsche, Ibsen, and Shaw" that helped to resolve my major adolescent identity crisis by formulating an ideal of authentic yea-saying selfhood that creates human meaning in an otherwise bleak and Godless universe. (The Ibsen I examined was *Peer Gynt*; the Shaw, *Man and Superman*.) Reading and rereading Maslow for the present purpose, I realized with a shock how significant Nietzsche also must have been to him (e.g., Maslow,

Reprinted by permission from the *Journal of Humanistic Psychology*, 1973, *13*, 17–33.
Written at the invitation of Bertha Maslow and originally intended for a volume of critical essays on Maslow's work.

1954, p. 201; 1971, p. 37). Not only does he share Nietzsche's concern about a nontheological basis for human values, but the Superman reappears in the guise of the self-actualizing person. There are even echoes of Nietzsche in the aphoristic style of Maslow's later, less self-censored writings. Be that as it may, over the years I have been drawn again and again to the problem of the psychological status of values, how to avoid the twin perils of ethnocentric (or theological) *absolutism* with its vulnerable dogmas and of a *relativism* that undercuts the significance of human choice. (Self-actualization in its various meanings is intrinsically concerned with values. For Maslow, the doctrine bridged the gulf between value and fact.)

As I came to focus these persisting concerns in an attempt to clarify the nature and criteria of psychological well-being or "positive mental health," I arrived at a skeptical view that nevertheless seemed to me to be liberating. I argued (Smith, 1969a, pp. 179–190) that "mental health" is not a scientific concept at all, but more in the nature of a chapter heading under which any and all evaluative perspectives on human personality can be placed. Proposed criteria of mental health—like the ability to love and work, realistic perception, integration, and active mastery—are values in terms of which personality may be appraised. Scientific psychology cannot settle *which* values people should live by, and psychological arguments about criteria of mental health are therefore fruitless. But psychologists make a distinctive contribution to the discussion when they discover developmental and situational conditions under which particular values can be realized and consequences or side effects of pursuing particular values. This was not quite a relativistic position, since I assumed that in the light of such evidence and of human experience people's value choices might converge. My plea to those concerned with "mental health" was to be explicit about which values they had in mind, and not to use the global concept as a cover to impose their own idiosyncratic values in the name of science. This still seems to me good advice, and, as I will shortly make clear, it underlies a major bone that I have to pick with Maslow.

As it turned out, I could not remain comfortable with this uncommitted, skeptical position, since it gave me no help with my sociopolitical concerns for human betterment (another point where I feel a strong resonance with Maslow). (He too was a basically optimistic reformist.) In the moral atmosphere of the War on Poverty, it appeared that the public interest in mental health criteria dictated a primary focus on human effectiveness as a successor to the gross value of not-illness (appropriate to the institutional psychiatry of an earlier day) of that of personal adjustment and fulfillment (appropriate to the private client in the consulting room) (Smith, 1969b). I drew upon Robert White's (1959) motivationally based concept of competence for the key to a reformulated conception of "positive mental health" that seemed more adequate to the needs of the times.

Mulling over what seemed to me the requirements for survival at our critical juncture in human history, my own direct experience with Peace Corps volunteers and college youth, and directly cogent new research by Rotter (1966) and De Charms (1968), I came to refocus my thinking about "competence" upon processes of *self-determination* (Smith, 1972a). Some people more than others seem to be in charge of their lives—to be Agents or "Origins" of personal causation rather than Pawns. The unprecedented human situation with its headlong trends toward multiple disaster sets a high premium upon Agency, upon the rearing of people who will not passively take these trends for granted. A view of self-determination as an empirical variable in which people differ also appealed to me as cutting through the philosophical deadlock between determinists and voluntarists in psychology. If, in the realm of the reflexive self, the "self-fulfilling prophecy" is a causal mechanism, then people's causally rooted conceptions of themselves as Origins or as Pawns may make the crucial difference as to whether they actively *live* their lives or merely suffer them. Many people who were previously not self-determining—blacks and Chicanos, former colonials, women, even students—were demanding self-determination as against external constraint, and achieving the inner basis of self-determination through redefinition of their identities. A scientific social psychology of personality could help to understand this humanly important process and perhaps to advance it.

These considerations still strike me as compelling. (Incidentally, they do not appear to fit very easily with Maslow's [1954] otherwise attractive hierarchical conception of human motivation. Events have shown that people who are still suffering from gross Deficiency [D] motivation are capable of acting to promote self-determination for themselves and the groups with which they identify [though their leaders, to be sure, are unlikely to be dominated by D-motives]. Maslow's D-motive of Respect is related to the quest for self-determination, but does not seem to encompass it.) I have come to realize, however, that a specialized focus upon self-determination, understandable and appropriate as it may be for minority activists or radical feminists, is a one-sided, biased perspective for the psychologist who is concerned with optimal human functioning.

Even in the essay (Smith, 1972a) in which I developed these ideas, I noted as an afterthought that they probably reflect a male bias. The Promethean, instrumental, "coping" emphasis of what I had to say about competence and self-determination has a characteristic flavor of male aspirations and hangups (some self-analysis here!). It probably requires some modulation to fit the ways that females, on the average, will find most fitting to live their lives as the cultural pressures that limit them are relaxed. Reflection on my own experiential sources of value and protracted discussions with Santa Cruz students in seminar (a majority of whom had biases complementary to my instrumentalism) convinced me that the one-sidedness is more fundamental. In the terms of Rollo May's (1969) provocative book, for one thing, I had been focusing single-mindedly on Will. What about Love? But Maslow had long been asserting the insufficiency of coping and competence as criteria of the "fully human." A long, close look at the inkblot of self-actualization, under which he dealt with the criterion problem, thus takes high priority on my agenda.

LARGE DETAILS IN THE INKBLOT

Among the many contexts in which Maslow discusses self-actualization, I find three major ones, which of course are closely interrelated. Initially, and throughout his subsequent writings, Maslow (1950) talked about *self-actualizing people* as rare specimens of psychological health who can be used as a kind of touchstone to explore human potentialities. He refers repeatedly to the examination of *peak experiences* of transcendent value, which he finds common among self-actualizing people. For more ordinary humanity, these may be regarded as moments of self-actualization. He also refers to a self-actualizing *growth process* governed by "metamotives" that take over when deficiency motivation is satisfied. As a basis for subsequent discussion, I will briefly (because of the familiarity of Maslow's writings) characterize each of these nodes of meaning.

Self-Actualizing People

In a very modestly presented informal study (Maslow, 1950, 1954)—regrettably informal considering the speculative weight it was subsequently called upon to support —Maslow examined the characteristics that he discerned as shared among 51 public or historical figures, contemporaries, and carefully screened young people who seemed to him to exemplify or to approach the ideal of psychological health. (Later [e.g., Maslow, 1971, p. 34], he preferred to substitute "full or diminished humanness" for the medical terminology of health and illness.) Maslow (1954) wrote that

> the positive criterion for selection was positive evidence of self-actualization (SA), as yet a difficult syndrome to describe accurately. For the purposes of this discussion, it may be loosely described as the full use and exploitation of talents, capacities, potentialities, etc. Such people seem to be fulfilling themselves and to be doing the best that they are capable of doing, reminding us of Nietzsche's exhortation, "Become what thou art [pp. 200–201]!"

The following, in brief, are the characteristics of Maslow's self-actualizing people:

> superior perception of reality; increased acceptance of self, of others and of nature; increased spontaneity; increase in problem centering; increased detachment and desire for privacy; increased autonomy, and resistance to enculturation; greater freshness of appreciation, and richness of emotional reaction; higher frequency of peak experiences; increased identification with the human species; changed (the clinician would say, improved) interpersonal relations; more democratic character structure; greatly increased creativeness; certain changes in the value system [Maslow, 1968, p. 26].

Many of his later statements elaborate upon and add to the traits listed in this summary. Maslow is explicit that self-actualization in this defining sense is an uncommon achievement attained only in late maturity.

Peak Experiences

As just noted, Maslow found that his self-actualizers were especially likely to report transcendent, even ecstatic or mystical experiences that they regard as imbued with the greatest intrinsic value, in which awareness of the self and its boundaries is eclipsed by immersion in larger meanings. Not all self-actualizers are "peakers," as Maslow later (1971) observed. Many people who fall short of attaining his criterion of self-actualization nevertheless have peak experiences, which Maslow suggests are transient moments of self-actualization, of "Being." Because they involve a transcendence of the self, they also provide the link for him to a "transpersonal" psychology.

Growth Process

Self-actualization can be viewed not only as a life achievement and as a momentary state, but also as the normal process of psychological growth that occurs (in Maslow's [1954] theory of a hierarchy of motives) when a person's deficiency motives are satisfied and his defenses are not mobilized by present threats. "Self-actualization is not only an end state but also the process of actualizing one's potentialities at any time, in any amount [Maslow, 1971, p. 47]." Maslow (1968) suggests:

> that growth takes place when the next step forward is subjectively more delightful, more joyous, more intrinsically satisfying than the previous gratification with which we have become familiar and even bored; that the only way we can ever know what is right for us is that it feels better subjectively than any alternative. The new experience validates *itself* rather than by any outside

criterion. It is self-justifying, self-validating. . . . This is the way in which we discover the Self and answer the ultimate questions Who am I? What am I [p. 45]?

Of course this formulation of growth-through-delight commits us to the necessary postulation that what tastes good is also, in the growth sense, ''better'' for us. We rest here on the faith that if free choice is *really* free and if the chooser is not too sick or frightened to choose, he will choose wisely, in a health and growthward direction, more often than not [p. 48].

It is here that Maslow espouses what the critic Kurt Back (1972) identifies as the central model upon which the whole personal growth movement is based,

the model of a prisoner in a cage. Underlying most of the thought is the idea of man (or whatever the essential man is) as being imprisoned by different layers of circumstances which do not allow him to reach his full potentialities. Allied to this image is also the supposition that, if he could escape, everything would be good, and he would only use his potentialities for creative and beneficial results [p. 110].

My quotation of Back suggests that I see problems in this faith. It is time to turn to the difficulties that I encounter with Maslow's formulations.

DIFFICULTIES

The difficulties that make Maslow's doctrine of self-actualization stick in my craw, much as I would like to swallow it whole, touch upon central and perennial issues concerning human nature. Since I generally agree with him about which is the side of the Angels, since I entirely agree with him (and with Chein, 1972) in espousing an Image of Man as an actor, not a mechanism, and since most of the bones that I have to pick bear on other humanistic psychologies as much as Maslow's, I hope that a vigorous argument about points of disagreement may contribute to a reconstruction of humanistic psychology along lines that preserve the humanism but improve the chances for a rapprochement with science.

Methodological Difficulty

First I have to note a petty methodological problem that seriously affects my reading of Maslow's study of self-actualizing people. Maslow is so modest about its inadequacies and technical flaws and so informal about reporting it that it seems quite unfair to criticize—like turning a howitzer on a butterfly. But it is necessary, since the study provides the foundation for so much of what Maslow has to say about self-actualization.

The crucial flaw, one that I noted in 1959 (Smith, 1969a, p. 169), and so far as I am aware Maslow never acknowledged, has to do with the boot-straps operation by which he selected his ''sample'' of self-actualizing people. In effect, Maslow eliminated people with gross pathology—the Dostoyevskis and Van Goghs—and selected people for whom, after close scrutiny, he had the highest admiration as human specimens. His empirical definition of psychological health or self-actualization thus rests, at root, on his own implicit values that underlie this global judgment. The array of characteristics that he reports must then be regarded not as an empirical description of the fully human (the value-laden facts that he claims to have established), but rather as an explication of his implicit conception of the fully human, of his orienting frame of human values. This is still interesting because of our respect for Maslow's discriminations of human quality, but it is not the factual foundation for humanistic values that he claims it to be.

The trouble is apparent when we look at the names of his seven cases of "fairly sure" or "highly probable" public and historical figures: Abe Lincoln in his last years, Thomas Jefferson, Albert Einstein, Eleanor Roosevelt, Jane Addams, William James, and Spinoza. Why not also George Washington in *his* later years, Casanova in his earlier years, Napoleon, Thomas Edison, or Lenin? All of these could equally be said to be making, in the phrasing of Maslow's criterion statement of self-actualization, "the full use . . . of talents, capacities, potentialities, ... to be fulfilling themselves and to be doing the best they were capable of doing, reminding us of Nietzsche's exhortation, 'Become what thou art!'" In the inherent nature of the case, the dice are loaded toward Maslow's own values. I like them, but that is beside the point.

The Problem of Potentialities

The methodological point shades into a theoretical one. How, indeed, are we to understand the "human potentialities" that get actualized? The term is most at home in an Aristotelian, finalistic conception, in which development is conceived as the realization of potentialities that are in some sense uniquely predetermined. As I subsequently suggest, that is not so bad a fit to the biological facts when we are dealing with the adaptive products of long-term evolution (even though most biologists do not regard it as a viable theoretical formulation). Maslow (1968) stretches the biological analogy to cover the case of human psychology, as in the following:

> Man demonstrates *in his own nature* a pressure toward fuller and fuller Being, more and more perfect actualization of his humanness in exactly the same naturalistic, scientific sense [sic] that an acorn may be said to be "pressing toward" being an oak tree, or that a tiger can be observed to "push toward" being tigerish, or a horse toward being equine. . . . The environment does not give him potentialities or capacities; he *has* them in inchoate or embryonic form, just as he has embryonic arms and legs [p. 160].

This will hardly do. Except for some universals of the human species like language and symbolization, constructiveness, interdependence, and maybe reactive aggression that have an entrenched evolutionary status and probably fit the acorn-oak tree model as well as the plant itself does (which is to ignore the complex interactive processes of epigenesis), the young person has an extremely broad range of multiple potentialities. The course of life, including the choices of the emerging self, excludes some of them, sets limits on others, and elaborates upon still others. Vice and evil are as much in the range of human potentiality, I would argue, as virtue; specialization as much as "well-rounded" development. Our biology cannot be made to carry our ethics as Maslow would have it.

I see that I am resorting here to sheer assertions to counter Maslow's. But the burden of proof is upon him. The kinds of people that he excludes from his self-actualizing sample, its bias toward Maslovian values, undermine his case for the *distinctive* humanness of the particular human potentialities that his sample exemplifies. These are among the attractive possibilities of human existence; its interest, its tragedy, and I think its glory lie in the fact that they are not "built in" but exist as possibilities among a range of very different ones, any of which can be regarded as an actualization of potentiality, though trivially so, when it occurs.

Generally, I think the doctrine of potentiality is more misleading than helpful (see also Chein, 1972).

Self-Actualization: What Is the Self?

The difficulties that I have just examined lead me to reject (unambivalently) a part of Maslow's doctrine. Now I come to a matter that remains a problem for me, though I think it can be clarified beyond the point where Maslow leaves it: How do our conceptions of the *self* affect our view of self-actualization?

Although conceptual attention to the Self as actor, as reflexive object, and in its relations to other selves is a hallmark of humanistic psychology, our theories about the self remain primitive and underdeveloped. Plausible fragments from Schilder, G. H. Mead, Jung, Erikson, Allport, and others lie scattered and unintegrated. My own thinking about the self is not in good order, and so far as I can tell, Maslow's is mainly implicit. Yet one attractive meaning of self-actualization, as experience or action that is in deep accord with the self or carries forward its projects, depends entirely on what we assume about the self. Two radically contrasting versions are current, with many variants.

One version can be identified with the Socratic dictum, "The unexamined life is not worth living." Selfhood from this perspective inheres in the uniquely human gift of reflexive *self*-awareness. Actions "actualize" the self when they are done reflectively and responsibly to correspond to the value priorities that comprise the core of the person's self-accepted identity. Self-actualization is the cumulative product of such action, and is accompanied by self-understanding.

Quite a contrary version of the self can be identified with Jung who has elaborated it most richly: an "iceberg" conception according to which the true, essential self, the source of creativity, of authenticity and value, lies mostly outside of awareness. Only partly can one aspire to know and understand the self, but one can still be sensitive to and guided by the self's dictates. Self-actualizing *experience*, from this perspective, erupts for the prepared person if he is properly receptive to it—as in "peak experiences." Action is likely to be self-actualizing if it is spontaneous and *un*reflective. Thus the term self-actualization can be employed to designate empirical phenomena and ethical prescriptions that are diametrically opposed. The growth movement in humanistic psychology, and Maslow with it, seems heavily committed to the iceberg version.

I see no need to negotiate between these contrasting interpretations of selfhood, which I would rather understand as partial accounts of what it is to be human, that reflect competing realms of human value. I am sympathetic to what Maslow (1971, Appendix A) says, in a slightly different context, about Appolonian (orderly) and Dionysian (impulsive) versions of self-actualization. As he puts it, the current Dionysian excesses of the encounter movement and the counter-culture counterbalance the massive Apollonian emphasis of our technological society. But if I agree with this, I must also note that the major drift of Maslow's theoretical and quasi-empirical writings about self-actualization is one-sidedly Dionysian. Taken as a new, "scientific" gospel, it is open to the charge of anti-intellectualism and romantic impulsivity.

Human nature *is* multipotential. A dazzling choice of options is available. There is no cosmic requirement, nor biological necessity, that our choices be well balanced. But they have consequences, all the same, in the inner world of experience and the outer world of practical affairs.

Self-Actualization and Transcendence

What I have just said about Maslow's Dionysian bias (an emphasis on the *daimonic,* in May's [1969] terms, though for May the daimonic carries more multivalent, potentially tragic overtones than the Dionysian in Maslow's optimistic, rather sanguine version) has implications for the meaning of "peak experiences" as glimpses or criteria of self-actualization. Peak experiences belong on the nonrational, Dionysian side; if one grants the co-reality of the more Apollonian forms of self-actualization, their authority diminishes. In a purportedly general "Psychology of Being," it seems to me questionable to give as much weight as Maslow does to insights "validated" by the content of such experiences. Maslow notes that among his self-actualizing sample, Eleanor Roosevelt was a "non-peaker." Had his sample been drawn to follow his explicit criterion more faithfully, less according to his implicit value preferences, peak experiences would figure less prominently as a characteristic of self-actualization. In question, particularly, is the raising of mysticism to a more honored status than rationality among the possible competing realms of value between which human choice historically has oscillated.

For myself, I think I understand what Maslow is talking about when it comes to peak experiences in love, nature, and music. They contribute very much to the personal richness and value of life, to the feeling that life is worthwhile and that one could die knowing that one had lived fully. They remain great mysteries that make religion imaginable to me. I wish a scientific psychology could encompass them; they surely reflect something unique to man and exceedingly important to him. It is to Maslow's great credit that he has brought them back into psychology. But the high value that I set upon these experiences does not persuade me to regard the "gut feel" as more enduringly valid than the considered thought, the passively eruptive as "higher" and "truer" than the actively sought. There are many *varieties* of human experience, religious and otherwise, all of which deserve respect and study. In a warranted pendulum swing against the prevailing emphasis in psychology, Maslow has opted for inspiration over perspiration. But a pendulum swing should not be mistaken for the revelation of a higher truth.

Peak experiences "transcend" ordinary selfhood, which they temporarily obliterate. Another of the senses in which Maslow employs the term "transcendence" I can only applaud. In an introduction to "Being-values," Maslow (1971) writes:

> Self-actualizing people are, without one single exception, involved in a cause outside their own skin, in something outside themselves. They are devoted, working at something, something which is very precious to them—some calling or vocation in the old sense, the priestly sense . . . so that the work-joy dichotomy in them disappears [p. 43].

This, of course, is only a restatement of the Christian wisdom that he who would find his life must lose it—that happiness is a by-product that eludes direct pursuit. I think the observation has validity beyond Maslow's biased sample, and I conjecture that it will remain as an enduring truth about selfhood and its fulfillment. It needs to be fitted into a conceptually articulated self-psychology.

Self-Actualization: Biology or History?

In my earlier discussion of the doctrine of potentiality, I questioned Maslow's biologism that projects a determinate course of self-actualization as rooted in man's biological nature. Here Maslow is faithful to his mentor, the holistic neurologist Goldstein (1939), who wrote:

> Normal behavior corresponds to a continual change of tension, of such a kind that over and again that state of tension is reached which enables and impels the organism to actualize itself in further activities, according to its nature. Thus, experiences with patients teach us that we have to

assume only one drive, the drive of self-actualization, and that the goal of the drive is not a discharge of tension [p. 197].

Goldstein anticipated the current trend in motivational theory in his attack on the principle of tension-reduction. But his concept of self-actualization according to the *nature* of the organism seems to me to have limited applicability at the level of human action. What is the *nature* of the human "organism" or, better, of the human person? Perennial problems of philosophy and psychology are involved.

The member of a subhuman animal species, stably adapted to a well-defined ecological niche as the result of long evolutionary process, *has* a nature the fulfillment of which is likely to result in adaptation and the survival of the individual (until reproduction). As a higher primate that also passed through a long evolutionary period of stable adaptation, man too has a biological nature, though what it is and what constraints it puts upon present human action are just now important controversial questions. The chances are that it has to do with such problematic matters as male enjoyment of hunting and a good fight, such essential safeguards as mothers' irresistible attraction to babies (embarrassing to the new feminists), and such important but motivationally neutral propensities as preprogrammed readiness to learn the elaborate symbol system of a human language. The "further reaches of human nature," in Maslow's phrase, are still beyond the reach of evolutionary process: historical time is so short. All the more so must this be the case because (according to Maslow's hierarchical theory of motivation) "B-" or "Metamotives," the sphere of self-actualization, take over only after Deficiency motives have been satisfied.

Maslow's is a psychology for the affluent, postindustrial society. The eons of protohuman evolutionary history must all have been lived mainly at the lower Deficiency levels when life was indeed nasty, brutish, and short. Protopeople were in ecological equilibrium with their resources (which means the edge of hunger) and with their internal parasites (which does not mean health). How, indeed, could a biological human nature of "instinctoid" metamotives of the kind Maslow regards as inherent in self-actualization get established in evolution?

These considerations raise questions as to whether the "wisdom of the body" (and of the untutored mind) is sufficient for the valid guidance of significant human choice, as Maslow's faith would have it. Just as our gut reactions of pleasure may mislead us about saccharine and more dangerous drugs that had no part in our evolution, so they may lead us astray or, what amounts to the same thing, into difficult and destructive conflicts in the human relations of an interdependent urban society. In evolutionary terms, these are almost as new as saccharine.

The trouble is, I think, that in this respect Maslow's psychology is pseudo-biologistic; it is inadequately humanistic in the sense long defended by spokesmen for the humanities. Maslow neglects the discontinuity in the biological record that came with language, culture, self-consciousness, and the accompanying moral order of society. What a humanist would regard as historical human action he persists in regarding as the instinctoid expression of biological propensities. His misguided attempt to arrive at a naturalistic basis for human values rules out any serious consideration of the ethics and politics of human action.

Darwin's principle of natural selection provides the equivalent of an Unseen Hand that gradually (though cruelly) shapes biological nature toward adaptiveness. In history and culture there is no Unseen Hand; there is human action. Human action can succeed or fail, it can be constructive or destructive of self and others, it creates a miraculous variety of values and must choose among them. This is the essence of human hope, of human tragedy, of human dignity. "Becoming fully human" is a personal-cultural-historical adventure. The biological metaphor is ill-suited to grasp it, but a humanistic psychology should.

Self-Actualization and the Common Good

If an Unseen Hand is absent in human history, then self-actualization in the sense of growth process does not inevitably lead to the common good. "Doing what comes naturally" is not enough. The emphasis in Maslow's writings is on the fulfillment of the individual, and the encounter movement that draws upon his writings has become much more flagrantly individualistic.

Yet Maslow's (1971) own view is more complex. Not only do self-actualizing people tend to be altruists, but he notes that "the basic needs can be fulfilled *only* by and through other human beings, i.e., society [p. 347]." Further, societies differ in the extent to which they make it possible for people to transcend the conflict between selfishness and altruism. Maslow (p. 202) adopts from Ruth Benedict the concept of "synergy" for this characteristic of societies according to which the social institutions either tend to make virtue pay or, instead, tend to structure social life as a zero-sum game. The concept plays a central role in his Utopian (or "Eupsychian") thinking.

There is a suggestive basis here for political and ethical analysis and empirical inquiry. In spite of Maslow's preoccupation with humane institutions and management in his later writings (see especially Maslow, 1965), however, his thought was essentially unpolitical. He was an optimist about the extent to which "Eupsychian" arrangements could indeed provide the equivalent of an Unseen Hand. Maslow did not actually deny the irreducible reality of conflict, either in the unconscious psyche or in society, but he was not disposed to dwell upon it or to take it very seriously.

TOWARD RECONSTRUCTION

I have dealt severely with several aspects of Maslow's doctrine of self-actualization because I think it deserves to be taken seriously. For my own use, I should like to salvage the *process* conception of self-actualization. I would interpret it as characterizing a person's actions or experiences when they are in congruence with his existing self (rather than dictated by external constraint or conformity, or driven by inner compulsions that are alien to the self). Such actions or experiences feed back in their consequences to enrich the self, to express its values, or to further its enterprises. This, I take it, is the crux of Maslow's concept. It is also a major part of his rationale for psychological growth. I think that it is important, and a more adequate psychology of the self can build upon it.

I would insist, however, upon an open conception of selfhood until our personological knowledge is more firmly based and better formulated—one with a place both for the creative depths of the "iceberg" theory and for the reflective commitments emphasized by a view that sets greater stock on rational consciousness. Therefore, I would stress the many routes that are open to self-actualization (corresponding to the rich variety of human nature and its personal and cultural expressions). I would not expect, however, to find a single syndrome of virtues in the "self-actualized people" who are nearing the end of the journey.

Self-actualization, so conceived, seems to me a precious psychological value, but I would want to appreciate it in the context of other psychological and social realities. Since I do not believe that self-actualizing action can dependably be counted upon to produce the common good (short of Eupsychia, which I fear would be as dull as Walden II or the classless society), I see it as in necessary and desirable interplay with social norms and sanctions, on the one hand, and with internalized principles and perhaps even taboos, on the other. These are essential if a degree of social and psychological order is to be attained which people need and which does not "come naturally." For both individuals and societies the pendulum swings between order and expressiveness. Individual differences in personal priorities (Apollonian and Dionysian) are to be expected and valued.

Because social realities are at best imperfectly synergic in Maslow's sense, conflict will remain; there is need for politics. And because "gut-feeling" and delight can be misleading guides to the common good (though valuable if fallible ones to individual self-actualization), ethics is needed as well. Neither ethics nor politics is bestowed upon man by any instinctoid biology, though workable versions of ethics and politics have to take his biological nature as well as his historically developing situation into account. Both ethics and politics are the emergent, historical creations of conscious actors who by their new human nature—a "nature" that is transformed in the dialectics of human action—are interdependent and have to take one another into account. They involve human choices about difficult matters with uncertain outcomes.

A psychology is humanistic to the extent that it takes serious account of man as an experiencing actor. We know from man's history and from appreciative acquaintance with his cultural products that even a minimally adequate account must be very complex. Maslow's corpus of writing certainly goes far toward evoking this complexity. But some of his ideas about self-actualization seem to me to purvey a one-sided, though admirable, vision of human potentiality and to fall short of full justice to the distinctively human nature of the historical domain of human choice.

REFERENCES

Back, K. *Beyond words. The story of sensitivity training and the encounter movement.* New York: Russell Sage Foundation, 1972.

Chein, I. *The science of behavior and the image of man.* New York: Basic Books, 1972.

DeCharms, R. *Personal causation.* New York & London: Academic Press, 1968.

Goldstein, K. *The organism.* New York: American Book, 1939.

Maslow, A. H. Self-actualizing people: A study of psychological health. In *Personality Symposia: Symposium No. 1 on Values.* New York: Grune and Stratton, 1950.

Maslow, A. H. *Motivation and personality.* New York: Harper, 1954.

Maslow, A. H. *Religions, values, and peak-experiences.* Columbus, Ohio: Ohio State University Press, 1964.

Maslow, A. H. *Eupsychian management: A journal.* Homewood, Ill.: Irwin-Dorsey, 1965.

Maslow, A. H. *The psychology of science: A reconnaisance.* New York: Harper & Row, 1966.

Maslow, A. H. *Toward a psychology of being.* (2nd ed.) Princeton, N.J.: Van Nostrand, 1968.

Maslow, A. H. *The farther reaches of human nature.* New York: Viking, 1971.

May, R. *Love and will.* New York: Norton, 1969.

Rogers, C. *On becoming a person.* Boston: Houghton Mifflin, 1961.

Rotter, J. B. Generalized expectancies for internal versus external control of reinforcement. *Psychological Monographs,* 1966, *80*(1, Whole No. 609).

Smith, M. B. Review of A. H. Maslow, The psychology of science: A reconnaissance. *Science,* 1966, *153,* 284–285.

Smith, M. B. *Social psychology and human values.* Chicago: Aldine-Atherton, 1969.(a)

Smith, M. B. Competence and "mental health": Problems in conceptualizing human effectiveness. In S. B. Sells (Ed.), *The definition and measurement of mental health: A symposium.* Washington, D.C.: National Center for Health Statistics, USPHS, 1969.(b)

Smith, M. B. Normality: For an abnormal age. In D. Offer and D. X. Freedman (Eds.), *Modern psychiatry and clinical research: Essays in honor of Roy R. Grinker, Sr.* New York: Basic Books, 1972.(a)

Smith, M. B. Toward humanizing social psychology. In T. S. Krawiec (Ed.), *The psychologists.* Vol. 1. New York: Oxford University Press, 1972.(b)

White, R. W. Motivation reconsidered: The concept of competence. *Psychological Review,* 1959, *66,* 297–333.

Part 5
COGNITIVE THEORY

Ten
GEORGE A. KELLY

George A. Kelly's (1905–1967) theory of constructive alternativism proposes that people be seen from a radically different angle—as scientists rather than as beasts or objects. For Kelly, the most essential characteristic of human beings is that they *construe* their environment, giving meaning, or interpretation, to the social and physical events that surround them. It is by means of these *cognitive constructions* that people make predictions about their world—predictions that they use as guides for acting and moving about in their world. Consequently, to understand human behavior, it is not nearly so important to know what "pushes" and "pulls" impinge on human beings as it is to know what and how they think about these pushes and pulls.

The *act of construing* involves bringing some order to one's experience, which at first appears to be a continuous and fortuitous flow. In order to predict and control, people must make some sense of their experiences, and one way of doing so is by classifying them in terms of likenesses and differences. Once events have been classified in this way, generalizations can be formed. In other words, people *abstract* certain similarities from many different events and thus become able to categorize (recognize) events. In this way, people's experiences (events) become meaningful to them, and people become able to generate hypotheses (predictions) about what will happen next. Construing, then, means anticipating events; because anticipation governs human behavior, one's behavior is determined by how one construes the world.

The product of this act of construing is the *personal construct*. Constructs are categories of thought that have developed as a result of people's classification of events in *dichotomous* ways. (For Kelly, constructs are dichotomous by nature.) It is this system of personal constructs that enables us to predict and control events.

Since, in Kelly's theory, behavior is determined solely by how the individual constructs the events of his or her world, the concept of motivation (central to almost all theories of personality) is rejected. *Motivated* means alive; *nonmotivated* means inert. Because being alive is an essential human property, there is no reason to study motivation as a cause of human behavior. People should be studied as people moving about in their world, Kelly says, rather than as organisms that move around in their world because they are motivated to do so.

In the first selection in this chapter, Kelly presents his argument against the continued use of the concept of motivation and then goes on to show how motivational phenomena are dealt with by the theory of personal constructs. In the remainder of the paper, Kelly discusses his rejection of other conventional psychological concepts and how his personal-construct theory makes it unnecessary to conceptualize human beings in these conventional ways.

The concept of *cognitive complexity* is typical of the kinds of concepts that are central to Kelly's theory—concepts dealing with cognitive styles. This particular concept refers to the degree of differentiation in the system of constructs that is employed by an individual in understanding his or her world. An individual may use only a few gross constructs or may interpret the environment in terms of many finely delineated meanings.

The research report by James Bieri demonstrates the use of Kelly's *Role Construct Repertory Test*, or *Rep Test*—an instrument devised specifically to measure a person's cognitive complexity or simplicity. The Rep Test procedure places more faith in subjects' ability (and willingness) to report the important determinants of their behavior than is usual in measures of personality, but this faith is totally in keeping with Kelly's view of human beings as governed by thought and perception rather than by pushes and pulls of drives and stimuli. In Kelly's view, the person who uses many constructs in describing people on the Rep Test is cognitively complex, whereas the person who uses only a few constructs is cognitively simple. It follows that the cognitively complex person should be more accurate than the cognitively simple person in predicting the behavior of other people *and* in perceiving the behavior of others as different from his or her own when in fact it is different. Bieri set out to test this prediction.

The subjects in the Bieri experiment were 34 college undergraduates—22 women and 12 men. The subjects were first administered the Rep Test and then rank ordered, on the basis of their individual scores, along a continuum of cognitive complexity simplicity. The higher the score, the more cognitively complex the individual; the lower the score, the more cognitively simple the individual. Then Bieri administered a second test, called the *Situations Questionnaire*. On this test, various social situations that demand responses are described. Each of Bieri's subjects was instructed to select from among various alternatives the response that he or she would make to each situation. The questionnaire was also administered to classmates of each subject, and each of the 34 experimental subjects was asked to predict the responses of two of his or her classmates to the Situations Questionnaire. The predictive accuracy of each subject was thus determined.

Scores on the Rep Test were then correlated with predictive accuracy on the Situations Questionnaire. Bieri found that, as predicted, cognitive complexity was *positively correlated* with a person's accuracy in predicting the behavior of others. This means that, the higher the subject's score on the Rep Test, the more accurate were his or her predictions of classmates' responses on the Situations Questionnaire. Bieri also found that cognitive complexity was *negatively correlated* with inaccurate perception. This means that, the lower the subject's score on the Rep Test (the more cognitively simple), the less accurate his or her predictions on the Situations Questionnaire. Thus, the theory was supported: cognitively complex individuals were more accurate in predicting the behavior of others, and cognitively simple persons tended to wrongly perceive similarities between themselves and others (*assimilative projection*).

Critics of Kelly feel that he has placed too great an emphasis on cognitive variables in his theory. In the third selection of this chapter, both Jerome S. Bruner and Carl R. Rogers take Kelly to task for ignoring human emotions in an attempt to do full justice to human intellect. Rogers addresses himself to the method of psychotherapy that Kelly derives from his personality theory, deploring Kelly's inattention to the emotional relationship between therapist and patient. Although Bruner would certainly agree with Rogers's criticism of Kelly's psychotherapeutic approach, he levels his criticism at Kelly's personality theory—in particular, at its failure to deal with what Bruner considers to be the essence of the human condition: emotionality.

SUGGESTIONS FOR FURTHER READING

Kelly's definitive work is *The Psychology of Personal Constructs*, published in two volumes by Norton in 1955. Volume 1 presents his theory of personality, and Volume 2 deals with his theory of psychotherapy. Both volumes are highly recommended to the serious student.

For consideration of research on Kelly's theory, consult the chapter by James Bieri in *Functions of Varied Experience,* edited by S. Maddi and D. W. Fiske (Dorsey Press, 1961), and the chapter by J. C. J. Bonarius in *Progress in Experimental Research,* edited by B. A. Maher (Academic Press, 1965).

A collection of some of Kelly's papers is contained in an excellent volume edited by Brendan Maher: *Clinical Psychology and Personality,* published by Wiley in 1969.

If you want to delve more deeply into personal-construct theory, two interesting books on it have been published by Academic Press (London). *The Evaluation of Personal Constructs,* by D. Bannister and J. M. M. Mair, was published in 1968. *Perspectives in Personal Construct Theory,* edited by D. Bannister, was published in 1970 and contains some interesting essays on Kelly's theory as well as two papers by Kelly.

George A. Kelly
MAN'S CONSTRUCTION OF HIS ALTERNATIVES

Some twenty years or more ago a group of us were attempting to provide a traveling psychological clinic service to the schools in the State of Kansas. One of the principal sources of referrals was, of course, teachers. A teacher complained about a pupil. This word-bound complaint was taken as prima-facie grounds for kicking the bottle—I mean, examining the pupil. If we kicked the pupil around long enough and hard enough we could usually find some grounds to justify any teacher's complaint. This procedure was called in those days, just as it is still called, "diagnosis." It was in this manner that we conformed to the widely accepted requirements of the scientific method—we matched hypothesis with evidence and thus arrived at objective truth. In due course of time we became quite proficient in making something out of teachers' complaints, and we got so we could adduce some mighty subtle evidence. In short, we began to fancy ourselves as pretty sensitive clinicians.

Now, as every scientist and every clinician knows and is fond of repeating, treatment depends upon diagnosis. First you find out what is wrong—really wrong. Then you treat it. In treatment you have several alternatives; you can cut it out of the person, or you can remove the object toward which the child behaves improperly, or you can remove the child from the object, or you can alter the mechanism he employs to deal with the object, or you can compensate for the child's behavior by taking up a hobby in the basement, or teach the child to compensate for it, or, if nothing better turns up, you can sympathize with everybody who has to put up with the youngster. But first, always first, you must kick the bottle to make it either confirm or reject your diagnostic hunches. So in Kansas we diagnosed pupils, and having impaled ourselves and our clients with our diagnoses, we cast about more or less frantically for ways of escape.

After perseverating in this classical stupidity—the treatment-depends-on-objective-diagnosis stupidity—for more years than we like to count, we began to suspect that we were being trapped in some pretty fallacious reasoning. We should have liked to blame the teachers for getting us off on the wrong track. But we had verified their complaints, hadn't we? We had even made "differential diagnoses," a way of choosing up sides in the name-calling games commonly played in clinical staff meetings.

Two things became apparent. The first was that the teacher's complaint was not necessarily something to be verified or disproved by the facts in the case, but was, rather, a construction of events in a way that, within the limits and assumptions of her personal construction system, made the most sense to her at the moment. The second was the realization that, in assuming diagnosis to be the independent variable and treatment the

From G. A. Kelly, "Man's Construction of His Alternatives," in G. Lindzey (Ed.), *Assessment of Human Motives*, pp. 33–64. Copyright © 1958 by Gardner Lindzey. Reprinted by permission of Holt, Rinehart and Winston, Inc.

dependent variable, we had got the cart before the horse. It would have been better if we had made our diagnoses in the light of changes that do occur in children or that can be made to occur, rather than trying to shape those changes to independent but irrelevant psychometric measurements or biographical descriptions.

What we should like to make clear is that both these difficulties have the same root—the traditional rationale of science that leads us to look for the locus of meaning of words in their objects of reference rather than in their subjects of origin. We hear a word and look to what is talked about rather than listen to the person who utters it. A teacher often complained that a child was "lazy." We turned to the child to determine whether or not she was right. If we found clear evidence that would support a hypothesis of laziness, then laziness was what it was—and diagnosis was complete. Diagnosis having been accomplished, treatment was supposed to ensue. What does one do to cure laziness? While, of course, it was not quite as simple as this, the paradigm is essentially the one we followed.

Later we began to put "laziness" in quotes. We found that a careful appraisal of the teacher's construction system gave us a much better understanding of the meaning of the complaint. This, together with some further inquiry into the child's outlook, often enabled us to arrive at a vantage point from which we could deal with the problem in various ways. It occurred to us that we might, for example, help the teacher reconstrue the child in terms other than "laziness"—terms which gave her more latitude for exercising her own particular creative talents in dealing with him. Again, we might help the child deal with the teacher and in this way alleviate her discomfort. And, of course, there was sometimes the possibility that a broader reorientation of the child toward himself and school matters in general would prove helpful.

We have chosen the complaint of "laziness" as our example for a more special reason. "Laziness" happens to be a popular motivational concept that has widespread currency among adults who try to get others to make something out of themselves. Moreover, our disillusionment with motivational conceptualization in general started with this particular term and arose out of the specific context of school psychological services.

Our present position regarding human motives was approached by stages. First we realized that even when a hypothesis of laziness was confirmed there was little that could be said or done in consequence of such a finding. While this belief originally appeared to be less true of other motivational constructs, such as appetite or affection, in each instance the key to treatment, or even to differential prediction of outcomes, appeared to reside within the framework of other types of constructs.

Another observation along the way was that the teachers who used the construct of "laziness" were usually those who had widespread difficulties in their classrooms. Soon we reached the point in our practice where we routinely used the complaint of "laziness" as a point of departure for reorienting the teacher. It usually happened that there was more to be done with her than there was to be done with the child. So it was, also, with other complaints cast in motivational terms. In general, then, we found that the most practical approach to so-called motivational problems was to try to reorient the people who thought in such terms. Complaints about motivation told us much more about the complainants than it did about their pupils.

This generalization seems to get more and more support from our clinical experience. When we find a person who is more interested in manipulating people for his own purposes, we usually find him making complaints about their motives. When we find a person who is concerned about motives, he usually turns out to be one who is threatened by his fellow men and wants to put them in their place. There is no doubt that the construct of motives is widely used, but it usually turns out to be a part of the language of complaint about the behavior of other people. When it appears in the language of the client himself, as it does occasionally, it always—literally always—appears in the context of a kind of rationalization apparently designed to appease the therapist, not in the spontaneous utterances of the client who is in good rapport with his therapist.

One technique we came to use was to ask the teacher what the child would do if she did not try to motivate him. Often the teacher would insist that the child would do nothing —absolutely nothing—just sit! Then we would suggest that she try a nonmotivational approach and let him "just sit." We would ask her to observe how he went about "just sitting." Invariably the teacher would be able to report some extremely interesting goings-on. An analysis of what the "lazy" child did while he was being lazy often furnished her with her first glimpse into the child's world and provided her with her first solid grounds for communication with him. Some teachers found that their laziest pupils were those who could produce the most novel ideas; others, that the term "laziness" had been applied to activities that they had simply been unable to understand or appreciate.

It was some time later that we sat down and tried to formulate the general principles that undergirded our clinical experiences with teachers and their pupils. The more we thought about it, the more it seemed that our problems had always resolved themselves into questions of what the child would do if left to his own devices rather than questions about the amount of his motivation. These questions of what the child would do seemed to hinge primarily on what alternatives his personal construction of the situation allowed him to sense. While his construed alternatives were not necessarily couched in language symbols, nor could the child always clearly represent his alternatives, even to himself, they nonetheless set the outside limits on his day-to-day behavior. In brief, whenever we got embroiled in questions of motivation we bogged down, the teachers bogged down, and the children continued to aggravate everybody within earshot. When we forgot about motives and set about understanding the practical alternatives which children felt they were confronted by, the aggravations began to resolve themselves.

What we have said about our experiences with children also turned up in our psychotherapeutic experiences with adults. After months or, in some cases, years of psychotherapy with the same client, it did often prove to be possible to predict his behavior in terms of motives. This, of course, was gratifying; but predictive efficiency is not the only criterion of a good construction, for one's understanding of a client should also point the way to resolving his difficulties. It was precisely at this point that motivational constructs failed to be of practical service, just as they had failed to be of service in helping children and teachers get along with each other. Always the psychotherapeutic solution turned out to be a reconstruing process, not a mere labeling of the client's motives. To be sure, there were clients who never reduced their reconstructions to precise verbal terms, yet still were able to extricate themselves from vexing circumstances. And there were clients who got along best under conditions of support and reassurance with a minimum of verbal structuring on the part of the therapist. But even in these cases, the solutions were not worked out in terms of anything that could properly be called motives, and the evidence always pointed to some kind of reconstruing process that enabled the client to make his choice between new sets of alternatives not previously open to him in a psychological sense.

APPROACH TO A NEW PSYCHOLOGICAL THEORY

Now, perhaps, it is time to launch into the third phase of our discussion. We started by making some remarks of a philosophical nature and from there we dropped back to recall some of the practical experiences that first led us to question the construct of motivation. Let us turn now to the formulation of psychological theory and to the part that motivation plays in it.

A half-century ago William McDougall published his little volume *Physiological Psychology* (1905). In the opening pages he called his contemporary psychologists' attention to the fact that the concept of *energy* had been invented by physicists in order to account for movement of objects, and that some psychologists had blandly assumed that they too would have to find a place for it in their systems. While McDougall was to go on in his lifetime to formulate a theoretical system based on instinctual drives and thus, it seems to us, failed to heed his own warning, what he said about the construct of energy still provides us with a springboard for expounding a quite different theoretical position.

The physical world presented itself to pre-classical man as a world of solid objects. He saw matter as an essentially inert substance, rather than as a complex of related motion. His axes of reference were spatial dimensions—length, breadth, depth—rather than temporal dimensions. The flow of time was something he could do very little about, and he was inclined to take a passive attitude toward it. Even mass, a dimension which lent itself to more dynamic interpretations, was likely to be construed in terms of size equivalents.

Classical man, as he emerged upon the scene, gradually became aware of motion as something that had eluded his predecessors. But for him motion was still superimposed upon nature's rocks and hills. Inert matter was still the phenomenon, motion was only the epiphenomenon. Action, vitality, and energy were the breath of life that had to be breathed into the inertness of nature's realities. In Classical Greece this thought was magnificently expressed in new forms of architecture and sculpture that made the marble quarried from the Greek islands reach for the open sky, or ripple like a soft garment in the warm Aegean breeze. But motion, though an intrinsic feature of the Greek idiom, was always something superimposed, something added. It belonged to the world of the ideal and not to the hard world of reality.

The Construct of Motivation Implies that Man Is Essentially Inert

Today our modern psychology approaches its study of man from the same vantage point. He is viewed as something static in his natural state, hence something upon which motion, life, and action have to be superimposed. In substance he is still perceived as like the marble out of which the Greeks carved their statues of flowing motion and ethereal grace. He comes alive, according to most of the psychology of our day, only through the application of special enlivening forces. We call these forces by such names as "motives," "incentives," "needs," and "drives." Thus, just as the physicists had to erect the construct of energy to fill the gap left by their premature assumption of a basically static universe, so psychology has had to burden itself with a construct made necessary by its inadequate assumption about the basic nature of man.

We now arrive at the same point in our theoretical reasoning at which we arrived some years earlier in appraising our clinical experience. In each instance we find that efforts to assess human motives run into practical difficulty because they assume inherently static properties in human nature. It seems appropriate, therefore, at this juncture to reexamine our implied assumptions about human nature. If we then decide to base our thinking upon new assumptions we can next turn to the array of new constructs that may be erected for the proper elaboration of the fresh theoretical position.

In This Theory the Construct of Motivation Is Redundant in Explaining Man's Activity

There are several ways in which we can approach our problem. We could, for example, suggest to ourselves, as we once suggested to certain unperceptive classroom teachers, that we examine what a person does when he is not being motivated. Does he turn into some kind of inert substance? If not—and he won't—should we not follow up our observation with a basic assumption that any person is motivated, motivated for no other reason than that he is alive? Life itself could be defined as a form of process or movement. Thus, in designating man as our object of psychological inquiry, we should be taking it for granted that movement is an essential property of his being, not something that has to be accounted for separately. We should be talking about a form of movement—man—not something that has to be motivated.

Pursuant to this line of reasoning, motivation ceases to be a special topic of psychology. Nor, on the other hand, can it be said that motivation constitutes the whole of psychological substance, although from the standpoint of another theoretical system it might be proper to characterize our position so. *Within our system,* however, the term "motivation" can appear only as a redundancy.

How can we further characterize this stand with respect to motivation? Perhaps this will help: Motivational theories can be divided into two types, push theories and pull theories. Under push theories we find such terms as drive, motive, or even stimulus. Pull theories use such constructs as purpose, value, or need. In terms of a well-known metaphor, these are the pitchfork theories on the one hand and the carrot theories on the other. But our theory is neither of these. Since we prefer to look to the nature of the animal himself, ours is probably best called a jackass theory.

Thus far our reasoning has led us to a point of view from which the construct of "human motives" appears redundant—redundant, that is, as far as accounting for human action is concerned. But traditional motivational theory is not quite so easily dismissed. There is another issue that now comes to the fore. It is the question of what directions human actions can be expected to take.

The Construct of Motivation Is Not Needed to Explain Directionality of Movement

We must recognize that the construct of "motive" has been traditionally used for two purposes; to account for the fact that the person is active rather than inert, and also for the fact that he chooses to move in some directions rather than in others. It is not surprising that, in the past, a single construct has been used to cover both issues; for if we take the view that the human organism is set in motion only by the impact of special forces, it is reasonable to assume also that those forces must give it direction as well as impetus. But now, if we accept the view that the organism is already in motion simply by virtue of its being alive, then we have to ask ourselves if we do not still require the services of "motives" to explain the directionality of the movement. Our answer to this question is "No." Let us see why.

Here, as before, we turn first to our experiences as a clinician to find the earliest inklings of a new theoretical position. Specifically, we turn to experiences in psychotherapy.

Clinical experience. When a psychologist undertakes psychotherapy with a client he can approach his task from any one of a number of viewpoints. He can, as many do, devote most of his attention to a kind of running criticism of the mistakes the client makes, his fallacies, his irrationalities, his misperceptions, his resistances, his primitive mechanisms. Or, as others do, he can keep measuring his client; so much progress today, so much loss yesterday, gains in this respect, relapses in that. If he prefers, he can keep his attention upon his own role, or the relation between himself and his client, with the thought that it is not actually given to him ever to know how the client's mind works, nor is it his responsibility to make sure that it works correctly, but only that he should provide the kind of warm and responsive human setting in which the client can best solve his own problems.

Any one of these approaches may prove helpful to the client. But there is still another approach that, from our personal experience, can prove most helpful to the client and to the psychotherapist. Instead of assuming, on the one hand, that the therapist is obliged to bring the client's thinking into line, or, on the other, that the client will mysteriously bring his own thinking into line once he has been given the proper setting, we can take the stand that client and therapist are conjoining in an exploratory venture. The therapist assumes neither the position of judge nor that of the sympathetic bystander. He is sincere about this; he is willing to learn along with his client. He is the client's fellow researcher who seeks first to understand, then to examine, and finally to assist the client in subjecting alternatives to experimental test and revision.

The psychologist who goes at psychotherapy this way says to himself, "I am about to have the rare opportunity of examining the inner workings of that most intricate creation in all of nature, a human personality. While many scholars have written about the complexity of this human personality, I am now about to see for myself how one particular personality functions. Moreover, I am about to have an experienced colleague join me in this venture, the very person whose personality is to be examined. He will help me as best he can, but there will be times when he cannot help, when he will be as puzzled and confused as I am."

When psychotherapy is carried out in this vein the therapist, instead of asking himself continually whether his client is right or not, or whether he himself is behaving properly, peers intently into the intimate psychological processes which the unusual relation permits him to see. He inquires rather than condemns. He explores rather than rejects or approves. How does this creature, man, actually think? How does he make choices that seem to be outside the conventionalized modes of thought? What is the nature of his logic—quite apart from how logicians define logic? How does he solve his problems? What ideas does he express for which he has no words?

Conventional psychological concepts. Out of this kind of experience with psychotherapy we found ourselves becoming increasingly impatient with certain standard psychotherapeutic concepts. "Insight" was one of the first to have a hollow sound. It soon became apparent that, in any single case, there were any number of different possible insights that could be used to structure the same facts, all of them more or less true. As one acquires a variety of psychotherapeutic experience he begins to be amazed by how sick or deviant some clients can be and still surmount their difficulties, and how well or insightful others can be and yet fall apart at every turn. Certainly the therapist who approaches his task primarily as a scientist is soon compelled to concede that unconventional insights often work as well or better than the standardized insights prescribed by some current psychological theory.

Another popular psychotherapeutic concept that made less and less sense was "resistance." To most therapists resistance is a kind of perverse stubbornness in the client. Most therapists are annoyed by it. Some accuse the client of resisting whenever their therapeutic efforts begin to bog down. But our own experiences with resistance were a good deal like our experiences with laziness—they bespoke more of the therapist's perplexity than of the client's rebellion. If we had been dependent entirely on psychotherapeutic experiences with our own clients we might have missed this point; it would have been too easy for us, like the others, to blame our difficulties on the motives of the client. But we were fortunate enough to have opportunities also for supervising therapists, and here, because we were not ourselves quite so intimately involved, it was possible to see resistance in terms of the therapist's naïveté.

When the so-called resistance was finally broken through—to use a psychotherapist's idiom—it seemed proper, instead of congratulating ourselves on our victory over a stubborn client, to ask ourselves and our client just what had happened. There were, of course, the usual kinds of reply, "I just couldn't say that to you then," or "I knew I was being evasive, but I just didn't know what to do about it," etc.

But was this stubbornness? Some clients went further and expressed it this way, "To have said then what I have said today would not have meant the same thing." This may seem like a peculiar remark, but from the standpoint of personal construct theory it makes perfectly good sense. A client can express himself only within the framework of his construct system. Words alone do not convey meaning. What this client appears to be saying is this: When he has the constructs for expressing himself, the words that he uses ally themselves with those constructs and they make sense when he utters them. To force him to utter words which do not parallel his constructs, or to mention events which are precariously construed, is to plunge him into a chaos of personal nonsense, however much it may clarify matters for the therapist. In short, our experience with psychotherapy led us to believe that it was not orneriness that made the client hold out so-called important therapeutic material, but a genuine inability to express himself in terms that would not appear, from his point of view, to be utterly misconstrued.

Perhaps these brief recollections of therapeutic experiences will suffice to show how we began to be as skeptical of motives as direction-finding devices as we were skeptical of them as action-producing forces. Over and over again, it appeared that our clients were making their choices, not in terms of the alternatives we saw open to them, but in terms of the alternatives they saw open to them. It was their network of constructions that made up the daily mazes that they ran, not the pure realities that appeared to us to surround them. To try to explain a temper tantrum or an acute schizophrenic episode in terms of motives only was to miss the whole point of the client's system of personal dilemmas. The child's temper tantrum is, for him, one of the few remaining choices left to him. So for the psychotic, with his pathways structured the way they are in his mind, he has simply chosen from a particular limited set of alternatives. How else can he behave? His other alternatives are even less acceptable.

We have not yet fully answered the question of explaining directionality. We have described only the extent to which our therapeutic experiences led us to question the value of motives. But, after all, we have not yet found, from our experience, that clients do what they do because there is nothing else they can do. We have observed only that they do what they do because their choice systems are definitely limited. But even by this line of reasoning, they do have choices, often bad ones, to be sure, but still choices. So our question of directionality of behavior is narrowed down by the realization that a person's behavior must take place within the limited dimensions of his personal construct system. Yet, as long as his system does have dimensions, it must provide him with some sets of alternatives. And so long as he has some alternatives of his own making we must seek to explain why he chooses some of them in preference to others.

"Neurotic paradox." Before we leave off talking about clinical experience and take up the next and most difficult phase of our discussion, it will do no harm to digress for a few moments and talk about the so-called neurotic paradox. O. H. Mowrer has described this as "the paradox of behavior which is at one and the same time self-perpetuating and self-defeating" (1950, p. 486). We can state the paradox in the form of a question, "Why does a person sometimes persist in unrewarding behavior?" Reinforcement theory finds this an embarrassing question, while contiguity theory, to which some psychologists have turned in their embarrassment, finds the converse question equally embarrassing, "Why does a person sometimes not persist in unrewarding behavior?"

From the standpoint of the psychology of personal constructs, however, there is no neurotic paradox. Or, to be more correct, the paradox is the jam which certain learning theorists get themselves into rather than the jam their clients get themselves into. Not that clients stay out of jams, but they have their own ingenious ways of getting into them and they need no assistance from us psychologists. To say it another way, the behavior of a so-called neurotic client does not seem paradoxical to him until he tries to rationalize it in terms his therapist can understand. It is when he tries to use his therapist's construction system that the paradox appears. Within the client's own limited construction system he may be faced with a dilemma but not with a paradox.

Perhaps this little digression into the neurotic paradox will help prepare the ground for the next phase of our discussion. Certainly it will help if it makes clear that the criteria by which a person chooses between the alternatives, in terms of which he has structured his world, are themselves cast in terms of constructions. Not only do men construe their alternatives, but they construe also criteria for choosing between them. For us psychologists who try to understand what is going on in the minds of our clients it is not as simple as saying that the client will persist in rewarding behavior, or even that he will vacillate between immediate and remote rewards. We have to know what this person construes to be a reward, or, still better, we can bypass such motivational terms as "reward," which ought to be redefined for each new client and on each new occasion, and abstract from human behavior some psychological principle that will transcend the tedious varieties of personalized motives.

If we succeed in this achievement we may be able to escape that common pitfall of so-called objective thinking, the tendency to reify our constructs and treat them as if they were not constructs at all, but actually all the things that they were originally only intended to construe. Such a formulation may even make it safer for us to write operational definitions for purposes of research, without becoming lost in the subject-predicate fallacy. In clinical language it may enable us to avoid concretistic thinking—the so-called brain-injured type of thinking—which is what we call operationalism when we happen to find it in a client who is frantically holding on to his mental faculties.

Now we have been procrastinating long enough. Let us get on to the most difficult part of our discussion. We have talked about experiences with clients who, because they hoped we might be of help to them, honored us with invitations to the rare intimacies of their personal lives and ventured to show us the shadowy processes by which their worlds were ordered. We turned aside briefly in our discussion to talk about the neurotic paradox, hoping that what we could point to there would help the listener anticipate what needed to come next. Now we turn again to a more theoretical form of discourse.

Man Links the Past with the Future—Anticipation

If man, as the psychologist is to see him, exists primarily in the dimensions of time, and only secondarily in the dimensions of space, then the terms which we erect for understanding him ought to take primary account of this view. If we want to know why man does what he does, then the terms of our whys should extend themselves in time rather than in space; they should be events rather than things; they should be mileposts rather than destinations. Clearly, man lives in the present. He stands firmly astride the chasm that separates the past from the future. He is the only connecting link between these two universes. He, and he only, can bring them into harmony with each other. To be sure, there are other forms of existence that have belonged to the past and, presumably, will also belong to the future. A rock that has rested firm for ages may well exist in the future also, but it does not link the past with the future. In its mute way it links only past with past. It does not anticipate; it does not reach out both ways to snatch handfuls from each of the two worlds in order to bring them together and subject them to the same stern laws. Only man does that.

If this is the picture of man, as the psychologist envisions him—man, a form of movement; man, always quick enough, as long as he is alive, to stay astride the darting present—then we cannot expect to explain him either entirely in terms of the past or entirely in terms of the future. We can explain him, psychologically, only as a link between the two. Let us, therefore, formulate our basic postulate for a psychological theory in the light of this conjunctive vision of man. We can say it this way: *A person's processes are psychologically channelized by the ways in which he anticipates events*.

The Nature of Personal Constructs

Taking this proposition as a point of departure, we can quickly begin to sketch a theoretical structure for psychology that will, undoubtedly, turn out to be novel in many unexpected ways. We can say next that man develops his way of anticipating events by construing, by scratching out his channels of thought. Thus he builds his own maze. His runways are the constructs he forms, each a two-way street, each essentially a pair of alternatives between which he can choose.

Another person, attempting to enter this labyrinth, soon gets lost. Even a therapist has to be led patiently back and forth through the system, sometimes for months on end, before he can find his way without the client's help, or tell to what overt behavior each passageway will lead. Many of the runways are conveniently posted with word signs, but most of them are dark, cryptically labeled, or without any word signs at all. Some are rarely traveled. Some the client is reluctant to disclose to his guest. Often therapists lose patience and prematurely start trying to blast shortcuts in which both they and their clients soon become trapped. But worst of all, there are therapists who refuse to believe that they are in the strangely structured world of man; they insist only that the meanderings in which they are led are merely the play of whimsical motives upon their blind and helpless client.

Our figure of speech should not be taken too literally. The labyrinth is conceived as a network of constructs, each of which is essentially an abstraction and, as such, can be picked up and laid down over many different events in order to bring them into focus and clothe them with personal meaning. Moreover, the constructs are subject to continual revision, although the complex interdependent relation between constructs in the system often makes it precarious for the person to revise one construct without taking into account the disruptive effect upon major segments of the system.

In our efforts to communicate the notion of a personal construct system we repeatedly run into difficulty because listeners identify personal constructs with the classic view of a concept. Concepts have long been known as units of logic and are treated as if they existed independently of any particular person's psychological processes. But when we use the notion of "construct" we have nothing of this sort in mind; we are talking about a psychological process in a living person. Such a construct has, for us, no existence independent of the person whose thinking it characterizes. The question of whether it is logical or not has no bearing on its existence, for it is wholly a psychological rather than a logical affair. Furthermore, since it is a psychological affair, it has no necessary allegiance to the verbal forms in which classical concepts have been traditionally cast. The personal construct we talk about bears no essential relation to grammatical structure, syntax, words, language, or even communication; nor does it imply consciousness. It is simply a psychologically construed unit for understanding human processes.

We must confess that we often run into another kind of difficulty. In an effort to understand what we are talking about, a listener often asks if the personal construct is an intellectual affair. We find that, willy-nilly, we invite this kind of question because of our use of such terms as thought and thinking. Moreover, we are speaking in the terms of a language system whose words stand for traditional divisions of mental life, such as "intellectual."

Let us answer this way. A construct owes no special allegiance to the intellect, as against the will or the emotions. In fact, we do not find it either necessary or desirable to make that classic trichotomous division of mental life. After all, there is so much that is "emotional" in those behaviors commonly called "intellectual," and there is so much "intellectualized" contamination in typical "emotional" upheavals that the distinction becomes merely a burdensome nuisance. For some time now we have been quite happy to chuck all these notions of intellect, will, and emotion; so far, we cannot say we have experienced any serious loss.

Now we are at the point in our discourse where we hope our listeners are ready to assume, either from conviction or for the sake of argument, that man, from a psychological viewpoint, makes of himself a bridge between past and future in a manner that is unique among creatures, that, again from a psychological viewpoint, his processes are channelized by the personal constructs he erects in order to perform this function, and, finally, that he organizes his constructs into a personal system that is no more conscious than it is unconscious and no more intellectual than it is emotional. This personal construct system provides him with both freedom of decision and limitation of action—freedom, because it permits him to deal with the meanings of events rather than forces him to be helplessly pushed about by them, and limitation, because he can never make choices outside the world of alternatives he has erected for himself.

The Choice Corollary

We have left to the last the question of what determines man's behavioral choices between his self-construed alternatives. Each choice that he makes has implications for his future. Each turn of the road he chooses to travel brings him to a fresh vantage point from which he can judge the validity of his past choices and elaborate his present pattern of alternatives for choices yet to be made. Always the future beckons him and always he reaches out in tremulous anticipation to touch it. He lives in anticipation; we mean this literally; *he lives in anticipation!* His behavior is governed, not simply by *what* he anticipates—whether good or bad, pleasant or unpleasant, self-vindicating or self-confounding—but by *where* he believes his choices will place him in respect to the remaining turns in the road. If he chooses this fork in the road, will it lead to a better vantage point from which to see the road beyond or will it be the one that abruptly brings him face-to-face with a blank wall?

What we are saying about the criteria of man's choices is not a second theoretical assumption, added to our basic postulate to take the place of the traditional beliefs in separate motives, but is a natural outgrowth of that postulate—a corollary to it. Let us state it so. *A person chooses for himself that alternative in a dichotomized construct through which he anticipates the greater possibility for extension and definition of his system.*

Such a corollary appears to us to be implicit in our postulate that a person's processes are psychologically channelized by the ways in which he anticipates events. For the sake of simplification we have skipped over the formal statement of some of the intervening corollaries of personal construct theory: the corollary that deals with construing, the corollary that deals with the construct system, and the corollary that deals with the dichotomous nature of constructs. But we have probably covered these intervening ideas well enough in the course of our exposition.

What we are saying in this crucial *Choice Corollary* gives us the final ground for dismissing motivation as a necessary psychological construct. It is that if a person's processes are channelized by the ways in which he anticipates events he will make his choices in such a way that he apparently defines or extends his system of channels, for this must necessarily be his comprehensive way of anticipating events.

At the risk of being tedious, let us recapitulate again. We shall be brief. Perhaps we can condense the argument into three sentences. First we saw no need for a closet full of motives to explain the fact that man was active rather than inert; there was no sense in assuming that he was inert in the first place. And now we see no need to invoke a concept of motives to explain the directions that his actions take; the fact that he lives in anticipation automatically takes care of that. Result: no catalogue of motives to clutter up our system and, we hope, a much more coherent psychological theory about living man.

Footnotes

At this point our discourse substantially concludes itself. What we have left to offer are essentially footnotes that are intended to be either defensive or provocative, perhaps both. Questions naturally arise the moment one begins to pursue the implications of this kind of theorizing. One can scarcely take more than a few steps before one begins to stumble over a lot of ancient landmarks that remain to serve no purpose except to get in the way. Perhaps it is only fair that we spotlight some of these relics in the hope of sparing our listeners some barked intellectual shins.

Is this a dynamic theory? This is the kind of question our clinical colleagues are likely to ask. We are tempted to give a flat "No" to that question. No, this is not what is ordinarily called a dynamic theory; it intentionally parts company with psychoanalysis, for example —respectfully, but nonetheless intentionally. However, if what is meant by a "dynamic theory" is a theory that envisions man as active rather than inert, then this is an all-out dynamic theory. It is so dynamic that it does not need any special system of dynamics to keep it running! What must be made clear, or our whole discourse falls flat on its face, is that we do not envision the behavior of man in terms of the external forces bearing upon him; that is a view we are quite ready to leave to the dialectic materialists and to some of their unwitting allies who keep chattering about scientific determinism and other subject-predicate forms of nonsense.

Is this rationalism revisited? We anticipated this question at the beginning of our discussion. We are tempted to answer now by claiming that it is one of the few genuine departures from rationalism, perhaps the first in the field of psychology. But here is a tricky question, because it is not often clear whether one is referring to extrapsychological rationalism or to an essential-psychological rationalism that is often imperfect when judged by classical standards and often branded as "irrationality," or whether the question refers simply to any verbalized structure applied to the behavior of man in an effort to understand him.

Certainly ours is not an extrapsychological rationalism. Instead, it frankly attempts to deal with the essential rationalism that is actually demonstrated in the thinking of man. In doing so it deals with what is sometimes called the world of the irrational and nonrational.

But, in another sense, our interpretation, in its own right and quite apart from its subject matter, is a psychologist's rationale designed to help him understand how man comes to believe and act the way he does. Such a rationale approaches its task the way it does, not because it believes that logic has to be as it is because there is no other way for it to be, not because it believes that man behaves the way he does because there is no other way for him to react to external determining forces, nor even because the rationale's own construction of man provides him with no alternatives, but, rather, because we have the hunch that the way to understand all things, even the ramblings of a regressed schizophrenic client, is to construe them so that they will be made predictable. To some persons this approach spells rationalism, pure and simple, probably because they are firmly convinced that the nether world of man's motives is so hopelessly irrational that anyone who tries to understand that world sensibly must surely be avoiding contact with man as he really is.

Finally, there is the most important question of all; how does the system work? That is a topic to be postponed to another time and occasion. Of course, we think it does work. We use it in psychotherapy and in psychodiagnostic planning for psychotherapy. We also find a place for it in dealing with many of the affairs of everyday life. But there is no place here for the recitation of such details. We hope only that, so far as we have gone, we have been reasonably clear, and a mite provocative, for only by being both clear and provocative can we give our listeners something they can set their teeth into.

ADDENDUM

The invitation to prepare this paper was accompanied by a list of nine issues upon which, it was presumed, would hinge the major differences to be found among any group of motivational theorists. On the face of it such a list seems altogether fair. But one can scarcely pose even one such question, much less nine of them, without exacting hostages to his own theoretical loyalties. And if a correspondent answers in the terminology of the questions posed, he in turn immediately bases his discourse on the assumptions of an alien theory. Once he has done that he will, sooner or later, have to talk as if the differences he seeks to emphasize are merely semantical.

Yet the nine questions need to be met, if not head on, at least candidly enough to be disposed of.

How important are conscious as opposed to unconscious motives in understanding human behavior? We do not use the conscious-unconscious dichotomy, but we do recognize that some of the personal constructs a person seeks to subsume within his system prove to be fleeting or elusive. Sometimes this is because they are loose rather than tight, as in the first phase of the creative cycle. Sometimes it is because they are not bound by the symbolisms of words or other acts. But of this we are sure, if they are important in a person's life, it is a mistake to say they are unconscious or that he is unaware of them. Every day he experiences them, often all too poignantly; the point is that he cannot put his finger on them or tell for sure whether they are at the spot the therapist has probed for them.

When does a person fall back upon such loosened thinking? Or when does he depend upon constructs that are not easily subsumed? Ordinarily when one is confronted with confusion (anxiety) the first tendency is to tighten up; but beyond some breaking point there is a tendency to discard tight constructions and fall back upon constructs that are loose or which have no convenient symbolizations. It is in the human crises that it becomes most important to understand the nature of a person's secondary lines of defense.

What is the relative importance of direct as opposed to indirect techniques for assessing human motives? Let us change the word "motives" to "constructs." They are not equivalent, of course, but "motives" play no part in our system, whereas "constructs" do. If we ask a person to express his constructs in words, and we take his words literally, then we may say, perhaps, that we are assessing his constructs "directly." If we assume that his words and acts have less patent meanings and that we must construe him in terms of a background understanding of his construct system, shall we say that we have used a more "indirect" technique? But is anything more direct than this? Perhaps the method that takes literal meanings for granted is actually more indirect, for it lets the dictionary intervene between the client and the psychologist. If time permits, we vote for seeking to understand the person in the light of his personal construct system.

Is it essential in assessing motives to provide some appraisal of the ego processes, directive mechanisms, or cognitive controls that intervene between the motive and its expression? "Ego" is a psychoanalytic term; we still don't know what it means. "Cognitive" is a classical term that implies a natural cleavage between psychological processes, a cleavage that confuses everything and clarifies nothing; let's forget it. The notion of a "motive," on the one hand, and "its expression," on the other, commits one to the view that what is expressed is not the person but the motivational gremlins that have possessed him. Finally, if the term "directive mechanisms" is taken in a generic sense, then we can say that we see these as in the form of constructs formulated by the person himself and in terms of which he casts his alternatives. What we need to assess are these personal constructs, if we wish to understand what a person is up to.

In assessing human motives how important is it to specify the situational context within which the motives operate? Each of a client's constructs has a limited range of convenience in helping him deal with his circumstances. Beyond that range the construct is irrelevant as far as he is concerned. This is the point that was so long obscured by the law of the excluded middle. Knowledge, therefore, of the range of convenience of any personal construct formulated by a client is essential to an understanding of the behavior he structures by that construct.

How necessary is knowledge of the past in the assessment of contemporary motivation? It is not absolutely necessary but it is often convenient. Events of the past may disclose the kind of constructions that the client has used; presumably he may use them again. Events of the past, taken in conjunction with the anticipations they confirmed at the time, may indicate what has been proved to his satisfaction. Again, events of the past may indicate what the client has had to make sense out of, and thus enable us to surmise what constructions he may have had to formulate in order to cope with his circumstances. Finally, since some clients insist on playing the part of martyrs to their biographical destinies, therapy cannot be concluded successfully until their therapists have conducted them on a grand tour of childhood recollections.

At this time is the area of motivation more in need of developing precise and highly objective measures of known motives or identifying significant new motivational variables? Neither.

In attempting to understand human motivation is it advisable at present to focus upon one or a small number of motivational variables, or should an effort be made to appraise a wide array of variables? Human impetus should be assumed as a principle rather than treated as a variable or group of variables.

What is the relative importance of detailed studies of individual cases as compared to carefully controlled experimental research and large-scale investigations? All three have their place in the course of developing psychological understanding. The detailed case studies provide excellent grounds for generating constructs. Experimental research, in turn, permits us to test out constructs in artificial isolation. Large-scale investigations help us put constructs into a demographic framework.

Is there a unique and important contribution to the understanding of human motives that can be made at present through the medium of comparative or lower-animal studies that cannot be duplicated by means of investigations utilizing human subjects? No.

REFERENCES

Kelly, G. A. *The psychology of personal constructs*. New York: Norton, 1955.
McDougall, W. *Physiological psychology*. London: Dent, 1905.
Mowrer, O. H. *Learning theory and personality dynamics*. New York: Ronald, 1950.

James Bieri
COGNITIVE COMPLEXITY-SIMPLICITY
AND PREDICTIVE BEHAVIOR

A common focus of problems in current research has been concerned with what is variously called social perception (Gage, 1953; Scodel and Mussen, 1953), interpersonal perception (Bieri, 1953b; Lundy and Bieri, 1952), understanding others (Cronbach, 1954), empathy (Dymond, 1949), or social sensitivity (Bender and Hastorf, 1953). In these studies, social perceptions often are defined operationally as responses on a questionnaire or rating scale which represent the *predictions* of how the subject (*S*) felt some other individual responded to the questionnaire or scale. By comparing these predictions with *S*'s own responses and with the other's own responses, certain hypotheses about the accuracy of the perceptions are tested. The multiplicity of findings in this area have been reviewed and discussed elsewhere (Bruner and Tagiuri, 1954). The purpose of this paper is to present a tentative theoretical framework into which these diverse empirical findings can be placed. From this framework, several predictions will be evolved, and empirical evidence relative to these predictions will be presented.

It is suggested that what is involved in the studies cited above is primarily the *predictive accuracy* of an individual's behavior. That is, one perceives another accurately to the extent that his predictions of the other's behavior are accurate. The position taken here is that predictive behavior, and its accuracy or inaccuracy, may be fruitfully viewed as a function of certain behavioral variables within a conception of personality structure. In this sense, predictive behavior is akin to expectancy behavior, as postulated in certain theories of learning and personality (Rotter, 1954).

In the present discussion, those aspects of personality functioning which set the necessary conditions for predictive behavior are construed within a general perceptual or cognitive framework. Following the theoretical orientation developed by G. A. Kelly (1955), it is assumed that a basic characteristic of human behavior is its movement in the direction of greater predictability of an individual's interpersonal environment. It is further assumed that each individual possesses a system of constructs for perceiving his social world. These constructs are invoked and form the basis for making predictions. The constructs composing the system are the characteristic modes of perceiving persons in the individual's environment. Thus, under the supposition that person X is perceived as "hostile" (construct), an individual may make one kind of prediction about his behavior, while if he were perceived as "friendly," another kind of prediction might be made. The relative success or failure of these predictions are postulated as affecting the constructs upon which they are based. Thus, unsuccessful predictions are presumed to cause greater changes in the construct sys-

From J. Bieri, ''Cognitive Complexity-Simplicity and Predictive Behavior,'' *Journal of Abnormal and Social Psychology*, 1955, *51*, 263–268. Reprinted by permission of the American Psychological Association.

tem than successful predictions. Research results to date have generally substantiated these notions concerning construct change (Bieri, 1953a; Poch, 1952).

Assuming these constructs or modes of perceiving persons are fundamental in predictive behavior, the problem arises of determining the predictive efficiency of the individual's system of constructs. A partial answer to this problem should lie in the versatility of the individual's construct system. Inasmuch as constructs represent differential perceptions or discriminations of the environment, it would be expected that the greater the degree of differentiation among the constructs, the greater will be the predictive power of the individual. In other words, there should be a positive relationship between how well an individual's system of constructs differentiates people in the environment and how well the individual can predict the behavior of these people. For our present purposes, we have designated the degree of differentiation of the construct system as reflecting its *cognitive complexity-simplicity*. A system of constructs which differentiates highly among persons is considered to be cognitively complex. A construct system which provides poor differentiation among persons is considered to be cognitively simple in structure.

The first general hypothesis would be: Among a group of Ss, there should be a significant positive relationship between degree of cognitive complexity and accuracy of predictive behavior.

In analyzing predictive behavior, a comparison may be made between the similarity of the predictor's own responses and his predictions of another individual. This similarity has been referred to as a tendency to perceive others as similar to oneself (Bieri, 1953b), as projection (Bender and Hastorf, 1953), and as assumed similarity (Fiedler, 1954). In the attempt to incorporate predictive behavior into the broader realm of personality functioning, it would seem wise to apply more specific terminology to this projective process. Cameron's concept of *assimilative projection* would appear to approximate the type of projection occurring here. That is, the individual assumes others are the same as oneself, often on the basis of insufficient evidence. In reference to persons prone to indulge in assimilative projection, Cameron states (1947, p. 167): "The less practiced a person is in the social techniques of sharing the perspectives of others, the less opportunity he will have of finding out how different from himself other ordinary people can be. The less his opportunities for finding out and sharing in such individual differences, the more likely is he to extend assimilative projection farther than the actual conditions warrant." Thus, the individual who has not made finer discriminations among his perceptions of other individuals is posited as having a greater tendency to engage in assimilative projection in reference to his perception of other individuals.

This forms the basis for the second general hypothesis: Among a group of Ss, there should be a significant negative relationship between degree of cognitive complexity and the tendency to engage in assimilative projection in one's predictive behavior.

METHOD

Subjects

The Ss in this study were a group of 22 female and 12 male university undergraduates. This group was composed of College of Education sophomores and juniors whose vocational interests centered around primary and secondary teaching.

Cognitive Complexity

   A technique for measuring the degree of cognitive complexity among one's perceptions of others is afforded by the Role Construct Repertory Test (RCRT) developed by Kelly. A detailed description of this test can be found elsewhere (Kelly, 1955). Briefly, it consists of a matrix or grid across the top of which S lists a certain number of persons in his social environment. The S is asked successively to consider three of these persons at a time and to decide in what important personal way two of them are alike and different from the third. In this manner, a series of constructs or modes of perceiving others is formed which is assumed to be relatively characteristic of him as an individual. Each time a construct is formed, check marks are placed in the grid under the names of the persons perceived as similar in some way and the name of the construct entered next to the grid. After all these sorts have been completed, and a certain number of constructs established, the individual is asked to go through each construct row again and check all the other persons in that row, in addition to the two already checked, whom he considers that particular construct applies to most. No limits are placed upon how many others in each construct row the subject may check. This procedure yields a matrix of check patterns which represents how S perceives and differentiates a group of persons relative to his personal constructs. By considering how similar each construct row is to every other construct row in the matrix, in terms of similarity of check patterns, one can objectively ascertain the degree of differentiation the constructs have for the persons in the matrix. That is, if two construct rows have identical check patterns, then these two constructs are presumed to be functionally equivalent, regardless of the verbal labels given the constructs by S. Should many of the construct rows have identical or highly similar check patterns, then the person would be said to have low cognitive complexity (i.e., cognitive simplicity) in his perceptions of others. At the opposite extreme, if an individual's construct rows have check patterns which are all quite dissimilar to one another, then he is considered as having high cognitive complexity in his perceptions of others.
   The actual scores of cognitive complexity-simplicity in this study were derived in the following way. Each time a construct check pattern was repeated in its identical form in the matrix, it was given a score of -2. Each time a construct check pattern was repeated save for a difference of *one* check mark, it was given a score of -1. The summation of these scores for the entire matrix yielded the individual's cognitive complexity score. The lower the algebraic score, the lower was the cognitive complexity. Although the use of the -2 and -1 scores was somewhat arbitrary, it had its basis in several considerations. First, a 12×12 grid or matrix was employed in the study. That is, there were 12 persons being perceived according to 12 possible constructs. Practical time considerations in the experimental situation were primary in determining the use of this number of constructs. The cognitive complexity scores obtained ranged from 0 (one case) to -22 (one case) and approximately a normal distribution. Determining the reliability of these scores posed certain problems due to the nature of the construct formation task. Thus, it would be tenuous to assume the equivalence of items for either a split-half or odd-even procedure. However, as part of a larger research project (Bieri, 1953a), retest data on these 34 Ss were available. The time interval between administrations was short, the check pattern data having been collected at the beginning and at the end of the same experimental session. However, as part of the experimental procedure, a set was produced in each S for changes to be made on the second matrix which conceivably would lower the reliability. A test-retest reliability coefficient of .78 was obtained under these conditions. Thus, even with a set to change, Ss were highly consistent in their cognitive

complexity scores over this short period of time. Further evidence is available indicating a high degree of consistency in constructs formed by *S*s over longer periods of time (Hunt, 1951).

Predictive Instrument

The predictive instrument employed was a Situations Questionnaire consisting of 12 items depicting social situations in which four reasonable behavioral alternatives were presented. A representative item is listed below:

You are working intently to finish a paper in the library when two people sit down across from you and distract you with their continual loud talking. Would you most likely:

    a. Move to another seat
    b. Let them know how you feel by your facial expression
    c. Try to finish up in spite of their talking
    d. Ask them to stop talking

Each *S* completed this questionnaire by selecting one of the four alternative responses and in addition predicted the responses of two of his classmates who had previously taken the questionnaire. Thus, a total of 24 predictions were made by each *S*. These two classmates were also used in the construct sortings on the RCRT. The degree of familiarity with a person would conceivably affect one's predictive ability of his behavior. An attempt was made to control this variable by collecting the data early in the quarter while the students were still developing their class acquaintanceships. Each *S* was asked to list six classmates and then rank them one through six in terms of how well he felt he knew them. In every case, two classmates with the intermediate ranks were used in making the predictions (i.e., ranks 3 and 4). Each *S* was encouraged to use his filled-in construct matrix to assist him in making his predictions.

Scores

Three types of data from the questionnaire are used in deriving the scores of predictive behavior. These are (a) the responses which *S* himself gave to the questionnaire, (b) the responses the other person being predicted (*O*) gave to the questionnaire, and (c) the predictions made by *S* of *O*'s responses on the questionnaire. By considering the relation between these responses, three major scores can be derived, i.e., predictive accuracy, assimilative projection, and actual similarity.

Predictive accuracy scores were obtained by summing the correct number of predictions made by each *S* on both *O*s, the criterion for accuracy being the agreement of *S*'s prediction with the responses given by *O*. *Assimilative projection* scores were obtained by totaling the number of accurate and inaccurate predictions made by an *S* which were identical to the responses given by *S* himself. The scores of predictive accuracy and assimilative projection were used in testing Hypotheses I and II, respectively.

Each of these three scores can be broken down into component scores, some of which are shared by the major scores. Analysis of the predictive accuracy score indicates it is composed of two components: (a) those accurate predictions representing responses identical to those *S* made himself (*accurate projections*) and (b) those accurate predictions which are different from the responses given by *S* (*accurate perceived differences*). Similarly, the assimilative projection score contains the accurate projection component plus an *inaccurate projection* component (i.e., S and O gave different responses but S predicted that O gave a similar response). If we consider the *actual.similarity* between S's own responses and O's responses, we find this score to be composed of the accurate projection component plus those *inaccurate* predictions which are different from the responses given by S (*inaccurate perceived differences*). In this latter case, S and O have identical responses but S predicts a difference. We may schematize these scores and their components as indicated below:

Predictive accuracy = accurate projection + accurate perceived differences.
Assimilative projection = accurate projection + inaccurate projection.
Actual similarity = accurate projection + inaccurate perceived differences.

For purposes of this study, three component scores were utilized, namely accurate projection, inaccurate projection, and accurate perceived differences. The relationships of these scores to the cognitive complexity measure will be discussed relative to the experimental hypotheses.

RESULTS

Using the Pearson product-moment coefficient, the various scores discussed above relative to predictive behavior were correlated with the cognitive complexity measure. Inasmuch as directional predictions were made, one-tailed significance tests were employed in assessing results for Hypotheses I and II. Hypothesis I states that a significant positive relationship exists between cognitive complexity and predictive accuracy. From Table 1, it is observed that the relationship is significant at the .05 level. Considering the two component scores subsumed under predictive accuracy, it is apparent that accurate projection shows no relationship ($r = .02$) to cognitive complexity. However, the correlation between accurate perceived differences and cognitive complexity ($r = .35$) is significant at the .05 level (two-tailed test). Thus, it appears that the cognitive behavior measured here relates more directly to the accurate prediction of *differences* between self and others than to the accurate prediction of similarities between self and others.

Hypothesis II states that a significant negative relationship will exist between degree of cognitive complexity and the tendency to engage in assimilative projection in one's predictions. Reference to Table 1 suggests that this is the case. The assimilative projection score correlates negatively ($r = -.32$) with the cognitive complexity score ($p < .05$). It will be noted that the correlations of the two component scores of assimilative projection, namely accurate projection and inaccurate projection, with cognitive discrimination are .02 and $-.40$ respectively. The latter significant negative correlation implies that the tendency for cognitively simple Ss to engage in assimilative projection is largely a function of their tendency to perceive unwarranted or inaccurate similarities between themselves and others.

The correlation between cognitive complexity and actual similarity yields a positive but insignificant correlation ($r = .20$). This suggests there was some tendency for cognitively complex Ss to predict persons who were relatively more similar to themselves in terms of questionnaire responses. However, the accurate projection component of this score contains the only predictive accuracy measure for actual similarity. Since this component correlates only .02 with cognitive complexity, we may infer that actual similarity played no significant role in producing greater predictive accuracy for cognitively complex Ss.

It may reasonably be asked what relationship general intelligence may have to these

Table 1. Correlations of cognitive complexity with measures
of predictive behavior ($N = 34$)

	Predictive behavior	Cognitive complexity
Predictive accuracy		.29
Assimilative projection		−.32
Accurate projection		.02
Accurate perceived differences		.35
Inaccurate projection		−.40
Actual similarity		.20

Note: One-tailed *p* values: 1% = .40, 5% = .29.
      Two-tailed *p* values: 1% = .44, 5% = .34.

measures, particularly cognitive complexity. For 28 of the 34 *S*s, it was possible to obtain total scores on the Ohio State Psychological Examination (OSPE), which is considered to be primarily a measure of verbal intelligence. The correlations between OSPE scores and the various scores in Table 1, including cognitive complexity, were insignificant and low, ranging from .01 to .12.

DISCUSSION

The above results are construed as offering tentative evidence as to the interrelationship of three forms of behavior: (a) the degree of complexity in one's perceptions and differentiations of other persons, (b) the degree of accuracy with which one can predict the behavior of these other persons and (c) the degree to which assimilative projection is invoked in one's predictive behavior. The underlying formulation has been that making adequate differentiations in one's perceptions of others is basic to an optimum predictability of their behavior. Although the relationships posited in the experimental hypotheses are supported at a statistically significant level by the empirical results, the magnitude of the correlations obtained suggests that additional factors must be operating.

Let us consider the relationship between cognitive complexity and predictive accuracy. In this study, our primary concern has been to explain predictive behavior in terms of organismic variables to the partial exclusion of the external behavioral realm to be predicted. Cronbach (1954) and others have pointed out that the complexity of the behavioral situation to be predicted may affect accuracy of prediction. Thus, bringing complex differentiations into a simple situation may lead to lower accuracy than would be the case if simple differentiations were invoked. Undoubtedly, there are many situations in which a response based upon a simple yes-no, this-or-that discrimination would be preferable to responses based upon more elaborate cognitive differentiations. We must not infer, however, that the capacity to make complex differentiations in situations is necessarily equivalent to invoking complex behavior in dealing with the situation. Developmentally, we may assume that complex differentiations arise from more simple ones, and that the presence of the former implies the presence of the latter. Thus, the cognitively complex individual has versatility in both simple and complex behavioral realms, so to speak, while the cognitively simple individual is versatile in only one realm. In addition to these situational factors, it is evident that *qualitative* differences are important in terms of the adequacy of interpersonal differentiations. When the paranoid reacts to an insignificant gesture with an elaborate delusional structure, his complex reaction is considered inappropriate to the objectively simple gesture. Something in addition to degree of cognitive complexity is involved in determining the adequacy of this response. In line with these considerations, the effect of differing modes of adjustment upon both the adequacy and degree of cognitive differentiations is currently being studied.

The results of this study cast light upon the importance of assimilative projection in predictive behavior. When we consider the components of assimilative projection, we find no apparent relationship between accurate projection and degree of cognitive complexity. The significant relationship exists between inaccurate projection and cognitive simplicity. These findings reinforce the belief that the condition of cognitive simplicity reflects an incomplete differentiation of the boundaries between self and the external world, leading to unwarranted assumptions of similarity between self and others. Here again, the implicit role of adjustment and developmental factors would appear to warrant further study.

The similarity between the conceptual framework underlying the present study and related research in the area of *meaning* should be noted. Osgood's semantic differential (1952) contains certain characteristics of the personal construct. Thus, it is a bipolar dimension ranging from a characteristic to its opposite (e.g., hard to soft) upon which *S*s are asked to perceive other individuals. The essential difference between the two approaches rests upon the *source* of the dimensions invoked in perceiving others. Personal constructs represent the individual's own dimensions for differentiating his world, while Osgood, Cronbach, and others use standard, nomothetically derived dimensions. For purposes of conceptual integration into the broader framework of personality functioning, using the person's own perceptions may offer more utility.

SUMMARY

A theoretical approach which conceives predictive behavior to be a function of one's perceptions of others is presented as a means of unifying certain empirical data ordinarily subsumed under the labels of social perception, empathy, or social sensitivity. The viewpoint taken is that all these forms of behavior rest operationally upon the predictive behavior of the individual. Further, this predictive behavior is assumed to be dependent upon the interpersonal discriminations or constructs which the individual invokes in making his predictions. The complexity of an individual's cognitive system relative to the degree of differentiation among his perceptions of others should thus affect his predictive behavior. Two major hypotheses were derived: (a) There should be a significant positive relationship between degree of cognitive complexity and predictive accuracy, and (b) there should be a significant negative relationship between cognitive complexity and assimilative projection. These hypotheses were tested on a sample of 34 *S*s, each of whom predicted the behavior of two classmates on a Situations Questionnaire. Both of the hypotheses were supported by the data. By considering the component scores of predictive accuracy and assimilative projection, these relationships were further explored. Thus, cognitive complexity relates especially to the tendency to predict accurately the differences between oneself and others. Similarly, the tendency to engage in inaccurate projections concerning the similarity between self and others relates significantly to cognitive simplicity. It is concluded that the complexity of one's cognitive system for perceiving others is effectively related to one's ability to predict accurately the behavior of others and to one's tendency to engage in assimilative projection in such behavior. Certain suggestions for further investigation are discussed.

REFERENCES

Bender, I. E., and Hastorf, A. H. On measuring generalized empathic ability (social sensitivity). *J. abnorm. soc. Psychol.*, 1953, *48*, 503–506.

Bieri, J. A study of the generalization of changes within the personal construct system. Unpublished doctor's dissertation, Ohio State Univ., 1953a.

Bieri, J. Changes in interpersonal perceptions following social interaction. *J. abnorm. soc. Psychol.*, 1953b, *48*, 61–66.

Bruner, J. S., and Tagiuri, R. The perception of people. In G. Lindzey (Ed.), *Handbook of social psychology*. Cambridge, Mass. Addison-Wesley, 1954, Pp. 634–654.

Cameron, N. *The psychology of behavior disorders*. Boston: Houghton Mifflin, 1947.

Cronbach, L. J. Processes affecting "understanding of others" and "assumed similarity." *Tech. Rep. No. 10, Group Effectiveness Research Laboratory* (Contract N6ori-07135). Urbana: Univ. of Illinois, 1954. (Mimeograph)

Dymond, Rosalind F. A scale for the measurement of empathic ability. *J. consult. Psychol.*, 1949, *13*, 127–133.

Fiedler, F. E. Assumed similarity measures as predictors of team effectiveness. *J. abnorm. soc. Psychol.*, 1954, *49*, 381–388.

Gage, N. L. Accuracy of social perception and effectiveness in interpersonal relationships. *J. Pers.*, 1953, *22*, 128–141.

Hunt, D. E. Studies in role concept repertory: Conceptual consistency. Unpublished master's thesis, Ohio State Univ., 1951.

Kelly, G. A. *The psychology of personal constructs*. New York: Norton, 1955. 2 vols.

Lundy, R. M., and Bieri, J. Changes in interpersonal perceptions associated with group interaction. *Amer. Psychologist*, 1952, *7*, 306. (Abstract)

Osgood, C. E. The nature and measurement of meaning. *Psychol. Bull.*, 1952, *49*, 197–237.

Poch, Susanne M. A study of changes in personal constructs as related to interpersonal prediction and its outcomes. Unpublished doctor's dissertation, Ohio State Univ., 1952.

Rotter, J. B. *Social learning and clinical psychology*. New York: Prentice-Hall, 1954.

Scodel, A., and Mussen, P. Social perceptions of authoritarians and nonauthoritarians. *J. abnorm. soc. Psychol.*, 1953, *48*, 181–184.

Jerome S. Bruner and Carl R. Rogers
TWO CRITICAL COMMENTS ON KELLY'S PSYCHOLOGY OF PERSONAL CONSTRUCTS

A COGNITIVE THEORY OF PERSONALITY

These excellent, original, and infuriatingly prolix two volumes easily nominate themselves for the distinction of being the single greatest contribution of the past decade to the theory of personality functioning. Professor Kelly has written a major work.

The book is an effort to construct a theory of personality from a theory of knowledge: how people came to know the world by binding its diverse appearances into organized construct systems which vary not only in organization but in their goodness of fit to the bricks and mortar of reality. The point of view that dominates the work—the author labels it "constructive alternativism"—is one that the author applies both to himself as a science-maker and to his troubled clients. In a deep sense, the book reflects the climate of a generation of nominalistic thinking in the philosophy of science.

Let me summarize the major theoretical elements of the work—a task made somewhat easier than usual by the author's admirable use of a Fundamental Postulate and a set of elaborating corollaries. The Fundamental Postulate is that "A person's processes are psychologically channelized by the ways in which he anticipates events." In short, man's effort is to gain prediction and control over his environment—much as a scientist. Does not man "have his theories, test his hypotheses, and weigh his experimental evidence"—and each in his own way? The author contrasts this point of view with one that he feels is prevalent among personality theorists: "I, being a *psychologist* and therefore a *scientist*, am performing this experiment in order to improve the prediction and control of certain human phenomena; but my subject, being merely a human organism, is obviously propelled by inexorable drives welling up within him." If it was Freud's genius to cut through the rationalistic cant of nineteenth-century Apollonianism, George Kelly's talent is to outstare the fashionable Dionysianism of the twentieth.

The Eleven Corollaries provide ways of describing or chronicling the vicissitudes of man's fumbling efforts at predicting and controlling his world. The first, or Construction Corollary, has to do with the process of cognitive working-through: "A person anticipates events by construing their replications." It is not from experience but from its reconstruing that we learn. The next two corollaries deal with the idiosyncratic nature of each man's construct world and man's construing acts.

The next corollary leads to some highly original and striking ideas about psychodiag-

From J. S. Bruner, "A Cognitive Theory of Personality," and C. R. Rogers, "Intellectualized Psychotherapy," reviews of George A. Kelly's *Psychology of Personal Constructs* in *Contemporary Psychology*, 1956, *1*, 355–358. Reprinted by permission of the American Psychological Association.

nostic testing. It is the notion of dichotomization that has proved so fruitful in communication theory and in modern structural linguistics. "A person's construction system is composed of a finite number of dichotomous constructs." The dichotomized construct is inferred from triadic judgments. That is to say, given events A, B, and C, A and B are judged similar to each other in the same respect in which C is in contrast to both of them. A construct is not understood unless one grasps the two construct poles that form it, one of which may often be unrecognized by the construing person.

The Choice Corollary gets the author, I think, into a conceptual trap. "A person chooses for himself that alternative in a dichotomized construct through which he anticipates the greater possibility for extension and definition of his system." That is to say, an event is construed or "placed" at one or the other alternative poles of a construct ("good" or "bad," "healthy" or "hostile," or whatever) depending upon "which seems to provide the best basis for anticipating the ensuing events." One object of categorizing the world in terms of a construct system is to minimize the disruptive surprises that it can wreak on us. This, I think, is the principal doctrine of "motivation" in the book—an implicit one, but one stamped on every page. It is the author's counterproposal to the Law of Effect, to the Pleasure Principle, to the watered-down hedonisms and tension reductions of such various Yale thinkers as Neal Miller, John Dollard, and David McClelland.

But must event-construing or categorizing always be guided by the need to extend cognitive control over one's environment? Need man be viewed *either* as the pig that reinforcement theory makes of him *or* the professor that Kelly implies as a model? I think not: in categorizing events, there is more to be maximized that predictiveness. Here is an example of the folly. "No matter how obvious it may be that a person would be better off if he avoided a fight . . . , such a course of action would seem to him personally to limit the definition and extension of his system as a whole." I rather suspect that when some people get angry or inspired or in love, they couldn't care less about their "system as a whole." One gets the impression that the author is, in his personality theory, over-reacting against a generation of irrationalism.

The next four corollaries have to do with what might be called the dynamics of construct utilization and change. Any given construct anticipates only a finite range of events, and effective action depends upon recognizing this "range of convenience." Construct systems change with time, experience, and the reconstruing of replicates, and they vary in their permeability to the influence of new events. As he goes through life, a person may develop a construct system with high or low degrees of integration, fragmentation, or incompatibility.

So much, then, for the axiomatic apparatus in terms of which Professor Kelly construes the world. What does he make of it?

For one thing, and a very considerable thing, I believe, he has found a way of ungluing the eye of psychology from the keyhole of projective techniques. His REP test (Role Construct Repertory Test) is a simple and elegant way of determining the manner in which significant figures in the person's life are fitted into a construct system. Take a list of the significant kinds of people with whom a person interacts: parents, boy friends, teachers, sweethearts, bosses, "a person who dislikes you," etc. The client thinks of specific people who fill these roles in his life. He is then given triads of these and asked to indicate which two are most alike, in what respects, and how the third differs from these: the method of getting at the dichotomized contrast poles of the construct. The constructs that emerge from the sorting of the triads are then reduced mathematically and intuitively to get at the nature of general constructs used, the range they comprise, their degree of preemptiveness, etc.

The author then sets forth a subtle and interesting set of dimensions for describing the

constructs of patients: looseness-tightness, constriction-dilation, level of cognitive awareness, and then proceeds to redefine some classic concepts in terms of these. He redefines
anxiety as awareness that events to be coped with lie outside the range of convenience of one's
construct system, and *hostility* as an effort to extort validational evidence for an anticipatory
prediction already recognized as failing.

I have said nothing about Professor Kelly's approaches to therapy, nor am I particularly
qualified to do so. One point I must make, however, for it is at the core of his theoretical
approach. The effort in therapy is not to give the patient "insight" which, according to the
author, too often means getting the patient's construct system to conform to that of the
therapist. Rather the process of therapy is considered as an occasion for learning—for testing
the fit of one's own (not the therapist's) construct system to the world. To do this, a kind of
role-playing approach is employed, much in the spirit of characters in a Pirandello or O'Neill
play who learn of themselves partly through the experience of contrasting or confusing (or
both) what they are with the mask they are wearing in different life situations.

Where does the book succeed and where fall down? Who are the ancestors? What is
portended by the appearance of this extraordinary and original work? The book succeeds, I
think, in raising to a proper level of dignity and importance the press that man feels toward
cognitive control of the world. It succeeds too in recognizing the individuality and "alternatives" of the routes to mental health. It succeeds in providing a diagnostic device strikingly in
keeping with its presuppositions.

The book fails signally, I think, in dealing convincingly with the human passions. There
was a strategy in Freud's choice of Moses or Michelangelo or Little Hans. If it is true that
Freud was too often the victim of the dramatic instance, it is also true that with the same coin
he paid his way to an understanding of the depths and heights of *la condition humaine*. By
comparison, the young men and women of Professor Kelly's clinical examples are worried
about their dates, their studies, and their conformity. If Freud's clinical world is a grotesque of
fin de siècle Vienna, Kelly's is a gloss on the post-adolescent peer groups of Columbus, Ohio,
who are indeed in the process of constructing their worlds. Which is more "real"? I have no
idea. I wish Professor Kelly would treat more "most religious men in their most religious
moments," or even just Nijinsky or Gabriel d'Annunzio.

With respect to ancestry, Professor Kelly seems to care little for it. One misses reference
to such works as Piaget's *The Child's Construction of Reality*, the early work of Werner, and
the writings of Harry Stack Sullivan, Lewin, and Allport—all of whom are on his side and
good allies to boot.

The book is a theory of cognition extrapolated into a theory of personality—a genuine
new departure and a spirited contribution to the psychology of personality.

INTELLECTUALIZED PSYCHOTHERAPY

This is a man's life work. In this enormous outpouring of 1200 pages (broken into two
volumes only because of its bulk) George Kelly has endeavored to express the thinking which
has grown out of twenty years of clinical experience, teaching, and supervision of research.
Here is his philosophical base, the theory of personality which has emerged in his thinking, a
new diagnostic instrument he has developed, a new therapeutic method, plus his extended
views on all phases of psychodiagnosis and psychotherapy. In these half-million words he is
saying "Here I am." It is a good solid figure which emerges, even if the question grows ever
stronger as one reads on, whether any man has 1200 pages to express at one time.

In Kelly's view the framework of the book is provided by his theory of personality and behavior, largely presented in the first three chapters. To this reviewer these 183 pages were much the freshest, most original, most valuable. Kelly takes off from no current theory, but solely from the distillation of his own informed experience with individuals. He attempts to build a theoretical system which looks forward, not backward—which sees behavior as anticipatory, not reactive. He is attempting to hold persons as processes, not objects. He emphasizes phenomenological information, but his theory superimposes normative thinking upon the phenomenological data.

His basic concept is that the individual's behavior is channelized by the way he anticipates events, and that the individual anticipates events by the constructions (interpretations, meanings) he has placed upon his experience. The careful, rigorous logic with which Kelly works out the way in which these constructs are formed, the implications which flow from their mode of organization, and the ways in which they may change, make stimulating and thought-provoking reading. There emerges a picture of man as being not "a victim of his past, only the victim of his construction of it." This view, in Kelly's opinion, allows for the "determinism" which is a part of science, yet permits a concept of "constructive alternativism," or choice, in the way in which the individual construes his world.

It is gratifying to learn that this carefully formulated theory, presented in terms which can be given operational definition, is already being tested in small ways by a very considerable number of doctoral researches at Ohio State University (most of them unfortunately unpublished).

Since the space limits of this review severely restrict the reviewer, he must omit many areas of the book to comment on Kelly's views on psychotherapy.

It is in his chapter on *Fixed-Role Therapy* that the author becomes most personally expressive. It is clear that in this new method he has found an approach congenial to his personality, which is perhaps the basic aim of every therapist. Essentially, a diagnosis is made of the client's psychological constructs as they operate in his most significant interpersonal relationships. Then a number of clinicians (to avoid the bias of any one) develop a sketch of a new person, one that this client might become if his constructs were altered constructively. The aim is to get him to "play-act" this role for several weeks, without any notion that it represents a goal for him. The hope is that by shaking loose the organization of his psychological constructs, by giving him a new role, he will be more able to choose a role for himself built around an altered set of personal hypotheses, which will be confirmed or disconfirmed in his continuing experience.

Kelly shows real zest in his description of the way the client is kept from knowing the purpose of this "play-acting," and the enthusiastic manner in which he coaches the client in his new role, playing the parts, one after another, of the individuals with whom the client will interact. Kelly's statement that the therapist needs "a great deal of enthusiastic momentum" and "some measure of verbal fluency and acting skill" to succeed in this effort seems a decided understatement, but it is clear that Kelly enjoys it. He describes his clinical experience with the use of this method both in individual and in group therapy (where a role sketch is devised for each person), but there are as yet no research studies of its effectiveness. One point which is unmentioned by Kelly is that this method could not be used with any client who had read about it or heard about it, since it is very important that the client regard the new role initially as simply an exercise, not in any sense as a possible pattern for his personality.

There are many other chapters, including the last five of Volume II, which deal with Kelly's psychotherapeutic observations. It is impossible to do more than indicate briefly some reactions to them.

An overwhelming impression is that for Kelly therapy is seen as almost entirely an intellectual function, a view which should be comforting to many psychologists. He is continually thinking about the client, and about his own procedures, in ways so complex that there seems no time or room for entering into an emotional relationship with the client. One small example. There are ten types of weeping to be differentiated. In dealing with one of them or with some other problem the client is expressing, there are nine techniques for reducing anxiety, twelve techniques (in addition to role playing) for encouraging the client to move or experiment in therapy, fifteen criteria to consider regarding the client's readiness to explore new areas, etc., etc. One has the impression of an incredibly "busy" therapist. This reviewer cannot help but wonder about the relation between "busyness" and effectiveness in therapy.

This approach to therapy is also highly eclectic. The therapist in appropriate situations manipulates the transference, prescribes activities, gives interpretations, uses "non-directive reflecting," confrontation, the discussion of dreams, the playing back of previous recorded interviews, etc. What the effect will be of setting this enormous cookbook of therapy before students who are preparing to undertake therapy is problematical. Certainly they will find almost every problem of therapy mentioned in its pages, but what a student should do about a particular problem with a particular client will depend upon whether he construes the difficulty as "controlling guilt feelings" or "loosening constructs." The recipes are very different. Kelly believes that his views on therapy are given unity by his initial theory, but such unity consists largely in the fact that anything done to the client affects his psychological constructs in some way.

In the beginning of the theoretical presentation Kelly pays tribute to the strength of each individual as a private "scientist" who tests out hypotheses in his own behavior. In the chapters on therapy, however, the wisdom all lies in the mind of the therapist. Since the client's perceptions of therapy and therapist are mostly false, therapy can only reach its proper goal if the therapist carefully chooses the role which should be played with this client at this time and appropriately manipulates the multitudinous aspects of the therapeutic process as suggested above. Confidence in the client as the "scientist" of his own life does not here find much operational expression.

Another disappointing element in this clinician, who has undoubtedly been of help to many individuals, is the lack of any sense of depth in his discussions of therapy. The chapters on theory clearly show an author who has thought deeply about his experience. The chapters on therapy seem to present meager evidence that he has lived deeply with his clients, and the bulk of the anecdotal examples seem to describe but superficial change. This reviewer had the feeling that perhaps Kelly was not doing justice to this phase of his experience. Actually the work might have a stronger impact if much of the last section were omitted.

However any one reader may see their strengths and weaknesses, these two volumes are clearly the measure of a man. They are written with modesty, with occasional humor, with brilliance in the theoretical sections, with earnestness and essential open-mindedness in the diagnostic and therapeutic sections. In spite of being too wordy, they show a person who is not afraid to launch out on his own in the development of theory, who looks to his experience rather than to authority for the source and the confirmation of his ideas. They show a man who believes deeply in the scientific method and who expects his views to be changed by research findings. Psychologists, perhaps especially young ones, will profit greatly from reading these chapters because they will find their own psychological constructs loosened by the experience. And, while any reader will find a great many pages which seem to him of dubious value, that still leaves many pages, ample enough to constitute highly rewarding reading.

Eleven
LEON FESTINGER

Leon Festinger's (1919–   ) theory of cognitive dissonance is not intended as a formal personality theory. Rather, it is an attempt to clarify the various roles that cognitions and motivations play in the psychological resolution of conflict following the occurrence of an emotionally significant event. Central to Festinger's theory are the clusters of opinions, attitudes, and bits of knowledge that compose an individual's cognitive system. When any of these cognitive elements is inconsistent (dissonant) with another, the psychological system may—depending on the proximity and strength of the conflicting elements—be thrown into a state of disequilibrium. Because this state of imbalance is an uncomfortable, presumed to be tension-creating experience, the individual is thought to seek to reduce the tension by attempting to resolve the apparent contradiction. The simplicity suggested by this capsule statement of Festinger's theory is deceptive; the theory has been used to explain a wide variety of complex social and individual behavioral phenomena.

The paper presented in this volume is the first chapter in Festinger's major work, *A Theory of Cognitive Dissonance*. Festinger systematically outlines his theory in this paper, beginning with the two hypotheses that are basic to his theoretical position. The first hypothesis is that, because the state of dissonance is an uncomfortable psychological experience, people will try to reduce dissonance and achieve consonance. Consonance is the opposite of dissonance and represents a conflict-free cognitive state. When consonance exists, a person's opinions and attitudes are consistent with one another. The second hypothesis is that a person will try in various ways to reduce dissonance and to avoid situations and information that might tend to increase dissonance. The crucial point made by Festinger is that people are motivated to reduce dissonance and that, therefore, cognitive dissonance will motivate dissonance reduction in the same way that hunger motivates hunger reduction. A consideration of the motivational aspect of Festinger's theory leads to many interesting speculations about the relationship between cognitive dissonance and personality style. Festinger's theory has thus provided the framework for many ingenious research studies.

The research paper by Dana Bramel describes an attempt to explain the psychoanalytic defense mechanism of projection by means of the experimental application of cognitive dissonance theory. Bramel hypothesized that, when individuals are exposed to undesirable information about themselves, the more incompatible with their level of self-esteem this information is, the greater their tendency to use projection as a defense. Bramel offered an additional hypothesis: that reduction of dissonance will occur when undesirable traits attributed to oneself are projected onto respected, favorably evaluated persons.

In the first part of Bramel's study, one group of subjects was given fraudulent favorable self-esteem information, and the other group was given fraudulent unfavorable self-esteem information. Then both the favorable and unfavorable groups were exposed to information suggesting the presence in them of homosexual tendencies. (All of the subjects were men.) This set was ingeniously reinforced through the use of falsified galvanic skin response feedback during the presentation of pictures of nearly nude men. In this phase of the experiment, all subjects were arranged in pairs; each subject was asked to estimate his partner's galvanic skin response to the pictures of men that were being projected on a screen before them. Thus, each subject received false galvanic skin response feedback about himself and was at the same time required to judge his partner's response to the same stimuli.

The chief measure of the attribution of homosexual tendencies to the partner was the numerical difference between the subject's false galvanic skin response score and his estimation of his partner's galvanic skin response score. In the final phase of the experiment, additional rating scales were administered to test the subject's judgment of his own and his partner's masculinity and to test his self-esteem.

The results tended to confirm both of the experimenter's expectations. Projection was greatest when the information presented to the subject was most dissonant with his self-concept. Thus, subjects in the favorable self-concept set attributed higher reactions to the threatening stimuli to their partners than did subjects in the undesirable self-concept set. The data also revealed that the high-dissonance group (favorable self-concept set) only projected when the target was another individual who had previously been evaluated favorably.

The final paper in this chapter, by Daryl J. Bem, is a detailed review of a sample of cognitive dissonance experiments, offering an alternative interpretation of some of the findings. This critique paper is particularly interesting because Bem applies a "radical" behavioral analysis associated with the work of B. F. Skinner to the theory of cognitive dissonance, which is basically a phenomenological cognitive theory. Bem does not question the social phenomena Festinger describes, only the explanations.

In his analysis, Bem also reports his own empirical data. He replicated a few of the classical cognitive dissonance experiments and in each replication added a special experimental detail designed to clarify the theoretical issue he was interested in. (A replication is an experiment that duplicates the basic conditions of the original research. Replications of experiments are necessary in science because they provide verification that the results obtained were not chance phenomena or unique events from which one can't generalize.) Bem concludes, on the basis of his experiments, that a behavioral interpretation—one based on observable behavior rather than on inferred mental phenomena—is a more powerful analysis than a theoretical position, such as cognitive dissonance, that relies on an "appeal to hypothetical internal states of the organism."

SUGGESTIONS FOR FURTHER READING

A Theory of Cognitive Dissonance, published by Stanford University Press in 1957, is Festinger's classic work. Further elaborations of theory and research can be found in Brehm and Cohen, *Explanations in Cognitive Dissonance*, published by Wiley in 1962, and in Festinger, *Conflict, Decision, and Dissonance*, published by Stanford University Press in 1964.

An interesting group of studies that relate the theory of cognitive dissonance to biological drives such as thirst, hunger, and pain and to social motives and personality variables is presented in *The Cognitive Control of Motivation*, edited by Philip G. Zimbardo. The book was published by Scott, Foresman in 1969.

Leon Festinger
THE THEORY OF COGNITIVE DISSONANCE

It has frequently been implied, and sometimes even pointed out, that the individual strives toward consistency within himself. His opinions and attitudes, for example, tend to exist in clusters that are internally consistent. Certainly one may find exceptions. A person may think Negroes are just as good as whites but would not want any living in his neighborhood; or someone may think little children should be quiet and unobtrusive and yet may be quite proud when his child aggressively captures the attention of his adult guests. When such inconsistencies are found to exist, they may be quite dramatic, but they capture our interest primarily because they stand out in sharp contrast against a background of consistency. It is still overwhelmingly true that related opinions or attitudes are consistent with one another. Study after study reports such consistency among one person's political attitudes, social attitudes, and many others.

There is the same kind of consistency between what a person knows or believes and what he does. A person who believes a college education is a good thing will very likely encourage his children to go to college; a child who knows he will be severely punished for some misdemeanor will not commit it or at least will try not to be caught doing it. This is not surprising, of course; it is so much the rule that we take it for granted. Again what captures our attention are the exceptions to otherwise consistent behavior. A person may know that smoking is bad for him and yet continue to smoke; many persons commit crimes even though they know the high probability of being caught and the punishment that awaits them.

Granting that consistency is the usual thing, perhaps overwhelmingly so, what about these exceptions which come to mind so readily? Only rarely, if ever, are they accepted psychologically *as inconsistencies* by the person involved. Usually more or less successful attempts are made to rationalize them. Thus, the person who continues to smoke, knowing that it is bad for his health, may also feel (a) he enjoys smoking so much it is worth it; (b) the chances of his health suffering are not as serious as some would make out; (c) he can't always avoid every possible dangerous contingency and still live; and (d) perhaps even if he stopped smoking he would put on weight which is equally bad for his health. So continuing to smoke is, after all, consistent with his ideas about smoking.

But persons are not always successful in explaining away or in rationalizing inconsistencies to themselves. For one reason or another, attempts to achieve consistency may fail. The inconsistency then simply continues to exist. Under such circumstances—that is, in the presence of an inconsistency—there is psychological discomfort.

Reprinted from *A Theory of Cognitive Dissonance* by Leon Festinger with the permission of the publishers, Stanford University Press. © 1957 by Leon Festinger. Pp. 1–31.

The basic hypotheses, the ramifications and implications of which will be explored in the remainder of this book, can now be stated. First, I will replace the word "inconsistency" with a term which has less of a logical connotation, namely, *dissonance*. I will likewise replace the word "consistency" with a more neutral term, namely, *consonance*. A more formal definition of these terms will be given shortly; for the moment, let us try to get along with the implicit meaning they have acquired as a result of the preceding discussion.

The basic hypotheses I wish to state are as follows:

1. The existence of dissonance, being psychologically uncomfortable, will motivate the person to try to reduce the dissonance and achieve consonance.

2. When dissonance is present, in addition to trying to reduce it, the person will actively avoid situations and information which would likely increase the dissonance.

Before proceeding to develop this theory of dissonance and the pressures to reduce it, it would be well to clarify the nature of dissonance, what kind of a concept it is, and where the thoery concerning it will lead. The two hypotheses stated above provide a good starting point for this clarification. While they refer here specifically to dissonance, they are in fact very general hypotheses. In the place of "dissonance" one can substitute other notions similar in nature, such as "hunger," "frustration," or "disequilibrium," and the hypotheses would still make perfectly good sense.

In short, I am proposing that dissonance, that is, the existence of nonfitting relations among cognitions, is a motivating factor in its own right. By the term *cognition* I mean any knowledge, opinion, or belief about the environment, about oneself, or about one's behavior. Cognitive dissonance can be seen as an antecedent condition which leads to activity oriented toward dissonance reduction just as hunger leads to activity oriented toward hunger reduction. It is a very different motivation from what psychologists are used to dealing with but, as we shall see, nonethcless powerful.

THE OCCURRENCE AND PERSISTENCE OF DISSONANCE

Why and how does dissonance ever arise? How does it happen that persons sometimes find themselves doing things that do not fit with what they know, or having opinions that do not fit with other opinions they hold? An answer to this question may be found in discussing two of the more common situations in which dissonance may occur.

1. New events may happen or new information may become known to a person, creating at least a momentary dissonance with existing knowledge, opinion, or cognition concerning behavior. Since a person does not have complete and perfect control over the information that reaches him and over events that can happen in his environment, such dissonances may easily arise. Thus, for example, a person may plan to go on a picnic with complete confidence that the weather will be warm and sunny. Nevertheless, just before he is due to start, it may begin to rain. The knowledge that it is now raining is dissonant with his confidence in a sunny day and with his planning to go to a picnic. Or, as another example, a person who is quite certain in his knowledge that automatic transmissions on automobiles are inefficient may accidentally come across an article praising automatic transmissions. Again, at least a momentary dissonance is created.

2. Even in the absence of new, unforeseen events or information, the existence of dissonance is undoubtedly an everyday condition. Very few things are all black or all white; very few situations are clear-cut enough so that opinions or behaviors are not to some extent a mixture of contradictions. Thus, a midwestern farmer who is a Republican may be opposed to

his party's position on farm price supports; a person buying a new car may prefer the economy of one model but the design of another; a person deciding on how to invest his money may know that the outcome of his investment depends upon economic conditions beyond his control. Where an opinion must be formed or a decision taken, some dissonance is almost unavoidably created between the cognition of the action taken and those opinions or knowledges which tend to point to a different action.

There is, then, a fairly wide variety of situations in which dissonance is nearly unavoidable. But it remains for us to examine the circumstances under which dissonance, once arisen, persists. That is, under what conditions is dissonance not simply a momentary affair? If the hypotheses stated above are correct, then as soon as dissonance occurs there will be pressures to reduce it. To answer this question it is necessary first to have a brief look at the possible ways in which dissonance may be reduced.

Since there will be a more formal discussion of this point later on in this chapter, let us now examine how dissonance may be reduced, using as an illustration the example of the habitual cigarette smoker who has learned that smoking is bad for his health. He may have acquired this information from a newspaper or magazine, from friends, or even from some physician. This knowledge is certainly dissonant with cognition that he continues to smoke. If the hypothesis that there will be pressures to reduce this dissonance is correct, what would the person involved be expected to do?

1. He might simply change his cognition about his behavior by changing his actions; that is, he might stop smoking. If he no longer smokes, then his cognition of what he does will be consonant with the knowledge that smoking is bad for his health.

2. He might change his "knowledge" about the effects of smoking. This sounds like a peculiar way to put it, but it expresses well what must happen. He might simply end up believing that smoking does not have any deleterious effects, or he might acquire so much "knowledge" pointing to the good effects it has that the harmful aspects become negligible. If he can manage to change his knowledge in either of these ways, he will have reduced, or even eliminated, the dissonance between what he does and what he knows.

But in the above illustration it seems clear that the person may encounter difficulties in trying to change either his behavior or his knowledge. And this, of course, is precisely the reason that dissonance, once created, may persist. There is no guarantee that the person will be able to reduce or remove the dissonance. The hypothetical smoker may find that the process of giving up smoking is too painful for him to endure. He might try to find facts and opinions of others to support the view that smoking is not harmful, but these attempts might fail. He might then remain in the situation where he continues to smoke and continues to know that smoking is harmful. If this turns out to be the case, however, his efforts to reduce the dissonance will not cease.

Indeed, there are some areas of cognition where the existence of major dissonance is customary. This may occur when two or more established beliefs or values, all relevant to the area of cognition in question, are inconsistent. That is, no opinion can be held, and no behavior engaged in, that will not be dissonant with at least one of these established beliefs. Myrdal (1944), in the appendix of his classic book, states this quite well in connection with attitudes and behavior toward Negroes. In discussing the simultaneous existence of opinions and values concerning human beings in general, Negroes in general, specific groups of Negroes, and so on, Myrdal states:

A need will be felt by the person or group, whose inconsistencies in valuations are publicly exposed, to find a means of reconciling the inconsistencies. . . . The feeling of need for logical consistency within the hierarchy of moral valuations . . . is, in its modern intensity, a rather new phenomenon. With less mobility, less intellectual communication, and less public discussion, there was in previous generations less exposure of one another's valuation conflicts (pp. 1029, 1030).

While I find myself in disagreement with Myrdal in the importance he places on the public exposure of the dissonance, I feel it is a good statement of some of the reasons why strong dissonance exists in this area.

The notions introduced thus far are not entirely new; many similar ones have been suggested. It may be of value to mention two whose formulation is closest to my own. Heider (1958) discusses the relationships among people and among sentiments. He states:

> Summarizing this preliminary discussion of balanced, or harmonious, states, we can say that they are states characterized by two or more relations which fit together. If no balanced state exists, then forces toward the [balanced] state will arise. Either there will be a tendency to change the sentiments involved, or the unit relations will be changed through action or cognitive reorganization. If a change is not possible, the state of imbalance will produce tension, and the balanced states will be preferred over the states of imbalance.

If one replaces the word "balanced" with "consonant" and "imbalance" with "dissonance," this statement by Heider can be seen to indicate the same process with which our discussion up to now has dealt.

Osgood and Tannenbaum (1955) published a paper in which they also formulated and documented a similar idea with respect to changes in opinions and attitudes. In discussing the "principle of congruity," as they call it, they state: "Changes in evaluation are always in the direction of increased congruity with the existing frame of reference" (p. 43). The particular kind of "incongruity" or cognitive dissonance with which they deal in their study is produced by the knowledge that a person or other source of information which a subject regards positively (or negatively) supports an opinion which the subject regards negatively (or positively). They proceed to show that under such circumstances there is a marked tendency to change either the evaluation of the opinion involved or the evaluation of the source in a direction which would reduce the dissonance. Thus, if the source were positively evaluated and the opinion negatively evaluated, the person might end up reacting less positively to the source or more positively to the issue. It is also clear from their data that the particular outcome depends on whether the evaluation of the source or of the issue is initially more firmly rooted in the person's cognition. If his attitude toward the source is highly "polarized," then the opinion is more likely to change, and vice versa. Indeed, by careful initial measurement of the attitudes toward the sources and toward the opinions before the dissonance is introduced, and by careful measurement of how resistant each of these is to change, the authors are able to predict quite nicely the direction, and in some instances the amount, of change in evaluation.

The important point to remember is that there is pressure to produce consonant relations among cognitions and to avoid and reduce dissonance. Many other writers have recognized this, although few have stated it as concretely and as succinctly as the authors we have mentioned. The task which we are attempting in this book is to formulate the theory of dissonance in a precise yet generally applicable form, to draw out its implications to a variety of contexts, and to present data relevant to the theory.

DEFINITIONS OF DISSONANCE AND CONSONANCE

Most of the remainder of this chapter will deal with a more formal exposition of the theory of dissonance. I will attempt to state the theory in as precise and unambiguous terms as possible. But since the ideas which constitute this theory are by no means yet in a completely precise form, some vagueness is unavoidable.

The terms "dissonance" and "consonance" refer to relations which exist between pairs of "elements." It is consequently necessary, before proceeding to define these relations, to define the elements themselves as well as we can.

These elements refer to what has been called cognition, that is, the things a person knows about himself, about his behavior, and about his surroundings. These elements, then, are "knowledges," if I may coin the plural form of the word. Some of these elements represent knowledge about oneself: what one does, what one feels, what one wants or desires, what one is, and the like. Other elements of knowledge concern the world in which one lives: what is where, what leads to what, what things are satisfying or painful or inconsequential or important, etc.

It is clear that the term "knowledge" has been used to include things to which the word does not ordinarily refer—for example, opinions. A person does not hold an opinion unless he thinks it is correct, and so, psychologically, it is not different from a "knowledge." The same is true of beliefs, values, or attitudes, which function as "knowledges" for our purposes. This is not to imply that there are no important distinctions to be made among these various terms. Indeed, some such distinctions will be made later on. But for the definitions here, these are all "elements of cognition," and relations of consonance and dissonance can hold between pairs of these elements.

There are further questions of definition one would like to be able to answer. For example, when is an "element of cognition" *one* element, or a group of elements? Is the knowledge, "the winter in Minneapolis is very cold" an element, or should this be considered a cluster of elements made up of more specific knowledge? This is, at present, an unanswerable question. Indeed it may be a question which does not need answering. As will be seen in those chapters where data are presented and discussed, this unanswered question does not present a problem in connection with measurement.

Another important question concerning these elements is, how are they formed and what determines their content? At this point we want to emphasize the single most important determinant of the content of these elements, namely, *reality*. These elements of cognition are responsive to reality. By and large they mirror, or map, reality. This reality may be physical or social or psychological, but in any case the cognition more or less maps it. This is, of course, not surprising. It would be unlikely that an organism could live and survive if the elements of cognition were not to a large extent a veridical map of reality. Indeed, when someone is "out of touch with reality," it becomes very noticeable.

In other words, elements of cognition correspond for the most part with what the person actually does or feels or with what actually exists in the environment. In the case of opinions, beliefs, and values, the reality may be what others think or do; in other instances the reality may be what is encountered experientially or what others have told him.

But let us here object and say that persons frequently have cognitive elements which deviate markedly from reality, at least as we see it. Consequently, the major point to be made is that *the reality which impinges on a person will exert pressures in the direction of bringing the appropriate cognitive elements into correspondence with that reality*. This does not mean that the existing cognitive elements will *always* correspond. Indeed, one of the important consequences of the theory of dissonance is that it will help us understand some circumstances where the cognitive elements do not correspond with reality. But it does mean that if 'the cognitive elements do not correspond with a certain reality which impinges, certain pressures must exist. We should therefore be able to observe some manifestations of these pressures. This hypothesized relation between the cognitive elements and reality is important in enabling measurement of dissonance, and we will refer to it again in considering data.

It is now possible to proceed to a discussion of the relations which may exist between pairs of elements. There are three such relations, namely, irrelevance, dissonance, and consonance. They will be discussed in that order.

Irrelevant Relations

Two elements may simply have nothing to do with one another. That is, under such circumstances where one cognitive element implies nothing at all concerning some other element, these two elements are irrelevant to one another. For example, let us imagine a person who knows that it sometimes takes as long as two weeks for a letter to go from New York to Paris by regular boat mail and who also knows that a dry, hot July is good for the corn crop in Iowa. These two elements of cognition have nothing to do with one another; they exist in an irrelevant relation to each other. There is not, of course, much to say about such irrelevant relations except to point to their existence. Of primary concern will be those pairs of elements between which relations of consonance or dissonance can exist.

In many instances, however, it becomes quite a problem to decide a priori whether or not two elements are irrelevant. It is often impossible to decide this without reference to other cognitions of the person involved. Sometimes situations will exist where, because of the behavior of the person involved, previously irrelevant elements become relevant to one another. This could even be the case in the example of irrelevant cognitive elements which we gave above. If a person living in Paris was speculating on the corn crop in the United States, he would want information concerning weather predictions for Iowa but would not depend upon boat mail for getting his information.

Before proceeding to the definitions and discussion of the relations of consonance and dissonance which exist if the elements are relevant, it may be well to stress again the special nature certain cognitive elements have—usually those cognitive elements which correspond to behavior. Such a "behavioral" element, by being relevant to each of two irrelevant cognitive elements, may make them in fact relevant to each other.

Relevant Relations: Dissonance and Consonance

We have already acquired some intuitive notion of the meaning of dissonance. Two elements are dissonant if, for one reason or another, they do not fit together. They may be inconsistent or contradictory, culture or group standards may dictate that they do not fit, and so on. It is appropriate now to attempt a more formal conceptual definition.

Let us consider two elements which exist in a person's cognition and which are relevant to one another. The definition of dissonance will disregard the existence of all the other cognitive elements that are relevant to either or both of the two under consideration and simply deal with these two alone. *These two elements are in a dissonant relation if, considering these two alone, the obverse of one element would follow from the other.* To state it a bit more formally, x and y are dissonant if not-x follows from y. Thus, for example, if a person knew there were only friends in his vicinity and also felt afraid, there would be a dissonant relation between these two cognitive elements. Or, for another example, if a person were already in debt and also purchased a new car, the corresponding cognitive elements would be dissonant with one another. The dissonance might exist because of what the person has learned or come to expect, because of what is considered appropriate or usual, or for any of a number of other reasons.

Motivations and desired consequences may also be factors in determining whether or not two elements are dissonant. For example, a person in a card game might continue playing and losing money while knowing that the others in the game are professional gamblers. This latter knowledge would be dissonant with his cognition about his behavior, namely, continuing to play. But it should be clear that to specify the relation as dissonant is to assume (plausibly enough) that the person involved wants to win. If for some strange reason this person wants to lose, this relation would be consonant.

It may be helpful to give a series of examples where dissonance between two cognitive elements stems from different sources, that is, where the two elements are dissonant because of different meanings of the phrase "follow from" in the definition of dissonance given above.

1. Dissonance could arise from logical inconsistency. If a person believed that man will reach the moon in the near future and also believed that man will not be able to build a device that can leave the atmosphere of the earth, these two cognitions are dissonant with one another. The obverse of one follows from the other on logical grounds in the person's own thinking processes.

2. Dissonance could arise because of cultural mores. If a person at a formal dinner uses his hands to pick up a recalcitrant chicken bone, the knowledge of what he is doing is dissonant with the knowledge of formal dinner etiquette. The dissonance exists simply because the culture defines what is consonant and what is not. In some other culture these two cognitions might not be dissonant at all.

3. Dissonance may arise because one specific opinion is sometimes included, by definition, in a more general opinion. Thus, if a person is a Democrat but in a given election prefers the Republican candidate, the cognitive elements corresponding to these two sets of opinions are dissonant with each other because "being a Democrat" includes, as part of the concept, favoring Democratic candidates.

4. Dissonance may arise because of past experience. If a person were standing in the rain and yet could see no evidence that he was getting wet, these two cognitions would be dissonant with one another because he knows from experience that getting wet follows·from being out in the rain. If one can imagine a person who had never had any experience with rain, these two cognitions would probably not be dissonant.

These various examples are probably sufficient to illustrate how the conceptual definition of dissonance, together with some specific meaning of the phrase "follow from," would be used empirically to decide whether two cognitive elements are dissonant or consonant. It is clear, of course, that in any of these situations, there might exist many other elements of cognition that are consonant with either of the two elements under consideration. Nevertheless, the relation between the two elements is dissonant if, disregarding the others, the one does not, or would not be expected to, follow from the other.

While we have been defining and discussing dissonance, the relations of consonance and irrelevance have, of course, also been defined by implication. If, considering a pair of elements, either one *does* follow from the other, then the relation between them is consonant. If neither the existing element nor its obverse follows from the other element of the pair, then the relation between them is irrelevant.

The conceptual definitions of dissonance and consonance present some serious measurement difficulties. If the theory of dissonance is to have relevance for empirical data, one must be able to identify dissonances and consonances unequivocally. But it is clearly hopeless to attempt to obtain a complete listing of cognitive elements, and even were such a listing available, in some cases it would be difficult or impossible to say, a priori, which of the three relationships holds. In many cases, however, the a priori determination of dissonance is clear and easy. (Remember also that two cognitive elements may be dissonant for a person living in one culture and not for a person living in another, or for a person with one set of experiences and not for a person with another.) Needless to say, it will be necessary to cope with this problem of measurement in detail in those chapters where empirical data are presented and discussed.

The Magnitude of Dissonance

All dissonant relations, of course, are not of equal magnitude. It is necessary to distinguish degrees of dissonance and to specify what determines how strong a given dissonant relation is. We will briefly discuss some determinants of the magnitude of dissonance between two elements and then turn to a consideration of the total amount of dissonance which may exist between two clusters of elements.

One obvious determinant of the magnitude of dissonance lies in the characteristics of the elements between which the relation of dissonance holds. *If two elements are dissonant with one another, the magnitude of the dissonance will be a function of the importance of the elements.* The more these elements are important to, or valued by, the person, the greater will be the magnitude of a dissonant relation between them. Thus, for example, if a person gives ten cents to a beggar, knowing full well that the beggar is not really in need, the dissonance which exists between these two elements is rather weak. Neither of the two cognitive elements involved is very important or very consequential to the person. A much greater dissonance is involved, for example, if a student does not study for a very important examination, knowing that his present fund of information is probably inadequate for the examination. In this case the elements that are dissonant with each other are more important to the person, and the magnitude of dissonance will be correspondingly greater.

It is probably safe to assume that it is rare for no dissonance at all to exist within any cluster of cognitive elements. For almost any action a person might take, for almost any feeling he might have, there will most likely be at least one cognitive element dissonant with this "behavioral" element. Even perfectly trivial cognitions like knowing one is taking a walk on a Sunday afternoon would likely have some elements dissonant with it. The person who is out for a walk might also know that there are things around the house requiring his attention, or he might know that rain was likely, and so on. In short, there are generally so many other cognitive elements relevant to any given element that some dissonance is the usual state of affairs.

Let us consider now the total context of dissonances and consonances in relation to one particular element. Assuming momentarily, for the sake of definition, that all the elements relevant to the one in question are equally important, *the total amount of dissonance between this element and the remainder of the person's cognition will depend on the proportion of relevant elements that are dissonant with the one in question.* Thus, if the overwhelming majority of relevant elements are consonant with, say, a behavioral element, then the dissonance with this behavioral element is slight. If in relation to the number of elements consonant with the behavioral element the number of dissonant elements is large, the total dissonance will be of appreciable magnitude. Of course, the magnitude of the total dissonance will also depend on the importance or value of those relevant elements which exist in consonant or dissonant relations with the one being considered.

The above statement can of course be easily generalized to deal with the magnitude of dissonance which exists between two clusters of cognitive elements. This magnitude would depend on the proportion of the relevant relations between elements in the two clusters that were dissonant and, of course, on the importance of the elements.

Since the magnitude of dissonance is an important variable in determining the pressure to reduce dissonance, and since we will deal with measures of the magnitude of dissonance repeatedly in considering data, it may be well to summarize our discussion concerning the magnitude of dissonance.

1. If two cognitive elements are relevant, the relation between them is either dissonant or consonant.

2. The magnitude of the dissonance (or consonance) increases as the importance of value of the elements increases.

3. The total amount of dissonance that exists between two clusters of cognitive elements is a function of the weighted proportion of all relevant relations between the two clusters that are dissonant. The term ''weighted proportion'' is used because each relevant relation would be weighted according to the importance of the elements involved in that relation.

THE REDUCTION OF DISSONANCE

The presence of dissonance gives rise to pressures to reduce or eliminate the dissonance. The strength of the pressures to reduce the dissonance is a function of the magnitude of the dissonance. In other words, dissonance acts in the same way as a state of drive or need or tension. The presence of dissonance leads to action to reduce it just as, for example, the presence of hunger leads to action to reduce the hunger. Also, similar to the action of a drive, the greater the dissonance, the greater will be the intensity of the action to reduce the dissonance and the greater the avoidance of situations that would increase the dissonance.

In order to be specific about how the pressure to reduce dissonance would manifest itself, it is necessary to examine the possible ways in which existing dissonance can be reduced or eliminated. In general, if dissonance exists between two elements, this dissonance can be eliminated by changing one of those elements. The important thing is how these changes may be brought about. There are various possible ways in which this can be accomplished, depending upon the type of cognitive elements involved and upon the total cognitive context.

Changing a Behavioral Cognitive Element

When the dissonance under consideration is between an element corresponding to some knowledge concerning environment (environmental element) and a behavioral element, the dissonance can, of course, be eliminated by changing the behavioral cognitive element in such a way that it is consonant with the environmental element. The simplest and easiest way in which this may be accomplished is to change the action or feeling which the behavioral element represents. Given that a cognition is responsive to ''reality'' (as we have seen), if the behavior of the organism changes, the cognitive element or elements corresponding to this behavior will likewise change. This method of reducing or eliminating dissonance is a very frequent occurrence. Our behavior and feelings are frequently modified in accordance with new information. If a person starts out on a picnic and notices that it has begun to rain, he may very well turn around and go home. There are many persons who do stop smoking if and when they discover it is bad for their health.

It may not always be possible, however, to eliminate dissonance or even to reduce it materially by changing one's action or feeling. The difficulty of changing the behavior may be too great, or the change, while eliminating some dissonances, may create a whole host of new ones. These questions will be discussed in more detail below.

Changing an Environmental Cognitive Element

Just as it is possible to change a behavioral cognitive element by changing the behavior which this element mirrors, it is sometimes possible to change an *environmental* cognitive element by changing the situation to which that element corresponds. This, of course, is much more difficult than changing one's behavior, for one must have a sufficient degree of control over one's environment—a relatively rare occurrence.

Changing the environment itself in order to reduce dissonance is more feasible when the social environment is in question than when the physical environment is involved. In order to illustrate rather dramatically the kind of thing that would be involved, I will give a rather facetious hypothetical example. Let us imagine a person who is given to pacing up and down in his living room at home. Let us further imagine that for some unknown reason he always jumps over one particular spot on the floor. The cognitive element corresponding to his jumping over that spot is undoubtedly dissonant with his knowledge that the floor at that spot is level, strong, and in no way different from any other part of the floor. If, some evening when his wife is away from home, he breaks a hole in the floor at that exact spot, he would completely eliminate the dissonance. The cognition that there is a hole in the floor would be quite consonant with the knowledge that he jumps over the place where the hole exists. In short, he would have changed a cognitive element by actually changing the environment, thus eliminating a dissonance.

Whenever there is sufficient control over the environment, this method of reducing dissonance may be employed. For example, a person who is habitually very hostile toward other people may surround himself with persons who provoke hostility. His cognitions about the persons with whom he associates are then consonant with the cognitions corresponding to his hostile behavior. The possibilities of manipulating the environment are limited, however, and most endeavors to change a cognitive element will follow other lines.

If a cognitive element that is responsive to reality is to be changed without changing the corresponding reality, some means of ignoring or counteracting the real situation must be used. This is sometimes well-nigh impossible, except in extreme cases which might be called psychotic. If a person is standing in the rain and rapidly getting soaked, he will almost certainly continue to have the cognition that it is raining no matter how strong the psychological pressures are to eliminate that cognition. In other instances it is relatively easy to change a cognitive element although the reality remains the same. For example, a person might be able to change his opinion about a political officeholder even though the behavior of that officeholder, and the political situation generally, remain unchanged. Usually for this to occur, the person would have to be able to find others who would agree with and support his new opinion. In general, establishing a social reality by gaining the agreement and support of other people is one of the major ways in which a cognition can be changed when the pressures to change it are present. It can readily be seen that where such social support is necessary, the presence of dissonance and the consequent pressures to change some cognitive element will lead to a variety of social processes.

Adding New Cognitive Elements

It is clear that in order to eliminate a dissonance completely, some cognitive element must be changed. It is also clear that this is not always possible. But even if it is impossible to eliminate a dissonance, it is possible to reduce the total magnitude of dissonance by adding new cognitive elements. Thus, for example, if dissonance existed between some cognitive elements concerning the effects of smoking and cognition concerning the behavior of continuing to smoke, the total dissonance could be reduced by adding new cognitive elements that are consonant with the fact of smoking. In the presence of such dissonance, then, a person might be expected to actively seek new information that would reduce the total dissonance and, at the same time, to avoid new information that might increase the existing dissonance. Thus, to pursue the example, the person might seek out and avidly read any material critical of the research which purported to show that smoking was bad for one's health. At the same time he would avoid reading material that praised this research. (If he unavoidably came in contact with the latter type of material, his reading would be critical indeed.)

Actually, the possibilities for adding new elements which would reduce the existing dissonances are broad. Our smoker, for example, could find out all about accidents and death rates in automobiles. Having then added the cognition that the danger from smoking is negligible compared to the danger he runs driving a car, his dissonance would also have been somewhat reduced. Here the total dissonance is reduced by reducing the *importance* of the existing dissonance.

The above discussion has pointed to the possibility of reducing the total dissonance with some element by reducing the proportion of dissonant as compared with consonant relations involving that element. It is also possible to add a new cognitive element which, in a sense, "reconciles" two elements that are dissonant. Let us consider an example from the literature to illustrate this. Spiro (1953) gives an account of certain aspects of the belief system of the Ifaluk, a nonliterate society. The relevant points for our purposes here are as follows:

1. In this culture there is a firm belief that people are *good*. This belief is not only that they should be good but that they *are* good.

2. For one reason or another, young children in this culture go through a period of particularly strong overt aggression, hostility, and destructiveness.

It seems clear that the belief about the nature of people is dissonant with the knowledge of the behavior of the children in this culture. It would have been possible to reduce this dissonance in any number of ways. They might have changed their belief about the nature of people or have modified it so that people are wholly good only at maturity. Or they might have changed their ideas about what is and what is not "good" so that overt aggression in young children would be considered good. Actually, the manner of reducing the dissonance was different. A third belief was added which effectively reduced the dissonance by "reconciliation." Specifically, they also believe in the existence of malevolent ghosts which enter into persons and cause them to do bad things.

As a result of this third belief, the knowledge of the aggressive behavior of children is no longer dissonant with the belief that people are good. It is not the children who behave aggressively—it's the malevolent ghosts. Psychologically, this is a highly satisfactory means of reducing the dissonance, as one might expect when such beliefs are institution-alized at a cultural level. Unsatisfactory solutions would not be as successful in becoming widely accepted.

Before moving on, it is worthwhile to emphasize again that the presence of pressures to reduce dissonance, or even activity directed toward such reduction, does not guarantee that the dissonance will be reduced. A person may not be able to find the social support needed to change a cognitive element, or he may not be able to find new elements which reduce the total dissonance. In fact, it is quite conceivable that in the process of trying to reduce dissonance, it might even be increased. This will depend upon what the person encounters while attempting to reduce the dissonance. The important point to be made so far is that in the presence of a dissonance, one will be able to observe the *attempts* to reduce it. If attempts to re-duce dissonance fail, one should be able to observe symptoms of psychological discom-fort, provided the dissonance is appreciable enough so that the discomfort is clearly and overtly manifested.

RESISTANCE TO REDUCTION OF DISSONANCE

If dissonance is to be reduced or eliminated by changing one or more cognitive elements, it is necessary to consider how resistant these cognitive elements are to change. Whether or not any of them change, and if so, which ones, will certainly be determined in part by the magnitude of resistance to change which they possess. It is, of course, clear that if the various cognitive elements involved had no resistance to change whatsoever, there would never be any lasting dissonances: Momentary dissonance might occur, but if the cognitive elements involved had no resistance to change, the dissonance would immedi-ately be eliminated. Let us, then, look at the major sources of resistance to change of a cognitive element.

Just as the reduction of dissonance presented somewhat different problems depending upon whether the element to be changed was a behavioral or an environmental one, so the major sources of resistance to change are different for these two classes of cognitive elements.

Resistance to Change of Behavioral Cognitive Elements

The first and foremost source of resistance to change for *any* cognitive element is the responsiveness of such elements to reality. If one sees that the grass is green, it is very difficult to think it is not so. If a person is walking down the street, it is difficult for his cognition not to contain an element corresponding to this. Given this strong and sometimes overwhelming responsiveness to reality, the problem of changing a behavioral cognitive element becomes the problem of changing the behavior which is being mapped by the element. Consequently, the resistance to change of the cognitive element is identical with the resistance to change of the behavior reflected by that element, assuming that the person maintains contact with reality.

Certainly much behavior has little or no resistance to change. We continually modify many of our actions and feelings in accordance with changes in the situation. If a street which we ordinarily use when we drive to work is being repaired, there is usually little difficulty in altering our behavior and using a different route. What, then, are the circumstances that make it difficult for the person to change his actions?

1. The change may be painful or involve loss. A person may, for example, have spent a

lot of money to purchase a house. If for any reason he now wants to change, that is, live in a different house or different neighborhood, he must endure the discomforts of moving and the possible financial loss involved in selling the house. A person who might desire to give up smoking must endure the discomfort and pain of the cessation in order to accomplish the change. Clearly, in such circumstances, there will be a certain resistance to change. The magnitude of this resistance to change will be determined by the extent of pain or loss which must be endured.

2. The present behavior may be otherwise satisfying. A person might continue to have lunch at a certain restaurant even though they served poor food if, for example, his friends always ate there. Or a person who is very domineering and harsh toward his children might not easily be able to give up the satisfactions of being able to boss someone, even if on various grounds he desired to change. In such instances, of course, the resistance to change would be a function of the satisfaction obtained from the present behavior.

3. Making the change may simply not be possible. It would be a mistake to imagine that a person could consummate any change in his behavior if he wanted to badly enough. It may not be possible to change for a variety of reasons. Some behavior, especially emotional reactions, may not be under the voluntary control of the person. For example, a person might have a strong reaction of fear which he can do nothing about. Also, it might not be possible to consummate a change simply because the new behavior may not be in the behavior repertory of the person. A father might not be able to change the way he behaves toward his children simply because he doesn't know any other way to behave. A third circumstance which could make it impossible to change is the irrevocable nature of certain actions. If, for example, a person has sold his house and then decides he wants it back, there is nothing that can be done if the new owner refuses to sell it. The action has been taken and is not reversible. But under circumstances where the behavior simply cannot change at all, it is not correct to say that the resistance to change of the corresponding cognitive element is infinite. The resistance to change which the cognitive element possesses can, of course, not be greater than the pressure to respond to reality.

Resistance to Change of Environmental Cognitive Elements

Here again, as with behavioral cognitive elements, the major source of resistance to change lies in the responsiveness of these elements to reality. The result of this, as far as behavioral elements go, is to tie the resistance to change of the cognitive element to the resistance to change of the reality, namely, the behavior itself. The situation is somewhat different with regard to environmental elements. When there is a clear and unequivocal reality corresponding to some cognitive element, the possibilities of change are almost nil. If one desired, for example, to change one's cognition about the location of some building which one saw every day, this would indeed be difficult to accomplish.

In many instances, however, the reality corresponding to the cognitive element is by no means so clear and unambiguous. When the reality is basically a social one, that is, when it is established by agreement with other people, the resistance to change would be determined by the difficulty of finding persons to support the new cognition.

There is another source of resistance to change of both behavioral and environmental cognitive elements. We have postponed discussion of it until now, however, because it is a more important source of resistance to change for environmental elements than for others. This source of resistance to change lies in the fact that an element is in relationship with a number of other elements. To the extent that the element is consonant with a large number of other elements and to the extent that changing it would replace these consonances by dissonances, the element will be resistant to change.

The above discussion is not meant to be an exhaustive analysis of resistance to change or a listing of conceptually different sources. Rather, it is a discussion which attempts to make distinctions that will help operationally rather than conceptually. In considering any dissonance and the resistance to change of the elements involved, the important factor in the attempt to eliminate the dissonance by changing an element is the total amount of resistance to change; the source of the resistance is immaterial.

LIMITS OF THE MAGNITUDE OF DISSONANCE

The maximum dissonance that can possibly exist between any two elements is equal to the total resistance to change of the less resistant element. The magnitude of dissonance cannot exceed this amount because, at this point of maximum possible dissonance, the less resistant element would change, thus eliminating the dissonance.

This does not mean that the magnitude of dissonance will frequently even approach this maximum possible value. When there exists a strong dissonance that is less than the resistance to change of any of the elements involved, this dissonance can perhaps still be reduced for the total cognitive system by adding new cognitive elements. In this way, even in the presence of very strong resistances to change, the total dissonance in the system could be kept at rather low levels.

Let us consider an example of a person who spends what for him is a very large sum of money for a new car of an expensive type. Let us also imagine that after purchasing it he finds that some things go wrong with it and that repairs are very expensive. It is also more expensive to operate than other cars, and what is more, he finds that his friends think the car is ugly. If the dissonance becomes great enough, that is, equal to the resistance to change of the less resistant element, which in this situation would probably be the behavioral element, he might sell the car and suffer whatever inconvenience and financial loss is involved. Thus the dissonance could not exceed the resistance the person has to changing his behavior, that is, selling the car.

Now let us consider the situation where the dissonance for the person who bought a new car was appreciable but less than the maximum possible dissonance, that is, less than the resistance to change of the less resistant cognitive element. None of the existing cognitive elements would then be changed, but he could keep the total dissonance low by adding more and more cognitions that are consonant with his ownership of the car. He begins to feel that power and riding qualities are more important than economy and looks. He begins to drive faster than he used to and becomes quite convinced that it is important for a car to be able to travel at high speed. With these cognitions and others, he might succeed in rendering the dissonance negligible.

It is also possible, however, that his attempts to add new consonant cognitive elements would prove unsuccessful and that his financial situation is such that he could not sell the car. It would still be possible to reduce the dissonance by what also amounts to adding a new cognitive element, but of a different kind. He can admit to himself, and to others, that he was wrong to purchase the car and that if he had it to do over again, he would buy a different kind. This process of divorcing himself psychologically from the action can and does materially reduce the dissonance. Sometimes, however, the resistances against this are quite strong. The maximum dissonance which could exist would, in such circumstances, be determined by the resistance to admitting that he had been wrong or foolish.

AVOIDANCE OF DISSONANCE

The discussion thus far has focused on the tendencies to reduce or eliminate dissonance and the problems involved in achieving such reduction. Under certain circumstances there are also strong and important tendencies to avoid increases of dissonance or to avoid the occurrence of dissonance altogether. Let us now turn our attention to a consideration of these circumstances and the manifestations of the avoidance tendencies which we might expect to observe.

The avoidance of an increase in dissonance comes about, of course, as a result of the existence of dissonance. This avoidance is especially important where, in the process of attempting to reduce dissonance, support is sought for a new cognitive element to replace an existing one or where new cognitive elements are to be added. In both these circumstances, the seeking of support and the seeking of new information must be done in a highly selective manner. A person would initiate discussion with someone he thought would agree with the new cognitive element but would avoid discussion with someone who might agree with the element that he was trying to change. A person would expose himself to sources of information which he expected would add new elements which would increase consonance but would certainly avoid sources which would increase dissonance.

If there is little or no dissonance existing, we would not expect the same kind of selectivity in exposure to sources of support or sources of information. In fact, where no dissonance exists there should be a relative absence of motivation to seek support or new information at all. This will be true in general, but there are important exceptions. Past experience may lead a person to fear, and hence to avoid, the initial occurrence of dissonance. Where this is true, one might expect circumspect behavior with regard to new information even when little or no dissonance is present to start with.

The operation of a fear of dissonance may also lead to a reluctance to commit oneself behaviorally. There is a large class of actions that, once taken, are difficult to change. Hence, it is possible for dissonances to arise and to mount in intensity. A fear of dissonance would lead to a reluctance to take action—a reluctance to commit oneself. Where decision and action cannot be indefinitely delayed, the taking of action may be accompanied by a cognitive negation of the action. Thus, for example, a person who buys a new car and is very afraid of dissonance may, immediately following the purchase, announce his conviction that he did the wrong thing. Such strong fear of dissonance is probably relatively rare, but it does occur. Personality differences with respect to fear of dissonance and the effectiveness with which one is able to reduce dissonance are undoubtedly important in determining whether or not such avoidance of dissonance is likely to happen. The operational problem would be to independently identify situations and persons where this kind of a priori self-protective behavior occurs.

SUMMARY

The core of the theory of dissonance which we have stated is rather simple. It holds that:

1. There may exist dissonant or "nonfitting" relations among cognitive elements.

2. The existence of dissonance gives rise to pressures to reduce the dissonance and to avoid increases in dissonance.

3. Manifestations of the operation of these pressures include behavior changes, changes of cognition, and circumspect exposure to new information and new opinions.

Although the core of the theory is simple, it has rather wide implications and applications to a variety of situations which on the surface look very different.

REFERENCES

Heider, F. *The psychology of interpersonal relations*. New York: Wiley, 1958.

Myrdal, G. *An American dilemma*. New York: Harper, 1944.

Osgood, C. W., and Tannenbaum, P. The principle of congruity and prediction of attitude change. *Psychol. Rev.*, 1955, *62*, 42–55.

Spiro, M. Ghosts: An anthropological inquiry into learning and perception. *J. abnorm. soc. Psychol.*, 1953, *48*, 376–382.

Dana Bramel
A DISSONANCE THEORY APPROACH TO DEFENSIVE PROJECTION

Ego defensive processes, as discussed in psychoanalytic theory, often seem to bear some resemblance to the cognitive changes dealt with in Festinger's (1957) dissonance theory. This observation has led to a comparison of the two theories and to consideration of the possibility that certain of the Freudian defense mechanisms might occur in response to dissonance. Especially interesting from the point of view of social psychology is the concept of projection, since it clearly has implications for interpersonal relations.

Consider those situations, described in psychoanalytic theory, in which the individual's perception of some aspect of himself is contrary to his internalized standards of right and wrong (the superego). According to the theory, the perception of this information arouses fear of punishment, perhaps especially a fear of painful guilt feelings (Fenichel, 1945). In order to avoid further anxiety and guilt feelings, the ego is said to initiate defensive measures.

In order to determine the relevance of dissonance theory to this phenomenon, one must ask whether dissonant relations would be expected to exist among the cognitions involved. Imagine, for example, a person who considers homosexuality a bad and disgusting thing; on some occasion he is suddenly exposed to information strongly implying that he has homosexual tendencies. According to classical psychoanalytic theory, the crucial relation is the conflict between the information or impulse and demands of the superego. Is the new cognition—that one has homosexual tendencies—necessarily dissonant with one's belief that such tendencies are bad and that one should not have them? The answer is no. People who conceive of themselves as possessing a mixture of good and bad traits, or a preponderance of bad traits, would not generally expect that new information would be favorable to themselves or consistent with superego standards. It follows that a discrepancy between the new information and superego standards, although threatening in the psychoanalytic sense, would not necessarily be dissonant.

This is not to say, however, that dissonance would be completely absent from the cognition of the person who recognizes that he is not perfect. For example, when he discovers he has homosexual tendencies, this knowledge may be dissonant with his specific belief that he is really quite masculine, even though it is not dissonant with his conviction that homosexuality is a bad thing.

The point can be clarified by a hypothetical example. Imagine two people, A and B. Both consider homosexuality a very bad thing, and both believe they are quite lacking in such motivation. A believes he is an extremely fine person in general; B sees himself as possessing almost no favorable characteristics. Both are then confronted with information that they have

From D. Bramel, "A Dissonance Theory Approach to Defensive Projection," *Journal of Abnormal and Social Psychology*, 1962, *64*, 121–129. Reprinted by permission of the American Psychological Association.

strong homosexual tendencies. For both, this information is contrary to superego standards and dissonant with their belief that they are not homosexual. However, for A, the information is also strongly dissonant with his belief that he is a nearly perfect person. For B, on the other hand, the information is quite consonant with his belief that he is a failure. The new information produces more dissonance for the person with high self-esteem, even though the conflict with the superego is substantially the same for the two people. This emphasis upon the actual self-concept in the dissonance theory approach reveals a difference in focus of the two theories.

Can dissonance involving the self-concept be reduced by projecting the offending trait onto other people? Perhaps the most effecitve mode of dissonance reduction would be to deny the implications of the information. Let us assume, however, that the information is so unambiguous that successful denial is not possible for the person. He is compelled to ascribe the undesirable trait to himself. Under these circumstances, attributing the trait to other persons might reduce dissonance in several ways. By attributing it to respected people, the projector may enable himself to re-evaluate the trait. If respected persons possess it, then perhaps it is not so bad a thing after all. Then possession of the trait would not be contradictory to a favorable level of self-esteem. Another possibility is that the person may attribute the trait to members of his reference or comparison group (Festinger, 1954). In this way he could convince himself that he does not deviate from the persons with whom he ordinarily compares himself. If he is only average in his possession of the trait, then subjectively his favorable level of self-esteem is not so strongly negated.

These possibilities suggest that indeed projection may be used as a means of reducing dissonance. There are several studies in the literature (for example, Murstein, 1956; Wright, 1942) which are specifically relevant and show positive results, but all leave certain important issues unresolved. Consequently, the experiment reported here was conducted to test whether projection occurs in response to dissonance and to throw some light on the particular ways in which this attribution may reduce dissonance.

The hypotheses to be tested were these:

1. If a person is exposed to information strongly implying that he possesses an undesirable characteristic, he is more likely to attribute the trait to others if the information is dissonant with his level of self-esteem; the greater the dissonance, the more likely it is that projection will occur.

2. If a person is compelled to ascribe an undesirable and dissonant characteristic to himself, he will be motivated to attribute the characteristic to favorably evaluated persons and/or to persons with whom he ordinarily compares himself.

METHOD

Overview

Subjects in the Favorable condition received falsified personality test results aimed at temporarily increasing their general level of self-esteem; subjects in the Unfavorable condition received parallel information intended to lower their general self-esteem. Subsequently, all subjects were privately exposed to further falsified information of an undesirable nature about themselves. It was hypothesized that this information, being more dissonant with the self-concept of subjects in the Favorable condition, would lead to more projection in that condition. Attribution was measured by asking each subject to rate another subject with whom he was paired.

First Session

Each subject who signed up for the experiment appeared individually for the first session. He was told that the first part of the experiment was designed to discover what kinds of people had insight into themselves. He was asked to take a number of personality tests, which, he was told, would be carefully and confidentially analyzed by three members of the clinical psychology staff. He was informed that, after the tests were scored, he would learn the results in an interview, during which time his self-insight was to be measured. Among the tests included were the Taylor Manifest Anxiety scale, the *F, K,* and *L* scales from the MMPI, and an adjective checklist self-concept measure.

At the end of the hour, the subject was told that the second session would also include a measure of his ability to judge the personality of another person on the basis of a first impression.

Second Session

On the basis of the self-concept measure subjects were paired for the second session by matching their level of self-esteem and their concept of their own masculinity.

At the beginning of the second session the two unacquainted subjects scheduled for the hour were introduced to each other. In order to aid subjects in forming an impression of each other, the experimenter asked each in turn (in the presence of the other) a set of questions about himself and his attitudes toward certain current events. At the conclusion of this meeting the subjects were separated and interviewed privately regarding the results of their personality tests.

Unknown to the subject, the ''results'' which he received had been prepared with no reference whatsoever to his actual test performance. There were only two test reports used in the experiment, one very favorable, the other very unfavorable. The reports covered the personality ''dimensions'' of creativity, hostility, egocentricity, and over-all maturity. Each section of the report gave a rather detailed discussion of the test results bearing upon the particular dimension. The tone was objective and the general favorability was very consistent throughout the report. The two reports were very similar in form, but the specific contents were directly opposite in implication.

After having been assigned randomly to his experimental condition, the subject was read the report in private by the experimenter, and its discrepancies from the subject's present self-concept were explicitly pointed out by the experimenter. The report was finished in approximately 20 minutes. In each pair of subjects, one was assigned to the Favorable condition, one to the Unfavorable condition. Two interviewers were used for this part of the experiment, alternating between the two conditions.

Following the test report, the two subjects were brought together in another room, where they expected to make some personality judgments about each other. Each was then given a questionnaire consisting of 11 polar adjective seven-point scales to be used to rate the other person. An over-all favorability score could be computed across the scales. Examples were masculine-feminine, friendly-hostile, competent-incompetent, and mature-immature. A self-concept measure followed, consisting of 16 polar adjective scales similar to those included in the prior rating of the other person. These were selected partially to tap dimensions covered in the personality reports and to serve as a check on the manipulation of self-esteem. As in the previous set, they included the item masculine-feminine, and could be summated to provide a general favorability score. Emphasis was placed upon the anonymity of the questionnaires and upon the earnest request that the subject respond "as *you* see yourself, from your own point of view at the present time."

Introducing the Undesirable Cognition

It was expected that informing a male undergraduate that he has homosexual tendencies would be sufficiently dissonant under certain conditions to provoke defensive behavior. Care was taken to ensure that the degree of threat was not extreme and that no damaging effects would remain at the end of the experiment. These precautions will be discussed in more detail below.

At this point in the experiment, while making ratings of partner and self, the two subjects were seated along one side of a long table, separated by about 4 feet, both facing a projection screen 6 feet in front of them. On the table in front of each subject was a small plywood box containing a galvanometer dial facing him. Issuing from the box were two wires with electrodes on the ends. Each box, with its dial, was completely shielded from the other persons in the room. Thus, each subject perceived his apparatus immediately in front of him and could not see the other subject's apparatus.

Next, the experimenter read a set of instructions to set the stage for the undesirable cognitions about homosexuality. These instructions were largely of a deceptive nature. It was explained that this part of the experiment would be concerned with the perception of sexual arousal. An elaborate explanation of the physiology of sexual arousal and the sensitive techniques for its measurement followed. Care was taken to distinguish the galvanometer response to sexual arousal from that commonly associated with anxiety reactions by pointing out the unmistakable signs of the former. Considerable emphasis was placed on the unconscious nature of sexual arousal and the impossibility of exerting conscious control over its expression in the "psychogalvanic skin response." It was further explained that the experimenter was investigating the perception of homosexual rather than heterosexual arousal. The task set for the subject was to observe his own sexual arousal response on his galvanometer for each of a series of photographs of men which would be projected onto the screen. He was to record this figure on a page of a small anonymous booklet. After he had recorded his own arousal level for the particular picture on the screen, he was to make an estimate of the needle indication of the other subject's apparatus for the same photograph. All subjects were explicitly told that movements of the dial would indicate homosexual arousal to the photographs. As a precaution against excessive threat, they were told that persons with very strong homosexual tendencies would consistently "go off the scale." Further, the anonymity and privacy of the situation were carefully spelled out, with the intention of convincing the subject that no one but he would know what his own responses had been.

Unknown to the subject, the supposed "psychogalvanic skin response apparatus" was not actually responding to changes in his own level of sexual arousal to the pictures. Rather, the galvanometers in each of the two boxes were controlled remotely by the experimenter. Concealed wires led from the galvanometers, in a direct current series circuit, to a calibrated variable resister. Thus, the experimenter exerted complete control over the movements of the needles, which were identical for the two subjects. Each photograph had been assigned an "appropriate" needle reading in advance, so that those depicting handsome men in states of undress received more current than did those depicting unattractive and fully clothed men. Both subjects were, thus, led to believe that they were sexually aroused by certain pictures and not by others, according to a consistent pattern. Both subjects were confronted with exactly the same stimulus input at this point of the experiment.[1]

It was expected that the instructions would be so impressive to the subject that denial of the fact that homosexual arousal was being indicated would be very difficult. By closing off certain alternative avenues of dissonance reduction, such as the cognition that the apparatus was untrustworthy, it was intended that the situation would be conducive to the appearance of defensive projection. According to the hypothesis, subjects in the Favorable condition should experience considerable dissonance when observing their needle jump in response to photographs of attractive males. For subjects in the Unfavorable condition there would be many cognitions consonant with the new information concerning homosexuality, and not so many dissonant cognitions. For most subjects there would, no doubt, be some dissonance due to their prior belief that they are not homosexual, but the two conditions would not differ in this respect. Since the test reports contained no material concerning sexuality, subjects in the two conditions were not expected to differ in their concepts of their own masculinity or in their superego standards.

Fifteen photographs of men were used. Many of the men were almost entirely nude and had physiques somewhat more delicate and posed than those typically found in physical culture magazines. These photographs were chosen on the assumption that subjects might perceive them as being the type toward which homosexuals would be attracted.

Measuring Attribution

It seemed that the most meaningful measure for testing the hypotheses would be a score representing the difference between the subject's own recorded score and his estimate of his partner's galvanic skin response. This should most accurately reflect the subject's comparison between himself and his partner. Therefore, a total score was computed for each subject, taking the algebraic sum of the differences between own and attributed scores across the 15 photographs. This summary score (P score) would be positive if the subject attributed (on the average) higher needle indications to his partner than to himself (i.e., attributed greater homosexual arousal). It would be zero if on the average there was no difference between own and attributed scores. It would be negative if the subject attributed lower needle indications to the other subject than to himself.

Following the threatening material, the subject responded to anonymous questions about his own and his partner's degree of possession of homosexual tendencies, and about his attitude toward the "psychogalvanic skin response" as a measure of such tendencies.

A considerable amount of time at the end of the experiment was allocated to explaining the true nature of the study and demonstrating in detail that the personality reports and the apparatus were incapable of giving a correct evaluation of a person. The expression of relief which often followed the unveiling of the deceptions indicated that the manipulations had been effective. The necessity for the deceptions used in the experimental analysis of such delicate processes was carefully explained, and all questions were answered. Not until the subjects seemed quite restored and satisfied was the session ended. All available evidence indicates that the subjects considered the experiment interesting and worthy of their participation.

---

[1]A similar experimental technique was independently devised by Harold Gerard (cf. Gerard, 1959; Gerard and Rabbie, 1960).

Subjects

All subjects in the experiment were undergraduate men registered in the introductory psychology course. Not all of those who took part in the first session were selected to finish the experiment. Those who scored very high on the Taylor Manifest Anxiety scale and at the same time very low on the defensiveness scale of the MMPI were excluded from the second session, since there was the possibility that the manipulations might be too threatening for them. Of the 98 subjects who participated in both sessions of the experiment, 14 were excluded from the analysis—8 for suspicion regarding the procedure, 3 for excessive age (over 30), and 3 for failure to obey the instructions. Of those excluded, 7 were in the Favorable and 7 in the Unfavorable condition.

RESULTS

Adequacy of Experimental Operations

The major independent variable was the level of self-esteem, or the number of favorable self-referent cognitions. A checklist measure of self-esteem administered before the manipulations revealed no initial difference between the groups. The effectiveness of the personality reports was determined by comparing the Favorable and Unfavorable groups on self-esteem as measured by adjective scales shortly after the manipulation. Mean favorability scores could range from a low of 1 to a high of 7. The results are shown in Table 1. The mean for the Favorable group was significantly higher than for the Unfavorable group ($t = 8.35$, $p < .001$).[2] We may infer, therefore, that the desired difference in self-esteem was successfully created by the fraudulent test reports.

Table 1. Means and standard deviations of variables measured prior to introduction of the undesirable cognition

Variable	*Favorable* (n = 42)	*Unfavorable* (n = 42)
Before self-esteem manipulation		
Initial self-esteem (checklist)		
M	14.5	15.1
SD	3.6	3.3
After self-esteem manipulation		
Self-esteem (seven-point scales)		
M	5.52	4.20
SD	.54	.86
Favorability of rating of partner		
M	4.79	4.90
SD	.69	.68
Rating of masculinity of partner		
M	5.39	5.30
SD	1.11	1.32
Rating of own masculinity		
M	5.87	5.56
SD	1.00	1.02

[2]All reported significance levels are based upon two-tailed tests.

Another important problem of experimental control had to do with the favorability of the subjects' ratings of each other prior to introduction of the cognitions concerning homosexuality. A score was calculated for each subject, taking the mean of his ratings of his partner (scored for favorability) across 10 polar adjective scales, excluding the item masculine-feminine (considered separately below). The first half vs. second half reliability of the score was .57. Possible scores could range from 1 (very unfavorable) to 7 (very favorable). As shown in Table 1, there was no significant difference between the two conditions in favorability of rating of partner.

On the masculine-feminine scale, 1 indicated ''very feminine'' and 7 indicated ''very masculine.'' Mean scores of the two groups did not differ on this scale, as shown in Table 1. Further, the groups did not differ significantly in their rating of their own ''masculinity-femininity.''

On the basis of these comparisons, it seems justifiable to conclude that the Favorable and Unfavorable groups did not differ regarding these possible artifactual effects of the self-esteem manipulations.

Self-Esteem and Projection

Before comparing the two experimental conditions on the attribution of homosexual arousal, let us check the reliability of the measure, the P score. For the first 23 subjects used in the experiment, the series of 15 photographs was repeated, yielding a set of 30 judgment situations for each subject. The discrepancies between his own recorded dial readings and his estimates of his partner's dial were summed separately for the first 15 and the second 15 exposures of the photographs. The correlation between these two sums (P scores) was .95. For subsequent analyses, only the P score for the first 15 photographs was used.

Subjects in the two conditions did not differ, on the average, in their own recorded scores. That is, they were equal in the accuracy with which they recorded their own needle indications. Therefore, the P scores, which were partially derived from the subjects' own recorded dial readings, could not differ between the two groups simply as a function of differences in own recorded scores.

For evidence concerning the relation between dissonance and projection, let us look first at the gross differences between the experimental conditions. As shown in Table 2, the mean P score for the Favorable condition was -2.95; the mean for the Unfavorable condition was -11.45. Thus, subjects in the high dissonance condition tended to say that their partner's arousal level was about the same as their own, while those in the low dissonance condition tended to say their partner's arousal was somewhat less than their own. Attributing one's own

Table 2. Means and standard deviations of attribution measured after manipulation of self-esteem

Attribution	Favorable (n = 42)	Unfavorable (n = 42)
Raw P score		
M	−2.95	−11.45
SD	25.52	27.96
P score adjusted for pre-threat judgment of masculinity of partner		
M	+4.65	−4.76
SD	24.28	23.99

characteristic to others was therefore more frequent in the high dissonance, or Favorable, group. The difference between the means yielded a *t* (for correlated means, due to matching) of 1.52, which is at the .13 level of significance. In order to arrive at a more firm conclusion regarding the outcome of this comparison, let us look at another source of variance which can be taken out of the gross variance in the *P* scores.

It has been anticipated that part of the variance in *P* scores would be due to the impression of masculinity created by the partner prior to the introduction of the undesirable cognition. If the subject rated his partner as very masculine on the masculine-feminine scale, then he would be likely to make somewhat lower (less homosexual) needle estimates for his partner than if he had rated him as very feminine. Correlations were therefore calculated between perceived masculinity of the partner (prethreat) and attribution of homosexual arousal to the photographs (*P* score). Within the Favorable group the resulting product-moment correlation was $-.32$ ($p < .05$); in the Unfavorable group the correlation was $-.52$ ($p < .01$). It will be remembered that the two groups did not differ in their mean (prethreat) rating of the masculinity of the partner (as measured by the masculine-feminine scale); in addition, the distributions of these ratings were very similar in the two groups. Therefore, it was decided that the rather similar within-groups correlations would justify combining the groups, calculating the correlation between the two variables in the total sample, and computing adjusted *P* scores as deviations from the regression line. By means of this procedure the variance associated with how masculine the partner appeared (*prior* to the threat) could be partialed out. Within the total sample ($N = 84$) the correlation between "masculinity" (prethreat) and *P* score was $-.42$. Each subject's *P* score deviation from the regression line was calculated, and the resulting scores were then interpreted as reflecting differences in attribution due to factors other than the initial perceived masculinity of the partner. The adjusted means for the groups are shown in Table 2. A *t* test for correlated means yielded a *t* of 2.04 ($df = 40$), significant beyond the .05 level. On the basis of these results one may conclude that the groups differed in attribution in the direction predicted by the hypothesis relating dissonance and projection.

In all subsequent comparisons, the original, unadjusted *P* scores were used. The use of the simpler score should make interpretations clearer and more direct, especially in the case of within-conditions analyses.

It is of interest to look at the relation between self-esteem and attribution of arousal within the two experimental conditions. The product-moment correlation within the Favorable group was $+.29$ ($p < .07$); within the Unfavorable group the correlation was $+.10$ ($p < .55$). The relations are presented graphically in Figure 1, showing the mean raw *P* scores within each condition as a function of increasing self-esteem. The lack of correlation in the Unfavorable condition suggests that projection as a means of reducing dissonance occurred only when the amount of dissonance was quite high. From the point of view of the theory, this is not surprising. For the person with low self-esteem the undesirable information is actually consonant with his general self-evaluation (although dissonant with his specific cognitions about his adequate masculinity). Only for the person who believes he is consistently good will the undesirable information be strongly dissonant with his general self-esteem.

In Figure 1 it can be seen that the two groups show considerable continuity where they overlap in level of measured self-esteem. This fact is important because it implies that the self-esteem manipulations did not have strong opposed artifactual effects upon the amount of attribution of homosexual arousal. If the personality test report interviews had had effects on attribution in ways other than through the self-esteem variable, then differences between conditions might have appeared when considering subjects in the two groups with equivalent

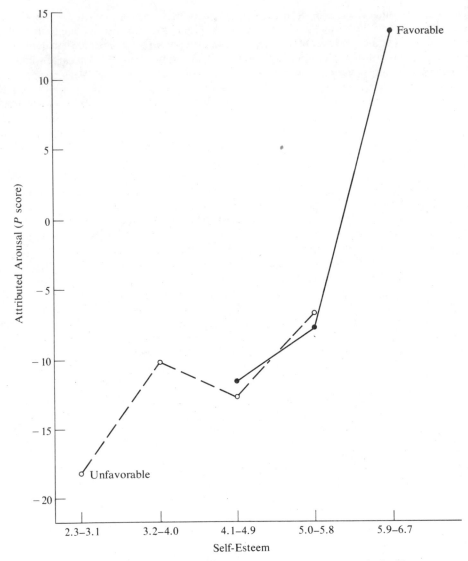

Figure 1.   Mean attribution of homosexuality as a function of level of self-esteem.

levels of self-esteem. Judging from Figure 1, persons in the two groups who had equivalent measured self-esteem levels apparently reacted similarly to the undesirable cognition.

Projection and Attitude toward Available Social Objects

There is a well known judgmental tendency which leads a person to perceive others as possessing traits consistent with his general evaluation of those others (a halo effect). On the basis of the halo effect alone, one would expect a tendency to attribute homosexuality (an unfavorable trait) to persons who are evaluated in general relatively negatively. However, the presence of dissonance resulting from self-ascription of homosexuality should introduce a contrary tendency. To the extent that projection, of the type defined in this report, occurs, it should be aimed primarily at persons who are relatively favorably evaluated. Since in this experiment projection was expected to occur to a greater extent in the Favorable group, it follows that the empirical pattern of attribution in that condition should be some compromise between the projection pattern and the halo pattern, since one may expect both forces to be operating. In the Unfavorable condition, on the other hand, one would expect to find a pattern more closely resembling the pure halo pattern, due to the absence of large amounts of dissonance.

In Figure 2 the results are shown separately for the two conditions. Mean P scores are shown as a function of increasingly favorable evaluation of the partner, as measured independently and prior to the introduction of the cognitions regarding homosexuality. It can be seen that the results are consistent with the hypothesis. For relatively negative and moderate levels of evaluation of the partner, subjects in the Favorable and Unfavorable conditions attributed homosexual arousal consistent with a halo effect. The less favorably they rated the other subject, the more homosexuality they attributed to him. However, when the partner had been evaluated very favorably, subjects in the two experimental conditions reacted in quite different ways. The Unfavorable group continued to follow the halo pattern, attributing very low homosexuality to the partner. The Favorable group, in contrast, exhibited no decrease in attribution when confronted with favorably evaluated objects. In fact, there was a slight but insignificant increase. The difference between the mean P scores of the Favorable ($n = 9$) and Unfavorable ($n = 12$) groups at the high respect point (5.4 to 6.4 in Figure 2) was significant beyond the .05 level by the t test. Since the subject's respect for his partner was not experimentally manipulated, it is possible that via self-selection other variables may be contributing to the observed difference. It should be pointed out, for example, that the measured self-esteem level of subjects in the Favorable group (with respected partner) was slightly higher than that of other subjects in the Favorable group, so that some of the tendency of these particular subjects to project may be traceable to their higher self-esteem rather than to their attitude toward their partner. Unfortunately, the number of cases is too small to allow an internal analysis to throw light on this question. All things considered, one can be fairly confident that the difference between the conditions does reflect a tendency for projection to be directed toward favorably evaluated persons under these circumstances.

DISCUSSION

The results provided good support for the central hypothesis, that projection can be a response to dissonance involving the self-concept. Subjects in the Favorable condition, for whom the undesirable information about homosexuality was more dissonant with the self-concept, attributed more arousal to other persons. It is very unlikely that this difference was due to differences between conditions in severity of superego standards concerning homosexuality. In designing the experimental manipulations, care was taken to avoid any implications about the good or bad aspects of homosexuality. Since subjects were assigned randomly to conditions, it appears safe to assume that the groups did not differ on the average in their moral evaluation of homosexuality as such. The experiment was therefore capable of demonstrating the role of dissonance in projection while controlling the superego variable.

The finding that projection resulting from dissonance was aimed primarily at respected persons supported the second hypothesis. A number of defensive projection processes have been summoned in order to explain phenomena of prejudice toward out-groups (for example,

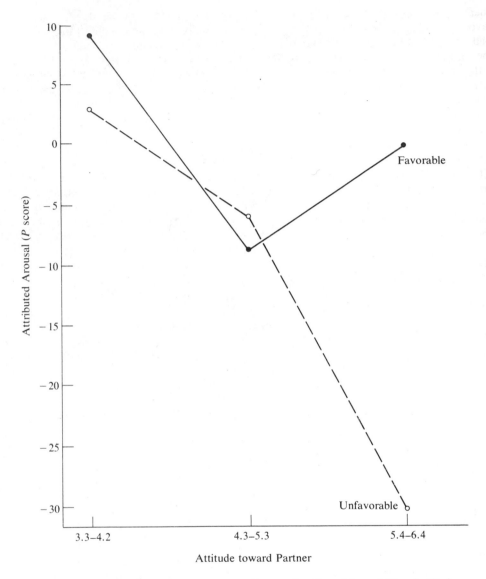

Figure 2.   Mean attribution of homosexuality as a function of favorability of attitude toward partner.

Ackerman and Jahoda, 1950; Adorno, Frenkel-Brunswik, Levinson, and Sanford, 1950). It is important to note that in most cases projection is said to be aimed at persons and groups who are disliked and considered incomparable and inferior to the projector. This is, of course, quite different from the kind of projection revealed in the present experiment.

Let us consider possible alternative explanations for the results shown in Figure 2. Perhaps the dissonance introduced by the undesirable information in the Favorable condition led directly to a re-evaluation of homosexuality. That is, perhaps these subjects were able to change their attitude toward the trait without the intermediate step of associating it with favorably evaluated persons. This re-evaluation prior to attribution might then affect the pattern of attribution in such a way as to give the appearance, deceptively, of projection. Once the undesirability of the trait was reduced, there would be less tendency to attribute it differentially to disliked persons (halo effect). The effect of such a process would be to attenuate the halo pattern in the Favorable condition, and might be revealed in part as a greater tendency to attribute homosexuality to respected persons, as compared with subjects in the Unfavorable condition. Is this hypothesis capable of explaining the results of the experiment without resort to the hypothesis of defensive projection?

The data show that subjects in the Favorable condition did tend to follow the halo pattern when the partner was evaluated unfavorably or moderate in favorability. In Figure 2, the difference between the unfavorable ($n = 9$) and moderate ($n = 24$) points within the Favorable group was significant beyond the .10 level by the t test, and was at least as striking as the pattern for the Unfavorable group. If in fact the high dissonance in the Favorable condition had led directly to re-evaluation of homosexuality (without projection), then the halo effect would have been attenuated in this condition at all points in Figure 2. There is no apparent reason for supposing that re-evaluation of the trait (without defensive projection) would have occurred among Favorable subjects confronted with respected partners more so than among other subjects in the Favorable group.

Consider another alternative explanation of the results. Perhaps the personality test report led subjects in the Favorable condition to conclude that they were generally better than other people, while those in the Unfavorable condition concluded they were worse than other people. Both groups of subjects then were given information that they possessed some degree of homosexual arousal. If subjects in the Favorable condition believed they were generally superior people, they might then have deduced that their partner was likely to be less worthy than themselves. This could result in rating the partner as possessing a greater amount of homosexual motivation. Persons in the Unfavorable condition would, by similar reasoning, conclude that their partner possessed a smaller amount of homosexual arousal. Such non-defensive processes could account for the overall difference in attribution between the two experimental conditions.

The data, as presented in Figure 2, cast doubt upon this alternative explanation. If the over-all difference between conditions were due to nondefensive deductions from the personality test reports, one would expect to find differences between the Favorable and Unfavorable conditions at all points along the attitude-toward-partner dimension. It is apparent, on the contrary, that the difference between conditions occurred only when the partner had been rated favorably.

It is interesting to speculate about the conditions under which dissonance with the self-concept will lead to projection onto favorably evaluated persons. In this experiment the dissonance-producing information was probably quite striking and unambiguous to the subjects. With great care the experimenter had explained that movement of the needle in response to looking at the photographs was a clear and indisputable sign of homosexual arousal. The situation was such that outright denial of the meaning of the needle movements would have been quite difficult for persons in reasonable touch with reality. It is very likely that these subjects were forced to accept the information as implying some degree of homosexual arousal in themselves. Under these circumstances of self-ascription, a good way to reduce the dissonance remaining was to try to get desirable people "into the same boat."

However, if the subjects had been able to deny the direct implications of the galvanic skin response, then a different pattern of attribution might have been observed. If the information were sufficiently ambiguous, so that partial denial occurred, then it would no longer be so comforting to attribute the undesirable trait to persons with whom the subject ordinarily classes himself. That is, when one is attempting to avoid self-ascription, it probably does not help to ascribe the trait to others who are seen as generally similar to one's self. Whether, when denial is possible, projection tends to be directed toward undesirable persons or out-groups, is an interesting question for further experimental exploration.

SUMMARY

A laboratory experiment was conducted to investigate some of the conditions affecting the occurrence of defensive projection. It was hypothesized that such projection is a positive function of the amount of cognitive dissonance resulting from the introduction of a self-referent cognition of negative valence. Further, it was hypothesized that certain types of defensive projection are likely to be selectively aimed at persons who are favorably evaluated by the threatened individual. Two groups of normal subjects were prepared in such a way that different amounts of dissonance would result from their exposure to the same undesirable information about themselves. All subjects received fraudulent information to the effect that they possessed homosexual tendencies. During the presentation of the disturbing material, each subject made estimates of the degree of homosexual arousal of another subject with whom he was paired, and whom he had met only rather briefly just prior to this part of the experiment.

The results supported the hypotheses. On the average, subjects in the high dissonance condition attributed to their partner about the same degree of arousal as they themselves appeared to be having. Those in the low dissonance condition in general attributed to their partner a level of arousal less than their own. The evidence suggested that the high dissonance group projected only when confronted with a partner whom they had previously evaluated quite favorably on adjective rating scales.

The relation between the psychoanalytic and dissonance theory approaches to defensive processes was discussed. It was proposed that study of the selection of objects should throw light upon the possible existence of distinct varieties of defensive projection.

REFERENCES

Ackerman, N. W., and Jahoda, Marie. *Anti-Semitism and emotional disorder*. New York: Harper, 1950.

Adorno, T. W., Frenkel-Brunswik, Else, Levinson, D. J., and Sanford, R. N. *The authoritarian personality*. New York: Harper, 1950.

Fenichel, O. *The psychoanalytic theory of neurosis*. New York: Norton, 1945.

Festinger, L. A theory of social comparison processes. *Hum. Relat.*, 1954, *7*, 117–140.

Festinger, L. *A theory of cognitive dissonance*. Stanford, Calif.: Stanford Univ. Press, 1957.

Gerard, H. B. A specific study: Conflict and conformity. *Amer. Psychologist*, 1959, *14*, 413. (Abstract)

Gerard, H. B., and Rabbie, J. M. Fear, affiliation, and social comparison. *Amer. Psychologist*, 1960, *15*, 409. (Abstract)

Murstein, B. I. The projection of hostility on the Rorschach and as a result of ego-threat. *J. proj. Tech.*, 1956, *20*, 418–428.

Wright, Beatrice A. Altruism in children and the perceived conduct of others. *J. abnorm. soc. Psychol.*, 1942, *37*, 218–233.

Daryl J. Bem
SELF-PERCEPTION:
AN ALTERNATIVE INTERPRETATION
OF COGNITIVE DISSONANCE PHENOMENA

A theory of self-perception is proposed to provide an alternative interpretation for several of the major phenomena embraced by Festinger's theory of cognitive dissonance and to explicate some of the secondary patterns of data that have appeared in dissonance experiments. It is suggested that the attitude statements which comprise the major dependent variables in dissonance experiments may be regarded as interpersonal judgments in which the observer and the observed happen to be the same individual and that it is unnecessary to postulate an aversive motivational drive toward consistency to account for the attitude change phenomena observed. Supporting experiments are presented, and metatheoretical contrasts between the "radical" behavioral approach utilized and the phenomenological approach typified by dissonance theory are discussed.

If a person holds two cognitions that are inconsistent with one another, he will experience the pressure of an aversive motivational state called cognitive dissonance, a pressure which he will seek to remove, among other ways, by altering one of the two "dissonant" cognitions. This proposition is the heart of Festinger's (1957) theory of cognitive dissonance, a theory which has received more widespread attention from personality and social psychologists in the past 10 years than any other contemporary statement about human behavior. Only 5 years after its introduction, Brehm and Cohen (1962) could review over 50 studies conducted within the framework of dissonance theory; and, in the 5 years since the appearance of their book, every major social-psychological journal has averaged at least one article per issue probing some prediction "derived" from the basic propositions of dissonance theory. In popularity, even the empirical law of effect now appears to be running a poor second.

The theory has also had its critics. Reservations about various aspects of the theory have ranged from mild (e.g., Asch, 1958; Bruner, 1957; Kelly, 1962; Osgood, 1960; Zajonc, 1960) to severe (Chapanis & Chapanis, 1964), and alternative interpretations have been offered to account for the results of particular studies (e.g., Chapanis & Chapanis, 1964; Janis & Gilmore, 1965; Lott, 1963; Rosenberg, 1965). No theoretical alternative to dissonance theory has been proposed, however, which attempts both to embrace its major phenomena and to account for some of the secondary patterns of results which have appeared in the supporting experiments but which were not predicted by the theory. This article proposes such an alternative.

Like many theories in psychology, the theory of cognitive dissonance attempts to account for observed functional relations between current stimuli and responses by postulat-

Reprinted by permission from the *Psychological Review*, 1967, *74*, pp. 183–200. Copyright 1967 by the American Psychological Association.

ing some hypothetical process within the organism, in this case, an inferred process of the arousal and reduction of dissonance. Like many other contemporary personality and social psychological theories, dissonance theory is further characterized by an emphasis on the individual's current phenomenology; the explanatory account in the theory itself is ahistorical.

In contrast, the alternative formulation to be presented here eschews any reference to hypothetical internal processes and seeks, rather, to account for observed functional relations between current stimuli and responses in terms of the individual's past training history. Such an approach has been called "radical" behaviorism (see Scriven, 1956), a position most often associated with the name of B. F. Skinner. In analyzing a complex behavioral phenomenon, the radical behaviorist attempts to establish it as a special case of some previously substantiated functional relation discovered in the experimental analysis of simpler behaviors. His functional analysis is thus based on empirical generalization and, accordingly, is frankly inductive not only in its experimental execution, but in its formal presentation.

A functional analysis characteristically begins by inquiring into the ontogenetic origins of the observed dependent variable and attempts to ascertain the controlling or independent variables of which that behavior is a function. The present analysis of dissonance phenomena proceeds in the same way by noting first that the dependent variable in cognitive dissonance studies is, with very few exceptions, a subject's (S's) self-descriptive statement of an attitude or belief. Indeed, this is the dependent variable in nearly all of contemporary social psychology. But how are such self-descriptive behaviors acquired? What are their controlling variables? It is to these questions that the analysis turns first.

SELF-PERCEPTION: A SPECIAL CASE OF INTERPERSONAL PERCEPTION

Self-perception, an individual's ability to respond differentially to his own behavior and its controlling variables, is a product of social interaction (Mead, 1934; Ryle, 1949; Skinner, 1957). Verbal statements that are self-descriptive are among the most common responses comprising self-perception, and the techniques employed by the community to teach its members to make such statements would not seem to differ fundamentally from the methods used to teach interpersonal perception in general. The community, however, does face severe limitations in training the individual to make statements describing internal events to which only he has direct access. Skinner (1953, 1957) has analyzed the limited resources available to the community for training its members thus to "know themselves," and he has described the inescapable inadequacies of the resulting knowledge.

Skinner suggests that some self-descriptions of internal stimuli can be learned through metaphor or stimulus generalization. The child, for example, can easily learn to describe "butterflies in the stomach" without explicit discrimination training. More often, however, a socializing community must teach the descriptive responses more directly. In training a child to describe pain, for example, the community, at some point, must teach him the correct response at the critical time when the appropriate private stimuli are impinging upon him. But the community itself must necessarily identify the "critical time" on the basis of observable stimuli or responses and implicitly assume that the private stimuli are, in fact, accompanying these public events.

This analysis suggests that many of the self-descriptive statements that appear to be exclusively under the discriminative control of private stimuli may, in fact, still be partially controlled by the same accompanying public events used by the training community to infer the individual's inner states. Private stimuli may play a smaller role than the individual himself suspects. For example, by manipulating the external cues of the situation, Schachter and Singer (1962) were able to evoke self-descriptions of emotional states as disparate as euphoria and anger from Ss in whom operationally identical states of physiological arousal had been induced. It appears that these Ss utilized internal stimuli only to make the gross discrimination that they were emotional, but that the more subtle discrimination of *which* emotion they were experiencing was under the control of external cues.

A similar division of control between internal and external stimuli appears to operate in the domain of attitude statements. Osgood, Suci, and Tannenbaum (1957) theorize that a pattern of internal responses elicited by a word or an object comprises the connotative or "emotional" meaning of the stimulus for an individual, including his attitude toward it. Using the Semantic Differential technique, these investigators report that an individual's verbal descriptions of these hypothesized internal responses can be factor analyzed into a very small number of factors, factors which appear to have extensive cross-cultural generality as well (Osgood et al., 1957). These findings, too, are consistent with the view that an individual is unable to make more than a small number of independent discriminations among stimuli that have never been publicly available to a socializing community, and it is suggested that the many subtle discriminations which individuals do make when describing their attitudes are based, rather, on the kinds of cues that are potentially available to an outside observer. In particular, it is suggested that self-descriptive attitude statements can be based on the individual's observations of his own overt behavior and the external stimulus conditions under which it occurs. A number of recent experimental studies provide support for this proposition.

Several studies have shown that an individual's belief and attitude statements can be manipulated by inducing him to role-play, deliver a persuasive communication, or engage in any behavior that would characteristically imply his endorsement of a particular set of beliefs (Brehm & Cohen, 1962; King & Janis, 1956; Scott, 1957, 1959). A recent experimental analysis of these phenomena of "self-persuasion" demonstrates that an individual bases his subsequent beliefs and attitudes on such self-observed behaviors to the extent that these behaviors are emitted under circumstances that have in the past set the occasion for telling the truth (Bem, 1965, 1966). For example, in one of three studies reported in Bem (1965), Ss were first trained to tell the truth in the presence of a colored light and to tell lies in the presence of another. Later in the experimental session, Ss were required to state attitudes with which they disagreed; one of the two colored lights was illuminated as each attitude statement was made. It was found that Ss subsequently endorsed the attitude statements they had uttered in the presence of the "truth light" significantly more than attitude statements they had made in the presence of the "lie light"; the lights, in short, determined the degree to which Ss believed what they had heard themselves say. Furthermore, no S could report any awareness of the control exerted by his statements or the lights over his subsequent attitudes.

In another study, the same technique was employed to demonstrate that an individual can be induced to believe in "false confessions" he has made if there are external cues present that characteristically set the occasion for telling the truth (Bem, 1966). These several studies have also illustrated that the control over an individual's beliefs and attitudes exerted by his overt behavior is vitiated to the extent that cues are present implying that the behavior is deceitful or, more generally, is being emitted for immediate specific reinforcement. For example, just as a communicator is more persuasive to others if he is known to be receiving no payment for his communication, so, too, it is found that he is more likely to believe himself under such circumstances (Bem, 1965). The effectiveness of self-persuasion can thus be altered by many of the techniques typically used to manipulate the credibility of any persuasive communicator.

The major implication of these findings is that, to the extent that internal stimuli are not controlling, an individual's attitude statements may be viewed as inferences from observations of his own overt behavior and its accompanying stimulus variables. As such, his statements are functionally similar to those that any outside observer could make about him. When the answer to the question, "Do you like brown bread?" is "I guess I do, I'm always eating it," it seems unnecessary to invoke a fount of privileged self-knowledge to account for the reply. In such a case the reply is functionally equivalent to one his wife might give for him: "I guess he does, he is always eating it." Only to the extent that "brown bread" elicits strongly conditioned internal responses might he have additional evidence, not currently available to his wife, on which to base his self-descriptive attitude statement.

The present analysis of dissonance phenomena, then, will rest upon the single empirical generalization that an individual's belief and attitude statements and the beliefs and attitudes that an outside observer would attribute to him are often functionally similar in that both sets of statements are partial "inferences" from the same evidence: the public behaviors and accompanying stimulus cues upon which the socializing community has relied in training him to make such self-descriptive statements in the first place.

PHENOMENA OF DISSONANCE THEORY

The major phenomena of dissonance theory have been classified into three main categories (Brehm & Cohen, 1962, p. 21): (*a*) forced-compliance studies; (*b*) free-choice studies; and (*c*) exposure-to-information studies. Within each category, this discussion will treat the major functional relation predicted and subject the data from a single dissonance experiment to detailed analysis. Two sets of secondary findings will also be discussed.

Because the literature of dissonance theory has now become so large that it would be impossible to discuss all the experimental paradigms that have been employed, the specific experiments selected for detailed analysis had to satisfy certain criteria. First, whenever possible, they had to be illustrative of several others in the same category so that the applicability of the self-perception analysis to studies not explicitly discussed would be apparent. Second, for each experiment there had to be at least one other study in the literature that had successfully replicated the same conceptual phenomenon employing different experimental procedures if possible. These first two criteria together attempt to ensure that the analysis avoids "explaining" phenomena that are artifactual, while at the same time not requiring that the particular study under analysis be invulnerable to methodological criticism. Finally, the studies selected are those which are best known and most widely reprinted or cited.

There will be no discussion of studies that simply use the vocabulary of dissonance theory but which explore functional relations that are not derivations from the major propositions of the theory (e.g., studies of postdecision regret; Festinger, 1964). There will also be no additional discussion of phenomena which, although derivable from dissonance theory propositions, are already considered by the dissonance theorists themselves to be as parsimoniously accounted for by straightforward empirical generalizations concerning the interpersonal judgmental skills of *S*s (e.g., attitude change phenomena produced by persuasive communication). (See Brehm & Cohen, 1962, pp. 105–111.) Indeed, the primary purpose of the present analysis is to extend this same kind of empirical generalization to the very phenomena that the dissonance theorists claim to be "entirely closed to the judgmental interpretation and rather unequivocally explainable by the dissonance formulation [Brehm & Cohen, 1962, p. 111]."

THE FORCED-COMPLIANCE STUDIES

The most frequently cited evidence for dissonance theory comes from an experimental procedure known as the forced-compliance paradigm. In these experiments, an individual is induced to engage in some behavior that would imply his endorsement of a particular set of beliefs or attitudes. Following his behavior, his "actual" attitude or belief is assessed to see if it is a function of the behavior in which he has engaged and of the manipulated stimulus conditions under which it was evoked. The best known and most widely quoted study of this type was conducted by Festinger and Carlsmith (1959). In their experiment, 60 undergraduates were randomly assigned to one of three experimental conditions. In the $1 condition, S was first required to perform long repetitive laboratory tasks in an individual experimental session. He was then hired by the experimenter as an "assistant" and paid $1 to tell a waiting fellow student (a stooge) that the tasks were enjoyable and interesting. In the $20 condition, each S was hired for $20 to do the same thing. Control Ss simply engaged in the repetitive tasks. After the experiment, each S indicated how much he had enjoyed the tasks. The results show that Ss paid $1 evaluated the tasks as significantly more enjoyable than did Ss who had been paid $20. The $20 Ss did not express attitudes significantly different from those expressed by the control Ss.

Dissonance theory interprets these findings by noting that all Ss initially hold the cognition that the tasks are dull and boring. In addition, however, the experimental Ss have the cognition that they have expressed favorable attitudes toward the tasks to a fellow student. These two cognitions are dissonant for Ss in the $1 condition because their overt behavior does not "follow from" their cognition about the task, nor does it follow from the small compensation they are receiving. To reduce the resulting dissonance pressure, they change their cognition about the task so that it is consistent with their overt behavior: they become more favorable toward the tasks. The Ss in the $20 condition, however, experience little or no dissonance because engaging in such behavior "follows from" the large compensation they are receiving. Hence, their final attitude ratings do not differ from those of the control group.

In contrast with this explanation, the present analysis views these results as a case of self-perception. Consider the viewpoint of an outside observer who hears the individual making favorable statements about the tasks to a fellow student, and who further knows that the individual was paid $1 ($20) to do so. This hypothetical observer is then asked to state the actual attitude of the individual he has heard. An outside observer would almost certainly judge a $20 communicator to be "manding" reinforcement (Skinner, 1957); that is, his behavior appears to be under the control of the reinforcement contingencies of the money and not at all under the discriminative control of the tasks he appears to be describing. The $20 communicator is not credible in that his statements cannot be used as a guide for inferring his actual attitudes. Hence, the observer could conclude that the individual found such repetitive tasks dull and boring in spite of what he had said. Although the behavior of a $1 communicator also has some mand properties, an outside observer would be more likely to judge him to be expressing his actual attitudes and, hence, would infer the communicator's attitude from the content of the communication itself. He would thus judge this individual to be favorable toward the tasks. If one now places the hypothetical observer and the communicator into the same skin, the findings obtained by Festinger and Carlsmith are the result. There is no aversive motivational pressure postulated; the dependent variable is viewed simply as a self-judgment based on the available evidence, evidence that includes the apparent controlling variables of the observed behavior.

If this analysis of the findings is correct, then it should be possible to replicate the inverse functional relation between amount of compensation and the final attitude statement by actually letting an outside observer try to infer the attitude of an *S* in the original study. Conceptually, this replicates the Festinger-Carlsmith experiment with the single exception that the observer and the observed are no longer the same individual.

AN INTERPERSONAL REPLICATION OF THE FESTINGER-CARLSMITH EXPERIMENT

Seventy-five college undergraduates participated in an experiment designed to "determine how accurately people can judge another person." Twenty-five *S*s each served in a $1, a $20, or a control condition. All *S*s listened to a tape recording which described a college sophomore named Bob Downing, who had participated in an experiment involving two motor tasks. The tasks were described in detail, but nonevaluatively; the alleged purpose of the experiment was also described. At this point, the control *S*s were asked to evaluate Bob's attitudes toward the tasks. The experimental *S*s were further told that Bob had accepted an offer of $1 ($20) to go into the waiting room, tell the next *S* that the tasks were fun, and to be prepared to do this again in the future if they needed him. The *S*s then listened to a brief conversation which they were told was an actual recording of Bob and the girl who was in the waiting room. Bob was heard to argue rather imaginatively that the tasks were fun and enjoyable, while the girl responded very little except for the comments that Festinger and Carlsmith's stooge was instructed to make. The recorded conversation was identical for both experimental conditions in order to remain true to the original study in which no differences in persuasiveness were found between the $1 and the $20 communications. In sum, the situation attempted to duplicate on tape the situation actually experienced by Festinger and Carlsmith's *S*s.

All *S*s estimated Bob's responses to the same set of questions employed in the original study. The key question required *S*s to rate the tasks (or for Bob's attitude toward them) on a scale from −5 to +5, where −5 means that the tasks were extremely dull and boring, +5 means they were extremely interesting and enjoyable, and 0 means they were neutral, neither interesting nor uninteresting.

Results

Table 1 shows the mean ratings for the key question given by *S*s in all three conditions of both the original experiment and the present replication.

The results show that in both studies the $1 and control conditions are on different sides of the neutral point and are significantly different from one another at the .02 level of

Table 1. Attitude ratings and interpersonal estimates of attitude ratings toward the tasks for each condition

Study	Control	Experimental condition	
		$1 compensation	$20 compensation
Festinger-Carlsmith	−0.45	+1.35	−0.05
Interpersonal replication	−1.56	+0.52	−1.96

Note.—For the Festinger-Carlsmith study, $N = 20$ in each condition; for the Interpersonal replication study, $N = 25$ in each condition.

significance ($t = 2.48$ in the original study; $t = 2.60$ in the replication).[1] In both studies, the $1 condition produced significantly more favorable ratings toward the tasks than did the $20 condition ($t = 2.22$, $p < .03$ in the original study; $t = 3.52$, $p < .001$ in the replication). In neither study is the $20 condition significantly different from the control condition; and, finally, in neither study were there any significant differences between conditions on the other questions asked of Ss about the experiment. Thus, the inverse relation between amount of compensation and the final attitude rating is clearly replicated; and, even though the present analysis does not require the attitude judgments themselves of the interpersonal observers to duplicate those of Ss in the original experiment, it is seen that the two sets of ratings are quite comparable on the 10-point scales.

Since the above replication was conducted, Jones (1966) has reported a study in which Ss' attitudes and observers' judgments were compared directly in the same experiment. Again, the observers' judgments not only replicated the inverse functional relation displayed by the attitude statements of Ss themselves, but the actual scale positions of observers and Ss were again similar.

These successful replications of the functional relation reported by Festinger and Carlsmith provide support for the self-perception analysis. The original Ss may be viewed as simply making self-judgments based on the same kinds of public evidence that the community originally employed in training them to infer the attitudes of any communicator, themselves included. It is not necessary to postulate an aversive motivational drive toward consistency.

These interpersonal replications are illustrative of others which have been reported elsewhere (Bem, 1965). It has been shown that the present analysis applies as well to forced-compliance experiments which utilize compensations much smaller than $20, to studies which manipulate variables other than the amount of compensation, and to studies which evoke different behaviors from S. Alternative dependent variables have also been considered. For example, Brehm and Cohen show that S's rating of how hungry he is can be manipulated by inducing him to volunteer to go without food for different amounts of compensation (1962, pp. 132–137), and a successful interpersonal replication of that experiment, again supports the present self-perception analysis of these forced-compliance phenomena (Bem, 1965).

The merits of alternative formulations to an established theory are often sought in their ability to explicate functional relations about which the original theory must remain mute. Accordingly, the analysis now turns to a pattern of related findings which have not been adequately accommodated by dissonance theory: the observed relationships between the *amount* of behavior evoked from S in a forced-compliance setting and his final attitude statements.

A number of forced-compliance experiments have demonstrated that the differential effects of the stimulus manipulations on attitude statements can be obtained even before any of the behavior to which the individual has committed himself is actually emitted (Brehm & Cohen, 1962, pp. 115–116). That is, the behavior of volunteering to emit the behavior is sufficient to control the individual's subsequent self-judgment of attitude. (The self-perception interpretation of this effect has also been confirmed by an interpersonal replication, Bem, 1965.) In fact, in an experiment in which Ss volunteered to write essays against their initial opinions, Rabbie, Brehm, and Cohen (1959) report that the mean of attitude ratings obtained before the essays were actually written was not significantly different from the mean of attitude ratings obtained after the essays were written. But the variance across Ss

---

[1] All significance levels in this article are based on two-tailed tests.

was much greater in the latter case. That is, actually writing the essays increases *and* decreases the initial effect of volunteering. In addition, there was a negative relationship between the number of arguments *S* wrote and the degree to which his final attitude statement agreed with the position advocated in the essay. On the other hand, Cohen, Brehm, and Fleming (1958) report a positive relationship between "original arguments" and amount of attitude change, but this relationship appeared in only one of the experimental conditions. Unpublished data from the Festinger-Carlsmith experiment show a negative correlation in one condition between attitude ratings and "number and variety" of arguments and a positive correlation in the other (reported by Brehm & Cohen, 1962, p. 119). Finally, when *S*s themselves rate the quality of their persuasive communications, the confusion is further compounded. Brehm and Cohen conclude that "the role of discrepant verbal behavior in the arousal and reduction of dissonance remains unclear [p. 121]." How might the self-perception analysis treat these effects?

If an outside observer begins with the discrimination that a communicator is credible, then the more arguments put forth, the more persuasive the speaker might well become, *if* nothing intervenes to change the observer's judgment of the communicator's credibility. If, however, the observer discriminates the communicator as manding reinforcement, then it seems likely that the more insistent the speaker becomes in pushing his point of view, the more it appears to the observer that he "doth protest too much," and the less likely it is that the speaker's statements will be taken to express his "actual" attitudes.

Now consider the self-observer. If *S*s in the dissonance experiments begin with the discrimination that they are not manding (*S*s in the low compensation conditions, for example), then the more arguments they put forth, the more self-persuasive they might become. For any given *S*, however, presenting a communication counter to his initial position might itself provide him with the cues that he is manding and hence destroy the initial effect of volunteering under nonmand conditions; he will become less self-persuasive as he continues. This analysis, then, leads one to expect the increased variability in postessay as compared to pre-essay measures of attitude. It is equally clear, however, that to confirm this analysis, the hypothesized discrimination of credibility must be brought under experimental control rather than being left under the control of the unique past histories of individual *S*s. To do this, the Festinger-Carlsmith experiment is again used as an illustrative example.

AN EXTENDED INTERPERSONAL REPLICATION OF THE FESTINGER-CARLSMITH EXPERIMENT

Festinger and Carlsmith found that within the $1 condition, the greater the number and variety of arguments stated by *S* about the tasks, the more favorable his final evaluation was of them. Within the $20 condition, however, the greater the number and variety of arguments, the less favorable his final rating. The following study thus seeks to replicate this pattern of results with interpersonal observers.

Method

In the earlier replication, the persuasive communication heard by *S*s was identical for both conditions. All *S*s heard the speaker present a fairly imaginative and lengthy set of reasons as to why he had enjoyed the tasks. For the present extension, a second communication was designed, which was somewhat shorter and contained comparatively unimaginative arguments. The replication was then rerun on an additional 50 *S*s assigned either to a $1 or a $20 condition. The Ss were again asked to estimate the actual attitude of the speaker. Thus, except for the length and variety of arguments in the communication, this replication is identical with the earlier one. The total design, then, contains four experimental groups: $1-long communication, $1-short communication, $20-long communication, and $20-short communication.

If the present analysis is correct, then within the $1 condition, where the communicator is more likely to be perceived as credible, the long communication should lead interpersonal observers to infer that the communicator enjoyed the tasks more than the short communication would. Within the $20 condition, however, the long communication should be *less* persuasive than the short one; the longer the speaker carries on, the harder he appears to be trying to earn his $20. He "doth protest too much." Thus, an interaction effect is predicted between the two variables of communication length and amount of compensation. It will be noted that this is equivalent to saying that the "dissonance" effect, the inverse functional relation between compensation and attitude change, is itself a function of communication length. The shorter the communication, the smaller the inverse relationship should become, perhaps even reversing itself at very short communication lengths.

Results

Tables 2 and 3 display the results and their analysis, respectively. It will be recalled that scores can range from -5 to $+5$; the higher the score, the more favorable the communicator is judged to be toward the tasks.

It is seen that the interpersonal interpretation of self-perception is supported by these results. By employing attitude estimates of outside observers, the study has replicated Festinger and Carlsmith's positive correlation between number of arguments and attitude change within the $1 condition and the negative correlation between these two variables within the $20 condition. The main effect of compensation seen in Tables 2 and 3 is, of course, the primary "dissonance" effect reported earlier. As also noted earlier, however, the

Table 2. Interpersonal estimates of attitude ratings toward the tasks

Experimental condition	Long communication	Short communication
$1 compensation	+0.52	−1.04
$20 compensation	−1.96	−0.64

Note.—$N = 25$ in each cell.

Table 3. Summary of analysis of variance of interpersonal estimates of attitude ratings toward the tasks

Source of variation	Sum of squares	df	Mean square	F
Long versus short	0.360	1	0.360	0.05
$1 versus $20	27.040	1	27.040	4.07*
Interaction	51.840	1	51.840	7.80**
Within cells	637.920	96	6.645	

*$p < .05$
**$p < .01$

"dissonance" effect is itself a function of communication length, and the main effect is due entirely to the inverse relation appearing in the conditions employing the long communication, the communication designed to duplicate these found in the original Festinger-Carlsmith experiment. A nonsignificant reversal actually appears when very short communications are employed. It may be that communication length is thus one of the confounding parameters responsible for the conflicting findings, including reversals, reported in forced-compliance experiments, a point noted by Aronson (1966). If this is so, then the present conceptualization might provide a reconciliation of the conflicting predictions made by a reinforcement theory (e.g., Scott, 1957, 1959), "incentive" theories (Janis & Gilmore, 1965), and dissonance theory within a single theoretical framework (cf. Bem, 1965).

NONVERBAL DEPENDENT VARIABLES

Both dissonance theory and the present analysis can be characterized as dealing with cognitions, attitudes, beliefs, or self-descriptive statements as the dependent variables. There is, however, a long history of evidence demonstrating that an individual's beliefs and attitudes can function as antecedent or independent variables as well, exercising partial control not only over his instrumental and consummatory behaviors, but over many of his physiological responses as well. Accordingly, the same "dissonance" manipulations that can produce attitude change should be expected to produce changes in some of these nonverbal behaviors too, an expectation that has now been well confirmed (e.g., Brehm, Back, & Bogdonoff, 1964; Brock & Grant, 1963; Cohen, Greenbaum, & Mansson, 1963; Freedman, 1965; Zimbardo, Cohen, Weisenberg, Dworkin, & Firestone, 1966). It should be clear, however, that, although either theory could claim to anticipate these "noncognitive" effects, neither formulation contains the theoretical machinery for "explaining" them in any nontrivial sense; this is especially true for the striking physiological effects (e.g., Zimbardo et al., 1966). In addition, Weick (in press) has persuasively argued that the apparent motivational effects of dissonance manipulations on the intensity of nonverbal instrumental behavior often fail to show the predicted attitude change that should accompany such effects and that these effects are more parsimoniously accounted for by propositions drawn from frustration theory and cue-utilization theory.

In sum, it is suggested that the interpersonal model of self-perception provides a viable alternative to the theory of cognitive dissonance in accounting for the attitudinal phenomena that have emerged from the forced-compliance experiments.

THE FREE-CHOICE STUDIES

In the second major category of data on dissonance theory, an S is permitted to make a selection from a set of objects or courses of action. The dependent variable is his subsequent attitude rating of the chosen and rejected alternatives. Dissonance theory reasons that any unfavorable aspects of the chosen alternative and any favorable aspects of the rejected alternatives provide cognitions that are dissonant with the cognition that the individual has chosen as he did. To reduce the resulting dissonance pressure, the individual exaggerates the favorable features of the chosen alternative and plays down its unfavorable aspects. This leads him to enhance his rating of the chosen alternative. Similar reasoning predicts that he will lower his rating of the rejected alternatives. These predictions are confirmed in a number of studies. (See Brehm & Cohen, 1962, p. 303; see also Festinger, 1964).

A number of secondary predictions concerning parameters of the choice have also been confirmed. In an experiment by Brehm and Cohen (1959), school children were permitted to select a toy from either two or four alternatives. Some children chose from qualitatively similar toys; others chose from qualitatively dissimilar alternatives. The children's postchoice ratings of the toys on a set of rating scales were then compared to initial ratings obtained a week before the experiment. The main displacement effect appeared as predicted: Chosen toys were displaced in the more favorable direction; rejected toys were generally displaced in the unfavorable direction. In addition, however, the displacement effect was larger when the choice was made from the larger number of alternatives. This is so, according to dissonance theory, because "the greater the number of alternatives from which one must choose, the more one must give up and consequently the greater the magnitude of dissonance [p. 373]." Similarly, the displacement effect was larger when the choice was made from dissimilar rather than similar alternatives because "what one has to give up relative to what one gains increases [p. 373]," again increasing the magnitude of the dissonance experienced.

To interpret these findings within the framework of self-perception, consider an observer trying to estimate a child's ratings of toys; the observer has not seen the child engage in any behavior with the toys. Now compare this observer with one who has just seen the child select one of the toys as a gift for himself. This comparison parallels, respectively, the prechoice and the post-choice ratings made by the children themselves. It seems likely that the latter observer would displace the estimated ratings of the chosen and rejected alternatives further from one another simply because he has some behavioral evidence upon which to base differential ratings of these toys. This is the effect displayed in the children's final ratings.

The positive relation between the number of alternatives and the displacement effect can be similarly analyzed. If an observer had seen the selected toy "win out" over more competing alternatives, it seems reasonable that he might increase the estimated displacement between the "exceptional" toy and the group of rejected alternatives. Finally, the fact that the displacement effect is larger when the alternatives are dissimilar would appear to be an instance of simple stimulus generalization. That is, to the extent that the chosen and rejected alternatives are similar to one another, they will be rated closer together on a scale by any rater, outside observer, or the child himself.

In sum, if one regards the children as observers of their own choice behavior and their subsequent ratings as inferences from that behavior, the dissonance findings appear to follow. The following demonstration illustrates the point.

AN INTERPERSONAL REPLICATION OF THE TOY STUDY

Twenty-four college students served as control *S*s by estimating how an 11-year-old boy might rate several different toys. These toys were selected from the list reported by Brehm and Cohen (1959) and were rated on the same rating scales. The toys to be rated in the subsequent experiment were then selected on the basis of these ratings according to the same criteria of selection employed by the original investigators.

For the experiment itself, 96 college students were given a sheet of paper with the following information: "In a psychology experiment, an 11-year-old boy was asked to rate how well he liked toys that are typically popular with this age group. He was then permitted to select one of these toys to keep for himself. We are interested in how well college students can estimate his ratings." Each sheet also informed *S* which toy the child had chosen and from which alternatives he was permitted to choose. He then made his estimates of the child's ratings. The *S*s were randomly assigned to one of four conditions corresponding to the combinations of number of alternatives (two or four) and similarity of alternatives (similar or dissimilar).

Results

Table 4 lists the toys employed, the control group means, and the displacements from those means of the corresponding experimental group means for the chosen and rejected alternatives in each condition. Scores can range from 0 to 5, where a higher number indicates greater liking for the toy; a positive displacement indicates increased liking for the toy. To facilitate comparisons among conditions, the toy rated as most popular by the control group, the swimming snorkel, was employed as the "chosen" toy in all experimental conditions. In addition, it will be noted that it was possible to match closely the combined mean ratings of the rejected alternatives in the four-alternative conditions; unfortunately this could not be done for the two-alternative conditions.

Table 4. Mean displacement in toy ratings from control group means for chosen and rejected alternatives in each condition

Experimental condition			Similar alternatives			Dissimilar alternatives		
		Toy	Control	Displacement	Toy	Control	Displacement
Two alternatives	Chosen	Swimming snorkel	3.45	+.35	Swimming snorkel	3.45	+.22
	Rejected	Swimming mask	3.44	−.39	Archery set	2.79	−.42
Four alternatives	Chosen	Swimming snorkel	3.45	+.69	Swimming snorkel	3.45	+.99
	Rejected	Swimming mask			Archery set		
		Swimming fins	2.54	−.01	Bowling game	2.58	−.26
		Life jacket			Ship model		

Note.—$N = 24$ in the control and each experimental condition.

It is seen in Table 4 that the chosen alternative was rated higher and the rejected alternatives were rated lower than the corresponding control group means in every condition. In both of the two-alternative conditions, the total displacement effect is significant at the .01 level ($t = 3.66$ and 2.81 for the similar and dissimilar conditions, respectively); for both of the four-alternative conditions, it is significant at the .001 level ($t = 5.26$ and 9.18, respectively). Some of the downward displacement of the rejected alternatives in the two-alternative conditions can be attributed to regression effects since the initial means of these alternatives are above the grand mean, but this problem has been avoided in the four-alternative conditions by combining the ratings of the three rejected alternatives; in this case the predicted displacement effect is opposite in direction to that due to regression, as is the upward displacement of the chosen alternative in all four conditions. Thus, the main displacement effect is clearly replicated by interpersonal judgments.

Similarity of alternatives. From simple considerations of stimulus generalization, it was predicted that the displacement effect should be greater in the dissimilar than in the similar conditions. Because of the differential effects of regression, mentioned above, however, the analysis must be confined to the four-alternative conditions where it was possible to match the control group means of the rejected alternatives. Within this condition, the mean total displacement is .70 in the similar condition and 1.25 in the dissimilar condition, a difference significance at the .05 level ($t = 2.22$). The hypothesis is confirmed insofar as it is possible to test it with these data.

Number of alternatives. The present experiment is attempting to replicate the positive relation found between the displacement and the number of alternatives. Again, the displacements of the rejected alternatives in the two-alternative conditions cannot be legitimately incorporated into the comparison. The present analysis, therefore, is confined to the upward displacement of the chosen alternative. For the four-alternative conditions, the mean upward displacement of the swimming snorkel is seen to be .84; for the two-alternative conditions, it is .28. This difference is significant at the .01 level ($t = 3.29$). The dissonance findings are again replicated by interpersonal observers.

Although it would have been desirable to test the predictions unconfounded by the noncomparability of the two-alternative base lines, this would have required departing from the toys employed in the original experiment. More importantly, however, this would still not have yielded a more direct comparison between the replication and the original experiment because the results reported by Brehm and Cohen are themselves confounded by uncorrected regression effects. The present replication actually provides clearer evidence for the predicted effects than the original study.

It is suggested that this same kind of analysis can be applied to the other studies in this category of dissonance experiments. Once again, it seems unnecessary to invoke a motivational construct to account for the data.

EXPOSURE-TO-INFORMATION STUDIES

The third category of dissonance studies includes two general paradigms: experiments in which an individual is involuntarily exposed to information that is discrepant with information he already possesses, and studies that examine an individual's willingness to expose himself voluntarily to dissonant information.

An experiment of the first type in which male Ss received information discrepant with their "self-images" was conducted by Bramel (1962). Each S was first led to view himself favorably or unfavorably on a number of personality characteristics and then given information that implied that he was sexually aroused by homoerotic pictures. This information was in the form of numerical readings from a meter which was supposedly measuring S's sexual arousal to the stimulus pictures; actually, all Ss received the same meter readings. The dependent variable of the study was S's prediction of the meter readings that were obtained from his "partner," another male S who was participating in the experiment concurrently.

Bramel reasons from dissonance theory that the arousal information would be quite dissonant for Ss who had been led to view themselves favorably. In order to reduce this dissonance, these Ss would "project" or attribute a higher amount of homosexual arousal to their partners than would Ss in the Unfavorable condition, who would find the information less dissonant with their self-image. The results are consistent with this prediction. The data show that the higher S's measured self-esteem, the more arousal he attributed to his partner.

This study may be reanalyzed by considering the nature of the task set *S*. He is asked to make a comparative judgment of another person along a numerical scale. His only standard of reference is his own meter reading. In addition, he knows that high meter readings are to be associated with a negative attribute, and he can again use himself as the reference for a standard of "good" and "bad." It would appear to follow that the more an *S* judges himself as "good," the higher an arousal number, relative to his own, he would assign to another person on whom he has no additional data, precisely the relationship reported by Bramel.[2]

This straightforward "psychophysical" interpretation is further supported by the observed relationship between *S*'s prediction of his partner's arousal and his overall evaluation of the partner which he had made prior to receiving the experimental manipulation. A simple "halo effect" is evident: *S*s attribute high readings to partners toward whom they had generally unfavorable attitudes; they attribute moderate readings to moderately esteemed partners; and, with one exception, they attribute low readings to highly esteemed partners. This monotonic relation is violated at only one point: *S*s who have high self-esteem appear to use their own meter reading as a lower bound of "goodness" and simply assign a similar level of arousal to partners whom they also regard favorably. This finding, too, is consistent with the judgmental interpretation of Bramel's data.

A number of other experiments examine the effects of giving *S*s information that is dissonant with their self-images. Unfortunately, the more remarkable effects (e.g., Aronson & Carlsmith, 1962) are apparently difficult to reproduce, and it is still possible that the original findings are artifactual. (See McGuire, 1966, for a review.)

Throughout this discussion, it has been argued that the data under analysis could be accounted for without postulating an aversive motivational drive. The second kind of exposure-to-information studies may be viewed as a direct test for the existence of such a drive. If cognitive dissonance is, in fact, an aversive state, then a person should avoid exposure to sources of dissonant information and seek out nondissonant sources. Compared with the theoretical chain of reasoning behind the other studies discussed, this deduction from dissonance theory is by far the most direct, the easiest to test, and the most crucial for justifying a motivational construct like dissonance. The available evidence, however, is not supportive. In an extensive review of the relevant studies, most of which were conducted by investigators whose theoretical orientation would lead them to look for selective exposure to nondissonant information, Freedman and Sears (1965) conclude that "clearly experimental evidence does not demonstrate that there is a general psychological tendency to avoid nonsupportive and to seek out supportive information."

There is, of course, nothing within the behaviorist's functional framework that would rule out a motivational phenomenon. For example, it is not implausible to suppose that punishment is often contingent upon being inconsistent, illogical, or just plain wrong in our highly verbal culture. This would be particularly true for the college students who typically serve as *S*s in cognitive dissonance experiments. Accordingly, evidence demonstrating that it is aversive for such *S*s to maintain incompatible responses in their verbal repertoires might well be forthcoming. Such a phenomenon is appropriately labeled motivational, but it would be the consequence of a particularly common cultural practice and would not, it is suggested, justify the reification of a new internal drive that is assumed to be an inherent characteristic of behaving organisms. In any case, the assumption of any motivational process to account for the data reviewed in this discussion would seem gratuitous.

---

[2]Bramel briefly considers a similar interpretation, but rejects it in favor of the dissonance interpretation.

SOME METATHEORETICAL CONSIDERATIONS

In the opening remarks, some contrasts were noted between the conceptual approach typified by dissonance theory and the behavioral approach represented here by the functional analysis of self-perception. It was pointed out that the behaviorist's goal is to account for observed relations between current stimuli and responses in terms of an individual's past training history and a small number of basic functional relations discovered in the experimental analysis of simpler behaviors. The behaviorist's functional analysis of complex behaviors like dissonance phenomena was thus seen to be based on empirical generalization, a feature which infuses it with an inductive flavor and spirit.

In contrast, the dissonance theorists clearly prefer the "deductive" nature of their theory and explicitly derogate the "weakness of an empirical generalization as compared with a true theoretical explanation [Lawrence & Festinger, 1962, p. 17]." This criticism of the behaviorist's functional analysis, namely, that it has no deductive fertility or predictive power, is often expressed. The radical behaviorist, so the criticism goes, will not venture a specific prediction without knowing the complete reinforcement history of the organism. He cannot provide a "true theoretical explanation."

It is suggested here that a functional analysis appears to have limited predictive power only because it makes explicit the kinds of knowledge about the past and present controlling variables that any theorist must have if he is to predict behavior accurately. How, for example, do the dissonance theorists conclude that dissonance is present in a particular case? That is, how do they decide when one cognition does not "follow from" another? According to Festinger, "the vagueness in the conceptual definition of dissonance—namely, two elements are dissonant if, considered alone, the obverse of one follows from the other—lies in the words 'follows from'. . . . One element may follow from another because of logic, because of cultural mores, because of things one has experienced and learned, and perhaps in other senses too [1957, p. 278]." Five years later, Brehm and Cohen note that "the 'follows from' relationship can sometimes be determined empirically but is limited by our abilities to specify and measure cognitions and the relationships among them . . . the 'follows from' relationship is not always clear and specifiable [1962, pp. 11–12]."

In actual practice, however, the dissonance theorists do not experience difficulty in inferring the existence of dissonance from their stimulus operations. But this is so precisely because in that inference the dissonance theorists sneak through the back door the very knowledge they claim to do without. It is in that inference that they implicitly make use of the fact that they have been raised by the same socializing community as their Ss. The dissonance theorists can thus infer that a \$1 compensation will produce more dissonance than a \$20 compensation, just as it has been *our* common history with these same Ss that permits *us* to speculate that the difference in compensation represents a difference in the mand properties of the induced behavior. Interpersonal observers are successful in replicating dissonance phenomena for the same reason. Dissonance theorists and radical behaviorists need the same kinds of knowledge. Only the behaviorists, however, take as their explicit obligation the necessity for accounting for both their own and their Ss' differential response to such controlling variables.

In sum, it is concluded that the greater "deductive fertility" of dissonance theory is largely illusory. In the process of adequately explicating the phrase "follows from" in their fundamental statement, the dissonance theorists will necessarily have to perform the explicit functional analysis they had hoped to finesse. It remains our conviction that the appeal to hypothetical internal states of the organism for causal explanations of behavior is often heuristically undesirable. Such diversion appears only to retard and deflect the thrust of the analysis that is ultimately required.

REFERENCES

Aronson, E. The psychology of insufficient justification: An analysis of some conflicting data. In S. Feldman (Ed.), *Cognitive consistency: Motivational antecedents and behavioral consequents*. New York: Academic Press, 1966. Pp. 109–133.

Aronson, E., & Carlsmith, J. M. Performance expectancy as a determinant of actual performance. *Journal of Abnormal and Social Psychology, 1962, 65,* 178–182.

Asch, S. E. Review of L. Festinger, *A theory of cognitive dissonance. Contemporary Psychology,* 1958, *3,* 194–195.

Bem, D. J. An experimental analysis of self-persuasion. *Journal of Experimental Social Psychology,* 1965, *1,* 199–218.

Bem, D. J. Inducing belief in false confessions. *Journal of Personality and Social Psychology,* 1966, *3,* 707–710.

Bramel, D. A dissonance theory approach to defensive projection. *Journal of Abnormal and Social Psychology,* 1962, *64,* 121–129.

Brehm, J. W., & Cohen, A. R. Re-evaluation of choice alternatives as a function of their number and qualitative similarity. *Journal of Abnormal and Social Psychology,* 1959, *58,* 373–378.

Brehm, J. W., & Cohen, A. R. *Explorations in cognitive dissonance*. New York: Wiley, 1962.

Brehm, M. L., Back, K. W., & Bogdonoff, M. D. A physiological effect of cognitive dissonance under stress and deprivation. *Journal of Abnormal and Social Psychology,* 1964, *69,* 303–310.

Brock, T. C., & Grant, L. D. Dissonance, awareness, and motivation. *Journal of Abnormal and Social Psychology,* 1963, *67,* 53–60.

Bruner, J. S. Discussion of L. Festinger, The relationship between behavior and cognition. In J. S. Bruner (Ed.), *Contemporary approaches to cognition.* Cambridge: Harvard University Press, 1957. Pp. 151–156.

Chapanis, N. P., & Chapanis, A. Cognitive dissonance: Five years later. *Psychological Bulletin,* 1964, *61,* 1–22.

Cohen, A. R., Brehm, J. W., & Fleming, W. H. Attitude change and justification for compliance. *Journal of Abnormal and Social Psychology,* 1958, *56,* 276–278.

Cohen, A. R., Greenbaum, C. W., & Mansson, H. H. Commitment to social deprivation and verbal conditioning. *Journal of Abnormal and Social Psychology,* 1963, *67,* 410–421.

Festinger, L. *A theory of cognitive dissonance*. Stanford: Stanford University Press, 1957.

Festinger, L. *Conflict, decision and dissonance*. Stanford: Stanford University Press, 1964.

Festinger, L., & Carlsmith, J. M. Cognitive consequences of forced compliance. *Journal of Abnormal and Social Psychology,* 1959, *58,* 203–210.

Freedman, J. L. Long-term behavioral effects of cognitive dissonance. *Journal of Experimental Social Psychology,* 1965, *1,* 103–120.

Freedman, J. L., & Sears, D. O. Selective exposure. In L. Berkowitz (Ed.), *Advances in experimental social psychology*. Vol. 2. New York: Academic Press, 1965. Pp. 57–97.

Janis, I. L., & Gilmore, J. B. The influence of incentive conditions on the success of role playing in modifying attitudes. *Journal of Personality and Social Psychology,* 1965, *1,* 17–27.

Jones, R. G. Forced compliance dissonance predictions: obvious, non-obvious, or nonsense? Paper read at American Psychological Association, New York, September 1966.

Kelly, G. Comments on J. Brehm, Motivational effects of cognitive dissonance. In M. R. Jones (Ed.), *Nebraska symposium on motivation: 1962*. Lincoln: University of Nebraska Press, 1962. Pp. 78–81.

King, B. T., & Janis, I. L. Comparison of the effectiveness of improvised vs. non-improvised role-playing in producing opinion change. *Human Relations,* 1956, *9,* 177–186.

Lawrence, D. H., & Festinger, L. *Deterrents and reinforcement*. Stanford: Stanford University Press, 1962.

Lott, B. E. Secondary reinforcement and effort: Comment on Aronson's "The effect of effort on the attractiveness of rewarded and unrewarded stimuli." *Journal of Abnormal and Social Psychology,* 1963, *67,* 520–522.

Mead, G. H. *Mind, self, and society*. Chicago: University of Chicago Press, 1934.

McGuire, W. J. Attitudes and opinions. *Annual Review of Psychology,* 1966, *17,* 475–514.

Osgood, C. E. Cognitive dynamics in human affairs. *Public Opinion Quarterly,* 1960, *24,* 341–365.

Osgood, C. E., Suci, G. J., & Tannenbaum, P. H. *The measurement of meaning*. Urbana: University of Illinois Press, 1957.

Rabbie, J. M., Brehm, J. W., & Cohen, A. R. Verbalization and reactions to cognitive dissonance. *Journal of Personality,* 1959, *27,* 407–417.

Rosenberg, M. J. When dissonance fails: On eliminating evaluation apprehension from attitude measurement. *Journal of Personality and Social Psychology,* 1965, *1,* 28–42.

Ryle, G. *The concept of mind*. London: Hutchinson, 1949.

Schachter, S., & Singer, J. Cognitive, social, and physiological determinants of emotional state. *Psychological Review,* 1962, *69,* 379–399.

Scott, W. A. Attitude change through reward of verbal behavior. *Journal of Abnormal and Social Psychology,* 1957, *55,* 72–75.

Scott, W. A. Attitude change by response reinforcement: Replication and extension. *Sociometry,* 1959, *22,* 328–335.

Scriven, M. A study of radical behaviorism. In H. Feigl & M. Scriven (Eds.), *Minnesota studies in philosophy of science,* Vol. 1. *Foundations of science and the concepts of psychology and psychoanalysis*. Minneapolis: University of Minnesota Press, 1956. Pp. 88–131.

Skinner, B. F. *Science and human behavior*. New York: Macmillan, 1953.

Skinner, B. F. *Verbal behavior*. New York: Appleton-Century-Crofts, 1957.

Weick, K. E. Dissonance and task enhancement: A problem for compensation theory? *Organizational Behavior and Human Performance,* in press

Zajonc, R. B. The concepts of balance, congruity, and dissonance. *Public Opinion Quarterly,* 1960, *24,* 280–296.

Zimbardo, P. G., Cohen, A. R., Weisenberg, M., Dworkin, L., & Firestone, I. Control of pain motivation by cognitive dissonance. *Science,* 1966, *151,* 217–219.

NAME INDEX

SUBJECT INDEX

443